D0163578

Routledge History of Philosophy
Volume V

European philosophy from the late seventeenth century through most of the eighteenth is broadly conceived as 'the Enlightenment', a period of reaction against the ambitious metaphysical systems of the seventeenth-century Rationalists.

This volume begins with Herbert of Cherbury and the Cambridge Platonists and with Newton and the early English Enlightenment. Locke is a key figure in later chapters, as a result of his importance both in the development of British and Irish philosophy and because of his seminal influence in the Enlightenment as a whole. *British Philosophy and the Age of Enlightenment* includes discussion of the Scottish Enlightenment and its influence on the German *Aufklärung*, and consequently on Kant. French thought, which in turn affected the late radical Enlightenment, especially Bentham, is also considered here.

This survey brings together clear, authoritative chapters from leading experts and provides a scholarly introduction to this period in the history of philosophy. It includes a glossary of technical terms and a chronological table of important political, philosophical, scientific and other cultural events.

Stuart Brown is Professor of Philosophy at the Open University. He has written extensively on seventeenth and eighteenth century philosophy and is the author of a book on Leibniz. He has edited several collections, including *Philosophers of the Enlightenment* (1979) and *Nicholas Malebranche: his Philosophical Critics and Successors* (1991).

Routledge History of Philosophy
General Editors – G. H. R. Parkinson and S. G. Shanker

The *Routledge History of Philosophy* provides a chronological survey of the history of Western philosophy, from its beginnings in the sixth century BC to the present time. It discusses all major philosophical developments in depth. Most space is allocated to those individuals who, by common consent, are regarded as great philosophers. But lesser figures have not been neglected, and together the ten volumes of the *History* include basic and critical information about every significant philosopher of the past and present. These philosophers are clearly situated within the cultural and, in particular, the scientific context of their time.

The *History* is intended not only for the specialist, but also for the student and the general reader. Each chapter is by an acknowledged authority in the field. The chapters are written in an accessible style and a glossary of technical terms is provided in each volume.

Each volume contains 10–15 chapters by different contributors

Routledge History of Philosophy
Volume V

British Philosophy and the Age of Enlightenment

EDITED BY
Stuart Brown

London and New York

Mohawk Valley Community College Library

First published 1996
by Routledge
11 New Fetter Lane, London EC4P 4EE

Simultaneously published in the USA and Canada
by Routledge
29 West 35th Street, New York, NY 10001

selection and editorial matter © 1996 Stuart Brown
individual chapters © 1996 the contributors

Phototypeset in Garamond by
Intype, London

Printed and bound in Great Britain by
TJ Press (Padstow) Ltd, Padstow, Cornwall

All rights reserved. No part of this book may be reprinted or reproduced or
utilized in any form or by any electronic, mechanical, or other means, now
known or hereafter invented, including photocopying and recording, or in any
information storage or retrieval system, without permission in writing from the
publishers.

British Library Cataloguing in Publication Data
A catalogue record for this book is available from the British Library

Library of Congress Cataloguing in Publication Data
A catalogue record for this book has been requested

ISBN 0–415–05379–X

Ref
B
72
.R68
1993
v. 5

Contents

General editors' preface

The history of philosophy, as its name implies, represents a union of two very different disciplines, each of which imposes severe constraints upon the other. As an exercise in the history of ideas, it demands that one acquire a 'period eye': a thorough understanding of how the thinkers whom it studies viewed the problems which they sought to resolve, the conceptual frameworks in which they addressed these issues, their assumptions and objectives, their blind spots and miscues. But as an exercise in philosophy, we are engaged in much more than simply a descriptive task. There is a crucial critical aspect to our efforts: we are looking for the cogency as much as the development of an argument, for its bearing on questions which continue to preoccupy us as much as the impact which it may have had on the evolution of philosophical thought.

The history of philosophy thus requires a delicate balancing act from its practitioners. We read these writings with the full benefit of historical hindsight. We can see why the minor contributions remained minor and where the grand systems broke down: sometimes as a result of internal pressures, sometimes because of a failure to overcome an insuperable obstacle, sometimes because of a dramatic technological or sociological change, and, quite often, because of nothing more than a shift in intellectual fashion or interests. Yet, because of our continuing philosophical concern with many of the same problems, we cannot afford to look dispassionately at these works. We want to know what lessons are to be learned from the inconsequential or the glorious failures; many times we want to plead for a contemporary relevance in the overlooked theory or to consider whether the 'glorious failure' was indeed such or simply ahead of its time: perhaps even ahead of its author.

We find ourselves, therefore, much like the mythical 'radical translator' who has so fascinated modern philosophers, trying to understand an author's ideas in their and their culture's eyes, and, at the same time, in our own. It can be a formidable task. Many times we fail in the historical undertaking because our philosophical interests are so strong, or lose sight of the latter because we are so enthralled by the former. But the nature of philosophy is such that we are compelled to master both techniques. For learning about the history of philosophy is not just a challenging and engaging pastime: it is an essential element in learning about the nature of philosophy – in grasping how philosophy is intimately connected with and yet distinct from both history and science.

The *Routledge History of Philosophy* provides a chronological survey of the history of western philosophy, from its beginnings up to the present time. Its aim is to discuss all major philosophical developments in depth, and, with this in mind, most space has been allocated to those individuals who, by common consent, are regarded as great philosophers. But lesser figures have not been neglected, and it is hoped that the reader will be able to find, in the ten volumes of the *History*, at least basic information about any significant philosopher of the past or present.

Philosophical thinking does not occur in isolation from other human activities, and this *History* tries to situate philosophers within the cultural, and in particular the scientific, context of their time. Some philosophers, indeed, would regard philosophy as merely ancillary to the natural sciences; but even if this view is rejected, it can hardly be denied that the sciences have had a great influence on what is now regarded as philosophy, and it is important that this influence should be set forth clearly. Not that these volumes are intended to provide a mere record of the factors that influenced philosophical thinking; philosophy is a discipline with its own standards of argument, and the presentation of the ways in which these arguments have developed is the main concern of this *History*.

In speaking of 'what is now regarded as philosophy', we may have given the impression that there now exists a single view of what philosophy is. This is certainly not the case; on the contrary, there exist serious differences of opinion, among those who call themselves philosophers, about the nature of their subject. These differences are reflected in the existence at the present time of two main schools of thought, usually described as 'analytic' and 'continental' philosophy respectively. It is not our intention, as general editors of this *History*, to take sides in this dispute. Our attitude is one of tolerance, and our hope is that these volumes will contribute to an understanding of how philosophers have reached the positions which they now occupy.

One final comment. Philosophy has long been a highly technical subject, with its own specialized vocabulary. This *History* is intended not only for the specialist but also for the general reader. To this end, we have tried to ensure that each chapter is written in an accessible style; and since technicalities are unavoidable, a glossary of technical terms is provided in each volume. In this way these volumes will, we hope, contribute to a wider understanding of a subject which is of the highest importance to all thinking people.

G. H. R. Parkinson
S. G. Shanker

Notes on contributors

number of articles on ethics, and on the philosophy of

David Berman is Associate Professor of Philosophy and Fellow of Trinity College, Dublin. He is the author of *A History of Atheism in Britain: from Hobbes to Russell* (1988) and *George Berkeley: Idealism and the Man* (1994) as well as the editor of *George Berkeley's Alciphron in Focus* (1993).

Stuart Brown is Professor of Philosophy at the Open University. He wrote *Leibniz* (1984) for the 'Philosophers in Context' series and is the author of a number of articles on late seventeenth and eighteenth century philosophy. The books he has edited include *Philosophers of the Enlightenment (1979)*, and *Malebranche: Philosophical Critics and Successors* (1991).

Ian Harris is Lecturer in Political Theory at the University of Leicester. He is the author of *The Mind of John Locke: a study of political theory in its intellectual setting* (1994) and editor of *Edmund Burke: Pre-Revolutionary Writings* (1993). He has also written on the theory of international relations.

Rosalind Hursthouse is Senior Lecturer in Philosophy at the Open University. She is the author of several articles on virtue ethics and of *Beginning Lives* (1987), a book on abortion.

Sarah Hutton is Reader in the School of Humanities and Education at the University of Hertfordshire. She is editor of *Henry More (1614–1687): Tercentenary Studies (1989)*; co-editor of *New Perspectives on Renaissance Thought (1990)*; and Director of the series *International Archives in the History of Ideas*. She has also revised Marjorie Nicolson's edition of the correspondence of Henry More and Anne Conway, *The Conway Letters* (1992).

Anne Jaap Jacobson is Associate Professor of Philosophy at the University of Houston. In addition to her several articles on Hume, she has published papers on topics in metaphysics, epistemology and philosophy of mind. Some of her recent work also reflects issues in feminism/postmodernism.

Peter Jimack is Emeritus Professor of French at the University of Stirling. He has written books on Diderot and Rousseau, and a number of articles on aspects of eighteenth century French thought, also mostly concerning Diderot and Rousseau.

Manfred Kuehn is Associate Professor of Philosophy at Purdue University, Lafayette, Indiana, and is the author of *Scottish Common Sense in Germany, 1768–1800* (1987).

David McNaughton is Senior Lecturer in the Philosophy Department at Keele University. He is the author of *Moral Vision* (1988) and of a number of articles on ethics, and on the philosophy of religion.

Antonio Pérez-Ramos is Professor Titular at the University of Murcia. He is the author of *Francis Bacon's Idea of Science and the Maker's Knowledge Tradition* (1988) and a number of articles and contributions to collective works on the history of philosophy and of science.

G. A. J. Rogers is Professor of Philosophy at Keele University and the Editor of the *British Journal for the History of Philosophy*. He is the Editor (with the late Peter Nidditch) of *Drafts for the 'Essay Concerning Human Understanding' and Other Philosophical Writings* (vol. 1 1990, vols 2 and 3 forthcoming). He has also edited (with Alan Ryan) *Perspectives on Thomas Hobbes* (1989) and, most recently, *Locke's Philosophy: Content and Context* (1994). He is the author of numerous articles on the history of seventeenth century philosophy.

M. A. Stewart is Professor of the History of Philosophy at the University of Lancaster. He has worked extensively on the intellectual history of Scotland and Ireland in the eighteenth century, and has edited *Studies in the Philosophy of the Scottish Enlightenment* (Oxford, 1990).

Ian Tipton is Reader in Philosophy at the University of Wales, Swansea. His publications include *Berkeley: The Philosophy of Immaterialism* (1974), and he edited *Locke on Human Understanding: Selected Essays* (1977) in the Oxford Readings in Philosophy series.

Chronology

	Politics and religion	The arts
1620	Pilgrim Fathers sail for North America	Monteverdi, *Seventh Book of Madrigals*
1621	Huguenot rebellion against Louis XIII Cardinal Bellarmine d.	Van Dyck, *Rest on the Flight to Egypt*
1622	James I dissolves English parliament	Molière b.
1623	Maffeo Barberini becomes Pope Urban VIII	Byrd d. Bernini sculpture of David
1624	Donne, *Devotions upon Emergent Occasions*	Hals, *The Laughing Cavalier*
1625	James I of England (James VI of Scotland) d. Succeeded by Charles I	Orlando Gibbons d.
1626	Richelieu suppresses Chalais conspiracy	Façade of St Peter's, Rome, finished
1627	Huguenot uprising in France	Rembrandt, *The Money Changers*
1628	Bunyan b. Ignatius Loyola canonized	Velázquez, *Christ on the Cross*
1629	Charles I dissolves parliament (which does not meet again till 1640)	Rubens knighted by Charles I
1630	John Winthrop, English Puritan leader leads an expedition of 1,000 settlers and founds Boston	Beginning of the High Baroque period in Italy
1631		Donne d. Dryden b.
1632	Charles I issues charter for the colony of Maryland	Christopher Wren b.

Unless otherwise specified, the dates assigned to books or articles are the dates of publication, and the dates assigned to musical or stage works are those of first performance. The titles of works not written in English have been translated, unless they are better known in their original form.

Science and technology	Philosophy	
Alsted, *Encyclopaedia*	Bacon, *Novum Organum*	1620
Kepler's Epitome of the Copernican Astronomy banned by Catholic Church		1621
	Böhme, *The Signature of All Things*	1622
	Pascal b. Bacon, *Of the Advancement and Proficience of Learning*	1623
Briggs, *Logarithmical Arithmetic*	Bacon, *New Atlantis* Gassendi, *Exercises in the Form of Paradoxes against the Aristotelians* Herbert of Cherbury, *On Truth [De veritate . . .]*	1624
	Grotius, *On the Law of War and Peace [De Jure Belli ac Pacis]*	1625
Human temperature measured by thermometer	Bacon d.	1626
Boyle b. Kepler compiles Rudolphine Tables	Boyle b.	1627
Harvey, *Anatomical Exercise on the motion of the heart and the blood*	*c.* 1628 Descartes, *Rules for the Direction of the Mind* written Thomas Spencer, *The Art of Logick*	1628
Huygens b.		1629
Kepler d.		1630
		1631
Leeuwenhoek b. Galileo, *Dialogue on the Two Chief World Systems*	Spinoza b. Locke b.	1632

	Politics and religion	The arts
1633	First Particular (or Calvinistic) Baptist Church formed at Southwark, London	Van Dyck, *Charles I*
1634	Oberammergau Passion Play given for the first time	Milton, *Comus*
1635	Peace of Prague reduces combatants in Thirty Year's War	Poussin, *Kingdom of Flora*
1636	Dutch settle in Ceylon	1636–7 Mersenne, *Universal Harmony*
1637	Introduction of new liturgy in Scotland causes riots	Buxtehude b. Ben Johnson d.
1638	Scottish Covenant drawn up and signed	Milton, *Lycidas* Hobbema b. Poussin, *Et in Arcadia ego*
1639	First Bishops' War in Scotland	Monteverdi, *Adone* Rubens, *Judgment of Paris*
1640	Short Parliament and Long Parliament (–1653) in England Second Bishops' War in Scotland	Rembrandt, *Self Portrait at the age of 34*
1641	Catholic rebellion in Ireland	Van Dyck d.
1642	English Civil War begins All theatres in England closed by order of Puritans (–1660)	Monteverdi, *L'incoronazione di Poppea* Rembrandt, *Night Watch*
1643	Accession of Louis XIV	Frescobaldi d. Monteverdi d.
1644	Queen Christina begins her reign in Sweden	Rembrandt, *Woman taken in Adultery*
1645	Peace talks between Holy Roman Empire and France	Milton, *L'Allegro, Il Penseroso*
1646	First English Civil War ends	Henry Vaughan, *Poems*
1647–8	Second English Civil War	Henry More, *Philosophical Poems*
1648	Peace of Westphalia ends Thirty Years' War George Fox starts to preach about 'inner light'	Schütz, *Musicalia ad chorum sacrum*
1649	Charles I beheaded. Scots proclaim Charles II as king England declared a Commonwealth, Cromwell invades Ireland	William Drummond of Hawthornden d.
1650	Charles II lands in Scotland	Murillo, *The Holy Family with the Little Bird* Jan van Goyen, *View of Dordrecht*

Science and technology	Philosophy	
Galileo forced by Inquisition to abjure the theories of Copernicus		1633
Founding of the University of Utrecht		1634
Richelieu founds Académie Française Robert Hooke b.		1635
Harvard College founded	Joseph Glanvill b.	1636
Descartes, *Geometry* Swammerdam b.	Descartes, *Discourse on Method*	1637
Galileo, *Mathematical Discourses and Demonstrations* or/ *Discourses concerning two new sciences*	Malebranche b.	1638
Désargues publishes book on geometry		1639
Coke made from coal for first time	Hobbes, *The Elements of Law Natural and Politic*	1640
Cotton goods begin to be manufactured in Manchester	Descartes, *Meditations*	1641
Newton b. Galileo d.	Hobbes, *De Cive* White, *Three Dialogues on the World*	1642
Torricelli invents barometer		1643
	Descartes, *Principles of Philosophy* Digby, *Of the Immortality of Man's Soul* Gassendi, *Metaphysical Disquisition*	1644
Preliminary meetings of London scientists which leads to formation of Royal Society (1662)	Grotius d. Herbert of Cherbury, *On the causes of errors*	1645
Kircher constructs first projection lantern	Leibniz b.	1646
Torricelli d.	Bayle b.	1647
John Wilkins, *Mathematical Magic* J. B. van Helmont (posth.), *Ortus medicinae*	Mersenne d. Herbert of Cherbury d.	1648
Isbrand de Diemerbrock publishes a study of the plague Harvey, *Two Anatomical Exercises on the Circulation of the Blood*	Descartes, *The Passions of the Soul* Gassendi, *An Introduction [Syntagma] to the Philosophy of Epicurus*	1649
	Descartes d. Hobbes, *The Elements of Law, Moral and Political*	1650

XV

	Politics and religion	The arts
1651	Charles II crowned King of Scots: defeated by Cromwell at Worcester and flees to France English Navigation Act	Potter, *Landscape with Cows*
1652	Royalists pardoned English defeat Dutch at Battle of the Downs	Inigo Jones d. First opera house in Vienna
1653	Cromwell becomes Lord Protector Pascal joins Jansenists	Corelli b.
1654	Treaty of Westminster ends Anglo-Dutch War Queen Christina becomes a Catholic and abdicates	Webster (posth.), *Appius and Virginia*
1655	Cromwell dissolves Parliament Cromwell re-admits Jews into England	Cyrano de Bergerac d. Colgrave, *The English Treasury of Literature and Language*
1656	Spinoza excommunicated Harrington, *The Commonwealth of Oceana* Bunyan, *Some Gospel Truths Opened*	Cyrano de Bergerac (posth.), *The Other World Comical History of the States and Empires of the Moon* Opening of the first London opera house
1657	Richard Baxter, *A Call to the Unconverted*	Rembrandt, portrait of his son Titus
1658	Cromwell d. Succeeded as Lord Protector by his son Richard (–1659) Harrington, *The Prerogative of Popular Government*	
1659	Peace of Pyrenees between France and Spain	
1660	Charles II enters London Harrington, *Political Discourses*	Dryden, *Astrea Redux* Velásquez d.
1661	Louis XIV begins personal rule Coronation of Charles II	
1662	Act of Uniformity gives assent to revised English prayer book	Molière, *L'Ecole des femmes*
1663	Writings of Descartes put on Index	Lully, *Le Ballet des arts*
1664	English annex New Netherlands and rename New Amsterdam as New York	Molière, *Le Tartuffe* Wren's Sheldonian Theatre, Oxford, begun Schütz, *Christmas Oratorio*
1665	Bunyan, *The Holy City*	*Journal des Savants* started in Paris

Science and technology	Philosophy	
Riccoli's map of the moon Harvey, *Two Anatomical exercises concerning the Generation of Animals*	Hobbes, *Leviathan*	1651
Guericke invents air pump	Culverwell, *An Elegant and Learned Discourse of the Light of Nature*	1652
Johann Schultes' book on surgical instruments and procedures published	More, *An Antidote against Atheisme*	1653
Jacques Bernoulli b. Pascal and Fermat develop theory of probability	Charleton, *Physiologia Epicuro-gassendo-Charltonia: a Fabrick of Science Natural upon the Hypothesis of Atoms . . .*	1654
	Hobbes, *De Corpore* Gassendi d. 1655–62 Stanley, *A History of Philosophy*	1655
Edmund Halley b.	White, *Peripatetical Institutions*	1656
Huygens designs first pendulum clocks	1657–9 More's correspondence with Descartes (conducted 1648–9)	1657
Swammerdam observes red corpuscles	Gassendi, *Elements of Logic* Hobbes, *De homine*	1658
	More, *The Immortality of the Soul*	1659
	Pufendorf, *Two Books on the Elements of Universal Jurisprudence* Smith, *Select Discourses*	1660
Boyle, *The Sceptical Chemist*	Glanvill, *The Vanity of Dogmatizing*	1661
Royal Society founded	Arnauld and Nicole, *Logic, or the Art of Thinking*	1662
Boyle, *Concerning the Usefulness of Experimental Philosophy*		1663
	Clauberg, *The Union of Body and Soul in Man*	1664
Newton discovers differential and integral calculus Hooke, *Micrographia*	Glanvill, *Scepsis Scientifica* White, *An Exclusion of Sceptickes from all Title to Dispute*	1665

	Politics and religion	The arts
1666	France and Holland declare war on England	Molière, *Le Misanthrope*
1667	Peace of Breda between Holland, France and England	Milton, *Paradise Lost*
1668	Murder of brothers De Witt in the Netherlands	Buxtehude becomes organist of St Mary's, Lübeck
1669	Locke's constitution for Carolina approved, S. Carolina founded	Rembrandt d. Racine, *Britannicus*
1670	William of Orange made Captain-General of United Provinces	Molière, *Le Bourgeois gentilhomme* Racine, *Bérénice*
1671	Bunyan, *A Confession of my Faith*	Aphra Behn, *The Forced Marriage* Milton, *Paradise Regained*
1672	France invades Netherlands Declaration of Indulgence issued by Charles II (withdrawn 1673)	Addison b. Dryden, *Marriage à la mode* Molière, *Les Femmes savantes*
1673	Test Act excludes Roman Catholics from office in England	Molière d.
1674	Office of Stadholders of the United Provinces becomes hereditary in the House of Orange	Lully, *Alceste* Milton d.
1675		Vermeer d. Wren begins rebuilding St Paul's Cathedral
1676	Nathaniel Bacon, *Declaration of the People of Virginia*	Murillo, *Madonna purissima*
1677	William III of Orange marries Princess Mary of England Webster, *The Displaying of Supposed Witchcraft*	Racine, *Phèdre*
1678	Popish Plot leads to further restrictions on Roman Catholics Simon, *Critical History of the Old Testament*	Bunyan, *The Pilgrim's Progress*, Part I Aphra Behn, *Oroonoko*
1679	Habeas Corpus Amendment Act in England Gilbert Burnet, *History of the Reformation of the Church of England, Vol. I*	Scarlatti's first opera performed in Rome

Science and technology	Philosophy	
Newton measures moon's orbit Académie Royale des Sciences founded	De La Forge, *Treatise on the Soul of Man* Cordemoy, *The Distinction between Body and Soul*	1666
Sprat, *The History of the Royal Society of London*	More, *Enchiridion Ethicum* Samuel Parker, *A Free and Impartial Censure of the Platonick Philosophie*	1667
Hooke, *Discourse on Earthquakes* Newton constructs reflecting telescope Van Leeuwenhoek describes red corpuscles	Glanvill, *Plus Ultra* More, *Divine Dialogues*	1668
Swammerdam, *History of the Insects* Malpighi studies life and activities of silkworms		1669
Typical symptoms of diabetes first described	Spinoza, *Tractatus Theologico-Politicus*	1670
Rohault, *Treatise on Physics*	Third Earl of Shaftesbury b. Glanvill, *Philosophia Pia* More, *Enchiridion Metaphysicum*	1671
Josselyn, *New England's Rarities Discovered*	Cumberland, *Philosophical Disquisition on the Laws of Nature* Pufendorf, *On the Laws of Nature and of Nations*	1672
French explorers reach headwaters of Mississippi River		1673
	1674–5 Malebranche, *Search after Truth*	1674
Leibniz's independent discovery of the differential and integral calculus Newton begins to write his *Optics*	1675–9 More, Complete Works (in Latin)	1675
Sydenham, *Medical Observations*	Cuperus, *The Secrets of Atheism Revealed . . . through an Examination of the Tractatus Theologico-Politicus*	1676
Isaac Barrow d.	Spinoza d. Knorr von Rosenroth, *Kabbala denudata*, Vol. I Rust, *A Discourse of Truth* Spinoza, *Ethics* (posth.)	1677
Hugyens writes *Treatise on Light*	Bernier, *Epitome [Abrégé] of the Philosophy of Gassendi* Cudworth, *The True Intellectual System of the Universe*	1678
Halley, *Catalogue of Australian Stars*	Hobbes d. Wolff b.	1679

	Politics and religion	The arts
1680	French colonial empire in North America Filmer, *Patriarcha*	Purcell becomes organist of Westminster Abbey
1681	Royal Charter of Pennsylvania	
1682	Revocation of Edict of Nantes: 58,000 French Huguenots forced to conversion	Murillo d. Van Ruisdael d.
1683	Rye House Plot to assassinate Charles II discovered	Purcell made court composer to Charles II
1684	Bermudas become crown colony	Bunyan, *The Pilgrim's Progress* Part II Bayle, *Nouvelles de la République des Lettres* first published in Amsterdam
1685	Charles II d. Succeeded by his brother as James II Monmouth's Rebellion Louis XIV revokes Edict of Nantes Many Protestants flee France	J. S. Bach d. Handel b. Scarlatti b.
1686	League of Augsburg against Louis XIV	Lully, *Armide et Renaud*
1687	James II issues Declaration of Indulgence for liberty of conscience	Fénelon, *Treatise on the Education of Girls* Lully d.
1688	William of Orange invited to accept English throne, lands at Torbay and enters London. James II escapes to France	Bunyan d. Pope b.
1689	Declaration of Rights William and Mary proclaimed King and Queen of England and Scotland Louis XIV declares war on Britain	Aphra Behn d. Richardson b. Purcell, *Dido and Aeneas*
1690	William III defeats James II at the Battle of the Boyne	*Athenian Gazette* founded in London

Science and technology	Philosophy	
Swammerdam d.	Malebranche, *Treatise of Nature and of Grace*	1680
Academy of Sciences founded in Moscow Thomas Burnet, *Sacred Theory of the Earth*		1681
Acta eruditorum first published in Leipzig	F. M. Van Helmont, *A Cabbalistical Dialogue in Answer to the Opinion . . . that the World was made out of Nothing*	1682
Newton explains mathematical theory of tides	Arnauld, *True and False Ideas* Rust, *A Discourse of the Use of Reason in Matters of Religion* Spinoza/Blount? *Miracles no Violation of Laws of Nature*	1683
	Leibniz, 'Meditations on Knowledge, Truth and Ideas' Malebranche, *Treatise on Ethics*	1684
	Berkeley b.	1685
Willughby, (*Historia piscium*) Fontenelle, *Dialogues on the Plurality of Worlds*	Fontenelle, *Doubts about the Physical System of Occasional Causes* Leibniz writes *Discourse on Metaphysics* (not published till nineteenth century)	1686
Newton, *Principia*		1687
	Malebranche, *Dialogues on Metaphysics and Religion* Norris, *The Theory and Regulation of Love*	1688
	First English translation of Spinoza's *Tractatus Theologico-Politicus* Norris, *Reason and Religion*	1689
Huygens, *Treatise on Light*	Locke, *Essay concerning Human Understanding* Locke, *Two Treatises of Civil Government* Norris, 'Cursory Reflections upon a Book call'd An Essay concerning Human Understanding', appended to *Christian Blessedness*	1690

	Politics and religion	The arts
1691	Treaty of Limerick: William III King of Ireland Ray, *The Wisdom of God in the Works of Creation*	
1692	French fleet destroyed by English at La Hogue First Boyle lectures on natural theology given by Richard Bentley	Purcell, *The Fairy Queen*
1693	French defeat English merchant fleet at Battle of Lagos Blount, *Summary Account of the Deist's Religion*	Congreve, *The Old Bachelor*
1694	Death of Queen Mary, William III accepted as King in his own right	Voltaire b.
1695	Locke, *The Reasonableness of Christianity* End of government press censorship in England	Henry Vaughan d. Purcell d.
1696	Habeas Corpus Act suspended in England Toland, *Christianity not Mysterious*	
1697	French attempt to colonize west Africa Stillingfleet, *A Letter to a Deist* Matthias Earbery, *Deism Examined and Confuted*	Canaletto b. Hogarth b.
1698	Blasphemy Act in England Society for Promoting Christian Knowledge founded in London William Sherlock, *The Present State of the Socinian Controversy*	
1699	Gilbert Burnet, *Exposition of the Thirty-nine Articles*	Fénelon, *Télémaque* Racine d.

Science and technology	Philosophy	
Boyle, d. Leibniz, *Protogaea*	Régis, *Complete Course of Philosophy,* or *General System, according to* *Descartes' Principle*	1691
Burnet, *Archaeologiae philosophicae* Malebranche, *The Laws of the* *Communication of Motion*	Joseph Butler b. Conway, *The Principles of the Most* *Ancient and Modern Philosophy*	1692
	Latin orations by Addison and other Oxford students defending the new philosophy Locke writes his *Examination of P.* *Malebranche's Opinion of Seeing All* *Things in God* (published in 1704)	1693
Camerarius, *Letters on the Sex of* *Plants*	Hutcheson b. Locke writes his *Remarks on Some of* *Mr Norris's Books* (published 1720) Translations of Malebranche's *Search* *after Truth* and *Treatise on Nature and* *Grace* James Lowde, *A Discourse concerning* *the Nature of Man*	1694
Huygens d. Woodward, *Essay towards a Natural* *History of the Earth*	Leibniz, *New System* Norris and Mary Astell, *Letters* *concerning the Love of God*	1695
	Blount, *Anima Mundi* Damaris Masham, *A Discourse* *Concerning the Love of God* John Sergeant, *The Method to Science* 1696–7 Controversy between Locke and Stillingfleet	1696
	Bayle, *Historical and Critical* *Dictionary* Burgersdijck, *Monitio Logica, an* *Abstract of Logic* (trans. of 1626 edition of *Institutionum logicarum*) Sergeant, *Solid Philosophy Asserted,* *against the Fancies of the Ideists . . .*	1697
	Fardella, *The Nature of the Human* *Soul as Revealed by Augustine*	1698
Dampier explores north-west coast of Australia	Malebranche, *A Treatise of Morality* (trans. of 1684 book) Lowde, *Moral Essays: Wherein some of* *Mr Locke's and Monsr Malebranche's* *Opinions are Briefly examined*	1699

	Politics and religion	The arts
1700	Pope Innocent XII d. Gian Francesco Albani becomes Pope Clement XI (–1721)	Congreve, *The Way of the World*
1701	Act of Settlement provides for Protestant succession in England of House of Hanover	Steele, *The Funeral, or Grief à la Mode*
1702	William III d. succeeded by Queen Anne Toland (anon.), *Reasons for Addressing His Majesty to Invite into England Their Highnesses*	
1703	John Wesley b. Jonathan Edwards b.	
1704	British take Gibraltar	Swift, *The Battle of the Books* Handel, *St John Passion* J. S. Bach writes his first cantata
1705	Gildon, *Deist's Manual* Tolard (anon.), *Socinianism Truly Stated*	
1706	Tindal, *Rights of the Christian Church* Marlborough conquers Spanish Netherlands	Johann Pachelbel d.
1707	Union of England and Scotland as Great Britain Collins, *An Essay Concerning the use of Reason*	Henry Fielding b. Dietrich Buxtehude d.
1708	British capture Minorca and Sardinia Charles Leslie, *The Socinian Controversy Discuss'd*	Professorship of Poetry founded at Oxford University
1709	Marlborough and Prince Eugene take Tournai and Mons and defeat French at Malplaquet Collins, *Priestcraft in Perfection*	Samuel Johnson b. Meindert Hobbema d. Invention of the pianoforte First issue of *The Tatler*
1710	Mauritius becomes French	*The Examiner* issued for first time
1711	French capture Rio de Janeiro Swift, *An Argument against Abolishing Christianity*	Pope, *Essay on Criticism* Handel, *Rinaldo* *Spectator* begun by Addison and Steele

Science and technology	Philosophy	
Berlin Academy of Sciences founded		1700
Yale College founded	1701–4 Norris, *An Essay towards the Theory of the Ideal or Intelligible World*	1701
	Henry Lee, *Anti-Scepticism* Catharine Trotter, *A Defence of Mr Locke's Essay on Human Understanding*	1702
Isaac Newton elected President of the Royal Society	1703–5 Leibniz's *New Essays on Human Understanding* written	1703
Newton, *Optics*	Locke d. Clarke, *A Discourse Concerning the Being and Attributes of God* Toland, *Letters to Serena*	1704
Halley predicts return in 1758 of the comet seen in 1682 John Ray d.	Astell, *The Christian Religion as Profess'd by A Daughter of the Church* 1705–29 Mandeville, *Fable of the Bees* Clarke, *A Discourse Concerning the Unchangeable Obligations of Natural Religion . . .*	1705
Römer's catalogue of astronomical observations	Boyle d. William Carroll, *A Dissertation upon the Tenth Chapter of the Fourth Book of Mr Locke's Essay Concerning Human Understanding* P. King (ed.) *Posthumous Works of Mr John Locke*	1706
Linnaeus (Carl von Linné) b.	1707–8 Berkeley writes his *Philosophical Commentaries* Leibniz writes comments on Locke's 'Examination' of Malebranche's seeing all things in God	1707
Hermann Boerhaave, *Medical Principles*	Norris, *A Philosophical Discourse concerning the Natural Immortality of the Soul*	1708
	Berkeley, *New Theory of Vision* Shaftesbury, *The Moralists; a philosophical Rhapsody* Vico, *The Ancient Wisdom of the Italians*	1709
Jacob Christoph Le Blon invents three-colour printing	Leibniz, *Theodicy* Berkeley, *Principles of Human Knowledge* Thomas Reid b.	1710
	Shaftesbury, *Characteristics* Hume b. Norris d.	1711

	Politics and religion	The arts
1712	Last execution for witchcraft in England Peace congress opens at Utrecht	Swift, *A Proposal for Correcting the English Language*
1713	Peace of Utrecht signed. King Frederick I of Russia d. (succeeded by Frederick William I) Collins, *A Discourse on Freethinking* Bentley, *Remarks upon the Late Discourse on Freethinking*	Addison, *Cato* Laurence Sterne b.
1714	Queen Anne d. succeeded by George Louis, Elector of Hanover, as George I	Gluck b.
1715	Jacobite rebellion Louis XIV d. followed by regency of the Duke of Orleans	Early beginning of rococo
1716	Treaty of Westminster (between Britain and Emperor Charles VI) Christian religious teaching prohibited in China	Lancelot 'Capability' Brown b.
1717	Peter the Great in Paris United (Masonic) Grand Lodge of England founded	Handel's *Water Music* first performed on Thames
1718	Quadruple Alliance signed by France, the Empire, Britain and Holland	Voltaire imprisoned in the Bastille
1719	France declares war on Spain Jesuits expelled from Russia	Defoe, *Robinson Crusoe* Handel, director of Royal Academy of Music
1720	'South Sea Bubble' bursts Prince Charles Edward Stuart, the 'Young Pretender' b.	Old Haymarket Theatre opens in London Canaletto b.
1721	Peter I proclaimed Emperor of All the Russias	J. S. Bach, *The Brandenburg Concertos* Telemann arrives in Hamburg as Director of music
1722		Defoe, *Moll Flanders*
1723	Louis XV attains majority	J. S. Bach, *St John Passion* Wren d. Joshua Reynolds b.
1724	Pope Innocent III d. Pierro Francesco Orsini becomes Pope Benedict XIII	Longman's (publishers) founded

Science and technology	Philosophy	
	Rousseau b. Berkeley, *Passive Obedience*	1712
Newton, *Principia (2nd edn)*	Berkeley, *Dialogues between Hylas and Philonous* Collier, *Clavis universalis* Shaftesbury d. Wolff, *Rational Thoughts on the Powers of the Human Understanding* Derham, *Physico-Theology* Diderot b.	1713
Fahrenheit constructs mercury thermometer	Baumgarten b. Leibniz writes his *Monadology*	1714
Brooke Taylor invents calculus of finite differences	Malebranche d. Crusius b. Helvétius b. 1715–16 Leibniz engaged in correspondence with Samuel Clarke Collins, *Philosophical Inquiry concerning Liberty*	1715
	Leibniz d.	1716
Innoculation against smallpox introduced in England	d'Alembert b.	1717
First bank notes in England Porcelain manufactured for first time in Vienna		1718
		1719
Charles Bonnet, Swiss entomologist b.	Wolff, *German Metaphysics* Toland, *Pantheisticon*	1720
Regular postal service established between London and New England	Berkeley, *De motu* Montesquieu, *Persian Letters*	1721
R. A. Ferchault de Réaumur writes on steel making	Wollaston, *The Religion of Nature Delineated*	1722
Anthony van Leeuwenhoek d.	Adam Smith b. Richard Price b. d'Holbach b.	1723
Boerhaave, *The Elements of Chemistry*	Kant b.	1724

	Politics and religion	The arts
1725	Peter the Great d. succeeded by his wife, Catherine	James Thompson, *The Seasons* Canaletto, *Four Views of Venice* Alessandro Scarlatti d.
1726	St John of the Cross canonized	First circulation library established by Allan Ramsey in Edinburgh Voltaire flees to England Swift, *Gulliver's Travels*
1727	George I d. succeeded by son as George II Catherine I d. succeeded by grandson as Peter II Britain at war with Spain Quakers call for abolition of slavery	Gainsborough b.
1728	William Law, *A Serious Call* Madrid Lodge of Freemasons founded but soon suppressed by the Inquisition	Pope, *The Dunciad* Robert Adam b. John Gay, *Beggar's Opera*
1729	Treaty of Seville between France, Spain and Britain Founding of Baltimore	Congreve d. Steele d. J. S. Bach, *St Matthew Passion* Lessing b.
1730	Peter II d. succeeded by Anne Tindal, *Christianity as Old as the Creation*	Hogarth, *Before and After*
1731	Treaty of Vienna between Britain, Holland, Spain and the Holy Roman Empire Mass expulsion of Protestants from Salzburg	Defoe d. William Cowper b.
1732	George Washington b. King Frederick William I of Prussia settles 12,000 Salzburg Protestants in east Prussia	Haydn b.
1733	First German Masonic Lodge founded in Hamburg	1733-4 Pope, *An Essay on Man* J. S. Bach, *B Minor Mass* Couperin d.
1734	Swedenborg, *Prodromus philosophiae*	1733-5 Hogarth, *A Rake's Progress* Voltaire, *Letters on the English*

Science and technology	Philosophy	
Catherine I founds St Petersburg Academy of Science	Franklin, *Dissertation on Liberty and Necessity* Vico, *The New Science* Hutcheson, *Inquiry into the Original of Our Ideas of Beauty and Virtue*	1725
James Hutton, geologist b.	1726–9 Voltaire banished to England Butler, *Sermons*	1726
American Philosophical Society founded in Philadelphia Isaac Newton d.	Woolston, *A Discourse on the Miracles of our Saviour*	1727
James Cook, navigator and explorer b. Behring Strait discovered by Vitus Behring	1728–9 Balguy, *The Foundation of Moral Goodness* Hutcheson, *An Essay on the Nature and Conduct of the Passions and Affections* Wolff, *Rational Philosophy, or Logic*	1728
Newton's *Principal* translated into English Academia de buenas letras founded in Barcelona	Wolff, *First Philosophy, or Ontology* Moses Mendelssohn b. Burke b. Collins, *Dissertation on Liberty and Necessity* Mandeville, *The Fable of the Bees*, part 2	1729
Réaumur constructs alcohol thermometer Joseph Wedgwood b.	Collier, *A Specimen of True Philosophy*	1730
Erasmus Darwin b. John Hadley invents quadrant for use at sea	Cudworth (posth.), *A Treatise Concerning Eternal and Immutable Morality* Boulainvilliers, *Refutation of the Errors of Benedict Spinoza*	1731
	Berkeley, *Alciphron* Chubb, *The Sufficiency of Reason in Matters of Religion further considered* Wolff, *Empirical Psychology*	1732
John Kay patents his flying shuttle loom	Balfour, *An Enquiry into the Nature of the Human Soul* Balguy, *The Law of Truth* Campbell, *An Enquiry into the Original of Moral Virtue*	1733
	Balguy, *A Collection of Tracts, Moral and Theological* Wolff, *Rational Psychology* Voltaire, *Letters on the English* Voltaire, *Treatise on Metaphysics*	1734

	Politics and religion	The arts
1735	John Wesley writes his *Journals*	
1736	Porteous riots in Edinburgh William Warburton, *The Alliance between Church and State* English statutes against witchcraft repealed	Pergolesi d.
1737	Wesley, *Psalms and Hymns*	Gibbon b. Censorship introduced for London stage
1738	Papal bull against Freemasonry Conversion of John Wesley	
1739	Charles VI signs peace treaty as Turks approach Belgrade Mormon Church founded in America	Handel oratorios *Saul* and *Israel in Egypt*
1740	England and Spain at War in West Indies Charles VI d. succeeded by Maria Theresa Frederick the Great succeeds to throne of Prussia	James Boswell b. Richardson, *Pamela* Scarlatti in London and Dublin
1741	Frederick the Great conquers Silesia	Vivaldi d.
1742	Peace of Berlin ends First Silesian War	Handel, *The Messiah* Fielding, *Joseph Andrews* Pope, *The New Dunciad*
1743	Maria Theresa crowned in Prague George II defeats French at Dettingen	Hogarth, *Marriage à la mode* Boccherini b. B. Newmann begins Baroque Vierzehnheiligen church
1744	France declares war on England Second Silesian War begins	Pope d. Gluck, *Iphigénie en Aulide*
1745	Second Jacobite Rebellion begins	Swift d. Rousseau's opera, *Les Muses galantes*
1746	Charles Edward Stuart and his supporters routed at Culloden Annet, *Deism Fairly Stated*	Canaletto in England
1747	William IV of Orange becomes hereditary Stadholder of the seven provinces of the Netherlands	Johnson, *Plan of a Dictionary of the English Language*

Science and technology	Philosophy	
Linnaeus, *System of Nature*		1735
First successful operation for appendicitis Manufacture of glass begins in Venice James Watt, inventor, b.	*c.* 1736 Tetens b. 1736–7 Wolff, *Natural Theology* Butler, *Analogy of Religion*	1736
Réaumur, *History of the Insects*		1737
William Herschel b. First spinning machines patented in England	Voltaire, *Elements of the Philosophy of Newton*	1738
John Winthrop publishes his *Notes on Sunspots*	Baumgarten, *Metaphysics* 1739–40 Hume, *Treatise of Human Nature*	1739
University of Pennsylvania founded Frederick the Great founds the Berlin Academy of Sciences Huntsman invents crucible steel process in Sheffield	Chubb, *An Enquiry into the Ground and Foundation of Religion*	1740
Linnaeus founds Botanical Garden, Uppsala	Chubb, *A Discourse on Miracles . . .* Turnbull, *A Discourse upon the Nature and Origin of Moral and Civil Laws*	1741
Celsius invents centigrade thermometer	1742–7 Brucker, *Critical History of Philosophy* Henry Dodwell, *Christianity Not Founded on Argument*	1742
French explorers reach Rocky Mountains d'Alembert, *Treatise on Dynamics*	Jacobi b. Crusius, *On the Use and Limits of the Principle of Determining Reason* Saint-Hyacinthe, *Philosophical Enquiries . . .* Voltaire, *Philosophical Letters*	1743
Lamarck b. Sir George Anson returns from voyage around the world	Vico d. Berkeley, *Siris*	1744
Bonnet, *Treatise on the Study of Insects* Colden, *An Explication of the First Causes of Action in Malts*	Crusius, *A Sketch of the Necessary Truths of Reason* La Mettrie, *Natural History of the Soul*	1745
First geographical map of France	Hutcheson d. Condillac, *Treatise on Systems* Condillac, *Essay on the Origin of Human Knowledge*	1746
Hartley, *Observations on Man*	Crusius, *The Way to the Certainty and Reliability of Human Knowledge* Gerdil, *The Immateriality of the Soul Demonstrated against Locke*	1747

	Politics and religion	The arts
1748	Peace of Aix-la-Chappelle ends War of Austrian Succession	Richardson, *Clarissa* Smollett, *Roderick Random* Voltaire, *Zadig*
1749	First settlement of Ohio Company	Fielding, *Tom Jones* J. S. Bach, *The Art of Fugue* Goethe b. Gainsborough, *Mr and Mrs Robert Andrews*
1750	Spanish-Portuguese treaty on S. America Frederick the Great, *Works of the Philosophy of Sanssouci*	J. S. Bach d. Neoclassicism spreading over Europe
1751	Britain joins Austro-Russian alliance against Prussia	Thomas Gray, *Elegy written in a Country Churchyard* Fielding, *Amelia*
1752	Gregorian calendar adopted in Britain	Voltaire, *Micromégas*
1753	French troops from Canada seize Ohio Valley Turgot, *Lettres à un grand vicaire sur la tolérance*	British Museum founded Horace Walpole begins Gothic revival building *Strawberry Hill*
1754	British and French troops clash in the Ohio Valley and contest for North America resumed	Hume, *History of England* (1754–62) John Wood begins Circus at Bath Hogarth, *The Election* Fielding d.
1755	Great Lisbon earthquake	Johnson, *Dictionary* Winckelmann, *On the Imitation of Greek Painting and Sculpture*

Science and technology	Philosophy	
La Mettrie, *The Man Machine* Invention of wool-carding machine	Bentham b. Hume, *Enquiry Concerning Human Understanding* Maupertuis, *Philosophical Reflections on the Origin of Languages and the Meaning of Words* Montesquieu, *The Spirit of Laws*	1748
Hartley, *Observations on Man* Buffon, *Natural History Vols 1–3* Euler, *Analysis of Infinites*	Diderot, *Letters on the Blind* Maupertuis, *Essay on Moral Philosophy*	1749
J. T. Mayer, *Map of the Moon*	Baumgarten, *Aesthetics* vol. I Rousseau, *Discourse on the Arts and Sciences* La Mettrie, *Discourse on Happiness* Maupertuis, *Essay on Cosmology* Turgot, *Philosophical Panorama of the Progress of the Human Mind*	1750
Invention of breech-loading gun Linnaeus, *Philosophia Botanica* 1751–80 *Encyclopédie* of Diderot	d'Alembert, *Preliminary Discourse to the Encyclopedia of Diderot* Diderot, *Letter on the Deaf and Dumb* Hume, *Essays on the Principles of Morality and Natural Religion* Hume, *Enquiry Concerning the Principles of Morals* Maupertuis, *System of Nature*	1751
Franklin invents the lightning conductor	Butler d.	1752
Linnaeus, *Species of Plants*	Berkeley d. Dugald Stewart b.	1753
First iron-rolling mill at Fareham in Hampshire	Wolff d. Bonnet, *Essay on Psychology* Condillac, *Treatise on Sensations* Diderot, *On the Interpretation of Nature* 1754–6 Leland, *A View of the Principal Deistical Writers...*	1754
Joseph Black, *Experiments upon Magnesia, Quicklime, and other Alkaline Substances* Kant, *General Natural History and Theory of the Heavens*	Condillac, *Treatise on Animals* Condillac, *Dissertation on the Existence of God* Mendelssohn, *On Feelings* Rousseau, *Discourse on the Origin of Inequality* Reimanus, *The Principal Truths of Natural Religion Defended and Illuminated* (English translation 1766) Hutcheson, *A System of Moral Philosophy*	1755

	Politics and religion	The arts
1756	Start of Seven Years' War French drive British from the Great Lakes	Mozart b.
1757	Execution of Admiral Byng Clive wins at Plassey and takes control of Bengal Far East India Company	William Blake b. Fontenelle d. Scarlatti d.
1758	British capture Louisbourg (Cape Breton Island) from the French	Johnson starts the periodical *The Idler* John Carr and Robert Adam, *Harewood House* begun
1759	Jesuits expelled from Portugal British victory at Quebec	Handel d. Voltaire, *Candide* Johnson, *Rasselas*
1760	Accession of George III British capture Montreal	Macpherson's 'Ossian' Fragments Sterne, *Tristram Shandy* books 1 & 2
1761	British capture Cuba, the French Antilles and Pondicherry	Diderot, *Rameau's Nephew* Rousseau, *The New Héloise* Richardson d.
1762	British capture Martinique, Grenada, Havana and Manila Accession of Catherine the Great Jesuits expelled from France	Gluck, *Orpheus and Euridice* Stuart and Revett, *Classical Antiquities of Athens* Mozart tours Europe as infant musical prodigy
1763	Voltaire, *Treatise on Toleration* Seven Years' War ends	Boswell meets Johnson for first time
1764	Beccaria, *On Crimes and Punishments* Meslier (posth.), 'The Testament of Jean Meslier', in Voltaire, *The Gospel of Reason*	Work begun on Pantheon in Paris Mozart writes his first symphony Hogarth d.
1765	Stamp Act imposed on American colonies	Thomas Percy and William Shenstone, *Reliques of Ancient English Poetry*
1766	Declaratory Act asserts Britain's right to tax American Colonies	Goldsmith, *The Vicar of Wakefield* Lessing, *Laocoön*
1767	First Mysore War Jesuits expelled from Spain and Portugal d'Holbach, *Christianity Unmasked*	Edward Craig's plan for the new town of Edinburgh accepted Rousseau settles in England
1768	France buys Corsica from Genoa Boston citizens refuse to quarter British troops	Sterne, *Sentimental Journey* Founding of Royal Academy of Art

Science and technology	Philosophy	
Cotton velvet first made at Bolton, Lancashire	Burke, *Vindication of Natural Society* Godwin b.	1756
Réaumur d.	Burke, *The Origins of Our Ideas of the Sublime and the Beautiful* Hume, *Natural History of Religion*	1757
Quesnay, *Economic Table* Bridgewater Canal between Liverpool and Leeds begun	Baumgarten, *Aesthetics* vol. II Helvétius, *On the Spirit* Price, *Review of the Principal Questions in Morals* Jermyn, *A Free Inquiry into the Nature and Origin of Evil*	1758
Bavarian Academy of Science founded British Museum opened (at Montagu House)	Gerard, *An Essay on Taste* Smith, *Theory of Moral Sentiments*	1759
Botanical Gardens at Kew opened Wedgwood founds pottery works at Etruria (Staffs)	Bonnet, *Analytical Essay on the Faculties of the Mind*	1760
Süssmilch initiates study of statistics		1761
Cast iron converted into malleable iron at Carron, Stirlingshire Bridgewater Canal opened Bonnet, *Reflections on Organised Bodies*	Rousseau, *Social Contract* Rousseau, *Émile* Fichte b.	1762
	Campbell, *A Dissertation on Miracles* Mendelssohn, *Philosophical Conversations*	1763
Hargreaves invents spinning-jenny 1764–5 Bonnet, *Contemplation de la nature*	Mendelssohn, *Essays on Evidence in Metaphysical Science* Reid, *Inquiry into the Human Mind on the Principles of Common Sense* Voltaire, *Philosophical Dictionary*	1764
Turgot, *Reflections on the Formation and Distribution of Wealth*	Leibniz (posth.), *New Essays concerning Human Understanding*	1765
Cavendish discovers hydrogen Bougainville circumnavigates the globe	Ferguson, *Essay on Civil Society*	1766
Priestley, *The History and present State of Electricity*	Mendelssohn, *Phaedon*	1767
Cook embarks on his first voyage of discovery in the South Seas	Naigeon, *The Military Philosopher, or Difficulties concerning Religion, proposed to Father Malebranche* Priestley, *Essays on the First Principles of Government* 1768–77 Tucker, *The Light of Nature Pursued*	1768

	Politics and religion	The arts
1769	Napoleon b. Arthur Wellesley, future Duke of Wellington, b.	Adam Brothers, Adelphi, London Diderot writes *The Dream of d'Alembert* (pub 1830)
1770	Dauphin marries Marie-Antoinette 'Boston Massacre' Edmund Burke, *Thoughts on the Cause of the Present Discontents*	Goldsmith, *The Deserted Village* Beethoven b. Wordsworth b.
1771	Russia and Prussia agree over partition of Poland	Walter Scott b. Bougainville, *A Voyage round the World*
1772	Inquisition abolished in France Priestley, *Institutes of Natural and Revealed Religion*	Samuel Taylor Coleridge b. Friedrich von Novalis b.
1773	'Boston Tea Party'	Goethe, *Goetz von Berlichingen*
1774	Accession of Louis XVI in France First American Continental Congress	Goldsmith d. Caspar David Friedrich b. Goethe, *Werther*
1775	American Revolution begins Peasants revolt in Bohemia	Jane Austen b. Charles Lamb b. Johnson, *A Journey to the Western Isles of Scotland* Sheridan, *Rivals*
1776	American Declaration of Independence Americans driven out of Canada Price, *Observations on the Nature of Civil Liberty*	Gibbon, *Decline and Fall of the Roman Empire*, vol. I John Constable b. Mozart, *Haffner Serenade*
1777	British surrender at Saratoga	Sheridan, *The School for Scandal*
1778	Franco-American Alliance	William Hazlitt b.
1779	Washington defeats British at Monmouth, N.J.	Lessing, *Nathan the Wise* Thomas Chippendale d. Chardin d.

Science and technology	Philosophy	
Watt's steam engine patented Alexander von Humboldt b. First lightning conductors on high buildings G. L. Cuvier b.		1769
Euler, *Introduction to Algebra* Cook discovers Botany Bay in Australia	Hegel b. Beattie, *An Essay on the Nature and* *Immutability of Truth* Bonnet, *Palingénesie philosophique* d'Holbach, *System of Nature* Kant, *Inaugural Dissertation*	1770
Arkwright founds first spinning mill in England First edition of *Encyclopaedia* *Britannica*		1771
Daniel Rutherford discovers nitrogen	Ferguson, *Institutes of Moral* *Philosophy* Herder, *Treatise on the Origin of* *Language* Meiners, *Revision of Philosophy* Hemsterhuis, *Letter on Man and his* *Relationships*	1772
	Helvétius (posth.), *On Man* d'Holbach, *Social System*	1773
Priestley discovers oxygen		1774
Priestley discovers hydrochloric and sulphuric acids James Watt perfects his invention of the steam engine	Herder, *Philosophy of History and* *Culture* Tetens, *On Universal Speculative* *Philosophy* Crusius d.	1775
Smith, *Wealth of Nations*	Bentham, *Fragment on Government* Hume d. d'Holbach, *Universal Ethics*	1776
Howard, *Enquiry into the Present State* *of Prisons*	Priestley, *Disquisitions Relating to* *Matter and Spirit* Priestley, *The Doctrine of Philosophical* *Necessity Illustrated* Tetens, *Philosophical Essays*	1777
Cook discovers Hawaii Buffon, *The Epochs of Nature*	Rousseau d. Voltaire d.	1778
Spallanzani proves that semen is necessary for fertilization. First cast-iron bridge, near Coalbrookdale in Shropshire	Hume (posth.), *Dialogues concerning* *Natural Religion* Schiller, *Philosophy of Physiology*	1779

	Politics and religion	The arts
1780	Henry Grattan demands Home Rule for Ireland Serfdom abolished in Bohemia and Hungary Rebellion in Peru against Spanish rule	Sébastien Erard makes first modern pianoforte Lessing, *On the Education of the Human Race*
1781	Warren Hastings deposes Rajah of Benares	Lessing d. Schiller, *The Robbers*
1782	Spanish capture Minorca from Britain Priestley, *A History of the Corruptions of Christianity*	Fanny Burney, *Cecilia* Cowper, *Poems* Laclos, *Les Liaisons dangereuses*
1783	Britain concedes legislative independence to Irish Parliament Peace of Versailles ends war between Britain, France, Spain and America and establishes American independence	Mozart, *Mass in C minor* Beethoven's first works published
1784	Pitt's India Act brings East India Company under government control John Wesley's Deed of Declaration	Johnson d.
1785	Diamond Necklace Affair in Versailles discredits Marie Antoinette	Boswell, *Journal of a Tour of the Hebrides with Samuel Johnson*, D.D. J. L. David, *The Oath of the Horatii*
1786	Frederick the Great d.	Robert Burns, *Poems* Mozart, *The Marriage of Figaro*
1787	Association for the abolition of the slave trade founded in Britain Turkey declares war on Russia	Goethe, *Iphigenia in Tauris* Gluck d. Mozart, *Don Giovanni*
1788	U.S. constitution, ratified by New Hampshire, the ninth state, comes into force New York declared federal capital of the U.S.	Goethe, *Egmont* Gainsborough d.
1789	Fall of Bastille. Beginning of French Revolution Austrian Netherlands declare independence as Belgium	Blake, *Songs of Innocence*

Science and technology	Philosophy	
American Academy of Sciences founded	Schiller, *Essay on the Connections between Man's Animal and His Spiritual Nature*	1780
Herschel discovers planet Uranus	Kant, *Critique of Pure Reason* (1st edn)	1781
	Rousseau (posth.), *Confessions* vols 1–6	1782
Herschel, *Motion of the Solar System in Space* Ascent of Montgolfier air-balloon	d'Alembert d. Kant, *Prolegomena to Any Future Metaphysics* Mendelssohn, *Jerusalem, or on Religious Power and Judaism*	1783
First iron-rolling mill Andrew Meikle invents threshing machine	1784–91 Herder, *Ideas towards the Philosophy of the History of Mankind* Kant, 'What is Enlightenment?' Reinhold, 'Thoughts on Enlightenment'	1784
Seismograph for measuring earthquakes invented Hutton, *Theory of the Earth*	Mendelssohn, *Morning Hours, or Lectures on the Existence of God* Kant, *Foundations of the Metaphysics of Morals* Jacobi, *On the Doctrine of Spinoza* Diderot d. Reid, *Essays on the Intellectual Powers of Man* Paley, *Principles of Morals and Political Philosophy*	1785
First gas lighting Buffon, *Natural History of Birds*	Mendelssohn, *To the Friends of Lessing*	1786
Steamboat launched on Delaware River Lavoisier, *Method of Chemical Nomenclature*	Herder, *God: Some Conversations* Jacobi, *David Hume on Belief* Madison and Hamilton, *The Federalist* Kant, *Critique of Pure Reason* (2nd edn)	1787
Hutton, *New Theory of the Earth* Laplace, *Laws of the Planetary System*	Kant, *Critique of Practical Reason* Schopenhauer b. 1788–93 Feder (ed), *Philosophical Library* Reid, *Essays on the Active Powers of Man*	1788
Jussieu, *Species of Plants (Genera plantarum)* Louis Daguerre, pioneer of photography, b.	Bentham, *Introduction to the Principles of Morals and Legislation* Holbach d.	1789

	Politics and religion	The arts
1790	Austrians in Brussels, suppress Belgian revolution Burke, *Reflections on the Revolution in France*	Wollstonecraft, *Original Stories from Real Life* Mozart, *Così fan tutte*
1791	Paine, *The Rights of Man* part I Slave revolt in St Dominique (Haiti) Wilberforce's motion for abolition of slave trade carried through Parliament Unitarian Society founded in England	Mozart, *The Magic Flute* Boswell, *Life of Johnson*
1792	Wollstonecraft, *Vindication of the Rights of Women*	Haydn, *Sinfonia Concertante* Rossini b. Robert Adam d.
1793	Execution of Louis XVI and Marie-Antoinette Reign of Terror begins in France	David, *The Murder of Marat*
1794	Habeas Corpus Act suspended in Britain (–1804) Freedom of worship in France Paine, *The Age of Reason* part I	Blake, *Songs of Experience* Godwin, *Caleb Williams*
1795	Kant, *Perpetual Peace*	Boswell d. John Keats b. Thomas Carlyle b. Beethoven, three piano trios Op. 1
1796	Napoleon defeats Austrians at Lodi and enters Milan Freedom of Press in France	Burns d. Goya, *Los Caprichos*
1797	Napoleon defeats Austrians at Rivoli and advances on Vienna Nelson and Jervis defeat Spanish fleet at Cape St Vincent	Coleridge writes *Kubla Khan* Goethe, *Hermann and Dorothea* Turner, *Millbank, Moon Light* Haydn, *Emperor Quartet*
1798	French capture Rome and declare Roman Republic Battle of the Pyramids makes Napoleon master of Egypt Nelson destroys French fleet at Abukir Bay	Wordsworth and Coleridge, *Lyrical Ballads*
1799	Austria declares war on France Kingdom of Mysore divided between Britain and Hyderabad Church Missionary Society founded in London	Godwin, *St Leon* Beethoven, *Symphony No. 1* Haydn, *The Creation*

Science and technology	Philosophy	
Lavoisier, *Table of 31 Chemical Elements*	Kant, *Critique of Judgment* Maimon, *Examination of Transcendental Philosophy* Adam Smith d. 1790–93 Beattie, *Elements of Moral Science*	1790
London School of Veterinary Surgery founded Metric system proposed in France	Price d. Reinhold, *On the Foundations of Philosophical Knowledge*	1791
Gas used for lighting in England	Ferguson, *Principles of Moral and Political Science* Fichte, *Attempts at a Critique of all Revelation* Stewart, *Elements of the Philosophy of the Human Mind*	1792
Eli Whitney invents the cotton gin	Crombie, *An Essay on Philosophical Necessity* Godwin, *Enquiry concerning Political Justice* Kant, *Religion within the Limits of Reason Alone* Stewart, *Outlines of Moral Philosophy*	1793
Erasmus Darwin, *Zoonomia, or the Laws of Organic Life*	1794–9 Fichte, *Foundation of the Complete Theory of Knowledge* Paley, *Evidences of Christianity*	1794
Joseph Bramah invents hydraulic press		1795
Cuvier establishes science of comparative zoology	Reid d.	1796
Thomas Bewick, *British Birds* L. N. Vauquelin discovers chromium	Kant, *Metaphysics of Morals* Schelling, *Ideas for a philosophy of Nature* (1st edn) Burke d.	1797
Malthus, *Essay on the Principle of Population* Laplace, *Exposition of the System of the World*	Comte b. Green, *An Examination of the Leading Principle of the New System of Morals*	1798
Perfectly preserved mammoth discovered in Siberia 1798–1825 Laplace, *Treatise on Celestial Mechanics*		1799

	Politics and religion	The arts
1800	Napoleon establishes himself as First Consul in the Tuileries Jefferson wins U.S. presidential election British capture Malta	Goya, *The Two Majas* David, *Napoleon at Grand Saint-Bernard* Haydn, *The Seasons* Beethoven, *First Symphony*

Science and technology	Philosophy	
Gauss, *Arithmetical Disquisitions* Royal College of Surgeons founded Richard Trevithick constructs light- pressure steam engine	Fichte, *The Vocation of Man* Schelling, *System of Transcendental Idealism*	1800

Introduction
Stuart Brown

This volume is concerned with European philosophy from the late seventeenth century through most of the eighteenth – the period of the Enlightenment, as broadly conceived. Some apology is due for the overall emphasis on what is commonly referred to as 'British philosophy', but the attention to English early Enlightenment figures, such as Newton and Locke, is easily justified, since they were important influences on the Enlightenment elsewhere. Philosophy flourished in Britain and Ireland in the eighteenth century. Wales produced Richard Price', while Ireland could boast of Berkeley and Burke.' Ireland also produced Francis Hutcheson, to whom Hume and the Scottish Enlightenment owed a considerable debt.' The Scots in turn had a considerable influence on the Enlightenment or *Aufklärung* in Germany, not least on the thought of Kant.

The opening chapter focuses on the Cambridge Platonists, in whose thought the Enlightenment emphasis on reason and toleration is already prefigured. The concluding chapter deals with the beginnings of the reaction against Enlightenment concepts and values towards the end of the eighteenth century. 'Enlightenment' is thus something of a unifying concept. At the same time it should be acknowledged that histories of philosophy do not always make use of it. Sometimes, rather, they use the term 'empiricism' to characterize the philosophy of the period and to contrast it with the 'rationalism' of the earlier period.

There are indeed other notions that have been or might be put forward as central to understanding the development of philosophy in this period. For instance, the development of the laity or the use of ordinary language as the vehicle for articulating philosophical ideas are possible centres of focus. Alternatively one might attend to the secularization of philosophy or the growth of the demand for rational religion. But, while each of these perspectives can enrich our understand-

Introduction
Stuart Brown

This volume is concerned with European philosophy from the late seventeenth century through most of the eighteenth – the period of 'the Enlightenment' as broadly conceived. Some apology is due for the overall emphasis on what is commonly referred to as 'British philosophy'. But the attention to English early Enlightenment figures, such as Newton and Locke, is easily justified, since they were important influences on the Enlightenment elsewhere. Philosophy flourished in Britain and Ireland in the eighteenth century. Wales produced Richard Price,[1] while Ireland could boast of Berkeley and Burke.[2] Ireland also produced Francis Hutcheson, to whom Hume and the Scottish Enlightenment owed a considerable debt.[3] The Scots in turn had a considerable influence on the Enlightenment or *Aufklärung* in Germany, not least on the thought of Kant.[4]

The opening chapter focusses on the Cambridge Platonists, in whose thought the Enlightenment emphasis on reason and toleration is already prefigured. The concluding chapter deals with the beginnings of the reaction against Enlightenment concepts and values towards the end of the eighteenth century. 'Enlightenment' is thus something of a unifying concept. At the same time it should be acknowledged that histories of philosophy do not always make use of it. Sometimes, rather, they use the term 'empiricism' to characterize the philosophy of the period and to contrast it with the 'rationalism' of the earlier period.

There are indeed other notions that have been or might be put forward as central to understanding the development of philosophy in this period. For instance, the development of the laity or the use of ordinary language as the vehicle for articulating philosophical ideas are possible centres of focus. Alternatively one might attend to the secularization of philosophy or the growth of the demand for rational religion. But, while each of these perspectives can enrich our understand-

I

ing of the period, serious distortions can result from focussing on a single perspective to the exclusion of others. For this reason there are some scholars who distrust the application of any period and 'school' labels. Descartes, Spinoza, Malebranche and Leibniz, for instance, are often classed as 'rationalists',[5] on the one hand, and Locke, Berkeley and Hume as 'empiricists', on the other. But critics consider that these labels distort historical realities and misrepresent at least some of the individual philosophers concerned.[6] There are also those who think the period of the so-called 'Enlightenment' is too diverse to be accurately presented as if it were a coherent and unified cultural phenomenon.

Though I will address these doubts later in this introduction, my main purpose is not so much to lay them entirely to rest as to set the scene for the individual chapters that comprise the substance of the volume. The reader will find that some of these chapters are devoted to a major figure, as are the chapters on Berkeley and Vico, or even, in the case of Locke and Hume, to part of the thought of an individual philosopher. More commonly, the chapters deal with two or more figures as a group. Thus there are two chapters on the *philosophes* of the French Enlightenment and a chapter each on the Enlightenment in Scotland and in Germany. Had space permitted there might have been chapters on the Enlightenment in other countries.[7] The various national Enlightenment movements took place at rather different times and in widely different circumstances.

This introduction will concentrate to a large extent on the Enlightenment in England. English intellectual and political culture was much admired by Voltaire and other *philosophes* of the early French Enlightenment. Attention to it can be a way of announcing some of the themes of the volume as a whole and also linking together some of the figures dealt with in later chapters.

∽ THE ENGLISH 'ENLIGHTENMENT' ∽

Defenders of what is called 'the Enlightenment', such as the *philosophe* d'Alembert, commonly used the metaphor of spreading light to refer to the kind of intellectual and cultural progress they believed in. Furthermore there was a debate in Germany as to what '*Aufklärung*' (usually translated 'Enlightenment') was. So enlightenment was a concept wich was establishing itself during the period as one in terms of which the *avant garde* thought of themselves and their projects. But the phrase 'the Enlightenment' itself was not adopted until the nineteenth century, when it began to be used in retrospect of a period as a whole.[8] Historians have challenged the extent to which, as had previously been supposed, the Enlightenment can be represented as a single

European cultural phenomenon. But there is no doubt there were important interconnections, such as the English influence on the *philosophes*.[9] At the same time the Enlightenment in England itself, for instance, followed a quite different course from that in France.

The English Enlightenment was in some respects prefigured by Herbert of Cherbury and the Cambridge Platonists. But it is convenient, customary and defensible to fix 1688 – the year of the Whig revolution – as a starting-date. Until then the High Church party had dominated. Books had been subject to censorship and religious diversity had been discouraged. After the 'Revolution', when William and Mary were offered the British crowns, liberals had more influence in politics and the 'latitudinarians', as they wre known, in the Church. Symbolically perhaps, Spinoza's *Tractatus Theologico-Politicus*, which argued the case for freedom of expression in religious matters, appeared for the first time in English tradition in 1689. That work was published anonymously and illegally. But, by the middle of the 1690s, controversial works could be published legally. Though anonymity was still usual, it was no secret that Locke was the author of *The Reasonableness of Christianity* or John Toland the author of *Christianity not Mysterious*. These words were denounced as dangerous but they were not suppressed and no action was taken against the authors. Books could still be burned[10] and a Blasphemy Act was passed by the English Parliament in 1698. Yet there was a new tolerance of theological deviation, moderately expressed. For instance, Samuel Clarke – remembered by philosophers for his translations and defences of Newton – had a successful career as an Anglican clergyman notwithstanding the suspicion and even charge of heresy certain of his publications gave rise to.[11]

The early English Enlightenment is marked by vigorous controversy between two extremes – the anti-authoritarian 'deists' and the High Church defenders of hierarchy and othodoxy. The latitudinarians and the moderate Whig intellectuals sought to distance themselves from either extreme but sometimes found themselves accused of 'deism'.[12] Though there had been, in the 1690s, anti-clerical materialists who were inclined to republicanism, by the middle decades of the eighteenth century there were few prominent English intellectuals who defended such extreme positions. The philosophical scene came to be dominated by moderate opinion. The leading figures included moderate Anglican clergy, such as Joseph Butler and William Paley.[13] Deism declined and Thomas Chubb, one of its last representatives, was so moderate that he even retained some Church connections. Radicalism re-emerged later on and is represented, for instance, by the scientist and Unitarian minister, Joseph Priestley (1733–1804). The radical Enlightenment is also reflected later in the writings of William Godwin (1756–1836) and

3

Mary Wollstonecraft (1759–97). But during the peak of the French Enlightenment in the mid-eighteenth century English philosophy generally lacked the anti-clerical, anti-Establishment materialism common amongst the French *philosophes*.

The *philosophes*, as we have noted, developed what they took from Locke and others in a radical way.[14] But the English radicals in the late eighteenth and early nineteenth century were themselves influenced by their French counterparts. For instance, Jeremy Bentham (1748–1832) was indebted to Helvétius, from whom he derived some of his utilitarian ideas. Utilitarianism became a feature of the Enlightenment and Bentham might be regarded as a late Enlightenment figure. In fact he is a transitional figure who, particularly in relation to his later thoughts, can be treated as the beginning of a new phase of British philosophy. He is so treated in this series and is, accordingly, discussed in a later volume. But it is worth noting that the anti-metaphysical character of the 'positivist' movement of the nineteenth century (which Bentham helped to encourage) was also shared by some of the Enlightenment philosophers, such as Condillac and Hume. This anti-metaphysical tendency reflects one point of continuity between the periods covered by this volume and that on *The Nineteenth Century*.

The Enlightenment as it has emerged so far was characterized by more weight being given than formerly to certain values, such as toleration, freedom and reasonableness. It was associated with opposition to authoritarianism. Its rejection of an excessive emphasis on the authority of the clergy was combined with a greater respect for lay opinion. In this way it is also linked, as I have already indicated, with what was known as 'deism' as well as with scepticism. Confidence in the progress being made in the sciences was matched by scepticism about dogmatic ('rationalist') metaphysical systems. Both were associated with a broad empiricism.

By focussing on one or other of these features we may obtain different perspectives on our period and I will attend to each in turn. The perspectives they provide may serve to provide some background to at least the secondary figures of the period. As in other periods, the great thinkers of the Enlightenment are, in one way or another, not entirely typical. But at least sometimes they can be better understood once it is seen where they are deviant or out of step with their times. This is true mostly obviously of Kant, who is certainly an Enlightenment figure (and wrote an essay on '*Was ist Aufklärung?*'), but who is the focus of a separate volume in this series.

❧ LAY INVOLVEMENT IN THE NEW ❧ PHILOSOPHY

The growth of Protestantism in parts of northern Europe was accompanied by strong anti-clerical movements amongst the laity. The Catholic tradition had its Latin Bible and a clerical hierarchy who laid down how it was to be understood. But, in the wake of the Protestant Reformation, it was often replaced by a diametrically opposed tradition committed to a vernacular Bible that the common people were supposed to be able to understand just by reading. While most Protestant groups retained clergy and attached importance to their mission as teachers, they encouraged the laity, in varying degree, to learn to read and understand the Bible for themselves.

An authorized English version of the Bible was in use from 1611. A whole spectrum of religious parties and sects offered a variety of encouragements and discouragements to lay people who wished to engage in religious speculation and to that extent in philosophy. At one end of the spectrum was the High Church party of the Church of England, which believed in clerical authority and tended to favour censorship. At the other extreme there were sects like the Seekers and the Ranters, who had no clergy and who came to be associated in various ways with political radicalism. A home-spun metaphysics might serve as a way of integrating theology and politics. Thus, for example, the leader of one of the groups which was active in the aftermath of the Civil War in England – the Diggers – used a pantheistic metaphysics to underpin his rejection of all hierarchy, whether in religion or politics, and to make radical democratic and communist demands.[15] At a more sophisticated level were the metaphysical ideas developed in the Quaker group centred on Ragley Hall, the home of Anne, Viscountess Conway.[16]

Those to whom I have been referring as 'the laity' included all those who were not clergymen. They also included 'lay philosophers', that is to say, those who were not trained in a university. The training of clergy (as well as doctors and lawyers) was a major part of the business of the universities throughout this period and, for some of them, through much of the nineteenth century as well. Students at Oxford and Cambridge had to subscribe to the doctrines of the Anglican church as expressed in the Thirty Nine Articles. The concept of 'academic freedom' was as yet unknown in the seventeenth century and universities were not generally associated with free-thinking. The place for any free exchange of ideas was either in a club, a salon or a private house; or, again, if less respectably, in the coffee-houses or taverns frequented by others of like mind.[17]

The participation of lay people in philosophy was not new in the

Enlightenment. For centuries lay men and women, especially those from privileged backgrounds, might occasionally benefit from an education which brought them in touch with scholastic philosophy.[18] But, without learning Latin, they could not hope to progress far, and it was not until humanist education diffused this learning more widely in the fifteenth and sixteenth centuries that it became available to a significant minority. By the beginning of the period covered in this volume, lay participation in philosophy was already noticeable and was set to increase considerably.[19]

Universities were not merely theologically correct but, for the most part, intellectually conservative places in the seventeenth century.[20] New ideas were not likely to take root quickly in such an environment. The early history of modern philosophy shows how some laypeople were more receptive than most academics were. Philosophy had been written in French before Descartes, whose philosophy is discussed in a previous volume. What was new with Descartes was that he used French as a vehicle, not just for popular works, but to express and argue for a difficult and demanding set of doctrines. By writing in his native language he was able to win for his philosophy the support and patronage of influential lay people – women as well as men – and this helped Cartesianism to survive and even flourish despite being banned from French universities.

As well as writing in a vernacular language, Descartes sometimes adopted a literary style, as in his *Meditations* and *Discourse on Method*, that was more accessible to the laity than formal academic works. Indeed his conception of philosophy was that of a subject in which lay people were already equipped. Good sense was not the prerogative of the learned but, on the contrary, as Descartes announced right at the beginning of his *Discourse*, it 'is the best distributed thing in the world'. Everyone had ideas and Descartes played down any obstacles there were to learning how to distinguish those that are 'clear and distinct' and which could therefore give true knowledge. Scholastic philosophy required a long period of initiation, not only into a technical Latin but into a special way of thinking. Modern philosophy, by contrast, sought to deal in a currency ('ideas') which the whole of humankind was supposed to have in common.

Descartes's approach was taken further by Nicholas Malebranche (see Volume IV in this series), who not only wrote exclusively in French but very largely for a lay readership, especially when he wrote in the dialogue form. Philosophical discussion thus began to look continuous with the social world of conversation between equals, in which there is due consideration for how one's utterances may be received, respect for the judgement of others, and so on. This was not the philosophy of the cloister or the schoolroom but of the salon or country house.

By such means philosophy was becoming available to lay people in an unprecedented way. French replaced Latin as the language of modern philosophy in much of continental Europe. The use of the vernacular became more common in England and, by the end of the seventeenth century, the leading modern philosophers, such as Locke and Norris, were publishing exclusively in their native language.

These changes involved not only a new language but a new style of philosophy, in which liveliness and clarity were regarded as particular virtues. Thus Locke, in his Epistle to the Reader at the beginning of his *Essay*, thought it appropriate to apologize to his reader for the difficulties that remained because of the way the work had been composed. He had *not* written it for academics but for what he called 'polite company'. He hoped it would bring some pleasure to his reader and, most significantly, told his reader that 'this Book must stand or fall with thee, not by any Opinion I have of it, but thy own'.[21]

Locke's writings were not only accessible in the sense that lay people could follow them but also in the sense that they made available to lay people a method of doing philosophy which they could replicate. Thus the reader was invited to refer to his or her own 'observation and experience' as part of a process of clarifying his or her ideas. His friend and pupil, Damaris, Lady Masham, published books in which she used a Lockean method in order to resolve, at least to her own satisfaction, a controversy with Mary Astell about the meaning of the word 'love' in a religious context.

There was a marked increase in the number of books by lay philosophers in the eighteenth century. But no less significant was the potentially large lay readership that had been established for philosophical works. New careers became possible for philosophical writers who wrote for this readership. The most striking success of this kind was Pierre Bayle's *Historical and Critical Dictionary*.[22] With such writings the world of philosophy became part of the world of letters. Even the more difficult professional or semi-professional philosophers, like Berkeley and Hume, consciously sought to produce more accessible versions of their philosophy.[23] The leading *philosophes* of the French Enlightenment, such as Voltaire and Diderot, were men of letters as much as they were philosophers, concerned to entertain as well as instruct and convince.[24]

One important difference between the contexts of French and English philosophy in the eighteenth century was that the *philosophes* were subject to censorship laws. Such laws dogged the publication of their great collaborative project, the *Encyclopédie*. Moreover, philosophers were discouraged from extending their speculations into areas bordering on religion. In England, on the other hand, the censorship laws lapsed in 1695 and were never renewed. In this relatively free political climate there was, at least initially, a spate of heterodox publications, such as Toland's *Christianity Not Mysterious*.[25] It was at this point that the deist movement, with its stress on the sufficiency of reason in matters of religion, came to the fore.[26]

⚫⚫ DEISM AND 'THE AGE OF REASON' ⚫⚫

There is no consistent usage for the term 'deism' in our period nor a complete consensus as to who the deists were. That is hardly surprising, since those who used the term of what they subscribed to often had no more in mind than a reasonable Christianity: whereas those who used it of their enemies had in mind a tendency that was subversive of true religion. The deists commonly dropped several of the core features of church Christianity like revelation, miracles, the means of grace, the Incarnation, the divine inspiration of Scripture and a divinely-ordained ecclesiastical hierarchy. At the same time they clung onto those beliefs they regarded as rationally defensible: for example, in a first cause, an intelligent general providence, immortality and, sometimes, retribution for wrong-doing. When we consider, however, that Spinoza was commonly regarded as the quintessential deist, and yet he did not believe in providence or immortality (as usually understood) or retribution, we see how difficult it is to define deism by doctrines.[27] The best we can do is to note the desire for a wholly rational religion or a rational replacement for Christianity. The deists were characteristically anti-clerical and they usually went well beyond mere heresy by rejecting the Bible or revelation as sources of truth. As to their politics, they rejected the idea that monarchs are divinely appointed – the so-called 'divine right of kings' – and, if they were not republican, they were often inclined to hold that the authority of the monarch was derived ultimately from the consent of the people.

Some of the 'rationalist' philosophers discussed in the previous volume could either readily be identified as deists, as in the case of Spinoza, or showed some tendency in that direction, as did Leibniz and Malebranche.[28] For all that it was a rationalizing tendency within religion, however, deism was not a necessary accompaniment of 'rationalism' in the special sense used of certain philosophers, especially of the seventeenth century but also later. The rationalists, in the special sense, accepted an ideal of a system of knowledge built up, as geometry was taken to be, by demonstrations from self-evident truths. Moreover, the major rationalists of the seventeenth century believed it was possible to make some headway in building up a system of metaphysics that approximated to this ideal. But not all of them were led to encroach on theology, to depart from orthodoxy or to aspire to a kind of philosophical religion. Descartes was careful not to do so. Thus being a rationalist in philosophy did not necessarily mean being a rationalizer in matters of religion and hence being deistical in tendency.[29]

To add to the confusion, the philosophers of the Age of Reason tended to reject the aspiration after metaphysical systems of the kind produced by the seventeenth-century rationalists. Philosophers often continued to espouse such rationalism in other areas. Thus, for instance, Locke and Richard Price are said to have been rationalists about ethics.[30] There were those too, like Samuel Clarke, who were rationalists in natural theology. None the less rationalism in metaphysics (and natural science) was characteristically rejected. The roots of rationalism in the special sense lie in the Aristotelian ideal of *scientia*[31] and therefore in the Latin-based university philosophical tradition. That ideal had been attacked by sceptics as unattainable and the attack was continued in Locke's influential *Essay*. The certainty which sufficed for the purposes of practical life came to be regarded as sufficient also for our understanding of the world. Those who claimed more, especially in metaphysics and natural science, were no longer taken seriously. D'Alembert could write, in 1751, that 'the taste for systems . . . is today almost entirely banished from works of merit . . . a writer among us who praised systems would have come too late'.[32]

Leibniz's 'optimism', i.e. his theory that this is the best of all possible worlds, is one example of what d'Alembert took to be a 'system' in an uncomplimentary sense. It resulted from Leibniz's belief – which he thought he could demonstrate – that the world has a perfect creator.[33] Voltaire lampooned such optimism in his enormously successful *Candide* and philosophies like that of Leibniz were largely rejected by the *philosophes*.[34] Again, the Cartesians rejected Newton's theory of gravity because it involved action at a distance. They thought they had a clear and distinct idea of matter on the basis of which action at a distance could be ruled out. The controversy dragged on for some time. But the Newtonian cause, of which Voltaire was one of the champions, prevailed. Systems that prescribed the nature of the world a priori fell into disrepute.

For all that rationalism in the more technical sense used by philosophers was in decline in the eighteenth century, the deists were rationalists in a perfectly clear sense, i.e. rationalizers of religion. Thus Matthew Tindal (1657?–1753), author of what came to be referred to as 'the Bible of Deism', suggested that Christianity was not new but already contained in 'the religion of Nature'.[35] Its truths, such as Tindal could accept, were ones that reason could discover without the need of revelation.

There was a large deist literature in early eighteenth century England and an even greater volume of refutations, especially books from the Anglican clergy. But by the mid-century deism had declined and the controversy it aroused had subsided. It is sometimes suggested that the deists lost the arguments. More probably, however, Anglican Christianity itself had become less authoritarian or fideistic than it had been a century before and those who might otherwise have been tempted to deism could more readily be accommodated within the church. The liberal or latitudinarian wing of the Church of England became much stronger in the eighteenth century. From the Boyle lecturers on, the philosophical sermon became an established genre.[36] Though sermons were commonly published at that time, they were delivered in the first place to a captive audience. That church-goers should have been offered the arguments of natural religion is some evidence that the demand for a rational religion had taken root amongst the faithful as well as the dissenters. Whatever the extent of this demand, many of the clergy seemed intent on meeting it. Sophisticated arguments became available to support belief in miracles and in a providence.

Perhaps because the demand for a rational religion was in some measure being met by Anglican apologetics, the controversy about deism abated. In 1790 Burke claimed that no one read any of the deists any more and had not done so for some time.[37] Deism moderated and declined in England during a period when it became more radical and conspicuous in France. When it reappeared in England, for instance in Tom Paine's *Age of Reason* (1794–5), it assumed a more revolutionary form, hostile to organized religion, which the author claimed was a means 'to terrify and enslave mankind, and monopolize power and profit'. But, though there was a late flowering of the Enlightenment, in Britain and America, the excesses of the French Revolution provoked a reaction to the mechanistic, materialistic and egalitarian philosophies that had previously predominated.

❧ SCEPTICISM AND THE REJECTION OF ❧ METAPHYSICAL SYSTEMS

Deism involves scepticism about traditional beliefs and a demand for critical reconstruction. Scepticism, or what was taken to be such, was widespread during the Enlightenment – especially in relation to metaphysics. But there were few philosophers who were tempted by radical doubts about the possibiity of knowledge.

Radical scepticism had been adopted by some of the ancient Greek philosophers and was codified by Sextus Empiricus in the third century AD. It had been revived during the religious turmoil of the sixteenth century, by Montaigne and others.[38] What emerged was a marriage of scepticism with 'fideism' (from the Latin word for 'faith'), in which all reliance on reason was totally demolished and the need for a total dependence on faith proposed instead. Doubts, if pressed far enough, were supposed to lead to a strengthening of faith. Such thinking was, however, subversive of the emerging sciences. And, in any case, the idea that faith might be confirmed by destroying all its rational bases did not sit well with the Catholic intellectual tradition, in which, following Aquinas and others, it was supposed that reason could make a good beginning in establishing the truths of religion. Descartes took upon himself the role of defeating the sceptics on their own terms. But no one seems to have been convinced by his *Meditations* and, ironically, they came to be valued more for the arguments they gave in favour of scepticism than for refuting it. Scepticism not only survived but was stimulated by Descartes's attempt to refute it.

One late seventeenth century French sceptic, Simon Foucher (1644–97) made a point of identifying the assumptions underlying the metaphysical writings of Descartes and his successors and then insisting that they neither had been nor could be demonstrated – hence that the system being offered was inadequately founded.[39] Foucher addressed himself critically to contemporary philosophy but the titles and contents of his books were off-putting. He presented himself unfashionably within a late Renaissance tradition of reviving ancient scepticism and he did not receive the attention he deserved from contemporaries. None the less, he anticipated or influenced the arguments of the best known sceptic of the late seventeenth century – Pierre Bayle.

Bayle (1647–1706) enjoyed a literary success rivalled by only a few other philosophers of his time. He wrote for a wide range of readers and could be witty as well as profound. At a time when being frank or direct was to court trouble he acquired the art of burying his most contentious remarks where his reader might least expect to find them. He could expound the most outrageous views or relate the most licentious stories and yet put an authorial distance between himself and the views and events he wrote about. His *Historical and Critical Dictionary*[40] aimed to be nothing less than a survey of human folly. Of the works first published in the late seventeenth century few had such a marked effect on eighteenth century philosophy. Bayle used his scepticism to defend tolerance towards those with whom one disagreed (still very controversial in religious matters in his time) and to underline the necessity of faith. His stress on faith was understood by the *philosophes* (almost certainly wrongly) as a mere subterfuge. And such a subterfuge of concealing total scepticism about revealed religion under the pretence of defending the necessity of faith became a convention.[41]

Typical of Bayle was the way he seized upon what was perceived as Descartes's failure to demonstrate the existence of a material world and Malebranche's insistence that, since it was taught in the Bible, the existence of such a material world must be received on faith even though it could not be demonstrated by philosophy. Bayle observed:

> it is useful to know that a Father of the Oratory [Malebranche], as illustrious for his piety as for his philosophical knowledge, maintained that faith alone can truly convince us of the existence of bodies. Neither the Sorbonne, nor any other tribunal, gave him the least trouble on that account. The Italian inquisitors did not disturb Fardella, who maintained the same thing in a printed work. This ought to show my readers that they must not find it strange that I sometimes point out that, concerning the most mysterious matters in the Gospel, reason gets us nowhere, and thus we ought to be completely satisfied with the light of faith.[42]

Of the Enlightenment philosophers, none apart from Hume took scepticism as far as Bayle did. And, if Hume had any antidote to scepticism, it was to be found in his belief in natural judgement.[43] The *philosophes*, for the most part, were sceptical about religion and metaphysics but not about science. Theirs was a moderate scepticism which followed more in the path trodden by Locke. Locke's French disciple, Condillac, wrote a critique of metaphysical systems of the kind produced by Malebranche and Leibniz.[44] Such systems had, as Hume claimed, been dismissed from science and it was time they were dismissed elsewhere:

> Men are now cured of their passion for hypotheses and systems in natural philosophy, and will hearken to no arguments but those which are derived from experience. It is full time they should attempt a like reformation in all moral disquisitions; and reject every system of ethics, however subtle or ingenious, which is not founded on fact and observation.[45]

In these remarks Hume links scepticism about 'systems' and 'hypotheses' with a preference for empirical arguments. And indeed the eighteenth century is sometimes represented as a period when empiricism became prevalent, at any rate amongst those regarded as the most progressive thinkers. It is worth considering, briefly and in conclusion, how far this is true.

❧ EMPIRICISM ❧

The term 'empiricist' is used broadly of anyone who thinks that all knowledge *of the world* is based upon experience – or, slightly more narrowly, of anyone who thinks that all *substantive* knowledge is based upon experience. Those who are empiricists in the broad sense might allow that there is substantive knowledge not based upon experience if, for instance, they believed (as Locke did) that the existence of a God or the truths of ethics could be demonstrated. They might none the less believe the truths about the natural world could only be established by observation and experiment. Hume, in saying that 'men . . . will hearken to no arguments [in natural philosophy] but those which are derived from experience' might be understood as claiming that, by the middle of the eighteenth century, empiricism had established itself as the methodology for the natural sciences. He also thought, as the same passage makes clear, that people ought to go further, and be empiricists in moral philosophy as well as natural. And indeed he defended empiricism in a narrower, more rigorous sense, rejecting all rationalist metaphysics as well as ethics. For Hume, as for any strict empiricist, no substantive question could be settled except by reference to experience. Thus, in his *Dialogues Concerning Natural Religion*, he is brief and dismissive about the traditional a priori arguments for the existence of God. The argument discussed sympathetically and at length in the *Dialogues* is an argument from experience.

Hume was more thorough-going in his empiricism than Locke, in whom, as we have seen, it is possible to detect rationalist elements. But this is not to say that Locke was inconsistent inasmuch that such elements are compatible with a broad empiricism. Insofar as empiricism was widespread in the eighteenth century, it was of the broader sort. This is the empiricism or 'experimental philosophy' defended by members of the Royal Society.[46] Though it is natural to extend the demand that arguments are only drawn from experience into ethics and natural theology, there is no necessity to do so.

The best known defender of rationalism in ethics and natural theology in eighteenth century England was Samuel Clarke (1675–1729). In the first of his two series of Boyle lectures,[47] Clarke argued a priori for the existence of God and, in the second, he sought to argue that there were eternal truths of ethics which, like those of mathematics, were grasped by reason. Clarke generated a very considerable controversy which lasted long after his death.[48] Some critics objected, not only to the details of his arguments, but to his use of a priori arguments to demonstrate the existence of God. Their point was that only a posteriori, i.e. empirical arguments, were appropriate to establish the existence of anything. And this view seems to have gained ground during the eighteenth century. The only argument for the existence of God Hume was willing to take seriously was the a posteriori one.[49] That was the argument used by apologists, such as Butler and Paley.[50]

Clarke's rationalism in ethics was criticized by Francis Hutcheson amongst others. Hume regarded him as the leading exponent, after Malebranche and Cudworth, of the 'abstract theory of morals' he sought to undermine. Clarke's 'eternal law of righteousness' did not commend itself to the sceptical, secular and empirical thinkers of the mid-eighteenth century. Their temper was suited by one or another form of utilitarianism. The utilitarian ethics of Hume and of certain of the *philosophes* (including Helvétius) was a direct influence on Bentham.

The association of empiricism with utilitarianism in ethics is a natural, though not a necessary one. Historically both are associated with the sceptical Epicurean tradition and so with both hedonism and materialism. Locke was mistaken by many of his critics for an adherent of this tradition. He was attacked by Aristotelians as a 'sceptic'.[51] He was also commonly interpreted as a materialist, partly because of the agnosticism he expressed about whether matter could think, which occasioned a considerable controversy.[52] Though Locke was not a materialist, his thought was taken in that direction, both by his British followers, such as Toland and Collins, and also the *philosophes*, such as Condillac and Helvétius, who developed his ideas in their own ways.[53] The empiricist tradition, as inherited by Bentham later in the century, was hedonistic and materialist. It is only one strand in Enlightenment thinking and was always controversial. But, after Locke, it had an intellectual respectability that it never had before.

One important contribution Locke made to developing empiricism as a philosophical doctrine was in relation to the theory of ideas. Whereas Descartes and others had held that certain ideas were 'innate', Locke held that all our ideas are ultimately derived from experience, either from the senses or from our mind turning 'its view inward upon itself'.[54] Against Descartes and others who held the concept of God to be innate Locke insists that we arrive at a concept of God through reflection. The concept of 'an eternal, most powerful, and most knowing being' is a complex one. Locke agreed with Descartes that the existence of such a being could be demonstrated a priori. His empiricism is not, therefore, straightforwardly to be contrasted with Descartes' rationalism. None the less, his rejection of innate ideas was taken up by many philosophers in the eighteenth century and became one of the hallmarks of the Enlightenment.

In this respect Kant was a typical product of the Enlightenment as well as a philosopher who pointed beyond it. In general Kant accepted as uncontroversial the Lockean view of the origin of our ideas in experience. Though he added the all-important qualification that this was not absolutely true, that there were certain categories that humans bring to experience, he accepted the need to argue for such a priori concepts. To that extent Kant's philosophy starts from a presumption of empiricism. But Kant and his philosophy lie beyond the scope of this volume.

❧ NOTES ❧

1 Price is discussed in chapter 8, together with two English moralists, Shaftesbury and Joseph Butler.

2 The Irish context of Berkeley's writings, which is often played down, is brought out by David Berman in chapter 5 below. Burke is discussed in chapter 14.

3 See chapters 7 and 11 below.

4 See chapter 12 below.

5 The previous volume of the current series – *The Renaissance and Seventeenth Century Rationalism* – so classifies them. See also John Cottingham's *The Rationalists*, paired with R. S. Woolhouse, *The Empiricists* (Oxford, Oxford University Press, 1988) in the History of Western Philosophy series.

6 Louis E. Loeb, for instance, rejects the standard division of the major figures of seventeenth and eighteenth century philosophy into either 'continental rationalists' or 'British empiricists'. See his *From Descartes to Hume: Continental Metaphysics and the Development of Modern Philosophy*, Ithaca, NY, Cornell University Press, 1981. Loeb groups Berkeley with Malebranche and Leibniz (and others) as a 'continental metaphysician'.

7 It is regrettable, for instance, that there was no space for a chapter on the American Enlightenment, which included representative figures such as Thomas Paine and Jefferson.

8 There is a vast literature on the Enlightenment. As an introduction Norman Hanson's *The Enlightenment* (London, Penguin, 1968) can still be recommended, as can Peter Gay's fuller *The Enlightenment: An Interpretation* (2 vols, New York, Knopf, 1966, 1969). See also *The Blackwell Companion to the Enlightenment*, ed. John W. Yolton *et al.*, Oxford, Blackwell, 1991.

9 See chapter 10 below. See also N. L. Torrey, *Voltaire and the English Deists*, New Haven, Yale University Press, 1930.

10 Toland's book was indeed burned by the common hangman in Ireland. This fate befell books by the deist Matthew Tindal in England in 1709.

11 Clarke, in his Boyle Lectures, had established himself as one of the leading defenders of natural religion in the country. It was claimed that his heresy was what prevented him, despite being favoured at Court, from becoming Archbishop of Canterbury. He had, however, secured the comfortable living and fashionable pulpit of St James, Piccadilly. And the protracted campaign by the heresy-hunters within the Church of England failed to dislodge him. See J. P. Ferguson, *Dr. Samuel Clarke: An Eighteenth Century Heretic*, Kineton, The Roundwood Press, 1976.

12 For a fuller account of some of these controversies see my ' "Theological politics" and the Reception of Spinoza in the early English Enlightenment', *Studia Spinozana* 9 (1994).

13 Butler is discussed in chapter 8. William Paley (1743–1805) offered arguments from design in spite of Hume's critique of such arguments in his *Dialogues*

concerning Natural Religion. None the less Paley was very influential and his books were set reading at Cambridge when Charles Darwin was there in 1829 and the years following.

14 See chapters 9 and 10.

15 For instance, Gerrard Winstanley's tracts *The Law of Freedom* and *The New Law of Righteousness* (1648), see *The Works of Gerrard Winstanley*, ed. G. H. Sabine, Ithaca, NY, Cornell University Press, 1941. Radical sects seem to have been responsible for disseminated metaphysical ideas (like pantheism) amongst lay people during the early modern period.

16 See chapter 1.

17 Locke was a founder of such a club, the Dry Club, in London and had been a member of a similar club in Rotterdam. When, due to ailing health, he retired to a country house (Oates, in Essex, the home of Lady Damaris Masham), he was visited by a wide range of liberal-minded thinkers. Salons, like country houses, enable women to play a more prominent part in philosophical discussion. They flourished in Paris. The free-thinker John Toland was disapproved of for discussing serious subjects in coffee-houses and taverns.

18 This period shows a marked increase in the participation by English women in philosophical discussion. Some of the debates of the period, particularly between Norris and his critics, were pursued in print by women – notably Mary Astell, Damaris Masham (discussed in chapter 1) and Catharine Trotter. Access for women to the world of learning remained very limited right to the end of the nineteenth century. See Mary E. Waite (ed.), *A History of Women Philosophers*, Dordrecht, Kluwer Academic, 1991, vol. 3 (1600–1900).

19 Herbert of Cherbury, who is discussed in chapter 1, is an early example and Shaftesbury was a later one. Shaftesbury, one of the major English moral philosophers of the period, is discussed in chapter 8 below.

20 Big changes were, however, in motion towards the end of the century. Modern philosophy was being championed in the early 1690s by Oxford students, including the essayist Joseph Addison and the disciple of Malebranche, Thomas Taylor. There were attempts at Oxford to ban Locke's books but he seems to have been widely read by students. He was taught to the young Berkeley at Trinity College, Dublin at the turn of the century. Other universities, such as Edinburgh (attended by Hume), were reformed in the early eighteenth century.

21 *Essay*, ed. P. H. Nidditch, Oxford, Clarendon Press, 1975, p. 7.

22 Bayle's work went into many editions, including English editions, and seems to have been a significant influence on Hume. Some of the philosophically most important and interesting entries are included in *Pierre Bayle: Historical and Critical Dictionary: Selections*, trans. with an introduction by R. H. Popkin, Indianapolis, Hackett, 1991.

23 Berkeley's *Treatise concerning the Principles of Knowledge* (1710) did not have the reception its author had hoped for and he sought to popularize it by writing his *Three Dialogues between Hylas and Philonous* (1713). Hume's formidable *Treatise of Human Nature* (1739) was initially a flop – it 'fell still-born from the press', according to its author – and he produced simplified versions that correspond to two of the three main parts of the original work: *An Enquiry Concerning Human Undestanding* (1748) and *An Enquiry concering the Principles of Morals* (1752).

24 D'Alembert, who sought to act as a spokesman for the *philosophes*, took it for granted that philosophy aims to please, though he also insisted that it was intended principally to instruct. See *Preliminary Discourse to the Encyclopedia*, trans. R. N. Schwab, Indianapolis, Bobbs-Merrill, 1963.

25 John Toland (1670–1722) concocted the word 'pantheism', though his philosophical views derive from, amongst others, Giordano Bruno. See R. E. Sullivan, *John Toland and the Deist Controversy: A Study in Adaptations*, Cambridge, Mass., Harvard University Press, 1982.

26 Herbert of Cherbury (see chapter 1) was reputed to be 'the father of deism' and others, like Voltaire, were also deists. Others, like Berkeley and Burke (see chapter 14), reacted against it.

27 Leslie Stephen, in his *History of English Thought in the Eighteenth Century* (London, 1876), claimed that 'the whole essence of the deist position may be found in Spinoza's Tractatus Theologico-Politicus' (London, Harbinger, 1962, p. 27). Some of the critics of deism around the turn of the eighteenth century, such as Matthias Earbury and William Carroll, would have agreed. But Hobbist and Lockean doctrines were often more prominent in summaries of deism by English authors.

28 See my 'The Regularization of Providence in Post-Cartesian Philosophy', in R. Crocker (ed.), *Religion, Reason and Nature*, Dordrecht, Kluwer Academic, forthcoming.

29 'Rationalism' is often used as a close synonym of 'deism'. Bernard Williams, in his entry on 'Rationalism' in the *Encyclopedia of Philosophy*, ed. P. Edwards, New York, Macmillan, 1967, acknowledges Enlightenment 'rationalism' and 'rationalism in theology' as 'two other applications' of the term in addition to the philosophically most important one, namely, to refer to 'the philosophical outlook or program which stresses the power of a priori reason to grasp substantial truths about the world' (op. cit., vol. VII, p. 69). Deism, though not essentially connected with rationalism in this sense, connects these two lesser applications of the term.

30 Locke wrote that he was 'bold to think, that Morality is capable of Demonstration, as well as Mathematicks' (Essay III, xi. 16) Ian Tipton, in chapter 3, comments further on the 'strong rationalist streak in Locke'. Price's ethics are discussed in chapter 8.

31 *Scientia* simply means 'knowledge' or 'science'. *Scientia*, according to the Aristotelian view, is arrived at on the basis of correct syllogistic reasoning on the basis of premises which are both necessary and certain. It is both universal and necessary. For a helpful account of *scientia* see R. S. Woolhouse, *Locke*, Brighton, Harvester, 1983, chapter 8.

32 *Preliminary Discourse to the Encyclopedia of Diderot*, ed. R. Schwab, Indianapolis: Bobbs-Merrill, 1963, p. 94. For a further account, see my 'Leibniz and the Fashion for Systems and Hypotheses' in P. Gilmour (ed.), *Philosophers of the Enlightenment*, Edinburgh, Edinburgh University Press, 1989, pp. 8–30.

33 Though Leibniz, in his book on the subject – his *Theodicy* of 1710 – was content to show that the existence of evil in the world could be made consistent with belief in a perfect creator, other writings suggest he was not content personally to accept belief in a perfect creator merely as a matter of faith. For instance, in a paper of 1697 'On the Ultimate Origin of Things' argues that it

Mohawk Valley Community College Library

is 'evident *a priori*' from considerations about the necessary origins of things that, contrary to the appearance of a chaotic world in which divine wisdom had no part, 'the highest perfection there could possibly be ... is secured' (*Gottfried Wilhelm Leibniz: Philosophical Writings*, ed. and trans. G. H. R. Parkinson, London, Dent (Everyman), 1973, p. 141).

34 Voltaire's reaction to optimism is discussed in chapter 10 below.

35 The title of the book, in the obliging fashion of the period, declares its contents: *Christianity as Old as the Creation: Or, The Gospel A Republication of the Religion of Nature* (1730).

36 Some of the sermons of Joseph Butler became a classic of eighteenth-century moral philosophy. See chapter 8 below.

37 'Who born within the last forty years has read one word of Collins, and Toland, and Tindal, and Chubb, and Morgan, and that whole race that call themselves freethinkers? Who now reads Bolingbroke? Who ever reads him through?' ('Reflections', *Works* V: 172). Burke's attitude to deism is discussed in chapter 14 below.

38 See R. H. Popkin, *The History of Scepticism from Erasmus to Spinoza*, Berkeley, University of California Press, 1979.

39 See, for instance, his *Critique de la recherche de la vérité*, 1675, repr. New York, Johnson Reprint, 1969 and the editorial introduction by R. A. Watson. Watson regards Foucher as an important critic of Cartesianism. See his *The Breakdown of Cartesian Metaphysics*, Atlantic Highlands, NJ, Humanities Press International, 1987.

40 The *Dictionnaire historique et critique* was first published in 1697 and Bayle made many alterations in the editions that went through during his lifetime.

41 Hume, for instance, seems to have adopted such a conventional subterfuge at the end of his essay 'Of Miracles' when he concluded that 'the *Christian Religion* not only was at first attended with miracles, but even at this day cannot be believed by an reasonable person without one' (*An Enquiry Concerning Human Understanding*, section X).

42 Op. cit., p. 376.

43 The question as to how radical Hume's scepticism was is discussed by Anne Jaap Jacobson in chapter 6 below.

44 His *Traité des Systèmes*. See chapter 9.

45 *An Enquiry Concerning the Principles of Morals*, sect. I.

46 See chapter 2. See also R. S. Woolhouse, *The Empiricists* (History of Western Philosophy series), Oxford, Oxford University Press, 1988, chapter 5.

47 Clarke's two sets of lectures were published as *A Demonstration of the Being and Attributes of God: more particularly, in answer to Mr. Hobbs, Spinoza, and their followers*, London, Knapton, 1705 and *A Discourse concerning the Unchangeable Obligations of Natural Religion*, London, Knapton, 1706.

48 The controversy is described in J. P. Ferguson, *The Philosophy of Dr. Samuel Clarke and its Critics*, New York, Vantage Press, 1974.

49 In his posthumously published *Dialogues concerning Natural Religion*, Hume gave careful consideration to the argument from design but was peremptory in his treatment of the a priori arguments.

50 See Butler's *Analogy of Religion, Natural and Revealed, to the Constitution and Course of Nature*, London, 1736 and Paley's *Natural Theology: or Evidences*

of the Existence and Attributes of the Deity, Collected from the Appearances of Nature, London, 1802.

51 For instance by Henry Lee in *Anti-Scepticism*, London, 1702 (repr. New York, Garland, 1978).

52 See Yolton, John, *Thinking Matter: Materialism in Eighteenth Century Britain*, Minneapolis, University of Minnesota Press, 1984 and *Locke and French Materialism*, Oxford, Clarendon Press, 1991.

53 See chapter 9 below.

54 *Essay concerning Human Understanding*, book IV, ch. X, sect. 6.

CHAPTER 1

Lord Herbert of Cherbury and the Cambridge Platonists

Sarah Hutton

The philosophy of Lord Herbert of Cherbury (1582/3–1648) and of the Cambridge Platonists exemplifies the continuities of seventeenth-century thought with Renaissance philosophy. At the same time, they were very much engaged with new developments in philosophy of the seventeenth century. Together they represent the development of philosophy outside the Aristotelian tradition. And each illustrates one aspect of what were to become interconnected features of seventeenth-century philosophy: its lay character and the use of the vernacular as the language of philosophical discourse. Although he wrote in Latin, still the *lingua franca* of intellectual exchange, Lord Herbert was a lay practitioner of philosophy. The Cambridge Platonists were all university men, although they wrote in English.

❧ LORD HERBERT OF CHERBURY ❧

Lord Herbert of Cherbury is normally placed in a category of his own as a philosopher, separate from the philosophical groupings of the seventeenth century. He was neither the successor to, nor the founder of a school. His reputation as a philosopher derives from his epistemo-logical treatise *De veritate* (1624, begun 1617) and his work of religious philosophy, *De religione laici* (published with the third edition of *De veritate* in 1645). His motivation in writing these works was as much religious irenicism as a wish to confront the problem of scepticism. Having travelled in Europe and served as English ambassador to France 1619–24, he undoubtedly benefited from his contact with European intellectuals – Grotius, Tilenus, Casaubon, and especially the Mersenne circle. Indeed Mersenne is credited with the French translation of *De veritate*.[1] Herbert was acquainted with Gassendi and appears to have known Descartes personally (Descartes presented a copy of his *Méditations* to him (1.60) and Herbert commenced an English translation of the *Discours*). Both Descartes and Gassendi wrote comments on the second edition of *De veritate* (1633) at his request or that of Mersenne.[2]

De veritate is a blend of Stoic, Neoplatonic and Aristotelian elements, founded on the Renaissance microcosmic/macrocosmic analogy between man and nature: everything knowable in the world has its corresponding faculty in the mind. Nothing can be known except through those faculties. True knowledge consists in conformity between the faculties of the mind and the objects of knowledge: 'Truth is a harmony between objects and their faculties' ([1.34], 148). While he insists that certainty of knowledge is possible, Herbert recognises the limitations of human knowledge and accepts that not everything can be known. He distinguishes four classes of truth: truth of the thing itself (*veritas rei*), truth of appearance (*veritas apparentiae*) truth of concepts (*veritas conceptus* or subjective truth), and truth of the intellect (*veritas intellectus*), each of which is able to grasp truth according to its own nature. The main faculties of the mind are: natural instinct, internal perception (equivalent to will or conscience), external perception (equivalent to sensation) and discursive thought (reason). Over and above these he posits the presence in the mind of common notions, 'imprinted in the soul by dictate of nature' ([1.34], 106). These *koinai ennoiai* (to use the Stoic term Herbert adopts) 'are the principles without which we should have no experience at all' ([1.34], 132). These common notions are implanted in the mind by Divine Providence. Indeed they constitute an important part of the image of God in man. And their truth is attested by universal consent.

Among the faculties of the mind, Natural Instinct is the highest, able to grasp truth intuitively, with absolute conviction. Reason or discursive thought (*discursus*) is the lowest faculty of all, most liable to error through misapplication, but of enormous value when properly applied in accordance with the common notions. Reason is to be guided by the application of a set of rules or 'zetetica', not dissimilar to Aristotle's categories, which help it to discern the common notions and perform its functions of generalization, analysis, reflection. Along with internal and external perception, reason is part of a cumbersome apparatus for processing subjective classes of truth in order to ascertain the certainty of the thing in itself in accordance with the common notions. Herbert's epistemology is integrally connected to his religious concerns. He does not supply a comprehensive list of the common notions apart from the five pertaining to religious belief. In *De veritate*, *De religione gentilium* and his argument for religious tolerance in *De religione laici* he proposes a minimum number of fundamental beliefs, arrived at by examining the common elements in all religions. These religious common notions are that there is a god, that god is to be worshipped, that virtue and piety are the chief parts of worship, that we should repent of our sins, and that the afterlife brings reward or punishment. Thus the essentials of religion may be arrived at by reason without the need for revelation.

Herbert's most eminent contemporary critics (Descartes and Gassendi)[3] were quick to point out that the certainty of his method for arriving at truth is fatally dependent on universal consent and therefore inadequate as an answer to scepticism. He is the one philosopher actually named by Locke in his critique of innatist epistemology. But, as R. H. Popkin points out ([1.42], 155), Herbert anticipates many of the objections levelled at him by Locke and he appears to suppose that knowledge is derived from empirical observation of the world outside the mind.

Herbert's standing as a philosopher in the later seventeenth century was occluded by posthumous association with deism and irreligion. His reputation as father of deism derived in large part from his posthumously published *De religione gentilium* (Amsterdam, 1663) which discusses religion in distinctly non-Christian terms and has affinities with the religious views of Bruno and Campanella. Herbert's deism seemed more obvious in the wake of hostile reaction to developments in philosophy in the later seventeenth century, especially to the work of Hobbes and Spinoza's *Tractatus theologico-politicus*. On the one hand, Christian Kortholt in *De tribus impostoribus* (Cologne, 1680)[4] and Michael Berns in *Altar der Atheisten* (Hamburg, 1692) read Herbert, along with Hobbes, as a forerunner of Spinozistic atheism. On the other hand, the deist Charles Blount professed himself to be a disciple of Herbert and plagiarized Herbert's *De religione laici* in his own work of that name (1683). The imputation of deism lead to *De veritate* being regarded as the theoretical underpinning of natural religion, and Herbert as a forerunner of the Enlightenment. This posthumous standing as a kind of *proto-philosophe* should not obscure the fact that, with its eclectic blend of elements of ancient philosophy (Stoic, Neoplatonic and Aristotelian) along with its emphasis on free will and *consensus gentium* arguments, Herbert's philosophy is a product of the humanist tradition of Renaissance philosophy. His concern with the problem of scepticism places it within the new philosophical climate of the seventeenth century. This blend of Renaissance elements with seventeenth-century philosophical concerns, as well as arguments for free will and arguments based on universal consent, are all characteristics of the diffuse group of English thinkers known as the Cambridge Platonists, although none of them were actually followers of Herbert.

❧ THE CAMBRIDGE PLATONISTS ❧

The term 'Cambridge Platonist' is a label of convenience for a cluster of philosophical divines, liberal in their theology and educated at the University of Cambridge in the first half of the seventeenth century. The most prominent members of this group were Henry More (1614–87) and Ralph Cudworth (1617–88). Other contemporaries associated with the group were also Cambridge dons: Nathaniel Culverwell (1619–51), John Smith (1618–52), Peter Sterry (1613–72) and the man traditionally regarded as their forerunner, Benjamin Whichcote (1609–83). Their younger followers include George Rust (d. 1670), John Norris (1657–1711), Anne Conway (c. 1630–79) and the group of liberal churchmen now known as the latitudinarians, especially Simon Patrick (1626–1707) and Edward Fowler (1632–1714). Two kindred spirits, that might also be mentioned in this connection are Joseph Glanvill (1636–80) and Jeremy Taylor (1613–67). The Cambridge Platonists are too heterogenous a group to be considered a philosophical school: the common element in their thinking is a liberal theological outlook rather than a consistent set of philosophical doctrines. Indeed their philosophical concerns must be understood in relation to their primary concerns with religious apologetics. In theology, their emphasis on the role of reason in religion and on the freedom of the will, contrasted with the prevailing Calvinist predestinarian orthodoxy of the first half of the century, suggesting that their theological roots lie with Erasmian humanism. Reason was conceived as a safeguard against the excesses of the fanaticism of self-proclaimed prophets, or 'enthusiasts' as such 'private spirits' were then known. This is a reminder that Cambridge Platonism developed in the context of a period of religious strife and uncertainty of belief. The Platonism of their sobriquet was an eclectic Neoplatonism, reminiscent of Florentine Neoplatonism and strikingly receptive to those aspects of seventeenth-century philosophy and science which appeared compatible with their rational theology, though hostile to the materialistic philosophies inconsistent with it. More, Cudworth and Smith were all attracted by Cartesianism (albeit with differing degrees of reservation). More and Cudworth were implacable in their opposition to Hobbes and Spinoza. Thus their theological stand against voluntarism and predestinarian Calvinism corresponds to their philosophical opposition to the materialism of Hobbes and Spinoza. Behind both their religious and philosophical concerns, the challenge of scepticism is apparent. The same blend of Ficinian Neoplatonism and anti-determinism is to be found in their Oxford predecessor, Thomas Jackson (1579–1640).[5] In Jackson's work, as later in that of the Cambridge Platonists, eclectic Neoplatonism serves as a philosophical alternative to prevailing but increasingly outmoded Aristotelianism. Peter Sterry, on the other hand, combines his visionary Neoplatonism with denial of free will in his *Discourse of the Freedom of the Will* (1675). And Nathaniel Culverwell's *An Elegant and Learned Discourse of the Light of Nature* (Cambridge, 1652) is critical of aspects of Platonism, especially the doctrine of the pre-existence of souls, preferring instead to draw on scholastic sources, especially Thomas Aquinas and Suarez. His use of Aquinas is consistent with his rationalizing theology. (Ficino before him had used Aquinas in his *Theologica platonica*).

In their emphasis on reason, the Cambridge Platonists were careful to acknowledge its limitations in fallen human nature. While affirming the compatibility of faith and reason, they never elevated reason above faith. Reason is the pre-condition of faith (faith without reason is blind), but it is also illuminated by faith. Right reason is affective reason, directed by love towards God. Furthermore, by reason, the Cambridge Platonists do not mean mere abstract speculation (logic too, is blind, according to Smith), but a more elevated capacity of the mind than discursive reason. Reason corresponds to *mens* or *nous*, deriving its power from either reflection of or participation in the divine. Moreover, their concept of reason emphasises practical reason: the mind contains within it the principles of moral conduct. Thus, moral purification is the best way to obtain true knowledge. In advancing the claims of reason in religion, Whichcote, Culverwell and Smith appear to be addressing fellow-believers who deny reason a role in religious matters. Cudworth and More, by contrast, set out to defend religious belief against un-believers, conscious of the need to defend religion in a 'seculum philosophicum'. But they were careful to define its role so that it did not conflict with faith. *The Apology of Henry More* (1664) gives a set of rules for the use of reason in matters of religion, insisting that the apologist should choose 'Philosophick theorems' which are 'solid and rational in themselves, nor really repugnant to the word of God'.[6]

It is a mark of their repudiation of Aristotelianism as the philosophical groundbase of theology that the Cambridge Platonists each adopt some version of innatism. This also, perhaps, explains part of the attraction of Cartesianism for them. For Culverwell, the mind is furnished with 'clear and indelible Principles' through which the mind can recognize the law of nature or *nomos graphos* written in the heart of man. These principles include moral principles. But while he accepts that they are innate, he denies that they are 'connate' (that is, present from the moment of the creation of the soul) – a view which he associates with the Platonic doctrine of pre-existence of souls. These innate ideas or principles are often referred to as common notions, as for example by John Smith who calls the common notions 'praecognita' or 'the Radical Principles of Knowledge' imprinted in the soul ([1.27],

13). These *logoi spermatikoi* include the idea of God and of virtue as well as the principles of mathematical demonstration. The doctrine of common notions is not in itself attributable to Herbert's influence, since it derives from Cicero through whom it became a commonplace of Renaissance humanism.[7] When, in *The Immortality of the Soul* (London, 1657), Walter Charleton proposes, in opposition to Aristotle's conception of the soul as a *tabula rasa*, a set of 'Proleptical and Common Notions' innate to the mind he is echoing the Cambridge Platonists. Charleton's common notions include ideas of 'Motions and Figures' and the means whereby the mind can form ideas of things when stimulated by external objects.[8] Later in the same work he links this concept of proleptical and innate ideas with Descartes' demonstration of the existence of God from the idea of God in the mind. It is none the less true that the Cambridge Platonists were aware of Herbert's theory of truth: Whichcote and Rust both draw on his theory of truth. Cudworth and Culverwell are critical of Herbert ([1.25], 31–6; [1.26], 193; [1.10], 160).

In 'The True Way or Method of Attaining to Divine Knowledge' John Smith argues that knowledge of God is possible by inward meditation rather than external ([1.27]). The innate knowledge of the mind is obscured by the body, and is therefore to be attained by closing the eyes of sense and opening the eyes of understanding. While Smith subordinates sense-perception to intellection in this way, he none the less insists that knowledge of the external world is conducive to religious belief. Far from being antithetical to developments in contemporary science, the Cambridge Platonists accommodated them. Culverwell is open in his admiration of Francis Bacon in *The Light of Nature*, while Cudworth and More used contemporary natural philosophy in their construction of a *philosophica perennis* that combined both the Renaissance idea of a *prisca theologia* and a concomitant *prisca scientia*. From a philosophical point of view, the most important of the Cambridge Platonists were Ralph Cudworth and Henry More.

RALPH CUDWORTH

The only major philosophical work which Cudworth published in his lifetime was his *True Intellectual System of the Universe* (1678). The published part constitutes the first book of a treatise originally conceived as a more extensive work which was never completed. None the less, book 1 stands on its own as a self-contained unit. Of the papers Cudworth left behind on his death, two treatises were published posthumously: his *Treatise Concerning Eternal and Immutable Morality* (1731) and his *Treatise of Free Will* (1838). For all the humanistic antiquarianism of his writings, Cudworth was a modern in natural philosophy, in that he accepted the mechanical philosophy, albeit with important modifications to safeguard dualism and ensure its compatibility with Christian teaching. He maintains that matter is inert, 'Extended bulk' of which the principle attributes are 'Divisibility into Parts, Figures, and Position, together with Motion or Rest, but so as that no part of Body can ever Move it Self; but is alwaies moved by something else' ([1.9], 7). These properties are deducible from the very idea of matter, and hence intelligible without the otiose and untintelligible apparatus of intentional species, and substantial forms of scholasticism. Since the properties of matter by definition exclude mental operations, to posit the existence of matter endowed with these properties and no others is to imply the existence of incorporeal substance: 'neither can Life and Cogitation, Sense, and Consciousness, Reason and Understanding, Appetite and Will, ever result from Magnitudes, Figures, Sites and Motions, and therefore they are not Corporeally generated and Corrupted'. ([1.9], 36). Hence it is that 'the same Principle of Reason which made the Ancient Physiologers to become Atomists, must needs induce them also to be Incorporealists' ([1.9], 40). Furthermore, since true atomism leads to the recognition of an intellectual faculty able to judge the appearances of things, it is an antidote to scepticism ([1.9] (1845), 3: 554–5).

True Intellectual System of the Universe is a work of immense classical erudition. Most of it is taken up with *consensus gentium* arguments showing the prevalence among ancient philosophers of belief in a supreme deity. Insofar as Cudworth sets out the philosophical schemes of ancient atomists, *The True Intellectual System* can be considered as a history of philosophy. The purpose of this antiquarian exercise is in large measure to vindicate corpuscularean natural philosophy from the charge of atheism. The underlying conception of philosophy is of a *philosophia perennis* deriving ultimately from Moses and transmitted to all nations of the world where it resurfaces in more or less partial or imperfect forms. *The True Intellectual System* thus presupposes the homogeneity of philosophy, its systematic unity and the singleness of truth. True philosophy combined atomistic, mechanistic natural philosophy and a metaphysics positing the existence of spirit and of God. In its pure totality it was taught by Pythagoras, and less perfectly by Empedocles, Anaxagoras, Plato and Aristotle. Degeneracy set in with the separation of the metaphysical and ethical aspects (the 'Theology or Pneumatology') from natural philosophy (the 'Atomical or Mechanical Physiology'), with philosophers like Plato (excusably) opting for the former. Leucippus, Democritus and Epicurus rejected the metaphysical component, thereby promoting dangerous atheistic versions of the original atomic mechanism. Cudworth distinguishes four distortions of mosaic atomism in four varieties of atheism: as atomical atheism (in which all things came about by chance), hylozoic atheism (initiated by Strato of Lampsacus, which imputes life to matter), hylopathian atheism (deriving from Anaximander, in which all things are derived from matter as the highest *numen*), and cosmo-plastic atheism (which entails a concept of the world soul, but without positing a guilding mind). These have their contemporary proponents: Spinoza by imputing the properties of spirit to matter is a hylozoist; Hobbes, by denying the existence of spirit altogether, but not denying the existence of God is a material atheist of the hylopathian variety. Cartesianism appears to occupy a somewhat ambiguous position in Cudworth's estimation. In many respects Cudworth appears to have adopted Cartesianism implicitly, but regarded its compatibility with the true, spiritualized mechanism propounded by Cudworth as inconsistent, necessitating the modifications Cudworth advances to secure its orthodoxy. In large measure, Cudworth's critique of Cartesianism is grounded in theological objections to Cartesian voluntarism and denial of final causes, with the philosophical consequences attendant upon that. Descartes is in some respects worse than the ancient pagans since he did not recognize the argument from design, and obstinately refused to see the hand of the deity in the orderly universe he described.

The vindication of ancient atomism in *The True Intellectual System* is part of the demonstration of the belief in the existence of God by an appeal to universal consent. To this end the evidence of pagan polytheism as well as pagan philosophy is mustered and interpreted to prove that belief in a divinity is natural to all human kind, even if it is expressed in corrupt form as polytheism. Cudworth is concerned not simply to prove the existence of God, but to demonstrate the true idea of God. In this respect his project is aimed not just at atheists and philosophers but also at Christian theologians. The idea of God, in Cudworth's conception, is integrally linked to the rational order of the universe, and therefore to the intelligibility of the universe. Just as atheism is characterized by deterministic notions of causality, so misconceptions of the deity, pagan and Christian alike, are characterized by misplaced emphasis on divine will, and elevation of divine omnipotence above other attributes. According to Cudworth, voluntaristic conceptions of God mean that the deity acts in an arbitrary manner. In consequence there is no criterion of truth, no secure grounds of morality, no providential government of the universe, since goodness, right and wrong, truth and falsehood would all depend on the arbitrary whim of the almighty. Voluntarism thus opens the way to scepticism. Instead, Cudworth stresses God's goodness and knowledge, above His omnipotence, arguing that this follows from the idea of God as 'a being absolutely perfect'. It follows from such an idea of God that divine

justice and moral principles are not arbitrary, but founded in the goodness and rationality of God. The laws of morality and God's providential design, being thus evidently rational, it also follows that human
beings must bear responsibility for their actions. Cudworth is also at
pains to emphasize divine providence, the visible hand of God in His
creation being clear demonstration of the wisdom and goodness of God.
It is in this connection that he puts forward his distinctive doctrine of
'Plastic Nature'. Derived ultimately from the Platonic *anima mundi*,
the 'Plastic Nature' is a spiritual agent of God, the chief instrument of
His government of the physical universe. Plastic nature is 'an Inferior
and Subordinate Instrument doeth Drudgingly Execute that Part of his
providence, which consists in the Regular . . . and Orderly Motion of
Matter' ([1.9], 150). Its existence implies that nature is not the supreme
numen but is subordinate to a Perfect Mind. It is the means whereby
God imprints His presence on His creation, displaying His wisdom
and goodness and rendering it intelligible. It is comparable to human
art, though superior to it. In positing 'plastic nature' as the intermediary
between God and the world, Cudworth was attempting to defend
divine providence by steering a course between mechanistic determinism, which explained all physical phenomena as the result of chance,
and occasionalism, which required the intervention of God in even the
minutest details of day-to-day natural occurrences. Determinism is as
irrational as it is impious: its theistic version, which admits the existence
of the deity, reduces the role of God to that of an 'idle Spectator',
rendering divine wisdom useless and irrelevant. In fact, what the mech-
anist identifies as the laws of motion, are actually the operations of
plastic nature putting divine purposes into effect. Occasionalism dispen-
ses with divine providence, making it 'operose, Sollicitous and Distracti-
ous', thereby opening the door to atheism. The occasionalist's god is
an undignified god obliged to intervene directly in the most menial
minutiae of the day-to-day running of the universe. As a buttress
against atheism, Cudworth's doctrine of Plastic Nature failed to satisfy
Pierre Bayle (1647–1706) who saw it as a reworking of the peripatetic
doctrine of substantial forms and inconsistent with the idea of a provi-
dentially ordered universe because it meant that God is ignorant of
what He does. Bayle's criticisms were based on the extracts translated
into French by Jean Leclerc and published in the *Bibliothèque choisie*
(1703–6).[9]

If Cudworth's Christian Platonism is evident in his making the
good the chief attribute of the deity, his debt to Neoplatonism is evident
in the fundamentals of his epistemology. His theory of knowledge is
scattered through *The True Intellectual System* but is most systematically set out in *A Treatise Concerning Eternal and Immutable Morality*.
The ultimate objective is a confutation of the materialistic concept of

mind and the ethical relativism of Hobbes. It is also integrally related to his idea of God. The underlying Neoplatonism is apparent in his conception of the relationship of the soul (and hence mind) to God, and of God to the world. The human mind not only mirrors the divine, but its capacity for knowledge comes about through its participation in the divine: 'The first Original Knowledge is that of a Perfect Being. Infinitely Good and Powerful, Comprehending itself'. 'The Divine Word is the Archetypal Pattern of all Truth', and it is 'by a Participation of the Divine Mind' that 'Created Minds' are 'able to know Certainly'. Knowledge is therefore innate to the mind which is like a microcosm of the world: 'The Minde and Understanding is as it were a Diaphanous and Crystalline Globe, or a kind of Notional World, which hath some Reflex Image, and correspondent Ray or Representation in it, to whatsoever is in the True and Real World of Being' ([1.9], 638; cf. [1.9] (1845), 3: 581). To comprehend is thus, in a sense, to contain all knowable things as ideas. The common notions are the *noemata* or 'intelligible' of things within the mind, the 'seeds' of certain knowledge derived from God by virtue of the fact that created intellects are 'ectypal models or derivative compendiums of the mind of God' ([1.9] (1845), 3: 581). The truth to which we have access in this way is one and eternal.

As the archetype of all things the mind of God precedes both the human mind and the world. Mind is thus antecedent to things, the intellect precedes intellection ([1.9], 733). Hence the common notions are *prolepses* or 'anticipations' of knowledge. Furthermore, the mind is not the passive recipient of knowledge, whether this is derived from God or from the external world. Cudworth conceives of the mind as active in obtaining knowledge: the 'cognoscitive' power of the soul is 'a power of raising intelligible ideas and conceptions of things from within itself' ([1.9] (1845), 3: 572). Thus knowledge is an inward and active energy of the mind itself. Cudworth rejects the image of the soul as a container to be filled (mere mental capacity) preferring an image of mental activity which also implies that knowledge is present in the mind potentially: knowledge is 'not be poured into the soul like liquor, but rather to be invited and gently drawn forth from it; nor the mind so much to be filled therewith from without like a vessel, as to be kindled and awakened' ([1.9] (1845), 3: 582).

Furthermore, the ectypal character of the natural world means that it bears the stamp of the divine ideas from which it derives, in the same way that a building, in its structure and the arrangement of its parts, corresponds to the plan of the architect. The design of the building, which differentiates it from a heap of bricks, displays the mind of the architect.

... no man that is in his wits will say that a stately and royal palace hath therefore less reality, entity, and substantiality in it, than a heap of rubbish confusedly cast together; because forsooth, the idea of it partly consists of logical notions, which are thought to be mere imaginary things; whereas the totum, 'whole' is all solid matter without this notional form. For this logical form which is the passive stamp or print of intellectuality in it, the first archetypes contained in the idea or skill of the architect, and thence introduced into the thing that ... distinguishes it from mere dirt and rubbish, and gives it the essence of a house or palace. And it hath therefore the more of entity in it because it partakes of art or intellectuality.

([1.9] (1845), 2: 594)

In like manner, the cosmos bears the stamp of the creator: the order and harmony of the natural world constitute the *scheses* which render the natural world intelligible to the observing mind. The mechanical philosophy 'makes sensible things intelligible' because the properties of matter, 'magnitude, figure, site and motion' are 'intelligible principles' ([1.9] (1845), 3: 545).

This 'stamp of intellectuality' in the world is not apparent to the senses. Cudworth denies sense-perception can lead to knowledge, for the senses are passive and unreliable. With mathematics as his model he argues that the more abstract knowledge is, the closer it is to truth and that 'scientifical knowledge is best acquired by the soul's abstracting itself from outward objects of sense and retiring into itself, that so it may better attend to its own inward notions and ideas' ([1.9] (1845), 3: 581). Far from being an empirical philosophy atomism is the triumph of reason over sense ([1.9] (1845), 3: 555). None the less, he does not deny sense-perception a role. Sense-perception is in fact vital for making us aware of the existence of the external world, without which we could not be sure of the existence of any thing except God ([1.9] (1845), 3: 564). Empiricism has its place in his epistemology, but mind is necessary for making sense of sensory input, 'the active power of the mind exerting its own intelligible ideas upon that which is passively perceived'. The *noemata* act upon the *phantasmata* and *aisthemata* (sensations) produced by sense-perception.

HENRY MORE

Henry More was the most prolific of the Cambridge Platonists and the most famous in his own time: his international reputation stemmed in large measure from his correspondence with Descartes (as it does even today) and from the publication in Latin of his *Opera omnia* (1679). *Divine Dialogues* (1668) which present an accessible recension of his philosophical views in dialogue form, ensured him a non-academic contemporary readership at home. The Platonism of Henry More like that of Ralph Cudworth was a version of the eclectic and syncretic Neoplatonism of the Renaissance. He too subscribed to the notion of a *philosophia perennis* deriving from Moses/Moschus which he called a *cabala*, in which he became interested in his later years (1.69 and Katz in 1.72). This concept of philosophy and the transmission of philosophical ideas is given fullest expression in *Conjectura cabbalistica* (1653), which constitutes a three-fold commentary on the first book of Genesis: literal, moral and philosophical. In its main philosophical tenets, the perennial philosophy here described was receptive to certain aspects of seventeenth-century philosophy, notably Cartesianism and hostile to others, in particular Hobbism and Spinozism.

More's earliest writings, his poems (1642 and 1647) are Neoplatonic allegories of the soul which argue for the immortality, divine origin and pre-existence of the soul and for the infinity of the universe. The poems show not only his repudiation of scholasticism and his preference for Neoplatonism as the philosophical framework for his thought, but his awareness of the new astronomy and of Cartesianism: his notes to *Psychathanasia* and *Democritus platonissans* and *The Philosopher's Devotion* give up-to-date technical glosses on the references to astronomy in the poems. More's first philosophical prose treatise, his *Antidote against Atheism* (1653) sets out the main themes which were to dominate his thought: the existence of spirit and the immortality of the soul. His metaphysical crusade against philosophical materialism, was the equivalent in his philosophy to his crusade against religious enthusiasm in which he advanced the role of reason in religion as a safeguard against sectarian fanaticism. In *An Antidote* he sets out to combat atheism by using arguments 'compiled of no Notions but such as are possible according to the Light of Nature'. *The Immortality of the Soul* develops many of these points adopting an axiomatic mode of argument in imitation of Descartes, proposing some thirty-two axioms which are designed to follow one from another or which are supposedly self-evidently rational. This is a method he adopts again in his *Enchiridion ethicum* (1667). Conceived as the introduction to a larger work of metaphysics which he never completed, *Enchiridion metaphysicum* (1671) is a reiteration rather than a development of arguments, which had been put forward in the *Antidote* and the *Immortality* and in More's letters to Descartes and to 'V.C.'.

From his poems through to his mature metaphysical writings, More develops and elaborates the pneumatology which formed the mainstay of his critique of the mechanical philosophy. He consistently proposed the existence of incorporeal substance and a spiritual explanation of causality. In his letters to Descartes (1648–9) and in his apologetic *Epistola . . . ad V.C.* (1664) he argues that there is immaterial extension as well as material. He tries to persuade Descartes to adopt his own distinction between material and immaterial extension: that the former is divisible and impenetrable, and the latter indivisible and penetrable. In the *Immortality* More defends his contention that the idea of spiritual substance is easy to define, entailing the properties of 'Self-penetration, Self-motion, Self-contraction and Dilatation, and Indivisibility'. More refines his concept of Spirit as extension with properties obverse to those of matter: where matter is divisible ('discerpible') and impenetrable, spirit is indivisible ('indiscerpible') but penetrable. In the *Immortality* he also gives his most developed account of his concept of the Spirit of Nature ('principium hylarchicum') which he had first described in his philosophical poems. The hylarchic spirit is More's answer to purely mechanistic explanations of 'all these Sensible Modifications in Matter'. It is 'a substance incorporeal, but without Sense and Animadversion, pervading the whole Matter of the Universe, and exercising a Plastical power therein according to the sundry predispositions and occasions in the parts it works upon, raising such *Phaenomena* in the World, by directing the parts of the Matter and their Motion, as cannot be resolved into mere mechanical powers' ([1.18], bk. 3, ch. 2, sect. 1). As the immaterial agent of God in the physical world, the spirit of nature is the equivalent in More's philosophy of Plastic Nature in Cudworth's: deriving from the Platonic world soul, it offered a means of explaining natural phenomena without recourse to the mechanism of the moderns or the substantial forms and occult qualities of the scholastics. In the *Immortality* More reserves its operations to cover the explanatory weaknesses of mechanistic theory, to account for phenomena such as the sympathetic vibration of lute strings 'which cannot be resolved into any *Mechanical* Principle'. In his *Enchiridion metaphysicum* (1671) More extends the operations of the spirit of nature to all phenomena which had hitherto been ascribed to mechanical causes. In the anti-mechanical cause, More marshals a wide array of physical and metaphysical phenomena from tidal motion and magnetic attraction to the operations of the soul and records of apparitions as well as experiments described in Boyle's *An Hydrostatical Discourse*. More criticizes Descartes for over-reliance on the argument for the existence of God from the idea of God, and for failing to take account of God's providence: innatism shorn of final causes is a recipe for misbelief, even disbelief in God, the deity being reduced to a mere philosophical abstraction, or at best the initial impetus that set creation in motion. More dubs Cartesians 'nullibists', as it were 'nowhere-ists', because they argued that God existed but failed to recognize that spiritual substance (God included) was extended and operative throughout creation.

The finality of More's opposition to mechanism of *Enchiridion metaphysicum* should not obscure the fact that, with important metaphysical qualifications, he accepted tenets of Cartesian mechanism as the best available natural philosophy, concerned as he was to oppose any manifestation of the materialism promoted by atheistical atomists like Epicurus. The worst contemporary manifestations of what he saw as atheistic materialism were the philosophies of Hobbes (which he attacked consistently and especially in *Immortality*) and Spinoza (attacked in two short treatises styled 'Epistolae': *Ad V.C. Epistola altera, quae brevem Tractatus Theologico Politici confutationem complectitur* and *Demonstrationum duarum propositionum . . . confutatio*) (in 1.32). More was one of the first promoters of Cartesianism in England (1.41; 1.70). He has been credited with the first English translation of the *Discours*[10] though this attribution has not been established with certainty. In the preface to his *Antidote against Atheism* he urges that Cartesianism should be taught in the universities. Initially Cartesianism seemed an ally in the battle against atheism. It appeared to offer a system of natural philosophy to replace discredited Aristotelianism, as well as an invincible innatist argument for the existence of God. In the preface *An Antidote against Atheism* More acknowledges his debt to Descartes, but rejects all his arguments for demonstrating the existence of God except the ontological argument claiming that the others are not such as would persuade atheists. In *Immortality of the Soul* More restates his admiration of Descartes and makes explicit that Hobbesian materialism is his chief target. However, More's Cartesianism was never pure Cartesianism. Much as he admired Descartes' natural philosophy, he consistently sought to enlarge the metaphysical dimension of Cartesianism. (cf. *Immortality of the Soul*). He points to the problem of transmission of motion from one object to another, if motion like shape is merely a mode of body. He argues that motion can only be imparted to matter by divine contagion, that is, if God is literally contiguous to it ('Quo modo enim motum imprimeret materiae . . . nisi proxime quasi attingeret marteriam universi aut saltem aliquando attigisset?').[11] He contests Descartes' denial of the existence of a vacuum, by advancing his own conception of divinized space: the sides of a vacuum-sealed jar are prevented from collapsing, not because the jar is filled with subtle matter, as in the Cartesian account, but because it is filled with divine extension ('divinam contendo interiacere extensionem'). He rejects Descartes' mechanical conception of animals, arguing that animals have souls. By no means all of the points that More raises are founded on a dogmatic a priori commitment to existence of a spirit of nature. He points up a number of areas where Descartes is not fully self-consistent, or does not appear to have the courage of his convictions to state his position clearly: for example, he criticizes him for side-stepping Copernicanism and for not admitting the infinity of the universe. On Descartes' own argument, the vortices should be cylindrical in shape and celestial bodies oblong, not round. More's criticisms of Descartes are revealing because they throw into relief key points of his own system. His 'Cartesianism' was less a conversion to the French philosophy, than an attempt to assimilate Descartes to More-ism, an attempt most vividly represented by his incorporation of Descartes in his *philosophia perennis* as a Neo-Pythagorian atomist in *Conjectura cabbalistica*. Underlying the fluctuations in More's assessment of Cartesianism was a consistent philosophy which entailed a natural philosophy dedicated to his religious apologetic.

The doctrine by which More is best remembered today, his conception of infinite space, is first discussed in his correspondence with Descartes. Against Descartes' view of extension, denial of the void and characterization of the extent of the universe as 'indefinite', More argues that space is a *res extensa* distinct from matter. Matter is mobile within space. If all matter were annihilated, space would remain. Furthermore, space, unlike matter, is infinite. As an immaterial *res extensa* space is thus analogous to spirit and to God Himself, whom More conceives as an infinitely extended spirit. The divinization of space is completed in *Enchiridion metaphysicum* where More describes space as 'an obscure shadow' of Divine extension, since the properties of space (immobility, immensity, immateriality etc.) correspond to most of the attributes of God. The conception of space as immaterial extension is important for More's argument for demonstrating the existence of incorporeal substances. His concept of space is thus formulated for primarily theological reasons. None the less, More's infinitization of space constitutes a significant contribution to the conceptual framework of the new philosophy of the seventeenth century, especially the new science. In certain important respects More anticipates Newton's concept of absolute space, though the question of More's direct influence on Newton continues to be disputed (Hall in [1.72]). It has also been argued that the pneumatology which accompanies More's concept of space may have a scientific afterlife, that More's concept of spirit may have contributed to the Newtonian concept of force.[12]

More's own excursions into empirical science were not entirely happy. While his poems bespeak a knowledge of contemporary scientific development, his letters to Samuel Hartlib (Hall in [1.72], and Webster [1.75]) document his antipathy to empirical investigation and a preference for the metaphysico-mathematical method of Descartes. In the 1662 edition of his *Antidote against Atheism* and again in *Enchiridium Metaphysicum*, More cited some of the experiments described in

Boyle's *New Experiments Physico-Mechanical* (London, 1660) as proof of the workings of the Spirit of Nature. His insistence on proffering a spiritual explanation for the results of the experiments incurred the public censure of Robert Boyle in his *An Hydrostatical Discourse* (London, 1672) (Henry in [1.72], and Greene [1.71]). A similar well-meaning attempt to harness empirical investigation to metaphysical enquiry was involved in the project for which he is most easily derided today: his compilation of instances of spiritual phenomena. Both *An Antidote against Atheism* and *The Immortality of the Soul* record the appearance of ghosts and poltergeists and examples of witchcraft. In this enterprise he found a willing ally in Joseph Glanvill whose *Sadducismus triumphatus* (1681) is just such a compendium of spiritual phenomena. While More's experiments in empiricism are wide open to criticism, the project was part of a philosophically-based religious apologetic which may be summed up in the motto which More himself supplied: 'No spirit no God'.[13] To twentieth-century minds to seriously propose the existence of witches, hobgoblins and ghosts savours of an irredeemably irrational occultism. In the seventeenth century such beliefs formed part of a logically coherent system of thought. Belief in evil spirits was not only consistent with belief in good spirits, but integral to the arguments for the existence of God based on the existence of spirit. Furthermore, it was widely accepted that the threat of Hell was necessary to ensure moral and law-abiding conduct. More was not an exception in his beliefs. Even Sir Francis Bacon suggested that cases of witchcraft should be recorded as a contribution to the natural history of marvels, and Lord Brereton proposed that the Royal Society should investigate supernatural effects (Coudert in [1.72]).

☙ ANNE CONWAY AND JOHN NORRIS ☙

The legacy of the Cambridge Platonists is most obvious in theology, especially among the more tolerant Anglicans known as the latitudinarians. Although these discarded the Neoplatonic underpinnings of Cambridge Platonism, their rational apologetic found a major exponent in John Ray whose *Wisdom of God manifested in the Works of Creation* (1691) acknowledges his debt to Cudworth and to More and became a model of its kind for Anglican religious apologetics based on the argument from design. In philosophy, there are echoes of the Cambridge Platonism in George Berkeley and Richard Price. Among their immediate followers in philosophy, particular mention should be made here of John Norris and Anne Conway, in both of whom distinctly Neoplatonic elements found new formulation.

Anne Conway (1630?-79) was a pupil of Henry More. Her

induction into philosophy was through his brand of Cartesianism. Later in her life she was influenced by the philosopher-physician, Francis Mercurius van Helmont[14]. In her posthumously published *Principia philosophiae antiquissimae et recentissimae* (1690) she posits a monistic ontology in which matter and spirit are conceived as one substance emanating from the Deity. The particles of this substance she calls monads. She denies the dualistic opposition of matter and spirit, asserting that what we take to be physical objects are composed of congealed particles of this one substance. The further this substance is from the perfection of God, the grosser or more corporeal it is. None the less, every particle is capable of regaining its original spiritual purity: 'even the vilest and most contemptible Creature, yea Dust and Sand, may be capable of all those perfections, sc. through various and succedaneous Transmutations from the one into the other' ([1.5], 225). She distinguishes two types of extension, 'Material and Virtual', the latter being the 'Internal Motion' or vital force of a body which may be transmitted from one body to another not mechanically but vitally, by a process she likens to propagation. In the course of her argument she attacks both the dualism of Descartes and More and the materialism of Hobbes and Spinoza, proposing a vitalistic explanation of causality more far-reaching than More's Spirit of Nature.

John Norris represents a different kind of development from Cambridge Platonism. He was an admirer of Henry More. Their brief correspondence, *Letters Philosophical and Moral* is appended to his *The Theory and Regulation of Love* (1688). His Cambridge-Platonist leanings predisposed him towards the philosophy of Malebranche,[15] of which he became the foremost English exponent ([1.76], [1.77], [1.78]). Norris himself denied that his encounter with Malebranche's philosophy lead to any great change in his philosophical views. Indeed in his early writings he argues for the existence of an ideal world and that God alone is the proper object of knowledge. The impact of Malebranche is evident in *The Theory and Regulation of Love* in which he defines love as 'a motion of the Soul towards good' and understands God to be the good in general. Norris distinguishes two kinds of love, love of God and love of things. The former is irresistible governing the direction of our will. Love of created things is derivative from the love for God but can be directed in its object by the will. *Reason and Religion* (1689) articulates Malebranche's theory of seeing all things in God. *Reflections on the Conduct of Human Life* (1689) adopts Malebranche's rules for guiding the mind which seeks truth. It is this Platonico-Malebranchean idealism which underlies Norris's critique of Locke's *Essay*, his *Cursory Reflections upon a Book Call'd an Essay Concerning Human Understanding*. Appended to his *Christian Blessedness* (1690) this takes Locke to task for trying 'to make the Idea of

God to come in by our Senses, and to be derived from Sensible Objects' (op. cit. p. 30). The influence of Malebranche on Norris is most fully developed in *An Essay towards the Theory of the Ideal or Intelligible World* (1701) which he originally planned as a work of Platonic metaphysics. Here Norris sets out to demonstrate the existence of an ideal world of necessarily existent entities which serves as the intelligible archetype of the natural world. It is 'the World of Truth, the great Type and Mould of external Nature'. ([1.22], p. 9). Material nature is modelled according to the archetypal plan of the ideal, but is contingent and mutable. The ideal world is 'necessary, permanent and immutable, not only Antecedent and Praeexistent to this [world], but also Exemplary and Representative of it, as containing in it Eminently and after an intelligible Manner, all that is in this Natural World, according to which it was made, and in conformity to which all the Truth, Reality, Order, Beauty and Perfection of its Nature does consist and is to be Measured' ([1.22], 8). The material world is an imperfect reflection of god, and cannot be known directly or with certainty. Only the ideal world as the 'omniform Essence' of God can be truly known. Our conceptions of physical nature derive from our seeing all things in God, not from sensory perception of physical bodies. Thus transmuted by Norris, Cambridge Platonism could be said to have enjoyed a kind of eighteenth-century afterlife in English Malebranchism.

❧ NOTES ❧

1 See [1.11]. On the attribution of the translation to Mersenne, [1.65], 529–35.

2 Descartes to Mersenne, 16 October 1639, in *Correspondence du P. Marin Mersenne*, ed. C. de Waard, Paris, 1963, vol. 8, p. 549–52. P. Gassendi, *Ad librum D. Edoardi Herberti angli de veritate epistola*, in Gassendi *Opera*, Lyon, 1658, vol. 3, pp. 411–19.

3 See previous note.

4 This was the first of several attacks on Herbert emanating from Germany. See Bedford, [1.59], 249.

5 S. Hutton, 'Thomas Jackson, Oxford Platonist and William Twisse, Aristotelianism', *Journal of the History of Ideas* 34 (1978): 635–52.

6 More, *Apology* appended to *A Modest Enquiry into the Mystery of Iniquity*, London, 1664.

7 Melancthon is credited with importing the idea of 'communa principia' or 'prolepses' into the arguments for the existence of God in reformation theology. See J. Platt, *Reformed Thought and Scholasticism. Arguments for the Existence of God, 1575–1650*, Leiden, 1982.

8 Walter Charleton, *The Immortality of the Soul*, London, 1657, pp. 92–6.

9 Bayle, *Œuvres diverses*, 1, pp. 216–7, 368 2, pp. 168–9. See R. Colie, 1.45,

chapter 7 and E. Labrousse, *Pierre Bayle*, 1964, vol. 2, pp. 214–6, 243–5 and footnotes.

10 *Discourse of a Method for the Well-guiding of Reason*, London, 1649. Crocker, [1.72], 235.

11 *Œuvres de Descartes* publiées par Charles Adam et P. Tannery, nouvelle presentation par B. Rochot, Paris, 1964–76) vol. 5, p. 236.

12 J. E. McGuire, 'Neoplatonism and Active Principles', in R. S. Westman and J. E. McGuire, *Hermeticism and the Scientific Revolution*, Los Angeles, 1977.

13 *An Antidote against Atheism*, [1.3], 142.

14 See vol. IV, ch. 1.

15 See vol. IV, ch. 10.

❧ BIBLIOGRAPHY ❧

Original Language Editions

(i) Complete and Selected Works

1.1 *The Cambridge Platonists*, ed. C. A. Patrides, London, Arnold, 1969.

1.2 Cudworth, Ralph, *Collected Works of Ralph Cudworth*, ed. B. Fabian, Hildesheim and New York, Olms, 1977.

1.3 More, Henry, *A Collection of Several Philosophical Writings*, London, 1662.

1.4 *Philosophical Writings of Henry More*, ed. F. L. MacKinnon, New York, Oxford University Press, 1925 (repr. 1969).

(ii) Separate Works

1.5 Conway, Anne, *Principia philosophiae antiquissimae et recentissimae*, Amsterdam, 1690.

1.6 *The Conway Letters Correspondence of Anne Viscountess Conway, Henry More, and their friends, 1642–1684*, ed. M. H. Nicolson, rev. S. Hutton, Oxford, Oxford University Press, 1992.

1.7 Cudworth, Ralph, *A Treatise of Freewill*, ed. J. Allen, London, 1838.

1.8 —— *A Treatise Concerning Eternal and Immutable Morality*, London, 1731.

1.9 —— *The True Intellectual System of the Universe*, London, 1678 (facsimile reprint, Stuttgart-Bad Cannstatt, 1964; edition with notes from J. L. Mosheim's 1733 Latin edition, London 1845; trans. (abbreviated version) Thomas Wise, London, 1706).

1.10 Culverwell, Nathaniel, *An Elegant and Learned Discourse of the Light of Nature*, London, 1652 (modern edition ed. R. A. Greene and H. McCallum, Toronto, University of Toronto Press, 1971).

1.11 Herbert of Cherbury, Edward, *De veritate prout distinguitur a revelatione, a verismili, a possibili, et a falso*, Paris, 1624 (2nd edn, London, 1633).

1.12 —— *De veritate . . . cui operi additi sunt duo alii tractatus: primus de causis errorum: alter, de religione laici*, London, 1645.

1.13 More, Henry, *An Antidote against Atheism*, London, 1652.

1.14 —— *Divine Dialogues*, London, 1668.

1.15 —— *Enchiridion ethicum*, London, 1667.

1.16 —— *Enchiridion Metaphysicum*, London, 1671.

1.17 —— *Epistola H. Mori ad V.C. quo complectitur apologia pro Cartesio, quaeque introductionis loco esse poterit ad universam philosophiam cartesianam*, Cambridge, 1664.

1.18 —— *The Immortality of the Soul*, London, 1659.

1.19 —— [Letters]: A. Gabbey, 'Anne Conway et Henry More. Lettres sur Descartes (1650–1651)', *Archives de Philosophie* 40 (1977): 379–404.

1.20 —— [Letters]: C. Clerselier, *Lettres de Mr. Descartes*, Paris 1657–9. (Vol. 1 contains the More Descartes correspondence reprinted in *Oeuvres de Descartes*, ed. C. Adam and P. Tannery, nouvelle présentation by B. Rochot, Paris, Vrin, 1957–8, vol. 5.

1.21 —— *Philosophical Poems*, Cambridge, 1647. Collected edition of poems previously published as follows: *Psychodia platonica* (Cambridge, 1642); *Democritus Platonissans* (Cambridge, 1645).

1.22 Norris, John, *An Essay towards the Theory of the Ideal or Intelligible World*, London, 1701–4 (repr., Hildesheim, 1974; New York, Olms, 1978).

1.23 —— *The Theory and Regulation of Love, a Moral Essay*, Oxford, 1688.

1.24 —— *A Philosophical Discourse concerning the Natural Immortality of the Soul*, London, 1708.

1.25 Rust, George, *A Discourse of Truth*, London, 1677.

1.26 —— *A Discourse of the Use of Reason in Matters of Religion*, London, 1683.

1.27 Smith, John, *Select Discourses*, ed. R. Worthington, London, 1660.

1.28 Sterry, Peter, *A Discourse of the Freedom of the Will*, London, 1675.

1.29 Whichcote, Benjamin, *Moral and Religious Aphorisms*, London, 1703.

1.30 —— *Select Notions*, London, 1685.

1.31 —— *Select Sermons*, London, 1694.

Translations

(i) Complete and Selected Works

1.32 More, Henry, *H. Mori Cantabrigiensis opera omnia*, London, 1675–9.

(ii) Separate Works

1.33 Conway, Anne, *The Principles of the Most Ancient and Modern Philosophy*, London 1692 (modern edition by P. Loptson, The Hague, Nijhoff, 1982).

1.34 Herbert of Cherbury, Edward *De veritate*, trans. M. H. Carré, Bristol, J. W. Arrowsmith, 1937.

1.35 —— *De religione laici*, ed. and trans. H. R. Hutcheson, New Haven, Conn., Yale University Press 1944.

Bibliographies

1.36 Crocker, R. 'A Bibliography of Henry More', in 1.72.
1.37 Pailin, D. S. 'Herbert von Cherbury', *Ueberwegs Grundriss der Geschichte der Philosophie: die Philosophie des 17. Jahrhunderts*, Basle, Schwabe & Co., 1988, vol. 3, pp. 223–4, 284–5.
1.38 Rogers, G. A. J. 'Die Cambridge Platoniker', *Ueberwegs Grundriss der Geschichte der Philosophie: die Philosophie des 17. Jahrhunderts*, Basle, Schwabe & Co., 1988, vol. 3, pp. 240–8, 285–90

Background and Influences on the Cambridge Platonists and Lord Herbert

1.39 Mintz, S. *The Hunting of Leviathan: Seventeenth-century Reactions to the Materialism and Moral Philosophy of Thomas Hobbes*, Cambridge, Cambridge University Press, 1962.
1.40 Nicolson, M. H. 'The Early Stages of Cartesianism in England' *Studies in Philology* 26 (1929): 35–53.
1.41 Pacchi, A. *Cartesio in Inghilterra, da More a Boyle*, Bari, Laterza, 1973.
1.42 Popkin, R. H. *The History of Scepticism from Erasmus to Spinoza*, Berkeley, University of California Press, 1979.
1.43 Rossi, M. M. *Alle fonti del deismo e del materialismo moderno*, Florence, 1942.

General Surveys and Aspects of the Cambridge Platonists

1.44 Cassirer, E. *The Platonic Renaissance in England*, trans. J. P. Pettigrove, Edinburgh, Nelson, 1953.
1.45 Colie, R., *Light and Enlightenment*, Cambridge, Cambridge University Press, 1957.
1.46 Lamprecht, S. P. 'Innate Ideas in the Cambridge Platonists', *The Philosophical Review* 35 (1926): 553–73.
1.47 Rogers, G. A. J. 'Die Cambridge Platoniker', *Ueberwegs Grundriss der Geschichte der Philosophie: die Philosophie des 17. Jahrhunderts*, Basle, Schwabe & Co., 1988, vol. 3, pp. 240–82.
1.48 Saveson, J. E. 'Differing Reactions to Descartes among the Cambridge Platonists', *Journal of the History of Ideas* 21 (1960): 560–7.
1.49 Stewart, J. A. 'The Cambridge Platonists', *The Encyclopaedia of Religion and Ethics* 3 (1911): 167–73.

Studies of Herbert and the Cambridge Platonists

Conway

1.50 Brown, S. 'Leibniz and More's Cabbalistic Circle', in 1.72.
1.51 Merchant, C. *The Death of Nature*, San Francisco, Harper Row, 1980.
1.52 Popkin, R. H. 'The Spiritualistic World of Anne Conway and Henry More', in Hutton, [1.72].
1.53 Walker, D. P. *The Decline of Hell*, London, Routledge, 1964.

Cudworth

1.54 Aspelin, G. 'Ralph Cudworth's Interpretation of Greek Philosophy. A Study in the History of English Philosophical Ideas', *Göthborgs Högskolas Arsskrift*, 49 (1943).
1.55 Carré, M. H. 'Ralph Cudworth', *Philosophical Quarterly* 3 (1953): 342–51.
1.56 Gregory, T. 'Studi sull'atomismo del seicento, III Cudworth e l'atomismo', *Giornale critico della filosofia italiana* 46 (1967): 528–41.
1.57 Hunter, W. B. 'The Seventeenth-century Doctrine of Plastic Nature' *Harvard Theological Review*, 43 (1950): 197–213.
1.58 Sailor, D. B. 'Cudworth and Descartes', *Journal of the History of Ideas* 23 (1962): 133–40.

Herbert

1.59 Bedford, R. D. *Herbert of Cherbury and the Seventeenth Century*, Manchester, Manchester University Press, 1979.
1.60 Fordyce, C. J. and T. M. Knox 'The Books Bequeathed to Jesus College Library, Oxford, by Lord Herbert of Cherbury', *Proceedings and Papers of the Oxford Bibliographical Society* 5 (1936–9).
1.61 Hutcheson, H. R. 'Lord Herbert and the Deists', *Journal of Philosophy* 43 (1946): 219–221.
1.62 Lagrée, J. Introduction to *Le salut du laïc. sur Herbert de Cherbury. Étude et traduction du 'De religione laïci*, Paris, Vrin, 1989.
1.63 Pailin, D. A. 'Herbert of Cherbury and the Deists', *The Expository Times* 94(1983): 196–200.
1.64 —— 'Herbert von Cherbury', *Ueberwegs Grundriss der Geschichte der Philosophie: die Philosophie des 17. Jahrhunderts*, Basle, Schwabe & Co., 1988, vol. 3, pp. 223–9.
1.65 Rossi, M. M. *La vita, le opere, i tempi di Edoardo Herbert di Cherbury*, Florence, Sansoni, 1947.
1.66 Sorley, W. R. 'The Philosophy of Lord Herbert of Cherbury' *Mind* n.s. 3 (1894): 491–508.
1.67 Walker, D. P. 'Edward Lord Herbert of Cherbury and Christian Apologetics', in *The Ancient Theology*, London, Duckworth, 1972.

More

1.68 Copenhaver, B. P. 'Jewish Theologies of Space in the Scientific Revolution: Henry More, Joseph Raphson, Isaac Newton and their Predecessors', *Annals of Science* 37 (1980): 489–548.

1.69 Coudert, A. 'A Cambridge Platonist's Kabbalist Nightmare', *Journal of the History of Ideas* 36 (1975): 633–52.

1.70 Gabbey, A. 'Philosophia cartesiana triumphata: Henry More, 1646–71', in T. M. Lennon *et al.* (eds) *Problems in Cartesianism*, Kingston and Montreal, Queens McGill, 1982.

1.71 Greene, R. A. 'Henry More and Robert Boyle on the Spirit of Nature', *Journal of the History of Ideas* 23 (1962): 451–74.

1.72 Hutton, S. (ed.) *Henry More, 1614–1687. Tercentenary Studies*, Dordrecht, Kluwer, 1990.

1.73 Koyré, A. *From the Closed World to the Infinite Universe*, Baltimore, Johns Hopkins University Press, 1957.

1.74 Power, J. E. 'Henry More and Isaac Newton on Absolute Space', *Journal of the History of Ideas* 31 (1970): 289–96.

1.75 Webster, C. 'Henry More and Descartes, some New Sources', *British Journal for the History of Science* 4 (1969): 359–77.

Norris

1.76 Acworth, R. 'Malebranche and his Heirs', *Journal of the History of Ideas* 38 (1977): 673–76.

1.77 —— *The Philosophy of John Norris of Bemerton (1657–1712)*, Hildesheim, Olms, 1979.

1.78 McCracken, C. J. *Malebranche and British Philosophy*, Oxford, Clarendon Press, 1983.

Smith

1.79 Micheletti, M. *Il pensiero religioso di John Smith, platonico di Cambridge*, Padua, La Garangola, 1976.

1.80 Saveson, J. E. 'Descartes' Influence on John Smith', *Journal of the History of Ideas* 20 (1959): 258–63.

Sterry

1.81 de Sola Pinto, V. *Peter Sterry, Platonist and Puritan 1613–1672*, Cambridge, Cambridge University Press, 1934.

Whichcote

1.82 Greene, R. A. 'Whichcote, the Candle of the Lord and Synderesis', *Journal of the History of Ideas* 52 (1991): 617–44.

CHAPTER 2

Science and British philosophy: Boyle and Newton

G. A. J. Rogers

~ INTRODUCTION ~

Achievements in the natural sciences in the period from Nicholas Copernicus (1473–1543) to the death of Isaac Newton (1642–1727) changed our whole understanding of the nature of the universe and of the ways in which we may acquire knowledge of it. These innovations had unprecedented implications for philosophy, and in Britain John Locke, George Berkeley and David Hume, were only the most famous of those philosophers whose work in large part reflected the scientific developments and the issues that they generated.

Copernicus's vision of a moving earth and a heliocentric universe found strong support in the observations of Galileo with the telescope in 1609, but the full intelligibility of the heliocentric view awaited a comprehensive physics to replace that of Aristotle. This new physics gradually took shape during the seventeenth century with Galileo and René Descartes prominent in its formulation. The zenith of this development was the publication in 1687 of Newton's *Mathematical Principles of Natural Philosophy*, the *Principia*, which provided a comprehensive mechanics that gave physical sense to the idea of a moving earth and provided a deep understanding of central physical concepts. It also generated an accuracy in scientific calculation and prediction scarcely previously conceived.

The birth of the new cosmology and the new physics was accompanied by a revival of ancient atomist theories of matter. Like the new cosmology and physics, the new atomism came to the fore at the expense of Aristotle's plenist theories of matter and space. The new atomism, suitably modified to minimize conflict with standard Christian theology, was most ably advocated in mid-century by Pierre Gassendi as part of a concerted attack on traditional Aristotelian or Scholastic philosophy. Other thinkers, before and after Gassendi, took up the campaign for atomism or some form of corpuscular theory of matter. Amongst these were Galileo, Thomas Hobbes and Descartes, indicative of a fruitful marriage between the new mechanics and corpuscularianism that remained at the heart of scientific achievement for the next two hundred years. In England the great advocate of the new atomism was the leading natural philosopher of the group who came to establish the Royal Society in 1660, Robert Boyle (1627–91). Boyle argued the case for 'the new corpuscular philosophy' in a series of works which were to have a great influence not only within matter theory but also, through the philosophy of John Locke, on epistemology.

An important strength of Gassendi's advocacy of atomism was that his version, whilst closely tied to that of Epicurus, was, nevertheless, argued from within a Christian theology. He was thus able to defuse the atomistic philosophy of what was standardly seen as its major liability, its association with atheism and an unacceptable hedonism. In England something similar was achieved by the Cambridge Platonists, especially Ralph Cudworth and Henry More. The former's *True Intellectual System of the Universe* (1678), which argued a Platonic-Christian atomism, and the latter in many of his writings, provided a basis from within Anglican theology for the acceptability of atomic theories. With a powerful group of like-minded enquirers into nature they helped to foster an atmosphere in which atomist theories of matter became acceptable. Concurrently with these philosophical works Boyle was not only producing argument but, importantly, presenting experiments in favour of the corpuscular theory. His findings were to be published through the 1660s and 1670s and became influential sources for the two most prominent thinkers of the end of the century, John Locke (1632–1704) and Isaac Newton.

Locke was not only a student of Boyle's writings, he was also a junior partner in Boyle's own scientific researches, conducted when they were both in Oxford in the 1660s. From an early point in his intellectual development Locke came to share Boyle's commitment to the corpuscular philosophy. Similarly, we can, through his early notebooks, trace Newton's close study of Walter Charleton's version of Gassendi's philosophy and the works of Boyle, and his early allegiance to a corpuscular account of matter.

The corpuscular theory raised fundamental questions about matter's basic properties which remain at the forefront of debate in the late twentieth century. It also raised in an acute form questions about how we can come to know what those properties are, or even if we have any reason to believe in an independent physical world at all. It was the implications of these accounts of matter that were to feature prominently in philosophy throughout the Enlightenment.

The natural philosophers had themselves often been conscious of these wider implications. Boyle, for example, was well aware that the generally empirically-based method for acquiring knowledge that he strongly favoured was open to various challenges from the sceptic. The most famous response to this scepticism in the seventeenth century was that of Descartes (1596–1650). But Boyle, whilst well aware of Descartes's achievement, was not himself attracted to the Cartesian solutions. Instead he chose to side-step the philosophical debate and pursue his researches in natural philosophy. Nevertheless, his account of matter and its properties both contained within it answers to philosophical questions and raised others that were to remain prominent and contentious issues.

Newton's *Principia* is famous for giving us the laws of motion and the theory of gravitation which provided a unified account of the physics of the heavens and the earth. But Newton also saw his science as exemplifying a method which he believed to be the most fruitful for enquiries into the physical world. Newton was himself influenced by the approach to nature that had emerged in England in the decades surrounding the English Civil War and which was much coloured by the programme for the investigation of nature that Bacon had advocated in the early part of the century. Newton added to that hard-headed empirical approach a mastery of mathematics which few have equalled. The combination was to produce the most powerful theory about the natural world than had ever been produced. Newton was himself aware of the debates about method that had dominated much seventeenth-century philosophy and he came down publicly very much in favour of an empirical methodology, even though he knew that it could never deliver that absolute certainty that could vanquish the committed sceptic. His final position emerged clearly in his later writings, especially in the second edition of the *Principia* (1713) and the later editions of the *Opticks*. In them he made his opposition to hypotheses, understood as empirically unsupported conjectures, very plain, and encouraged a commitment to the central place of careful observation, combined with minimal theory, a cornerstone of British physical science. Whether he was always quite consistent with his own principles is another, very interesting, question.

One issue that was to raise a great deal of debate was the exact status of Newton's claims for absolute space and time. Newton's account was to be challenged by the great German philosopher and mathematician Leibniz, in a fascinating exchange with Newton's spokesman, Samuel Clarke. Leibniz also challenged the acceptability of a central concept in Newton's system, that of gravitation. It was, Leibniz urged, an occult quality, as unacceptable as the occult qualities of the scholastics that Boyle and Newton were so eager to reject. It was a criticism that found echoes in the philosophy of George Berkeley, also writing in the early eighteenth century. The issues raised remain to this day subject to fruitful dispute in both science and philosophy.

❧ THE NATURE OF MATTER ❧

At the beginning of the seventeenth century the accounts of matter and its properties taught in the universities throughout Europe remained versions of Aristotle and his scholastic commentators. Central to these were a belief in the four elements of earth, water, air and fire, and the rejection both of the possibility of a vacuum ('Nature abhors a vacuum') and of any kind of atomic theory. The properties or qualities of bodies, of which there were supposed to be four *primary ones*, heat, cold, dryness and wet, were linked with the four elements. Thus water was a combination of prime matter plus the qualities of cold and wet. Water itself was regarded as a secondary matter. The qualities that objects may have are either the primary qualities or secondary qualities, and the latter are a function of the combination of the primary matter and the primary qualities. Examples of such secondary qualities would be lightness and heaviness, softness and hardness. It is worth underlining that the terminology of primary and secondary qualities, which was to feature so centrally in Boyle and Locke was not invented by them, but was taken over from their rejected predecessors. But the list of such qualities and the explanations offered for them were to be radically changed.

Another distinction drawn in the scholastic theory which was to be attacked by the corpuscularians was that between manifest and occult qualities. Whilst the scholastic primary and secondary qualities were all regarded as manifest, there were others, such as attraction, that were obscure or occult. Boyle was to see one of the great merits of the corpuscular account that it did away with these occult qualities of matter, explaining them as a function of more overt properties.

Dissatisfaction with the scholastic theory emerged outside the universities and in particular in iatrochemical theory. Thus Paracelsus in Switzerland added to the traditional four elements three 'principles', mercury, sulphur and salt, in his chemical medicine. His alternative account attracted a wide following throughout Europe in the late sixteenth and early seventeenth centuries and had a significant impact on the development of medical and chemical theory that is only now being fully appreciated.

At about the same time interest in classical atomism was revived with the publication of Lucretius' cosmological poem *De Rerum Natura*, and which itself led to a wider interest and enthusiasm for the philosophy, or such as had survived, of the Greek atomist Epicurus.

Epicurus had not only provided an alternative account of the properties of matter, he also offered a model of change which was radically different from that of Aristotle. For Aristotle changes in the properties of a given object were to be accounted for by the object itself acquiring or losing qualities, hotness, wetness, and the like. For the atomist, however, change in the properties of an object was generally to be accounted for by change in the arrangements of its parts, the atoms of various shapes, and the great source of such change was motion of those parts.[1]

This new conception of matter and its properties received early expression in Galileo's *Il Saggiatore* (1623). In a now famous passage he claimed that whenever he conceived of a material substance he had to think of it as having certain properties, of being bounded with a distinct shape and size and in some specific place, as being in motion or at rest, as touching or not touching other objects and as being one in number or few or many. These properties, he said, he could not separate from an object by any stretch of his imagination. It was, however, different with other properties such as taste, colour, sound and smell. These are not properties that one is compelled to regard an object as having and without our senses we would not have thought of them. So Galileo concluded that the latter qualities were not out there in the world but resided only in our consciousness and without living creatures they would not exist.[2]

Galileo's claims are often taken to be the first modern espousal of the primary-secondary quality distinction that was to be made famous by John Locke. For Galileo it meshed with his atomism and his commitment to the centrality of mathematics to a proper understanding of the world. The book of nature, he said, was written in the language of geometry, and it was for him important that the primary qualities of objects were amenable to quantified analysis.

Whether or not we see Galileo as the modern reviver of the distinction between primary and secondary qualities, the distinction itself must be seen as going together with the revival of Epicurean atomism or its near equivalent that was soon under way. This found particular expression in the writings of Pierre Gassendi, and the corpuscular philosophy of Descartes, where the primary-secondary quality distinction was most fully proposed in the latter's account of perception in the *Dioptrics*. Gassendi found an English spokesman in Walter Charleton, whose *Physiologia Epicuro-Gassendo-Charletoniana* (London, 1654) became a widely read statement in English of the new atomism.

Atomic theories of matter had begun to surface in England before the end of the sixteenth century, and in the works of Thomas Hariot, Walter Warner and Thomas Hobbes the theory received strong supporting argument. That argument, and more especially experimental evidence, for the corpuscular hypothesis was to reach an even greater level of sophistication in the writings of Robert Boyle. As a young man Boyle had travelled in Italy and was staying in Florence in January 1642, when Galileo died. Boyle was able to read Italian and he tells us that he studied Galileo's books,[3] but whether this included *Il Saggiatore* we do not know. It is, however, remarkable how close to that of the great Italian Boyle's account of matter's properties was later to be.

The most comprehensive treatment of Boyle's theory of matter was *The Origin of Forms and Qualities, According to the Corpuscular Philosophy* (1666, though much of it written many years earlier). In it Boyle expounds his reasons for rejecting the peripatetic explanation of matter's properties and for substituting it with the much richer corpuscular theory. Boyle emphasizes his lack of dogma, and says that he is not concerned to argue finer points of metaphysics. Nor does he wish to confine himself to one particular version of corpuscularian theory such as that there are indivisible particles called atoms, or the physical theory of Descartes, which identified matter with extension and claimed a vaccum to be impossible.[4] And neither does he intend to mix his exposition with matters of religion. Rather, he wishes his experiments and observations to be seen as leading naturally to the conclusions he draws.

Before turning to the experimental evidence, however, Boyle explains what his theory is, the 'hypothesis' that will be confirmed or disproved by the 'historical truths' or experiments that are to follow. It begins from the acceptance of a 'universal matter common to all bodies . . . a substance extended, divisible, and impenetrable'.[5] Second, the cause of the variety of matter is the motion of its parts, introduced, no doubt, Boyle is happy to allow, by God, for there is nothing necessary about matter having any kind or degree of motion.

With these 'two grand and most catholic principles of bodies, matter and motion' granted, Boyle is able to turn to matter and its properties or qualities. The matter of all natural bodies is, he says, the same, 'namely a substance extended and impenetrable'. Differentiation between bodies depends on differences in their 'accidents' or qualities. Motion, which is not part of the essence of matter, is the most important 'mood or affection' of matter, and it is this motion and the resultant collisions which divides matter into its various fragments, themselves often too minute to be perceivable. Each one of these minute parts (as well as all larger bodies) must have its own determinate size and shape and be either in motion or at rest. And out of the conglomeration of the different minute parts arises the texture of the gross perceivable object of experience.

These collections of particles – what we identify as particular material objects – come to our attention because they cause changes in us by ways which Boyle acknowledges remains problematic. But their affect is to produce in us the perceptions of such qualities as heat, colour, sound and odour. It is commonly imagined, says Boyle, that our perceptions 'proceed from certain distinct and peculiar qualities in the external object which have some resemblance to the ideas their action upon the senses excites in the mind.'[6] But this is not so, for all that there is in the body without us are the primary properties already listed. So Boyle is committed to saying that our ideas of such properties as colour and sound, although arising from real qualities of the perceived object, do not resemble their causes at all. They are, he says, 'but the effects of the oft-mentioned catholic affections of matter, and deducible from the size, shape, motion (or rest), order and the resulting texture, of the insensible parts of bodies'.[7]

Boyle anticipates what he perceives might be a serious difficulty for the corpuscular account of matter's properties. It is that the explication of colours, sounds and such like by reference to our senses is incompatible with something else that we take to be true, namely that the colour, say, of an object is an objective property of the body, and not dependent on our senses: 'snow (for instance) would be white, and a glowing coal would be hot, though there were no man or other animal in the world'.[8] Boyle's answer to this problem is to offer a dispositional account of the secondary qualities. There really is a difference between snow and coal, even in the dark, namely the dispositional property that if light were to shine on both one would cause the familiar experience of white in an observer and the other that of black, just as it is true, or not, that a particular musical instrument is in tune, whether or not it is actually being played.

So far Boyle's case for rejecting the scholastic account of properties in favour of his corpuscular theory is theoretical. But about half the *Origins of Forms and Qualities* consists of observations and experiments which Boyle argues can only be explained satisfactorily on the corpuscular hypothesis. Thus, drawing on his mastery of metallurgy and other chemically-based enquiries, he argues that what we now would see as examples of chemical change cannot be explained on the peripatetics' principles, whereas they are entirely intelligible on the corpuscular account.

In the 1650s Oxford was the scientific centre of England and even of Europe, and Boyle settled there in 1654. By this time he was already a skilled and knowledgeable chemist and wealthy enough to set up a laboratory in his house. He also initiated chemistry classes, and unsurprisingly came to occupy a dominant place in the scientific community. One of the people soon to be working most closely with him was the young John Locke, a professional contact that was to continue when they both moved to London in the late 1660s. It should not therefore come as any surprise to find that Locke was to draw on Boyle's scientific ideas in writing his major work on epistemology, the *Essay Concerning Human Understanding* of 1690.

A problem which arises from Boyle's account of qualities and our perception of them might be expressed like this. If objects in the world cause us to have our experiences of them, and if those objects are only known to us through the effects that they produce on us or in us, and those effects, our experiences of the secondary qualities such as colour and sound, for example, do not exist in the objects in the same way as we experience them, then is there not also a problem about knowing that our experiences of the primary qualities do resemble properties as they actually are in the objects? That, and related questions, have continued to concern philosophers since the seventeenth century, and although Boyle seems never to have considered the issue, we can be sure that it was one that does emerge from his and similar accounts and it was to be one that was to play a large role in philosophical discussion from this point on. It is worth underlining here that the problem arises out of the new corpuscular philosophy and its associated account of perception, and it is to feature strongly in the argument of Locke, Berkeley and Hume in Britain and, on the continent, it is central to the philosophy of Kant.

THE MECHANICAL PHILOSOPHY

Boyle's account of the properties of matter was part of his wider commitment to the mechanical philosophy. Various versions of this were already well known by the time that Boyle began to publish his own works. The two most powerful versions were Descartes's *Principles of Philosophy* (1644) and Hobbes's *Leviathan* (1651). But neither, for somewhat different reasons, was wholly convincing to British readers. The third great exponent of the mechanical philosophy in mid-century, Pierre Gassendi, was well known to the English exiles in Paris in the Civil War and Interregnum, and his philosophy reached a wider British audience with the publication in 1654 of Walter Charleton's *Physiologia Epicuro-Gassendo-Charltoniana*. The full title of the work well explained its content for it continued *Or a Fabrick of Science Natural, Upon the Hypothesis of Atoms, Founded by Epicurus, Repaired by*

Petrus Gassendus, Augmented by Walter Charleton. Essentially it was a translation of Gassendi's account of Epicurean physics, with supplements supplied by Charleton himself.

According to Charleton the physical world could be understood as a mechanical system governed by the following 'general Laws of Nature': '(1) That every effect must have its cause; (2) That no cause can act but by motion; (3) That nothing can act upon a distant subject... but by contact mediate or immediate'.[9] The last of these ruled out the possibility of 'action at a distance', with its language of sympathies and antipathies beloved of the natural magicians from whom Charleton and the atomists generally wished to distance themselves.

Charleton's work was undoubtedly influential, but it appeared at a time when another, altogether more powerful figure was in the ascendent, namely Boyle himself, and it was to be the account of the mechanical philosophy which he produced that was to become the most widely regarded, not least because Boyle was not only recognized as a leading natural philosopher in his own right, a position that Charleton never achieved, but also because his social standing and religious piety were never in question, matters of great importance to the acceptability of an account of nature which all too easily could be identified as subversive of state, church and morals.

What precisely Boyle understood by the mechanical philosophy has already in part been noticed in his claim that everything in the physical world may be understood in terms of matter in motion, but a fuller understanding of the new mechanical philosophy requires first of all a backward glance at Aristotle's explanation of change.

Fundamental to Aristotle's account of change was the principle that nature always acts for the sake of something. In other words, all natural change is goal directed. Such a teleological view of nature still has its place in some aspects of biological explanation. Thus we can ask of any particular organ of the body what its function is. And we can be told that, for example, the function of the heart is to pump the blood round the body. This characteristically biological explanation was generalized by Aristotle to the whole of the natural world. Thus he explained the falling of a stone towards the ground as manifesting the inclination of the stone to reach the centre of the universe, which was the 'natural place' towards which all objects made of earth matter – one of the four elements – were naturally inclined. Each element – the other three were water, air and fire – had its own natural place and objects would move according to their composition – objects made of liquid towards their natural place above the earth matter and below the air, and so on.

For some time before Boyle this account of the elements had been found wanting by a variety of natural philosophers. Amongst these were the followers of the sixteenth-century Swiss known as Paracelsus, who generated an alternative chemical theory that achieved a wide following in the early seventeenth century. Paracelsus and his followers were primarily interested in producing a new chemical medicine which was linked to their understanding that human beings were a microcosm of the wider universal macrocosm. The great debate about the merits of the Paracelsian theory was a feature of seventeenth-century chemistry that Boyle was party to and his own espousal of the mechanical philosophy was in conscious opposition to both the peripatetics and the Paracelsians, or, as he often calls them, the 'chemists'.

Boyle was happy to use the results obtained by the chemists if they were successful cures for ailments, but he was unpersuaded by their theory, at least for the most part. Instead, he proposed the mechanical philosophy as the best account of chemical change and other natural changes as well.

He abandoned also the Aristotelian commitment to final causes in nature and in one of his works, *A Free Enquiry into the Vulgarly Received Notion of Nature*, which remains a classic analysis of the concept, he comes close to abandoning completely any appeal to the concept of nature to explain anything. Rather, he holds that

> it seems manifest enough that whatever is done in the world, at least wherein the rational soul intervenes not, is really affected by corporeal causes and agents, acting in a world so framed as ours is, according to the laws of motion settled by the omniscient Author of things.[10]

It was this notion of the laws of motion that was central to the mechanical philosophy's account of change. Granted enough variety in the fundamental particles, variety of shapes and sizes, and a settled finite set of laws of motion, then it was possible, Boyle believed, to account purely on the basis of mechanical principles for the wide variety of events that can be observed. He included in this not only the gross movements of the planets and the other large objects but also what we now think of as chemical change and indeed also the way in which propagation of the species is achieved.[11]

The merits of the mechanical hypothesis were seen by Boyle to be many. Thus in contrast to the accounts of the peripatetics, the mechanical principles were very clear. Further, it was the simplest possible hypothesis, because there could not be fewer principles than those of matter and motion – there could not just be matter, for matter alone would be inactive. And, he held, neither matter nor motion can itself be resolved into anything simpler.

But for Boyle the clinching argument in favour of the mechanical hypothesis is its power of explanation, or, as he calls it, its comprehensiveness. With the assumption of a limited number of basic corpuscles of various shapes, moving at variable speeds, we can account for the vast number of varying properties that we discover in the world in rather the same way that the limited number of letters of the alphabet can account for all the works of literature written in various languages. Further, the mechanical hypothesis is not incompatible with many of the claims of other theories, for example the chemical theory of van Helmont, and their accounts can largely be comprehended within it.[12]

Under Boyle's influence especially, the mechanical philosophy became accepted by the virtuosi associated with the establishment of the Royal Society in Restoration England as the most plausible account of the natural world.

It might seem that the publication of Newton's *Principia* only added massive support to the mechanical hypothesis, for at first sight it seemed to provide an explanation of the motion of objects that was entirely in keeping with the mechanical model. But Newton himself rarely referred to the mechanical philosophy – the most famous occasion being in a letter to Boyle in 1679.[13] But he was very keenly aware that the introduction of the law of universal gravitation, whilst correctly reflecting the observed facts of motion, was not itself explained. Although he held that 'inanimate brute matter' could not affect other matter without mutual contact, thus ruling out action at a distance as a possible power of material objects, he made no claims to know what the cause of gravity might be. 'Gravity', he said, 'must be caused by an agent acting constantly according to certain laws, but whether this agent be material or immaterial I have left to the consideration of my readers.'[14] There is some reason to suppose that Newton actually believed that the direct cause of gravitation was indeed immaterial, and that it was God himself, a view linked to his belief that the Deity was co-present and co-extensive with the infinite universe.[15] There were, then, according to Newton, two kinds of things in the universe. There were particles of matter, which combined into gross material objects, and there were immaterial active agents.

In his *Opticks* Newton characterized matter in this way:

> it seems probable to me that God in the beginning formed matter in solid, massy, hard, impenetrable, movable particles, of such sizes and figures, and with such other properties and in such proportion to space as most conduced to the end for which he formed them; and that these primitive particles being solids are incomparably harder than any porous bodies compounded of them.[16]

These particles are moved, Newton went on, not only by the normal laws of contact dynamics, which flow from their natural inertial motion, but also by 'certain active principles' such as that of gravity and the forces which generate the cohesion of gross objects. With this we may see that Newton held, later in his life at least, a position quite different from that of the mechanical philosophy if this is supposed to suggest some simple allegiance to Epicurean atomism. His position was a long way away from Hobbes's materialist philosophy that the only things that exist are lumps of matter and the only cause of change is motion. Indeed Newton could not have accepted Boyle's view that, God and minds aside, the only principles are those of matter and motion. Rather, for Newton the immaterial principles that the mechanical philosophy thought had been ejected from physics, and even from the whole of creation, were, in his more speculative and secret thoughts, given a central role in his account of things. Why they were not as prominent in Newton's published works as they might have been is a matter that will be touched on later when we consider his attitude towards the possibility of achieving knowledge of the natural world.

Space and time

Newton's commitment to absolute space and time is a famous part of his account of the world and one which was to lead to considerable controversy. He appears to have been led to his absolutist position by a variety of considerations which included his admiration for the absolute theory of the Cambridge-Platonist philosopher, Henry More, who, incidently, like Newton, came from Grantham. More had argued against Descartes's relativist account of space that the existence of a Deity required the two absolutes of space and time in which God's existence could be placed. Indeed More went further, for he believed that everything that exists, whether material or immaterial, must be extended (i.e. must be a space-occupier with dimensions). In this he was very conscious of his disagreement with Descartes, who had identified matter and extension, and who held that all mind-substances, including ourselves and God, were necessarily *unextended* entities. But God, as an infinite being, was for More an infinitely extended being – i.e. He was omnipresent both spatially and temporally.

The extent and nature of More's account of space can only be gestured here, but the relevant points for understanding Newton's position are that More took space to be an absolute the properties of which can be described by geometry (though More was himself no great mathematician), and that it is directly linked with the nature of a Deity. More thus combined natural philosophy with theology in a commitment to absolute space and time. His account was, at the same time, an attack on the mechanical philosophy, and specifically on Robert

Boyle, for More was committed to establishing the impossibility of a purely mechanical (i.e. materialist) philosophy explaining all the phenomena of nature.[17]

These features were to reappear in Newton, but now cemented to the incomparably more powerful mathematical physics of the *Principia*. Essentially, he argued that physics required absolute space and time, and the existence of absolute space and time requires the existence of an infinite God. Thus in the scholium to Definition 8 he distinguished between absolute and relative space and time. That there was such a thing as absolute space and time followed, he said, from the existence of absolute motion, and absolute motion was known to exist because any object accelerating as a result of a force acting on it must be in absolute motion, for a force is precisely that thing that causes an object to change its state of rest or uniform motion. Such a state is exhibited, for example, whenever an object in rotation attempts to recede from the centre of rotation. We can only understand this to be an object which is absolutely rotating, i.e. moving in relation to absolute space.

In the General Scholium added to later editions of the *Principia* Newton explicitly linked his physics with his theology. God, Newton says, is the Lord of his creation and

> from his true dominion it follows that the true God is a living, intelligent, and powerful Being; and, from his other perfections, that he is supreme, or most perfect ... his duration reaches from eternity to eternity; his presence from infinity to infinity. ...
> He endures forever, and is everywhere present; and, by existing always and everywhere, he constitutes duration and space.[18]

So, in Newton's view, it is the existence of absolute space and time that entails the existence of an infinite deity and it is the new physics, Newton's new physics, that requires absolute space and time to explicate the central concept of force.

Newton's commitment to absolute space and time was one of the topics of a famous exchange between the English philosopher divine, Samuel Clarke and the German philosopher, Leibniz. Leibniz had several objections to the introduction of absolute space and time, some of which related to his understanding of what kind of universe God might create. But a central claim of his was that space and time were not real things which could exist separately from phenomena. They were essentially relational concepts and did not exist before a world was created, as Newton implied.[19]

A relativist position not too distant from that of Leibniz was also taken by George Berkeley, though for rather different reasons. The fullest expression of that position occurs in his work, *De Motu* (1721) in which Berkeley argues that the concepts of absolute space and time are empty since it is impossible to conceive of absolute motion. Motion can only be recognized or measured, he says, through observation, and since absolute space cannot affect the senses 'it must necessarily be quite useless for the distinguishing of motions'.[20] The debate about absolute space and time was to continue through the eighteenth century and well into the nineteenth, but in general the high standing of Newtonian science protected it from rejection until supplanted by the physics of Mach, Poincaré and Einstein at the end of the nineteenth century.

Knowledge and nature

The new science that developed in the sixteenth and seventeenth centuries challenged the understanding of knowledge and how it may be obtained in a variety of ways. Thus, to take but one, though important, example, Copernicus's suggestion that the earth rotates daily on its own axis and that in a year it circles the sun seemed quite at odds with our ordinary experience, where we see the sun rise in the east and set in the west and the earth itself feels stationary. Aristotle had himself stressed the empirical source of knowledge, and experience seemed to tell against Copernicus. Even if one granted that the Copernican system generated more accurate predictions, that in itself did not prove that it was true.

Those who sided with Copernicus, like Copernicus himself, were often strongly impressed with the power of mathematics to make sense of the world, and often went so far as to see mathematics as itself providing a criterion for truth between competing theories. In England this position was well represented in the 1570s by John Dee's Preface to the first English edition of Euclid's *Elements*. Geometry, Dee claimed, provided a bridge between the eternal and the transient, the mind of God and the changing world. Mathematics provided the key to the creation. We have already seen that something of that was later to find expression in Galileo, as it did also in Galileo's contemporary, the great astronomer, Kepler.

This emphasis on the power of mathematics stood in contrast with the general scholastic position which did not emphasize mathematics as a source of knowledge of the natural world. Indeed, for the most part Aristotle's natural philosophy rejected mathematics as irrelevant to understanding the truth about nature. Knowledge, it was held, was primarily a matter of identifying the true essence of natural kinds in terms of their essential properties by careful empirical investigation or, more often, mastering the truths that had been uncovered by the investigations of earlier thinkers, including, of course, Aristotle himself. According to Aristotle to have knowledge of a natural kind was to have arrived at a correct definition of that kind; to understand what a horse is, say, is to be able correctly to define the species.

The rejection of Aristotle's beliefs about the natural world was generally accompanied by rejection of his philosophy of science. And sometimes this included his understanding of what it was to explain something and his identification of the goal of enquiry with *scientia*, with known certain truth. Although central figures in the new approach to nature, of whom Francis Bacon, Galileo and Descartes are probably the most important examples, aspired to achieving certain knowledge in their enquiries, even Descartes saw that much of his account of the natural world should be regarded as reaching only some kind of high probability or 'moral certainty'.[21]

In England in the period around the establishment of the Royal Society in 1660, there was clear recognition that it was too easy to claim more certainty for one's science than was warranted. Boyle was just the leading figure in this circle, and his writings and practice provided a clear view of where he believed the limits of knowledge lay in matters of natural philosophy.

A central concept in his account was that of *hypothesis*. Part of its force was to suggest something of the notion that the claim made by the hypothesis was to some degree problematic, though the precise amount was open to enormous variation. Its problematic nature was, though, to be seen in sharp contrast with the *scientia* claimed by the Aristotelians. The latter were therefore always liable to be labelled dogmatists, a charge that had for the new thinkers a quite definite pejorative sense nicely captured in the title of Joseph Glanvill's defence of the new learning and its method, *The Vanity of Dogmatising* (1661).

Granted that hypotheses were a part of normal scientific enquiry, it was also very much Boyle's view that it was very easy, too easy, to assume as true something for which there was no substantial evidence. Something of this is to be found in his remarks about the Copernican theory of the universe. In an early letter Boyle complained of the dogmatic stances of the astronomers, 'Ptolemeans, Tychonians and Copernicans ... the one taking that ... for an undeniable demonstration, which the other will absolutely reject as a paralogism, or at least call in question as no more than a bare probability'.[22] At a later date Boyle made it clear that he regarded the Copernican system as a much superior *hypothesis* to the alternatives, because by it 'divers inconveniences are avoided' such as the assumptions by the Ptolemaic system of a firmament revolving about the earth at enormous speed every twenty-four hours, the need for epicycles to account for apparent retrograde motion, and so on.[23] Similarly the corpuscular philosophy was an 'hypothesis' which was to be 'either confirmed or disproved by, the historical truths [i.e. objective experimental facts] that will be delivered'.[24]

The contrast for hypotheses is with established empirical fact. And the gathering of such empirical data was the task of the natural philosopher. These were the histories of particular phenomena, the gathering of which Boyle, following Bacon, saw as the primary task of the virtuoso. Bacon had warned strongly against leaping to conclusions about the causes and nature of phenomena. In the *Novum Organum* (1620), his great work on scientific method that had such a high standing with the early Fellows of the Royal Society, he had argued that there are only two ways of searching into and discovering truth. 'The one flies from the senses and particulars to the most general axioms, and from these principles, the truth of which it takes for settled and immovable, proceeds to judgement and to the discovery of middle axioms.' This way, he says, is now in fashion, but the true way, as yet untried, 'derives axioms from the senses and particulars, rising by a gradual and unbroken assent, so that it arrives at the most general axioms last of all'.[25] The 'histories' of particular phenomena that Bacon recommended and Boyle was attempting to construct just were the evidence upon which the axioms might at a later stage be erected.

One such work was *The Experimental History of Colours* (1663) in which Boyle tells us that of all the theories about the nature of light and colours, he is inclined to take colour to be 'a modification of light: and would invite you chiefly to cultivate this hypothesis'. But he tells us that he proposes it only in a general sense and he does not pretend to choose between alternative views (one of which was Descartes's theory of rotating particles). He goes on to say that he does not pretend to know what light is, which is itself required to be known if we are to know what colour is.[26]

In an interesting short note amongst his many manuscript papers now preserved at the Royal Society Boyle sets out 'The Requisites of a *Good Hypothesis*' and 'The Qualities & Conditions of an Excellent Hypothesis'. For the former these include that it is intelligible, that it contains nothing impossible or manifestly false or that it supposes nothing unintelligible or absurd. It must be self-consistent and sufficient to account for the phenomena, and not contradict any other known phenomena.

An 'Excellent Hypothesis' must in addition have sufficient grounds in the nature of things; it must be the simplest of all the good hypotheses we can frame; it must explicate the phenomena better than any other; and it should provide a basis for making predications which can be tested by experiment.[27]

Boyle's requirements are not only of historical interest, but provide criteria which can as well be applied today. But they also reveal an important aspect of his approach to the natural world. Clearly Boyle did not aspire to the kind of science that begins from self-evident axioms and deduces consequences from these to produce a comprehensive account of nature. Equally clearly he did not reject a role for hypothetical explanation. But he did insist that not all hypotheses were equally acceptable, equally worthy of our attention. Very obviously, he wished to insist that there were rational criteria for choice, for theory choice, as philosophers of science might say today. Boyle, then, certainly cannot be accused of following a methodological path in science which some have seen as a fault in his mentor, Bacon, that of rejecting hypotheses as mere speculation and therefore unscientific. Many conjectures he no doubt did and would judge to be absurd. But this was because they failed to satisfy his criteria for good hypotheses and not because constructing hypotheses was itself pointless or worse.

Nor, it need hardly be urged, did Boyle subscribe to any kind of dogmatic empiricism and a rejection of any role for reason in human enquiries. 'Experience', he wrote, 'is but an assistant to reason, since it doth indeed supply information to the understanding; but the understanding remains still the judge.'[28]

Did Boyle believe that such enquiries would or could lead to knowledge? Precisely what epistemic status our judgements might be said to have is not something to which Boyle appears to have given us a direct answer, but it is fairly clear what his position was. He accepted that some things can be known to be true 'immediately and by intuition'. He would no doubt have included simple arithmetic as an example. But he also saw it to be true of claims made on the basis of experience 'as when by the bare evidence of the perception, [the mind] knows that this colour is red, and that other blue'.[29] But in many cases, he goes on to explain, the intellect judges with the aid of hypotheses 'such as are a great part of the theorems and conclusions in philosophy and divinity'.[30] In other words, the certainty of our conclusions, which cannot exceed the certainty of the premises from which they are derived, can be no more sure than the hypotheses which they assume, and therefore at best only probable. But Boyle was prepared to settle for that state of affairs. He was not just ready to admit, but keen to underline, that there were many truths that were beyond the human mind to grasp. He saw no reason, he said, 'that intelligibility to a human understanding should be necessary to the truth or existence of a thing, any more than that visibility to a human eye should be necessary to the existence of an atom, or of a corpuscle of air'.[31] And although we may rightly smile at the Aristotelians for thinking they have explained the qualities of bodies with their theory of substantial forms, we must recognize that whilst it remains true that we can give no satisfactory account of how it is that sensible objects are perceived or how mind and body are connected, we are in no position to claim superiority.[32] And in summary we may see in the following passage a reassertion of that Baconian position to which we have already referred. Men, he says, should be concerned 'to make experiments and collect observations without being over-forward to establish principles and axioms, believing it to be uneasy to erect such theories, as are capable to explicate all the phenomena of nature, before they have been able to take notice of a tenth part of those phenomena'. He continues with words that were to be echoed in Locke's *Essay Concerning Human Understanding*:

> it is sometimes conducive to the discovery of truth, to permit the understanding to make an hypothesis, in order to the explication of this or that difficulty, that by examining how far the phenomena are, or are not, capable of being solved by that hypothesis, the understanding, even by its own errors, be instructed.[33]

And again Boyle reminds us not to allow any hypotheses or systems that we do make to be regarded as so certain that we are not prepared to amend them in the light of further evidence.

Boyle's general approach to the possibility of knowledge of the natural world was to remain dominant for the remainder of the century and, with the fuller statement it was to receive in Locke's *Essay Concerning Human Understanding* in 1690, the position was consolidated well into the Enlightenment. It also appeared to be endorsed by Newton's methodology and by his pronouncements on method that appeared most overtly in the later editions of his works. Nor is this surprising when we remember that Boyle, Locke and Newton were, in their different areas, the leading intellectual figures of their time, united in their common commitment to the aspirations of the Royal Society. And Locke was a friend to both of them, as junior research partner to Boyle and his literary executor at his death, and as one of the few persons with whom Newton enjoyed a close personal and intellectual friendship.[34]

Newton's most famous statement of his philosophy of science was set out in the *Regulae Philosophandi* of the second edition of the *Principia* of 1713.[35] They appear to be a clear commitment to the empiricist account of natural science that we would expect from the President of the Royal Society. The first of the four embodies a principle of parsimony but which is qualified in an important way. The Rule reads: 'We are to admit no more causes of natural things than such as are both true and sufficient to explain their appearances'.[36] As explication Newton tells us that 'Nature is pleased with simplicity, and affects not the pomp of superfluous causes'.

Taken as a principle of parsimony and nothing more, reinforced by the second Rule which reads, 'Therefore to the same natural effects we must, as far as possible, assign the same causes', Newton's first Rule seems unproblematic enough. But it is important to note, first, that the Rule takes it for granted that the task of natural philosophy is to seek for the causes of phenomena, and therefore takes the concept of causation to be unproblematic. Newton was hardly the first person to do that, but within two decades David Hume was to subject the concept of causation to a critical examination which remains a classic in philosophical analysis.

Second, the Rule sets out two criteria which must be satisfied for the attribution of causes. It is not enough that the supposed causes explain the appearances, they must also be *true*. Newton does not tell us anything further about this, but it is easy enough to see what he had in mind. It was that the cause must not just be assumed to exist, there must be some evidence, and no doubt he had in mind empirical evidence, that the cause actually does exist. Thus, to take a simple example, if a ring disappears from a window sill by an open window, a sufficient explanation for its disappearance would be to assume that a magpie had taken it. But for Newton this would not count as a true explanation, unless we had some reason to believe that there was a magpie in the vicinity at the time. The ring's recovery from a neighbouring magpie's nest at a later stage, would be some (rather good) evidence that the supposed cause was the true one.

It is almost certain that Newton had a particular philosophy of science in mind to which he was opposed when he formulated his Rule in this way, and that was what he took to be the philosophy of Descartes. At the end of his *Principles of Philosophy*, which gave a comprehensive explanation for many of the phenomena of nature and was a work that Newton knew well, Descartes had written in defence of his system that 'if people look at all the many properties . . . and the fabric of the entire world, which I have deduced in this book from just a few principles, then, even if they think that my assumption of these principles was arbitrary and groundless, they will still perhaps acknowledge that it would hardly have been possible for so many items to fit into a coherent pattern if the original principles had been false'.[37] It was Newton's belief that we can make no such assumption. To do so would have been to accept an unwarranted hypothesis. As he expressed it in an important letter to Roger Cotes, it would be to accept 'a proposition as is not a phenomenon nor deduced from any phenomena, but assumed or supposed – without any experimental proof'.[38] He went on later in the same letter, 'hypotheses of this kind, whether metaphysical or physical, whether of occult qualities or mechanical, have no place in experimental philosophy. In this philosophy, propositions are deduced from phenomena, and afterwards made general by induction'.[39]

This last comment, the reference to induction, takes us to the fourth Rule (we shall return to consider Rule III below). In it Newton says that we should

> look upon propositions inferred by general induction from phenomena as accurately or very nearly true, notwithstanding any contrary hypotheses that may be imagined, till such time as other phenomena occur by which they may either be made more accurate or liable to exceptions.[40]

Newton is claiming that the way to proceed in experimental philosophy, or, as we would now call it, empirical science, is to make observations and then draw general conclusions based on those observations. It is important that the general conclusions are based on observations and not just plucked from the air (the kind of hypotheses that Newton rejected). But for Newton it was equally important to recognize that it was perfectly legitimate to generalize on this basis, even though he realized that there was no absolute certainty guaranteed by the method. He explained this latter point very clearly near the end of the Queries in the *Opticks*:

> And although the arguing from experiments and observations by induction be no demonstration of general conclusions, yet it is the best way of arguing that the nature of things admits of, and may be looked upon as so much the stronger, by how much the induction is more general.[41]

Newton, then, saw inductive generalization as central to proper scientific explanation, and although he clearly recognized that it did not guarantee truth, it was the best way open to us for reaching general claims about the world. Once again it was David Hume who was to give critical attention to this central concept in Newtonian science.

Newton's invocation of the concept of gravitation in the *Principia* had quickly brought his theory under critical scrutiny. And it was Leibniz, and from a different direction, Berkeley, who were again Newton's most important critics. Leibniz accused Newton of reintroducing occult qualities into philosophy because, Leibniz said, he was claiming that gravitation was the cause of the observed effects of bodies in motion, but gravity was only known by its effects and was therefore an unknown cause. In effect Leibniz was accusing Newton of just that intellectual sin that Newton himself so strongly opposed, namely assuming a cause without independent empirical evidence of its existence. The Rules of Reasoning were in part devised to meet such an objection, and it was Rule III in particular that was designed to do this. In it Newton says that the 'qualities of bodies which admit neither intensification nor remission of degree, and which are found to belong to all bodies within the reach of our experiments, are to be esteemed the universal qualities of all bodies whatsoever'.[42]

In his explication of the Rule Newton again underlines his commitment to empirical evidence as the legitimate source for our claims about the properties of bodies, against 'the dreams and vain fictions of our own devising'. And the qualities that we find in all bodies are, he says, those of extension, hardness, impenetrability, mobility and inertia, a list close to those primary qualities that we have already seen identified by Boyle and others. But Newton also points out that all bodies appear to gravitate towards one another, that is, all the objects that we come across have a tendency to move towards each other with increasing velocity. And this is an empirically identified property of all the bodies that we can investigate. But this property or tendency Newton says, is not claimed by him to be an essential property of matter. For it diminishes with distance, contrary to the first criterion for qualities in Rule III, namely, that it must not admit intensification or remission of degree. Still less was gravitation taken by Newton to be the *cause* of any action. And in many places Newton underlined that he did not have any sure explanation of the effect, the actual observed movement of objects towards each other.

The Rules, then, may be seen as part of Newton's deep commitment to the empirical approach to nature that he had early adopted and which not only found reinforcement in the success of his own enquiries but also in the philosophy of his friend, John Locke. But we also know that Newton sought an answer to that major question his account of motion raised, namely, what is it that causes objects to gravitate towards one another? Newton saw this as an issue related to several others, the nature and strength of chemical bonding, magnetic and electrical phenomena, for example, for which he had no satisfactory answer. But we have already seen that Newton was inclined to suspect that the cause of such observable forces in nature, such active principles, might be none other than the direct intervention of God himself. It was a conjecture, even an hypothesis, that Newton knew he was in no position to prove, and so he largely kept it to himself.

❧ NOTES ❧

1 Cf. Epicurus 'Letter to Herodotus' *passim* [2.12].
2 Cf. 'The Assayer' (1623) ([2.14], esp. 274–7).
3 Cf. Boyle's biography of his early years in 'The Life of the Hon. Robert Boyle', [2.2], vol. I, xxiv. Boyle was scarcely 15 at the time.

4 *Origin of Forms and Qualities*, [2.7], 7.

5 *ibid*, 18.

6 [2.7], 51.

7 [2.7], 37.

8 [2.7], 32.

9 [2.17], 343.

10 [2.7], 185.

11 See, for example, [2.7], 198–90 for Boyle's account of the creation and the principles required to maintain the world in being.

12 Cf. especially *About the Excellency and Grounds of the Mechanical Hypothesis* [2.7], 138–54.

13 [2.3], 2: 288–95.

14 [2.3], Newton to Richard Bentley, February 25 1692/3, vol. 3, 253–6.

15 Cf. B. J. T. Dobbs, [2.52].

16 *Opticks*, Fourth Edition, 1730, [2.9], 400.

17 For a fuller discussion of More on space and time and his relationship to Boyle see A. Rupert Hall, [2.30], Chs 9 and 10.

18 *Principia*, bk III, [2.8], 545.

19 Cf. *The Leibniz-Clarke Correspondence*, [2.24], especially the Fifth Letter.

20 *De Motu*, sect. 63, [2.25], 4: 49.

21 See, for example, Descartes, *Principles of Philosophy*, part 4, sects 204 and 205, [2.16], 289–90.

22 In a letter to Samuel Hartlib, 8 April 1647, [2.2], 1: xxxix.

23 Cf. *The Second part of the Christian Virtuoso*, [2.2], 6: 722–3.

24 *Origin of Forms and Qualities*, [2.7], 18.

25 *The New Organon*, Aphorisms – bk I, XIX, [2.15], 261.

26 [2.2], I: 695. Samuel Pepys was a great admirer of this work of Boyle, though he claimed not to be able to understand it.

27 Cf. [2.7], 119.

28 *The Christian Virtuoso* (1690), [2.2], 5: 539.

29 *Advices in judging of Things said to transcend Reason*, [2.2], 4: 460.

30 [2.2], 4, 461.

31 [2.2], 4, 450.

32 Cf. *The Excellence of Theology Compared with Natural Philosophy*, [2.2], 4: 45.

33 *Certain Physiological Essays*, [2.2], vol. 1, 302–3. Cf. Locke, *An Essay Concerning Human Understanding*, bk 4, ch. 12, sect. 13, [2.23], 648.

34 Not only did Newton go to stay with Locke at least twice at Oates in Essex but he invited Locke to visit him in London and in Cambridge. A favourite subject was their shared interest in theology and their secretly shared antitrinitarian commitments. On their close intellectual position see, for example, Rogers, [2.58]. On Boyle and Locke see Rogers, [2.48].

35 For accounts of the *regulae* and their place in Newton's thought see A. Koyré, 'Newton's "Regulae Philosophandi" ', [2.53], ch. 6, and G. A. J. Rogers, 'Locke's *Essay* and Newton's *Principia*', [2.59].

36 *Mathematical Principles of Natural Philosophy*, [2.8], 2: 398.

37 *Principles of Philosophy* IV, 205, [2.16], 1: 290.

38 [2.3], 5: 397.

39 *Ibid*.

40 [2.8], 400.
41 *Opticks*, [2.9], 404.
42 [2.8], 398.

❧ BIBLIOGRAPHY ❧

Standard Editions

2.1 *The Works of the Honourable Robert Boyle*, ed. Thomas Birch, London, 5 vols, 1744.

2.2 *The Works of the Honourable Robert Boyle*, ed. Thomas Birch, new edn, London, 6 vols, 1772.

2.3 *The Correspondence of Isaac Newton*, ed. H. W. Turnbull, *et. al.*, Cambridge, 7 vols, 1959–77.

2.4 Newton, Isaac *Philosophiae naturalis principia mathematica*, 1st edn, London, 1687, 2nd edn, 1713, 3rd edn, 1726.

2.5 ——— *Philosophiae naturalis principia mathematica, 3rd ed. 1726, with varient readings*, ed. A. Koyré and I. B. Cohen, 2 vols, Cambridge, 1972.

2.6 ——— *Opticks*, 1st edn, London, 1704, 2nd edn, 1717, 3rd edn, 1721, 4th edn, 1730.

Other Editions

2.7 *Selected Philosophical Papers of Robert Boyle*, ed. M. A. Stewart, Manchester, Manchester University Press, 1979.

2.8 Newton, Isaac *Mathematical Principles of Natural Philosophy and His System of the World*, trans. Andrew Motte in 1729, rev. Florian Cajori, 2 vols, Berkeley and Los Angeles, University of California Press, 1962.

2.9 ——— *Opticks*, New York, Dover, 1952.

Bibliographies

2.10 Fulton, J. F. *A Bibliography of the Honourable Robert Boyle*, Clarendon Press, Oxford, 2nd edn, 1961.

2.11 Wallis, P. and R. *Newton and Newtoniana, 1672–1975*, Folkstone, W. Dawson and Sons Ltd, 1977.

Important Primary Sources

2.12 Bacon, Francis *The Philosophical Works of Francis Bacon*, ed. J. M. Robertson from the text of Ellis and Spedding, London, George Routledge and Sons, 1905.

2.13 Berkeley, George *The Works of George Berkeley, Bishop of Cloyne*, ed. A. A. Luce and T. E. Jessop, 9 vols, London, Nelson, 1950–7.

2.14 Charleton, Walter *Physiologia Epicuro-Gassendo-Charletoniana: or A Fabrick of Science Natural upon the Hypothesis of Atoms, Founded by Epicurus, Repaired by Petrus Gassendus, Augmented by Walter Charleton*, London, 1654, repr. New York and London, Johnson Reprint Corporation, 1966.

2.15 Cudworth, Ralph *The True Intellectual System of the Universe*, London, 1678, repr. New York and London, Garland Press, 1978.

2.16 Descartes, R. *The Philosophical Writings of Descartes*, trans. John Cottingham, *et al.*, Cambridge, Cambridge University Press, 3 vols, 1985–91.

2.17 *Epicurus, The Extant Remains*, trans. C. Bailey, Oxford, The Clarendon Press, 1926.

2.18 Galilei, Galileo 'The Assayer' (Il Saggiatore) in *Discoveries and Opinions of Galileo*, trans., with Introduction and Notes by Stillman Drake, New York, Doubleday Anchor Books, 1957.

2.19 Hobbes, Thomas *The English Works of Thomas Hobbes*, ed. Sir William Moleworth, 11 vols, London, 1839–45, repr., with an Introduction by G. A. J. Rogers, London and Bristol, Thoemmes Press/Routledge, 1992.

2.20 *The Leibniz-Clarke Correspondence*, ed. H. G. Alexander, Manchester University Press, Manchester, 1956.

2.21 Locke, John *An Essay Concerning Human Understanding*, London, 1690, 2nd edn, 1694, 3rd edn, 1695, 4th edn, 1700, 5th edn, 1706.

2.22 —— *An Essay Concerning Human Understanding*, ed. P. H. Nidditch, Oxford, Clarendon Press, 1975.

2.23 Lucretius, *On Nature*, trans. R. M. Geer, New York, Bobbs Merrill, 1965.

2.24 More, Henry *A Collection of Several Philosophical Writings*, London, 1662, repr. New York and London, Garland Press, 1978.

2.25 —— *Enchiridion Metaphysicum*, London 1671.

Works on Science and Philosophy in Seventeenth- and Eighteenth-century Britain and Europe

2.26 Buchdahl, G. *Metaphysics and the Philosophy of Science*, Oxford, Blackwell, 1969.

2.27 Burtt, E. A. *The Metaphysical Foundations of Modern Physical Science*, Routledge and Kegan Paul, 2nd edn, London, 1932.

2.28 Clulee, N. H. *John Dee's natural Philosophy. Between Science and Religion*, London, Routledge, 1988.

2.29 Debus, A. G. *The English Paracelsians*, London, Oldbourne, 1965.

2.30 Hall, A. R. *Henry More. Magic, Religion and Experiment*, Oxford, Blackwell, 1990.

2.31 Kargon, R. H. *Atomism in England from Hariot to Newton*, Oxford, Clarendon Press, 1966.

2.32 McMullin, E. (ed.) *the Concept of Matter in Modern Philosophy*, Notre Dame and London, University of Notre Dame Press, 1978.

2.33 Oldroyd, D. *The Arch of Knowledge. An Introductory Study of the History of the Philosophy and Methodology of Science*, New York and London, Methuen, 1986.

2.34 Osler, M. (ed.), *Atoms, Pneuma, and Tranquility. Epicurean and Stoic Themes in European Thought*, Cambridge, Cambridge University Press, 1991.

2.35 Schofield, R. E. *Mechanism and Materialism. British Natural Philosophy in an Age of Reason*, Princeton, Princeton University Press, NJ, 1970.

2.36 Shapiro, B. S. *Probability and Certainty in Seventeenth-Century England*, Princeton, Princeton University Press, NJ, 1983.

2.37 van Leeuwen, H. G. *The Problem of Certainty in English Thought. 1630–1690*, The Hague, Martinus Nijhoff, 1970.

2.38 Webster, C. *The Great Instauration. Science, Medicine and Reform 1626–1660*, London, Duckworth, 1975.

2.39 Yolton, J. W. (ed.) *Philosophy, Religion and Science in the Seventeenth and Eighteenth Centuries*, Rochester and Woodbridge, University of Rochester Press, 1990.

Works on Robert Boyle

2.40 Alexander, P. 'Boyle and Locke on Primary and Secondary Qualities', *Ratio* 16 (1974): 237–55.

2.41 Alexander, P. *Ideas, Qualities and Corpuscles. Locke and Boyle on the External World*, Cambridge, Cambridge University Press, 1985.

2.42 Hall, A. R. and Hall, M. B. 'Philosophy and Natural Philosophy, Boyle and Spinoza', in I. B. Cohen and R. Taton (eds), *Mélanges Alexandre Koyré. L'aventure de l'esprit*, Paris, 1964, pp. 241–56.

2.43 Jacob, J. R. 'Boyle's Atomism and the Restoration Assault on Pagan Naturalism', *Social Studies in Science* 8 (1978): 211–33.

2.44 Macintosh, J. J. 'Robert Boyle on Epicurean Atheism and Atomism' in [2.34].

2.45 Mandelbaum, M. *Philosophy, Science and Sense Perception*, Baltimore, Baltimore University Press, 1964.

2.46 McGuire, J. E. 'Boyle's Conception of Nature', *J. of the History of Ideas* 33 (1972): 523–42.

2.47 O'Toole, F. J. 'Qualities and Powers in the Corpuscular Philosophy of Robert Boyle', *J. of the History of Philosophy* 12 (1974): 295–315.

2.48 Rogers, G. A. J. 'Boyle, Locke and Reason', *J. of the History of Ideas* XXVII: 206–16, repr. in [2.39].

2.49 Shapin, S. and Schaffer, S. *'Leviathan' and the Air-Pump. Hobbes, Boyle and the Experimental Life*, Princeton, Princeton University Press, 1985.

Works on Isaac Newton

2.50 Austin, W. H. 'Isaac Newton on Science and Religion', *J. of the History of Ideas* XXXI (1970): 521–42.

2.51 Butts, R. E. and Davis, J. W. *The Methodological Heritage of Newton*, Oxford, Blackwell, 1970.

2.52 Dobbs, B. J. T. 'Stoic and Epicurean Doctrines in Newton's System of the World' in [2.34].

2.53 Hall, A. R. *Philosophers at War. The Quarrel between Newton and Leibniz*, Cambridge, Cambridge University Press, 1980.

2.54 Koyré, A. *Newtonian Studies*, London, Chapman, 1968.

2.55 Kubrin, D. C. 'Newton and the Cyclical Cosmos. Providence and the Mechanical Philosophy', *J. of the History of Ideas* 28 (1967): 325–46.

2.56 McGuire, J. E. 'Atoms and the "Analogy of Nature". Newton's third Rule of Philosophizing', *Studies in the History and Philosophy of Science* 1 (1970): 154–208.

2.57 McGuire, J. E. and Tamny, M. *Certain Philosophical Questions. Newton's Trinity Notebook*, Cambridge, Cambridge University Press, 1983.

2.58 Rogers, G. A. J. 'The Empiricism of Locke and Newton' in S. C. Brown (ed.) *Philosophers of the Enlightenment*, Brighton, Harvester Press, 1979, pp. 1–30.

2.59 —— 'Locke's *Essay* and Newton's *Principia*', *J. of the History of Ideas* 39 (1978): 217–32. Repr. in [2.39].

2.60 Westfall, R. S. 'The Foundations of Newton's Philosophy of Nature', *British J. for the History of Science*, 1 (1962): 171–82.

2.61 —— *Force in Newton's Physics. the Science of Dynamics in the Seventeenth Century*, London, Macdonald and New York, American Elsevier, 1971.

2.62 —— *Never at Rest. A Biography of Isaac Newton*, Cambridge, Cambridge University Press, 1980.

CHAPTER 3

Locke: knowledge and its limits

Ian Tipton

I

That John Locke's *Essay concerning Human Understanding* is one of the philosophical classics is something nobody would deny, yet it is not easy to pinpoint precisely what is so special about it. Locke himself has been described as the founder of British empiricism, but labels of this sort are increasingly treated with suspicion, and some affinities to Descartes, usually regarded as the first of the great rationalist philosophers, have also been widely acknowledged. Students studying his philosophy will spend some time pondering on his advocacy of a distinction between primary and secondary qualities, but they will also be told that the doctrine had a long history and that, in Locke's own day, it was central to the theorizing of Robert Boyle and the 'new science' generally. They may dwell too on his talk of a material *substratum* of qualities, but they may also be told that his thinking here was confused, and that at this point anyway he was strongly influenced by the scholastic philosophy he saw himself as trying to break away from. They are likely to be puzzled by his talk of 'ideas' as the 'objects' of thought – he tells us at one point that 'the Mind . . . perceives nothing but its own *Ideas*' (IV.iv.3)[1] – if only because, on the face of it, this poses the obvious problem that, as Berkeley was to stress, it seems to rule out the possibility of the very knowledge of the 'real' world that Locke clearly took it for granted we have. Locke himself confesses that the *Essay* is too long – 'the way it has been writ in, by catches, and many long intervals of Interruption, being apt to cause some Repetitions' (Epistle to the Reader) – and his style makes it neither easy nor attractive to read; yet it richly rewards study. That this would be agreed both by those who have thought him guilty of fundamental errors throughout and by those who see him as belonging most decidedly to our age, and as characteristically judicious and sane, merely adds to the fascination of his work and encourages deeper study. This fascination is increased when we realize that in his own time he was often considered a dangerous and subversive thinker.

Locke was born at Wrington, Somerset, in 1632. He attended Westminster School and Christ Church, Oxford, where he retained his Studentship until 1684. After an introduction to the world of diplomacy when he was involved in a mission to Brandenburg he set out to qualify in medicine, working at one stage with Thomas Sydenham, the great physician whom, in the Epistle to the Reader which prefaces the *Essay*, he describes, along with Robert Boyle, Christiaan Huygens, the Dutch astronomer and physicist, and 'the incomparable Mr. Newton', as one of the 'Master-Builders, whose mighty Designs, in advancing the Sciences, will leave lasting Monuments to the Admiration of Posterity'. Locke had worked with Boyle too, and Boyle was clearly one important influence on the *Essay*, just as Lord Ashley, afterwards Earl of Shaftesbury, to whom he became personal physician in 1667 and also a political adviser, influenced his personal fortunes. Locke was to serve Shaftesbury in various capacities, becoming, eventually, Secretary to the Council of Trade and Plantations, of which Shaftesbury was President. This body was dissolved in 1675. In the same year Locke's deteriorating health led to him departing for France. He stayed first in Montpellier, but in Paris was able to make new contacts, including François Bernier, a leading disciple of Gassendi, a philosopher who had almost certainly influenced the development of his thinking, even before this period.[2] Locke returned to England, and to an increasingly troubled political scene, in 1679. Before long Shaftesbury was forced to flee to Holland, where he died in 1683, and later that year Locke himself left for Holland, returning only after James II had been deposed and William of Orange had secured the English throne. Locke's *Essay* was published not long after, in 1690, and it was regarded at once as both important and controversial. However, apart from engaging in a time-consuming controversy with Edward Stillingfleet, Bishop of Worcester, Locke showed little inclination to get involved in arguments with his critics, not even Leibniz, who attempted repeatedly to engage in correspondence with him, though his *New Essays on Human Understanding* was not published until long after the death of both men. Locke published other works after his return from Holland, including the *Two Treatises of Government*, discussed in the next chapter, but his health continued to fail. He was to spend the last years of his life in the house of Sir Francis Masham and his wife Damaris, daughter of the Cambridge Platonist Ralph Cudworth, and herself a woman of impressive intellect with whom Locke, a lifelong bachelor, had, it seems, once been in love. He died in 1704.

Even this brief sketch of Locke's life will be sufficient to show that it was an eventful one, and each stage had its impact on the development of Locke's intellectual life. He did not publish anything of importance until he was in his fifties, but his *Some Thoughts concerning Education* (1693) reflects his critical attitude to the sort of education he had himself encountered at Westminster School. His dissatisfaction with the sort of philosophy taught at Oxford when he was there, which he described as 'perplexed with obscure terms and useless questions', influenced the development of the *Essay*, as, more positively, did his reading of Descartes who, he was to tell Stillingfleet, offered him 'my first deliverance from the unintelligible way of talking' of the schools. His association with Shaftesbury involved him in practical affairs, and it is no surprise that his publications should include *Some Considerations of the Consequences of the Lowering of Interest, and Raising the Value of Money* (1692), as well as *A Letter concerning Toleration* (1689), which championed religious toleration, of which Shaftesbury had been a proponent. The likely influence of Gassendi, which probably antedated Locke's acquaintance with Bernier, has already been mentioned, and R. I. Aaron is one commentator who has stressed the influence of the Cambridge Platonists, claiming that 'Much of the fourth book of the *Essay* might have been written by one of the Cambridge School'.[3] One could go on, even in a way that might suggest that Locke was hardly an original thinker at all, though that would be grossly unfair. A fairer estimate would be to see him as a child of his time, certainly, but as making a major contribution to the debates and disputes which characterized the period in a way which led to a recognition of his importance at the time, though not always for the reasons that have been most widely stressed since. In very general terms, he can be seen as a spokesman for his age who also helped mould that age. In addition, he was to come to be seen, somewhat distortedly, as the originator of a school, the British empiricists, diametrically opposed to the rationalism stemming from the philosophy of Descartes. From either point of view his *Essay concerning Human Understanding* will be seen as an important legacy, and to that we now turn.

～ II ～

There are two well-known passages in the Epistle to the Reader which help focus our minds on the aims and purposes of the *Essay*, one being that in which Locke praises the 'Master-Builders', scientists such as Boyle, with respect to whom he contrasts himself as 'an Under-

Labourer ... clearing Ground a little, and removing some of the Rubbish, that lies in the way to Knowledge'. This passage makes his project look modest, but it also suggests that, in so far as he sees himself as having opponents, these are not so much the Cartesians as the Aristotelians, or those proponents of the debased scholasticism which for many still constituted learning, but which was characterized by the 'frivolous use of uncouth, affected, or unintelligible Terms' which Locke goes on to complain of. There is much in the *Essay* that could be described as rubbish-removal, from the attack on innate principles in Book I, to, for example, criticism of the doctrine of substantial forms. However, this passage does suggest that Locke's project is negative, so it must be added both that, in practice, rubbish-removal usually goes along with positive alternative doctrines, and that in the other passage in the Epistle he gives a rather different account of his aims. Here he tells us how the *Essay* came to be written, referring to a meeting with friends – usually thought to have taken place in the winter of 1670–1 – when an issue 'very remote' from that discussed in the *Essay* was being debated and they 'found themselves quickly at a stand, by the Difficulties that rose on every side'. Locke's response, he tells us, was to consider whether the question that perplexed them was one they could hope to resolve. More generally, he suggested, 'it was necessary to examine our own Abilities, and see, what Objects our Understandings were, or were not fitted to deal with'. This topic set the agenda for the *Essay*. Locke could indeed have given his work the title 'Human Knowledge: Its Scope and Limits', which was the title which, over two hundred years later, Bertrand Russell gave to one of his books.

Even this, however, can make Locke's project look very negative, but what he goes on to stress in the first chapter of Book I is the positive advantages of this approach which are, first, that an enquiry into the limits of the understanding will enable us to concentrate our minds upon matters we can tackle with some hope of success, and second, and as a consequence, that we will not retreat into a general scepticism because *some* issues are beyond human resolution. The same chapter makes it clear that Locke does not take the thought that there are areas in which we cannot expect to have *knowledge* to imply that in all such areas we must expect to remain *ignorant*, and that he is as interested in cases where certainty is not possible for us but in which we may have reasonable beliefs. Hence his announced programme, which is 'to enquire into the Original, Certainty, and Extent of humane Knowledge; together, with the Grounds and Degrees of Belief, Opinion, and Assent'. Hence too a feature of the *Essay*, that where others might see their inability to solve some problem arising from their overall position on some topic as at least a prima facie objection to that position, Locke may see such difficulties as simply confirming that our powers of comprehension are limited. Sometimes this may strike the tough-minded critic as simply dodging the issues that matter, but this is certainly not Locke's attitude.

So far, then, we know something of Locke's purpose, but nothing of his strategy for achieving it which he sets out in I.i.3 as being, first, to 'enquire into the *Original* of those *Ideas*, Notions, or whatever else you please to call them, which a Man observes, and is conscious to himself he has in his Mind; and the ways whereby the Understanding comes to be furnished with them'; then 'to shew, what *Knowledge* the Understanding hath by those *Ideas*'; and finally to 'make some Enquiry into the Nature and Grounds of *Faith*, or *Opinion*'. However, while this may seem superficially clear, it in fact gives only an imperfect guide to the overall structuring of the *Essay*, and it leaves certain questions unanswered, one of these being precisely what Locke means by 'idea'. This question has vexed commentators ever since, who have not been greatly helped by the knowledge that Locke inherited the term and some of the obscurities that go with it. Locke offers some sort of explanation in I.i.8, but the overall impression one gets is that it strikes him as just obvious *that* we have 'ideas' in our minds – the ideas of, for example, whiteness, thinking, an elephant or an army – and that he is not concerned with what an idea *is*. Thus the important question becomes simply how we *come by* our ideas. His reply – 'To this I answer, in one word, From *Experience*' (II.i.2) – is what has marked him out as an 'empiricist', or as one committed, using a dictionary definition, to 'The theory which regards experience as the only source of knowledge'. One need not quarrel with this ascription – Locke goes on to stress that 'In that, all our Knowledge is founded; and from that it ultimately derives it self' – so long as one appreciates that, for Locke, it is experience that is the origin of *ideas*, or what he calls the 'materials' of knowledge, and that when, in book IV, he considers 'what *Knowledge* the Understanding hath by those *Ideas*', it might seem as appropriate to judge him a rationalist. Nor should we assume that because Locke takes it as evident that we have 'ideas', or conceptions, such as those of an elephant, existence or God, there is nothing problematic about his talk of 'ideas'. Locke encourages us to take a relaxed attitude to them, and it would indeed be rash to assume at the outset that they must be *images* as some have thought,[4] but it would be just as rash to assume that questions don't arise concerning them. For the moment, however, we must just be clear that Book II of the *Essay* is not concerned with knowledge and belief as such, but with the 'ideas' that ground these. Locke will consider, for example, how we come by the ideas of God and existence. If we have *knowledge* that God exists, this will emerge in Book IV.

~~ III ~~

Though Locke announces his programme at the beginning of Book I by saying that his first concern will be with how we acquire our ideas, he in fact doesn't address this question directly until Book II. Instead, after the first chapter in Book I, which introduces the *Essay* as a whole, three chapters are devoted to what may strike the modern reader as a tiresome digression: an attack on innate principles. It is important to realize, then, both that the attack on innatism was deemed highly controversial at the time, and that these chapters complement the rest of the *Essay*. Putting it simply, Locke's positive claim that all our knowledge derives from experience really amounts to a claim that no knowledge is prior to it, and this would have been seen by his contemporaries as in itself denying that some knowledge is innate. The direct attack on innatism in Book I and the working out of his empiricism in the rest of the *Essay* are thus two sides of one coin, and both were judged subversive, even by those who insisted that he attacked too crude a version of innatism, leaving more sophisticated versions intact. Whatever precisely they *meant* by this, many felt it imperative to hold that certain principles which Locke calls 'practical', including the fundamental principles of morality and religion, were innate if their authority was not to be jeopardised, and many were convinced that certain 'speculative' principles, for example 'Whatever is, is' must equally be 'native' to the mind, and indeed fundamental to knowledge in general. When, much later in the *Essay* Locke attacks the scholastic notion that 'all Reasonings are *ex praecognitis, et praeconcessis*', explaining that this means that certain supposedly innate maxims are 'those Truths that are first known to the Mind' and those upon which 'the other parts of our Knowledge depend' (IV.vii.8), we have an illustration of how Locke could see himself as 'removing some of the Rubbish, that lies in the way to Knowledge'. We can also see that his attack on innatism was not peripheral to his programme.

In the event Locke devotes one chapter to the supposedly innate speculative truths, one to practical truths, and, finally, one largely to innate ideas on the basis that if, for example, the knowledge that God is to be worshipped were innate, the ideas of God and worship would have to be innate too. That the ideas are not innate Locke takes to be evident. As he says,

> If we will attentively consider new born *Children*, we shall have
> little Reason, to think, that they bring many *Ideas* into the
> World with them. For, bating, perhaps, some faint *Ideas*, of
> Hunger, and Thirst, and Warmth, and some Pains, which they

may *have* felt in the Womb, there is *not* the least appearance of any settled *Ideas* at all in them.

(I.iv.2)

Infants, then, patently lack them, but so too do some adults, both of which would be impossible were they innate.

To the modern reader, one problem with Locke's polemic is likely to be that what he takes to be obvious here – and he takes much the same line on supposedly innate principles – will seem just that, obvious, so that his attack on innatism is likely to seem unnecessarily prolix, particularly given that it might seem that nobody could seriously have held the view he attacks. Thus Descartes, for example, who we know did hold that the idea of God was innate, surely didn't believe that every infant, or indeed every adult, has the idea consciously formed in his mind. To be fair, Descartes can be found writing in a way that suggests that the idea will be there, fully formed but not attended to – the infant

> has in itself the ideas of God, itself, and all truths which are said
> to be self-evident; it has these ideas no less than adults have
> when they are not paying attention to them, and it does not
> acquire them afterwards when it grows up

but elsewhere he takes the view that what is innate is, rather, a capacity or disposition, comparable to a natural disposition to gout.[5] Both notions are designed to take account of the fact that the infant does not entertain conscious thoughts about God, which might seem to cut the ground from under Locke's objection. In fact, it is clear that neither move would trouble Locke. His tactic throughout the polemic is to take the claim that certain items of knowledge (or ideas) are in the mind from the first quite literally, so that the infant for example should be conscious of them, and then to represent any watering down of the doctrine as a retreat into obscurity or triviality. For example, dealing with the notion that what is innate is a natural capacity, he argues that 'if the Capacity of knowing be the natural Impression contended for, all the Truths a Man ever comes to know, will, by this Account, be, every one of them, innate', for, trivially, we must always have had the capacity to acquire any knowledge we eventually acquire, so that 'this great Point will amount to no more, but only to a very improper way of speaking' (I.ii.5). At this level, indeed, Locke's attack on innatism is quite effective; it was clearly necessary, for in one form or another the doctrine that there was innate knowledge was widely received; and even if it did not once and for all end any talk of innate impressions (Leibniz for one attempted to defend it against Locke) it increasingly lost its hold. It has been claimed that 'there has been no trace of it in recent thought'.[6]

IV

As already stated, Book I complements the rest of the *Essay* in the sense that the denial of innate knowledge is merely the negative face of the positive claim announced at the beginning of Book II. It follows that Locke himself sees the direct attack as in a way superfluous to his programme (see I.ii.1), though, by the same token, he sees that the attack in Book I will be 'more easily admitted' once it has been shown how experience does provide a sufficient basis for our ideas (II.i.1). What follows in the rest of the *Essay* is thus, in part, an account of how experience gives rise to our ideas, and the knowledge based on them, though, and in a way more importantly, it is an exploration of the implications of this account. The fascination of the work as a whole thus lies in large part in what Locke has to say on a variety of issues, ranging from what sorts of achievement we can expect in natural science, to the nature of the human mind and its relation to the body, personal identity, the status of moral truths, and whether God's existence can be proved. The emphasis throughout is of course epistemological – on what we can know and what we can reasonably surmise in this or that area – but firm conclusions are drawn, including that there is a God and that this can be proved. For the moment, however, we must stay with Locke's basic empiricist claim.

This is that all our knowledge derives from 'experience', but the gloss Locke immediately puts on this is important for three reasons. First, he makes it clear that there are *two* sources of experience, sensation and what he calls 'reflection', which provides the mind with ideas of its own operations, such as perception, thinking and doubting; second because the derivation of an idea from experience is not seen as always a simple matter (on the model of deriving the idea of green from seeing green things), in that it will be necessary to take 'a full survey' of our ideas, including 'their several Modes, Combinations, and Relations', or as they are 'with infinite variety compounded and enlarged by the Understanding' (II.i.5); and, third, because, from the outset, the existence of external objects is apparently taken for granted. Ideas of sensible qualities, such as that of yellow, are thus *introduced* as those conveyed into the mind 'from external Objects' (II.i.3), and it is not until much later (IV.xi) that Locke dwells on the notion, which he even there treats as absurd, that there may be no external objects at all. This may seem surprising given that scepticism on this matter was very much in the air at this time, and indeed that, since Berkeley at least,

76

we have been encouraged to see Locke's own philosophical position as positively inviting scepticism, so it needs stressing that Locke himself shows no such anxieties. It is worth noting too that the examples of ideas derived from sensation given in II.i.3 – yellow, white, heat, cold, soft, hard, bitter, sweet – are all what Locke will call 'simple' ideas, and that this is no accident. It is an essential part of what is known as Locke's 'compositionalism' that 'simple' ideas are as it were the basic data, and that, given these, other, complex ideas can be formed, such as those of gold, a centaur or a lie. It would be possible to spend quite a lot of time on the distinction between simple and complex ideas, for there is no doubt that it is, at best, not as clear and straightforward as Locke seems to suggest and it has even been argued that he tacitly abandoned it when it becomes embarrassing. Here we can only note that chapters ii to viii of Book II are officially devoted to 'simple' ideas, that chapters ix to xi cover various faculties and operations of the mind, and that from chapter xii on Locke turns to 'complex' ideas. That it is not, however, the issue of Locke's basic compositionalism that is of most interest or importance is suggested by the fact that many of the topics that have most engaged readers then and since can be examined without paying special attention to it.[7] There is much in Book II we could linger on, and some things that we shall.

Book II of the *Essay* is in fact a mine of interesting and often important material, though the significance of much of it can only be fully understood in terms of the philosophical concerns of the time, and even then the significance may not be immediately recognizable, at least from the titles of the relevant chapters. Thus, the unpromising title of chapter xiii, for example, is *'Of simple Modes; and first, of the simple Modes of Space'*, but it includes Locke's rejection of the Cartesian claim that a vacuum is inconceivable, building on a distinction between the ideas of body and space established in chapter iv, as well as observations on the notion of substance, though this will not be the main focus of interest until chapter xxiii. Similarly, chapter viii has the unexciting title *'Some farther Considerations concerning our Simple Ideas'*, but it is here that we find Locke's classic defence of a distinction between primary and secondary qualities. Chapter xxi – *'Of Power'* – includes a long discussion of human freedom; while if we want to know how Locke takes the idea of God to be derived from experience, we must look to four sections (33–6) almost hidden away towards the end of chapter xxiii. One could go on. Suffice it to say that, though the *Essay* as whole can strike one as rambling and diffuse, so that it becomes tempting to focus on the isolated topics which interest one, the work is better approached as a whole. Certainly, one needs to be alert to various developing *themes*.

Just which themes are the most important must be to some extent a matter of opinion, and it is certainly true that what was judged most significant in Locke's own day often differs from what has most exercised commentators more recently. This is hardly surprising, given Locke's successes in removing what he saw as rubbish, which has meant that what seemed to be important issues then have often ceased to exercise our minds since. Indeed this may be the point to reiterate that in his own time Locke was often regarded as subversive,[8] to the extent that some were inclined to suspect a not too well hidden agenda. Stillingfleet or Leibniz could be cited here, but as good an example as any would be another critic, Thomas Burnet, who devoted the first of three sets of published *Remarks* on the *Essay* to polite queries, but who concluded the third set by laying his cards on the table and accusing Locke of not doing the same. The 'key' to deciphering Locke's philosophy, indeed 'the mystery aimed at all along', is he suggests, the supposition 'that God and matter are the whole of the universe'. For Burnet, Locke emerges as a deist, whose system provides for only an inadequate conception of both God and the human soul. Shortly afterwards Berkeley was yet another to be struck by what he saw as dangers implicit in Locke's philosophy, but he was only one of many to be struck by Locke's suggestion that matter might think. In fact, this particular suggestion occurs in just one section (IV.3.6), where Locke presents it only as an illustration of how limited our knowledge is, and it would be rash to assume that there was a hidden agenda. However, the suggestion can be seen as a natural culmination of much that had gone before. It provides one key, though certainly not the only one, to unravelling some of the intricacies of the *Essay*.

Thus the modern reader approaching even the first chapter of Book II may find it odd that, in defending his claim that we are dependent on experience for our ideas, Locke devotes many sections to an attack on the notion that the soul always thinks, either prior to an individual's first sensory experiences, or during the course of his life. For, while there is an obvious connection here with Locke's basic empiricist programme and his rejection of innatism, what we may miss is the significance of the fact that Locke is also undermining the notion that thought is the soul's *essence*. For Descartes at least, this notion was central to a proof that the soul was immaterial, so it is unsurprising that those immersed in this tradition could see Locke's attack on it, and indeed his attack on innatism too, as closely connected with doubts about the soul's immateriality. Indeed, the dangers could only become more apparent when, in II.xxiii, Locke makes it clear that we are ultimately in the dark about what the soul's essence is. Here there is a link between his observations on *corporeal* substance, or the supposed substratum of sensible qualities, which we shall return to, and his comments on the substance underlying mental operations, when he claims that, like the substance of body, 'The substance of Spirit is unknown to us' (sect. 30). Admittedly, chapter xxvii, which was added in the second edition, is for the most part devoted to an account of personal identity which attempts to disentangle the idea of the continuance of a *person* from that of the persistence of *any* particular sort of substance, and he will hold in IV.iii.6 that our belief in immortality is not threatened whatever the nature of the soul. But the upshot is that Locke can find no *proof* of the natural immortality of the soul. For Locke, of course, this emerges as one illustration of the limits of human knowledge. For many readers, the dangers were clear.[9]

❧❧ VI ❧❧

There is, however, a much more dominant theme running through the *Essay*, which connects indeed with the last but underlies much that Locke says in Books II, III and IV, for many of Locke's concerns centre on what might best be described as an exploration of the implications of the corpuscular science associated in particular with Boyle. In Book II, two topics to which this concern is clearly very central are his treatment of primary and secondary qualities in II.viii, and of our idea of substance in II.xxiii. Both have given rise to much discussion, and indeed – with the possible addition of II.xxvii (on personal identity) – these have probably been the most widely discussed chapters in Book II. They are, I think, best treated together, though very often they have been treated separately.

Certainly, that Locke's concern in II.viii is with the implications of the new science can hardly be denied given what he himself says in section 22 where, after noting that 'I have in what just goes before, been engaged in Physical Enquiries a little farther than, perhaps, I intended', he adds that this was

> necessary, to make the Nature of Sensation a little understood, and to make the *difference between the Qualities in Bodies, and the* Ideas *produced by them in the Mind*, to be distinctly conceived, without which it were impossible to discourse intelligibly of them.

Nor is it deniable that the natural philosophy Locke has in mind here is the corpuscular system, which, as Locke explicates it, entails that our ideas of colours, odours and tastes for example correspond to secondary qualities, which are but powers in objects depending on 'the Bulk,

Figure, Texture, and Motion of their insensible parts' (sect. 10). There is indeed much that is problematic in II.viii – for example the implications of his claim that our ideas of primary qualities, but not of secondary qualities, are 'resemblances' of them, but the centrality of the new science to what Locke says is evident. What this *opposes* is, basically, Aristotelian science, which would account for our perception of colours for example by reference to the *forms* of the colours in the objects, so it seems reasonable to suppose that when Locke complains that

> Men are hardly to be brought to think, that *Sweetness and Whiteness are not really in Manna*; which are but the effects of the operations of *Manna*, by the motion, size, and figure of its Particles on the Eyes and Palate
>
> (sect. 18)

the men he has in mind will include, not just ordinary folk, but supporters of a soon to be defunct metaphysics.

Even if we accept that, however, there is much that could be discussed. It might be asked, for example, what right Locke had to appeal to the new science for the distinction, given that the new science remained controversial; how, if the 'minute parts' which are central to the story are 'insensible', we could know anything at all about them; and how Locke's view that some of our ideas are, and some are not, 'resemblances' of qualities could ever be established, given, what he will say later, that 'the Mind ... perceives nothing but its own *Ideas*'. Here, so far as the first of the questions is concerned, it must suffice to say that Locke's general attitude to the corpuscular hypothesis is that it is the best available (IV.iii.16); that, so far as the particles being 'insensible' goes, Locke takes this insensibility to be a merely contingent matter, which would be overcome if our senses were more acute; and that, ultimately it seems, his claims about which ideas are and which are not resemblances of qualities could be justified only in terms of an acceptance of the underlying scientific theory. All we need to add perhaps is that this acceptance was not simply dogmatic. Given this theory, and the distinction between ideas that goes with it, facts such that the same water can feel warm to one hand and cool to the other could be accounted for (II.viii.21).[10] The question of what exactly Locke *means* when he says that 'the Mind ... perceives nothing but its own *Ideas*', is perhaps better left for a while. There is more than one way of understanding it.

For the moment it is more important that we note that notions that figure prominently in II.viii do re-emerge in II.xxiii, where the attention of commentators has often been focused more on what Locke says about our idea of substance *in general*, particularly in the earlier sections, than on the topic suggested by the title, which is 'Of our *Complex* Ideas *of Substances*'. On the first of these issues Locke talks of our 'obscure and relative *Idea* of Substance in general' as 'something... *standing under*', or supporting qualities; but on the second, where his concern is with our ideas of particular *sorts* of substances such as gold, his claim is that we form these 'by collecting such Combinations of simple *Ideas*, as are by Experience and Observation of Men's Senses taken notice of to exist together, and are therefore supposed to flow from the particular internal Constitution, or unknown Essence of that Substance'. As is so often the case with Locke's *Essay*, there has been no clear concensus on precisely what is going on in this chapter,[11] but there is growing agreement that what he is struck by is the unhelpful-ness of philosophical theorizing in terms of the abstract categories of *substance* and *accident*, even though he sees our ordinary ways of talking about objects as reflecting an idea of 'something' underlying the *observable* qualities of things. Suggestions such as that if we had 'Senses acute enough' we would 'discern the minute particles of Bodies, and the real Constitution on which their sensible Qualities depend' (sect. 11) give us a very obvious link with II.viii, and underwrite the view that, for Locke, speculations about substance in general bring us to the area of 'obscure terms and useless questions', contrasting with the intelligible theorizing of the new science. It remains the case, how-ever, that we have here an area where, in Locke's reasonable seven-teenth-century view, the limits of human understanding are clear. Had we 'Senses acute enough' we would indeed be able to penetrate into the inner natures of things, but the truth is that we don't.

❧ VII ❧

The programme announced in I.i.3 would lead one to expect that, having dealt with the 'materials' of knowledge, Locke would next consider knowledge itself. But, as he says at the very end of Book II, he has been struck by the fact that 'there is so close a connexion between *Ideas* and Words... that it is impossible to speak clearly and distinctly of our Knowledge... without considering, first, the Nature, Use, and Signification of Language'. In Book III, therefore, he gives us his account of language.

The basic picture he offers in the first two chapters in Book III is fairly simple. Words are not necessary for thought itself, but primarily in order for men to communicate their thoughts to others, or 'to record their own Thoughts for the Assistance of their own Memory' (III.ii.2). Words, or significant sounds, are therefore signs of our internal concep-tions, and can 'properly and immediately signify nothing but the *Ideas*, that are in the Mind of the Speaker' (sect. 4). Men do, however, give them a secondary or 'secret' reference in that, precisely because language is used to communicate, they assume that the words they use to signify their own ideas mark the same ideas in the minds of those they converse with, while, 'Because *Men* would not be thought to talk *barely* of their own Imaginations, but of Things as they really are' they often take them to stand for '*the reality of Things*' (sect. 5). Locke's cautionary words at this point – 'it is a perverting the use of Words, and brings unavoidable Obscurity and Confusion into their Signification, whenever we make them stand for any thing, but those *Ideas* we have in our own Minds' – may strike us as simply perverse – surely if I say 'John is bald' I do mean to refer to John himself, but the implications of the remark become much clearer later. Sticking for the moment with the opening chapters, it is necessary only to add that Locke is very conscious that most words do not signify only particular, individual things. Many stand for general ideas.

There are, however, nine chapters still to come in Book III, and it must be said at once that here, as quite often in the *Essay*, one becomes conscious of a mismatch between what probably most interests Locke himself – the points he most wants to get across – and what has most caught the attention of critics and commentators since. This can indeed be illustrated by the fact that Book III ends with three chapters on the 'abuses' and 'imperfections' of words, and the 'remedies' for these, which are clearly important to Locke, given his overall aims, though they have concerned commentators less. It is, however, also apparent even if one turns to chapter iii, which is certainly the most widely discussed. It is entitled '*Of General Terms*'.

Clearly the topic of general terms, and the general ideas which they signify, is important to Locke, if only because, as will become plain in Book IV, most of our knowledge will be found to consist in general propositions; but, since Berkeley at least, what has most caught the attention of commentators has been his account of what might be termed the mechanics of abstraction, or the process by which Locke takes it we form general ideas. Taking the word 'man' as an example, Locke holds that children will start with the ideas of individuals – Peter, James, Mary and Jane – and then, having noted certain resemblances, frame an idea in which they 'leave out . . . that which is peculiar to each, and retain only what is common to them all'. Berkeley was to devote the bulk of the Introduction to the *Principles* to attacking abstraction, insisting, for example, that 'the idea of man that I frame to my self, must be either of a white, or a black, or a tawny, a straight, or a crooked, a tall, or a low, or a middle-sized man' and that 'I cannot by any effort of thought conceive the abstract idea above described', and his criticisms have often focused minds on this aspect of Locke's thought. By contrast, what seems to matter most to Locke is the distinction between real and nominal essences which he spells out later on in the chapter, to which the account of abstraction is a prolegomenon.

Certainly, this distinction brings us right back to a dominant theme which we have already looked at, for 'the real Essences of corporeal Substances' are located in the 'real, but unknown Constitution of their insensible Parts, from which flow those sensible Qualities, which serve us to distinguish them one from another' (sect. 17). And the dominant notion that emerges now is that we rank things into sorts, neither on the basis of these real essences, which we do not know, nor on the basis of the real essences of the scholastics, which they think of as 'a certain number of Forms or Molds, wherein all natural Things, that exist, are cast, and do equally partake' (ibid.), but rather according to what Locke calls 'nominal' essences. These are, indeed, the abstract ideas already covered, but the crucial thought is that we categorize things into sorts on the basis of certain *observed* properties which we choose to associate as constituting one sort. Negatively, then, the dominant concern of the chapter is another piece of rubbish-removal, in this case the 'real essences' or 'forms' of the schools;[12] positively it is an account of classification according to which 'the sorting of Things, is the Workmanship of the Understanding' (sect. 12). More generally, and as we shall see, the account prepares the way for what Locke will say about the science of nature in Book IV.

There is of course much more in Book III, including treatments of the names of simple ideas in chapter iv, of the names of mixed modes and relations ('adultery' and 'gratitude' are among the examples) in chapter v, of the names of substances again in chapter vi, and of particles (words such as 'but' and the 'is' of predication) in chapter vii, but this book concludes with the three chapters on remedying 'abuses' and 'imperfections'. Recalling the concern Locke expressed in his Epistle to the Reader about 'the learned but frivolous use of uncouth, affected, or intelligible Terms', we can understand that these chapters are not peripheral to Locke's purposes, and his reference here to 'gibberish' such as the Epicurean notion of *endeavour towards Motion in their Atoms, when at rest*' (III.x.14) can serve as just one example of the sort of thing he has in mind. In fact he casts his net wide. His observation that, in common use, 'body' and 'extension' stand for distinct ideas, but that 'there are those who find it necessary to confound their signification' (sect. 6) is an obvious reference to the Cartesians.[13]

∾ VIII ∾

Given that one of the main aims of the *Essay* is to determine the scope of human knowledge, it perhaps comes as something of an anticlimax that, in the event, Locke allows very little that he will count as knowledge. That this will be so is strongly suggested by the very first chapter in Book IV where he defines 'knowledge' as *'the perception of the connexion and agreement, or disagreement and repugnancy of any of our Ideas'*, giving as the first two examples *'White is not Black'* and *'the three Angles of a Triangle are equal to two right ones'*. Locke in fact holds that the first of these involves one of four sorts of agreement or disagreement on which knowledge can be based – *'Identity, or Diversity'* – while the second is based on what he calls *'relation'*. The other sorts of perceived agreement are *'Co-existence, or necessary connexion'* (one example given is that *'Iron is susceptible of magnetical Impressions'*, which, in so far as we know it, will turn out to be construed as what we would now term an analytic proposition), and *'Real Existence'*, the one example given in IV.i being *'GOD is'*. When we find that in chapter ii he tells us that the primary ways of knowing are 'intuition' (anyone who has the two ideas will simply see that white is not black) and 'demonstration', of which mathematical proofs are the favoured model, the strong rationalist streak in Locke becomes apparent. Indeed, for him, 'intuition', or self-evidence, lies at the root of nearly all he recognizes as 'knowledge', for demonstration turns out to be based on nothing more than a series of intuitions. A good illustration of how this is supposed to work would be the series of supposed intuitions which he offers in IV.x as constituting a demonstration that God exists.

Locke, then, offers a very restrictive account of 'knowledge', and as the chapters proceed we find as much attention being given to things we cannot hope to know with certainty as to what we can. Examples of things lying beyond the scope of our knowledge thus turn out to include that man cannot be nourished by stones (IV.vi.15) – the explanation here being that our idea of man is that of 'a Body of the ordinary shape, with Sense, voluntary Motion, and Reason join'd to it' and we can neither intuit nor demonstrate by our reason any 'necessary connexion' between that and what will nourish him – and that opium will make a man sleep (IV.iii.25), but these could be multiplied. The proposition that gold is malleable for example *is* indeed certainly known to be true, but only if, as Locke puts it, *'Malleableness* be a part of the complex *Idea* the word *Gold* stands for'. If we happen not to include malleability in the definition of gold, or in the abstract idea, this again is something that cannot certainly be known (IV.vi.9). As he puts it in IV.viii.9, the general *Propositions* that are made *about Substances, if they are certain, are for the most part but trifling*; and if they are instructive, are uncertain, and such as we can have no knowledge of their real Truth, how much soever constant Observation and Analogy may assist our Judgments in guessing.

There are indeed *some* areas where Locke's insistence that we lack 'knowledge' is, if not uncontroversial, at least such as to reflect a not unreasonable caution, as for example his denial that we know that matter cannot think, but equally there are many that seem surprising. If I am not now perceiving any men, for example, Locke will deny that I 'know' there are other men in the world (IV.xi.9).

One question that arises here, then, is precisely why Locke tolerates an account of knowledge that is as restrictive as this. And here no doubt at least part of the answer must be that he simply accepts a tradition whereby 'knowledge' does require a very high degree of certainty, and is indeed tied to the notion of necessity. However, this judgement must be tempered by three further observations. One is that, for all his parsimony when it comes to recognizing 'knowledge', he does allow some items that, to us, may seem less certain than they did to him. The second is that in some cases where he is bound to say we do and perhaps always will lack 'knowledge', he is still guided by a view of what acquiring knowledge in these cases would be like. And the third is that, though he sees that, with the requirements for 'knowledge' set this high, our 'knowledge' will be very limited, he also insists that what we are then bound to call 'probability' may be of a very high order indeed. These three points are essential to an understanding of Locke's overall position, so I shall elaborate on them briefly in turn.

First, then, it is indeed true that Locke denies that we 'know' certain things we would normally suppose we knew, but what we also find is that there are two areas of fundamental importance in which he believes demonstrability is attainable. The obvious example here is his supposed proof of the existence of God which, though flawed, he took to be a sound demonstration, but we should note too his repeated claim that *'Morality is capable of Demonstration, as well as Mathematicks'* (III.xi.16, cf. IV.iii.18, IV.iv.7 and IV.xii.8). To be sure, Locke never claimed to have developed the system he envisaged, but the mere fact that he thought it possible in principle is significant. For if, starting from God's existence, and the supposed self-evidence of a creature's obligations to his creator, man could come by certainty in this area at least, 'knowledge' would certainly transcend the trivial. As he put it as early as I.i.5,

How short soever [men's] Knowledge may come of an universal, or perfect Comprehension of whatever is, it yet secures their great Concernments, that they have Light enough to lead them to the Knowledge of their Maker, and the sight of their own Duties.

Indeed, the second point connects with this, for if Euclidean geometry is seen as providing the model for a demonstrative morality, it is also the model of what it would be like to have certainty in natural philosophy. For here, Locke's insistence that we don't for example 'know' that hemlock will always kill is combined with thoughts about what would be knowable to one who *could* penetrate into the real essences of substances. Hence his observation in IV.iii.25 that could we but penetrate into the internal structure of things 'we should know without Trial several of their Operations one upon another, as we do now the Properties of a Square, or a Triangle' (IV.iii.25). His assertion that 'Could any one discover a necessary connexion between *Malleableness*, and the *Colour* or *Weight* of *Gold* . . . he might make a *certain* universal Proposition concerning *Gold* in this respect' thus goes along with pessimism about the possibility of *our* discovering any such a connection, but also with a view about what such a discovery would be like. As he has it, 'That *all Gold is malleable*, would be as *certain* as of this, *The three Angles of all right-lined Triangles, are equal to two right ones*' (IV.vi.10).

The strong rationalist streak in Locke is thus evident here, in his pessimism about *our* acquiring much by way of 'knowledge' in this area, quite as much as it is in his optimism about the possibility of a demonstrative morality, but it also connects with his lack of any deep concern that our 'knowledge' is, on his view, limited. And this brings us to the third point, which concerns the stress he put on the notion that 'probability' is not to be despised. For, on Locke's account, to deny that I 'know' that man cannot be nourished by stones turns out to be no more than to assert that this truth is not self-evident or demonstrable, not that 'constant Observation and Analogy' don't justify the high degree of assurance we in fact have, let alone that there are reasonable grounds for doubt. The tone here was in fact set back in I.i.5 with his observation that we should 'not peremptorily, or intemperately require Demonstration, and demand Certainty, where Probability only is to be had, and which is sufficient to govern all our Concernments', and the same note is struck later, in IV.xi.10. A truth may be 'plain and clear', though not strictly 'known'.

~ IX ~

It would thus be a mistake to describe Locke as a sceptic, at least solely on the basis that he denies us 'knowledge' in certain areas where we would normally suppose we had it.[14] Admittedly there are areas in which he thinks our lack of understanding goes deep – 'We have the *Ideas* of *Matter* and *Thinking*, but possibly shall never be able to know, whether any mere material Being thinks, or no' (IV.iii.6), and we simply don't understand for example 'how any *size*, *figure*, or *motion* of any Particles, can possibly produce in us the *Idea* of any *Colour*, *Taste*, or *Sound* whatsoever' (IV.iii.13) – but in matters that affect our practice, such as that stones will not nourish us, all we lack is demonstrative *proofs*. The most that can be said is that there may be one particular area where Locke should have been more sceptical than he was. This brings us back to the area of 'real existence', and in particular to sensitive knowledge.

The truth here is that, though when he introduces his account of knowledge in IV.i the only example Locke gives of our knowledge of real existence is our demonstrative knowledge that God exists, he in fact recognizes not only our supposedly intuitive knowledge of our own existence (IV.ix.3), but knowledge of the existence of external objects. Admittedly, the scope of this knowledge turns out to be very limited – broadly I 'know' that an object exists only when I actually sense it – but all the same it has often been questioned whether Locke is entitled to claim even this. There are two difficulties here. One is that Locke defines 'knowledge' as the perception of the agreements and disagreements of *ideas*, and it seems doubtful that this can allow for 'knowledge' of the existence of *anything* which is not itself an idea, whether God, oneself, or any external thing; and the second is whether he is entitled to claim even an assurance of the existence of bodies, given his apparent belief that we never perceive any. This second difficulty is at best tangentially connected with the definition of 'knowledge', and would arise even without it. His notorious comment in IV.iv.3 that 'the Mind . . . perceives nothing but its own *Ideas*' raises it very forcibly, while bringing us back to the topic of Locke's idea of 'idea'.

On the first of these supposed difficulties, all that can be said here is that it seems that Locke himself did not think that his definition ruled out any knowledge of 'real existence', in that he supposed the existence of God at least could be demonstrated by attending solely to our ideas. What is supposedly established here is, apparently, still a relationship between two ideas, those of God and of real existence. He makes a similar point to Stillingfleet in defending his position on sensitive knowledge,[15] though in the *Essay* itself there are indications that he does have some misgivings about whether, strictly, this should count as 'knowledge' at all.[16] Even there, however, he certainly claims that in this area 'we are provided with an Evidence, that puts us past doubting', so the real issue is whether he was entitled to claim even that. At this stage it is the second difficulty that becomes acute. Very often, traditionally even, Locke has been seen as adopting a Representative Theory of Perception which positively invites scepticism in this area. If 'the Mind . . . perceives nothing but its own *Ideas*' it seems we do *not* perceive tables and chairs, and this appears to make their existence genuinely questionable. That Locke himself shows little sign of anxiety about this hardly lessens the difficulty.

Unfortunately we can do little more than note this apparent problem, apart from observing that it is of some historical importance (Berkeley's idealism will have it as its starting-point) and that there has been much controversy on just what view of perception Locke is committed to. Whether those commentators are right who claim that Locke's ideas of sense are 'objects' or 'entities', and indeed the only objects of which we are ever aware, rather than 'perceptions', or states of awareness *of the things themselves*, lies beyond the scope of an introductory essay. What must at least be conceded, however, is that there is undeniably a strong streak of what might be called 'perceptual realism' in Locke; that in many passages he does talk of perceiving the external things, and that even the claim that 'the Mind . . . perceives nothing but its own *Ideas*' can be interpreted in the light of his talk of ideas as being 'found' in the things themselves.[17] Perhaps, but only perhaps, Locke is simply inconsistent, but claims such as that 'we immediately by our Senses perceive in *Fire* its Heat and Colour' (II.xxiii.7) and suggestions that what we do *not* perceive is the corpuscular structuring on which these qualities depend are significant. A strong case can be made for the view that the key to Locke's thinking lies there.

✎ X ✎

It goes without saying that there is much in Locke's *Essay* that has not been discussed here. That however is inevitable. His interest is perennial and his importance clear, but just what most interests a particular reader will depend on a number of factors. To his contemporaries his attacks on what he saw as 'rubbish' lying in the way to knowledge were of genuine significance, while the perceived implications of his epistemology for theology could and did cause deep concern. The importance he himself attached to, for example, his attack on 'enthusiasm' in religion in IV.xix is, though it was only introduced in the fourth edition, evident from its vigour, but the chapter is omitted from a recent abridgement. We now know that Berkeley was soon to attack the very notion of 'matter', or of bodies existing without the mind, and though he certainly wasn't just addressing Locke, Locke has often been seen as his prime target. Locke's doctrines concerning ideas have thus come to be seen as a stepping-stone to Berkeley's idealism and indeed to Hume's scepticism. His accounts of abstract ideas, primary and secondary qualities, substance and so on have been examined over and over again in the light of Berkeley's criticisms, while others see them as significant in their own right. Again, Locke's account of personal identity has been no more than touched on here, but he was the first to raise the issue in the form in which it continues to be discussed today, and his contribution is admired and, still, widely discussed. Other features of his position have been warmly praised – one commentator claims that he handles the notion of real essence 'almost flawlessly'[18] – yet often he has been used for target practice, and Gilbert Ryle once suggested, though perhaps not wholly seriously, that 'nearly every youthful student of philosophy both can and does in about his second essay refute Locke's entire Theory of Knowledge'.[19] I imagine that few, certainly few who have delved at all deeply into his thinking, would now second that sort of judgement, but for all that the correct interpretation of his position remains a matter of controversy at almost every point. This is perhaps hardly surprising, for Locke stands at a crucial point in the development of the history of philosophy, epitomizing the shift from ways of thinking that have become largely foreign to us, to ways that seem familiar. University courses entitled 'History of Modern Philosophy' thus customarily have Locke's *Essay* as their first text originally written in English. His problems have become, in a sense, our problems. Yet we find them emerging from a background that has become less familiar. Getting the most out of Locke's philosophy will therefore involve using hindsight, for we know its fruits, but also understanding the world from which it emerged. It is only if we do both that Locke's true genius can be seen.

NOTES

1 References to the *Essay* are to the Clarendon Edition, [3.3], and cite book, chapter and section number. Except in the case of the Epistle to the Reader the italics have been left unchanged.

2 In his *John Locke* ([3.22], 31–5), first published in 1937, R. I. Aaron noted Leibniz's comment that Locke 'writes obviously in the spirit of Gassendi', and argued that the influence of Gassendi's thought on him was considerable. Further discussions include Kroll, [3.52], and Michael, [3.56].

3 Aaron, [3.22], 27. However, both he and Gibson, [3.25], 236–41, also draw

attention to important differences of view. For one thing, most of the Cambridge Platonists held that there were innate ideas, and as Gibson notes 'nothing, Cudworth declared, could more directly promote atheism than the Aristotelian maxim, "Nihil est in intellectu quod non fit prius in sensu" '.

4 As will emerge, for Locke we have ideas in sense experience, and also in thinking and reasoning. The question of whether ideas are images can therefore emerge at two levels. Some have held that he takes the immediate object of perception when we see or otherwise perceive an object to be itself an image, or an entity which somehow stands proxy for the object, while others seem more concerned with whether the ideas that we might now call concepts are images. No doubt the relationship between these two issues is important, but it seems fair to say that most often it has been his view of sense perception that has exercised his readers, though it is ideas as concepts that feature most prominently in the *Essay*. When, however, Ayers claims ([3.21], 1:44) that, 'the grounds for holding him an imagist are conclusive', it is clear from the context both that he regards this judgement as controversial, and that his eye is fixed on ideas as they function in thought. Certainly, the nature of Locke's idea of 'idea' continues to be much discussed.

5 For an examination of Descartes's doctrine of innate ideas, which includes the relevant passages, see Anthony Kenny, *Descartes: A Study of His Philsophy*, New York, Random House, 1968, ch. 5.

6 Mabbott, [4.26], 80. Even when this was published, however, a debate was in progress over Noam Chomsky's claim that his work in linguistics vindicated the rationalists on this issue. This claim was controversial, and it was widely criticized. See, for example, D. E. Cooper, 'Innateness: Old and New', *Philosophical Review* 81 (1972): 465–83.

7 Which is not to say that nothing is lost. Aaron, [3.22], 110–14, and Gibson, [3.25], ch. 3, are among commentators who have played down its importance, but for a survey which takes it seriously, see Stewart, [3.58]. Locke's compositionalism and its historical background also looms large in, for example Schouls, [3.38], and Ayers, [3.44].

8 This notion did not rest only on what he wrote in the *Essay*, nor simply on the issue I shall concentrate on here. His publication of a work entitled *The Reasonableness of Christianity* in 1695 fuelled doubts as to his orthodoxy, particularly on doctrines such as those of original sin and the Trinity, while his correspondence with Stillingfleet focused attention on the supposed theological implications of the *Essay*.

9 This is well documented by Yolton, [3.15], 148–66, cf. [3.40], ch. 1 and *passim*, and [3.41]. If, from our standpoint it might seem absurd that Locke's contemporaries made so much of a suggestion that is far from prominent in the *Essay*, we should be clear that things looked very different then, as they did to Leibniz for example. His reaction is examined by Jolley, [3.37], who argues that 'For all its apparent randomness and lack of direction, the *New Essays on Human Understanding* is a book dedicated to defending the idea of a simple, immaterial and naturally immortal soul' (p. 7).

10 This is among a number of phenomena instanced in II.viii.16–21, which have, since Berkeley at least, often been read as revealing Locke's acceptance of what is called 'the argument from the relativity of perception' to *prove* or *demonstrate*

the subjectivity of certain supposed qualities. For a quite different, and more plausible account, see Alexander, [3.35], 124–9.

11 See for example Ayers, [3.43], including the references given on p. 78, n. 2.

12 This is just one of a number of references in the *Essay* to the substantial forms of the schools. For example, in IV.iv.13 Locke again protests the view that 'there were a certain number of these Essences, wherein all Things, as in Molds, were cast and formed'. It is strongly arguable that commentators who fail to attach due importance to Locke's dissatisfaction with this scholastic notion can only misunderstand many of Locke's better known pronouncements, including not only a problem he raises earlier in IV.iv – that of how we can know that our ideas 'agree with Things themselves' – and his answer to it as it relates to our ideas of substances, but also his insistence that words signify ideas, the account of knowledge given in Book IV, and even the content of II.xxiii. There too, in section 3, we find a significant reference to the suspect 'substantial forms' of the schools. (For a brief account of the doctrine, as understood by Locke and his contemporaries, see Woolhouse, [3.33], sect. 12.)

13 These examples are of 'abuses', but Locke's treatment of the 'imperfections' of words is also important. His initially puzzling insistence that 'Words ... can properly and immediately signify nothing but the *Ideas*, that are in the Mind of the Speaker' underlies his analysis of the difficulties we get into with the names of mixed modes (such as 'murder') and substances, and the remedies for these. An illustration is a dispute between physicians he reports on in III.ix.16 over 'whether any Liquor passed through the Filaments of the Nerves'. This was largely resolved when they saw that 'each of them made [the term 'liquor'] a sign of a different complex *Idea*'.

14 References to Locke as a sceptical philosopher that are found in the literature are, however, not wholly unjustified if they are linked to his observations about the limits of human understanding and, in particular, to his claims about our inability to penetrate into the real essences of things. The one point I want to insist on is that, for Locke, the claim that I don't 'know' for example that stones won't nourish me does not entail suspension of judgement, nor any suggestion that there are reasonable grounds for doubt.

15 Locke, [3.2], 4: 360.

16 Thus Locke's account of the 'degrees' of our knowledge in IV.ii dwells on intuition and demonstration, and he observes at the beginning of section 14 that 'These two ... are the degrees of our Knowledge; whatever comes short of one of these, with what assurance soever embraced, is but Faith, or Opinion, but not Knowledge'. On the face of it, this *should* rule out knowledge of the existence of things 'without us', for in the same section he admits that this falls short of 'either of the foregoing degrees of certainty'. All the same, it 'passes under the name of Knowledge', and this is something Locke immediately endorses. Similarly, his observation in IV.xi.3 that in this area we have 'an assurance that *deserves the name of Knowledge*' is not unnaturally read as conceding that he is making it 'knowledge' by special dispensation.

17 Locke's only sustained treatment of our knowledge of the existence of things 'without us' is in IV.xi, so it should be noted that here as in other key passages (e.g. II.viii.12) there is no suggestion that we do not perceive such objects. Indeed, it is said at the outset that it is 'when by actual operating upon him, it

makes it self perceived by him' that a man knows that an external object exists. This is the sort of thing one has in mind when one talks of a strong streak of perceptual realism in Locke, but it has of course been recognized by those who hold that it cannot be taken at face value. The issue then becomes, I think, whether other things Locke says suggest that, really, all we are aware of is mind-dependent items, or whether the dominant thought is simply that, though we are aware of the things, the way they appear to us will depend in large part on facts about our sensory apparatus. For an analysis of the issues that divide commentators here, see Tipton, [3.59].

18 Bennet, [3.36], 120.

19 Ryle [3.57], 147. The remark, made in conversation with Bertrand Russell, was set in the context of a recognition that 'Locke made a bigger difference to the whole intellectual climate of mankind than anyone had done since Aristotle'. The paper in which he reports it is thus not dismissive, but rather Ryle's attempt to explain what Locke's great contribution was.

❧ BIBLIOGRAPHY ❧

Collected Works

3.1 In progress: *The Clarendon Edition of the Works of John Locke*, Oxford, Clarendon Press, 1975–.

3.2 *The Works of John Locke*, London, T. Tegg, *et al.*, 1823, 10 vols.

Editions of the Essay

3.3 Nidditch, P. H. (ed.) *An Essay concerning Human Understanding*, Oxford, Clarendon Press, 1975.

3.4 Yolton, J. W. (ed.) *An Essay Concerning Human Understanding* (abr. edn), London, Dent, 1976.

Early Criticisms

3.5 Burnet, Thomas *Remarks upon an Essay concerning Humane Understanding*, London, 1697, *Second Remarks* (1697), and *Third Remarks* (1699); ed. G. Watson as *Remarks on John Locke*, Doncaster, Brynmill Press, 1989.

3.6 Carroll, William *A Dissertation upon the Tenth Chapter of the Fourth Book of Mr. Locke's Essay (etc.)*, London, 1706; repr. Bristol, Thoemmes, 1990.

3.7 Lee, Henry *Anti-Scepticism: Or, Notes upon each Chapter of Mr. Locke's Essay (etc.)*, London, 1702; repr. New York, Garland, 1978.

3.8 Leibniz, G. W. *New Essays on Human Understanding*, first pub. 1765, trans. and ed. P. Remnant and J. Bennett, Cambridge, Cambridge University Press, 1981.

3.9 Lowde, James *A Discourse concerning the Nature of Man...*, London, 1694; repr. New York, Garland, 1979.

3.10 Norris, John *Cursory Reflections upon a Book call'd, an Essay concerning Human Understanding.* Appended to his *Christian Blessedness*, London, 1690; repr. New York, Garland, 1978.

3.11 Sergeant, John *Solid Philosophy Asserted, against the Fancies of the Ideaists*, London, 1697; repr. New York, Garland, 1984.

3.12 Stillingfleet, Edward *A Discourse in Vindication of the Doctrine of the Trinity*, London, 1696.

3.13 —— *The Bishop of Worcester's Answer to Mr. Locke's Letter, concerning some Passages relating to his Essay (etc.)*, London, 1697.

3.14 —— *The Bishop of Worcester's Answer to Mr. Locke's Second Letter...*, London, 1698.

3.15 Yolton, J. W. *John Locke and the Way of Ideas*, Oxford, Oxford University Press, 1956. (A survey of many early responses.)

Bibliographies

3.16 Christophersen, H. O. *A Bibliographical Introduction to the Study of John Locke*, Oslo, 1930; repr. New York, Franklin, 1968.

3.17 Hall, R. and Woolhouse, R. *Eighty Years of Locke Scholarship*, Edinburgh, Edinburgh University Press, 1983.

3.18 *The Locke Newsletter*, published annually since 1970 by Roland Hall of the Department of Philosophy at the University of York, contains a 'Recent Publications' section.

Biographies

3.19 Fox Bourne, H. R. *The Life of John Locke*, London, 1876; repr. Bristol, Thoemmes, 1991.

3.20 Cranston, M. *John Locke: A Biography*, London, Longmans, 1957.

General Surveys

3.21 Ayers, M. R. *Locke*, 2 vols, London, Routledge, 1991.

3.22 Aaron, R. I. *John Locke*, 1st edn 1937; 3rd edn, Oxford, Clarendon Press, 1971.

3.23 Brandt, R. (ed.) *John Locke: Symposium Wolfenbüttel 1979*, Berlin, de Gruyter, 1981.

3.24 Duchesneau, F. *L'Empirisme de Locke*, The Hague, Nijhoff, 1973.

3.25 Gibson, J. *Locke's Theory of Knowledge and its Historical Relations*, Cambridge, Cambridge University Press, 1917.

3.26 Mabbott, J. D. *John Locke*, London, Macmillan, 1973.

3.27 Mackie, J. L. *Problems from Locke*, Oxford, Clarendon Press, 1976.
3.28 O'Connor, D. J. *John Locke*, New York, Dover, 1967.
3.29 Squadrito, K. *Locke's Theory of Sensitive Knowledge*, Washington, University Press of America, 1978.
3.30 Tipton, I. C. (ed.) *Locke on Human Understanding: Selected Essays*, Oxford, Oxford University Press, 1977.
3.31 Webb, T. E. *The Intellectualism of Locke*, Dublin, 1857; repr. Bristol, Thoemmes, 1990.
3.32 Woolhouse, R. S. *Locke's Philosophy of Science and Knowledge*, Oxford, Blackwell, 1971.
3.33 —— *Locke*, Brighton, Harvester, 1983.
3.34 Yolton, J. W. *Locke and the Compass of Human Understanding*, Cambridge, Cambridge University Press, 1970.

Comparative Studies and Special Themes

3.35 Alexander, P. *Ideas, Qualities and Corpuscles: Locke and Boyle on the External World*, Cambridge, Cambridge University Press, 1985.
3.36 Bennett, J. *Locke, Berkeley, Hume: Central Themes*, Oxford, Clarendon Press, 1971.
3.37 Jolley, N. *Leibniz and Locke: A Study of the New Essays on Human Understanding*, Oxford, Clarendon Press, 1984.
3.38 Schouls, P. A. *The Imposition of Method: A Study of Descartes and Locke*, Oxford, Clarendon Press, 1980.
3.39 Yolton, J. W. *Perceptual Acquaintance from Descartes to Reid*, Oxford, Blackwell, 1984.
3.40 —— *Thinking Matter: Materialism in Eighteenth-Century Britain*, Oxford, Blackwell, 1984.
3.41 —— *Locke and French Materialism*, Oxford, Clarendon Press, 1991.

Articles and Chapters

3.42 Ashworth, E. J. 'Locke on Language', *Canadian Journal of Philosophy* 14 (1984): 45–73.
3.43 Ayers, M. R. 'The Ideas of Power and Substance in Locke's Philosophy', first pub. 1975, repr. in [3.30], above.
3.44 Ayers, M. R. 'Locke's Logical Atomism', in *Rationalism, Empiricism and Idealism*, ed. A. Kenny, Oxford, Clarendon Press, 1986.
3.45 Barnes, J. 'Mr. Locke's Darling Notion', *Philosophical Quarterly* 22 (1972): 193–214.
3.46 Bennett, J. 'Substratum', *History of Philosophy Quarterly* 4 (1987): 197–215.
3.47 Buchdahl, G. 'Locke: Narrowing the Limits of Scientific Knowledge', ch. 4 in his *Metaphysics and the Philosophy of Science*, Oxford, Blackwell, 1969.
3.48 Curley, E. M. 'Locke, Boyle, and the Distinction between Primary and Secondary Qualities', *Philosophical Review* 81 (1972): 438–64.

3.49 Flew, A. 'Locke and the Problem of Personal Identity', *Philosophy* 26 (1951): 53–68.

3.50 Harris, J. 'Leibniz and Locke on Innate Ideas', first pub. 1974, repr. in [3.30], above.

3.51 Kretzmann, N. 'The Main Thesis of Locke's Semantic Theory', first pub. 1968, repr. in [3.30], above.

3.52 Kroll, R. W. F. 'The Question of Locke's Relation to Gassendi', *Journal of the History of Ideas* 45 (1984): 339–59.

3.53 Jackson, R. 'Locke's Distinction between Primary and Secondary Qualities', *Mind* 38 (1929): 56–76.

3.54 Laudan, L. 'The Nature and Sources of Locke's Views on Hypotheses', first pub. 1967, repr. in [3.30], above.

3.55 Mandelbaum, M. 'Locke's Realism', Essay 1 in his *Philosophy, Science and Sense Perception*, Baltimore, John Hopkins Press, 1964.

3.56 Michael, F. S. and E. 'The Theory of Ideas in Gassendi and Locke', *Journal of the History of Ideas* 51 (1990): 379–99.

3.57 Ryle, G. 'John Locke', first pub. 1967, repr. in his *Collected Papers*, vol. 1, London, Hutchinson, 1971.

3.58 Stewart, M. A. 'Locke's Mental Atomism and the Classification of Ideas' (in two parts), *The Locke Newsletter* 10 (1979): 53–82, and 11 (1980): 25–62.

3.59 Tipton, I. C. ' "Ideas" and "Objects": Locke on Perceiving "Things" ', in *Minds, Ideas, and Objects: Essays on the Theory of Representation in Modern Philosophy*, ed. P. D. Cummins and G. Zoeller, Atascadero, Calif., Ridgeview Publishing Company, 1992.

3.60 Wilson, M. D. 'Superadded Properties: The Limits of Mechanism in Locke', *American Philosophical Quarterly* 16 (1979): 143–50.

3.61 Winkler, K. P. 'Locke on Personal Identity', *Journal of the History of Philosophy* 29 (1991): 201–26.

CHAPTER 4
Locke's political theory
Ian Harris

The author of *Two Treatises of Government* also wrote *An Essay concerning Human Understanding*. This is an elementary fact, but one with an important implication for understanding Locke's political theory. For *Two Treatises* is an explanatory work. Its objective is to explain the proper character of political authority (or, in the Latinate usage Locke preferred, political power).[1]

To consider Locke's political theory in this way is to place it within the framework of his other intellectual concerns. This is not the only way of writing about theories of politics, but it has a special relevance to Locke. *Two Treatises* is one of the most studied works in political theory. Yet the design of its argument has not been much considered. The picture which the student may form is one of disorder within the text.[2] This impression is unfortunate, because a modest examination of Locke's political argument in the light of his broader thought will yield a much clearer picture: and a justified clarity, after all, is the best assistance that scholarship can give to the reader.

One word of caution should be added, indicating a way in which *one* philosophical approach to Locke's political theory would give a misleading impression of the author in his time. Locke is often supposed to be a progenitor of modern liberalism. Now liberalism assumes as many guises as an imaginative chameleon, but the sort most prominent in philosophical thinking about politics presently is 'unLockean' in an important way. This thinking distinguishes between the right and the good, meaning by the former a basic organization of society according to some canon of justice (though the canon varies) and by the latter a view of how one is to run one's own life. The latter is to be decided by the individual in a manner satisfying to him or her, subject only to the protection or entitlements afforded to others in the name of the right. However the right is understood, there is present a belief that

96

the moral life is determined by and not for the individual: that there is no moral arbiter set over him or her.[3] This view is a complete inversion of Locke's fundamental position. To his mind the human condition was patterned by moral obligations imposed by God, patterned indeed in highly specific ways. This moral patterning has implications for politics, because Locke used the idea of God as a moral legislator to explain the sort of political organization he preferred.

The political doctrine of John Locke, briefly characterised, was founded on the assumption that God had ordered matters in a manner that aligns the force of theology and ethics behind responsible government. The Lockean God is taken to be mankind's superior: this means that He excels people in all salient aspects and, on the basis of these, is fitted to direct and guide them. The content of God's directions is manifold, but its fundamental points are straightforward. That is to say, first, that God wishes mankind to survive, to increase in number and to subdue the earth, and second, that He has promulgated laws, through both reason and revelation, that prescribe measures conducing to those ends. These laws, understood correctly, would conduct people to a sort of government that was limited to certain defined goals and accountable to its citizens.

We may contrast this doctrine of responsible government, limited and accountable, with absolutism. Absolutism is the doctrine that the ruler bears no responsibility to the ruled, and this because God is supposed to have ordered matters in a manner somewhat different to that which Locke attributed to Him. According to this view God either conferred authority directly upon the ruler (so that he was responsible to God rather than the ruled) or permitted the ruled to transfer whatever rights they had to the ruler, irrevocably and unconditionally.[4] Absolutism is a notion foreign to modern fashion: we are all used to the idea of responsible government. But it was *à la mode* in Locke's day and it is worth our while to see how his mind developed quite another cast.

❦ I ❦

It fell to Locke, as a young don at Christ Church, Oxford, to deliver a series of lectures on natural law. For our purpose the significance of the result, which we know as *Essays on the Law of Nature*,[5] is that it contained a theological and ethical position that would play an important role in Locke's political theory.

The primary supposition of these *Essays* was that God was the author of moral prescriptions to mankind. These prescriptions characteristically assumed two media, namely revelation and reason. Though revelation, essentially God's word in the Bible, was relevant to the whole human race it had been diffused to a section of people that was relatively small. Reason, on the other hand, was a faculty possessed by all humans: a code expounded through it could be said to be available to all. This code, called the law of nature, was obviously convenient to moralists who wished to give an explanation of ethical values by using theology. Thus natural law is found in the works of thinkers as various as Aquinas and Luther or Calvin and Culverwell.[6] Whilst the precise specification of its contents varied from writer to writer, its fundamental lines were clear. These took their rise from one central supposition of fact. This was that man was a creature constructed by God. On the one hand God had implanted in the human race certain natural drives. The chief of these were desires for self-preservation and the perpetuation of the species. But the human agent, considered individually, was unequal to the very task of surviving, so that the satisfaction of these desires implied co-operation with others in order to produce favourable conditions: that is to say, to produce society. Rational reflection on these facts suggested a series of precepts directing people to these ends – to preserve oneself and live in society (and, additionally, further precepts of the same tendency). On the other hand, reflecting on God's work in making mankind meant recognizing that He had conferred an incalculable benefit on it. This implied a debt of gratitude to Him, which was thought to be expressed fitly through worship. Thus to preserve oneself, to live socially and to worship were the basic terms of natural law.[7]

Locke's *Essays* were distinguished not by altering this content – indeed he endorsed it[8] – but by explaining its origin and binding force, and how mankind might know these things. That is to say, he argued that God was the moral legislator and that His precepts were always and everywhere of binding force. God was entitled to legislate because he was superior to man in the respects required for the proper direction of agents: not least in understanding, for God was understood to be omniscient. The notion of superiority, often conceived in terms of intelligence (and, when considering human superiors, birth, wealth and education) pervaded contemporary thought. Such attributes were supposed by contemporaries to be a title to direct others: as Obadiah Walker suggested, writing of the nobility, some had attributes 'rendring them eminent and conspicuous above other men, [which] sets them also at least as lights and examples to be followed by their Inferiors'.[9] The Lockean God not only provided directions but also complemented them with obligations. Locke understood obligation to imply not only a superior but also that superior's ability to bring sanctions to bear: God certainly qualified as an imposer of obligations, since He was omnipotent. The obligation to God's directions was universal in extent (for God was superior to all people) and perpetual in duration (since He was eternal).[10]

These theological and ethical points had a political relevance. They went most of the distance necessary to disbar the explanation of absolutism given by the notion of a transfer of right. That is to say, if we accept Locke's line of thought about obligation, people were bound to obey God's directions. They could not be entitled to surrender themselves without reservation to another human being's guidance. All Locke needed to add in order to rule such a transfer out of court was the assertion that God's directions would be undercut by those of absolute rulers (and others who threatened freedom), as we shall see.

⌒ II ⌒

Two Treatises of Government argued that absolutist explanations did not make sense and that the true explanation of political power is quite different. Its discourse was throughout tailored to these ends. Locke applied the word 'demonstration' to his own text and criticized Sir Robert Filmer, one of his principal absolutist targets, for preferring assertion to explanation. He criticized the quality of Filmer's work, terming it '*glib Nonsense*' and describing his reasoning as 'nothing but a Rope of Sand'. But though Locke expressed disdain for its quality, he regarded it as an explanation. Filmer's argument was '*his* Hypothesis' and its refutation provided 'premises' for Locke's conclusions; Locke's first book aimed to refute Filmer's *False Principles* and his second to reveal *The True Original, Extent, and End of Civil-Government*.[11]

Absolutism did not harmonize with the political prepossessions of the circle in which Locke moved. As early as 1675 Shaftesbury, Locke's patron, or an adherent of his had signalled his distaste of it, observing in particular that absolute governments were not entitled to unlimited obedience. *A Letter from a Person of Quality* distinguished 'bounded' from 'absolute' governments. A 'bounded' government was one 'limited by humane laws', denoting a contrast with absolute governments whose rulers were bound only by God's laws. The relevance of the distinction became clear when *A Letter* asked 'how can there be a distinction . . . between Absolute, and bounded Monarchys, if *Monarchs* have only the fear of *God* and no fear of humane Resistance to restrain them'. England, *A Letter* added, was a bounded government.[12]

Explanation is far from being the sole constituent of political discourse. Practical ends can be connected or annexed to theoretical writings. There has been some question about Locke's hypothesized involvement in political affairs and about the possible practical use of his *Treatises*.[13] But whatever the character of these, the work itself has an explanatory character. The work sets out to show how 'political power' is specific in its goals and limited in its authority, the latter being revocable.

We find argument also in two modes. Of course the argument has one primary subject, namely political power, but to this there were not one but two origins. All power was of God,[14] but derived from Him either directly or indirectly. The former source worked when God conveyed power by His command to some individual or group. This in effect meant conveyance through scripture. The latter source suggested that power was mediated through a longer route, as for instance popular consent. This would be discovered most characteristically through reason.

Locke had therefore to deal in the media of both scripture and reason and through these needed to both dispatch absolutism and establish 'bounded' government. This may sound a complicated agenda, but the structure of Locke's argument is straightforward enough. The first of his *Two Treatises* concerns primarily scripture and his second reason, though Locke deployed both media in each. He criticized absolutism and developed his alternative *pari passu*. For in his attack on Filmer throughout the first book Locke laid down several premises from which his own argument about government in the second proceeded, whilst that argument itself offered an alternative to the devices of absolutism by explaining a 'bounded' government. The two books of *Two Treatises of Government* form a continuous treatment of Locke's theme.

III

His *Two Treatises* were complementary, for each considered one of two routes. The first book considered one of the explanations that power is directly of God. This was the one developed in Locke's day by churchmen like Ussher and Sanderson, and found most extendedly in Filmer.[15] Locke set out to destroy Filmer's explanation of absolutism. Locke's second book provided an account of power on the other model by the 'indirect' route.

They were not merely complementary in subject matter, but also in their manner of treating it. For Locke's *First Treatise* provided a description of God's purposes which provides a large part of the basis of the *Second Treatise*. The *First*[16] is usually conceived as a refutation of one explanation of absolutism, and a rather tedious one at that. This judgement of tedium perhaps obscures the fact that the way in which Locke executed his attack on Filmer's view of political superiority involves also the rebuttal of Filmer's view of God's purposes: and brought with it a relocation of His intentions and, conformably, of political superiority.

Locke's method of dealing with superiorities, whether negatively or positively, was demonstrative in the sense that he set out to show the terms in which political superiority was created by tracing out connections amongst ideas. This method harmonized with his philosophical approach. By demonstration Locke intended 'noe thing else but shewing men how they shall see right'.[17] In his first book Locke was concerned to break the connections Filmer had set up, whilst in his second he aimed to establish connections of his own.

Filmer dealt essentially in one superiority, on the basis of which he attempted to establish a wide range of connections. In his view God had conferred on Adam a universal superiority over the earth and mankind. God's medium of expression was preserved in scripture and His conferral was direct. The contents of the grant comprised a superiority over the world as a whole: a power which was absolute over all Adam's descendants and unlimited in extent, as well as a parallel lordship over the whole earth and its creatures. This authority, Filmer argued, passed by descent to subsequent monarchs so that they enjoyed an absolute and unlimited power over person and property.[18]

Locke was not much amused by these connections. He required for the purposes of his own argument about government that man by nature be free from any superior (excepting God).[19] Filmer asserted that everyone had a superior, and that was one whose authority was complete in every way. Locke's first book was devoted to unpicking Filmer's connections. Sometimes his method was to suggest that these were insecurely grounded in scripture. At other times he argued that Filmer had not connected his ideas properly. These arguments are in their nature *ad hominem*. They are fairly exhaustive, though those who have not been exhausted before reaching section 80 know that Locke went beyond the text that found its way into print to discuss grant, usurpation and election as titles to government.[20] But in the course of breaking Filmer's connections Locke suggested some of his own. There were two points of especial importance here.

First, the absence of power given directly by God to one individual allows us to suppose that the same faculties presume the same moral standing for all, since God had made those faculties and their make reflected His intentions, because (Locke assumed) God acted purposively. That is to say, the similarity of people one to another afforded no grounds for setting one human above another: and so they should have the same status. As Locke put it,

> Creatures of the same species and rank promiscuously born to
> all the same advantages of Nature and the use of the same

faculties, should be equal one amongst another without Subordination . . . unless the Lord and Master of them all, should by any manifest Declaration of his Will set one above another.[21]

To this equality is correlated freedom from direction by others, for the faculties possessed were adequate to self-direction, and so direction by another was intellectually superfluous: or, in Locke's own words, people were in 'a *State of perfect Freedom* to order their Actions . . . as they think fit . . . without asking leave, or depending upon the Will of any other Man'.[22] Self-direction was the product of adequate and equal faculties, subject (of course) to God's superiority and His direction.[23]

This identity of status amongst people 'born to all the same advantages', as we shall see in a moment, was important in explaining the duty of preservation, which in its turn was integral to Locke's view of political organization. But central to many other matters is our second point.

Locke provided an explanation of a superiority common to the whole human race, a superiority over the world and its creatures, whether as dominion or as right, and suggests duties addressed to all. All these are cast in terms of the very point to which Locke alluded in his statement of equality, namely that the human intellect was a salient aspect of the image of man in God.

These are found in what Locke terms 'the great design of God'.[24] This design, as its name suggests, signified God's purpose for the human race. The direction was straightforward: people were required 'to promote the great Design of God, *Increase* and *Multiply*'. This language alluded to the narrative of God's setting the human race over lower animals recorded in the first chapter of *Genesis*. Indeed Locke adduced just this to emphasize the purpose. The specification in full runs as follows:

> *And God Blessed them, and God said unto them, be Fruitful and Multiply and Replenish the Earth and subdue it, and have Dominion over the Fish of the Sea, and over the Fowl of the Air, and over every living thing that moveth upon the Earth*
>
> [I Gen. 28]

and it is unambiguous. The God of Locke commanded the human race to propagate themselves, subdue the earth and have dominion over creatures. This was the 'great and primary Blessing of God Almighty'.[25]

Though the great design was cast as a command, it implied a right. To be specific, it explained how mankind collectively had a right to dominion and indeed property over the earth and over its creatures. Locke distinguished the concepts of dominion and property. But he was clear that the benediction of *Genesis* ix, 1–3, to Noah and his sons gave to the human race 'the utmost Property Man is capable of, which is to have a right to destroy any thing by using it'.[26] So mankind collectively had a right to property in the earth and its creatures.

How was the presence of a right made clear? We might say, simply, through revelation, but though true this would not be complete. The allusion to *dominion* makes the point clear. Dominion over animals, we may note, derived to mankind from their intellectual superiority. The common assumption of the day was that animals did not think or, if they did, that their thought was so conspicuously beneath man's that they were manifestly his inferiors. Thus he was their superior or, as Locke put it, had '*Dominion*, or Superiority'[27] over them. In the language of the piece known as *Draft B*, one of his early writings on the human mind, 'it is the Understanding that sets man above the rest of sensible beings & gives him all that dominion he hath over them'.[28] This was because mankind was like God, in that it had a superior understanding, 'for wherein soever else the *Image of God* consisted, the intellectual Nature was certainly a part of it'.[29] Thus the possession of the *imago dei* produced the right.

God made the grant, of course, for the sake of a purpose. A phrase common to both *Genesis* texts we have mentioned (1,28 and 9,1) specified the same purposes for mankind's performance in the same general terms, namely: be fruitful, and multiply, and replenish the earth. This general formula may be mediated into a number of particular forms. One of these is worth especial attention. The intention implicit in the grant required people to preserve themselves. Locke, indeed, indicated that there was a duty of self-preservation,[30] a duty which was matched by a desire for survival and whose content pointed towards the perpetuation of God's design.[31] We may infer that the great design gave people a right to the means of self-preservation; for example, to destroy an animal in order to eat it. Locke inferred as much himself, remarking that God would be unlikely to give property to Adam alone because

> it is more reasonable to think, that God who bid Mankind increase and multiply, should rather himself give them all a Right, to make use of the Food and Rayment, and other Conveniences of Life, the Materials whereof he had so plentifully provided for them[32]

In short the great design suggested that God had given the earth to all mankind, having in mind that it should survive and increase. A duty to preserve oneself was implicit in this.

Here we see Locke deploying conceptions gathered from the general thought of the day, not least his own. Self-preservation was a concern of writing about natural law, including his own *Essays*. The notion of the human dominion over animals had appeared in his writings on this understanding. These assumed also that God had equipped people with apprehensions fitting them to survive. We may add, if we care, that the design's prescription for the multiplication of mankind captured Locke's assumption, seen in his early writings on political economy, that large populations were best.[33] More pointedly, we may say that Locke had taken these motifs and formed from them a determinate pattern. That pattern, as we shall see, was central to his political thought.

We should attend to the generic form behind these formulations: that God had signified an intention for mankind. The design presents a teleology – an end or ends marked out by God for mankind to follow. The 'great Design' is an example of the sort of intentionality Locke had quietly attributed to God in constructing Draft B in 1671. The general principle that there was such a divine plan does not imply the content of the example of it Locke adduced in his *Treatises*, of course. But there is a continuity of thought between his early writings on the understanding and his political doctrine. For he assumed in the former that God had equipped mankind with apprehensions adapted to survival and to allow it to dominate the earth and its animals: in the latter the 'great Design' embodied these suppositions. For it was mankind's 'Senses and Reason', as well as his desires, that set it on the path God had indicated.[34] Thus Locke's view of the human understanding informed the bases of his politics. We should now turn to the superstructure.

❧ III ❧

These points were significant for Locke's larger intention. They provided some of the major bases for his argument about political power in his second book and concurrently about society too. The *Essay . . . of Civil-Government*, like the first book, was concerned with superiorities in society. Locke took care to distinguish these from each other. His prime concern was the superiority of the civil government (or, as he put it, magistrate over the citizen). This was differentiated carefully from the superiority of lord over slave (or, as Locke called it, absolute power).

To this end Locke distinguished types of power. He was concerned not just with demonstration but also with relations. Space precludes treating all of these here, but it is worth glimpsing the full extent of Locke's project. That is to say Locke wished to distinguish the relation between magistrate and subject from that between father and child or between master and slave, amongst others. In his own words:

> I think it may not be amiss, to set down what I take to be Political Power. That the Power of a *Magistrate* over a Subject, may be distinguished from that of a *Father* over his Children, a *Master* over his Servant, a *Husband* over his Wife, and a *Lord* over his Slave. All which distinct Powers happening sometimes together in the same Man, if he be considered under these different Relations, it may help us to distinguish these Powers one from another, and shew the difference betwixt a Ruler of a Common-wealth, a Father of a Family, and a Captain of a Galley.[35]

To these we might add the control which an owner enjoys over property, for Locke treated this in a manner congruent with his view of political power. Thus the *Essay ... of Civil-Government* presented an alternative to Filmer's conflation of these different relations. It did so, of course, in the interests of explaining 'bounded' government.

This argument required that people by nature have no superior. This meant a political superior. Locke was not disposed to deny the superiorities inherent in the society of his day, of parents over children or the owner over his property, for instance.[36] But Filmer had identified freedom by nature from a political superior as the central assumption of limited government.[37] Locke was as good as Filmer's word.

Locke's method of explaining the difference amongst different relations was to outline their source – in his vocabulary, their original. The original, in fact, was one, in that they were all referred to God's intentions. These are best understood by referring to the great design. All the relations important to Locke's argument are explained, wholly or partly, in terms of the great design, except for the relations of master and slave. It is this common explanation which united the terms of Locke's *Essay ... concerning Civil-Government*. Viewed as a list of contents, the principal items of the *Essay* might appear somewhat miscellaneous. Duties of self-preservation and preservation, slavery, property and political organization, to name no others, follow each other in a succession which does not seem entirely orderly at first blush. But there is a connection between these items. The laws of self-preservation and preservation explain the terms on which government is instituted, just as Locke's treatment of slavery illustrates how God's purposes limited these terms.

The great design had a major role in all of these arguments. The duty of self-preservation was part of the design. We shall see that the law of preservation follows from it, once set in conjunction with freedom, equality and the golden rule. God's superiority, prescribing self-preservation, excluded slavery (except in some marginal cases) and suggested that men must remain free. Property in general, we know from the *First Treatise*, derives to mankind from the great design. We shall see that property could be made private through an aspect of freedom; and that privatization was required by the terms of the design. Parental power Locke explained through the function of fitting children to be free and the design will explain the binding character of the function. After all this, it is natural to reflect that rights traditionally associated with Locke's name, all relate to the design. Government, of course, existed to protect them. In short, Locke's account of political power is related to the view of human purpose which he called the great design of God.

❧ IV ❧

If we start with government we soon find ourselves drawn back to the great design. Locke argued that civil government was empowered by two rights – rights belonging to the individual and whose exercise he or she delegated to ensure that they would be applied efficiently. These were the rights to execute the law of nature and to preserve oneself. These rights themselves derive from two duties, to preserve others and to preserve oneself.[38]

We have seen the duty to preserve oneself in book one, but what of duty to preserve others? The idea of a duty to preserve others is quite intelligible in itself. Its explanation is another matter. It does not figure in scripture. Locke argued that because we have a duty to preserve others: that 'Every one as he is *bound to preserve himself* . . . so by the like reason . . . ought he, as much as he can, *to preserve the rest of Mankind*'.[39] How can we explain it?

Locke, as often in his *Treatises*, may seem to write elliptically in explaining the law of preservation. But he had no need to be more than allusive because he employed an idea well known to his contemporaries. The law of preservation he explained by combining man's desire for self-preservation with the golden rule. The golden rule was a central item in the thought of the day. The agent's duty, therefore, could be summarized in the form: love God, and thy neighbour as thyself. This thought figured in a variety of Christian sources, from St. Matthew to Hooker (to go no further). So habitual was its use that there was evidently little need to set it out in explicit language. But its role becomes clear as we pursue the reasoning in chapter 2 of his *Essay on . . . Civil-Government*.[40]

Locke reminded the reader that men were in a state of freedom and equality and went on to say that Hooker had made 'this *equality* of Men by Nature' 'the Foundation of that Obligation to mutual Love amongst Men, on which he Builds the Duties they owe one another'.[41] Hooker had argued that each man should expect no more from his neighbour than he himself performed, for they were equal by nature and so in that respect there was no ground for differentiating between them. He also wrote of taking care to satisfy what one supposed one's neighbour to desire. This follows on the ground of equality. Let us put these considerations more formally.

The conjunction of the golden rule with desire we may describe first in very general terms. It implies the procedure of putting oneself, mentally, in another's place. There one considers how one would like to be treated if really in his or her shoes. One formulates one's conclusion as a rule and one should treat others according to it if one wishes to deserve like conduct from them towards oneself. The procedure could be stated formally in these terms: it cannot be right for A to treat B in a manner in which it would be wrong for B to treat A, merely on the ground that they are two different individuals, and without there being any difference between the nature or circumstances of the two which can be stated as a proper ground for any difference of treatment.

Locke chose to adduce the 'strong desire of Self-preservation', which we have seen correlated to the great design, 'the desire, strong desire of Preserving his Life and Being . . . Planted in him, as a Principle of Action by God himself'.[42] This desire, joined with the golden rule, brings us to the law of preservation.

There is a further significance to self-preservation: on Locke's terms it prevented absolutism on the terms preferred by modern thinkers. To trace power directly from God was one route to the absolutist destination. But the same result could be had by an unreserved transfer of right from free men, as we have noted. These arguments presupposed that people were free to transfer their rights.

Locke precluded this by asserting that people answerable to God and that God required of them conduct incompatible with an unreserved transfer of freedom. God required man to preserve himself and self-preservation was ensured by freedom from absolute power. According to Locke the only reason why anyone would attempt to gain absolute power over another was to threaten his life.[43] To subordinate oneself to a superior without reservation was therefore out of the question:

> *Freedom* from Absolute, Arbitrary Power, is so necessary to, and closely joyned with a Man's Preservation, that he cannot part with it . . . For a Man, not having the Power of his own Life, *cannot*, by Compact, or his own Consent, *enslave himself*

to any one, nor put himself under the Absolute, Arbitrary Power of another, to take away his Life, when he pleases. No body can give more Power than he has himself; and he that cannot take away his own Life, cannot give another power over it.[44]

So people could not countenance submission to absolutism in this mode because they were answerable to God and because the content of God's purposes required them to retain their natural freedom. Freedom, that is to say, cannot be utterly alienated. We shall see that it could be transferred in order to execute other purposes, but that only on conditions which admitted recall. Thus the operations Locke attributed to God restricted the range of possible governments.

❧ V ❧

Locke had not only to explain political power but also to explain those values his society prized. Once the ability to direct oneself and so the basis of civil freedom had been established, property was the most important of these. Hence the second of *Two Treatises* passes from freedom (in chapters 2–4) to property (in chapter 5). This ordering had a logic beyond psychological linkage (it has the latter because liberty and property were key values in politics in Locke's day). For having established political power in terms of God's design, including intellect and freedom, it was incumbent upon him to explain property in a like manner.

Locke placed the retention of freedom significantly, for freedom in his hands would be the instrument of explaining how property could be private. To explain it so was important, for the prevalent style of explanation founded private property on terms that admitted absolutism. To substitute a version that grounded private property in freedom rather than subjection would be a major coup.

What was the task before Locke? The great design of God gave property in the earth and its creatures to mankind collectively. The question, then, was how to move from that to private property. Locke explained this in terms of freedom, for he argued that it was an attribute of a free man that his labour was his own. It was free labour, under the auspices of the great design once more, that produced appropriation and was present in the accumulation of more sophisticated forms of property.

A dictionary of the seventeenth century distinguished an individual's property by its independence from others' control, defining it as 'the highest right that a man hath or can have to any thing, which is no way depending vpon any other mans courtesie'.[45] The writer followed the usage we employ today by applying this definition only to material possessions. Locke is well known for construing the term in a broader way. He embraced not only property as land and goods but also the property each man had in his person. This dual usage is important because it situated 'property' in his wider political explanation.

Locke needed to treat private property in a certain way in order to sustain his own political theory. His *Second Treatise* undertook to explain political power in a way which distinguished it from other sorts of power. He wished to do so in a way incompatible with absolutism. The plausibility of his doctrine to contemporary readers would depend not just on his reasoning about political power itself but also on showing that property could be explained adequately within the terms Locke proposed. His wider argument would not be acceptable if it did not base their cherished property soundly.

Political theory likewise explained property in terms which made it easy to refer it to government. The most powerful explanation was Grotius'. He assumed that mankind originally held property in common and subsequently agreed to partition it amongst themselves, thus producing private property. Pufendorf added the refinement of classifying the original ownership by the whole community in two ways, as negative (which was common because not marked out by any action) and positive (which was common to a given group but not to outsiders), but he did not modify the fundamental theory.[46] Whilst this view of itself implies nothing about government, the two combined easily in the suggestion that only government could produce an enforceable and therefore stable partition. Hobbes asserted that 'there be no Propriety, no Dominion, no *Mine* and *Thine* distinct' without government.[47] Hence private property turned out to be the creation of governmental power.

That the most persuasive criticism of Grotius came from a source radically hostile to natural freedom did not help. Filmer had pointed out an acute difficulty in producing a division of common property because he disliked the implications of the natural freedom it implied.[48] Such a division, he argued, would require a consent of all mankind. Hobbes's view that the state of nature could hardly sustain a viable agreement about property was equally unhelpful to anyone who wished to explain property without relying on government. Their arguments in effect required a new explanation of private property from one who wished both to uphold natural freedom and to explain property in terms free of governmental attachments. Locke noted the difficulty[49] and proceeded to solve it. The *Second Treatise* set out an explanation of property which is founded on natural freedom and is *incompatible* with absolutism. Locke reasoned from the assumption that man was by nature free of a political superior: he retained his natural freedom. That left open the way to set property in terms of freedom. How was this accomplished?

If a human being were free it followed that 'every Man has a *Property* in his own *Person*'.[50] If a human being enjoyed freedom from another's control it followed that they had authority over themselves. As we have seen the seventeenth century called this exclusive control *dominium*. Sometimes too it was called property or *suum*. This control referred to the qualities inhering in a person and was thought to comprise his life, limbs, liberty and so on. Grotius described it as life, liberty, limbs, honour and reputation. Those who opposed absolutism emphasized that material possessions belonged with these, so that property in the ordinary sense was classified as *suum* rather than explained through government. Hence within the framework of *dominium* property in the sense of control over oneself came to include property in goods and estates. The Lockean trinity of life, liberty and property is only one example of this.[51]

It was one thing to move property in the concrete sense on the conceptual map and another to explain it in terms that would securely locate it there. Writers before Locke had not attempted this. He did so by suggesting that a deployment of the agent's *dominium*, his property in the wider sense, produced property in the narrower one. When Locke emphasized the property each had in his person, he added that the '*Labour* of his Body, and the *Work* of his Hands ... are properly his'.[52] That labour Locke used as the means to property. It was easy to describe this as appropriation, since it implied taking something to oneself. The activity had been mentioned by Grotius and Pufendorf, but only marginally.[53] Locke made appropriation the instrument of acquiring property.

But why should this use of the agent's property, his 'labour', produce property in the ordinary sense? It is a mystery why applying one's labour to something, even consuming it, makes the thing taken one's own.[54] After all we call one variety of this activity theft. The solution is that the world already belonged to God, who required mankind to use it for an end which necessitated labour.

Locke had argued for God's superiority in his *Essays* and assumed it in his *Treatises*: and indeed His ownership of the world was a datum common to all writers on the subject of property. They assumed, additionally, that He had given the world to man: Filmer argued one man, Adam, and Grotius and the rest all mankind. His donation was supposed, by Grotius and Filmer amongst others, to take the form declared in *Genesis*: *be Fruitful and Multiply and Replenish the Earth and subdue it*. Locke, of course, had used this passage to found his God's great design, and here we see its special bearing on property.

That lies in a point which is itself quite small, but which has important implications. Most writers treated this instruction of God's merely as a permission – Filmer described it officially as a blessing or benediction and Grotius as a right – which entitled people to live on the earth but did not demand anything of them. Locke by contrast treated it as a direction from God to man. This interpretation was crucial for his argument about property.[55]

The command was conveyed through both revelation and reason. The former, as we have seen, disclosed that God had set up 'the Dominion of the whole Species of Mankind, over the inferior Species of Creatures' and that this was entailed by His command. 'God who bid Mankind increase and multiply' intended to 'give them all a Right to make use of the Food and Rayment, and other Conveniences of Life, the Materials whereof he had so plentifully provided for them'.[56] The latter, we may add, was made as an inference from the nature of man and the world to the effect that God meant man to use the earth to preserve himself: 'God ... spoke to him, (that is) directed him by his Senses and Reason ... to the use of those things, which were serviceable for his Subsistence, and given him as means of his *Preservation*'.[57]

So God not only gave the world to man but also gave it for a purpose. That purpose, the preservation and increase of the human race, was integral to Locke's account of property.

In the first place it required appropriation as the means of God's design and therefore legitimated that activity. Locke was quick to insist that this required appropriation. 'God, who hath given the World to Men in common, hath also given them reason to make use of it to the best advantage of Life, and convenience', he remarked, and reason pretty soon concluded that 'there must of necessity be a means *to appropriate*' things before they could be used by anyone. The means of appropriation was labour. Hence the man who laboured in order to sustain life acquired property because He did as God willed with God's creation. 'The Law Man was under', in Locke's words, 'was rather for *appropriating*'.[58]

Whilst appropriation of itself suggested consumption or seizure, it could also be the instrument of service to the end attributed to God. His command to subdue the earth could be glossed to legitimate property in land. 'God and his Reason commanded him to subdue the Earth', we read, '*i.e.* improve it for the benefit of Life' which was achieved through appropriating land and farming it. The increase of mankind could be sustained, it seemed, by fencing in ground and more pointedly by improving land. Locke insisted eventually that at least 90 per cent 'of the *Products* of the Earth useful to the Life of Man' were 'the *effects of labour*'.[59]

The institution of money would encourage improvement still

more, for it removed the limit to rational labour and acquisition set by the perishable character of natural products: people could exchange their produce for money.[60] Thus both land and money turned out to be terms in God's design, for they both implied an increase in the resources available to sustain the human race.

Locke wrote near the end of his life that 'Propriety, I have no where found more clearly explain'd than in a Book intituled *Two Treatises of Government*'.[61] The outstanding immodesty of the assertion bespeaks the importance of a plausible explanation of property for his purpose. It accommodated the principal varieties of property in a way which relied upon man's natural freedom; it avoided the difficulties which Filmer and Hobbes had seen in the Grotian account; and it was incompatible with absolutism. So property and political power fell into the same pattern of explanation for Locke.

So the great design, because it involved freedom, made possible an explanation of private property in terms congruent with Locke's view of political power.

❦ VI ❦

Locke had indicated that political power resided in each agent. He had explained property in a way which showed that it was prior to civil government and unrelated to the underpinning of polity. Instead he referred both property to his view of God's intentions in the great design. But one great task remained: to treat government itself in the same terms.

For Locke's task was at once to explain government and to limit it. To explain government was necessary, because otherwise the obvious safeguard of liberty and property would be absent. For despite the suspicion of rulers built into the structure of *Two Treatises* both of its books assume the need for government. The explanation would have to be managed in terms of freedom too, in order to show how Locke's argument, which had begun without political superiors, conducted his reader to a secure government. That government had to be limited, in order to fulfil the aim of establishing 'bounded' government. One task, then, was to show how a polity could exist on his terms and the other was to show its limitations.

To show that government could exist legitimately was straight-forward enough. The rights of each and everyone to preserve themselves and to execute the law of nature, which we have seen flow from Locke's general views, explained government easily enough. Locke supposed that in order to secure the objectives corresponding to these rights people would consent to creation of a political society, that is to say a society whose governors were entitled to pursue just those objectives.[62] To suppose these rights inhered to each individual presupposed that everyone by nature was free of a political superior. So government was founded on terms compatible with freedom.

More positively he conceived that the agent's natural endowments, reason and will, could be used to establish political power on terms that suited him. First, setting up a government was a rational act. Civil government was a device designed to secure the ends embodied in God's design. It was supposed to secure them better than individual agents considered separately could secure them. For it made sense for people to do collectively what they could not individually.[63] Locke argued, in effect, that the creation of government was an exercise of rationality.

The very act of *setting up* a government implied adding something to nature. In this sense government for Locke was artifice. As such it appeared at an intelligible stage in the text. For having begun the second book of *Two Treatises* with natural matters, such as the endowments of mankind and their duties under natural law, Locke had moved to matters that required action, such as the acquisition of property and the exercise of parenthood. These activities, of course, accorded with God's prescriptions. But they involved people acting to better the nature they had received, whether by improving the earth or educating a child. Making a government, too, meant bettering the state of nature and was a deliberate act of artifice.

Yet it remains to ask, to what, precisely, did people consent? Locke's answer was cast in terms of reason and freedom.

❧ VII ❧

So far examination of political power has suggested that it was an instrument for securing certain ends, those connected with God's intent. His plans for mankind explained and defined its authority. It followed that an authority that was not defined so stood apart from this divinely warranted pattern. Absolutism, Locke felt able to conclude, was not a form of government at all.[64]

Having distinguished political power thus, Locke examined its character. Polity, according to him, had three aspects – executive, legislative and federative. The distinction, as stated in his text, was amongst functions. One agency was to legislate, another to execute the laws and so on, and another still to conduct foreign relations. These were not necessarily distinctions amongst personnel, for in government one agent might have more than one function.[65] It was the distinction of those functions that mattered, for it was integral to the responsible character of government. That is to say, Locke wished to subordinate the executive and federative to the legislative and to show that the latter depended on the consent of the governed.[66]

Locke specified that the purpose for which government existed was to sustain rights. How does this relate to the matters discussed so far? Right in Locke can be understood in relation to authority. In its root sense the latter involved an ability to direct. To say that A had authority over B would imply that A was able to direct B more successfully than B could have managed for himself. This would be partly a matter of intellect and partly of other faculties. Where faculties were in some sense equal, no one was better equipped by nature to guide others, as we have noted. But Locke maintained his general model. Hence, for example, God's authority over people derived from His superior ability to direct and to reward or punish them. This superiority, Locke thought, gave Him a right to deal with mankind as He chose.[67]

On this model, right would be an attribute of a bearer of authority. It would be attributable in respect of a superiority, meaning by that both that it accrued to a superior and referred to the aspect in which he or she excelled the inferior. Since God was superior to all forms of existence, His right held good over all aspects of creation. But we need not assume that the right enjoyed by a mere human agent over another would be so complete.

In particular we might emphasize that God's supereminent superiority gave Him a right over everything. It followed that His inferiors enjoyed a right only on terms of aspect and extent granted by Him. We have seen already that mankind enjoyed a right to the earth and its creatures because God decided it was so. We have seen, too, that God enlarged the extent of that grant (to embrace destroying the animals). It is worth adding the more striking illustration that people enjoyed life only as God chose.[68] On this basis, then, rights would be grants made by God.

This affects how we understand the concept of right. Most importantly, the attribution of right to an agent would relate to God's purposes. After all, God, if understood as wise, would not deal out rights without purpose. Rights would be attributed to those capable of doing His work and, by the same measure, discontinued if the capability were misused. Thus, for example, all human agents have the same faculties, faculties which were supposed to be adequate for self-direction. Hence each agent was entitled to direct himself or herself. This implies a right to be free from the direction of others, 'the Right of my Freedom'.[69] Again, each agent had a superiority over their persons, described by Locke as their right (and sometimes their property). The language suggests an exclusive possession, beyond the proper role of other human agents: but this self-direction was subject to direction by God. We find Locke's statement of the agent's independence was subject to natural law. By the same measure we find that those who contravened God's purposes decisively lost their rights, most dramatically by forfeiting their lives.[70]

Second, there may be an extension of usage, an extension relating to purpose. It happens several times in Locke's thought that rights are attributed to people by reason of the fact that they correspond to the means necessary to do God's work. Amongst these we can list the right to use the earth and its creatures as a means of self-preservation (without which the duty to preserve oneself would be impossible), and the right to punish aggressors (glossed immediately after its appearance as the right to execute the law of nature); without supposing this, as Locke pointed out, natural law could not be enforced terrestrially.[71]

This brings us to a further sense which right denoted, namely agreement with measures prescribing proper conduct. This was present generally in the seventeenth century, as in Hobbes's view that right existed where the laws were silent.[72] With Locke there is the special assumption that rights would not merely accord with law but would relate to the purpose for which the latter was made. This was true, for example, of the rights protected by government.

What was the subject matter of these? We say traditionally, life, liberty and property. These cohere as parts in God's design. Liberty was a condition of Locke's design, for the liberty it denoted was that of an agent independent of another's direction.[73] Property, as we have seen, was in its simplest form acquired in terms of the great design and in more sophisticated forms authorized by it. The generality of the formulation 'life' accords with the design. 'Life' is certainly general and seems oddly so, till we remember that activities to which it relates are as various as, preserve self and preserve others, charity and bring up children – and all of these in the best way possible.[74] Thus these rights refer to states of being integral to the purpose Locke attributed to God. So we see that the authorities on earth authorized by God – political, familial and so on – are to be explained in terms of His purpose, the great design.

In a like way the rights enjoyed by governors answered to the purpose Locke laid out. These rights issued directly from the rights enjoyed by every agent to preserve himself (and others) and to punish aggressors, which were themselves inferred from the law of preservation.[75] These rights proved difficult to exercise, and the point of government was to execute them where the individual could not do so easily.

Because the creation of a polity was an exercise in rationality, the same purposes for which it was created bounded its activity. This meant, first, that just as the agent had only a limited range of actions open to him or her legitimately, so too the government was restricted. The authority of polity came from the power an agent enjoyed over herself under the terms of the great design. That was limited and so polity at the utmost would enjoy no more. Locke put the matter with a clarity edging on pleonasm. 'No Body can transfer to another more power than he has in himself'; he wrote,

> and no Body has an absolute Arbitrary Power over himself or over any other, to destroy his own Life, or take away the Life or Property of another. A Man, as has been proved, cannot subject himself to the Arbitrary Power of another; and having in the State of Nature no Arbitrary Power over the Life, Liberty, or Possession of another, but only so much as the Law of Nature gave him for the preservation of himself, and the rest of Mankind; this is all he doth, or can give up to the Common-wealth.[76]

Where with Marvell the same arts that did a power gain must it maintain, with Locke the same power which did a power create bounded it.

Its boundaries were threefold. They lay with creation and function and forfeiture. Locke's agenda in the creation of a government did not admit of an unreserved contract, unlike Bodin, Grotius or Hobbes. These theorists had conceived that the agent was subject to no constraints on how he disposed of his or her person. For instance, it was permissible to enslave oneself. On these terms a transfer of right to a ruler could be complete and irreversible. But for Locke, because government was an instrument created for a specific end, it ceased to have validity when it ceased to serve that end. Thus polity loses its authority so soon as the purposes for which it was set up were violated.[77] Thus he made out his model of bounded government.

❧ VIII ❧

Locke's political theory took elements from his preceding thought and treated them in a manner that combined them with the devices and the needs of current thought in order to explain his preferred style of government. Locke wished to explain that government must be responsible, rather than absolute. Two items were especially significant in his project. These were his view of God as mankind's legislative superior, drawn from his moral theory, and his assessment of human faculties, based upon his writings on the human understanding, but not developed there in quite this direction. He used these devices, in company with his view of relations, to attribute a divinely-warranted purpose to mankind, which comprised an understanding of morality and of human life inconsistent with absolutism and favouring 'bounded' government.

This account suggests that Locke was a more powerful and single-minded theorist than the figure found in our textbooks. This may be a surprise, but should not be. For it should hardly be anticipated that the author of *An Essay concerning Human Understanding* would be less acute in dealing with politics: though this is not to say that his work is flawless.

❧ NOTES ❧

1 In the vocabulary of the seventeenth century 'power' connoted the Latin *potestas*, which embraces both authority and the ability to enforce one's will. Hence Locke's project of explaining political power has an emphasis on the normative. Note too that the century was reduced to describing power without right as power *de facto*. The author would like to thank Dr. Ian Tipton for commenting on an earlier draft.

2 E.g. [4.49], 537; the example could be matched by many others.

3 The outstanding specimen is now a classic: [4.54].

4 For different derivations of absolutism, cf. [4.20], chs 1–2 in [4.23]; [4.15] esp. 1.8, cf. [4.21] in [4.23], 172–83; [4.25], I.iii.viii.1–2; [4.26] II.xviii.

5 Locke's manuscripts were edited by Wolfgang Von Leyden under this title as [4.1] and re-edited by Robert Horwitz, Jenny Strauss Clay and Diskin Clay as [4.2]. This latter work expresses reservations about Von Leyden's edition: but these, if valid, would not affect the use of the text made here. The older edition (i.e. [4.1]) is cited because more accessible. Since Von Leyden's text is printed with a facing translation I have given the folio numbers printed in his edition in order to give a continuous numeration.

6 See [4.12], Ia, Iae.94 and generally 90–7 and Ia.IIae.10–12; [4.27], 40³: 612; [4.17], IV: 3–5; [4.19].

7 See e.g. [4.12], Ia.IIae.94.a.2. For an important commentary on the aspect of self-preservation, see [4.51].

8 [4.1], no. 4,ff. 60–1, pp. 156/158.

9 [4.33], I.iv: 31. Cf. II.v: 267: 'To admonish and reprehend is not an action of an Inferior'.

10 [4.1], no. 4, ff. 52–9, pp. 150–6.

11 [4.6], preface; I.i.1; II.i.1; title page: 153, 155, 159, 285.

12 [4.13], 1, 16.

13 See for this especially [4.38]. This fascinating volume has attracted a great deal of comment, much of which is used by [4.39]. Ashcraft replied to this in [4.40].

14 [4.59], xiii:1.

15 See [4.32], with a preface by Robert Sanderson.

16 Strictly there is no work entitled *First Treatise* and the expression *Second Treatise* appears as part of a larger title page. Locke regularly denominated both

as books (see the contents page, [4.6], 157 and 159, 285). The usage, however, is convenient.

17 [4.5], sect. 44: 153.

18 This is found most fully in the manuscript piece, given to the world after Filmer's death as [4.20].

19 The logic is well illustrated in [4.16], 1: 'It is certain, that the *Law of Nature* has put no difference nor subordination among Men ... so that ... all Men are born free'.

20 [4.6], I.viii.80: 220, a passage that, curiously, Dr Laslett and the other commentators have overlooked in trying to discover the contents of the lost ending of *First Treatise*.

21 [4.6], II.ii.4: 287.

22 Ibid.

23 For a fuller examination of this passage, including its intellectual background, see the present writer's [4.46], ch. 6.

24 [4.6], I.iv.41: 188.

25 [4.6], I.iv.41: 23, 33: 188, 174f., 182f.

26 [4.6], I.iv.39: 185.

27 Ibid.

28 [4.5], sect 1: 101. *Sensible* means accessible to sensation; a contrast is being drawn implicitly with angels and other spirits supposed to be usually beyond detection by human faculties.

29 [4.6], I.iv.30: 180.

30 [4.6], I.ix.86: 223:

> For the desire, strong desire of Preserving his Life and Being having been Planted in him, as a Principle of Action by God himself, Reason, *which was the Voice of God in him*, could not but teach him and assure him, that pursuing that natural Inclination he had to preserve his Being, he followed the Will of his Maker.

31 [4.6], I. ix. 86: 222f.:

> God having made Man, and planted in him ... a strong desire of Self-preservation, and furnished the World with things fit for Food and Rayment and other Necessaries of Life, Subservient to his design, that Man should live and abide for some time upon the Face of the Earth, and not that so curious and wonderful a piece of Workmanship by its own Negligence, or want of Necessaries, should perish again, presently after a few moments continuance.

32 [4.6], I.iv.41: 187.

33 See [4.5], sect. 39: 147,

> For our facultys being suited ... to the preservation of us to whome they are given or in whome they are & are accommodated to the uses of life, they serve to our purposes well enough if they will but give us certain notice of those things that either delight or hurt us, are convenient or inconvenient to us.

Also [4.3], 102f.; 'Trade' in [4.4], ii: 485; cf. [4.6], I.iv.33: 183 and I.iv.41: 188, on depopulation under absolutist regimes.

34 [4.6], I.ix.86: 223.

35 [4.6], II.i.2: 286.

36 See notably [4.6], II. vi.54: 322.

37 [4.20], I.i; [4.23], 2–5.

38 In logical sequence, [4.6], II.ii.8–11: 290–2; vii. 87–8: 341–3.

39 [4.6], II.ii.6: 289.

40 For a fuller explanation of this derivation, see [4.47].

41 [4.6], II.ii.5: 288.

42 [4.6], I.ix.86: 223.

43 [4.6], II.iii.17: 297.

44 [4.6], II.iv.23: 302.

45 [4.18], s.n. *Property.*

46 [4.25], II.2.ii, esp. 1,5; [4.29], IV.v.2,4.

47 [4.26], I.xiii: 63, cf. II.xxiv: 127.

48 For Filmer's objections, see [4.22], 234.

49 [4.6], II.v.25: 303f.

50 [4.6], II.v.27: 305.

51 For an objection to slavery, without Locke's argument against it, see [4.28], 36f.; for property as a quality inhering in a person, see [4.24], V.xiii: 409; for Grotius on *suum*, see [4.25], I.2.i.5 and II.17.2,1. It is worth remembering that Locke would admit slavery on other terms: see [4.6], II.iii-iv.

52 For instance Hobbes had included material possessions in his catalogue of 'propriety', but had been able to suggest that along with other examples of *suum* they were explained by the sovereign's actions: see [4.26], II.xxx: 179. [4.6], II.v.27: 305f..

53 Pufendorf only discussed appropriation after partition (see [4.29], IV.iv.12) and Grotius used the verb *arripere* to describe prior appropriation, which scarcely suggests a legitimate title to property (see [4.25], II.2.ii.1).

54 For some gaminesque queries, see [4.55], 174–82.

55 [4.22] in [4.20], 217; [4.25], II.2.ii.1.

56 [4.6], I.iv.28: 178f.; 41: 187.

57 [4.6], I.ix.86: 223.

58 [4.6], II.v.26: 304; v.35: 310; II.v.37: 312: 'he who appropriates land to himself by his labour, does not lessen but increase the common stock of mankind'.

59 See *seriatim* [4.6], II.v.28–9 (consumption), 30 (seizure), 32 (improvement), 40 (labour): 306–14.

60 [4.6], II.v.48; 50: 319, 320.

61 Locke to the Rev. Richard King, 25 August 1703 in [4.9], viii: 58.

62 See generally [4.6], II.vii-ix; [4.6], II.vii.78–88: 336–41.

63 [4.6], II.ix. esp. 131: 371.

64 [4.6], II.xv.169–74: 398–402.

65 [4.6], II.xii generally; for personnel see xii.148: 384 and xiii.151: 386.

66 As [4.6], II.xiii esp. 149: 384f..

67 [4.1], no. 4.

68 [4.6], I.iv.39: 185f.; [4.8], 8 for the fact that human life was understood to be God's: 'if God afford them a Temporary, Mortal Life, 'tis his Gift, they owe it

to his Bounty, they could not claim it as their Right, nor does he injure them when he takes it from them'. Cf. [4.1], no. 4, f. 56 (p.154).

69 [4.6], II.iii.17: 297.

70 E.g. [4.6], II.ii.4: 287, vi.63: 327; II.ii.11: 292.

71 [4.6], I.ix.86: 223; II.ii.7: 289f.: the supposition of the latter right obviated Hobbes' view that God's law was not enforced *as such* on earth (but only as a terrestrial sovereign's command): but the Lockean God gave people a legitimate title to enforce His commands.

72 E.g. [4.26], I.xiv: 64; [4.31], II.i: 167–8; [4.30], I.xiv.3: 194 and the young Locke [4.1], no. 1, f.11: 110.

73 See [4.46] for this.

74 For charity see [4.47], sect. 2.

75 See p.106 above.

76 [4.6], II.xi.135: 375.

77 See esp. [4.6], II.xix.211–19: 424–9.

❧ BIBLIOGRAPHY ❧

Works by Locke

4.1 *Essays on the Law of Nature*, ed. Wolfgang Von Leyden, Oxford, Oxford University Press, 1954, etc. See also

4.2 *Questions concerning the Law of Nature*, ed. Robert Horwitz, Jenny Strauss Clay and Diskin Clay, edition of the same mss as [4.1], London, Cornell University Press, 1990.

4.3 'An Essay concerning Toleration' (1667) in C. A. Viano (ed.) *Scritti Editi e Inediti sulla Toleranza*, Turin, Taylor Turino, 1961.

4.4 *Locke on Money*, ed. Patrick Kelly, 2 vols, Oxford, Oxford University Press, 1991.

4.5 *Draft B* in *Drafts for the Essay concerning Human Understanding and other philosophical writings*, ed. P. H. Nidditch and G. A. J. Rogers, vol. i, Oxford, Oxford University Press, 1990.

4.6 *Two Treatises of Government* ed. Peter Laslett, 2nd edn, Cambridge, Cambridge University Press, 1967.

4.7 *An Essay concerning Human Understanding* ed. P. H. Nidditch, Oxford, Oxford University Press, 1975.

4.8 *The Reasonableness of Christianity as delivered in the scriptures*, London, 1956.

4.9 *The Correspondence of John Locke* ed. E. S. de Beer, Oxford, 8 vols, Oxford University Press, 1976–89.

Amongst the works of Locke not mentioned here, especially important are

4.10 *Two Tracts of Government*, ed. Philip Abrams, Cambridge, Cambridge University Press, 1967 and

4.11 *Epistola de Tolerantia*, ed. Raymond Klibansky, Oxford, Oxford University Press, 1968.

Other Primary Works

4.12 Aquinas, Thomas *Summa Theologica*, trans. T. Gilby *et al*, London, Eyre and Spottiswoode, 60 vols, 1963–75.

4.13 Anon. *A Letter from a Person of Quality to his Friend in the Country*, n.p. [probably London], 1675.

4.14 Anon. *Vox Populi, Vox dei*, London, 1681.

4.15 Bodin, Jean *Les Six Livres de la Republique* (1576), ed. and trans. M. J. Tooley, Oxford, Blackwell, 1955.

4.16 Burnet, Gilbert *An Enquiry into the Measures of Submission to the Supream Authority*, London, 1688.

4.17 Calvin, Jean *Institutes of the Christian Religion*, trans. F. L. Battles, 2 vols, London, S.C.M. Press, 1962.

4.18 Cowell, John *The Interpreter*, Cambridge, 1607.

4.19 Culverwell, Nathaniel *A Learned and Elegant Discourse of the Light of Nature*, ed. R.A. Greene and H. Macallum, Toronto, Toronto University Press, 1971.

4.20 Filmer, Sir Robert *Patriarcha*,

4.21 *The Necessity of the Absolute Power of all Kings*,

4.22 *Observations concerning the Originall of Government* all in

4.23 *Patriarcha and Other Writings*, ed. J. P. Sommerville, Cambridge, Cambridge University Press, 1991.

4.24 Fuller, Thomas *The Holy State and the Prophane State*, Cambridge, 1642.

4.25 Grotius, Hugo *De Jure Belli ac Pacis*, Paris, 1625.

4.26 Hobbes, Thomas *Leviathan*, London, 1651.

4.27 Luther, Martin *Werke*, Weimar, 1883–.

4.28 Parker, Henry *Jus Populi*, London, 1644.

4.29 Pufendorf, Samuel *De Jure Naturae et Gentium*, Lund, 1672; edn Amsterdam, 1688.

4.30 *Elementa Jurisprudentiae Universalis*, 1660, edn, Cambridge, 1672.

4.31 Taylor, Jeremy *Ductor Dubitantium*, 1660; edn London, 1676.

4.32 Ussher, James *The Power Communicated to the Prince by God*, London, 1660, with a preface by Robert Sanderson.

4.33 Walker, Obadiah *Of Education*, Oxford, 1673.

Other Works

A full listing of secondary works will be found in

4.34 Hall, R., and Woolhouse, R. S. *Eighty Years of Locke Scholarship*, Edinburgh, Edinburgh University Press, 1983, which covers 1900–80. Subsequent work is listed annually in the

4.35 *Locke Newsletter*, ed. R. Hall. See too

4.36 Yolton, J. S. and J. W. *John Locke: A Reference Guide*, Boston, Hall, 1985. Works on Locke's political theory include:

4.37 Ashcraft, R. *Locke's Two Treatises of Government*, London, Unwin Hyman, 1987.

4.38 *Revolutionary Politics and Locke's Two Treatises of Government*, Princeton, NJ, Princeton University Press, 1986, on which see

4.39 Wootton, D. 'John Locke and Richard Ashcraft's *Revolutionary Politics*', *Political Studies* 40(1992): 79–98 and

4.40 Richard Ashcraft 'Simple Objections and Complex Reality', ibid. 40(1992): 99–115.

4.41 Colman, J. *John Locke's Moral Philosophy*, Edinburgh, Edinburgh University Press, 1983.

4.42 Dunn, J. *The Political Thought of John Locke*, Cambridge, Cambridge University Press, 1969.

4.43 *Locke*, Oxford, Oxford University Press, 1984.

4.44 Fagiani, F. *Nel crepuscolo della probilita*, Naples, Bibliopolis, 1983.

4.45 Franklin, J. *John Locke and the Theory of Sovereignty*, Cambridge, Cambridge University Press, 1978.

4.46 Harris, I. *The Mind of John Locke*, Cambridge, Cambridge University Press, 1994.

4.47 'Locke on Justice', *Oxford Studies in the History of Philosophy: 2; Seventeenth – Century Philosophy*, Oxford, forthcoming.

4.48 Parry, G. *John Locke*, London, Allen & Unwin, 1978.

4.49 Sabine, G. *A History of Political Thought*[3], London, Cassell, 1963.

4.50 Tuck, R. *Natural Rights Theories*, Cambridge, Cambridge University Press, 1979.
'The Modern Theory of Natural Law' in

4.51 Pagden, A. (ed.) *The Languages of Political Theory in Early Modern Europe*, Cambridge, Cambridge University Press, 1987.

4.52 Tully, J. *A Discourse of Property*, Cambridge, Cambridge University Press, 1980.

For articles, see

4.53 Ashcraft, R. (ed.) *John Locke: critical assessments*, 4 vols, London, Routledge, 1991. A list of writings about Locke's philosophy will be found in Dr Tipton's chapter (ch.3) in this volume. For modern liberal thought, see:

4.54 Rawls, J. *A Theory of Justice*, Oxford, Oxford University Press, 1971.

4.55 Nozick, R. *Anarchy, State and Utopia*, Oxford, Blackwell, 1974.

4.56 Ackerman, B. *Social Justice in the Liberal State*, New Haven, Conn., Yale University Press, 1980, and the commentaries in

4.57 Sandel, M. (ed.) *Liberalism and its Critics*, Oxford, Blackwell, 1982.

4.58 Campbell, T. *Justice*, London, Macmillan, 1988. In a distinct class is

4.59 St. Paul, *Epistle to the Romans*.

CHAPTER 5
George Berkeley
David Berman

BRITISH PHILOSOPHY AND THE AGE OF ENLIGHTENMENT

❧ BACKGROUND AND EARLY WORK ❧

George Berkeley was born on 12 March 1685 in Co. Kilkenny, where he spent his early years. His father was from England, his mother (very probably) was born in Ireland.[1] After attending Kilkenny College, he entered Trinity College, Dublin, in March 1700, where he became a Scholar in 1702 and received his B.A. in 1704. In 1707 he undertook the examination for a College Fellowship. In the same year he published his minor mathematical works, *Arithmetica* and *Miscellanea Mathematica*, probably in the hope of supporting his canditature for Fellowship, to which he was admitted on 9 June 1707. He then held such College positions as Librarian, Junior Dean, and Junior Greek Lecturer. In 1710 he was ordained into the Church of Ireland.

It was as a young Fellow in his early twenties that Berkeley developed his immaterialist philosophy, which he published in (what are now) three philosophical classics: *An Essay towards a New Theory of Vision* (1709), *The Principles of Human Knowledge* (1710), and *Three Dialogues between Hylas and Philonous* (1713). Much of his philosophy's complex development can be traced in the two philosophical notebooks he kept during this creative period, *c.* 1707–8. The notebooks, first printed in 1871 and now widely known as the *Philosophical Commentaries*, also enable us to see the influences on Berkeley's thinking. This is especially useful in Berkeley's case, since his three early works contain few references to the writings of other philosophers. It is clear from the *Philosophical Commentaries* that he was profoundly inspired by the work of John Locke and the Cartesians, particularly Nicolas Malebranche. Locke's *Essay concerning Human Understanding* (1690) had been put on the course at Trinity College as early as 1692 (see [5. 15], 149). That Berkeley read it carefully and appreciatively is evident from numerous references in his notebooks. Berkeley admired Locke's candour and concern for clarity. In the *Essay of Vision*, sect. 125, he describes Locke as 'this celebrated author', who has 'distinguished himself . . . by the clearness and significancy of what he says'. Berkeley also uses some of Locke's terminology, for example, when talking of 'primary and secondary qualities'. He also derived important theories from Locke, although he almost always modifies these in crucial ways. On certain issues, most notably abstract general ideas, he could be extremely critical of Locke.

The influence of Malebranche is harder to pin down. But since the publication of A. A. Luce's *Berkeley and Malebranche* in 1934, Berkeley's major debt to Malebranche's *Search after Truth* (1674/5) has been generally recognized. 'Ideas' play as central a role in Berkeley's *Principles* as they do in both Locke's *Essay* and Malebranche's *Search*. All three philosophers describe ideas as the immediate objects of the mind, when it experiences or thinks. But Berkeley is closer to Malebranche in characterizing ideas as having a certain substantial and independent reality. Summing up Berkeley's intellectual debt, Luce wrote: 'Locke taught him, but Malebranche inspired him' ([5. 18], 7).

There were other philosophers, however, who exerted a powerful, although less positive influence on Berkeley. Here Luce singled out Pierre Bayle, the great sceptic who 'alarmed and alerted' Berkeley, making him aware of the sceptical dangers inherent in Cartesianism. But the *Philosophical Commentaries* show that Berkeley was also reacting to the irreligious challenge of Hobbes and Spinoza – the two philosophers then most vilified by orthodox thinkers of Berkeley's theological sympathies. Hobbes's materialism and Spinoza's pantheism posed a formidable danger to theistic systems, and Berkeley felt that one great merit of his immaterialism was its effective response to this danger. As he notes in entry 824 of the *Commentaries*: 'My Doctrine rightly understood all that Philosophy of Epicurus, Hobbes, Spinoza &c wch has been a declared enemy of religion comes to ye ground'.[2] Of course, as this entry itself shows, Berkeley's philosophical horizon was not confined to (then) modern writers of the seventeenth and early eighteenth centuries. He was also responding to ancient Greek writers, notably Epicurus and Lucretius, as well as drawing inspiration from Plato, Aristotle, and other classic philosophers. Nor was Berkeley influenced only by philosophers. Like most astute thinkers, he was attentive to the revolutionary scientific and mathematical developments of the time, particularly to the mechanistic corpuscularianism of Isaac Newton, whose 'celebrated' *Principia* is the only book that Berkeley discussed and mentioned by name in the body of the *Principles*.

So far I have tried to situate Berkeley, as most histories of philosophy do, as the foremost philosopher after Locke (and before David

Hume), who was responding to the irreligious, sceptical and scientific challenges in seventeenth-century thought. Yet it is also important to see the local, Irish context of Berkeley's writings. It is probably no accident that Ireland's greatest philosopher emerged at the centre of Ireland's one great period of philosophical activity. This is, very briefly, the period that opens in the 1690s with William Molyneux, Robert Molesworth and John Toland; develops in the early eighteenth century with Berkeley, Francis Hutcheson, William King, Peter Browne; and culminates in the late 1750s with Edmund Burke and Robert Clayton (see [5. 15]). Neither before this sixty-year period, nor after it, has Ireland produced such continuous creative philosophy, or a philosopher of Berkeley's stature.

❧ THE *ESSAY OF VISION*: LIMITED ❧ IMMATERIALISM

The importance of the Irish context can be seen straightaway in Berkeley's first major work, *An Essay Towards a New Theory of Vision*, published in Dublin in 1709. Here the main influence was Molyneux, the Dublin polymath and friend of Locke, whose celebrated problem pervades much of Berkeley's argument in the *Essay*. Molyneux's problem was whether a man blind from birth would upon gaining his sight be able to distinguish (visually) a sphere and cube that he formerly knew by touch. Berkeley adverts again and again to this problem, which was first published in the second (1694) edition of Locke's *Essay*, II. ix. 8. Berkeley also made considerable use of Molyneux's *Dioprica Nova* (1692) – from which, for example, his *Essay's* key section 2 is drawn – as well as Molyneux's essay on the moon illusion. Another Irish influence on Berkeley's *Essay* was Archbishop King, a philosopher of European standing, whose criticisms prompted Berkeley to add an Appendix to the second edition, also published in 1709.

Berkeley's main aim in the *Essay* was to establish one part of his immaterialism, namely, that everything we *see* is mind dependent. He assumes here what he will deny in his next work, *The Principles of Human Knowledge* (1710), that there are tangible things independent of the mind. His strategy was to teach or convince his readers by stages. If he could show that the visual world was mind dependent, then that would be a crucial step towards the acceptance of full immaterialism: that the whole physical world – including what we touch – exists in the mind.

Another of Berkeley's objectives in his *Essay* was to explain how the mind judges visual distance, magnitude, and situation, and while doing this to solve three notable problems, associated with these topics, problems that seemed intractible on the (then) accepted theory of vision. One problem, concerned with the judgement of size, is why the moon looks larger on the horizon than in the zenith of the sky. According to the accepted theory, articulated in Descartes's *Dioptrics* (1637), most of our judgements of size are accomplished by a natural geometry. In short, rays coming from objects project onto the eyes angles by means of which the mind judges an object to be large or small, near or far away. Yet why, Berkeley asks, do we mistakenly see a large moon on the horizon? How can geometry lead us to false judgements? The moon illusion, Berkeley concludes, 'is a clear instance of the insufficiency of lines and angles for explaining the way wherein the mind perceives and estimates the magnitude of outward objects' (sect. 78). Berkeley's broader argument against the natural geometry theory is set out earlier in the *Essay* with reference to judgements of distance; but it can be reformulated to refer to size. In short:

(1) We do not immediately see the size of an object (cf. sect. 2).
(2) What we judge size by must itself be perceived (cf. sects 10–12).
(3) But we do not perceive projected lines or angles.
(4) Therefore, we do not judge size by a natural geometry.

In asserting (1) Berkeley was not distinguishing himself significantly from the received theory. Everyone seemed to agree that what we immediately see are variable patterns of visible points that change with the movement of our or other bodies; although for the accepted theory the visible points were immediately seen on the eye, whereas for Berkeley they are in the mind. But the important difference between the two positions is that for Berkeley the judgement of size is an inference based on what we immediately see, whereas for the innate-geometry theorist the judgement arises from the (unconscious) calculation of rays and angles.

Estimating the size of an object is, for Berkeley, like seeing that someone is angry or embarrassed. Although some people might say that they can directly see my anger, all they really see, according to Berkeley, are signs or expressions of it: my reddish face, flashing eyes, clenched fist. And if they were not able to see such perceptible signs, or connect them with the appropriate emotions, then they would not be able to infer that I am angry. So the innate geometry theorist is like someone who claims to know that I am angry, although he admits that he has not observed any behaviour expressive of anger.

Berkeley has another way of expressing this thesis which reveals his ultimate metaphysical position in the *Essay*: that what we see constitutes a language by means of which God tells us about the tangible world. This is the kernel of his so-called optic-language proof for the existence of God, a proof that Berkeley first presented in Dialogue

Four of *Alciphron, or the Minute Philosopher* (1732), to which he appended a revised (third) edition of the *Essay*. If his conclusion is correct – and I shall be considering his detailed argument below – then to claim that we can judge the size of an object by sight alone would be like asserting that we can be aware of what a sign or utterance signifies on first hearing it, and that there is a necessary or inner connection between, say, the English word 'table' and the table it signifies. This is clearly mistaken in the case of language, and Berkeley tries to show that it is equally wrong in the case of vision. For, according to him, the visual and the tangible are entirely different: it is only by correlating them over time that we learn to judge size, distance or shape by sight.

It is here that we can appreciate the importance of the Molyneux problem, mentioned above. For if the newly-sighted man could see straightaway which was the sphere, then this would show that the visual and tangible sphere have shape in common, that 'It is no more but introducing into his mind by a new inlet [sight] an idea he has been already well acquainted with [by touch]' (sect. 133). Hence a positive answer to the Molyneux problem consistently goes with the theory that there are common ideas underlying sight and touch. But Locke – who agreed with Molyneux's negative answer – also held that the sphere has one shape or figure, whether it is seen or touched; see, for example, Locke's *Essay* II. v. Berkeley's conclusion, then, is: 'We must therefore allow either that visible extension and figures are specifically distinct from tangible extension and figures, or else that the solution of this problem given by those two thoughtful and ingenious men is wrong' (sect. 133). Of course, for Berkeley their negative answer is correct; indeed, if anything, it does not go far enough. For when the newly-sighted man is asked the question – which is the sphere and cube? – he should be utterly perplexed and baffled, even by the question. He would be in a position similar to a person who was asked a question in Chinese, having never before heard that language spoken.

❧ COMPLETE IMMATERIALISM: *THE* ❧ *PRINCIPLES*

The authoritative statement of Berkeley's philosophy, generally called Immaterialism, is to be found in *The Principles of Human Knowledge* (1710). It contains his most complete defence of his 'immaterialist hypothesis' and its consequences, although it is supported by his earlier *Essay of Vision* and his later and more popular *Three Dialogues* (1713). Immaterialism has, broadly speaking, a negative and a positive side. It denies that matter or corporeal substance exists; it explains all existence in terms of minds and ideas. Although the *Principles* and *Dialogues* are mainly concerned with the negative side, Berkeley's original plan was to explicate the positive side of Immaterialism in a second part of the *Principles*. Thus in the *Commentaries*, 508, he writes: 'The two great Principles of Morality, the Being of a God & the Freedom of Man: these to be handled in the beginning of the Second Book.' And he had, as he informed his American friend, Samuel Johnson, on 25 November 1729, made considerable progress on Part Two, 'but the manuscript was lost about fourteen years ago [while travelling in Italy], and I never had leisure since to do so disagreeable a thing as writing twice on the same subject'. Berkeley never did publish Part Two of the *Principles*, although he made important additions in its second edition (1734), which is still described on the title-page as 'Part One'. He also probably introduced material from the projected part (or parts) in his later works, particularly *Alciphron* (1732) and the *Analyst* (1734). Thus in a letter of 1 March 1709/10, he mentions that one of the main topics of the *Principles* was to be the 'reconciliation of God's foreknowledge with the freedom of men' – a subject which is not discussed in the *Principles* (as we have it), but is examined at length in *Alciphron* VII. 16–23.

The negative thrust of the *Principles* begins in the Introduction, where Berkeley hopes 'to clear the first principles of knowledge, from the embarras and delusion of words' (sect. 25). Probably the two main delusions he has in mind are the dogma that (1) all meaningful words stand for ideas, from which it seemed to follow that (2) general words, such as 'extension', 'triangle' and 'motion', must stand for abstract general ideas. This conclusion was also based, according to Berkeley, on the nominalistic proposition, which he accepts, that (3) only particular triangles and specific instances of motion exist in nature, rather than (as Plato thought) triangularity or motion as such. The mistake was to infer from (3) and (1) that the mind must be able to form general ideas by a process of abstraction, that is, by eliminating those features which distinguish particular triangles, say, and retaining that which all triangles have in common. For Berkeley we can only abstract or form an idea of things that can exist separately. Thus we can abstract a lion's head from his body, but not the lion's colour from his (visual) shape.

Berkeley had previously attacked this influential theory of abstraction in the *Essay of Vision*, sections 122–5, as one of the sources of the (erroneous) view that there were ideas of shape, for example, in common between touch and sight. His strategy, both in the *Essay* and the Introduction, was to show the theory's absurdity by criticizing its most distinguished proponent – namely, Locke. Berkeley's 'killing blow' was to quote from Locke's *Essay* IV. vii. 9, a now well-known passage which describes the difficulties of abstraction:

For example, [writes Locke,] does it not require some pains and skill to form the general *idea* of a *triangle*, (which is yet none of the most abstract, comprehensive, and difficult) for it must be neither ... equilateral, equicrural, nor scalene; but all and none of these at once. In effect, it is something imperfect, that cannot exist; an *idea* wherein some parts of several different and inconsistent *ideas* are put together ...'

In arguing that no one could have such a contradictory idea, Berkeley does little more than allow Locke's description to speak for itself. For Berkeley a word becomes general 'by being made the sign, not of an abstract general idea but, of several particular ideas, any of which it indifferently suggests to the mind' (sect. 11); and this, Berkeley says, is sufficient for communication as well as demonstration.

Berkeley continues his attack on the dogma that every significant name stands for an idea by showing, more positively, how words can be used meaningfully which do not satisfy this semantic condition. Thus most of the time we use words like letters in algebra, or counters in a game, not thinking of their particular values or meanings, although we can do so, when – as in a card game – we encash the counters. There are also words which are used meaningfully that never inform or stand for ideas. Berkeley specifies three functions in section 20: non-cognitive words can evoke (1) emotions, (2) attitudes and (3) actions. I shall be saying more about this far-reaching thesis below, particularly when I consider its main deployment in *Alciphron*. Now we need to consider Berkeley's chief claim to fame, his rejection of matter.

Why, then, does Berkeley think that matter does not exist? Because, very briefly, every apparently feasible conception of it can be shown, according to him, to be either meaningless or self-contradictory. This is a very strong claim, which Berkeley tries to justify throughout the body of the *Principles*, but especially in sections 3–24, where he examines various theories of matter. Thus, matter is sometimes under-stood to be an inert, senseless substance in which subsist the so-called primary or intrinsic qualities, such as extension, solidity, shape, etc. (sect. 9). It is also defined as the substance that supports qualities, such as extension, where (unlike the previous case) the qualities are not part of the conception (sect. 16). Berkeley had many targets, because there were (and probably still are) many theories of matter. His strategy against matter differs radically from that against abstract general ideas. For it is not the case, as many histories of philosophy suppose, that his one target was Locke's theory of matter. Berkeley does not name his specific targets, either in the *Principles* or in the *Dialogues*. He is intentionally unspecific, as in section 9, where he speaks of 'some there are', or in section 16 where he describes the conception of matter considered there as 'the received opinion'. His aim was to refute all (seemingly plausible) theories of matter.

As the concept of matter changes, so does Berkeley's criticism. Thus the conception in section 16 is charged with meaninglessness, since in what sense can matter (which is supposedly different from extension) support extension? How can a non-extended thing or substance literally support anything? In section 9, on the other hand, matter is understood to be an extended substance, i.e. an inert substance in which extension, figure, etc., 'do actually subsist'; so this criticism would be inappropriate. Instead, Berkeley says that the conception is contradictory, since it asserts that qualities like extension inhere in an inert, senseless substance. Why is this contradictory? Berkeley's answer brings us to his fundamental positive insight, summed up in his famous axiom *'esse is percipi'* (sect. 3), that the existence of all physical things and qualities – extension, solidity, etc. – consists in being perceived. Berkeley traces the contrary belief – that one can separate the being of a physical thing from its being perceived – to the pernicious doctrine of abstraction, castigated in the Introduction.

For Berkeley the physical world is composed entirely of things perceptible, imprinted on the senses, which he calls variously sensible ideas, sensible objects, sensations, or ideas. As he expresses this in section 1:

> By sight I have the ideas of light and colours with their several degrees and variations. By touch I perceive, for example, hard and soft, heat and cold, motion and resistance . . . Smelling furnishes me with odours; the palate with tastes, and hearing conveys sounds to the mind in all their variety of tone and composition.

What else, after all, do we directly perceive? The widely-accepted philosophical and scientific answer was: mind-dependent sensory states, resulting from the impinging of external bodies (corpuscles) on the sense organs. Berkeley agreed with the initial part of this answer, but he rejects the sophisticated causal explanation in favour of what he calls the 'vulgar' or common view: that the things immediately perceived are the real things. Putting the two notions together, he says, constitutes the essence of his position, a marriage of philosophy and common sense, according to which the real physical qualities and objects are mind-dependent entities, idea-things (see [5. 3], 2: 262). Hence it follows that neither extension nor any physical quality can exist in a senseless or mindless substance any more than a thought or emotion can.

However, materialism, as Berkeley well recognized, takes many forms – one of the most important of which he confronts in section 8. This grants that what we immediately perceive are ideas, but it none the less asserts that these ideas are 'copies or resemblances' of the physical qualities that exist externally in unthinking substances. This account, sometimes called the representative theory of matter, involves these components:

(1) mind —— (2) ideas —— (3) physical objects.

Prima facie, this theory seems to evade the difficulties I mentioned earlier in connection with the theories of matter in sections 9 and 16. Against this theory, Berkeley brings another of his principles: that 'an idea can be like nothing but an idea' (sect. 8). In short, if physical objects are like ideas, then they are mind dependent; and in that case the theory is contradictory, as was that in section 16. If, on the other hand, a physical object is not like an idea, then what is it like? Can the materialist say anything meaningful? Berkeley thinks he cannot, since everything that he can say of physical objects must be drawn from what he perceives. But then the materialist's theory is empty, meaningless – as was that in section 9. And so Berkeley goes from target to target, arguing that every putative materialist theory is either meaningless or contradictory. As he puts it in section 24, 'Tis on this therefore that I chiefly insist, viz. that the absolute existence of things are words without a meaning, or which include a contradiction'. Of course, in saying that the word 'matter' can be meaningless, Berkeley is not saying that it lacks all meaning. For while 'matter' has no cognitive meaning, it does have, as he suggests in section 54, an emotive meaning: it makes people act as if the cause of their sensible ideas was material rather than spiritual. It also 'strengthened the depraved bent of the mind towards *atheism*' ([5. 3], 2: 261). 'Matter' is, in short, a perniciously emotive word, masquerading as a cognitive one.

Berkeley's positive claim, that there are only two beings in the world – minds and ideas – is in the dualistic tradition of Descartes; although Berkeley's system is more economical in that there is only one substance: mind. Apart from sensible ideas, described above, there are also ideas of memory and imagination, which are formed by 'either compounding, dividing or barely representing' sensible ideas (sect. 1), and are fainter and less orderly than them. But all ideas, according to Berkeley, are entirely passive or inert. It is the other sort of being, spirits or minds, that are active. They cause, will, perceive, or 'act about ideas'; hence Berkeley's more complete formula in *Commentaries*, 429: '*Esse* is *percipi* or *percipere*, or *velle*, i.e. *agere*'. To be is to be perceived or perceive or will, i.e., act. Minds and ideas are 'entirely distinct'. As with ideas, there are two species of spirits: finite and infinite. Section 2 is devoted to finite, human spirits. God, the infinite spirit, is introduced gradually, later in the *Principles*. As matter is vanquished so God comes to the fore, as the being which produces sensible ideas in finite minds.

❧ GOD REPLACES MATTER AND NATURE ❧

Berkeley offers a more or less formal proof for the existence of God in sections 145–9. An even more succinct proof of the immortality of human spirits is presented in section 141. Neither proof should be regarded as an afterthought. For, as is generally accepted, Berkeley's philosophy is directed primarily towards theological ends, particularly proving the existence of a religiously meaningful God and awakening his readers to a vivid sense of His presence. Setting out Berkeley's proof will help us to gain a clearer understanding of the philosophical infra-structure upon which it is based. Briefly then:

1 Physical objects are collections of inert sensible ideas.
2 Sensible ideas cannot produce or cause either themselves or other sensible ideas.
3 Physical objects must have some cause.
4 Matter cannot be that cause, since it cannot exist; and, in any case, matter is defined as an inert thing.
5 We finite spirits know that, although we can produce ideas of memory and imagination, we do not produce the world of physical bodies or collections of sensible ideas.
6 Hence, such a vast orderly world must be produced by an Infinite Spirit, God.

Berkeley's proof may be regarded as an immaterialistic version of the (then) popular argument – used, for example, by Locke in *Essay* IV. x – which combined the cosmological proof with the teleological. However, Berkeley gives his proof a distinctive twist by bringing to the fore, perhaps for the first time in the history of philosophy, the problem of other minds. While Descartes had adverted to the problem in his *Meditations*, Berkeley accords it major importance. That is:

7 We can not directly perceive another human mind, since a mind is an active being which perceives and wills rather than something that can be perceived (sect. 27).
8 I know that there other human spirits by inferring their existence from their orderly physical motions, which are collections of sensible ideas that I recognize to be similar to my own.
9 But these physical motions, which pick out finite spirits, are very slight compared with the orderly motions of the whole physical world.
10 Hence I have greater justification for believing in the existence of the Infinite Other Mind than in any other finite mind.

In effect, Berkeley is placing his reader in a dilemma: he must either accept theism or solipsism. If he demands rigorous proof, then he must be solipsist, believing, in other words, that only he and his ideas exist. However, if he does believe in other minds, then he must also accept that God exists.

God is very much at the centre of Berkeley's philosophy, replacing matter as the cause and orderer of the physical world, which is only a succession of ideas produced by God in finite minds. The orderly and regular appearance of sensible ideas displays God's wisdom and power, not that of matter or the laws of nature. Berkeley opposed the increasingly influential view, developed by Descartes and Newton, among others, that the world was a great machine, created and started by God but then left more or less to its own devices. Whereas this mechanistic world-view tended to marginalize God and spirits, Berkeley's idealistic world-view marginalizes the mechanistic, since for him physical objects are simply collections of inert sensible ideas. We impute activity to them in a way not dissimilar to the way that we seem to see action in a film or moving picture. Just as what we really see at the cinema are many independent, static frames or pictures; so what we really experience, according to Berkeley, are a succession of inert sensible ideas created and ordered in our minds by God.

Hence it is altogether appropriate, Berkeley holds (sect. 107), to speak of purpose behind nature, since the physical world is constantly being created by a Mind, not unlike our own, in accordance with its own wise rules, generally called the laws of nature. On the other hand, it is inappropriate, according to Berkeley, to speak of an autonomous physical world, existing in space and time. Berkeley opposes Newton's theory of absolute space, time and motion (in sects 111–17). Minds do not exist in the great containers, space and time; if anything, it is space and time that exist in minds. For space and time considered as independent beings are fictions thrown up by the pernicious tendency to reify abstractions. So time is only the succession of ideas in minds. Hence (as against Locke, but in accord with Descartes) minds always think. Berkeley outlines his philosophy of science in sections 101–32. Earlier, in sections 34–84, he had examined sixteen objections to his immaterialist philosophy as well as displaying its advantages over materialism. Thus he argues that materialism encourages scepticism, since if we accept matter, we can never be sure whether or to what extent our sensible ideas resemble the external material bodies.

Although the *Principles* is Berkeley's philosophical masterpiece, it was not well received. On the whole, it was either ignored or ridiculed. It was even suggested that its author was mentally unstable. As Berkeley's friend, John Percival, reported from London on 26 August 1710: 'A physician of my acquaintance undertook to describe your person, and argued you must needs be mad, and that you ought to take remedies'.[3] The *New Theory of Vision* had been somewhat more positively received. Believing that the *Principles* had failed mainly for reasons of presentation, Berkeley reformulated his case in the more accessible and elegant *Three Dialogues*, where Philonous defends Berkeley's immaterialism against the many-headed materialist enemy, represented by Hylas. The *Three Dialogues* was published in 1713. A year earlier Berkeley had issued his principal work on political theory, *Passive Obedience*, originally delivered as three sermons in the Trinity College Chapel. Here he tries to show that rebellion against the sovereign power is never morally justified, even if it exposes people to great suffering, hardship and death. Berkeley argues for this absolutist position on theological and utilitarian grounds.[4] He felt obliged to publish the sermons (which he did by combining them into one discourse) because of rumours that they constituted an insidious Jacobite attack on the Glorious Revolution.

❧ VARYING PERSPECTIVES ❧

In 1713 Berkeley left Ireland for London, where, in May, he published his *Three Dialogues*. The year 1713 brings to a close what may be seen as the first phase of his career. Although Berkeley was to publish other notable works – for example, on philosophical theology, mathematics, and economics – his fame and place in the history of philosophy is largely based on the three classics of this period. Hence it is worth trying to gain a deeper understanding of this work. Perhaps the safest approach here is to survey some of the major views, since, as with most great philosophers, there has been considerable disagreement. Although most commentators recognize that his non-materialist analysis of the physical world is Berkeley's main contribution, they differ in their interpretation and assessment of it. Thus it was held early on by Hume that Berkeley's position was sceptical, because his arguments 'admit of no answer and produce no conviction', but only produce 'momentary amazement and irresolution and confusion'.[5] Of course, Hume recognized that this was not Berkeley's own view, indeed, that he was writing against scepticism, as even his titles show.

Similarly, Thomas Reid maintained that despite Berkeley's intentions the logic of his position was to undermine not just matter, but also spirit, and hence that immaterialism represented an important phase in the disastrous movement towards Hume's scepticism and agnosticism – although, again, Reid realized that Berkeley would have been scandalized by such an accusation (see [5.16], 2: 166–7). But it was an accusation shared by later philosophers, some of whom – e.g., J. S. Mill, George Grote and A. J. Ayer – welcomed and applauded what they took to be the irreligious tendency of Berkeley's thought, the tendency towards phenomenalism, which one commentator has neatly character-ized as 'Berkeley without God' ([5.29]). Probably the more popular view was (and still is) that immaterialism is essentially untenable, because it undermines the objectivity of the physical world, transform-ing real things into mere appearances, thereby locking each of us into his or her subjective world. This reading of Berkeley as a subjective idealist, as it came to be called, was influentially supported in the eighteenth century by Kant and, in our own century, by Lenin.[6] Here again it was not supposed that 'the good Berkeley' actually intended or accepted this 'scandalous' position, but that this was where his theory logically led.

However, not all commentators have been so hostile, construing immaterialism as such an extreme form of idealism. Thus Berkeley's most distinguished twentieth-century biographer and editor, A. A. Luce, has argued forcibly that there is no justification for reading Berkeley either as a sceptic or a subjective idealist. Indeed, Luce goes so far as to deny that Berkeley has any significant kinship with the idealist tradition. 'Today [writes Luce] they even call him "the father of modern idealism." What a remarkable accident of birth this is! Berkeley is the putative father of modern idealism, and the child does not take after its father in the slightest degree' ([5.47], 26). Rather, according to Luce, Berkeley was a robust common sense realist, both theoretically and practically. For Luce not only defended Berkeley's philosophy as commonsensical, but in his masterful biography ([5.13]) also defends Berkeley the man against the charge that he was a visionary or unbalanced dreamer. While Luce's picture of Berkeley, the man, as 'sane, shrewd, efficient', has been almost universally accepted, this is not the case with his common sense reading of Berkeley's philosophy; although there have been some recent sympathizers here.[7] Yet even the critics, notably Geoffrey Warnock ([5.29]) and Ian Tipton ([5.49]), agree with the Luce interpretation in one respect: that Berkeley was deeply concerned to bring his philosophy into line with common sense and realism, and that this concern was perhaps as important to him as his religious aims.

For Luce and Tipton common sense seems to be the main focus. For Harry Bracken, however, the best way of understanding Berkeley is to see him as an Irish Cartesian, rather than as the second figure in the triumvirate of British empiricists (see [5.22]). For C. M. Turbayne, however, it is Berkeley's commitment to the language model and his rejection of the Cartesian-Newtonian machine model that makes most sense of Berkeley's work ([5.57] and [5.36]).

How is one to gain a fair, overall view of Berkeley's philosophy amidst such diverse perspectives? My general approach, following Berk-eley's own suggestion, is to present his work chronologically, pointing out its design and connections, and then to criticize it. For as he writes to Johnson on 24 March 1730: 'I could wish that all the things I have published on these philosophical subjects were read in the order wherein I published them; once, to take in the design and connexion of them, and a second time with a critical eye'. Let us continue, therefore, where we left off: with Berkeley's publication at 28 of his *Three Dialogues*, which marks the end of the first and heroic phase of his career.

❧ SECOND PHASE: THE 1732–4 SYNTHESIS ❧

In London in 1713 Berkeley soon became friendly with many of the leading literary and intellectual figures, among them Addison, Steele, Swift, and Arbuthnot. For Steele's periodical, *The Guardian* (1713), Berkeley wrote a number of essays, mostly attacking the freethinkers in the interest of religion and morality. He also (as we now know) collaborated with Steele on the *Ladies Library*, a three-volume educational anthology, published in the following year (see [5.10], 4: 4–13). In October 1713, he began his Continental travels, as Chaplain to Lord Peterborough. He visited Paris – where he probably met Malebranche – as well as Lyons and Leghorn. This first continental tour lasted about nine months. A second, more adventurous tour, extending from 1716 to 1720, was spent almost exclusively in Italy. Some of his travel diaries of this tour are still extant.

Returning to London in 1721, Berkeley published his *De Motu*, a short but searching work in the philosophy of science, in which he emphasizes the operational or pragmatic value of terms such as attraction and force. Berkeley had apparently submitted the essay to the Royal Academy of Sciences in Paris, which had offered a prize for the best essay on motion. Although *De Motu* failed to win the prize, it has been commended by Sir Karl Popper and others for anticipating the views of Mach and Einstein (see [5.56] and [5.54]). By late 1721 Berkeley was again in Dublin, teaching at Trinity College. He was not, however, to remain there long, since it was at this time that he conceived his ambitious plan to establish a missionary College in Bermuda. The College, as he explained in his *Proposal* (1724), was to educate the American colonists and train missionaries to the native Americans, becoming 'a fountain or reservoir of learning and religion' that would 'purify' the ill-manners and irreligion of the colonies ([5.3], vii: 358). He spent most of the period 1723–9 campaigning for his projected college. He received considerable private contributions; obtained a Royal Charter and was promised £20,000 by the British government. His financial position was also helped by his appointment in 1724 as

Dean of Derry, one of the richest livings in Ireland. In 1729 Berkeley set sail with his newly married wife, Anne, for Rhode Island, which was to be the American base for his College. Purchasing a farm near Newport, he spent nearly three years there, waiting in vain for the promised grant.

In late 1731 he returned to London, having been informed that the government grant would not be paid. During the next three years, he published a variety of works on theology and philosophy, as well as on vision and mathematics. *Alciphron* (1732), in seven dialogues, is the central work of this period. It is also Berkeley's main theological work, directed at what he saw as his principal enemy – irreligious free-thinking. Dialogues Four and Seven are philosophically most important. Dialogue Four sets out a novel proof for the existence of God, which, though similar to that in the *Principles*, does not draw on immaterialism. Instead, it develops the position of the *Theory of Vision*. Having argued that we can only know other thinking persons by inferring them from their bodily effects – 'hair, skin... outward form' – Berkeley then states (through his spokesman, Euphranor) that our inference to God is no less sound. Alciphron, the atheistic free-thinker, challenges this parity of reasoning: 'It is my hearing you talk that, in strict and philosophical truth, [says Alciphron,] is to me the best argument for your being' (sect. 6). Euphranor then argues, utilizing the main lines of the appended *Essay on Vision*, that God does indeed talk to us through the language of vision. Since it is accepted that language is 'the arbitrary use of sensible signs, which have no similitude or necessary connexion with the things signified' (sect. 7), Berkeley must prove that visual data and tangible things are entirely heterogeneous, which he tries to do in at least four different ways:

(1) He claims that it is confirmed by experimental evidence, citing, in section 15, the case of a boy made to see, 'who had been blind from his birth', reported in the *Philosophical Transactions* 402 (1728). In the *Theory of Vision Vindicated*, published in 1733, Berkeley quotes from this now famous case, reported by Chesselden, who performed the operation. 'When [the boy] first saw, he was so far from making any judgement about distances that he thought all objects whatever touched his eyes (as he expressed it) as what he felt did his skin... He knew not the shape of anything'. This is quoted in section 71, where, it may be noted, Berkeley is more cautious than in his earlier claim in *Alciphron* IV. 15.

(2) Berkeley argues for the heterogeneity thesis by conceptual argument. Thus if two things cannot be added, then they must be qualitatively different. And while one can add a line of two colours to make one continuous line; one cannot, Berkeley maintains, add a visible

and a tangible line together to form a continuous line (see *Essay*, sect. 131).

(3) Berkeley also, as we have seen above, makes use of an *ad hominem* argument, namely, that those who wish to return a negative answer to Molyneux's question – as did Locke and Molyneux himself – are logically committed to the heterogeneity thesis.

(4) Probably his main argument is that we can become aware that what we immediately perceive by sight are light and colours – a field of minimum visual points – entirely different from what we touch.

Having established his thesis, at least to his own satisfaction, Berkeley then ingeniously points out the correspondences between vision and a language such as English or French. (a) Both languages contain a vast variety of signs that can be combined to inform us about innumerable things. (b) Both languages need to be learned, although we are less aware of learning the visual language, mainly because it is a virtually universal language. (c) As English is ordered and explained by grammar, so there are God's laws of nature which govern the orderly appearance of visual data. (d) And violations are possible in each case. (e) One can also be deceived in both languages: an illusion is like a lie. (f) Context is important in both languages, as Berkeley shows in the case of the moon illusion. (g) Both languages usefully direct our actions, evoke attitudes and emotions, and can be entertaining. (h) In both languages we pay more attention to what the signs mean than to the signs themselves; thus we are scarcely able to hear the sounds as such in language we understand, rather than what the sounds mean. Similarly, it is hard for us to appreciate that what we see is not the same as what we may touch.

Berkeley's conclusion is that he has proven not merely a creator of the world, 'but a provident governor actually and intimately present and attentive to our interests'. For since we know that God speaks the 'optic language', we can know that He has 'knowledge, wisdom, and goodness' (*Alciphron* IV sect. 14). In short, Berkeley's *New Theory of Vision* enabled him to go further than the God of Deism – the distant absentee God whose main function was to create or activate the world. But this was not evident in the first two editions of the *Essay*, where the optic-language theory remains implicit. The crucial theological conclusion only became clear in the revised 1732 edition and, particularly, in its reformulation in *Alciphron* IV. Thus in the early editions of the *Essay*, section 147, Berkeley writes vaguely of 'an universal language of nature', whereas in the 1732 editions this is changed to 'an universal language of the author of nature'; also see section 152. Berkeley probably had a strategic aim here. He thought that his readers would be more likely to accept his theories if he revealed them gradually, saving the more radical conclusions till later. We have already seen how he presented only part of his immaterialism in the *Essay*, which he then followed in the next year with the full immaterialism of the *Principles*. And the *Principles* itself was written with strategic intent, as we learn from Berkeley's revealing letter to Percival of 6 September 1710: 'whatever doctrine contradicts vulgar and settled opinion had need be introduced with great caution into the world. For this reason I omitted all mention of the non-existence of matter in the title-page [of the *Principles*] dedication, preface and introduction, so that the notion might steal unawares on the reader'. By 1732, then, Berkeley was ready to reveal fully, or more fully, the significance of his *New Theory of Vision*.

Dialogue Four also discusses the status of God's attributes. Here Berkeley shows himself to be a tough-minded rational theologian, opposed not only to the vague Deism of free-thinkers, such as Shaftesbury, but also to the fideism and negative theology of fellow Christian philosophers, particularly his countrymen Archbishop King and Bishop Browne. In short, Berkeley attacked their position for basically the same reasons that he attacked materialistic representation (see [5. 15], 162–3). His acute criticisms call into question the popular accusation, alluded to above, that he was strong-minded about the material world, but weak-minded about the spiritual world.

Dialogue Seven is of considerable importance, as it contains Berkeley's most comprehensive and searching account of language. Here he reiterates (in the 1732 editions) his critique of abstract general ideas. More innovative, however, is the deployment of his theory of emotive meaning – that words and utterances can be meaningful even though they do not stand for ideas or inform, since they can be used to evoke emotions, attitudes and actions. Although we find little application of the theory in the *Principles*, we know from his more elaborate (1708) draft of the Introduction that he was aware of how it could be significantly applied in the areas of religious and (probably) moral discourse (see [5. 9]). His recognition that more needed to be published on this subject also comes out in his letter of 24 March 1730 (when he was, no doubt, at work on *Alciphron*) in which, after asking his friend Johnson 'to examine well what I have said about abstraction, and about the true sense and significance of words', he adds: 'though much remains to be said on that subject' (see [5. 3], 2: 293). Here again we seem to see Berkeley's strategy of publishing his more radical theories by degrees or stages. In *Alciphron* he uses the emotive theory to show how words standing for Christian mysteries, such as 'Holy Trinity' are to be understood. Free-thinkers, like John Toland, had argued that since mysteries do not stand for ideas, they must, according to the received theory of meaning, be meaningless. Hence, Toland maintained, Christianity either contained meaningless doctrines, or it was not mysterious. By showing that the received semantic theory, championed most notably by Locke, was narrowly restrictive, Berkeley was able to argue that doctrines such as the Holy Trinity were both meaningful and mysterious. For although, as he says in *Alciphron* VII. 8, a man can frame no 'distinct ideas of Trinity, substance or personality', the doctrine can 'make proper impressions on his mind, producing herein, love, hope, gratitude, and obedience, and thereby becomes a lively operative principle influencing his life and actions'.

It is perhaps ironic (and not generally recognized) that Berkeley's emotive account of religious utterances anticipates the similar account of religious discourse given by the Logical Posivitists in our own century. The irony is that Logical Posivitists such as A. J. Ayer – in many respects a modern Toland – used emotivism to explain away religion (see [5.58], 229). Berkeley, however, explained only religious mysteries emotively. He was entirely clear that doctrines of natural theology were to be understood cognitively and justified in a rigorous way. This point, as I noted earlier, is emphasized in the latter part of Dialogue Four, where Berkeley attacks the theological representationalism of King and Browne. In the area of natural theology, particularly concerning the proof of God's existence and nature, Berkeley was a hard-headed rationalist.

How, then, does Berkeley connect the cognitive statements of natural theology with the emotive utterances of religious mysteries? His approach is in line with the (at least then) orthodox view that natural religion forms the proper basis for revealed religion. In short, having accepted Berkeley's proof (or proofs) that a just and wise God exists, we should also recognize that it is right to respect Him; because He is good, it is also right to love Him. And the Christian mysteries, Berkeley believes, are the best ways of evoking these desirable attitudes and feelings. Thus the mystery of the future life is an excellent way of evoking fear of God's justice, and the symbolism of the Trinity of encouraging people to love God.

The Christian mysteries are also justified, according to Berkeley, because they are to be found in the Bible, whose privileged status he defends in Dialogues Five and Six. More important philosophically is the way that Berkeley defends emotive mysteries in Dialogue Seven by trying to show that 'there is nothing absurd or repugnant in our belief of those points' (sect. 33). His method here is to argue by parity of reasoning that while there may appear to be difficulties, even perhaps contradictions, in mysteries such as the Trinity, there are similar difficulties in, for example, the received (Lockean) theory of personal identity, according to which personal identity consists in identity of consciousness. For suppose, Berkeley says in section 8, that we divide a person's conscious life into three parts – A, B, and C. Suppose also that in B only half of A is remembered and in C half of B but none of A is remembered. Then it will follow according to Locke's theory (in *Essay* II. xxvii) that A is the same person as B and B is the same person as C, but A and C are not the same person. Is this any more absurd, Berkeley asks, than the Athanasian doctrine of the Trinity?

Berkeley presses this *ad hominem* defence of religious mysteries most effectively in his *Analyst* (1734), which examines, to quote its subtitle, 'whether the object, the principles, and inferences of the modern analysis are more distinctly conceived, or more evidently deduced, than religious mysteries and points of faith'. Berkeley's point is that mathematicians have no justification for rejecting mysteries, since the Newtonian account of infinitesimals can be shown to be equally obscure and contradictory. As he pointedly asks towards the end of the *Analyst*:

> Whether mathematicians, who are so delicate in religious points, are strictly scrupulous in their own science? Whether they do not submit to authority, take things upon trust, and believe points inconceivable? Whether they have not their mysteries, and what is more, their repugnances and contradictions?

Berkeley had criticized the theory of infinitesimals in the *Principles*, sections 126–32, which he alludes to in the *Analyst*, section 50 as the critical 'hints' which he is now 'deducing' and applying in detail against Newton. His earlier claim was that the infinite division of a finite line, for example, is an absurdity generated by false abstraction, since we cannot perceive infinitely small points. His attack now is directed particularly against the consistency and proof of Newton's account of fluxions.

The synthesis of 1732–4, which rivals that of 1709–13, is also supported by Berkeley's *Theory of Vision Vindicated* (1733), which elucidates the theory of vision that underpins his optic-language dem-onstration and also goes some way towards bringing the 1732–4 syn-thesis into line with the full immaterialism of the *Principles* and *Three Dialogues*. Two other works of the period, so far not mentioned, are Berkeley's *Defence of Freethinking in Mathematics* (1735) and his letter to Browne (circa 1733) on divine analogy. The first work responds to critics of the *Analyst* as well as continuing Berkeley's *ad hominem* defence of Christian mysteries. It concludes (as did the *Analyst*) with a series of 'ensnaring questions', which look ahead stylistically to Berke-ley's next work, *The Querist* (1735–7), composed entirely of queries. The letter to Browne develops points in *Alciphron* IV against Browne's extensive attack in his *Divine Analogy* (1733). Recently identified as by Berkeley – see [5. 63] – it shows his unwillingness to tolerate ambiguity in theological descriptions: God is either literally wise or (disastrously) He is not.

❧ FINAL PHASE: THE GOOD BISHOP ❧

In 1733 Berkeley was appointed Bishop of Cloyne, and in the following year he travelled with his family to Cloyne, in Co. Cork, where he was to reside until 1752. His main concerns were now with the spiritual, but also with the economic and physical needs of those under his care as well as with the wider population. Thus his main work on economics, *The Querist*, deals with the nature of wealth, the proper role of banks, credit and fashion. Perhaps its chief theoretical interest is the way Berkeley applies his emotive theory. For in the *Querist* he regards money as a system of operative signs. And just as he rejected the Lockean theory that every meaningful word stands for an idea, so in the *Querist* he rejected the mercantilist theory (also championed by Locke), according to which money had value only if it was made of precious metal or had a necessary connection with it. For Berkeley it is the efficient recording and manipulation of economic transactions, which facilitate prosperity, that gives money its value.

From social and economic matters Berkeley turned finally to medicine. In 1744 he published *Siris*, his last major work, in which he championed the drinking of tar-water, a medicine which he thought would cure or alleviate all physical ills. *Siris* is Berkeley's most puzzling and allusive book, moving from practical medical advice to pharmacology, then to chemistry, philosophy of science, metaphysics and finally to theology and speculations on the Trinity. The clear and close reasoning of the 1709–13 works has here given way to suggestive hints and allusive appeals to ancient authorities, particularly to Plato. (In this respect, *Alciphron* stands in a middle position between the 1709–13 works and *Siris*.) Some commentators, notably A. C. Fraser ([5. 2]) and John Wild ([5. 28]), have suggested that in *Siris* Berkeley abandoned his earlier empiricism and nominalism in favour of a more Platonic and pantheistic vision. One piece of evidence Fraser adduces to show that Berkeley relented on abstract ideas is his omission in the 1752 edition of *Alciphron* of the three sections (VII. 5–7) arguing against such ideas. *Siris*'s final section (367) also suggests that Berkeley was reassessing his earlier work. Thus he uses the term 'revise' and concludes that 'He that would make a real progress in knowledge must dedicate his age as well as youth, the later growth as well as first fruits, at the altar of truth'. Yet, typically, Berkeley is not specific here. The claim that Berkeley changed his mind is also vigorously opposed by Luce, who has argued at length for the unity of Berkeley's work ([5. 19]). Probably *Siris*'s main theoretical interest, at least for recent commentators, is its statements on the philosophy of science and corpuscularianism.[8]

In late 1752 Berkeley left Cloyne for Oxford, to supervise his son's education. His two last publications appeared in this year: *A*

Miscellany, Containing Several Tracts – nearly all previously published – and a revised edition of *Alciphron*. Berkeley died in Oxford on 14 January 1753.

❧ CRITICISMS ❧

Having surveyed Berkeley's work chronologically, with the aim of seeing its 'design and order', we must now briefly look at his philosophy 'with a critical eye'. In doing so, we will also be able to appreciate that his immaterialism is deeper and more complex than my account above might suggest. It is also appropriate to see its complexity within a context of criticisms, since that is how Berkeley himself proceeded. Thus his response to the sixteen self-imposed objections or difficulties – in *Principles*, sections 34–84 – fill in essential details of his account.

Probably the chief criticism of Berkeley's system has always been that it obliterates the real, objective, public world. If all I can perceive are my ideas, then am I not locked into my own subjective world? Hence – to take the most extreme and absurd possibility – will it not follow that only I (and my ideas) exist? That Berkeley would repudiate this solipsistic position is clear, but it is not so clear that the logic of immaterialism does not draw him towards it. For Berkeley is certainly and primarily anxious to prove that what we perceive is mind-dependent. But what can mind-dependent mean apart from being subjective in the way that emotions and pains are? But if all my sensible ideas are like pains, then am I not living in a world of 'mere illusion', as Kant put it – vivid and orderly, but still subjective? Some of Berkeley's best-known arguments lend weight to this subjective interpretation – for example, his assimilation of the experience of heat and pain in the first of the *Three Dialogues*, and his emphasis there on the relativity of our sensory experiences. His critique (mentioned above) of how matter supports qualities can also be turned against him here. For how can a sensible idea exist in a mind without being in the mind subjectively in the way that a pain is? Berkeley's response is to deny that such ideas exist in mind in this 'gross, literal' sense, by way of mode or attribute, but only as they are perceived (see [5. 3], 2: 250). But he does not clearly spell this out, or show that such a sense would not either undermine his arguments for the mind-dependence of ideas, or provide the materialist with an equally vague way of explaining how matter supports its properties.

Probably no interpretation is as anti-commonsensical as that of solipsism; but there are a range of less extreme positions with which Berkeley has been identified. Thus Andrew Baxter suggested as early as 1733 that Berkeley was logically committed to a world in which there was only me, my ideas and God as their cause (see [5. 41] and [5. 17]). Yet even if one allows Berkeley the existence of other finite minds, it does not follow that a common sense world is restored. For such a world seems to require independent, continuous, numerically-identical objects. But that is a far cry from the 'fleeting and variable' sensible ideas which, according to the usual reading of Berkeley, constitute physical objects. Berkeley struggles to bridge the gap, particularly in the *Three Dialogues*, but it is complicated, uphill work. And the more he succeeds in showing himself to side with common sense, the more he seems either to bring his immaterialist thesis into question, or to lose its vaunted advantages over materialism. Thus he is sometimes inclined to preserve the independence and permanence of real physical objects by claiming that they exist archetypally in the mind of God. Thus, to quote the well-known limerick, the tree in the quad 'will continue to be, since observed by . . . God' (see [5. 6], 16). But this solution only raises other problems, most notably the spectre of scepticism. For if the real, reassuringly permanent objects in God's mind are different from the fleeting ideas that I experience, then do I really perceive or know the real world? Is Berkeley not simply substituting one objectionable form of representationalism for another? To resist this Berkeley needs to show that God's archetypal tree is the same as mine. But how, given *esse* is *percipi*, could God's idea-tree be numerically the same as mine? In the *Dialogues*, Berkeley tries to play down this difficulty by maintaining that it is really verbal ([5. 3], 2: 247–8). Yet if this problem can be dismissed so easily, then why can't the materialist dismiss *esse* is *percipi* itself as merely verbal? Surely there is something substantive at issue, as Berkeley himself appears to recognize when he advises us 'to think with the learned and speak with the vulgar' (*Principles*, sect. 51). In this mood he does seem to allow (as does his fellow Immaterialist, Arthur Collier) that there is no (numerically) identical tree, but that each mind perceives a different idea-tree. Yet he might still insist that God's archetypal ideas are preferable to material bodies, because the former are meaningfully like human ideas. But are they? That God's idea of fire or salty food, for example, cannot be even qualitatively like mine seems to follow from Berkeley's argument in the *Dialogues*, according to which (1) experiencing the fire's heat cannot be separated from pain, and that (2) God, as a perfect being, does not experience pain ([5. 3], 2: 240). Hence God cannot perceive what we take to be heat. Furthermore, can we conceive what God's idea-tree could be like, since it must presumably contain all possible perceptions of 'the' tree – large, small, tube-shaped, circular-shaped, hard, soft – which makes it sound as incomprehensible as Locke's (impossible) triangle.

Berkeley's concept of mind or spirit also raises difficulties which, if anything, are even greater than those afflicting his account of bodies. Here, prima facie, Berkeley seems to be his own worst enemy, since he constantly says that we can have no idea or experience of minds, and that they are altogether different from ideas. But if we have no idea of mind, then why believe that it exists? Is it not as indefensible as matter? Berkeley considers this objection at length in the third edition of the *Dialogues*, where he states that his objection to matter is not merely that it is meaningless, but that it is also contradictory. Yet, as I noted earlier, Berkeley does attack some materialist theories as simply meaningless – as, for example, 'the idea of being in general, with the relative notion of its supporting accidents' (sect. 17). Yet if our grasp of matter is no more than that of spirit, then are not the two equally plausible or implausible?

Berkeley's main way of arguing for the greater plausibility of mind is by showing that it alone can be the source of activity or causality. (1) A sensible idea cannot cause either itself or other sensible ideas, since ideas are passive. (2) Yet sensible ideas must have some cause. (3) Imaginative ideas are crucial here; for we know that by willing we can produce them. (4) In doing so, we gain some notion of activity, and hence that minds (unlike material bodies) are active. (5) Thus Berkeley concludes that just as our (weak) imaginative ideas are caused by finite minds, so it is reasonable to infer that (vivid) sensible ideas are caused by the Infinite Mind. (3) and (4) are the decisive steps in this argument, and the question we need to ask is: how does Berkeley know that he produces imaginative ideas? There are two possibilities. He knows it by (a) direct experience, or (b) indirect inference. Although Berkeley occasionally seems to accept option (a), it is hardly tenable since it conflicts with his major principle that we can only directly experience passive ideas. While option (b) – which he generally prefers – is not in conflict with his major principles, it does not go far enough in justifying (4). For if I have no direct experience, then how do I know that my imaginative ideas are produced by my mind, rather than by my brain? Here again Berkeley's position does not seem any more intelligible or tenable than that of his materialist opponent.

⚬⚬ NOTES ⚬⚬

1 The authoritative biography is by Luce, [5. 13]; my references are to the 1992 edition, which contains a new Introduction with *addenda* and *corrigenda*; see pp. vi, x, 22.

2 All quotations from Berkeley are from the standard edition, edited by Luce and Jessop, of his *Works*, [5. 3]; for convenience, I refer to entry or section number or (in the case of his letters in vol. 8) date.

3 See B. Rand, *Berkeley and Percival*, Cambridge, Cambridge University Press, 1914, p. 80.

4 For useful discussion of Berkeley's moral and political views, see [5. 26], Broad in [5. 31], Warnock in [5. 39], and also [5. 62].

5 See Hume, *Inquiry concerning Human Understanding*, 1777, ed. C. W. Hendel, Indianapolis, Liberal Arts Press, 1955, p. 163 n.

6 See [5. 20] and Lenin, *Materialism and Empirio-Criticism*, 1909, Moscow, 1972), pp. 28 and 38.

7 See, for example, Pappas in [5. 48] and [5. 38]; also see [5. 37] and [5. 45].

8 See Garber in [5. 36], Wilson in [5. 37], and [5. 54].

I am grateful to Mr Ian Tipton for reading a draft of this chapter.

❧ BIBLIOGRAPHY ❧

Editions

(i) Complete and Selected Works

5.1 *The Works of George Berkeley... To which is Added, An Account of His Life, and Several of his Letters...*, ed. Joseph Stock, Dublin, John Exshaw, 2 vols, 1784. Repr. 1820 and 1837.

5.2 *The Works of George Berkeley... Including his Posthumous Works. With Prefaces, Annotations, Appendices, and An Account of his Life*, by A. C. Fraser, Oxford, Clarendon Press, 4 vols, 1901.

5.3 *The Works of George Berkeley*, ed. A. A. Luce and T. E. Jessop, London, Thomas Nelson, 9 vols, 1948–57; repr. 1964 and 1967; Kraus repr. 1979.

5.4 *Berkeley's Philosophical Writings*, ed. D. M. Armstrong, London, Collier, 1965.

5.5 *Berkeley: Philosophical Works including the Works on Vision*; introd. and notes by M. R. Ayers, London, Dent, 1975; repr. 1980, 1983, 1985, and 1989 with revisions and additions. (A useful volume, containing most of Berkeley's important works.)

5.6 *Principles and Three Dialogues*, ed. R. Woolhouse, London, Penguin, 1988.

(ii) Separate Works

5.7 *Philosophical Commentaries*, ed. G. H. Thomas, with notes by A. A. Luce, Alliance, Ohio, 1976; repr. New York, Garland, 1989.

5.8 *George Berkeley Alciphron, or the Minute Philosopher in Focus*, ed. D. Berman, London, Routledge, 1993. (Contains Dialogues 1, 3, 4 and 7 as well as critical commentaries from the eighteenth to the twentieth century.)

5.9 *George Berkeley's Manuscript Introduction, an editio diplomatica*, ed. B. Belfrage, Oxford, Doxa Press, 1987.

Bibliographies and Biographies

5.10 Berman, D. (ed.), *Berkeley Newsletter*, Dublin, 1977–.

5.11 Jessop, T. E. *A Bibliography of George Berkeley, with an inventory of Manuscript Remains* by A. A. Luce, Oxford, Oxford University Press, 1934; rev. edn 1973.

5.12 Keynes, G. *A Bibliography of George Berkeley*, Oxford, Clarendon Press, 1976.

5.13 Luce, A. A. *The Life of George Berkeley*, Edinburgh, Nelson, 1949; repr. 1969 and 1992 (with a new introduction by D. Berman).

5.14 Turbayne, C. M. 'A Bibliography of George Berkeley 1963–1979', in [6.36].

Influences and Reception

5.15 Berman, D. 'Enlightenment and Counter-Enlightenment in Irish Philosophy' and 'The Causation and Culmination of Irish Philosophy', in *Archiv für Geschichte der Philosophie* 2 and 3, 1982.

5.16 —— (ed.) *George Berkeley: Eighteenth-Century Responses*, New York, Garland, 2 vols, 1989.

5.17 Bracken, H. M. *The Early Reception of Berkeley's Immaterialism: 1710–1733*, The Hague, Martinus Nijhoff, 1959; rev. edn 1965.

5.18 Luce, A. A. *Berkeley and Malebranche*, Oxford, Clarendon Press, 1934; repr. 1967 and by Garland 1988.

5.19 —— 'The Alleged Development of Berkeley's Philosophy', *Mind* 206 (1943).

5.20 Walker, R. C. S. (ed.), *The Real in the Ideal: Berkeley's Relation to Kant*, New York, Garland, 1989.

5.21 Vesey, G. *Berkeley: Reason and Experience*, Milton Keynes, Open University Press, 1982.

General Surveys

5.22 Bracken, H. M. *Berkeley*, London, Macmillan, 1974.

5.23 Hicks, G. *Berkeley*, London, Ernest Benn Ltd., 1932.

5.24 Hone, J. M. and Rossi, M. M. *Bishop Berkeley: His Life, Writings and Philosophy*, with an introduction by W. B. Yeats, London, Faber and Faber, 1931.

5.25 Johnston, G. A. *The Development of Berkeley's Philosophy*, London, Macmillan, 1923; repr. New York, Garland, 1988.

5.26 Pitcher, G. *Berkeley*, London, Routledge and Kegan Paul, 1977.

5.27 Urmson, J. O. *Berkeley*, Oxford, Oxford University Press, 1982.

5.28 Wild, J. *George Berkeley. A Study of His Life and Philosophy*, 1936; repr. 1962.

5.29 Warnock, G. J. *Berkeley*, Harmondsworth, Pelican, 1953; repr. 1969.

Collections of Critical Essays

5.30 *George Berkeley Bicentenary*, issue of *The British Journal for the Philosophy of Science* 4, 13 (1953).

5.31 *George Berkeley 1985–1953*, in *Revue Internationale de Philosophie* 23–4 (1953).

5.32 *George Berkeley, Lectures Delivered before the University of California*, Berkeley, 1957.

5.33 Steinkraus, W. E. (ed.), *New Studies in Berkeley's Philosophy*, New York, Holt, Rinehart and Winston, 1966.

5.34 Martin, C. B. and Armstrong, D. M. (eds), *Locke and Berkeley*, Garden City, Doubleday, 1967; repr. New York, Garland, 1988.

5.35 Turbayne, C. M. (ed.), *Berkeley: Principles of Human Knowledge: Text and Critical Essays*, Indianapolis, Bobbs-Merrill, 1970.

5.36 —— *Berkeley: Critical and Interpretative Essays*, Minneapolis, University of Minnesota Press, 1982.

5.37 Foster, J. and Robinson, H. (eds) *Essays on Berkeley: A Tercentennial Celebration*, Oxford, Clarendon Press, 1985.

5.38 Berman, D. (ed.) *George Berkeley: Essays and Replies*, Dublin, Irish Academic Press, 1986; repr. from *Hermathena* cxxxix (1985).

5.39 Brykman, G. (ed.) *George Berkeley: 1685–1985*, Special Issue: *History of European Ideas* 7, 6 (1986).

5.40 Creery, W. (ed.), *George Berkeley: Critical Assessments*, London, Routledge, 3 vols, 1991.

Immaterialism

5.41 Baxter, A. *An Enquiry into the Nature of the Human Soul*, 3rd edn, 1745, vol. 2, sect. 2: 'Dean Berkeley's scheme against the existence of matter ... shewn inconclusive', repr. in [6. 16].

5.42 Bennett, J. *Locke, Berkeley, Hume: Central Themes*, Oxford, Clarendon Press, 1971.

5.43 Broad, C. D. 'Berkeley's argument about Material Substance', in [6. 34].

5.44 Dancy, J. *Berkeley: An Introduction*, Oxford, Blackwell, 1987.

5.45 Foster, J. *A Case for Idealism*, London, Routledge and Kegan Paul, 1982 (ch. 2 is on Berkeley).

5.46 Grayling, A. C. *Berkeley: the Central Arguments*, London, Duckworth, 1986.

5.47 Luce, A. A. *Berkeley's Immaterialism: A Commentary on his 'A Treatise ...'*, Edinburgh, Thomas Nelson, 1945; repr. 1967.

5.48 Pappas, G. 'Berkeley, Perception and Commonsense', in [6. 36].

5.49 Tipton, I. C. *The Philosophy of Immaterialism*, London, Methuen, 1974; repr. New York, Garland, 1988.

5.50 Winkler, K. P. *Berkeley: An Interpretation*, Oxford, Clarendon Press, 1989.

Vision, Science and Mathematics

5.51 Armstrong, D. M. *Berkeley's Theory of Vision*, Melbourne, 1960; repr. New York, Garland, 1989.

5.52 Atherton, M. *Berkeley's Revolution in Vision*, Cornell University Press, 1990.

5.53 Brook, R. J. *Berkeley's Philosophy of Science*, The Hague, Martinus Nijhoff, 1973.

5.54 Moked, G. *Particles and Ideas: Bishop Berkeley's Corpuscularian Philosophy*, Oxford, Oxford University Press, 1988.

5.55 Pitcher, G. (ed.) *Berkeley on Vision: A Nineteenth-Century Debate*, New York, Garland, 1988.

5.56 Popper, K. 'A Note on Berkeley as Precursor of Mach and Einstein', in [6. 34].

5.57 Turbayne, C. M. *The Myth of Metaphor*, New Haven, Yale University Press, 1962.

Theology, Ethics and Language

5.58 Berman, D. 'Cognitive Theology and Emotive Mysteries in Berkeley's *Alciphron*', *Proceedings of the Royal Irish Academy*, 1981.

5.59 Clark, S. R. L. (ed.) *Money, Obedience, and Affection: Essays on Berkeley's Moral and Political Thought*, New York, Garland, 1988.

5.60 Flew, A. 'Was Berkeley a Precursor of Wittgenstein?', in W. B. Todd (ed.) *Hume and the Enlightenment*, Edinburgh, Edinburgh University Press, 1974.

5.61 Mabbott, J. D. 'The Place of God in Berkeley's Philosophy', in [5. 34].

5.62 Olscamp, P. *The Moral Philosophy of George Berkeley*, The Hague, Martinus Nijhoff, 1970.

5.63 Pittion, J.-P. (with A. A. Luce and D. Berman), 'A New Letter to Browne on Divine Analogy', *Mind* (1969).

CHAPTER 6
David Hume on human understanding
Anne Jaap Jacobson

David Hume's *A Treatise of Human Nature*[1] was published before he was 30 years old. It is often said to be the greatest philosophical work written in English. Bold and ambitious, it is designed by its author to be a significant step in the construction of a science of human nature.

In his subtitle for the *Treatise*, Hume tells us that he will use the experimental method to develop this science. We learn elsewhere that he thinks of the experimental method in contrast to another method:

> we can only expect success, by following the experimental method, and deducing general maxims from a comparison of particular instances. The other scientific method, where a general abstract principle is first established, and is afterwards branched out into a variety of inferences and conclusions, may be more perfect in itself, but suits less the imperfection of human nature, and is a common source of illusion and mistake in this as well as in other subjects.[2]

Whether science is indeed best pursued by the experimental method or by starting with 'clear and self-evident principles'[3] was a matter being debated in Great Britain in the eighteenth century. Hume would have been aware of the debate while he was a student at the University of Edinburgh, during which time he appears to have conceived of the project issuing in the *Treatise*. Hume's declared intention to use the experimental method means, in effect, he is siding with Newton, as opposed to, among others, the continental philosophers Descartes and Leibniz, and the English philosopher, Clarke.

From Newton, and discussions of Newton, Hume derived not just a conception of method, but also a conception of success. Hume hopes to advance us towards an understanding of human nature that rivals in its systematicity the systematicity of Newton's mechanics. Locke and Berkeley also had a strong influence on Hume's philosophy. For example, Hume's theory of ideas is explicitly an amendment of Locke's. Hume's exposition of his theory of ideas is somewhat swift, an indication that he saw himself as largely modifying familiar claims. And Berkeley's philosophy shows up in several Humean theses, including Hume's attack on abstract ideas and his account of causation in terms of constant conjunction, as we will see below.[4] In addition, during his study at Edinburgh University, Hume clearly paid serious attention to other philosophers. Outstanding among these were those of the moral sense school of philosophy, particularly Hutcheson. The moral sense school of philosophy challenges the picture of human beings as at their best when functioning rationally, where rational functioning is a matter of arguing from truth to truths. In its place, Hutcheson *et al.* emphasize the role of the passionate side of human nature in our acquisition of some of our most important attitudes and beliefs.

At the same time, there is a decidedly continental influence on Hume's philosophy. The *Treatise* appeared after Hume had spent several years studying and writing in France; part of his time was spent at La Flèche, the school where Descartes was educated. Hume clearly absorbed work by Descartes and by his followers, most obviously Malebranche. Hume certainly rejects some of what he read in these sources. For example, Hume's conception of method is at times described in explicit opposition to Descartes'.[5] An additional example is Hume's discussion of personal identity which clearly attacks Descartes' account of the self. And Hume singles out some of Malebranche's views for explicit rebuttal.[6] None the less, Malebranche's philosophy also has a constant conjunction view of causality among material objects which is almost certainly the immediate ancestor of Berkeley's and Hume's; this is a matter to which we will return.[7] And Descartes has an account of natural belief, which is picked up by and elaborated by Malebranche and which will have reinforced the Hutchesonian influence on Hume.[8]

Despite the fact that Hume's philosophy is significantly influenced by his cultural context, it presents us with a systematic working out of a radical idea. The radical idea, greatly extending the claims of Hutcheson, is that in the most important aspects of human life – over a vast range of phenomena – we are and must be creatures ruled by the non-rational in our nature.

Our principle source in our following discussion will be Hume's *Treatise*. However, the *Treatise* undeservedly had a very poor reception (see the concluding section below) and Hume reworked and rewrote some of its most important parts. Those directly concerned with the understanding received their final articulation in *An Enquiry Concern-*

ing Human Understanding. The title 'the first *Enquiry*' is often used to distinguish it from his *An Enquiry Concerning the Principles of Morals.* The first *Enquiry* will be our second major source.

❧ THE THEORY OF IDEAS ❧

Hume's science of human nature starts with a theory of the understanding and the theory of the understanding starts with his theory of ideas. The theory of ideas is, to use Hume's terminology, a theory of *perceptions.* Perceptions include sensations, passions and emotions. The shock of cold as one falls into a icy pond is an example of a sensation. A person craving tobacco or someone angry at a rude comment will also have perceptions. Such perceptions, which Hume thinks of as particularly vivid and forceful, are *impressions.*

There is another class of perceptions. In addition to feeling cold, we can think about being cold. We can make plans about the best way to survive in a very cold place. Or we can remember the cold we felt on some occasion before. Or we can imagine being cold in the future. In such cases, Hume maintains, we have faint images of impressions. These faint images are called *ideas.*

Impressions come from either sensation or reflexion, the latter including passions, desires and emotions. Hume singles out two particular sources of ideas: memory and imagination. The imagination plays a very important role in Hume's philosophy, though its introduction in the theory of ideas does not really prepare us for this. Hume starts simply by remarking that the ideas of the imagination are less lively and strong than those of the memory and that the imagination, unlike the memory, is at liberty to transpose and change its ideas.

Hume's distinction between impressions and ideas is an explicit amendment of Locke's theory of ideas, which does not attempt a corresponding distinction. Hume does not tell us much at all about how to draw the distinction or decide a problem case, though he thinks that, in a few cases, we can have ideas nearly as vivid as impressions or impressions nearly as faint as ideas. None the less, he thinks the distinction is in general quite obvious and thus it is not 'very necessary to employ many words in explaining [it]'.[9]

Having introduced impressions and ideas, Hume gives us a distinction which applies to both categories. Both impressions and ideas can be *simple* or *complex.* Hume tells us that 'simple perceptions or impressions and ideas are such as admit of no distinction nor separation'.[10] As first examples Hume gives the colour, taste and smell of an apple. Colours are prominent in his discussions of simple ideas. For example, the idea of red and the idea of a particular shade of blue figure in his discussion in the *Treatise*.[11] The simple-complex distinction Hume employs is not actually entirely clear. We will see this below when we discuss abstract ideas.

For now we need to note that his simple-complex distinction allows Hume both to attempt to explain the creative powers of the human mind and to hold at the same time that in some sense all our ideas are derived from impressions. In the formation of our *impressions*, the human mind seems to be entirely passive; on the level of impressions there is no hint in Hume of the later, Kantian account of the mind making nature-as-we-experience-it.[12] But Hume is well aware of at least some of the creative powers of the human mind:

> To form monsters, and join incongruous shapes and appearances, costs the imagination no more trouble than to conceive the most natural and familiar objects. . . . What never was seen, or heard of, may yet be conceived; nor is anything beyond the power of thought, except what implies an absolute contradiction.[13]

Hume explains our ability to form complex ideas which are not directly derived from impressions as the ability to compound, transpose, augment or diminish the materials of experience.[14] He tells us that we can analyse our thoughts or ideas, however compounded or sublime, into simple ideas; each complex idea is composed of simple ideas which are and must be derived from impressions.[15] Thus, *simple* ideas are basic ingredients for the creations of the imagination, among other things.

We should want to understand, not just the major conclusions of Hume's science of human nature, but also the way he thinks a science should argue. Does Hume follow an experimental method? Hume gives us two arguments for the thesis that ideas depend on impressions. The first argument is a model causal argument. Simple ideas are constantly conjoined with corresponding simple impressions and vice versa. Such constant conjunctions *prove*[16] a causal dependence; and the direction of dependence is clear from our experience. One gives someone an idea of something by furnishing the opportunities for gathering an impression and not vice versa; hence, it is the impressions that are the causes. The second argument is based on 'the plain and convincing phenomenon' that people who lack a particular impression also lack the corresponding, resembling idea.[17] These arguments reflect a use of the experimental method as Hume conceives of it; they are based on observation and experience, as opposed to supposedly undeniable first principles.

Hume does qualify his thesis that all ideas are derived from impressions. The qualification concerns 'the missing shade of blue'. Suppose that one has had experience of all the shades of blue except one. Suppose further that a chart of all the shades of blue (except for the one not experienced) going from the lightest to the darkest is placed before one. Would it not be possible to spot the lack and have an idea of what is lacking? Interestingly, Hume answers in the affirmative and remarks that it is such a strange case that it should not lead him to alter his general maxim about the dependence of ideas on impressions. Possibly Hume thinks that merely imaginary cases have no bearing on the basic laws governing human cognition.[18]

Whatever the correct adjudication here might be, it remains the case that Hume thinks there are some universal principles and that he can tell us what some of them are. Hume's principles of association play a particularly crucial role. They are the source of much of the mind's creativity and they are the source of much in our ordinary beliefs. It is Hume's thesis that there are regular patterns to our thought and the principles of association give us his formulation of the patterns. There are three such principles: Resemblance, Contiguity and Causation. Given an impression or idea, our imagination naturally 'runs to' ideas resembling it. For example, one sees a horse and thinks of the horse one's neighbour owns. Similarly, the imagination also 'run[s] along the parts of space and time in conceiving its objects'; that is, an impression or idea of some object naturally leads us to ideas of spatially or temporally related objects.[19] For example, someone sees a picture of the Pope and thinks of the Vatican, which does not at all resemble the Pope, but which is usually fairly near him. By far the most important of the principles of association is cause and effect. '[T]here is no relation, which produces a stronger connexion in the fancy, and makes one idea more readily recall another, than the relation of cause and effect betwixt their objects'.[20] Thus, someone sees a vase being pushed off a table and then has an idea of the vase shattered into bits.

Underlying the creativity of the human mind is a systematic ability we have. If one has an idea of a orange circle and an idea of a brown equilateral triangle, one *therewith* becomes able to have the idea of an orange equilateral triangle. It seems Hume wants to explain this ability in terms of, in this case, our combining a simple idea of orange with an idea of an equilateral triangle. But what Hume says in his discussion of abstract ideas makes the use of the notion of 'simple idea' in such a context problematic. We will now turn to Hume's account of abstract ideas and then return to the question of how to understand the 'simple' of 'simple ideas'.

In his discussion of abstract ideas, Hume is attempting to account for the fact that we seem capable of uttering and understanding sentences which have an indefinite or even potentially infinite number of implications.[21] For example, (a) 'All human beings are mortal' and (b) 'X is a human being' imply 'X is mortal' for every fill-in for 'X'. Thus, 'Socrates is a human being and Elizabeth I is a human being', conjoined with (a), imply 'Socrates is mortal and Elizabeth I is mortal'. And so on for any fill-in for 'X' in 'X is a human being'. How do we manage to have such large thoughts? One answer is that we have abstract ideas; for example, an abstract conception of human being which applies equally to Socrates and Elizabeth I. Hume opposes such an account and instead locates generality in our language.

Hume aims to explain how we can have and use such terms. We only have specific ideas and so ideas attached to each general term are specific. But, Hume notes, we are also able to notice the similarity among, for example, various red objects that are correctly called 'red' or various objects that are correctly called 'globes'. In addition, when we use general terms, our imagination brings to mind lots of specific ideas of resembling objects, ideas of other red objects or ideas of other globes. The imagination here operates 'by custom'. Finally, if we make a mistake when using a general term, we are also so constituted that we are able to correct it. Should one think, 'No persons are snub-nosed', a counter-example will occur to one, if there are counter-examples one can be aware of. Note that this explanation of our use of general terms invokes the imagination at important points; below we will see other tasks the imagination performs.

In his arguments, Hume maintains that we cannot separate out features in the way proponents of abstract ideas appear to have thought we can. We cannot literally conceive, Hume thinks, of some abstract triangle which contains or models the triangularity every triangle (equilateral, isosceles, large, small, etc.) somehow is supposed to have. As he says, ''tis impossible to form an idea of an object, that is possest of quantity and quality, and yet is possest of no precise degree of either'.[22] Hume asserts, for example, 'When a globe of white marble is presented, we receive only the impression of a white colour dispos'd in a certain form, nor are we able to separate and distinguish the colour from the form'.[23] But this cannot be Hume's final word; if it were, then he would be denying himself access to the systematic ability underlying creativity which he is clearly aware we do have. To refer to a previous example: If one's idea of orange cannot be separated from an idea of circularity, then it is not a simple idea. This is so because, by definition, simple ideas are the ones that can be so separated. But then one is not going to be able to form an idea of *that* orange in a different shape. And now the theory leaves as highly questionable the thesis that if one has an idea of an orange circle and an idea of a brown equilateral triangle, one *therewith* becomes able to have the idea of an orange equilateral triangle.[24]

Not only do we lose our systematic ability to recombine such ideas, but, further, what Hume is saying *seems* to involve a staggering error, another sign that we may well not be interpreting him correctly. It is false that the colour of a particular circle one sees cannot be separated from that shape and size or that the colour of a particular globe cannot be separated from that globe. One could cut up the circle and rearrange the pieces; one could break off tile-like pieces from the globe and rearrange them. Further, Hume holds a thesis which entails, and could be used to explain, such possibilities.[25] According to Hume, extended surfaces are made up of physical points which are neither divisible nor extended; they are non-extended points. Any other extension, on Hume's account, can be regarded as decomposable into its points or atoms. Such an atomistic view makes it possible for the points to be rearranged. Further, according to Hume, our visual field is similarly constituted by such points. The thesis that our visual fields are so constituted makes the rearrangement particularly accessible to our imaginations. What this suggests is that when Hume says we cannot separate the colour from the form, he means that we cannot get the colour alone, without any shape. This is quite different from saying that we cannot get the colour without the particular shape it has at some one time.

It may be a mistake to push Hume further on the problem of reconciling a fruitful account of simple ideas with his denial of abstract ideas. For one thing, the area in which he is working is enormously difficult and it is arguable that every extant theory in the area is full of problems. More immediately concerned with our project is the fact that Hume has not pushed himself to a final explanation, as we can see from the fact that his account of abstract ideas simply invokes without explanation our ability to spot similarities.

We have looked at some of the central ingredients of Hume's theory of ideas. But what is the theory a theory *of*, what is it supposed to be explaining?

Of course, one thing the theory is telling us is what sensing and thinking are. The first is the having of impressions; the second the having of ideas. Hence, among other things, the theory is Hume's first move in building a theory of our perception of an external world. Hearing, seeing and feeling just are having impressions, as far as what goes on *inside* of us is concerned. But the theory is to tell us more than this. Thus the theory will deliver an account of belief, as we will shortly see. That is, the theory will tell us the difference between, for example, imagining it is cold outside and believing that it is. In addition, the theory yields quite directly a theory of meaning.[26] 'If you tell me, that any person is in love, I easily understand your meaning, and form a just conception of his situation', where understanding the meaning and forming a just conception consist in, it is clear from the context, having ideas.[27]

A major condition on meaningfulness which Hume proposes, one of his most important critical tools, follows from Hume's theses that all complex ideas are composed of simple ideas, that all simple ideas are derived from impressions and that meanings require ideas:

> When we entertain, therefore, any suspicion that a philosophical term is employed without any meaning or idea (as is but too frequent), we need but enquire, *from what impression is that supposed idea derived?* And if it be impossible to assign any, this will serve to confirm our suspicion.[28]

There are strict limits on the impressions we can have and these limits transfer into conditions on what ideas we can have and so on what we can intelligibly say.

There is a further aspect to the theory of ideas which needs emphasizing. From the start, Hume's examples of impressions give a prominent place to the impressions of reflection, our passions and emotions. This feature reflects the importance in Hume's philosophy of the non-rational aspect of human nature. In what follows we will be looking at Hume's descriptions of the mechanisms underlying many of our most important beliefs. As we will see, the roles of imagination and custom or instinct are very central. At the same time, some of Hume's discussion may make us wonder about whether, in Hume's philosophy, our ordinary beliefs are really all that likely to be true. Hence, it is very important to realize that Hume does not recommend that we abandon all these beliefs. What he in general is recommending will be discussed principally in the final section below.

We will next look at (i) Knowledge and Causation, (ii) The Existence of the External World and Personal Identity, and (iii) The Question of Humean Scepticism.

KNOWLEDGE AND CAUSATION

In the *Treatise*, Hume distinguishes between knowledge, proofs and probabilities.[29] Hume reserves the title 'knowledge' for those beliefs which cannot be false; for example, the belief that two plus two is four. The thesis that knowledge is restricted to what cannot be false is largely present in Locke and quite clearly derives from Descartes. *Proofs* belong to a species of belief commonly regarded as particularly well grounded and exceeding our merely probable beliefs. We could see 'knowledge' and 'proofs' as technical terms which together cover a significant amount of what we would ordinarily count as knowledge.

The distinction between knowledge and proofs stems from Hume's difficult theory of relations; similar material, in a more accessible form, can be found in the *Enquiry*. In the *Enquiry*, the corresponding material is introduced with a distinction between relations of ideas and matters of fact.[30] Relations of ideas, like knowledge in the *Treatise,* cannot be false; our discovery of them depends, Hume says, merely on the operation of thought. That $3 \times 5 =$ one half of 30, a relation of ideas, is something of which we can be wholly certain, however the course of nature unfolds. Matters of fact, on the other hand, *can* be false in the sense that they are not necessarily true. To use Hume's example, however sure we are that the sun will rise tomorrow, it is possible that our belief is false. We can always imagine what it would be like for such a belief to be false, Hume maintains. Hence, though our evidence for it can be great, it cannot measure up to that we can have for relations of ideas.

Those matter of fact beliefs for which our evidence is great include the 'proofs' of the *Treatise*. While Hume does allow that we do sometimes have proofs and that our evidence for matter of fact beliefs can be very great, he is typically seen as a sceptic about such beliefs. That is, he is typically interpreted as doubting or denying that we have any knowledge in such areas even when we use 'knowledge' in a much weaker sense than Hume uses it. He is so interpreted because he maintains that there cannot be any good arguments for our matter of fact beliefs. More precisely, he maintains this about our matter of fact beliefs which go beyond our beliefs about our present sensory environment, and our memories of such environments. Hume thinks that our matter of fact beliefs which are about things we do not and have not observed cannot be supported by any good arguments.[31]

In both the *Treatise* and the *Enquiry*, Hume's arguments for the claim that a host of our supposedly very probable matter of fact beliefs cannot be founded on argumentation begin with a discussion of necessary connexions and what we can know about them.[32] Hume's central claim in the *Enquiry* is that our matter of fact beliefs about the unobserved require connexions: 'And here it is constantly supposed that there is a connexion between the present fact and that which is inferred from it. Were there nothing to bind them together, the inference would be entirely precarious'.[33] If As are merely followed by and not connected with Bs, then the occurrence of an A places no restrictions on the occurrence of alternatives to B. If smoking is not connected to lung cancer, then the mere fact that someone is a smoker does not make lung cancer any more probable than not. If, as far as what we observe goes, there are no connections, then, as far as what we observe goes, B is no more probable than any alternative to B. But, Hume adds in, we do not observe any necessary connections. Thus, as far as what we do observe goes, for each cause there are a vast number of possible results each of which is, in an important sense, as possible as any other.

Suppose, then, one has observed an A followed by a B, where as far as anything one observed goes, there was a vast array of alternatives to B each of which was as likely as B. It would certainly be rash – and irrational – to expect a B before one occurs. Suppose, again, that one observes the conjunction repeating, though as far as observation goes, each time a B occurred, it had a host of equally likely alternatives. Let us add in (as Hume does) the fact that even our best reasoning by itself, and in operating on our observations, also failed to reveal any connections. Under such suppositions, can we really have strong reasons for thinking that a B will occur, given that an A has occurred? Remember, if there are no connections, then there are a host of alternatives to a B, each of which is as likely as a B. Just because of this, the prospects of one's getting a good argument securing the conclusion that a B will occur are very dim.

Hume does consider whether we might shore up an argument going from present and past observations to a conclusion about the unobserved by adding in a general belief about uniformity, namely, that the future will resemble the past (or the unobserved resembles the observed). The answer is that we do not really improve the argument. If there are no connections, the claim that the future will resemble the past is at least as doubtful as is the idea that a B will occur when an A next occurs. Hence, an argument for 'The future will resemble the past' has the same sort of problem that is had by an argument for the claim that a B will occur when an A next occurs. If 'The future will resemble the past' is needed to shore up an argument concluding that B will occur, it is every bit as much needed for any argument to show the general conclusion that the future will resemble the past. But, clearly, with the more general conclusion we have reached a position that cannot be shored up by 'The future will resemble the past', because that would make our argument circular.

We may worry that Hume is unnecessarily restricting what he is willing to count as a good argument. Even if we concede that we cannot construct a good argument *directly* from 'As and Bs have been conjoined in the past' to 'If an A occurs tomorrow, then a B will occur', might not there be some sort of legitimate argument from conjunctions to connections which would solve the problem Hume has located?

Hume has an argument against such an objection. The argument is an attack on the legitimacy of the notion of necessary connection. And his conclusion is that in so far as necessary connections are supposed to be more than constant conjunctions, they are in the observer, not the observed. Before we look at this attack, we need to consider Hume's positive account of how we do acquire beliefs about the unobserved.

How, then, does Hume think we manage to have any beliefs about the unobserved? Hume argues that our judgements are founded on our observations of constant conjunctions. Our belief that eating some piece of bread will nourish us depends on our having observed in the past a regular conjunction between eating bread and being nourished. When we have observed a series of conjunctions between two types of objects, we pronounce the one a cause of the other. And given an observation of the cause, we expect the effect. The details of this transition from the experience of a cause to an expectation of the effect are very important.

Such transitions draw on the imagination and custom or instinct. It just is a basic fact about the way our minds operate that our observations of a series of conjunctions among As and Bs will lead us to expect a B when we perceive an A. Further, there will be a transfer of vivacity from our impression of A to our idea of B. When vivacity is transferred to the idea of B, it counts as a belief, for beliefs just are more vivacious ideas in such a relation to a present impression.[34] The difference between merely raising the possibility that it is cold outside and believing it is cold outside is the fact that in the latter case, the idea has much more vivacity. 'Thus', Hume concludes, 'all probable reasoning is nothing but a species of sensation'.[35] It is a matter of how you feel.

How, then, does Hume argue that any connection which is more than constant conjunction is in ourselves, not in the objects we pronounce connected? The argument rests on the theory of ideas. If we have an idea, we must have had the relevant impression(s).[36] The only possible relevant impression sources for an idea of necessary connection are (i) our experience of constant conjunctions and (ii) our inferential reactions to such experiences. Thus, any content to our idea of necessary connection which goes beyond constant conjunctions comes from our inferential reactions. Hume concludes, 'Either we have no idea of necessity, or necessity is nothing but that determination of the thought to pass from causes to effects and from effects to causes, according to their experienc'd union.'[37] Hume accordingly gives two definitions of cause; the first gives us 'cause' in terms of constant conjunction, the second in terms of our inferences.[38]

Just as other philosophers, prominent among them Locke, have argued that colours-as-seen are really in the mind and merely projected onto the world, Hume holds that necessary connections are really just in the mind.

> 'Tis a common observation, that the mind has a great propensity
> to spread itself on external objects, and to conjoin with them
> any internal impressions, which they occasion, and which always
> make their appearance at the same time that these objects
> discover themselves to the senses ... Mean while 'tis sufficient

to observe, that the same propensity is the reason, why we suppose necessity and power to lie in the objects we consider, not in our mind, that considers them; notwithstanding it is not possible for us to form the most distant idea of that quality, when it is not taken for the determination of the mind, to pass from the idea of an object to that of its usual attendant.[39]

But, Hume holds, it is literally unintelligible to ascribe our inferential reactions to the things regarding which we are inferring. Hence, it is literally unintelligible to ascribe necessary connections to items we are saying are causally related.

> But when ... we make the terms of power and efficacy signify something, of which we have a clear idea, and which is incompatible with those objects, to which we apply it, obscurity and error begin then to take place, and we are led astray by a false philosophy. This is the case, when we transfer the determination of the thought to external objects, and suppose any real intelligible connexion betwixt them.[40]

To think of one thing as necessitating another is to think of one thing as a proof of another; that is, to think of one as a premise and the other as a conclusion.[41] And this is not, strictly speaking, something of which we can make sense.

From what we have just seen, one might well expect Hume to be a thorough sceptic about our beliefs about the unobserved and doubt or deny any statements which go beyond what we have observed. However, Hume's philosophy is full of causal generalizations which go way beyond what Hume could have observed. Hume in fact gives us rules by which we are to distinguish between good and bad causal judgements. Further, he does not take any doubts about our ability to know the unobserved to compel a silence about, for example, how human minds he has not observed do in fact work. Moreover, Hume uses his discussion of causation to propose a solution, in a frankly non-sceptical way, to the problem of freewill. In discussing freewill Hume gives us the first thorough articulation of a compatibilist position; that is, a position which says we can be both causally determined and morally responsible. Hume's arguments for compatibilism draw heavily on his two definitions of causation and Hume presents us as having a vast array of non-problematic beliefs about various constant conjunctions which go way beyond what we could have observed. Accordingly, we cannot simply assert that Hume was sceptical about all such beliefs.

None the less, Hume was acutely aware of the sceptical possibilities in his treatment of causation:

> The sceptic ... justly insists ... that nothing leads us to this

> inference [regarding the unobserved] but custom or a certain
> instinct of our nature; which it is indeed difficult to resist, but
> which, like other instincts, may be fallacious and deceitful.
> While the sceptic insists upon these topics, he shows his force,
> or rather, indeed, his own and our weakness; and seems, for
> the time at least, to destroy all assurance and conviction.[42]

At the same time, Hume does not conclude this discussion by endorsing
the scepticism. Rather, he maintains that the scepticism ought to be
rejected, because no durable good can come from it. (Notice, however,
that he does not attack the truth of the sceptic's premises or the power
of the sceptical arguments.)

As we have found, though Hume raises very serious, sceptical
questions about the content and justification of many of our ordinary
causal statements, he does make some causal statements himself. We
might well be tempted to see this as just inconsistent or, perhaps worse,
very sloppy. But Hume is much too good a philosopher for either
epithet to explain adequately a wide-spread feature of his thought.
Rather, what he is dealing with is a general and profound philosophical
problem. This is a topic we will return to in the final section below.

We have looked principally at the relation between Hume's
account of causation and his assessment of our beliefs about the unobserved. This is the emphasis in the *Enquiry*. There is another aspect of
Hume's discussion, part of which is placed more in the foreground in
the *Treatise*, which has been mentioned briefly and which we should
look at in a little more detail. Many seventeenth-and eighteenth-century
philosophers had, we might say, a problem about causation. Many had
reasons for believing that there are three domains in which causation
operates or *appears* to operate: (1) God causes events in the world; (2)
we cause our actions and (3) events in the world cause each other. It
is not easy to see how these three tasks can all be performed. For
example, if God causes physical events and physical events cause each
other (which already may look to be too much), there seems to be
little or no causation left for us to effect. And if there is nothing left
which requires our causing, how can we be responsible for any of
our actions? Hume's discussion of causation intersects with this larger
problem of causation at several points. As we have seen, Hume uses
his account of causation to argue that we can be both causally determined and morally responsible. And Hume attacks the seeming obvi-
ousness of some of the principles which create the problem of causation.
For example, he argues that the principle that every event has a cause,
which underlies many proofs for the existence of God, is not self-
evidently true.

We may feel, as some seventeenth- and eighteenth-century philosophers did, that causation by both God and worldly events is too much. Malebranche, and Berkeley in part under his influence, both did and both saw themselves as removing or downgrading causation among worldly events. What we think of as causation among worldly events is really just a matter of regularity or constant conjunction which is arranged by God, they each maintained. Genuine causation, which they thought of as embodying a kind of necessity, was reserved for another realm. It looks to be the case that Hume is in part reacting to just this picture. For Hume actively argues for the view that all there is to genuine causation among material objects is constant conjunction; what he adds is the denial that there are special necessitating connections anywhere.

❦ BODIES AND SELVES ❦

Hume tells us at the beginning of his discussion of body in the *Treatise* that 'We may well ask, *What causes induce us to believe in the existence of body?* but 'tis in vain to ask, *Whether there be body or not?* That is a point, which we must take for granted in all our reasonings'.[43] And Hume says that as a consequence he will restrict his attention to the question of what causes us to believe in bodies which are external to and independent of us, and which may continue to exist when we cease to perceive them. Hume's readers of this discussion have reason to wonder whether he is being disingenuous. For it very much looks as though Hume gives us an account which fails to reveal our belief in body as anything we would be willing to describe ourselves as in fact taking for granted. None the less, Hume is serious. And what we will come to see is that what we 'take for granted' may show the efficacy, in Hume's philosophy, of the imagination, even when it is at odds with reason.

There are strong similarities between Hume's discussion of our belief in body in the *Treatise* and the *Enquiry*. In each of them, Hume considers two accounts of what the belief in body is, what its content amounts to. The first is the belief held by the vulgar ('that is, all of us, at one time or other').[44] Their belief in continued and distinct bodies is really a belief about their perceptions. Hume tells us, '[T]he vulgar confound perceptions and objects, and attribute a distinct continu'd existence to the very things they feel or see'.[45] He maintains, 'The very image, which is present to the senses, is with us the real body'.[46] This is a very striking attribution and we need to ask why Hume thinks we do so confound.

In part the attribution is the result of Hume's general thesis that ideas and so meanings are determined by impressions. But we can also see two further components behind Hume's claim that we do so believe. In part he is representing us as direct realists; we believe that what we see – for example, a chair or a table – is immediately[47] present to us. Many philosophers would agree with Hume that the vulgar are such direct realists. Additional to this is Hume's account of how we come to believe this. It is really this last part which has the implication that our direct realism consists in beliefs about perceptions. According to Hume, the belief held by the vulgar is not the product of reasoning or argumentation; the vulgar do not reach the belief by 'reasoning beyond' their perceptions. As a consequence, the vulgar must be understood as having beliefs not based on their perceptions, but instead as in some sense *about* their perceptions. We will later look more at the details of this account.

At the same time, our belief that tables and chairs are directly present to us is unstable, at least for someone constructing a science of the mind.

> [T]he slightest philosophy ... teaches us, that nothing can ever be present to the mind but an image or perception, and that the senses are only the inlets, through which these images are conveyed, without being able to produce any immediate intercourse between the mind and the object. The table, which we see, seems to diminish, as we remove farther from it: but the real table, which exists independent of us, suffers no alteration: it was, therefore, nothing but its image, which was present to the mind.[48]

Thus our direct realism does not withstand the slightest scrutiny. It involves a fiction which Hume appears to count as literally false.[49]

Before we look more carefully at the details, we should consider Hume's second account of what the belief in body amounts to. Because the belief of the vulgar is so clearly problematic, philosophers tend to replace direct realism with a theory about two distinct existences. The philosophers' view is that there are internal images, directly present to us, which are caused by and resemble bodies which are external to us. This thesis of 'a double existence'[50] is what, on Hume's second account, a belief in bodies involves.

The philosophers' conception of body is hardly unproblematic. The universal opinion of us all – that is, the belief of the vulgar – is the product of primary instincts. It is something we find difficult to resist. But once we see its problems, and attempt to replace it, we end up unable to support the new view. We cannot simply maintain that, like our beliefs about the unobserved, the thesis of a double existence is merely a matter of custom and instinct. For, as we have seen, custom and instinct do not lead us to the philosophers' view; rather, they lead to the vulgar view. Neither, however, will we be able to produce a convincing argument for the philosophers' view. For we should argue for such a view as we would for any causal thesis. That is, we should start to observe whether the relevant constant conjunctions obtain. 'But here experience is, and must be entirely silent'.[51] All we have present to us, Hume maintains, is one sort of conjunct, the images. We cannot reach around our perceptions to see if they are constantly conjoined with resembling objects. Hence, we have *no* good argument for the causal thesis that our perceptions are caused by resembling objects.

When we take the existence of body for granted, then, we either believe something false or assent to something for which we cannot have a good argument. Further, in addition to the fact that we cannot successfully argue for the philosophers' view, that view seems plausible only because of our original assent to the vulgar view. If we had not started with a natural tendency to think we do perceive something which is independent of us, we never would have been tempted to construct the double existence view.[52]

Consequently, if it is vain to ask whether there is body, if that is something we *must* take for granted, it is not because the belief in body is luminously true. Rather, we must take it for granted the way a ball whose movement is unimpeded must move when struck. That is, our belief in body is causally fixed.

There are some aspects of Hume's description of how vulgar belief in bodies is causally fixed which particularly merit close attention. Hume argues that the belief in an external body which continues to exist even when not observed is not the product of the senses or of reason; instead it is the product of the imagination. What sets the imagination off is the fact that our perceptions have a coherence and constancy. Our perceptions cohere in that they appear according to regular patterns; the sight of a hand knocking on a door is regularly conjoined with the sound of a knock. Further, this coherence is much greater and more uniform if we suppose the directly perceived objects to have also continued existence when not perceived. And 'as the mind is once in the train of observing an uniformity among objects, it naturally continues, till it renders the uniformity as compleat as possible'.[53] Thus we naturally 'read' our experience as experience with continuing objects.

Even more influential is the constancy. Constancy consists in the great similarities among perceptions which leads us to judge that some object is being re-experienced. Hume notes, '[We find] that the perception of the sun or ocean, for instance, returns upon us after an absence or annihilation with like parts and in a like order, as at its first appearance'.[54] In such cases, we tend to think of the perceptions as really the same individual from one time to the next. Hume tells us, '[W]e are not apt to regard these interrupted perceptions as different, (which they really are) but on the contrary consider them as individually the same, upon account of their resemblance.'[55] We have such a tendency because their similarity means the imagination passes from one to the other with great ease and in such a case, surveying the different perceptions feels very like a surveying of a single object. As a consequence, we confound a succession with an identity and attribute sameness to every succession of such related objects.[56]

The claim that interrupted perceptions amount, none the less, to *the same thing* does ask that we account for how they can be both one thing and interrupted. We respond to this by 'feigning a continu'd being, which may fill those intervals, and preserve a perfect and entire identity to our perceptions'.[57] We in effect create the *fiction* of a continued existence: 'This propension to bestow an identity on our resembling perceptions, produces the fiction of a continu'd existence; . . . that fiction, as well as the identity, is really false, as is acknowledg'd by all philosophers'.[58]

As we have seen, the philosophers respond to such a view, by attempting to replace it with a thesis of double existence. But the philosophers' view is simply the monstrous offspring of two contrary principles: the imagination's propensity to ascribe an identity to distinct perceptions and reflection's insistence that 'our resembling perceptions are interrupted in their existence and different from each other'.[59]

The imagination's propensity to feign an identity is strong enough that we will succumb to it. However, when we return to Hume's critical perspective we may well want to say, with him, that

> I feel myself *at present* of a quite contrary sentiment, and am more inclin'd to repose no faith at all in my senses, or rather, imagination, than to place in it such an implicit confidence. I cannot conceive how such trivial qualities of the fancy, conducted by such false suppositions, can ever lead to any solid and rational system.[60]

There are several points at which one might object to what Hume is saying. For example, we might insist that he is wrong in describing our starting-point. We might insist that we start, not with our internal impressions, but with our shareable observations of a public world. Or we might question Hume's reasons for maintaining that we have no good reason for believing the philosophers' thesis of a double existence, with impressions on the one hand and resembling objects causing them on the other. His reason here is that we cannot verify this causal thesis the way we need to be able to; we cannot reach around our impressions to check on the existence of the resembling causes. One might object that Hume has placed his standards of proof too high. We often do, as a matter of fact, make inferences about classes of causes which we cannot observe. Such inferences are inferences about the best sort of explanation a phenomenon has. An example of such inferring was the inference to the existence of a gene in advance of our even being able to specify what its chemical composition is.[61]

Whatever the best philosophical position here is, it is important in understanding Hume that we realize that he has other attacks on body, on the coherence of a supposition that there is a publicly accessible world of material objects, which support his view. Hume argues that our thought regarding material objects is subject to further infections by imagination. Thus, Hume maintains, the imagination is apt to feign something unknown and invisible to make sense of our conviction that bodies are more than momentary and unstable clusters of qualities. This is *substance, or original and first matter*.[62] Such fictions are formalized in 'the antient philosophy',[63] but their effects are also present in ordinary thought.

In addition, Hume agrees with, and adds to, Berkeley's attack on the primary/secondary quality distinction. Hume takes learned opinion, 'modern philosophy', to assert that 'colours, sounds, tastes, smells, heat and cold ... [are] nothing but impressions in the mind, deriv'd from the operation of external objects'.[64] On this modern view, primary qualities – extension and solidity in their different mixtures and modifications – are the only properties really possessed by external, material objects. But, Hume objects, if secondary qualities are really in the mind, so also must primary qualities be. To suppose otherwise is to suppose the possibility of a kind of separating which, in his discussion of abstract ideas, Hume has argued is impossible.[65] Hume concludes:

> Bereave matter of all its intelligible qualities, both primary and secondary, you in a manner annihilate it, and leave only a certain unknown, inexplicable *something*, as the cause of our perceptions; a notion so imperfect, that no sceptic will think it worth while to contend against it.[66]

At several points in his discussion of bodies, some of which we have not explicitly considered, Hume appeals to the activity of the imagination. In the *Treatise* he contrasts the principles of the imagination which give rise to our reasonings concerning cause and effect with those principles which give us our belief in an external and independent world. The former are the more reputable; the latter are trivial.[67] (This contrast appears to be rejected in the *Enquiry*.)[68] As we will see, the less reputable principles of the imagination are also at work in our construction of our concept of ourselves.

Hume wants to place his discussion of the self in the context of a discussion of bodies. But the perspective in this discussion of bodies will be quite different from the discussion seen above. In discussing personal identity, Hume takes it for granted that there are planets, mountains, plants and animals. And he examines how we think about the identity of such things in order to extract some general principles to enlighten our discussion of the self.

We do think of plants and animals (and planets and mountains) as continuing to exist through a series of losses, or increments, of parts. Suppose someone removes a thorn from a rose bush. The rose bush is still there, we may feel very inclined to say, even though it now has one less thorn. Hume disagrees. He maintains that, strictly speaking, any mass of matter is the same mass only if there is no addition or subtraction of any matter.[69] Why do we think otherwise? The answer is one we have seen before: as long as the change is small, the passage of thought (the imagination) from the earlier to the later objects is so smooth and easy that we take the case to be one of identity.

Hume maintains that there are other describable general reasons why we disregard change and pronounce identity. For example, we do not take gradual and insensible change to interrupt identity. Another factor: we can even combine identity and a large change if the parts function toward some common end or purpose which is not destroyed by the changes. For example, an extensively repaired ship or remodeled house may be allowed to be the same ship or house. In addition, when the parts interact in promoting the common end, we can tolerate vast changes in matter. Thus, nearly all of the matter of a large tree will be different from that in a sapling planted, let us suppose, thirty years ago. This need not impede a judgement that the older tree *is* the tree planted thirty years ago. Finally, if the nature of the object is to be changeable, we may disregard change. Thus we speak of the same part of a river even when the river is rapidly flowing.

If Hume is right, then our ordinary talk of material objects is replete with error. None of the seemingly familiar objects in our present environment can have really existed for very long, despite our great inclination to believe otherwise. Given we make these errors, it is going to seem less odd to think we are making a similar error about ourselves. And Hume is going to maintain that we are wrong in the way we think about ourselves. Understanding what errors Hume thinks we make is made difficult by the fact that Hume appears to reject his initial discussion. In an appendix to the *Treatise*,[70] he seems to take it back, apparently telling us his two main principles are not consistent. Thus the account Hume gives us in the body of *Treatise* is presented with a confidence we need to regard as provisional.

Hume's discussion in 'Of personal identity' begins with an attack on Descartes, among others:

> There are some philosophers, who imagine we are every moment
> intimately conscious of what we call our SELF; that we feel
> its existence and its continuance in existence; and are certain,
> beyond the evidence of a demonstration, both of its perfect
> identity and simplicity. . . . [N]or is there any thing, of which
> we can be certain, if we doubt of this.[71]

Hume maintains that this description cannot be the description of a
genuine, contentful idea of the self. Such a self is supposed to exist at
every moment of our lives, yet we are without any awareness of such
a continuant. It is, further, something supposedly additional to our
perceptions, something which *has* the perceptions. Not only do we
lack any impression of such a continuant, all we do have are our
changing impressions. Nothing in our experience gives content to an
idea of, or provides evidence for, such a continuant.

Having attacked the idea that Cartesian self-reflection supports a
view of the self as that to which all our perceptions are referred, Hume
attempts, first, to explain why we have thought the Cartesian view of
the self is so plausible, and, second, to tell us what the truth is. We
find the Cartesian view plausible because of a tendency we have seen
Hume discuss above.[72] As we have seen in the case of body, when the
passage of the imagination is very smooth as it surveys a diversity of
perceptions or (what is for Hume) a series of trees, we have a tendency
to pronounce the case to be one of identity. Similarly in the case of
the mind, the easy transition of the imagination in its survey of our
perceptions leads us to think of the self in terms of identity, and not
diversity. In both such cases we 'substitute the notion of identity,
instead of that of related objects'.[73] Nor do we stop with the self at
'boldly assert[ing] that these different related objects are in effect the
same, however interrupted and variable'.[74] Rather,

> In order to justify to ourselves this absurdity, we often feign
> some new and unintelligible principle, that connects the objects
> together, and prevents their interruption or variation. Thus we
> feign the continu'd existence of the perceptions of our senses,
> to remove the interruption; and run into the notion of a *soul*,
> and *self*, and *substance*, to disguise the variation.[75]

As what we have just seen suggests, Hume thinks that our tendency to pronounce identity when we really have diversity does not
merely result in a verbal flourish. Rather, we take on a commitment to
a further kind of being. Thus, our propensity to declare identity when
there is really diversity is compounded by a tendency of ours to
think there is something more which is really unchanging and identical.
We do this with our creation of the fiction of the self or soul. But even

when our reaction to diversity is not as extreme as inventing a further thing to be there, we are still apt to 'imagine something unknown and mysterious, connecting the parts, beside their relation'.[76]

In the case of ourselves, as in the case of ordinary material objects, certain relations among the diverse elements leads us to pronounce identity. With ourselves, the diverse elements are perceptions and the relations are similarity and causation.[77] It is largely memory which accounts for the similarity among perceptions; and this similarity does promote an easy passage of the mind from one cluster of perceptions to another. Memory supplies us with copies of earlier perceptions and, as copies, they will be similar. In addition, our perceptions are causally interrelated, as again memory helps us to see. Impressions cause ideas which in turn can cause other impressions and ideas. The self is, then, an evolving cluster of perceptions related by similarity and causality.

In his famous misgivings in an appendix, Hume reviews his conception of the self and shows it to be anchored in two theses which he cannot renounce: '*that all our distinct perceptions are distinct existences*, and *that the mind never perceives any real connexion among distinct existences.*'[78]

Hume appears to say that these principles positively block any satisfactory account of the unity of the self, or at least that he cannot find a way to unite these principles with a needed, better account. The implication is that his earlier account of the self is defective and that he cannot do any better. His reaction to the resulting philosophical problem is to declare himself a moderate sceptic, who avoids any dogmatic conclusion and instead pleads the problem is too difficult for him to understand. That Hume declares himself a moderate sceptic is significant, as we will see.

❧ A CONCLUSION REGARDING ❧ SCEPTICISM

Hume's work is informed by the radical idea that in the most important aspects of human life – over a vast range of phenomena – we are and *must be* creatures ruled by custom and instinct, where this contrasts to being continuously guided by rational argumentation. To describe a set of beliefs, attitudes and actions as irrational in this way is not necessarily to denigrate them. In fact, one can easily and consistently hold that some patterns in our lives are very beneficial and even efficient in getting us true beliefs without thinking of them as consisting in rational arguments.

Hume's work has, however, often been regarded as negative and destructive. While Hume tells us that the remarkable outpouring of his own youth, *A Treatise of Human Nature, 'fell dead-born from the Press*, without reaching such distinction as even to excite a Murmur among the Zealots',[79] this comment looks like wishful thinking. The radical and ambitious *Treatise* in fact cost Hume dearly. As Mossner, his biographer, remarks:

> the *Treatise* was sufficiently alive in 1745 to lose for Hume the Professorship of Ethics and Pneumatical Philosophy at Edinburgh. . . . {And} after a quiescent period of more than a decade, the 'Murmur among the Zealots' began to rise in the 1750s, reaching something like a roar in the 1770s.[80]

The idea that Hume's work is full of perverse errors has persisted down to our own time. The latest such view of Hume is Antony Flew's. Flew refers to what he terms 'the strangeness, the often self-frustrating perversity'[81] of some of Hume's positions. He takes philosophical discussion of Hume to proceed best by reversing the arguments Hume gives for 'outrageous conclusions'[82] and turning them into disproofs of the premises.

Is Hume's work in the end perversely destructive? Or is he, like Kames and Turnbull,[83] other followers of Hutcheson, confident that our ideas unfold in harmony with the world they seem so obviously to represent? One way to decide this might be to see how much in our ordinary beliefs Hume wants us to discard.

The extent to which Hume thinks we do have satisfactory knowledge of the world around us is currently a matter of very considerable debate among Hume scholars. While some scholars view Hume's work as essentially sceptical,[84] others see Hume as principally a constructive philosopher[85] or as sharply limited in his scepticism.[86] Indeed, it is only recently that the philosophical community has begun to see that Hume's philosophy has many constructive features. In addition, the sort of naturalism Hume espouses – his picture of us as continuous with the brutes, acting and believing instinctively – seems to be increasingly confirmed by recent work in cognitive science. Hence, scholars are still in the process of re-examining the rich and subtle arguments Hume has given us. But at the same time, this ferment means that the community of Hume scholars has not reached a consensus on much at all. There is an ongoing, sometimes heated debate about how to understand Hume's arguments.

I am going to suggest a moderate, safe and easy answer to the question of whether Hume is a sceptic; then I am going to complicate things a bit. Before we approach the answer, however, we need to bring together some of what we have seen of Hume's philosophy. We have looked at some areas regarding which we make knowledge claims (in a less restricted sense of 'knowledge' than we saw Hume use in the

Treatise). That is, we do claim to have some knowledge about some things which we have not observed and about causal relations in which one thing *makes* something else occur. And we do claim to have some knowledge about our external environment. Further, we do think we can often tell quite easily that, for example, the coat we wore yesterday is the same as the one we have on today. Finally, most of us feel quite certain that our selves are substantial things which have mental states and are not just clusters of such states. Taking all these areas together, we should ask whether Hume is a sceptic regarding them.

The safest and easiest answer says that Hume is simply a moderate sceptic. The moderate sceptic eschews excessive or Pyrrhonic scepticism, which, according to Hume,[87] does maintain that we should suspend most or all of our beliefs in the areas we are discussing. A moderate sceptic also urges us to bear in mind our own and others' fallibility, to undertake our investigations cautiously, with the awareness that we are not going to get the answers we want to grand questions about the ultimate truth. In favour of this moderate-sceptic interpretation is the fact that Hume does clearly reject excessive scepticism and does say that his investigations do reveal limits on our ability to know. Indeed, we might say that Hume has a *healthy* scepticism regarding our claims to knowledge, where this means that he stresses that our knowledge is not boundless and that we are far from infallible. Finally, we might add that Hume assigns positive merit to the beliefs we have because of instinct and custom, to our natural beliefs.

Assigning such merit is not, however, a matter of seeing that the more extreme sceptic's arguments are based on false premises or are argued illicitly. Rather, the moderate sceptic offers us a *practical* solution to a problem we tend to think of as a purely theoretical problem. The moderate sceptic addresses issues about how to form our beliefs without continuing to attempt to defeat the claim that the beliefs may not be true.

There is a complication. One thing that Hume is also arguing is that ordinary thought proceeds on metaphysical assumptions that are philosophically indefensible. Our spreading necessity on nature, our fiction of external, resembling objects, and our fiction of a simple, continuing self are all *metaphysically questionable*. The slightest philosophy reveals that much in the beliefs of the vulgar cannot be justified philosophically. Whatever else one can say about the beliefs, we have no good reason to think them true. In addition, Hume's investigations have shown that the modern philosopher has failed to give us acceptable alternatives to the beliefs of the ordinary person.

Thus, taking Hume to be merely a moderate sceptic does not dispel all the tension in his work. Moreover, if we picture Hume as a moderate sceptic who is prepared to concede that truth may reside with the extreme sceptic, then the confidence with which the *Treatise* opens and the enthusiasm with which Hume continues his investigations in Books II and III become quite puzzling. It is hard to believe that Hume really is prepared to concede that most or all of what he says in Books II and III may be false.

A genuinely adequate model for the place of scepticism in Hume's work may have to put even more thoroughly into question the idea that a great philosopher must attempt to give us the final, true answer on the questions addressed. Such a model could pick out several different personas and perspectives in Hume's work, among them that of the vulgar, the modern philosopher, the extreme sceptic, the moderate sceptic and the scientist of the mind, the last being the persona who continues with Books II and III of the *Treatise*. The scientist of the mind, we could say, turns the moderate sceptic's practical solution of ignoring the excessive sceptic into a theoretical verdict against that sceptic's claim to have the truth.[88]

Somewhat similarly, we might question whether we need or can get the final truth about how best to understand Hume. Late twentieth-century post-modernism has put in question in many areas the insistence that there be one right answer. If we keep such a view in mind as we read Hume, we may see a philosopher who is even more radical than has been thought.

❧ NOTES ❧

1 [6.5]. Page references to the *Treatise* are to this edition.
2 [6.4], 174. Page references to *An Enquiry concerning Human Understanding* and those to *An Enquiry concerning the Principles of Morals* are to this edition. The second *Enquiry* begins with p. 167.
3 [6.4], 150.
4 I am indebted here to conversations with John Yolton. See [6.32].
5 See [6.4], section XII, part one.
6 [6.5], 159–60.
7 See [6.22], chs V and VI.
8 See [6.31], 221–30.
9 [6.5], 1.
10 [6.5], 2.
11 [6.5], 3, 6.
12 Though as we will see with the principles of association, there is considerable activity in the mind at other junctures.
13 [6.4], 18.
14 [6.4], 19.
15 Ibid.
16 Hume's word, [6.5], 4.

17 [6.5], 5.
18 For a useful discussion of this issue, see [6.29], 33–5.
19 [6.5], 11.
20 Ibid.
21 See [6.5], 24, 'they can become general in their representation, and contain an infinite number of ideas under them'.
22 [6.5], 20.
23 [6.5], 25.
24 One might see Hume as attempting to resurrect the thesis through distinctions of reason as he discusses them in [6.5], 24–5. There are, however, two reasons why this suggestion is faulty. First of all, the rhetoric Hume is employing is all wrong for a discussion of the fundamental ability which underlies all our creative cogitating. Second, the passage does not aim at explaining what is in question; namely, how we manage to recombine ideas of colors and shapes.
25 [6.5], 26–39.
26 As David Pears points out in [6.25], there is some controversy about whether Hume's theory of ideas is principally a theory of meaning or principally a theory of evidence. Like Pears, I think it is concerned with both meaning and evidence.
27 [6.4], 17.
28 [6.4], 22.
29 Hume is not completely consistent in his use of some of the terms central to this discussion, especially the terms 'reason' and 'reasoning' which are sometimes restricted to fairly formal arguments, consisting of premises and conclusions, and sometimes used to encompass a wider class of episodes of thinking. In addition, the distinction between proofs and the merely probable is not made consistently. Thus at points Hume includes proofs under 'probable reasoning'.
30 [6.4], 25–6. This distinction is an immediate ancestor of the now infamous analytic-synthetic distinction which has been the object of much scrutiny in the second half of the twentieth century. In [6.4] the distinction between proofs and probability is relegated to a footnote; see p. 57, n. 1.
31 My ascription to Hume of this negative assessment is a traditional interpretation; see [6.29]. Several commentators have recently argued against the interpretation. See [6.10] for a discussion of this disagreement.
32 The reader should know that the interpretation given below has a serious point of disagreement with the standard interpretation. On both my and the standard interpretation, Hume locates a problem in our beliefs about the unobserved. On the standard interpretation, the problem is that such beliefs rest on an unsupportable belief that the future will resemble the past. On my interpretation, the problem is fundamentally an ontological one about necessary connections. For a very good version of the standard interpretation, see [6.29], 42–67. I have defended my interpretation in [6.21].
33 [6.4], 26–7.
34 [6.5], 103.
35 Ibid.
36 The appeal I am making here to Hume's theory of ideas is controversial, though it is also the conventional reading. It has been challenged recently by, among others, [6.31] and [6.28]. However, it has been ably defended in [6.30].

37 [6.5], 166.
38 See [6.4], 76–7, and [6.5], 169–72.
39 [6.5], 167.
40 [6.5], 168.
41 [6.4], 76. My interpretation here is not the standard interpretation. The standard interpretation maintains that the determination is a kind of feeling. I have discussed the standard interpretation and argued that it is not fully accurate in [6.20].
42 [6.4], 159.
43 [6.5], 187.
44 [6.5], 205. 'Vulgar' here means just 'ordinary folk'.
45 [6.5], 193.
46 [6.5], 205.
47 Hume's word on [6.5], 212. In believing that what we see is directly present, we believe that we know what we are seeing without having to argue from some sort of visual clues.
48 [6.4], 152.
49 [6.5], 209. See my discussion below.
50 [6.5], 182 and 205.
51 [6.4], 153.
52 [6.5], 215.
53 [6.5], 198.
54 [6.5], 199.
55 [6.5], 199.
56 [6.5], 204.
57 [6.5], 208.
58 [6.5], 209. Of course, fictions do not have to be false, but Hume says that this one is. A work of fiction might tell a story which happens to be true. What makes something a fiction is, roughly, that there is little or no connection in the creator of the fiction between the existence of the fiction and its truth, if such there be.
59 [6.5], 215.
60 [6.5], 217.
61 It is immaterial to my point whether or not we want to say that we can now observe genes (with electron microscopes, for example); rather, the point is merely that we counted ourselves as knowing such genes existed before anyone was willing to say we observed them.
62 [6.5], 220.
63 [6.5], sect. III of part IV of book I.
64 [6.5], 226.
65 The separating in this sort of case would amount to separating colour from *any* shape.
66 [6.4], 155.
67 [6.5], 197 and 217.
68 [6.4], 159.
69 Hume's reasoning here seems at least in part to be a kind of slippery slope argument: In many or most cases, we would agree that subtracting or adding a large mass would destroy identity. Given this, one might argue, small changes

must destroy identity. Otherwise, a series of small changes will add up to a large change and we will have to say both that we do have identity (each small change preserved identity) and that we do not have identity (the large change occurred and, *ex hypothesis*, that destroys identity).

70 [6.5], 633–6.
71 [6.5], 251.
72 Jane McIntyre and Phillip Cummins have suggested to me in conversation that a very careful reading shows that Hume does not genuinely think that the vulgar – we – do have a Cartesian conception of the self. A more focused study would be needed to decide the issue.
73 [6.5], 254.
74 Ibid.
75 Ibid.
76 [6.5], 255.
77 Contiguity, Hume maintains, drops out.
78 [6.5], 636.
79 'Hume's *My Own Life*', quoted in [6.23], 612.
80 [6.23], 117.
81 [6.16], 3.
82 [6.16], 103.
83 See [6.24], 152–238.
84 See, in addition to Flew, [6.19], [6.24], [6.27]. See also [6.12].
85 See especially [6.10]. Both [6.26] and [6.29] are very important as initiating the current revision in our view of Hume.
86 See [6.14], [6.28] and [6.31].
87 Hume's interpretation of Pyrrhonism is questionable; see [6.18].
88 The view of Hume adumbrated here is developed further in my forthcoming 'A New Model of the Place of Scepticism in Hume's Philosophy'. An early version of this paper was presented at the Hume Society Conference in 1993.

❧ BIBLIOGRAPHY ❧

Works by Hume

6.1 *Philosophical Works*, 4 vols, ed. T. Hill Green and T. Hodge Grose, London, Longman, Green, 1875.
6.2 *The Letters of David Hume*, ed. J. Y. T. Grieg, New York and London, Garland Publishing, Inc., 1983.
6.3 *New Letters of David Hume*, ed. E. C. Mossner and R. Klibansky, Oxford, Oxford University Press, 1954. While the standard editions of Hume's works are the above Green and Grose editions, references in this chapter are to the commonly used Nidditch editions:
6.4 *An Enquiry Concerning Human Understanding and An Enquiry Concerning the Principles of Morals*, ed. L. A. Selby-Bigge, 3rd rev. edn by P. H. Nidditch, Oxford, Oxford University Press, 1975.

6.5 *A Treatise of Human Nature*, ed. L. A. Selby-Bigge, 2nd rev. edn by P. H. Nidditch, Oxford, Oxford University Press, 1978.

Other Historical Texts

6.6 *The Philosophical Writings of Descartes*, vols I & II, trans. J. Cottingham, R. Stoothoff, D. Murdoch, Cambridge, Cambridge University Press, 1985.

6.7 Locke, John, *An Essay Concerning Human Understanding*, ed. P. H. Nidditch, Oxford, Oxford University Press, 1975.

6.8 Malebranche, Nicolas *The Search after Truth, Elucidations of the Search after Truth, Philosophical Commentary*, trans. T. M. Lennon and P. J. Olscamp, Ohio, Ohio State University Press, 1980.

Twentieth-century Texts

6.9 Ardal, P. S. *Passion and Value in Hume's Treatise*, Edinburgh, Edinburgh University Press, 1989.

6.10 Baier, A. *A Progress of Sentiments Reflections on Hume's* Treatise, Cambridge, Mass., Harvard University Press, 1991.

6.11 Box, M. A. *The Suasive Art of David Hume*, Princeton, Princeton University Press, 1990.

6.12 Bricke, J. *Hume's Philosophy of Mind*, Princeton, Princeton University Press, 1980.

6.13 Chappell, V. C. (ed.), *Hume A Collection of Critical Essays*, London, MacMillan, 1966.

6.14 Craig, E. *The Mind of God and the Works of Man*, Oxford, Clarendon Press, 1987.

6.15 Danford, J. W. *David Hume and the Problem of Reason Recovering the Human Sciences*, Newhaven, Conn., Yale University Press, 1990.

6.16 Flew, A. *David Hume: Philosopher of Moral Science*, Oxford, Blackwell, 1986.

6.17 —— *Hume's Philosophy of Belief A Study of His First Inquiry*, New York, The Humanities Press, 1961.

6.18 Frede, M. 'The Skeptic's Beliefs', in *Essays in Ancient Philosophy*, Minneapolis, University of Minnesota Press, 1987, pp. 179–200.

6.19 Fogelin, R. J. *Hume's Skepticism in the* Treatise of Human Nature, London, Routledge and Kegan Paul, 1985.

6.20 Jacobson, A. J. 'Inductive Scepticism and Experimental Reasoning in Moral Subjects', *Hume Studies* (Nov. 1989): 325–38.

6.21 —— 'The Problem of Induction: What is Hume's Argument?' *Pacific Philosophical Quarterly* (Sept/Dec. 1987): 265–84.

6.22 Loeb, L. E. *From Descartes to Hume*, Ithaca, Cornell University Press, 1988.

6.23 Mossner, E. C. *The Life of David Hume*, 2nd edn, Oxford, Oxford University Press, 1980.

6.24 Norton, D. F. *David Hume Common-Sense Moralist, Sceptical Metaphysician*, Princeton, Princeton University Press, 1982.

6.25 Pears, D. *Hume's System An Examination of the First Book of his Treatise*, Oxford, Oxford University Press, 1990.

6.26 Smith, N. K. *The Philosophy of David Hume*, London, Macmillan & Co. Ltd., 1941. Repr. New York and London, Garland Publishing, Inc., 1983.

6.27 Stove, D. C. *Probability and Hume's Inductive Scepticism*, Oxford, Oxford University Press, 1973.

6.28 Strawson, G. *The Secret Connexion Causation, Realism, and David Hume*, Oxford, Oxford University Press, 1989.

6.29 Stroud, B. *Hume*, London, Routledge and Kegan Paul, 1977.

6.30 Winkler, K. P. 'The New Hume', *The Philosophical Review* (October 1991): 541–79.

6.31 Wright, J. P. *The Sceptical Realism of David Hume*, Minneapolis, University of Minnesota Press, 1983.

6.32 Yolton, J. *Perceptual Acquaintance from Descartes to Reid*, Oxford, Blackwell, 1984.

CHAPTER 7

Hume: moral and political philosophy

Rosalind Hursthouse

❧ INTRODUCTION ❧

Hume's moral and political philosophy, like his epistemology and meta-physics, originally appeared in *A Treatise of Human Nature*, (henceforth [7.1]), Book III of which, 'Of Morals', was published in 1740. He developed and recast it in a number of essays and dissertations published between 1741 and 1757, (collected together in Hume [7.3]) and in *Inquiry concerning the Principles of Morals* (henceforth [7.2]), published in 1751.

His moral philosophy borrows much from Hutcheson, and his political philosophy at least some from Hobbes and Mandeville.[1] His blending of these disparate elements is entirely his own, as is the *Treatise* attack on the role of reason in morals. The attack may be seen as a continuation of the scepticism of Book I (see chapter 6 of this volume) or even, despite the order of the Books, as having inspired it.[2] Or it may be played down. There is much debate amongst commentators about the extent to which the attack is mitigated in later stages of the Book III of the *Treatise*, and over whether it has been abandoned by the *Enquiry*, or retained in all essentials. Hence Hume has been interpreted as anything from a complete moral sceptic to at least as much of a moral realist as Aristotle. But its presence in the relevant sections of Book II and early sections of Book III is unmistakable, where it is heralded with the battle cry 'Reason is, and ought only to be the slave of the passions, and can never pretend to any other office than to serve and obey them' ([7.1] 415). Hume has reached this conclusion by a number of arguments, regarded by some commentators as conclusive, and by others as 'dreadful'.

179

❧ REASON AND PASSION ❧

Passions, according to Hume, following Locke, are 'secondary impressions' ([7.1], 275), or impressions of reflexion ([7.1], 8, 275). We might expect that *qua* impressions, they are all unmistakable ([7.1], 190) and possess, 'force and liveliness' ([7.1], 1); but this turns out not to be so (see below 'Moral Sentiments'). *Qua* secondary, they proceed from antecedent impressions or ideas, and 'mostly from ideas' ([7.1], 8). Once again following Locke, Hume takes it that all the familiar passions – love, hatred, joy, fear, anger, pride – arise directly or indirectly from the ideas (or impressions) of good or evil, which (unlike Locke), he does not bother to distinguish from the ideas or impressions of pleasure or pain, (*Treatise*, p. 276). Reason, or the understanding, operates with ideas, all of which are 'copy'd from our impressions' ([7.1], 72); it can never give rise to any new idea ([7.1], 164); reasoning is either *demonstrative*, concerned with abstract relations between ideas, or *probable*, concerned with matters of fact, i.e. with causes and effects.

This, in brief is the philosophical psychology that grounds Hume's attack on the role of reason in morals.[3] The historical setting of the attack is as follows. Hutcheson, without attempting to deny that reason is *an* essential determinant of correct moral approbation, had argued against the rationalists' claim that it was the *sole* determinant.[4] For Hutcheson, reason is essential for the very reason that Hume gives in the *Enquiry* ([7.2], 285); it is that faculty which enables us to judge, contrary to false appearances, the truly beneficial or pernicious tendencies of actions and qualities (character traits) to society. Hutcheson's point is that such reasoning would not motivate any creature which lacked our 'moral sense', namely our natural tendency to approve of benevolence, to discern 'beauty' in benevolent actions, or would motivate them differently.

But Hutcheson's claim that practical reasoning (reasoning that leads to action) must operate with the ideas of good and evil antecedently provided by our instincts, affections and moral sense is transmuted by Hume in the *Treatise* into the curious claim that reasoning, even about the probable outcome of action, cannot give rise to any action at all.

He begins by attempting to show '*first*, that reason alone can never be a motive to any action of the will' ([7.1], 413) (or produce any action, passion or volition, since he takes all these as equivalent in this context). Demonstrative reasoning alone is easily dismissed. Clearly it is never the cause of any action, since it is concerned with 'abstract relations', with 'the world of ideas' (ibid.), but the will is concerned with realities (ibid.).

He then considers 'the second operation of the understanding'

([7.1], 414). 'When we have the prospect of pain or pleasure from any object, we feel a consequent emotion or aversion or propensity'; we then cast around looking for ways to avoid or attain the object, i.e. for what action(s) will have these effects. This is (probable) reasoning and 'according as our reasoning varies, our actions receive a subsequent variation. But 'tis evident that the impulse arises not from reason, but is only directed by it' (ibid.).

As many commentators have noted, this argument, as it stands, is very weak.[5] He describes the cases in which 'an aversion or propensity' is already present, and then some reasoning takes place. Naturally, those passions or impulses do not arise from that reasoning which follows them. But this does nothing to show that they may not have arisen from some prior reasoning. Indeed, he seems committed to saying that they have. It is 'the prospect of pain or pleasure from some object' which has given rise to the passion or impulse in question, and this surely must, according to Hume, be the belief that the object will or would cause me pleasure or pain if 'embraced' or unless 'avoided'. And what is such a belief but the outcome of probable reasoning concerning causes and effects?

Taking himself to have established that reason 'alone' cannot produce any action (or volition or passion), Hume argues '*secondly*, that it can never oppose passion in the direction of the will' ([7.1,] 413). 'Nothing' he says, 'can oppose or retard the impulse of passion but a contrary impulse' ([7.1], 415). So, if reason could oppose a passion, it would have to do so by producing such a contrary impulse. But he has just shown (supposedly) that it cannot do this (alone). So it cannot oppose a passion.

He is fully aware that there are cases which we describe in terms of reason opposing passion, and indeed, winning out; for example when my passionate impulse to hit someone is conquered by the consideration that he is much stronger than I am, or that he is my old father and it would be wrong. Following Hutcheson[6] he claims that when we do so 'we speak not strictly and philosophically'. ([7.1], 415, cf. [7.1], 437–8). In truth, what happens in such a case is that a 'calm passion' determines the agent's will ([7.1], 417).

But in order to oppose a violent passion, a calm passion must be actually present, having been 'excited'; and belief, Hume allows, 'is a requisite circumstance to the exciting of all our passions, the calm as well as the violent' ([7.1], 427). Hutcheson, with no axe to grind about the slavishness of reason, is happy to say that 'calm desires' are the product of 'Reason or Reflection'. Of course, such reason employs, or reflects on, ideas of good and evil which are derived from our instincts, affections or moral sense, but it is no less reasoning for that. But Hume gives no account here of what excites the calm passions.

To make what Hume says in these two arguments plausible, we must assume that, unlike Hutcheson, he is using 'reason' in such a way as to exclude its operating with the ideas of *good* (pleasure) or *evil* (pain). That falling in the fire will cause me to feel great pain/evil is not, as we might have supposed, a conclusion of 'reasoning' concerning causes and effects.[7]

His further argument against reason (used at both [7.1], 415 and 458) is also close to one of Hutcheson's and directed against the same targets. The rationalists are taken to maintain that, in some sense, vicious actions (or the desire to do them), are an attempt 'to make (or will) things (to) be what they are not and cannot be', which is as contrary to reason as 'to pretend to alter the certain proportions of numbers' (Clarke) or that such actions declare that what is not so, is so (Wollaston).[8] Against this, Hume argues that a passion is an 'original existence' or 'fact'; as such 'it contains not any representative quality'. Hence it cannot be a *true* or *false* representation. But '(r)eason is the discovery of truth or falsehood' ([7.1], 458); so a passion cannot be 'contradictory to (...) reason', neither 'contrary (n)or conformable to reason.'

His three examples ([7.1], 416) – that it is 'not contrary to reason to prefer the destruction of the whole world to the scratching of my finger', to choose my total ruin to prevent the least uneasiness of a stranger, and to prefer, 'even my own acknowledg'd lesser good to my greater' – all run counter to variations of the principle that the greater good/lesser evil is to be preferred to the lesser good/greater evil, which Clarke regards as being akin to a mathematical axiom, discoverable by pure reason. But it has little bearing on what is supposed to be at issue, namely on whether reason can do anything but 'serve and obey' the passions, and indeed Hume immediately goes on to admit that, in two cases, 'our passions yield to our reason without any opposition' ([7.1], 416).

One case is unproblematic. (I may desire to do certain actions, supposing them to be the means to some desired good; if reason informs me that this supposition is false, the first desires (passions) will immediately cease ([7.1], 416–17). The second is not. Reason 'excites a passion by informing us of the existence of something which is a *proper* object of it' ([7.1], 459, my italics), i.e. something with a tendency to produce (as he says) pain or pleasure or (as he does *not* say here, but to be consistent, should) good or evil. Reason may subsequently discover that this supposition, of the existence of a proper object, is false, whereupon, once again, the passion yields. In this case, as in the former, 'No one can ever regard such errors as a defect in my moral character'. ([7.1], 460).

But this is a muddle. Reason, taking this to exclude any employment of the ideas of pleasure (good) or pain (evil), cannot excite any passion – this was the claim of the first argument. Taking it to include employment of such ideas of course it can – but then false suppositions about the tendencies of 'objects', or actions to produce good or evil, particularly long term good or evil, may well turn out to be 'the sources of all immorality' – as indeed Hutcheson seems to suppose but which Hume here denies ([7.1], 460).

The point of the lengthy discussion of the subservience of reason to passion in general has been to provide the ground for claiming, in Book III, that 'moral distinctions are not deriv'd from reason' ([7.1], 455) but from sentiments (a form of calm passions), so that '(m)orality is more properly felt than judg'd of' ([7.1], 470).⁹ Quite simply, 'morals have an influence' on our passions (and actions), and 'it follows, that they cannot be deriv'd from reason; and that because reason alone, as we have already prov'd, can never have any such influence' ([7.1], 457).

As has just been noted, 'reason alone' here has to be taken as meaning 'reason excluding any employment of the ideas of good or evil', and it was perhaps the extraordinary difficulty of making it mean that which lead Hume to some of the major changes in the *Enquiry*. Nothing is said there about what can, or cannot produce passions and the subservience claim has been dropped in favour of Hutcheson's view that reason must enter for a 'considerable share' in moral decisions ([7.2], 285).

The *Treatise* also contains a passage that is almost invariably quoted, the 'is/ought' passage ([7.1], 469–70), where Hume observes that in all 'systems of morality' he has met with, the authors begin with various *is*- and *is not*- statements, and then 'of a sudden', produce statements whose copula is *ought* or *ought not*. '(T)his *ought*, or *ought not*', he says, 'expresses some new relation or affirmation' which needs to be explained, but 'the authors commonly do not use this precaution.' Hume may be taken to be implying that no such explanation can be forthcoming; then the passage is interpreted as the claim 'No "ought" from an "is" ' and described as 'Hume's Law'. Alternatively, he may be interpreted as saying no more than that the authors in question (assumed to be the rationalists, who produce 'speculative systems' of morality) have not explained it, implying that an explanation in terms of human nature, such as he and Hutcheson give, can be given. Whichever interpretation is favoured, it must be acknowledged that the *Enquiry* does not contain any parallel passage.

However, some aspects of the *Treatise* position linger on. In both the *Treatise* and the *Enquiry* we are invited to consider an action agreed to be vicious (wilful murder in the *Treatise* ([7.1], 468), an act of ingratitude in the *Enquiry*, ([7.2], 287) and challenged to find that *matter of fact* wherein its vice or criminality lies. In both cases, it is taken as obvious that we cannot do so. But since, in both cases, we can obviously find a motive indicative of a character which, far from being useful or agreeable to its possessor or to others, has the contrary tendency, finding this cannot count as finding the sort of thing that 'reason' judges of – a *matter of fact*. So 'reason' here has to be *Treatise* reason: not the faculty which, according to Hutcheson and the *Enquiry* 'points out' the beneficial or harmful tendencies of personal qualities.[10]

❧ MORAL SENTIMENTS ❧

Having argued that 'moral distinctions are not deriv'd from reason', Hume claims that we 'mark the difference' between virtue and vice on the basis of a 'feeling or sentiment'. These are sometimes described as feelings of 'satisfaction or uneasiness' ([7.1], 471), sometimes as 'sentiments of approbation (or praise) or disapprobation (or blame)' ([7.1], 469), sometimes simply as 'sentiments of pleasure or pain' ([7.1], 472).

Avowedly 'subjectivist' accounts of moral judgements are faced with two standard problems. Firstly, if 'x is virtuous' just means (something like) 'I like x', and I like wine, why do I not say that wine is virtuous? And secondly, why am I charged with inconsistency or hypocrisy when I say that the truthfulness of my enemy, which prompts her to tell the truth about me or my friends, is vicious, but that our truthfulness is virtuous, if all I mean is that I dislike the former and enjoy the latter? Moral judgements have features which remarks of psychological autobiography lack.

Hume is sensible of these two features of moral judgement, though characteristically he treats them as psychological features of 'that *peculiar* kind (of feeling), which makes us praise or condemn' ([7.1], 472, cf. 517 and [7.2], §222). The sensations of pleasure we get from wine or music resemble each other just sufficiently to 'be express'd by the same abstract term' ([7.1], 472), but we can all recognize that they are very different. Similarly, the pleasure we get from the contemplation of character and actions is simply different from any of the others, so different that we never 'confound' them, that is, mistake one of the others for it ([7.1], 472, cf. [7.2], 213 n.1).[11]

Just as the moral sentiments are caused by characters and actions, never by music and wine, so they are caused 'only when a character (or action) is considered in general, without reference to our particular interest' never when the character or action is not so considered ([7.1], 472, cf. [7.2], §222–3). However, in this case Hume admits that the sentiments can be 'confounded'. The good qualities of my enemy may well give rise to a feeling of antipathy in me, despite the fact that the very same character traits in a person unconnected to me give rise to a feeling of pleasure, and I pronounce them virtuous. But if I think my enemy vicious, on account of my feeling of antipathy, this is because I am under an illusion, the illusion that the sentiment I have in contemplating the qualities of my enemy is indeed the moral sentiment, rather than one of the others.[12] But, though readily mistaken for non-moral sentiments, the moral sentiments are 'in themselves, distinct' and 'a man of temper and judgement may preserve himself from these illusions' ([7.1], 472).

How he does so is not entirely clear. To preserve myself from confounding a non-moral with a moral sentiment I place myself in 'a general point of view' and see what sentiment I have then. 'Experience soon teaches us this method of correcting our sentiments' ([7.1], 582) says Hume. However, it seems that this does not always work; the sentiment of aversion I feel towards the good qualities of my enemy may prove 'stubborn and inalterable' ([7.1], 582); for, in general 'the *heart* does not always take part with those general notions, or regulate its love and hatred by them' ([7.1], 603). What then? Well then we 'correct(. . .) our language' ([7.1], 582).

This may look like a move Hume should not allow himself to make, for what is the language in question, employing the epithets 'virtuous' and 'vicious', supposed to be about but the speaker's sentiments? Hume's answer to this is that, although I cannot love a remote historical character as much as I do someone present, I can know that I *would* feel much more strongly in favour of the former if he and the latter were both before me, and on that account I say the former is more virtuous (ibid.). So if, despite our rebellious sentiments, we 'correct our language' and pronounce the hurtful good qualities of our enemies to be virtues, 'the meaning of' this is that 'we know from reflexion' that they 'would excite strong sentiments' of pleasure if we found them in someone who was not an enemy (paraphrasing ([7.1], 584). And these sentiments would be the genuinely moral ones; the ones that are caused only when a character is considered 'without reference to our particular interest'.[13]

This is indeed an answer to the question 'what is the language in which we employ such terms as "virtuous" about?' but it is hardly consistent with his other oft-repeated claims that it is about those sentiments I find, *at the time*, in my own breast. Those 'peculiar' sentiments which make us praise or condemn are *not* always present when we do; it is not *only* when we feel them that we pronounce things to be virtuous; when, pronouncing wilful murder to be vicious, I look into my own breast, I may find all sorts of sentiments, but not necessarily the appropriate one, the moral sentiment of disapprobation. And this, although it does not entirely undercut the claim that morality is 'founded', ultimately, on sentiment as opposed to reason, does undercut his claim about the practical nature of morality, that it impels us to action ([7.1], 457).

Hume devotes far too little attention to the question of how people become wicked, and what their beliefs, desires and passions are.[14] Do the callous and ungrateful believe that they are really kind (but firm and not unduly indulgent of deserved misfortune) and grateful (when gratitude is *really* called for)? Or do they believe they are callous and ungrateful and not care? If so, do they not care because they believe these qualities are virtues not vices, or do they believe that they are vices, and the corresponding actions vicious, and still not care? Hume never expresses any views on these questions. But the overwhelmingly natural way to read him is as committed to the standard view that the latter, at least, is impossible. To pronounce (sincerely) that my killing my father is vicious is, *ipso facto*, to feel a strong aversion to killing him; this is precisely the sense in which morals have an influence on actions. But for morals to have this influence, the feeling must be *present*. If I can pronounce any possible action of mine to be vicious, not on account of what I actually feel about it, but on account of what I *would* feel about the same action *if* I saw someone else doing it, or indeed, *if* someone tried to do it to me, then the connection with impulses to action is lost. The 'fact' that I *would* feel an antipathetic sentiment if I saw someone else killing their father is, even if not a 'matter of fact' in Hume's restricted use of the phrase, certainly not a passion, and hence cannot explain what opposes my desire to kill my own when I hate him as my enemy.

So Hume copes with two of the standard objections to 'subjectivist' accounts of moral judgements only at some considerable cost. Further standard objections arise in the context of moral scepticism.

❧ SCEPTICISM AND SELF-LOVE ❧

Hume has been described as a 'moral sceptic', both in his own day and in ours. He himself denied that he was one. It is sometimes supposed that he did so only to avoid strife, and with a view to getting academic posts. It is more plausible to assume that 'moral scepticism' or 'the denial of the reality of moral distinctions' can be taken in a variety of ways, and that, in at least some ways of taking it, Hume was sincere when he claimed not to be a moral sceptic.

Amongst the writers described as moral sceptics by Shaftesbury[15] and Hutcheson were Hobbes, Locke and Mandeville, on the grounds that they all maintained that our sole passion or sentiment is that of self-love, or a concern for our private interest. It appears that there were two distinct ways in which such a claim about human nature was thought to amount to the denial of the 'reality' of moral distinctions and thereby to moral scepticism.

First, the moral distinctions we draw between actions are, strictly speaking, distinctions between the motives of those actions. But if there is only ever one motive, namely self-love, there are no such distinctions to be made; hence no real moral distinctions. Second, no philosopher who has embraced 'the selfish hypothesis' denies that, somehow, human beings are brought to distinguish between their own private interest and that of others, and, at least sometimes, to pursue the latter rather than the former. Given that this is contrary to (their) nature, it must be, in some sense, a convention, or artifice. But if moral distinctions arise from convention rather than nature, they are not real; hence, on 'the selfish hypothesis' they are not real.

Hume has little to say about self-love in the *Treatise* and makes little explicit attempt to dissociate himself from 'moral scepticism' except with regard to justice. Perhaps he did not expect to be charged with moral scepticism, since, after all, he concurred 'with all the ancient Moralists, as well as with Mr. Hutcheson, Professor of Moral Philosophy in the University of Glasgow'.[16]

However he is quite explicit about the rejection of moral scepticism in the *Enquiry*, maintaining at the very outset that 'those who have denied the reality of moral distinctions, may be ranked among the disingenuous disputants' ([7.2], 169) and producing much new material, not to be found in the *Treatise*, directed against 'the selfish hypothesis' ([7.2], 298). In part V he explicitly identifies this as a view of sceptics, who suppose, he says 'that all moral distinctions arise from education, and were, at first, *invented*, . . . by the art of politicians' ([7.2], 214, my italics) and in §175, he cites a number of 'instances', or experiments which compel us to renounce it ([7.2], 219). He returns to the attack in the *Enquiry*'s second Appendix 'Of Self-Love', where he names Hobbes and Locke as amongst those who maintain 'the selfish system of morals' ([7.2], 296) and produces several more arguments against it.

So if by a 'moral sceptic' we mean – as Shaftesbury and Hutcheson certainly meant – 'one who embraces "the selfish hypothesis" and is thereby committed to saying that no two actions have different motives and that moral distinctions are not natural but invented or matters of mere convention', then Hume was not a moral sceptic, and was not being disingenuous when he repudiated the charge.

❧ SCEPTICISM AND SUBJECTIVITY: THE ❧ STANDARD OF 'TASTE'

However, it may well be that there are tendencies to another sort of moral scepticism in Hume. Like Hutcheson, he compares virtue and vice to 'sounds, colours, heat and cold, which, according to modern philosophy, are not qualities in objects, but perceptions in the mind' ([7.1], 469, cf. [7.2], 294). A pure rationalist in morals may incline to saying that secondary qualities[17] such as sounds and colours are insufficiently real for the analogy to guarantee the reality of moral distinctions (and hence call both Hume and Hutcheson sceptics). But even if we grant that colours, for example, are sufficiently real, we may still wonder whether Hume's view of moral distinctions makes them sufficiently analogous. Regardless of whether or not colours are 'real powers', we can be right or wrong about them. That something looks red to me is not the end of the matter; if my vision is defective it may well *look* red, but *be* (as we say) yellow. Are virtue and vice sufficiently like colours in this respect – sufficiently real – for this to be true of them, according to Hume?

Hume's promise ([7.1], 547 n.) to consider '(i)n what sense we can talk either of a *right* or a *wrong* taste in morals, eloquence, or beauty', is not made good in the *Treatise* but, with respect to beauty at least, it is, in the Essay 'On the Standard of Taste'.

Here Hume explicitly raises, and tries to solve, the sceptical problem that founding aesthetics on sentiment seems to present. 'All determinations of the understanding are not right; because they have a reference to something beyond themselves, to wit, real matter of fact; and are not always conformable to that standard' ([7.3], I:268). But how can there be a Standard of Taste, according to which some aesthetic taste is right and some wrong, when 'all sentiment is right; because sentiment has a reference to nothing beyond itself, and is always real, wherever a man is conscious of it' (ibid.)?

Hume accepts that 'beauty and deformity (. . .) are not qualities in objects, but belong entirely to the sentiment'; but maintains that 'it must be allowed that there are certain qualities in objects, which are *fitted by nature* to produce those particular feelings' ([7.3], 273; my italics).[18] Supposing that there are such qualities, some 'calculated to please, and others to displease' ([7.3], 271), we may suppose that 'if they fail of their effect in any particular instance, it is from some apparent defect or imperfection in the organ' (ibid.).

Here we do have the parallel with colour judgements; which indeed, Hume draws.

> If, in the sound state of the organ, there be an entire, or a considerable, uniformity of sentiment among men, we may thence derive an idea of perfect beauty; in like manner as the appearance of objects in daylight, to the eye of a man in health, is denominated their true and real colour, even while colour is allowed to be merely a phantasm of the senses.
>
> ([7.3], 272)

So 'the true standard of taste and beauty' is the verdict of the person whose 'organ(s)' of aesthetic taste are 'sound' – the good critic. And '(S)trong sense, united to delicate judgement, improved by practice, perfected by comparison, and cleared of all prejudice, can alone entitle critics to this valuable character' ([7.3], 278). Such a standard may, of course, be very difficult to apply, since it requires a prior identification of a good critic; but the original sceptical challenge was not to produce a standard which was easy to apply, but any standard at all. 'It is sufficient for our present purpose, if we have proved, that the taste of all individuals is not upon an equal footing' ([7.3], 279).

A somewhat similar problem in relation to moral 'taste' is discussed in 'A Dialogue',[19] where, once again, Hume seeks to 'fix a standard' ([7.2], 333), this time for moral judgements, and to defend a 'universal standard of morals' ([7.2], 343). His problem here is not directly that 'all sentiment is right', and the wide difference in this respect between sentiment and understanding, but the 'wide difference,(...) in the sentiments of morals' which we find between different cultures, such as the ancient Greeks and contemporary Frenchmen ([7.2], 333).

Hume accounts for such differences by 'tracing matters a little higher' to what he calls 'first principles' (ibid.). Unlike the French, or Hume's contemporaries, the Greeks recommend pederasty. But they do so 'as the source of friendship, sympathy, mutual attachment and fidelity' and concerning these 'qualities' there is no disagreement. On the contrary they are 'esteemed in all nations and all ages' ([7.2], 334). Unlike the ancient Greeks, the French justify duelling, but they do so by appealing to courage, a sense of honour, fidelity and friendship, qualities which, again 'have been esteemed universally, since the foundation of the world' ([7.2], 335). Several other examples are given; the general point that is inferred from them is that 'the principles upon which men reason in morals are always the same' (ibid.); 'the original principles of censure and blame are uniform' ([7.2], 336).

Now this may be seen as a rather neat solution to 'cultural relativism' in morals; the moral disagreements we find between peoples is no proof that 'a universal standard of morals' is lacking, for they are mere surface disagreements concealing underlying agreement. In accordance with 'the original principles' of praise or blame 'erroneous conclusions can be corrected by sounder reasoning and larger experience' (ibid.). In the offing, we seem to have the promise of the 'good critic' in morals; someone whose wide experience, sound reasoning, freedom from parochial prejudice etc. would allow any action to produce 'its *due* effect' on her mind.

But the 'good critic' in morals thus envisaged is looking at *actions* such as duelling, not qualities such as courage. Indeed, to reach his conclusion, Hume has to assume (a) that human beings agree, and always have, on some fairly large list of qualities as virtues; and (b) that they never disagree about the criteria of virtue: 'never was any quality recommended by any one as a virtue (. . .) but on account of its being *useful*, or *agreeable* to a man *himself*, or to *others*', (ibid.). Has he simply overlooked the problem of disagreements about which qualities are virtues? Or does the 'good critic' determine the standard here too?

He is entitled, on his own terms, to assume (b) in 'A Dialogue', because the *Enquiry* has been devoted to proving it 'by the experimental method' ([7.2], 174). Its avowed intention is to 'collect and arrange' 'particular instances' of 'the estimable or blameable qualities of men', and to 'discover the circumstances on both sides, which are common to these qualities . . . and thence to reach the foundation of ethics, and find those universal principles, from which all censure or approbation is ultimately derived' (ibid.). Hume considers an impressively wide range (cf. [7.2], 277) of 'estimable qualities', i.e. virtues, (though fewer blameable ones), and, arranging them as 'qualities useful/agreeable to others/ourselves' etc. might well be taken to have proved to his point.

However, in following this procedure he makes a certain assumption about the content of the predicate 'useful', failing to notice that 'useful' is, quite generally, end-directed. If something is useful, it must be useful insofar as it promotes something or other, some end; and the end itself must be taken as good, or worth promoting, if that which is a means to it is to be counted as useful. And Hume simply assumes that a quality useful to its possessor is one 'which advance(s) a man's fortune in the world' ([7.2], 270); it is this assumption which enables him to dismiss 'celibacy, fasting, penance, mortification, self-denial, humility, silence, solitude, and the whole train of monkish virtues' (ibid.) as not being virtues at all *because* they are neither useful nor agreeable to their possessor or to others.

The 'monkish virtues' that he lists have rarely, if ever, been claimed to be useful because they 'advance a man's fortune in the world', but, given the Christian view of the nature of man, they can still be made out to be useful; this is not because they advance their possessor's fortune in *this* world, but because they preserve her soul for the next.

Hume thought, at least in his *Treatise* days, that he could give an account of morality which was neutral with respect to any view about the end of man;[20] he thought then, and continued to think, that an account of morality cannot bypass, but must be rooted in human nature. But it seems that questions about our end are, as Aristotle thought, inseparable from questions about our nature, and that Hume's account of the latter became much less neutral after the *Treatise* when he came to address the question of right and wrong 'taste' in morals.

Anyone who gives a religious or ascetic content to 'useful' and praises the 'monkish virtues' is a 'gloomy, hair-brained enthusiast' (ibid.); such people, under 'the illusions of religious superstition or philosophical enthusiasm' ([7.2], 343) lead 'artificial lives', wherein 'the natural principles of their mind play not with the same regularity, as if left to themselves' (ibid.).

Nor are these the only people who get things wrong. Those who think that avarice and dishonesty are virtues (because they are useful in securing money and thereby pleasure) are themselves 'the greatest dupes' ([7.2], 283) having 'sacrificed the invaluable enjoyment of a character, with themselves at least, for the acquisition of worthless toys and gewgaws' (ibid.).

So it seems that Hume's 'good critics' in morals, the ones whose verdicts (if we follow 'A Standard of Taste') provide the true standard of morals, would have to possess not only wide experience and sound reasoning, and *also* 'judge of things by their natural, unprejudiced reason, without the delusive glosses of superstition and false religion' ([7.2], 270), but further, have the *right* conception of happiness or pleasure, the conception which dismisses 'the feverish empty amusements of luxury and expense' ([7.2], 284) in favour of 'inward peace of mind, consciousness of integrity, (and) a satisfactory review of our own conduct' ([7.2], 283). And there is his problem, for where, in Hume's psychological or epistemological theory, is there room for the notion of right and wrong conceptions of happiness or pleasure? He may declare that the conceptions produced by the metaphysical speculations of religion or philosophy can be safely ignored, but it is not those that lead human beings to pursue 'luxury and expense', 'toys and gewgaws', instead of virtue. The pleasure we take in these worthless things seems all too natural, and it is not clear how Hume can dismiss it as in some sense 'false' without giving up his naturalism. If he believed in his 'good critic' in morals, he may have repudiated moral scepticism with sincerity, but not with consistency.

❧ POLITICAL PHILOSOPHY ❧

In both the *Treatise* and the *Enquiry* Hume devotes special attention to justice, claiming that in some way, or ways, it is significantly different from most of the other virtues. In the *Treatise* he tries to capture the difference by calling it an 'artificial' virtue, and the others 'natural'. This proved to be an unfortunate choice of words, since it immediately associated him with the most feared moral sceptics, Hobbes and Mandeville, (see above 'Scepticism and Self-love') and he dropped it in the *Enquiry*. The question of whether justice is natural is there relegated to a footnote, and dismissed as merely verbal ([7.2], 307–8). But it is clear that this does not signify any change in his position with regard to justice.

❦ NATURAL MOTIVES ❦

In the *Treatise*, the discussion of what distinguishes justice from (most of) the other virtues begins with a curiously difficult argument concerning *motives*. He begins by noting that 'when we praise any actions, we regard only the motives that produced them' ([7.1], 478); 'all virtuous actions derive their merit only from virtuous motives' ([7.1], 479). He immediately concludes

> that the first virtuous motive, which bestows a merit on any action, can never be a regard to the virtue of that action, but must be some other natural motive or principle. To suppose, that the mere regard to the virtue of the action, may be the first motive . . . is to reason in a circle.
>
> ([7.1], 478)

It is hard to see why.

What would be examples of virtuous motives? A parent's concern for her child; a concern for the well-being of others (ibid. ([7.2], 303)); these, we may note, are passions that occur in us naturally. But what about a *concern for virtue*? Suppose I want to do a benevolent action because it *is* benevolent. This might happen, but it could not always happen amongst human beings in general. For benevolent actions are so-called because they are taken as signs of benevolence, the (naturally occurring) concern for the well-being of others; if there were no such concern in human beings, but only a 'concern to do benevolent actions', there would not *be* any benevolent actions, and hence the 'concern' to do them would lack an object. So, before there can be a concern to do benevolent actions there must 'first' be a natural concern for the well-being of others.

Whether or not this argument works,[21] Hume is certain that it does, and turns to the question of our motive for just action, taking as his example the question of what motive I have for repaying a loan when my creditor demands it. If the argument works, the motive cannot in general be a 'regard to justice', that is, a concern to do a just action: before there can be such a concern there must 'first' be some other motive.

Hume rapidly rejects some suggestions favoured by other philosophers. It cannot be a concern for myself, i.e. self-interest ([7.1], 481) (since it may well not be in my interest to return the money), not even interest in my own reputation (since I may be able to preserve my reputation despite reneging on my debt). It cannot be a concern for the well-being of others, i.e. benevolence, for that might motivate me not to return the money. What if my debtor 'be a profligate debauchee, and would rather receive harm than benefit from large possessions?' ([7.1], 382). What about a concern for public interest? Hume has several objections to this ([7.1], 480–1), but his most trenchant mirrors his objection to benevolence as the motive. 'A single act of justice is frequently contrary to *public interest*' as in the case when a man disposed to spend his money in ways that benefit society restores 'a great fortune to a miser, or a seditious bigot' ([7.1], 497, cf. [7.2], 304 and 305). His action is just, but his concern for the public interest cannot be his motive, for that would motivate him to keep the fortune and spend it wisely in a way its rightful owners will not.

This seems to exhaust the possibilities of natural motives to justice, so we are driven to the conclusion that in some sense our motive to just acts must be a 'regard to justice'. By the circularity argument, this cannot occur naturally – cannot be 'first' – so it must arise 'artificially, though necessarily from education and human conventions' ([7.1], 483). Hence Hume is led to a consideration of the origin of justice.

❧ THE ORIGIN OF JUSTICE AND PROPERTY ❧

Hume appears to see justice as exclusively concerned with property rights and the obligation to honour a few sorts of promises or 'compacts'.[22] So he does not attempt to account for rules of justice which secure the 'natural rights' such as the right to life, or liberty, but concentrates on those which secure 'external goods'.[23] He begins by considering what the natural explanation is of the undoubted fact that 'man is a social animal', and identifies 'the first and original principle of human society' not as self-love, but as 'that natural appetite betwixt the sexes, which unites them together, and preserves their union, till a new tye takes place in their concern for their common offspring' ([7.1], 486, cf. [7.2], 192). Thus bonded into a little society by familial affections or 'limited generosity', human beings are enabled to become aware of something they could never work out, by pure reason, in isolation ([7.1], 486), namely that society is advantageous. Compared with other animals, we are ill-equipped to satisfy our need for food and shelter on our own, but banded together we may do so ([7.1], 485). So we are prompted to union.

But, advantageous as union is, it brings an attendant disadvantage. Those very external goods I can come to possess more easily when united with many other human beings are still in short supply, and moreover, more easily lost, prey no longer to the occasional wild animal, but to most of those other human beings. The 'tender regard' ([7.1], 494) my friends and family have for me keeps my possessions safe from them, but this 'generosity' with regard to me is confined to them. No one else has any motive to abstain from gratifying that 'insatiable, perpetual (and) universal' ([7.1], 492) avidity for possessions by taking mine. My possession of them is thus unstable.

So nature puts us in a quandary, from which we extract ourselves, inventive creatures that we are, by agreeing on a convention about abstaining from the possessions of others, a convention which restrains our insatiable avidity and thereby 'bestow(s) stability' ([7.1], 489) on our own, and every one else's possession. 'By this means, every one knows what he may safely possess' (ibid.). As soon as this agreement or convention is entered into 'there immediately arise the ideas of justice and injustice' (ibid.).

Hume nowhere explicitly defines justice or describes what it is an idea *of* and it is not clear how he would do so. However, it is clear that he rejects a number of familiar definitions as empty or circular. Justice cannot be defined as respecting others' property or rights because the ideas of *property* and *right* (as the singular of 'rights') arise *after* the idea of justice and are 'altogether unintelligible without first understanding (it)' ([7.1], 491).

To appreciate the plausibility of Hume's point here we must be particularly careful to give his terms their contemporary interpretation. My property, that which is mine in the *meum tuum* sense of 'mine', was commonly defined as anything I have a right to or in. Nowadays we find this odd, since we say we have a right to life, but do not regard our life as (our) 'property'. But Grotius, Pufendorf and Locke all find it perfectly natural to say that my life is my property – for it is, after all, mine.[24] So the ideas of *property* and *right* arise together, or not at all. But 'what is a man's property? Anything which it is lawful for him and him alone to use' ([7.2], 197), that is anything (and only those things) 'whose constant possession is established by the laws of society; that is, by the laws of *justice*' ([7.1], 491, my italics). So to understand the idea of *property* (and hence of *right*) we must first have understood the idea of justice as a convention according to which we abstain from taking – not another's property – but what they are actually possessed of. Prior to such a convention, actual possession is not even one-tenth of the law, because there is no law.

Hume has now given an explanation of how the motive to just acts can, despite the circularity argument, be 'regard to justice'. We respect the possessions of others because it would be unjust to take them (they are theirs, their property, they have a right to them) – but it would be unjust because it would violate an agreement that self-interest has lead us into.

He must now explain why justice is a virtue and injustice a vice – why, that is, the contemplation of them causes 'those peculiar sentiments'. Here the regard to public interest, (though not a motive to just acts) does come in. A violation of the agreement 'displeases us, because we consider it as prejudicial to human society' and we are concerned about that, not simply because of self-interest, but because 'we partake of (the uneasiness of others) by sympathy' ([7.1], 499). The contemplation of unjust acts we might do ourselves may, of course, cause only pleasure; but they are not thereby excused from being vicious, because the sentiment has not, as is requisite, been caused by taking the general point of view (see above, 'Moral Sentiments').

❧ THE ORIGIN OF GOVERNMENT AND THE ❧ SOURCE OF ALLEGIANCE

Hume mostly forgets that he has argued that the motive to performing individual acts of justice (rather than to establishing rules of justice in the first place) is not self-interest, but 'regard to justice' itself, enhanced by 'private education and instruction' ([7.1], 501), by which means 'the sentiments of honour (. . .) take root' in childrens' minds, 'and acquire such firmness and solidity' that they 'may fall little short' of natural principles (ibid.). Hence he accounts for our tendency to lapse into injustice, not as a motivational failure of our induced desire to be honourable or fulfill our obligations, but as an instance of the general human tendency to act against our long term (remote) personal advantage by seizing the present, or near, short term advantage.[25]

So natural to us is this tendency, that it cannot be changed or corrected; 'the utmost we can do is to change our circumstances and situation, and render the observance of the laws of justice our nearest interest' ([7.1], 537). Hence, having united into society, we go a step further and 'establish *political* society' or government, 'in order to administer justice' ([7.3], I: 113). '(C)ivil magistrates, kings and their ministers, our governors and rulers' ([7.1], 537) are instituted as people with an immediate interest in the observance of justice, and the power to 'inforce the dictates of equity thro' the whole society' (ibid.).

This 'new invention' ([7.1], 543) of government, is also the invention of a new obligation or duty ([7.3], I: 114) namely that of obedience or allegiance to the state; the source of this obligation is thus shown to be a mixture of natural and artificial elements, like the source of the obligation to justice. Having perceived the advantages of society, we invent justice (rules governing possessions) to secure them; now conscious of the advantages of justice, we invent government to secure them. But Hume says very little about this source – the psychological mechanisms by means of which we 'annex the idea of virtue' to civil obedience.[26]

❧ THE ORIGINAL CONTRACT AND THE ❧ OBLIGATION OF PROMISES

Many of Hume's predecessors[27] had maintained that the source of the obligation to obedience (or allegiance) to the state, was an 'original contract' or covenant. (The point of this, Hume notes ([7.1], 549, cf. 'Of the Original Contract', [7.3], I: 443) was to justify civil disobedience under 'an egregious tyranny in the rulers' ([7.1], 549),[28] something that could not be justified according to the rival account of the source of allegiance, namely, the divine right of kings.)[29] We all promise, or contract, to obey the state authorities, consenting to their rule, on the understanding that they will secure for us the advantages of being in society, namely the advantages of justice. The contract is conditional – 'I promise to obey – *if* you keep your side of the bargain and maintain justice'. Hence, 'as happens in all conditional contracts' ([7.1, 550), one is freed from the obligation to keep to it when the condition lapses; in this case, when the state authorities, instead of maintaining justice, act unjustly themselves, and attempt 'tyranny and oppression'.

When the condition is met, the (moral) obligation to obedience is the (moral) obligation to keep the promise – and herein lies Hume's objection to the account, for what is the source of the obligation to keep promises? Prior to embarking on his discussion of the origin of government, Hume has already, in the *Treatise*, argued that fidelity (to promises, or to one's word), like justice, is not a natural but an artificial virtue. His starting-point, as before, is the circularity argument concerning motives. It is clear that my motive for doing whatever I have promised you to do *is* (usually) my sense of (my) duty (to do so); I do it because I promised to, because I am under an obligation to, because you have a right to demand that I do. But it is clear from the content of this motive, however expressed, that it cannot be a natural one. Just as possessions without a convention governing abstention are not property, so a mere form of words, even a form of words attended by a peculiar act of the mind (such as the thought 'I resolve to do what I have just said I would do'), is not a promise, not something that puts the speaker under an obligation.

But if not natural, how does it arise? Like justice, by convention. We agree on the convention that 'a *certain form of words*' will just count as binding the speaker to the performance of a particular action

in the future, and '(t)his form of words constitutes what we call a
promise' ([7.1], 520). As with our agreement to abstain from others'
possessions, we see that such an agreement is, given our limited good-
will towards each other, necessary in order to secure certain advantages
that we unite into society to gain. (The advantages here are those of
the exchange of both goods and services. I promise to transfer my ten
bushels of corn to you, in exchange for your transferring five hogsheads
of wine to me; I promise to help you cut your ripe corn today in
exchange for your helping me to cut mine tomorrow ([7.1], 519–20)).

So we are prompted by self-interest to invent this convention,
'which create(s) a new motive' ([7.1], 520), and then (as with justice)
we 'annex the idea' of virtue to it, through '(p)ublic interest, education
and the artifices of politicians' ([7.1], 523).

Hence, the obligations to justice and fidelity to promise-keeping
arise first, according to Hume, and are quite distinct from the obligation
to civil obedience.[30] But if the latter is not simply the obligation to
keep one's 'original' conditional promise, can Hume explain the justifi-
ability of civil disobedience under 'egregious tyranny'? 'I flatter myself',
he says, 'that I can establish the same conclusion on more reasonable
principles' ([7.1], 550), but this may indeed be self-flattery. '(T)he
natural obligation to allegiance' is, he says, 'interest' (presumably the
coincidence of self and common interest) and hence lapses as soon as
the tyranny of the rulers ceases to promote it, in accordance with the
'maxim', 'when the cause ceases, the effect must cease also' ([7.1], 551).
But this maxim would be false when applied to 'the *moral* obligation
of duty'; to some extent Hume 'submit(s)' to the argument 'that men
may be bound by *conscience* to submit to a tyrannical government',
despite the fact that the cause of the moral obligation (said here to be
the natural obligation) has ceased. Hume's point here seems to be that,
once the idea of virtue has been annexed to civil obedience, so that the
peculiar moral sentiments are firmly associated with it, this is not
something that can quickly change. Despite knowing he is under tyranny, and that neither his own nor the common interest is being served,
the virtuous man, who has been well brought up, will still find himself
viewing obedience with moral approbation. Hume could say that he
also finds himself viewing the injustice of the rulers with moral disapprobation strengthened by self-interest, and thereby account for our
ceasing to ascribe viciousness to civil disobedience. But instead he
maintains, rather vaguely, that 'in all our notions of morals we never
entertain such an absurdity as that of passive obedience, but make
allowances for resistance in the more flagrant instances of tyranny'
([7.1], 552).

❧ CONCLUSION ❧

It can be seen, from the foregoing, that the resounding battle cry of Book II of the *Treatise* – 'Reason is, and ought only to be, the slave of the passions', – undergoes considerable modification, within the *Treatise* itself, as well as in its recasting in the second *Enquiry* and various essays. By the end of the modifications, neither the passions, nor reason, are quite what we, and Hume, initially took them to be. Many commentators have noted the essential role that reason plays in Hume's account of justice, (passed over in silence in the *Treatise* but explicitly acknowledged in the *Enquiry* ([7.2], 307); fewer have reflected this back in Book II. Here, the only passions discussed in connection with reason and action are the 'natural' ones – anger, fear, pride, hatred, which Hume thinks we basically share with other animals – which reason serves. The moral sentiments, initially introduced as felt passions which prompt us to action as the other 'animal' passions do, appear, eventually, to be transformed into the *correct* reactions of the 'good critic' in morals, with her correct conception of happiness. And, in Hume's discussion of justice, we find that, in virtue of our reason, unlike the other animals, we are able to invent new ideas which arouse passions – ideas such as those of *justice, property, right, promise, obedience*. Hume can indeed continue to maintain that reason serves the natural passion of self-love by coming up with these ideas. But in doing so, reason gains the whip hand. No longer a slave, it dictates what some of our passions will be, and thereby drives some of us to die for justice, to go to the stake rather than break a promise or contract, as no animal other than a rational animal could conceivably do.

❧ NOTES ❧

1 Thomas Hobbes, 1588–1679. His influential work in political philosophy, the *Leviathan*, was published in 1651. Bernard Mandeville (1670–1733) published a cynical satire, *The Fable of the Bees: or Private Vices, Public Benefits*, in 1714. Frances Hutcheson (1694–1746) developed a 'moral sense' theory – see Chapter 11 of this volume.

2 Kemp Smith argues that Book III of the *Treatise* was probably written first ([7.27], chapters 1–111), a view which is explicitly rejected by Norton, [7.20].

3 For discussion of the connections between Hume's discussion of the passions in Book II and of morals in Book III see Ardal, [7.8], and Baier, [7.10].

4 The main rationalists against whom Hutcheson and Hume argued were Ralph Cudworth (1617–1688) (see Chapter 1 of this volume), Samuel Clarke (1675–1729) and William Wollaston (1659–1724). Extracts from their writings are to be found in Raphael, [7.22], Selby-Bigge, [7.24] and Schneewind, [7.23]; their views are briefly discussed in Mackie, [7.19] and Sidgwick, [7.25].

5 See in particular Stroud, [7.29], 156ff.

6 Cf. Hutcheson in Raphael, [7.22], I: 317, or Selby-Bigge [7.24], I: 413.

7 That he intends such an exclusion is made clear by the only significant change he made when he recast Book II of the *Treatise* as *A Dissertation on the Passions*: 'reason, . . . can never, of itself, be any motive to the will, . . . Abstract relations of ideas are the object of curiosity, not of volition. And matters of fact, *Where they are neither good nor evil*, . . . cannot be regarded as any motive to action' ([7.3], II: 161, my italics).

8 See n.4 above.

9 Those who follow Kemp Smith in seeing Book I as arising from Hume's reflections on morals (cf. n. 2 above) compare this claim with *Treatise*, p. 183 – 'belief is more properly an act of the sensitive, than of the cogitative part of our natures'.

10 For a particularly challenging discussion of Hume's treatment of 'matters of fact' such as 'I owe you some money', see 'On Brute Facts' in Anscombe, [7.7].

11 This psychological account of the logical restrictions on moral approval or disapproval closely parallels his psychological treatment of the logical restrictions on pride. Cf. Foot, [7.13].

12 The disconcerting feature of all calm passions, including the moral sentiments, is that, despite their being impressions, we may not notice them. They 'are more known by their effects than by the immediate feeling or sensation' (*Treatise*, p. 417, cf. Stroud, [7.29], 163).

13 These are the passages that lead some commentators (cf. [7.11] and [7.14]) to ascribe an 'ideal observer' theory to Hume. The 'ideal observer' theory was developed by Hume's friend, Adam Smith, in *The Theory of Moral Sentiments*, published in 1759.

14 Strangely enough, he ignores Hutcheson's brief, but plausible account, (to be found in Selby-Bigge, [7.24], I: 124, quoted in Mackie, [7.19], 27).

15 The Earl of Shaftesbury (1671–1713) is generally regarded as the founder of the 'moral sense' or 'sentimentalist' school developed by Hutcheson and Hume; see Chapter 8 of this volume.

15a See *Treatise*, pp. 484, 500 and 620.

16 [7.5], 30.

17 For Locke's discussion of secondary qualities as 'real powers', see Chapter 4 of this volume.

18 It seems that Hume takes this to be established by the fact that '(a)ll the changes of climate, government, religion and language, have not been able to obscure (Homer's) glory' ([7.3], I: 271).

19 'A Dialogue' was originally published with the second *Enquiry* in 1751; page references are to Selby-Bigge, [7.2] which includes it. For an excellent discussion of it, see King, [7.18].

20 'For pray, what is the End of Man? Is he created for Happiness or for Virtue? For this Life or for the next? For himself or his Maker? your Definition of *Natural* depends upon solving these Questions, which are endless and quite wide of my Purpose.' (Letter to Hutcheson, 1739, [7.4], I: 33.)

21 One of the few philosophers to have found it to contain something important is G. E. M. Anscombe, in 'Rules, Rights and Promises' and 'On the Source of

the Authority of the State' in Anscombe, [7.7] and 'The Question of Linguistic Idealism' in [7.6]. See also Snare, [7.28].

22 Thomas Reid (1710–1796) criticized Hume for saying nothing about natural rights in *Essays on the Active Powers of the Human Mind* (1788), Essay V, chapter V, 'Whether Justice be a Natural or an Artificial Virtue'. But it may be argued that Hume's account covers natural rights as well as property rights – see Hursthouse, [7.17].

23 His account of how property rights arise has much in common with the accounts of two earlier writers on natural law, Hugo Grotius (1503–1645), and Samuel Pufendorf (1632–92); Hume indeed acknowledges his similarity to Grotius ([7.2], 307 n.). Nevertheless, he differs from each of them in respects which would make it quite inappropriate to describe him as a 'natural law theorist'.

24 For an illuminating discussion of the terms 'property' and 'right' in seventeenth century natural law theorists, see James Tully, *A Discourse on Property*, Cambridge, Cambridge University Press, 1980.

25 No doubt as a consequence of Hume's neglect of his own original view on the motive to particular just acts, most of Hume's commentators also overlook it, and discuss him as if he were inevitably committed to the 'free-rider problem'. For an unambiguous restatement of his original view on the motive to particular just acts, see 'Of the Original Contract' ([7.3], I: 455).

26 Presumably, he would suppose them to be similar to those by means of which 'we annex the idea of virtue to justice', but, if he had considered the matter, he would surely have said something too about the effects of state-enforced sanctions. He might have claimed, plausibly, that the idea of disobeying the laws will inevitably become associated in my mind with the unpleasant idea of punishment, and thereby lead me feel that disobedience is unattractive.

27 Most famously, Hobbes and Locke, but also Richard Hooker (1554?-1600), Benedict Spinoza (1632–77), Grotius and Pufendorf (see n. 23 above). Their idea of the original (or 'social') contract was subsequently supported by Jean Jacques Rousseau (1712–78).

28 This is not strictly true of Hobbes, whose sovereign is owed obedience however despotic; however Hobbes's covenant does allow for civil disobedience to a sovereign who lacks the power to protect the convenanters.

29 Locke's selected target in *Two Treatises of Civil Government* was the divine right theory of Robert Filmer, put forward in his *Patriarcha* (1680).

30 In 'Of the Original Contract' he even goes so far as to contrast 'the political or civil duty of allegiance' with 'the *natural* duties of justice and fidelity' ([7.3], I: 455).

❧ BIBLIOGRAPHY ❧

More comprehensive bibliographies are to be found in [7.15] below, and in 'The Hume Literature of the 1980's' by Nicholas Capaldi, James King and Donald Livingstone, in *American Philosophical Quarterly*, 1991.

Editions

7.1   *A Treatise of Human Nature*, ed. L. A. Selby-Bigge, Oxford, Clarendon Press, 1967.

7.2   *Enquiries Concerning the Human Understanding and Concerning the Principles of Morals*, ed. L. A. Selby-Bigge, Oxford, Clarendon Press, 1963. This edition also includes 'A Dialogue'.

7.3   *Essays, Moral, Political and Literary*, 2 vols, ed. T. H. Green and T. H. Grose, London, Longmans, Green and Co., 1889.

7.4   *The Letters of David Hume*, 2 vols, ed. J. Y. T. Grieg, Oxford, Clarendon Press, 1969.

7.5   *A Letter from a Gentleman to his friend in Edinburgh*, ed. E. C. Mossner and J. V. Price, Edinburgh, Edinburgh University Press, 1967.

Books and Articles

7.6   Anscombe, G. E. M. *From Parmenides to Wittgenstein*, Minneapolis, University of Minnosota Press, 1981.

7.7   —— *Ethics, Religion and Politics*, Minneapolis, University Of Minnesota Press, 1981.

7.8   Ardal, P. S. *Passion and Value in Hume's Treatise*, Edinburgh, Edinburgh University Press, 1966.

7.9   —— 'Some Implications of the Virtue of Reasonableness in Hume's *Treatise*' in D. W. Livingston and J. T. King (eds) *Hume: A Re-Evaluation*, New York, Fordham University Press, 1976, pp. 91–106.

7.10 Baier, A. *A Progress of Sentiments*, Cambridge (Mass.), Harvard University Press, 1991.

7.11 Firth, R. 'Ethical Absolutism and the Ideal Observer', *Philosophy and Phenomenological Research*, 1952.

7.12 Fogelin, R. *Hume's Skepticism in the Treatise of Human Nature*, London, Routledge and Kegan Paul, 1985.

7.13 Foot, P. 'Hume on Moral Judgement' in her *Virtues and Vices*, Oxford, Blackwell, 1978.

7.14 Glossop, R. J. 'Hume, Stevenson, and Hare on Moral Language' in D. W. Livingston and J. T. King (eds) *Hume: A Re-Evaluation*, New York, Fordham University Press, 1976, pp. 362–85.

7.15 Hall, R. *Fifty Years of Hume Scholarship*, Edinburgh, Edinburgh University Press, 1978.

7.16 Hudson, S. D. *Human Character and Morality*, Boston, Routledge and Kegan Paul, 1986.

7.17 Hursthouse, R. 'After Hume's Justice', *Proceedings of the Aristotelian Society* (1990–1).

7.18 King, J. 'Hume on Artificial Lives', *Hume Studies* XIV (1988), 1.

7.19 Mackie, J. L. Hume's Moral Theory, London, Routledge and Kegan Paul, 1980.

7.20 Norton, D. F. *David Hume, Common-sense Moralist, Sceptical Metaphysician*, Princeton, NJ, Princeton University Press, 1982.
7.21 Platts, M. 'Hume and Morality as a Matter of Fact', *Mind* (1988).
7.22 Raphael, D. D. *British Moralists 1650–1800*, 2 vols, Oxford, Clarendon Press, 1969.
7.23 Schneewind, J. B. *Moral Philosophy from Montaigne to Kant*, 2 vols, Cambridge, Cambridge University Press, 1990.
7.24 Selby-Bigge, L. A. *British Moralists*, 2 vols, Oxford, Clarendon Press, 1897.
7.25 Sidgwick, H. *History of Ethics*, London, Macmillan, 1931.
7.26 Smith, M. 'The Humean Theory of Motivation', *Mind* (1987).
7.27 Smith, N. K. *The Philosophy of David Hume*, London, Macmillan, 1941.
7.28 Snare, F. *Morals, Motivation and Convention*, Cambridge, Cambridge University Press, 1991.
7.29 Stroud, B. *Hume*, London, Routledge and Kegan Paul, 1977.

CHAPTER 8

British moralists of the eighteenth century: Shaftesbury, Butler and Price
David McNaughton

In this chapter I discuss the moral theories of three influential writers: Anthony Ashley Cooper, Third Earl of Shaftesbury (1671–1713); Joseph Butler (1692–1752) and Richard Price (1723–91). All three wrote extensively on issues in religion (Butler was an Anglican Bishop and Price a Dissenting Minister) but I shall only touch on their religious views where they bear on their ethical doctrines.

🙰 LORD SHAFTESBURY 🙰

I largely base my account of Shaftesbury's views on his most systematic ethical work, *An Enquiry Concerning Virtue or Merit*, in the version which was included in his *Characteristics*.

Shaftesbury was deeply influenced by Greek and Roman thought. In a letter he distinguishes two strands in Ancient philosophy:

> the one derived from Socrates . . . the other derived in reality from Democritus . . . The first . . . of these two philosophies recommended action, concernment in civil affairs, religion. The second derided all, and advised inaction and retreat, and with good reason. For the first maintained that society, right and wrong was founded in Nature, and that Nature had a meaning, and was herself, that is to say in her wits, well governed and administered by one simple and perfect intelligence. The second again derided this, and made Providence and Dame Nature not so sensible as a doting old woman.[1]

The former strand is the one to which Shaftesbury owes allegiance. It proceeds through Plato, Aristotle and the Stoics, to the Cambridge Platonists of the previous century, especially Cudworth, whose influence on Shaftesbury was considerable.[2] For Shaftesbury the universe is a well-ordered, intelligible system, in which humans have their proper place. By the use of unaided natural reason we can discover what role we are designed to play in that system and thus live virtuous and happy lives. That role is not arbitrary, but dictated by the very nature of things – by the way the world is organized.

This theme is developed in the first half of the *Inquiry*, which explores what it is to be a good or virtuous person, and how virtue is related to religion. The goodness of any creature, whether animal or human, must be judged, Shaftesbury holds, by its contribution to the good of the system of which it is a part. Just as each organ, if it is sound, is well-fitted to play its role in the functioning of the body, so each animal, if it is a good one of its kind, plays its part in a wider system. Each system is, in turn, part of a larger system, until we eventually reach the universe, which is the complete system comprehending all others. Thus each animal is a member of a species, and has a role to play in the preservation of the species as a whole. Each species, in its turn, makes a contribution to the welfare of other species, and so is a part of a system of animals. That system is itself a sub-system within the broader ecological system of the planet, and so on.

Each creature is ultimately to be judged good or bad by the contribution it makes to the good order of the universe. While a predator may appear bad from the point of view of the hunted, it is not really bad if, as Shaftesbury believes, it plays its proper part in the economy of the whole. It is, however, perfectly proper to judge an individual or a species bad, from the point of view of some sub-system of which it is a part, if it is injurious to the whole of the rest of that sub-system. Thus it is sufficient to show that a human being is bad if he is, by his nature, harmful to his fellow-humans.

In judging someone to be good or bad we are concerned only with his character. We look to see if what Shaftesbury calls his affections – his desires, motives and enjoyments – are good. Thus we do not think ill of someone because he has an infectious disease, though this may cause harm to others. Nor do we think well of someone who has only refrained from crime because she is imprisoned, or because of fear of punishment. This is as true of animals as it is of humans; a dog does not cease to be vicious because it is muzzled or cowed by its keeper. Neither do we think someone good if they act from a motive which, though it usually does harm, on this occasion happens to do good. 'A good creature is such a one as by the natural temper or bent of his affections is carried primarily and immediately, and not secondarily and accidentally, to good, and against ill.'[3] Shaftesbury is not as clear as he might be about what it is for an affection to carry an agent immediately (or, as he sometimes says, directly) to the good. The most charitable interpretation is that an affection is good if it has a natural tendency to promote the public good, even though particular circumstances may conspire to prevent the normal effects. It is certainly not necessary that what is desired is some good of the system to which one belongs. There are some instincts or desires, such as that for self-preservation, which, though their object is one's own good, normally and naturally contribute to the good of the species, since a species whose members lacked that instinct would be less likely to survive.

Both humans and other animals can be good, but only humans can be virtuous. What differentiates them from animals is that they are self-conscious. They have the capacity to reflect on their own actions and affections so that these in their turn can become the object of approval or disapproval. Our attitude will, of course, be determined by the contribution the action or affection in question makes to the public good. We cannot help forming these reflective affections. Shaftesbury, in typical eighteenth-century vein, goes so far as to maintain that, provided he has no personal interest in the case, even a morally corrupt person will approve of what is 'natural and honest' and disapprove of what is 'dishonest and corrupt'.[4] While we have no choice in forming these reflective affections their presence does enable humans to make choices about their actions in a way that is impossible for unreflective animals. Animals, because they lack a capacity for rational reflection, always act on the strongest unreflective desire. But a human being whose unreflective affections are not in the sort of harmony which would lead her naturally to do good can, nevertheless, resist the pull of any desire which reflection tells her is one on which she should not act. Thus rational reflection is capable of overcoming desire, and we can build a capacity for virtue which will withstand the assault of even the most alluring temptation.

Shaftesbury then turns to the relation between morality and religion. Like the Cambridge Platonists before him, he is opposed to theological voluntarism: the view that what is right or wrong depends on the will or decision of God. Voluntarism locates our obligation to obey God, not in any legitimacy which authorizes him to command and requires others to obey, but in His unchallengeable power, which compels our obedience through fear of the consequences of rebellion. It conflicts with both the central tenets of Shaftesbury's world-view because it denies that right and wrong are determined by the nature of the universe, independently of anyone's choice, and it denies that we can discover how we should live by rational reflection on our own nature and that of the world. If what is right or wrong depends on

God's will, then we require divine revelation to find out what our obligations are.

The rejection of voluntarism leaves open the question of whether religious belief, or the lack of it, has a good or a bad influence on one's virtue. Shaftesbury argues that false religion or superstition can certainly corrupt one's moral sensé by giving one a distorted sense of values. Atheism, by contrast, does better on this account since it does not itself prescribe the adoption of any particular values. Nor is it necessary to believe in God in order to distinguish right from wrong; our capacity to reflect on our own actions is sufficient for that. Belief in God might, nevertheless, strengthen our commitment to virtue. This is not, as the voluntarist supposes, because fear of divine wrath keeps us in check, since Shaftesbury has already argued that one who acts rightly through fear of punishment is not thereby virtuous. The recognition of God's moral perfection can, however, inspire us to develop our character so that it becomes more virtuous. It is easier, Shaftesbury concludes, to love the order or harmony of character in which virtue consists if one is convinced that the world is an orderly and harmonious system in which virtue has its proper place. Hence true theism has advantages, so far as the practice of virtue is concerned, over atheism.

Having defined virtue '[i]t remains to inquire, what obligation there is to virtue; or what reason to embrace it'.[5] Shaftesbury assumes, without argument, that he can only show that there is reason to be virtuous if he can show that it is in our interest to be so. In other words, Shaftesbury is a rational egoist; the justification of any way of life consists in showing how it would benefit the agent. He is not, as we have seen, a psychological egoist for he holds that we can be motivated by a concern, not for our own good, but for the good of the system of which we are a part. Nor is he an ethical egoist, for morality requires us to be motivated by a concern for others.

To be virtuous, as we have seen, an agent's affections must be so ordered as to dispose him to promote the common good. There are, Shaftesbury holds, three kinds of affections: natural affections which lead to public good; self-affections, which lead only to private good, and unnatural affections, which promote neither public nor private good, and may even have the opposite effect. Affections of the third type are intrinsically vicious; whether an affection of either of the first two kinds is good or bad depends on its strength; a desire can be bad in being either too strong or too weak for the constitution of that creature.

The distinction between the first two kinds of affection is unclear. His remarks seem most naturally to be taken as implying that a desire is a self-affection if, in the ordinary course of nature, indulging that affection tends to promote only the good of the agent and not the good of the species. But Shaftesbury includes among the self-affections self-preservation which, as we have seen, promotes the public good. Sometimes it seems that this distinction rests not on the causal tendency of the affection, but on whether the object of the affection is a good of the agent or of others.

His discussion of the correct classification of the delight some people take in mathematical and scientific discovery is an illustration of the latter point. He thinks it sufficient to show that this delight is not a self-affection to point out that it is quite disinterested. That is, its object is not some advantage to ourselves. In particular, its object is not the pleasure we gain from the contemplation. It is, he claims, a natural affection, because it is a delight in an admirable feature of the universe, namely its harmony and proportion.

Virtue consists in having no affections of the third kind, and in those of the first two sorts being neither too strong nor too weak. It is possible, though unusual, to have one's self-affections too weak, or one's natural affections too strong. To have an insufficient concern for one's own good or safety is a 'vice and imperfection'.[6] An over-strong natural affection can frustrate its own ends and is also a defect. Thus an excess of pity can simply paralyse, rendering one incapable of giving aid. Vice more usually consists, however, in any or all of the following: an insufficient concern for others, an excessive concern with oneself, or the presence of unnatural desires. To prove that virtue is in one's interest Shaftesbury must therefore show that to be in any of these three states is to be in an unenviable and miserable condition.

He begins with the natural affections. His strategy is to show that mental pleasures are vastly superior to bodily ones; he then argues that the mental pleasures are either identical with the natural affections or are their effects. There are difficulties with this strategy. First, the distinction between mental and bodily pleasures is not a clear one, yet Shaftesbury offers no help in drawing it. As examples of the sensual appetites, from whose satisfaction bodily pleasure arises, he apparently offers us the tired triumvirate of desires for food, drink and sex. Even here there is some unclarity, for he classifies sexual desire as a natural affection, because it has as its end the good of the propagation of the species. Unlike the other natural affections, however, its satisfaction gives rise to a sensual as well as a mental pleasure.

Second, Shaftesbury holds that it is only the natural affections which are, or can give rise to, the higher mental pleasures and thus make their possessor truly happy. But it is by no means clear that every desire or delight of an intellectual kind is to be classed as a natural affection, even if we think that he has successfully made out his case with respect to the joys of mathematics. There remains a suspicion that Shaftesbury cheats by suggesting that the only possible competition to the delights of virtuous living comes from the grubby sensual pleasures.

The pleasures of the virtuous life, Shaftesbury plausibly claims, are considerable. We are conscious of how delightful it is to be moved by such affections as 'love, gratitude, bounty, generosity, pity, succour, or whatever else is of a social or friendly sort'.[7] Not only are these feelings delightful in themselves but they are usually accompanied by equally delightful effects. The virtuous person derives a sympathetic pleasure from the good of others and is pleasantly conscious of the love and merited esteem of others. Finally, the virtuous person will be able to reflect on her own life with pleasure. The vicious person will still, as we have seen, disapprove of his own deeds and character, and will thus feel discomfort whenever he reviews, as he sometimes must, the conduct of his own life. In making this last claim Shaftesbury greatly underestimates the human capacity for self-deception. It is true that self-esteem is an important element in happiness, but those who lack any real worth are often not short of it.

Such are the rewards of virtue. How can we show them to be superior to the pleasures of sensual indulgence? Shaftesbury appeals, in a manner later to be made (in)famous by John Stuart Mill, to the verdict of qualified judges; that is, those who have had a full and proper experience of both kinds of pleasure. It turns out, however, that the verdict is a foregone conclusion, for whereas the temperance of the virtuous person makes him all the more able to savour keenly the delights of the flesh, 'the immoral and profligate man can by no means be allowed a good judge of social pleasure, to which he is so mere a stranger by his nature'.[8] This is too quick. It may be that a just appreciation of the social pleasures, like a taste for olives or opera, takes time and application to achieve. So we can reasonably demand that would-be judges give both kinds of pleasure a fair trial. But we cannot, without begging the question, assume that the sensualist only prefers his way of life because he has so little acquaintance with the alternatives.

Fortunately, Shaftesbury has a better point to make. The mere gratification of bodily appetite does not, in itself, offer any great satisfaction and soon palls. The real pleasures in the life of a bon viveur are social, the conviviality which comes from eating and drinking together. Nor should we assume that it is only the physical pleasures which make sexual relations enjoyable; much greater pleasure comes from the mutual passion and requited love of which sexual intimacy can be an expression. The sensualist misidentifies the source of much of the satisfaction that he obtains. We might add that the social pleasures that enter his life are, partly because of that misidentification, often second-rate; the conviviality forced and shallow and the passion feigned.

If a deficiency in the natural affections is not in one's interest, neither is an excess of self-love. An exaggerated concern for the prolongation of one's own life would lead one to cling to life even when illness or pain made this undesirable. The life of one who is excessively concerned about her own safety is full of the unpleasant emotions of fear and anxiety. Moreover, such a concern can be self-defeating, by robbing its victim of the capacity, when in peril, for sensible and resolute action which might save her life.

Among the unnatural passions are sadism, malice, envy, misanthropy and sexual perversion. To be prey to any of these is to be miserable. For the vicious person will not only be the object of the hostility and disapproval of others, but will also be aware, since he cannot extinguish his moral sense, that their attitude to him is justified. Nevertheless, we might object, there is surely this to be said for unnatural affections, that their satisfaction is pleasurable. Shaftesbury, however, following Plato, denies that these are true or genuine pleasures. Some states are only pleasurable in comparison to the unpleasantness of what went before. Thus recovery from an illness, or cessation of a headache, may be experienced as intensely pleasurable. In reality, we might think, there is no positive or real pleasure here, but only the relief of returning to a neutral state. No one would choose to have a migraine in order to experience the joy of its disappearance. Similar remarks can be made about cravings, addictions and even bodily appetites. There is nothing in itself particularly appealing about drinking a glass of water, but when one is parched with thirst it seems delicious, by contrast to the discomfort which preceded it. The trouble with cravings is that they are unpleasant in themselves and drive their possessor to satisfy them to gain that 'pleasure' which is, in effect, only the temporary removal of discomfort. Other pleasures are not preceded by discomfort; the delight of smelling an unexpected scent, or coming across a magnificent view, need not depend for their intensity on the quieting of some craving. Such, on this view, are the true pleasures.

If Shaftesbury were right in claiming that all unnatural desires are cravings, whereas the social affections give genuine pleasure, then he would have made a powerful case for his contention that anyone who encourages her unnatural affections will lead a miserable life. But we might doubt this claim. Contrast the natural affection of benevolence and the unnatural one of malice or ill-will. They seem mere mirror images of each other. The benevolent person is pleased when people flourish, pained when things go badly for them. The malicious person's reactions are the reverse. We need not think of the malicious, any more than the benevolent, as in the grip of some craving, from which he can only obtain occasional and temporary relief.

Despite these flaws in his arguments Shaftesbury has made out a strong case for saying that, in general, it is better to have the kind of sociable character that is sensitive to the rights and welfare of others, and that it is no good thing to be excessively self-absorbed. But is this enough to show that it is on every occasion in our interest to be virtuous? Surely the demands of morality sometimes involve a sacrifice for which there is no adequate compensation. And how can that be compatible with our self-interest?

Shaftesbury could acknowledge that morality may require individual acts which are not in our interest and yet defend his theory. He would have to claim that it is in our interest to develop a character in which the self-affections are not too strong and the natural affections not too weak. If we develop such a character we may sometimes be motivated to do an act which, on balance, damages our interests. But it will still be in our interest to develop such a character if there is no other character we could have developed that would serve those interests better.

Shaftesbury's influence on eighteenth-century thought was enormous. Of British philosophical works of the period only Locke's *Essay* went through more editions than the *Characteristics*. Among those who were most influenced was Hutcheson and, through him, Hume. This has no doubt occasioned the quite common view[9] that Shaftesbury was the founder of the sentimentalist school in ethics and the originator of the view that moral distinctions are known by a moral sense. I am inclined to think that this is mistaken. Shaftesbury's occasional use of the term 'moral sense' is casual and carries no implication that moral discernment is analogous to sensory awareness of secondary qualities. Nor would he side with those who held that morality is based on human sentiment or feeling rather than on reason. Moral distinctions are eternal and immutable, and the reflective faculty which discovers them is reason itself. Shaftesbury does indeed hold that, once we are capable of rational reflection on our affections, we shall immediately and inevitably develop reflective affections, but that may only be because, as a good Platonist, he holds that to recognise the good is to love it.

❦ JOSEPH BUTLER ❦

Butler's ethical doctrines are to be found in his *Fifteen Sermons* and in the later *Analogy of Religion*, particularly in the 'Dissertation on Virtue' which forms an Appendix to the latter. He is as much a practical as a theoretical thinker; his careful analysis is aimed at dispelling any intellectual confusions in his audience which may give them grounds, or at least excuse, for being less devoted to the cause of virtue than they should be. His central contention is that virtue consists in following human nature and vice in deviating from it, and that this reflection is sufficient to show why we should follow the path of virtue.

Like Shaftesbury, he conceives of the virtuous person as someone in whom the various motivational principles stand in the right relation to each other. For Butler, human nature is hierarchical; there are at least two principles which are by nature superior to the rest and whose verdicts must be respected. These are self-love, which considers what is in our interest, and conscience, which judges what is right or wrong. Butler's use of the term conscience is wider than ours – its verdicts embrace not only my own actions but those of others. Some commentators have contended, mistakenly in my view,[10] that Butler also thought of benevolence as a superior principle. At the bottom of the pecking order are the particular appetites, passions and affections, which can be thought of as desires for particular things – food, shelter, comfort, and so on.

Butler's account of superiority rests on a distinction between the strength and the authority of a principle of action. If there were no superior principles in our nature then we should be acting according to our natures in following the strongest impulse. A superior principle, however, has an authority which is independent of its strength, so that the question of whether we should act on its edicts is settled by appeal to its authority. That authority is a rational one; the verdict of a superior principle provides better reason to act than the promptings of an inferior one. To act deliberately in defiance of one's interest, or of what is right, is thus to violate one's own nature, for it is to follow a lower principle in preference to a higher, to prefer the worse reason to the better. Butler does not attempt to *argue* that moral and prudential requirements provide better reasons for action than those that stem from particular desires, rather he seeks simply to remind his readers of what he takes to be common knowledge. What chiefly seems to distinguish conscience and self-love from the other principles is that they are both reflective; they both survey our actual or proposed actions and pronounce upon their worthiness.

Though similar in their reflective authority, self-love and conscience differ in various ways. Butler classifies self-love, but not conscience, as an affection. It is hard to know what to make of this, but it seems to imply two things, both of which can be questioned. First, self-love, like any of the affections but unlike conscience, can be present in an immoderate degree, in which case it is liable to frustrate its own end. To this it might be objected that conscientiousness, as well as prudence, may perhaps be carried to excess. Second, Butler thinks of self-love, like any affection or desire, as having a distinctive feeling-tone of which we are aware when it is aroused in us. But in writing, as he sometimes does, of *cool* self-love Butler seems implicitly to acknowledge that a concern for our own good may be present and effective without manifesting itself as a feeling. Nor does it seem correct to deny that the promptings of conscience can have a feeling-tone; the pangs of conscience can be as searing as those of unrequited love.

More importantly, Butler contrasts the judgements of self-love, which require careful calculation of all the consequences of the actions open to us, with the deliverances of conscience, which are immediate, not in the sense that they require no thought, but that they are concerned only with the nature of the action itself, including the intention, and not with its consequences. Conscience 'pronounces determinately some actions to be in themselves just, right, good; others to be in themselves evil, wrong, unjust'.[11] Judgements of conscience, unlike those of self-love, are thus not hostage to fortune; we do not have to wait to see how things turn out in order to determine whether our moral judgement was correct.

In what relation do self-love and conscience stand to each other in Butler's hierarchical account of motivational principles? Are they equal or does one carry more authority than the other? This is a question to which Butler appears to give a variety of answers, and his apparent inconsistencies have much exercised commentators. Since he is generally concerned with theoretical matters only in so far as they bear on practice it might at first appear that he could, and perhaps should, have avoided the question altogether. For Butler is as convinced as Shaftesbury that there can never be a genuine conflict between duty and self-interest, at least if we take into account a future life.

> Conscience and self-love, if we understand our true happiness, always lead us the same way. Duty and interest are perfectly coincident; for the most part in this world, but entirely and in every instance if we take in the future and the whole; this being implied in the notion of a good and perfect administration of things.[12]

The question does not however, as Butler points out, lack practical application. Those who doubt Butler's claim can face a choice between what they believe to be two conflicting sources of obligation, and those who accept it may still find, because of the limitations of our knowledge, that self-love and conscience offer conflicting advice on some occasion.

Butler often writes as if conscience is pre-eminent, but there are places where he seems to rank the two equally and, in one notorious passage, self-love is given the power of veto.

> Let it be allowed, though virtue or moral rectitude does indeed consist in affection to and pursuit of what is right and good,

as such; yet, that when we sit down in a cool hour, we can neither justify to ourselves this or any other pursuit, till we are convinced that it will be for our happiness, or at least not contrary to it.[13]

This passage is generally considered not to represent Butler's considered views but to be a concession by him to his sceptical and wordly congregation. Even if Butler does not hold that we are not justified in pursuing some course unless we are convinced that it is not contrary to our interest, we should not however conclude that he holds that we would ever be justified in acting in a way that we were convinced was against our self-interest. For he nowhere states that moral obligations are, by their very nature, superior to prudential ones. What he does offer is an argument for holding that, when in doubt, we are obliged to follow the guidance of conscience rather than self-love. That argument is based, however, not on the superiority of moral to prudential reasons, but on the difference between the calculative nature of prudential reasoning and the immediacy of the verdicts of conscience.

> For the natural authority of the principle of reflection [i.e. conscience] is an obligation the most near and intimate, the most certain and known: whereas the contrary obligation can at the utmost appear no more than probable; since no man can be *certain* in any circumstances that vice is his interest in the present world, much less can he be certain against another: and thus the certain obligation would entirely supersede and destroy the uncertain one.[14]

Thus Butler holds, in conscious opposition to Shaftesbury, that our obligation to virtue remains even if we are completely sceptical about the coincidence of duty and interest. We do not have to appeal to something external to morality as our justification for doing what is right.

On what grounds does conscience determine that some course of action is the morally right one? Butler, in denying that benevolence is the whole of virtue, rejects the utilitarian position (strongly urged, for example, by Hutcheson) that the right action is the one which produces the most happiness. Butler advocates instead a pluralist deontology; that is, a theory in which there are several distinct duties, of which benevolence is merely one, each of which has its own claim on us. We disapprove, for example, of stealing and fraud in and of themselves, quite independently of their generally deleterious effects on the general happiness. Butler thinks that our other duties can be encompassed within three general headings: justice, veracity and, perhaps more controversially, prudence. Imprudence is, he holds, a vice because we not only regret our follies but disapprove of them as well.

Although Butler is clear that we are not, and should not be, utilitarians, he does appear at least to entertain the hypothesis that God might be a utilitarian, concerned only with maximizing the happiness of his creatures. If that were so, then He would have implanted a deontological conscience in us because 'He foresaw this constitution of our nature would produce more happiness, than forming us with a temper of more general benevolence'.[15] It is doubtful, however, if Butler would endorse this suggestion, for the following reason. He holds that to judge actions as morally good or evil carries with it the thought that they deserve reward or punishment respectively. God, as a morally righteous judge, must be supposed to reward and punish us according to our deserts. But to say that someone deserves ill is not to say 'that we conceive it for the good of society, that the doer of such actions should be made to suffer'.[16] Questions of desert look back to the quality of the action, but utilitarianism is essentially forward-looking, concerned only with the future effects of reward and punishment. In treating us according to our deserts God would be motivated not by benevolence but by justice.

Many commentators have criticized Butler for failing to give a more detailed account of the criteria which conscience might apply in determining what we ought to do on any specific occasion. In particular, he does not address a problem which faces anyone who holds that there is more than one duty, namely how we should decide in cases where duties conflict. His silence stems from his conviction that further guidance is not necessary.

> The inquiries which have been made by men of leisure, after some general rule, the conformity to, or disagreement from which, would denominate our actions good or evil, are in many respects of great service. Yet let any plain honest man, before he engages in any course of action, ask himself, Is this I am going about right, or is it wrong? Is it good or is it evil? I do not in the least doubt, but that this question would be answered agreeably to truth and virtue, by almost any fair man in almost any circumstance.[17]

While I share Butler's doubts about the utility of the reflections of the 'men of leisure', it is no longer possible to share Butler's confidence in the (almost complete) inerrancy of the pronouncements of conscience.

While benevolence may not be the whole of virtue it is a large part of it, and a correspondingly large part of Butler's defence of virtue is devoted to defending benevolence against two kinds of attack from those who think that self-love is, or ought to be, our only motive. He seeks to show, first, that benevolence is a genuine motive in human beings and, second, that there is no special antipathy between self-love and benevolence.

Benevolence is real only if people are sometimes directly motivated by a concern for the welfare of others. Two theories deny that this is the case: psychological egoism, which holds that all our actions are, at bottom, motivated by a concern for our own good, and psychological hedonism, which holds that what primarily motivates us is always the prospect of our own pleasure.

Butler's central argument against the psychological egoism of thinkers such as Hobbes and Mandeville draws on his analysis of the differences between self-love and the other, particular, affections. The particular affections are directed towards some specific object or state of affairs which we find attractive, for example, drinking a glass of beer, reading a novel or playing a round of golf. The object of self-love is not, however, any particular desirable state of affairs, but one's own happiness as such. Happiness is defined by Butler as consisting 'only in the enjoyment of those objects, which are by nature suited to our several particular appetites, passions, and affections'.[18] Self-love, the desire for our own happiness, is thus a reflective affection; it is a desire that our other desires attain their objects. But if that is so, then it cannot be the case that we are motivated solely by self-love. Self-love achieves its object through the satisfaction of our other affections; 'take away these affections and you leave self-love absolutely nothing at all to employ itself about'.[19] While we might question Butler's claim that happiness is to be identified with the satisfaction of our various affections, it cannot be doubted that getting what we want is an important element in happiness, and that is all Butler needs for this argument to be decisive.

The psychological hedonist claims that Butler has misdescribed the object of the particular affections; what motivates us to drink beer, play a round of golf, or relieve the distressed is always the pleasure we shall receive from these activities. Did they not please us we should not engage in them. So our primary object in helping others is not their welfare, but our pleasure. Making them happy is but a means to making ourselves happy. Butler argues in reply that the hedonist's account of the object of our affections is incoherent. We only derive pleasure from engaging in an activity or achieving a goal, Butler claims, if we want to engage in that activity or achieve that goal. I will only get pleasure from playing cricket if I want to play it; if I only wanted the pleasure and cared nothing for cricket my efforts to achieve pleasure that way would be self-stultifying. When I help others I may well get pleasure from doing so, but that does not show that my aim was to experience the pleasures of altruism. On the contrary, I must have wanted to help them in order to be pleased; my primary object must have been their good. Of course, given that I do experience pleasure from acting altruistically, self-love may encourage me to continue in that path in order to get more pleasure. But the pleasure will cease unless I continue to be motivated by a concern for the others' good.

This is a famous rebuttal but not, I think, a decisive one. It crucially depends on the claim that we cannot find pleasure in any activity unless we have a prior desire to engage in it. That claim is, however, false. Some pleasures come unbidden and unsought, as when we suddenly smell a delightful scent, or discover a fascinating programme while idly twiddling the radio tuner. The psychological hedonist can make use of this fact to construct a theory in which all intentional action is motivated by a desire for the associated pleasure. We are born, this theory runs, with some instincts which lead us to explore our environment in the search for food, warmth and so on, and a capacity to take pleasure in certain activities, while finding others distasteful. Our initial behaviour is thus instinctual but not intentional. We soon discover, however, that some activities are pleasant or bring pleasure in their wake. We then repeat the activity in order to experience the pleasure again. It is always the prospect of further pleasure which motivates the intentional repetition of what was not, initially, an intentional action. The correct response to this defence of hedonism is, I believe, to deny the distinction in terms of which the debate takes place; that is, to deny that we can here distinguish between our wanting to do some act and our wanting the pleasure that comes from doing it. But that would take us beyond Butler's argument.

Are benevolence and self-love incompatible? Butler has shown that the exercise of self-love requires us to be motivated by particular affections, and some of these affections, such as ambition and desire for esteem, have some good of our own as their primary end. Between such affections and self-love there would seem to be no essential conflict. Benevolence, however, appears directly opposed to self-love. The former aims at the good of others, the latter at my own good; so the more I am motivated by the one the less, it seems, I can be motivated by the other.

Butler's exposition of the mistake behind this line of thought is masterly. It falsely presupposes that if I am acting in your interests I cannot also be promoting my own. Butler's analysis has shown that, with respect to any desire of mine, my happiness consists in that desire being gratified. This is as true of a desire for the happiness of others as it is of any other desire. Insofar as I want you to be happy then my happiness depends on your being happy; my happiness is bound up with yours. We must not think of happiness by analogy with property, so that to give happiness to others is necessarily to diminish my own.

The truth is that benevolence, while distinct from self-love, is no more opposed to it than to any other particular passion. The gratification of any passion whatever will be seconded by self-love when it promotes my interest and vetoed by it when it conflicts with it.

Butler proceeds, in a Shaftesburian vein, to show both that to have a character in which benevolence is a strong motive is conducive to happiness, and that an excessive concern for one's own happiness is self-defeating. His discussion errs at only one point, and that is easily corrected. Butler equates selfishness with immoderate self-love, i.e. with an excessive calculating concern for one's own interest or advantage. But there is another type of person who is also properly regarded as selfish. As we have seen, some of our particular affections, such as ambition or covetousness, have as their end some good to ourselves; others, such as compassion or love of one's children, aim at the good of another. Someone in whom the former desires are too strong and the latter too weak is rightly seen as selfish, even if the attempt to satisfy his selfish desires leads him to ignore his real interest. Imprudence and selfishness are not incompatible.

Where does Butler fit into the eighteenth-century debate between rationalism and sentimentalism? Given his interest in moral instruction, rather than in metaphysical theory, Butler constructed a moral psychology which was neutral between rationalism and sentimentalism. Throughout his writings, however, there are clear indications that he sides with the rationalists in general and, almost certainly, with the position of Samuel Clarke in particular (with whom he corresponded on moral theory while he was a very young man).

❧ RICHARD PRICE ❧

Richard Price develops a rationalist theory which develops and improves on earlier theories, such as Clarke's. While indebted in many ways to both Shaftesbury and Butler, Price is chiefly distinguished from them by his interest in moral epistemology. The sentimentalists offer us an account of moral awareness which is modelled on what had been, since Locke, the orthodox account of our awareness of secondary qualities, such as colours, tastes, sounds and smells. The story runs like this. Through our sense-organs we are able to receive ideas of objects and events in our immediate environment. Some of these ideas, those of the primary qualities, such as shape, size and solidity, are both caused by and resemble those qualities in the objects of which they are ideas. There is nothing, however, in the objects themselves that resembles our ideas of colour, sound and so on. The story of what is going on in the physical world when someone sees red or smells coffee would not mention colours or smells at all. Rather, the object is so constituted that, under certain circumstances, it emits either waves or particles which stimulate the sense-organs in certain ways causing us to have the characteristic secondary quality experience. It follows that creatures whose sense-organs were unlike ours would have a quite different range of secondary quality experience.

When it comes, however, to the question of what colours, smells etc. actually are, we find two accounts current. First, there is the dispositional theory: colours etc. are properties of the object, but now understand as nothing more than a disposition of the object to cause characteristic ideas in normal human observers in standard perceptual conditions. Second, there is the subjective theory: colours, sounds etc. are not in the objects themselves but are identified with the ideas in the perceiving subject caused by those objects. Both accounts exist, in tension, in Locke, though it is now generally agreed that the former represents Locke's 'official' theory. But the latter account gained considerable currency through the work of Berkeley and Hume, who took it to be the one Locke was offering.[20] It is the account which Price accepts, and which he takes the sentimentalists to have used as their model for moral qualities. Thus the sentimentalists, represented for Price by Hutcheson, aided and abetted by Hume, maintain that '[m]oral right and wrong, signify nothing *in the objects themselves* to which they are applied, any more than agreeable and harsh; sweet and bitter; pleasant and painful; but only *certain effects in us*'.[21] We have within us a moral sense which finds certain actions (and characters) pleasing and others displeasing. It approves of the former and disapproves of the latter, and hence we call the former right (or good) and the latter wrong (or bad). It is clearly possible that there should be creatures whose moral sense is differently constituted from our own. Such beings would have different patterns of approval or disapproval from ours, but it would be idle to claim that one set of reactions might be closer to the truth or fit the facts better than another. The moral sense theory denies that there are distinctively moral facts and, if it allows for moral truth at all, can do so only relative to a particular type of moral sense.

In opposition to this view, Price offers us a realist conception of moral properties. An action is either right or wrong quite independently of our responses or choices, or those of any other being, including God. This position commits Price to rejecting not only the moral sense theory but also, like Shaftesbury and Butler before him, theological voluntarism. He sees that the prevailing Lockean epistemology forces one towards a moral sense theory and so sets about demolishing it, drawing extensively on Plato and the Cambridge Platonists, especially Cudworth.

Price agrees with the prevailing orthodoxy that all our ideas are either simple or complex, and that the latter are built out of the former. On the empiricist account, simple ideas, from which all our knowledge is built, are derived either from sense experience or from reflection on what passes in our own mind. Since our ideas of right and wrong are not sensory concepts, in the way in which squareness or redness might be thought to be, they must, on the empiricist story, be ideas of reflection. From what aspect of our inner life might they be derived? The obvious answer is from the feelings of pleasure or displeasure, approval and disapproval we experience when we contemplate action or character. Empiricism thus spawns a theory which offers an account of morality, not in terms of the nature of the object but in terms of our response to it.

Price defends several anti-empiricist theses which he does not always clearly distinguish. His main contention is that there is a third source of simple ideas, in addition to sense and reflection, namely the understanding, and that right and wrong are simple ideas derived from this third source. Sense and understanding have, on Price's view, quite different roles. Sense deals only with particulars – we are necessarily only aware, on any occasion, of one or more particular things and their properties – whereas understanding can grasp universals or abstract ideas and the relations between them. Sense is passive, while understanding is an active, discerning faculty, which, reflects, compares, judges and seeks to comprehend the nature of things. An idea which has its source in the understanding would be an a priori rather than an empirical concept; that is, a concept which could not be constructed by the standard Lockean method of abstraction from the contents of sense-experience.

Price's defence of the claim that right and wrong are simple a priori concepts is to search, as J. L. Mackie once put it, for companions in guilt. He produces many examples of ideas whose source, he claims, can only be the understanding, and these fall into different groups. They include: ideas applicable to objects of more than one sense, such as equality, resemblance and difference; ideas of what is unobservable, such as substance; ideas that involve modal notions, such as impenetrability and causation. (Modal notions include necessity and possibility. If something is impenetrable then it *cannot* be penetrated; if one thing causes another then, given the first, the second *must* follow. Experience can only tell us what does happen, not what cannot or must happen.)

We might concede, for the sake of argument, that all the items on this rather motley list are a priori concepts, but they are not all, on even the most generous interpretation, simple ideas, for many of them seem capable of further analysis. Price does not seem to be aware of this objection, but his argument may easily be developed to show that the understanding is the source of *simple* ideas. What Price is trying to show is that the complex concepts on his list cannot be built up in the standard empiricist manner, from simple ideas of sense or reflection. But then, given the traditional account of simple and complex within which Price is operating, that can only be because, of the simple ideas out of which they are built, at least one must itself be a priori. Thus, in the cases of concepts like impenetrability and causation, the argument would seem to be this. To hold that something is, say, impenetrable, is to hold that it is impossible for another body to occupy the space which it is occupying. The concept of impossibility is a plausible candidate, however, for being a simple a priori concept. Although there are other ways of saying that something is impossible – such as saying that it cannot happen – these do not provide an analysis of the concept into simpler elements. To understand that something cannot happen presupposes that one understands what it is for something to be impossible, and vice versa. So Price's argument can be construed as supporting the claim that there are simple a priori concepts.

If there are simple a priori concepts, then rightness and wrongness may certainly be among them. Since the consequence of believing they are not is the adoption of the counter-intuitive moral sense theory, we are justified in believing they do have this status. It has to be said, however, that Price makes the case for realism look stronger than he is entitled to by confronting it with a weak and implausible version of the moral sense theory. Because Price holds the subjective theory of secondary qualities he takes it that it is not only false but absurd to ascribe colours, sounds and so on to bodies.

> A *coloured body*, if we speak accurately, is the same absurdity with a *square sound*. We need no experience to prove that heat, cold, colours, tastes, etc. are not real qualities of bodies; because the ideas of matter and of these qualities are incompatible. But is there indeed any such incompatability between *actions* and *right*? Or any such absurdity in affirming the one of the other? Are the ideas of them as different as the idea of a sensation and its cause? [22]

But a sensible moral sense theorist would opt for the dispositional account of secondary qualities as his model and then argue, by analogy, that it is perfectly proper to speak of actions as right or wrong, just as it is to speak of objects as coloured. He would hope to give an account which did not require Price's kind of realism but which left our normal way of speaking and thinking unaltered.

Another of Price's favourite arguments against the moral sense theorist, which we might dub the indifference argument, is also too quick. It takes a theological turn in Price, but its implications are more general. If no actions are in themselves right and wrong then they are, in themselves, morally indifferent. God, who is not deceived, would recognize this and hence would be unable to approve or disapprove of any action, for He would see that nothing in reality could ground His approval or disapproval. But that would be to suppose that His concern for our happiness had no rational foundation and was the result of 'mere unintelligent inclination'[23] which would greatly detract from His moral perfection. The more general consequence of this line of thought is that, if the moral sense theory were true, it would be irrational to continue to make moral judgements once we had discovered this truth. This conclusion serves, once again, to make the rival theory look unpalatable. But the crucial premise, that the moral sense theory deprives us of any good reasons for approving of one course of action rather than another, is not supported.

The origin of our ideas of right and wrong is not the only issue between Price and the empiricists. For Price claims that we can have a priori knowledge of basic moral principles. The rightness or wrongness of an act springs from its nature. Thus an act may be wrong in virtue of its being, for example, cruel, or dishonest, or a breach of promise. The connection between the moral character of an act and those features on which its moral character depends is, Price maintains, a necessary one. If cruel actions are wrong then they are wrong in all possible circumstances. Empiricism claims, however, that all our knowledge of the world comes from experience and experience can, apparently, reveal only contingent connections between features. It can show only that they are connected, not that they must be. Price asserts, in contradiction to this, that we know of these connections through an intuitive act of reason; not, that is, through a process of reasoning, but by rational reflection on the propositions in question.

Empiricists classically allow that there is one kind of connection which is necessary and can be known a priori, and that is a connection between concepts – a doctrine which finds expression in Hume's account of relations of ideas. We can know a priori, to use a hackneyed example, the necessary truth that all bachelors are unmarried because to be a bachelor just is to be an unmarried man. If it could similarly be shown that the concepts of rightness and wrongness can be analysed into other, less philosophically puzzling, concepts then two contentious features of Price's account would be removed at a stroke. Suppose, to give a concrete example, it was claimed that to call an action right was simply to claim that it was productive of happiness. First, we would have to show that the word 'wrong' signified, not a mysterious a priori concept graspable only by understanding, but the familiar empirical notion of making people happy. Second, we could then accommodate, within an empiricist epistemology, the claim that it is a necessary truth, known a priori, that an action which produces happiness is right.

It is here that Price's claims that right and wrong are simple ideas comes to the fore. Rightness and wrongness are indefinable, and we can prove this by showing that any such analysis will produce untenable consequences. For if the proposed analysis were correct then it would be 'palpably absurd' to ask whether producing happiness is right, for that would be just to ask whether producing happiness produces happiness. But the question is not palpably absurd, and so the definition fails. This tactic was revived by G. E. Moore 150 years later and is now known as the Open Question Argument. Anyone familiar with the history of twentieth-century moral philosophy will be aware of the extent to which the epistemological issues which Price raises here have dominated the subject.

It is a corollary of his position, Price tells us, that morality is eternal and immutable. If lying and ingratitude are wrong they are so in virtue of the kinds of action they are and no one, not even God, can alter this truth. But that seems to raise an obvious difficulty. It seems reasonable to believe that an action that is in itself morally indifferent may become obligatory if commanded by God, or if I have promised to do it. Yet how can this be, if its moral nature is unalterable by the will of any agent? How could, for example, an action be indifferent before I promised to do it and obligatory after? Price's answer is that we must not suppose that, in promising to do the act, we have left the non-moral nature of the original act unchanged but changed its moral character; that is impossible. What we have done is to change the nature of the act; it is now, in addition to its earlier properties, an instance of promise-keeping and, as such, obligatory.

In the broad outlines of the remainder of his moral theory Price repeats and elaborates points already made by Butler. So I shall merely draw attention to one or two discussions where Price goes beyond anything we find in Butler.

We have seen that moral judgement is the work of reason. Our judgements of right and wrong are often accompanied, however, by feelings of delight or detestation respectively. These feelings are distinct from the judgement, but they are not merely arbitrarily connected with it in virtue of our particular human sensibilities. We feel revulsion *because* we judge the action to be wrong, and any rational agent would feel the same. Price, like Shaftesbury, is a Platonist, and holds that to love virtue it is only necessary to know it. Similarly, we should not suppose that all our desires are the product of instinctive drives which we just happen to have, but which other rational beings might lack. Some desires, such as hunger and thirst, are instinctive, and are properly called appetites. But rational creatures are so constituted that they will necessarily desire happiness and truth, once they understand the nature of these goods. Desires which are in this way the product of reason are best called affections. In imperfectly rational humans this rational desire for the happiness of ourselves and of others is strengthened by an instinctive concern for these ends; when so strengthened the resulting desire is properly called a passion.

Like Butler, Price rejects utilitarianism. We have a number of distinct duties, which he lists under six heads: (1) Duty to God; (2) Duty to self, or prudence; (3) Beneficence; (4) Gratitude; (5) Veracity; (6) Justice. Unlike Butler, Price does think that we need an account of what happens when duties conflict. In some cases, one duty is clearly weightier than another, and no perplexity arises. But there are many cases where it is not clear, and conscientious people may differ as to which duty should give way in these cases. There is always a determinate answer in such cases to the question What ought I to do? but we may lack penetration and wisdom to discern it. Doubt about what we should do in a particular case should not, however, infect our confidence in the existence of moral truth, for the fundamental principles which we bring to bear on individual cases are self-evident.

Does perfect virtue consist in performing all our duties or are there, as many have supposed, meritorious acts of heroism and saintliness which, while not morally required, are singled out for particular praise? Price maintains that there are no supererogatory acts, acts which go beyond the call of duty. Many of our obligations, such as that of being benevolent, are framed only in general terms; how we fulfil that duty is up to us. Since it is unclear how much is required of us by way of benevolence, truly virtuous persons will err on the side of generosity, but the praise we bestow on them will not be because they went beyond duty but because they showed such a great regard for their duty.

Finally, Price was apparently the first to draw the distinction, much discussed in the first half of the twentieth century, between what he called abstract and practical virtue, or what was later called objective and subjective duty. An agent's objective duty is determined by the actual facts of the case; his subjective duty by what he believes to be the facts of the case. It is for succeeding or failing to do one's subjective duty that one should be praised or blamed, for an imperfect agent cannot be required to avoid all errors of fact.[24]

❧ NOTES ❧

1 Rand [8.7], 359.
2 Although Shaftesbury was Locke's pupil, he rejected his ethics and his empiricism. See his scathing attack in a letter to Michael Ainsworth, 3 June 1709, in Rand [8.7], 403–5.

3 *Inquiry*, Book I, Part 2, sect. ii, p. 250 in [8.5]. All subsequent quotations from the *Inquiry* will appear in this form: I. 2. ii [8.5], 250.

4 *Inquiry*, I. 2. iii [8.5], 252.

5 *Inquiry*, II. 1. i [8.5], 280.

6 *Inquiry*, II. 1. iii [8.5], 288.

7 *Inquiry*, II. 2. i [8.5], 294.

8 *Inquiry*, II. 2. i [8.5], 295.

9 One might almost say, orthodoxy. See for example Selby-Bigge [8.10], xxxii; Hudson [8.12], 1.

10 I give my reasons for thinking this contention mistaken in [8.27].

11 References to Butler will be by Sermon number and paragraph number in Bernard [8.8] (reproduced in many other editions). The *Sermons* will be denoted by an *S*, the Preface, added in the second edition, by a *P*, and the *Dissertation on Virtue* by *D*. Then will come the page number in Bernard, [8.8]. Thus the present reference is *S* 2.8 [8.8], 45.

12 *S* 3.9 [8.8], I: 57.

13 *S* 11.20 [8.8], I: 151.

14 *P* 26 [8.8], I: 12.

15 *D* 8 [8.8], II: 293.

16 *D* 3 [8.8], II: 288–9.

17 *S* 3.4 [8.8], I: 53.

18 *S* 11.9 [8.8], I: 141.

19 *P* 37 [8.8], I: 17.

20 See Berkeley, *Principles*, sect. x ([8.31], 117), and Hume in Raphael [8.11], 2: 18–19.

21 Price [8.9], 15. (All future quotations from Price will just give a page number.).

22 [8.9], 46.

23 [8.9], 49.

24 I am greatly indebted to Jonathan Dancy and Eve Garrard for comments on an earlier draft of this piece.

❧❧ BIBLIOGRAPHY ❧❧

Last Edition of Cited Works in Author's Lifetime

8.1 Shaftesbury, Anthony, Lord *Characteristics of Men, Manners, Opinions, Times*, London, 3 vols, 2nd edn, 1714.

8.2 Butler, Joseph *Fifteen Sermons preached at the Rolls Chapel*, London, 4th edn, 1749.

8.3 —— *The Analogy of Religion, Natural and Revealed, to the Constitution and Course of Nature* with *Two Dissertations, On the Nature of Virtue and of Personal Identity*, London, 1736.

8.4 Price, Richard *A Review of the Principal Questions in Morals*, London, 3rd edn, 1787.

Modern Editions Cited in Notes

8.5 Shaftesbury, Anthony, Lord *Characteristics*, ed. J. Robertson, London, Grant Richards, 1900. Repr. Bobbs-Merrill, Indianapolis, 1964, with a new introduction by S. Green.

8.6 —— *An Inquiry Concerning Virtue, or Merit*, ed. D. Walford, Manchester, Manchester University Press, 1977.

8.7 *The Life, Unpublished Letters, and Philosophical Regimen of Anthony, Earl of Shaftesbury*, ed. B. Rand, New York, Macmillan, 1900.

8.8 *The Works of Bishop Butler*, ed. J. H. Bernard, London, Macmillan, 2 vols, 1900.

8.9 Price, Richard *A Review of the Principal Questions in Morals*, ed. D. D. Raphael, Oxford, Clarendon Press, 1974.

Predecessors and Successors

8.10 *British Moralists*, ed. L. A. Selby-Bigge, Oxford, Clarendon Press, 2 vols, 1897. Repr. Bobbs-Merrill, Indianapolis, 1964.

8.11 *British Moralists 1650–1800*, ed. D. D. Raphael, Oxford, Clarendon Press, 2 vols, 1969.

Books, and Parts of Books, on These Authors

(i) On all three authors

8.12 Hudson, W. *Ethical Intuitionism*, London, Macmillan, 1967.

8.13 Sidgwick, H. *Outlines of the History of Ethics*, London, Macmillan, 1949.

8.14 Stephen, L. *History of English Thought in the Eighteenth Century*, New York and London, G. P. Putnam's Sons, 2 vols, 1902.

(ii) Shaftesbury

8.15 Brett, R. L. *The Third Earl of Shaftesbury. A Study in Eighteenth Century Literary Theory*, London, Hutchinson's University Library, 1951.

8.16 Green, S. *Shaftesbury's Philosophy of Religion and Ethics*, Ohio, Ohio University Press, 1967.

(iii) Butler

8.17 Broad, C. D. *Five Types of Ethical Theory*, London, Routledge and Kegan Paul, 1930.

8.18 Cunliffe, C. *Joseph Butler's Moral and Religious Thought*, Oxford, Oxford University Press, 1992.

8.19 Duncan-Jones, A. *Butler's Moral Philosophy*, Harmondsworth, Penguin, 1952.

8.20 Penelhum, T. *Butler*, London, Routledge and Kegan Paul, 1985.

(iv) Price

8.21 Cua, A. S. *Reason and Virtue: A Study in the Ethics of Richard Price*, Athens Ohio, Ohio University Press, 1966.
8.22 Hudson, W. D. *Reason and Right: A Critical Examination of Richard Price's Moral Philosophy*, London, Macmillan, 1970.
8.23 Raphael, D. D. *The Moral Sense*, Oxford, Oxford University Press, 1947, ch. 4.
8.24 Thomas, D. O. *The Honest Mind*, Oxford, Clarendon Press, 1977.

Articles

(i) Shaftesbury

8.25 Darwall, S. 'Motive and Obligation in the British Moralists', *Social Philosophy and Policy* 7 (1989): 133–50. Issue of Journal reprinted as book: E. Paul *et al.* (eds) *Foundations of Moral and Political Philosophy*, Oxford, Blackwell, 1989.

(ii) Butler

8.26 Kleinig, J. 'Butler in a Cool Hour', *Journal of the History of Philosophy* 7 (1969): 399–411.
8.27 McNaughton, D. 'Butler on Benevolence', in Cunliffe [9.18], 269–91.
8.28 Raphael, D. D. 'Bishop Butler's View of Conscience', *Philosophy* 24 (1949): 219–38.
8.29 Sturgeon, N. 'Nature and Conscience in Butler's Ethics', *Philosophical Review* 85 (1976): 316–56.
8.30 Szabados, B. 'Butler on Corrupt Conscience', *Journal of the History of Philosophy* 14 (1976): 462–9.
8.31 White, A. 'Conscience and Self-Love in Butler's Sermons', *Philosophy* 27 (1952): 329–44.

(iii) Price

8.32 Aiken, H. D. 'The Ultimacy of Rightness in Richard Price's Ethics: A Reply to Mr. Peach', *Philosophy and Phenomenological Research* 14 (1954): 386–92.
8.33 Broad, C. D. 'Some Reflections on Moral Sense Theories in Ethics', *Proceedings of the Aristotelian Society* 45 (1944–5).
8.34 Peach, B. 'The Indefinability and Simplicity of Rightness in Richard Price's Review of Morals', *Philosophy and Phenomenological Research* 14 (1954): 370–85.

Other Works Cited

8.35 Berkeley, *A New Theory of Vision and Other Writings*, ed. A. D. Lindsay, London, Dent, 1963.

CHAPTER 9

The French Enlightenment I: science, materialism and determinism

Peter Jimack

The French Enlightenment is not just a convenient label devised by historians of philosophy, and the thinkers to be discussed in this chapter and the next were for the most part conscious of belonging to a movement. They shared to a remarkable degree, if in varying proportions, the negative and positive features which characterized it: on the one hand criticism, even rejection of traditional authority, especially that of the Church, and on the other a bold and constructive attempt to understand and explain man and the universe, and in particular to define man's place and role in society, both as it was and as it should be. On many topics (such as the origin of life, epistemology, natural law, religious toleration, political freedom), they held broadly similar views and differed only in matters of detail. The very term *'philosophes'* came to be used to designate the thinkers who held these views, and the *philosophes* actually saw themselves as a kind of brotherhood involved in a campaign, a group of 'frères' who shared the same attitudes and aspirations. Many of them were friends, or at least acquaintances, who met frequently, energetically exchanged ideas on such matters as metaphysics, morality, politics and economics – as well as gossip – and even contributed to each other's works in a variety of ways. Quite apart from the *Encyclopédie*, edited by Diderot and d'Alembert, which had over 130 contributors, several works were in a sense collective ventures, embodying the results of discussions within the group – or even, in the case of Raynal's *Histoire des deux Indes*, actual contributions by different individuals.

It has been argued that some of the principal figures of the French

Enlightenment were largely gifted vulgarizers, rather than original think-ers. While this is no doubt an exaggeration, it does draw attention to the way in which they picked up and developed ideas that had been expressed by sometimes lone voices in previous centuries. They them-selves often emphasized their links with the Ancients as a way of stress-ing their rejection of Christian tradition, though if their declared hero was Socrates, a more specific inspiration was probably provided by the materialism and evolutionary ideas of Lucretius. As for the modern world, Montaigne had adopted a relativist anthropological approach to morality two centuries before Montesquieu, and Descartes's rationalism had opened the way to the confidence in human reason and the rejection of traditional authority: his mechanistic account of man all but excluded the soul, and his mechanistic account of the universe all but dispensed with God. Pierre Bayle, a follower of Descartes in his use of reason, had ridiculed superstition (and by implication certain religious beliefs) in his *Pensées sur la Comète* (1682), which ended with a chapter envisag-ing, of all things, the possibility of a society of atheists. In his *Diction-naire historique et critique* (1697), which was to become an arsenal of material for use by Voltaire and others in the battle against the Church, he applied Cartesian scepticism to history, and more significantly, to biblical history. In the field of science, Bacon, a contemporary of Mon-taigne, had spelled out an ambitious programme of enquiry, based on investigation and experiment instead of the acceptance of authority, which would be one of the great inspirations of the *Encyclopédie*; and Newton's huge step forward in explaining the laws governing the uni-verse had made it ever easier to conceive of a world without God, despite his own deep religious convictions. Above all, perhaps, Locke's account in his *Essay concerning human understanding* (1690) of the origin of knowledge and genesis of the human faculties provided a starting-point both in content and in methodology for virtually all Enlightenment thought in this area.

It is in any case difficult to draw a precise dividing line between predecessors of the French Enlightenment and the movement itself. The very concept of an Enlightenment is no doubt a rather nebulous one, referring to a speeding up, an intensification of manifestations of certain currents of thought rather than a new departure. Voltaire (1694–1778), often seen as its most dominant figure, had begun writing long before what is usually thought of as the Enlightenment. Neverthe-less his work as a whole could legitimately be said to belong to the movement and some of his early individual works show many of its characteristics: his *Lettres philosophiques* ([9.15]), for example, pub-lished in 1734, which introduced Locke and Newton to the French public and praised English religious toleration and political freedom, implicitly contrasting them with the very different situation in France.

The same could equally be said of the *Lettres Persanes* by Montesquieu (1689–1755), a satirical account of French life, politics and religion as seen through the eyes of two Persian visitors, which was published as early as 1721. Nevertheless, it was the 1740s that saw the beginning of the great proliferation of works which constitute the French Enlightenment proper, while the movement could be said to have been brought to a natural close by the outbreak of the French Revolution. In many ways, of course, the Revolution was the outcome of this wave of intellectual attacks on authority, though retrospectively, the fact that it occurred has inevitably affected the way the intellectual movement itself is perceived – often as more revolutionary, and particularly more specifically political, than it actually was.

If there was one work which, more than any other, embodied the ideals and attitudes of the Enlightenment, it was the *Encyclopédie*. The origin of this virtual manifesto of the movement lay in a project to produce a French translation of Chambers's *Cyclopedia*, which had appeared in 1728. Denis Diderot (1713–84) – as yet merely a promising young writer, with some repute as a translator – was engaged to do some of the work, but in 1747 he was appointed co-editor, along with the distinguished mathematician Jean le Rond d'Alembert (1717–83). But from the very beginning, it was Diderot who was the dominant partner and the driving force behind the project. His vision and enthusiasm transformed it from being a mere translation into a vastly more ambitious enterprise, whose aims were set out in his own Prospectus and subsequent article 'Encyclopédie', as well as in his co-editor's 'Discours préliminaire': they wanted to make known to the public at large all the huge strides that had recently been made in human knowledge of every conceivable kind, and this comprehensive survey was to be written by appropriate experts in each field. Diderot and d'Alembert together amassed a veritable army of contributors, many of whom were – or were about to be – among the most eminent thinkers and foremost authorities of their day. The first seven volumes of the *Encyclopédie* appeared from 1751 to 1759, at which point the work was banned; the remaining ten were published clandestinely in 1765, under the sole editorship of Diderot.

Both in its conception and in its execution, the *Encyclopédie* reflected the emphatic anthropocentrism that was characteristic of the Enlightenment, and that was expressed in unambiguous terms in Diderot's article 'Encyclopédie': 'Man is the sole point from which one must start and to which one must bring everything back [...] Apart from my existence and the happiness of my fellow men, what does the rest of nature matter to me?'. Diderot and d'Alembert's admiration for the capacities and the achievements of the human race, their confidence in the progress of civilization, went hand in hand with a deeply felt desire to contribute to that progress and to work for the happiness of mankind. So that an important aspect of the knowledge that the Encyclopedists sought to popularize and disseminate was the critical thinking that was increasingly challenging received wisdom and established authority. Human reason was no longer a frail and unreliable prop in a world of mystery, but a sturdy guide in a universe that was gradually being understood and an environment that was gradually being mastered. Diderot and d'Alembert and many of their collaborators saw themselves as engaged in a campaign, fighting a battle against the forces of evil for the intellectual and material liberation of mankind. And this liberation truly involved enlightening men, changing the way they thought, as Diderot made clear in a letter written in 1762: 'In time this work will certainly bring about a revolution in men's minds . . . we shall have served humanity' ([9.6], 4: 172). Inevitably, in its concentration on man, its faith in reason, and its challenge to authority, the *Encyclopédie* was setting itself up as inherently opposed to Christianity, which required human reason to submit to authority. In fact, the Church came to be seen by many *philosophes* as the arch enemy of mankind, and in the articles of the *Encyclopédie* (as well as in many other works of the period), it was often represented not just as an obstacle to progress, but as a powerful agent of repression and restriction, an instrument of the forces of darkness which had for centuries sought to submerge the forces of enlightenment.

If Diderot was the principal inspiration of the *Encyclopédie*, it was d'Alembert who could be described as its theoretician. No doubt d'Alembert was not himself a brilliantly inventive thinker like Diderot; but this very fact helped to make him a representative figure of the movement. Though the admirably structured syntheses of the 'Discours préliminaire' of the *Encyclopédie* and of the later *Essai sur les Eléments de Philosophie* (1759) were d'Alembert's own, the ideas he was synthesizing represented for the most part the generally agreed position of the *philosophes*. He described the aims, the rationale and the methods of the work, expounding what one might describe as the philosophical starting point both of the *Encyclopédie* and of the Enlightenment as a whole.

D'Alembert was very conscious of his philosophical inheritance, of belonging to an embattled élite which had struggled towards enlightenment throughout the centuries and was only now coming into its own. He saw the history of human thought and endeavour as a never-ending war against oppressive forces, with the flag carried by a few great men, above all Bacon, Descartes, Newton and Locke. The aims of the Enlightenment reflected in the 'Discours préliminaire' were indeed vast – nothing less than an aspiration to understand and describe the whole of 'nature' and to give an account of every aspect of human knowledge. One of the most fundamental tenets of Enlightenment thought was the oneness of the universe, a principle which had been forcefully propounded the year before the publication of the first volume of the *Encyclopédie* in an *Essai de Cosmologie* by the gifted mathematician and natural scientist Pierre-Louis Moreau de Maupertuis (1698–1759): 'There is a universal connection between everything in nature, in the moral as well as in the physical' (quoted Goyard-Fabre [9.20], 158). D'Alembert argued in much the same way that the universe, if only we could understand it, would appear to be one single fact, and that there was some kind of unity underlying all natural phenomena. But his ambitious aims were accompanied by a characteristic humility, a recognition of the limitations of the human mind: he accepted, for instance, that first causes were almost always unknowable, and postulated as the only fruitful philosophical method the attempt to reduce phenomena to the smallest possible number of underlying principles, which he termed the 'esprit systématique'. But this method involved first and foremost the meticulous observation of facts, in contrast to the 'esprit de système' which had so often led thinkers astray with the creation of ingenious rational constructions not based on empirical evidence. To illustrate the point, he quoted the example of the magnet: it was a laudable philosophical enterprise to seek the single principle from which its various qualities stemmed, but this principle might well remain unknown for a long time. In the meantime, the only way forward lay in the amassing, ordering and cautious analysis of observations.

The best example of d'Alembert's organized approach to the ordering of data is perhaps his emphasis in the 'Discours préliminaire' on the interrelatedness of human knowledge. If all phenomena are linked in some way, then all knowledge must be similarly connected, though if the underlying unity of phenomena remains hidden, the true links between different areas of knowledge must remain at best speculative. While acknowledging therefore the arbitrariness of such theoretical divisions, he adopted, with slight modifications, the schematic tree of knowledge proposed by Bacon, with its three main branches the faculties of memory, reason and imagination, linked by the central stem of the understanding.

It may well be argued that the conviction that there is a unity underlying all natural phenomena and all human knowledge is itself an a priori assumption preceding empirical observation, and d'Alembert's position seems in fact to be a judicious blending of Cartesian rationalism with the emphasis on observation that derived from Newton and Locke. Be that as it may, his approach to the classification of knowledge can be seen both as pragmatic and, above all, as anthropocentric, in that it is based on human perception of phenomena rather than on their 'true' nature. Indeed, his whole discussion of knowledge is man-centred. He analyses, speculatively, the way in which all kinds of knowledge, from the elements of morality to the arts and sciences, have arisen organically as a response to human needs. D'Alembert's approach to philosophical enquiry is similarly based on human needs. Philosophy, he says in his *Eléments de philosophie*, should not be concerned with axiomatic truths like 'the part is smaller than the whole', since they are self-evident and thus useless; nor with vain metaphysical enquiry into such matters as the nature of movement. The true philosopher sensibly supposes the existence of movement and tries to discover how it operates in practice: our models should be the scientists who, from Archimedes to Newton, have discovered the laws according to which the universe functions.

Now it is true that d'Alembert was primarily a mathematician and physicist rather than a philosopher (though the distinction between philosophy and science in the eighteenth century was still rather imprecise), but his mistrust of what he saw as sterile metaphysical speculation about absolute reality and his emphasis on the scientific and the utilitarian were shared by many who were not scientists at all. Thinkers convinced of the ultimate intelligibility of the universe and imbued with confidence in man's capacities to decode it had little patience with the metaphysical theories of Spinoza or Leibniz, for example, about such matters as pre-established harmony. The knowledge that interested the thinkers of the Enlightenment was not metaphysical, but scientific, knowledge of the material world of nature.

Their principal inspiration in this field was undoubtedly Newton. The first writer in France to accept and expound his theory of gravitation was Maupertuis, in his *Discours sur les différentes figures des astres*, published in 1732, but after Maupertuis, Newton was taken up and popularized by Voltaire, particularly in his *Eléments de la philosophie de Newton* (1739) ([9.15]), and by the time the first volume of the *Encyclopédie* was published, the lavish praise bestowed on him by d'Alembert expressed a view which was widely shared in France.

It was above all Newton's methods which were to serve as a model for scientific investigation, the observation of phenomena followed by the attempt to discover the principles or laws underlying them. The most cogent exponent of this approach to science was no doubt the Abbé Etienne Bonnot de Condillac (1715–80), perhaps the most important philosopher – as distinct from *philosophe* – of the French Enlightenment, and certainly the most systematic one. In his *Traité des Systèmes*, published in 1749, supplemented by the 'Art de Raisonner', which formed part of a *Cours d'Etudes* (1769–73), he proposed a methodology of science which closely followed Newton. Like Newton, and like d'Alembert, he conceded that the ultimate reality of things was inaccess-

ible to the human mind, though he did believe both that our perception
of the universe in some way corresponded to its true reality, and that
it was indeed an ordered universe, consisting of a vast unified system.
Metaphysicians such as Descartes, Malebranche and Leibniz had gone
astray because the systems they had proposed were not based on
observation of the natural world: the proper procedure for the scientist
was not to construct systems, but to seek to discover as many elements
as possible of the true system of the universe. And the proper method,
said Condillac, was the analysis of a combination of two types of
evidence, the evidence of fact, based on the observation of phenomena,
and the evidence of reason, based as far as possible on a mathematical
model. Newton's system provided the perfect demonstration of such
an approach.

However, while there was general agreement that earlier philo-
sopher-scientists had gone too far in their construction of systems based
on a misguided use of hypotheses, it was beginning to be felt that some
disciples of Newton tended to go to the opposite extreme in their
reluctance to venture beyond the observation of phenomena. Mme du
Châtelet (Gabrielle-Emilie, Marquise du Châtelet, 1706–49, unjustly
better known to posterity as Voltaire's mistress, but in fact a serious
thinker in her own right who was largely responsible for making the
philosophy of Leibniz known in France), in her *Institutions de physique*
(1740), and Condillac, in the *Traité des Systèmes*, both advocated caution in the use of hypotheses, but they recognized their value as a part
of good scientific method: used correctly they should serve as a basis
for experimentation, suggesting further lines of enquiry in the quest to
discover the links between observed phenomena.

But Newton was a mathematician, and rather than the abstract
field of mathematics, it was the experimental domain of biological
science in which such methods were to be most productively employed.
If there was one work which both embodied the principles of the new
science and paved the way for the great strides it was to make in the
next century, it was surely the *Histoire naturelle* by Georges-Louis
Leclerc, Comte de Buffon (1707–88), which has been compared in its
importance to Newton's *Principia philosophiae naturalis* (Cassirer
[9.16], 104). Buffon's monumental work, the first three volumes of
which appeared in 1749, broke new ground both in its methods and in
its matter. To begin with, methodologically, while he remained Newtonian in his emphasis on observation and rejection of authority and
preconceptions, Buffon helped to liberate science from the over-restric-
tive requirement for mathematical type proof by envisaging a new
approach to scientific evidence: he saw that the repetition of identical
events, for instance, can lead one to postulate a theory which may not
have the certainty of mathematical proof, but which may legitimately

be based on such a degree of probability that it carries, in effect, moral conviction.

When Buffon applies such methods to the study of the natural world, his strikingly secular approach is firmly based on historicity. By considering the evidence of geology (and simply ignoring the Bible), he boldly drew conclusions about the immense age of the world. In his vision of an organically evolving universe, there was no room for final causes, which he rejected as misleading abstractions inhibiting true scientific enquiry. Whereas the great botanist Linnaeus, his exact contemporary, had a static view of nature, in which all plants and animals were created once and for all in permanent form for the glorification of God, Buffon emphasized the boundless creativity of 'nature' (rather than God): nature worked on a kind of trial and error basis, with its failures as well as its successes, producing monsters doomed to extinction as well as species equipped to survive and prosper by adapting to their environment. He stressed too, in volume two of the *Histoire naturelle*, the continuity in nature, pointing out that the categories we use to interpret the world – animal, vegetable, mineral – are merely convenient labels, corresponding only to 'general ideas', and that there are in reality no clear-cut distinctions between them. Thus no actual animal corresponds to the general idea animal, and some are further from it than others: an insect is less of an animal than a dog, an oyster than an insect, and so on through subtle gradations until we come, for example, to the egg, which is neither animal nor mineral. ('Histoire générale des animaux', ch. 8). As for man, if Buffon repeatedly emphasized his distance from the animals, this was in no sense a spiritual superiority based on theological arguments. He expressed a confidence in the capacity of human reason to discover 'the secrets of Nature' which was entirely characteristic of the Enlightenment, and he explained the nobility of man by a sound historico-biological demonstration. Man was originally an animal like the others, but endowed with certain characteristics which enabled him to develop in a spectacular fashion: an unusually long period of physical maturation led to the necessary creation of the family unit and of society, without which man could never have survived ('Les animaux carnassiers', [9.2], 7: 28–9); it was social life which led to the crucial creation of language, enabling man to preserve the intellectual heritage of his society and benefit from the cumulative transmission of knowledge and thought ('Nomenclature des singes', [9.2], 14).

Clearly Buffon's view of the universe was in many ways an evolutionary one. It has been argued that his thought was not really transformist, and that he had no true idea of the evolution of species [9.29], 577); nevertheless, by placing the study of biology in an historical perspective, by his vision of a dynamic, changing, natural world, he can truly be said to have anticipated Lamarck and Darwin. But such ideas were in the air. At almost exactly the same time as Buffon, Diderot too, first in his *Lettre sur les Aveugles* (1749) and then in the *Pensées sur l'interprétation de la nature* (1753), outlined a similar evolutionary account of the animal world ([9.5]): the apparently wonderful way in which existing forms of life are adapted to their needs and their environment, far from being evidence of final causes, is merely the result of a natural process, in which many created forms turned out to be blind alleys, unable to survive or simply unable to reproduce. It is true that this theory had been expounded by Lucretius in his *De natura rerum*, but its re-emergence in the eighteenth century, in the context of post-Bacon post-Newton science, gave it an entirely new significance.

However, there was one thinker at this time who went even further along the road towards Darwin. Having begun with the same Lucretian theory as Buffon and Diderot, Maupertuis developed it somewhat differently. One of the great scientific controversies of the period was the debate about the origin of life and procreation, which had been given a huge boost by the discoveries of John Needham, who thought he had observed the spontaneous generation of life in a test-tube. In his *Vénus physique* (1745), Maupertuis tackled the question of generation by the study of heredity, which, being observable, was a distinctly more feasible approach in the eighteenth century than by anatomical research, which was still very unreliable. The transmission of acquired parental and even ancestral characteristics appeared to confirm the theory that in procreation the seed came from both parents. When he developed these ideas further in his *Système de la nature* (1751), Maupertuis explained this process of transmission by a kind of memory retained by the component parts of the maternal and paternal seed, each of which comes from a different part of the body and is destined to reproduce a similar part in the new being. However, chance deviations can then lead to the transformation and multiplication of species:

> Could one not in this way explain how, starting from two single individuals, the multiplication of the most disparate species could have occurred? They would have owed their origin merely to a few chance productions [. . .]; and as a result of repeated deviations, there would have come about the infinite diversity of animals which we see today.
> [(*Système de la nature*, xlv, quoted Roger [9.29], 484)]

Now side by side with these developments in the field of biological science, an even more fundamental debate was being conducted about the nature of knowledge and the manner of its acquisition, one of the central issues of Enlightenment thought. The *philosophes* attempted earnestly – if not altogether consistently – to apply scientific method to the study of epistemology. To say, as d'Alembert had done, that knowledge is acquired in response to human need does not explain precisely how it was acquired: d'Alembert took it for granted that ideas, the building bricks of knowledge, are derived from the sensations, and his views were representative of French thought in the mid-eighteenth century. Descartes's innate ideas were totally discredited and the sensationalism of Locke was widely accepted. But if there was a general consensus accepting the broad lines of Locke's thought, opinions diverged when it came to the details, and these divergences were to have far-reaching implications.

The doctrine that all our knowledge originates in sense-experience was of course an ancient one, going back at least to Aristotle, but its development and analysis in Locke's *Essay concerning human understanding* went far beyond any previous version of it, and can truly be said to have laid the foundations of modern empirical psychology. There is, though, an inherent ambiguity in the celebrated maxim 'Nihil in intellectu quod non antea fuerit in sensu', which might seem to imply a totally materialist explanation of man. Locke did not go this far, and made a very clear distinction between sensation and reflexion, the capacity to organize the experience of the senses, thus retaining the activity of the mind – and the possibility of a spiritual soul. Even so, he had, as it were, opened a kind of Pandora's box, from which escaped not just the extreme doctrine of complete materialism, but also, curiously, what might seem to be its opposite, idealism.

If, as Locke argued, all our knowledge comes through our senses, how can we ever know with certainty anything at all about the outside world? How can we even know whether it exists, let alone whether it corresponds to our perception of it? In fact, however, this fundamental problem raised by Berkeley seemed to bother the French *philosophes* very little. A typical response was Voltaire's, in his *Traité de métaphysique* (written, though not published, about 1734). To begin with, he says, whether or not the external world really exists makes absolutely no difference to actual life. He then raises a number of common-sense objections to idealism, and concludes by declaring that he cannot help being more convinced by the existence of the material world than by many a geometrical truth. D'Alembert too dismissed Berkeleyan idealism with similar ease: if the external world *did* exist, then we should experience exactly the same sensations as we actually do; therefore, presumably, it does exist. The problem was taken rather more seriously and discussed at some length in the *Encyclopédie* article 'Existence', by Turgot, but the principal argument used boils down to saying that by far the most plausible cause of our sensations is the existence of the external world. This down-to-earth resolution of a complex metaphysical problem was in fact characteristic of the thinkers of the French

Enlightenment, whose approach to philosophy was pragmatic and relative, profoundly man-centred. Reliance on the perception of the world by the human senses seemed a perfectly sound starting point for the kind of enquiry that interested them.

Materialism, however, was quite another question, if only because of its implications for morality. At first, most thinkers retained Locke's dualism, invoking some kind of innate, active, non-physical power of the mind which was brought into play by the passive experience of the physical senses. This, for example, was the position adopted by d'Alembert, who maintained in the 'Discours Préliminaire' that the 'substance' in us which wills and thinks is self-evidently different from matter. But there was an increasing (though still minority) tendency to eliminate Locke's crucial distinction between sensation and reflexion, and to see all the operations of the mind as physiologically determined responses to the experience of the senses.

This shift away from Locke is to some extent epitomized in the thought of his principal heir, Condillac, who was certainly the most important French eighteenth century thinker in the field of epistemology (or 'metaphysics' as his contemporaries tended to call it). In his *Essai sur l'origine des connaissances humaines* (1746), Condillac set out to bring a greater precision to the thought of Locke, and consistently with the methodological aims which were to be enunciated by d'Alembert, to attempt to reduce the explanation of the human understanding 'to a single principle' – though it is debatable whether he succeeded in this. In the beginning was the sensation; but our physical needs cause us to experience pleasure or pain in response to certain sensations, and this creates the important phenomenon of attention. In turn, attention leads to the linking of sensations to form the association of ideas (needs are associated with their objects), and the association of ideas, by enabling a perception to be recalled in the absence of the object which caused it, constitutes the basis of memory. The development of the understanding thus far has been purely passive, an automatic response to outside stimuli, but at this point Condillac envisages the invention of signs (i.e. language) as the crucial step which endows man with the faculty of reflexion, the capacity to direct his attention at will, and it is this faculty which generates all the higher operations of the mind. As for Berkeley's idealism, Condillac virtually ignored it, and if he addressed the question of the unreliability of the information acquired through the senses, it was merely to point out that the errors of perception due to one sense can be corrected by recourse to others – thus apparently assuming the objective reality of the external world.

In the *Essai*, Condillac had already taken a substantial step towards a thoroughly materialist explanation of man. In contrast to Locke's sharp distinction between the static understanding, represented as a kind of *tabula rasa* on which sense impressions were 'written', and the innate active power of reflexion, Condillac's vision of the understanding was a dynamic one, conceived as a series of operations, thus facilitating its conversion to a self-sufficient system. The move towards materialism was taken a stage further in his most celebrated work, the *Traité des sensations* (1754). The *Traité* was rigorously systematic both in substance and in form. Whereas the *Essai* had followed Locke's dual scheme, retaining reflexion as a separate faculty, the *Traité* further simplified the explanation of man by making reflexion merely a product of the sensations. But the process of simplification and systematization was facilitated by the method Condillac used in this work. He imagined a statue which he then endowed successively with the five senses. The idea of a statue being given life as a way of studying the awakening of the human consciousness and understanding was not original – Buffon in particular had used it in the 'Histoire naturelle de l'homme' (in volume 3 of the *Histoire naturelle*, published in 1749); but Condillac's analysis was more systematic and more acute than Buffon's. He gave his statue one sense at a time, and with each sense he explored the range of ideas and feelings it would be able to acquire, first with that sense alone, and then, after the first sense, by combining that sense with those given to it previously. He began with the most humble, smell. Endowed with a sense of smell alone, the statue is presented with a variety of odours, causing it different degrees of pleasure or discomfort, and leading it to desire, to compare and to judge. However, Condillac notes, it will only experience desire when, as a result of a succession of sensations, it has realized that 'it can cease to be what it is and become again what it has been' (*Traité des sensations*, I,2,4, [9.3], 1: 225); when, in short, it has begun to remember, and it is the birth of memory which is a similar prerequisite for the development of comparison and judgement. After the sense of smell comes the turn of taste, which is dealt with similarly, and so on, through hearing, sight and finally touch. The whole process, from simple sensation to complex, abstract ideas, even to moral and aesthetic judgements, is an automatic one, determined by the interplay of sense impressions and the capacity for experiencing pleasure and pain. Remembering, reflecting, judging are all analyzed as different ways of being attentive. Judgement, for example, is the perception of a relationship, an automatic concomitant of comparison; but to compare 'is nothing other than to give one's attention to two ideas at the same time' (I,2,14–15, [9.3], 1: 226).

One of the most striking arguments in the *Traité* concerned the way in which man becomes aware of his own existence and of the outside world. Whereas Locke, and more recently Buffon, had appeared to take it for granted that perception was inseparable from self-awareness, Condillac maintained that initially, with only one sensation, the statue would have no sense of self at all. Only with a change of sensation, when it becomes aware (through memory, automatic for Condillac) of its own continuity despite the change, will it discover the concept 'I'. Even then, it will still necessarily identify with its sensations: it will seem to *be* the scent of the rose or the carnation, without any consciousness of a self distinct from its modifications. It will not, in other words, be conscious of the existence of a separate outside world which is responsible for causing its sensations. That consciousness will only come with the sense of touch and the experience of movement. There had long been a debate about the precise relationship between the senses of sight and touch and their relative importance. Condillac followed Berkeley, who in his *New Theory of Vision* (1709) had rejected Descartes's explanation of our perception of extension as a kind of intuitive calculation, and demonstrated that it could only result from movement. The other senses cannot by themselves convey the awareness of the outside world; it is only when the statue moves and becomes conscious of an obstacle to its movement that it will deduce the existence of space and otherness.

On the other hand, whether or not the 'real' outside world corresponded to our perception of it, whether even it was extended, was a matter on which Condillac would not commit himself. He shared Berkeley's view that we can know directly only our sensations and could see no evidence for assuming that the qualities we perceive actually exist in objects themselves. But this is not a reason for denying the existence of an outside world: the only sound inference we can draw from the available evidence is that 'bodies are beings which produce sensations in us, and which have properties about which we can make no sure judgement' (IV,5,1, [9.3], 1: 306n.).

Condillac's response to the problem of idealism highlights the ambiguous status of this kind of epistemological approach to psychology, on the borderline between science and metaphysics. He may have prided himself on his scientific methodology, but whilst it could justifiably be described as Newtonian in its quasi-mathematical rigour, it was scarcely scientific in the sense of empirical or experimental, and this was of course the case with the sensationalist debate in general. The acute observation and rigorous analysis of the *Traité* focused principally not on live human beings but on an imaginatively conceived ideal model. Condillac and his contemporaries did, however, make use of empirical investigation when it was possible. The ideal model itself, as well as other kinds of sensationalist speculation, must have been based on a good deal of largely unrecorded observation of real life, and sometimes there were opportunities for a more scientific, even experimental approach. A case in point was the actual functioning of the sense of sight. The English philosopher (and friend of Locke),

William Molyneux, had posed the following problem: would a person blind from birth who had learnt to distinguish by touch a cube from a sphere, and who had then had sight restored, be able, by sight alone, to recognize the two objects? Initially the debate was largely theoretical, but when the philosophically inclined London surgeon Cheselden pioneered and perfected the operation for the removal of cataracts, the opportunity was created to move it on to a more scientific basis: Cheselden's observation of a person born blind who was then given sight, reported in Voltaire's *Eléments de la philosophie de Newton*, appeared to confirm that the interpretation of visual sensations was not intuitive and had to be learned from experience in conjunction with other sense data.

Despite the fragility of its scientific foundations, sensationalist psychology reflected the spirit of the Enlightenment in being an attempted anatomical (if unproven) explanation of man, which ignored or was positively hostile to the traditional (Christian) explanation – another example of a field of knowledge being removed from the authority of theology towards (if not quite as far as) science. But there was also an indirect and perhaps more important way in which sensationalist psychology came into conflict with Christianity: it made much easier a totally materialist explanation of man, with the dire moral implications that we shall be examining in the next chapter. The most controversial point in sensationalist analyses of the understanding was the degree to which its operations were produced by an innate active element. If absolutely all mental processes are automatic, as they appear to be in the *Traité des Sensations*, resulting from pleasure- and pain-responses to sense impressions, then the mind is merely an extension of the body: not only is reflexion not an act of the will, but the will itself disappears. But Condillac was primarily a seeker after truth rather than a *philosophe*, and sought, if anything, to avoid controversy. Others, however, had distinctly more polemical intentions.

One of the most unambiguous expositions of the passivity of the understanding and of the will appeared in 1756 in the anonymous article 'Evidence', in the sixth volume of the *Encyclopédie*; the article was in fact by the physiocrat François Quesnay (1694–1774), though Rousseau, who profoundly disagreed with its central thesis, suspected it had been written by Buffon or Condillac (interesting indeed for his perception of their position in the matter). Quesnay argued that willing is merely a form of feeling: 'to want or to be willing is nothing other than to feel pleasantly; not to want or to be unwilling is similarly nothing other than to feel unpleasantly'. It was this thesis, developed at considerably greater length, which, two years later, served as the starting point of the scandalous *De l'esprit*, by Claude-Adrien Helvétius (1715–71): not only was the book banned, but the outrage it caused contributed to the definitive banning of the *Encyclopédie* itself. Helvét-ius began by arguing that remembering and even judging are merely forms of feeling, though his demonstration is neither very subtle nor very convincing as he deals with various possible objections. The central thesis of *De l'esprit* was that all minds are potentially equal, since all men (it is not entirely clear whether Helvétius intends this to include women or not) are endowed with the same capacity of attention which can enable them to attain to the most elevated ideas.

Helvétius, it may be argued, makes clear the materialism which had been latent in Locke. But sensationalism was not the only road to materialism, and the scientific progress discussed earlier also led a number of thinkers in a similar direction. In particular, despite New-ton's own views, gravitation came to be seen as a property of matter, alongside extent and impenetrability, so that matter was no longer passive, as for Descartes, but capable of moving itself, and this was to provide an obvious basis for materialist explanations of the world. But the first thoroughgoing materialist of the French Enlightenment, subsequently much admired by Marx, was not a physicist but a doctor, Julien Offroy de la Mettrie (1709–51). La Mettrie's approach was physiological: he extended the mechanism of Descartes to man, and transposed the determinism of the Newtonian universe to the sphere of human psychology.

His principal thesis, expounded mainly in his *Histoire naturelle de l'âme* (1745), otherwise known as *Traité de l'âme*, and developed further in *L'Homme machine* (1748), was that all man's mental functions are physiological in their origin. The *Traité de l'âme* attempts to destroy the case for the spirituality of the soul, arguing that there is no evidence whatsoever to lead one to suppose that the capacity for feeling belongs to a substance distinct from matter. If movement is an attribute of matter, why should this not also be true of feeling, thought, and will? Observation and experience confirm that the soul is material, says La Mettrie, whereas only metaphysical arguments are offered to support the contrary view. He admits he cannot understand precisely how matter feels and thinks, but points out that it is no easier to understand how it moves by itself, while the notion of an immaterial soul is even more inconceivable. He cites various examples which demonstrate that the memory can be affected by physical conditions and accidents, proving that it must be part of the material body and 'completely mechanical' (*Traité de l'âme*, ch. 10, X, [9.11], 87), and then goes on to argue that the exercise of liberty is similarly determined by sen-sations, and that the judgement is a passive acquiescence in the truth imposed by 'the evidence of the sensations'.

La Mettrie's principal point, to which he returns in *L'Homme machine*, is that the so-called soul, which falls asleep with the body and needs food to continue functioning, is merely a way of talking about certain functions of the body. Man, then, is just another animal. The instinct of animals is a product of their brain and nervous system; man's more complex behaviour is merely the result of having the most complex brain of all the animals: 'So that everything comes from the force of instinct alone, and the sovereignty of the soul is merely a figment of the imagination' (*Traité*, ch. 11, II, [9.11], 93). The parallel between man and the other animals is the central theme of *L'Homme machine*. Differences of character and mind between men are all physiological in origin, as are differences between men and animals: La Mettrie is convinced (wrongly, as we now know) that the only thing preventing monkeys from learning to speak is their inadequate organs. In *L'Homme plante* (1748), he went one stage further and extended the similarity of organization to all life forms, pointing out that the characteristics of animals, such as respiration and nutrition, are also to be found in plants.

Now it is clear that writers like Helvétius and La Mettrie were engaged in polemics. The implicit starting-point for both was the rejection not merely of the conventional Christian position, but of any religious or supernatural explanation of man and the universe, and they were consciously replying to the arguments of their adversaries: when La Mettrie attacked the doctrine of final causes, for example, together with the associated argument that the wonders of the universe provide incontrovertible proof of the existence of God, he was attacking the very foundation of the deism propounded by Voltaire and initially by Diderot, who for their part were explicitly refuting the arguments of the materialists. In fact, though atheist-materialists and deists tended to be equally hostile to Christianity, the thought of both has to be understood in the context of the continual debate that opposed them to each other.

It is perhaps in the early works of Diderot that this debate can be seen most clearly. Chiefly, this was because he started out as a deist and rapidly became a materialist. But it was also because most of what he wrote was in the form of a debate, often expressed as dialogue. It is not always easy, as a consequence, to know with certainty what exactly his ideas were. His writings reveal an endlessly inventive thinker, continually indulging in scientific and philosophical speculation, where the author's thought is sometimes to be found in the conflicting voices rather than in any single one: he was, in short, more given to raising and discussing difficult questions than to proposing answers. Yet despite the ambiguities of his thought, Diderot's materialism is historically much more significant than La Mettrie's. Perhaps because of his somewhat confrontational approach (the title 'L'homme machine' was surely intended to be provocative), La Mettrie was generally seen as a rather irresponsible extremist, and remained on the fringe of the philosophic movement. Diderot, in contrast, largely no doubt because of his role as principal editor of the *Encyclopédie*, was, more than anyone else, right at its centre, one of its acknowledged leaders. He was a friend of many of the most important thinkers of his day, meeting them frequently, mainly at Baron d'Holbach's house in Paris or his country estate of Grandval, and his later works in particular reflected the energetic discussions and exchanges of ideas that took place round the atheistic Baron's dinner table.

The debate between deism and atheism is quite explicit in Diderot's first original work, the *Pensées philosophiques* (1746), in which alternating 'Thoughts' present opposing views. The debate is a finely balanced one. In answer to the atheist's denial of God, Diderot proposes the standard deistic recourse to the manifest order and beauty of the physical world; but immediately afterwards, in response to the deist's claim that it is as inconceivable that the universe could have come into existence by the chance combination of atoms as that Homer's *Iliad* could have been produced by a chance combination of letters, he demonstrates that, taking into account the eternal duration of matter and movement, together with the infinity of possible combinations, it would be inconceivable if matter had not, by pure chance, ordered itself into some 'admirable arrangements' ([9.5], 1: 136).

By the time he wrote the *Lettre sur les Aveugles*, three years later, he had already begun work on the *Encyclopédie*, which helped to bring him into contact with the most advanced scientific thought of the age. The apparent uncertainty of the *Pensées* now seemed clearly to have given way to atheism and materialism. Much of the work is devoted to a discussion of sensationalism, in which Diderot anticipates the techniques of modern psychology by using the aberrant (here the blind) to provide clues to understanding the normal. Like La Mettrie, he emphatically dismisses the idea of a spiritual soul, declaring that a philosopher blind and deaf from birth trying like Descartes to locate the soul would surely place it not in the pineal gland, but at the tips of the fingers, the source of all his knowledge. But the most direct affirmation of Diderot's materialism and atheism is to be found in the centre-piece of the work, Saunderson's (fictitious) deathbed confession, which is mainly a refutation of the arguments of the deists. Just as ten years later, in *Candide*, Voltaire was to quote the harsh evidence of the real world against Leibnizian Optimism, so Diderot here cites the real world against Voltaire's wonders of the universe proof of deism: the blind Saunderson is a monster, living evidence of disorder in the universe. But in a materialist evocation of evolution, he then goes on to speculate that in the beginning, there was an abundance of such monsters, destined to disappear because of the inadequacy of their organs, so that only the fit survived. And using this biological process as an analogy, he proceeded to hypothesize about the world we inhabit, no doubt produced by a similar trial and error series of combinations of matter and movement.

After the *Lettre sur les Aveugles*, which led to his imprisonment as the author of an irreligious book, Diderot's materialist theories were elaborated, mostly speculatively, in his correspondence, in a number of *Encyclopédie* articles, and in several individual works, particularly the trilogy known as the *Rêve de d'Alembert*. They do not constitute a complete system, but they do present a corpus of more or less coherent ideas, reflecting consistent attitudes and a steadily growing preoccupation with biology.

The problem of the first cause is resolved once and for all by postulating that movement, a kind of energy, is a necessary and permanent attribute of matter – everything in nature is manifestly always in movement – and that matter is eternal. Like d'Alembert, Diderot emphasized the unity of the universe, which he described in the *Encyclopédie* article 'Animal' as 'a single, unique machine, in which everything is connected'. This article indeed attempted to give a unified account of all matter, organic and inorganic. Drawing principally on the ideas of Buffon, it nevertheless went considerably further in getting rid of the divisions between man and other animals, between animals and plants – Diderot quoted Trembley's recent observations on the fresh-water polyp, which did indeed seem to be neither – and even between animate and inanimate matter.

The conviction that there are no true divisions between the different categories in nature led Diderot to an idea he flirted with for many years but expressed most explicitly in the *Rêve de d'Alembert*, namely the hypothesis that 'sensibilité', the capacity to feel, is a 'general property of matter' ([9.5], 2: 116). This is not to say, of course, that all matter actually feels; sensibility is active in animals, and perhaps in plants, but inert, in other words potential, in inanimate matter. The hypothesis is confirmed for Diderot by the ease with which inanimate matter can cross the borderline to become living – the two obvious examples being the development of the egg in the process of generation, and the even more everyday process of eating: 'The plants feed on earth, and I feed on the plants' ([9.5], 2: 108).

The discussion of the active sentience of animate matter, a major issue in the *Rêve*, is in fact firmly based on the most recent developments in contemporary scientific thinking. A group of doctors based in Montpellier, which included not only Théophile de Bordeu (1722–76), one of the interlocutors in the *Rêve*, but also the young J.-J. Menuret de Chambaud (1739–1815), the *Encyclopédie*'s principal contributor in the field of medicine, were busy showing that all living matter is inherently sentient, a property which manifests itself in a variety of ways in the animal body, in reflexes, in the spontaneous contraction of muscles and organs, in the digestion – even in the response to stimuli of a muscle actually removed from the body. But if Diderot welcomed such scientific confirmation of his materialist theories, it still left many questions unanswered. In particular, if the formation of living beings can be explained by the successive accumulation of sentient 'molecules', how does the sentience of the component parts become transformed into a corporate consciousness and identity? Diderot suggests as a possible answer – which is more pleasing by its ingenuity than intellectually satisfying – a parallel between an animal and a swarm of bees clustered on a branch: if one imagines them becoming fused together by their legs, they pass from the state of contiguity to that of continuity, and this new state of the swarm is precisely that of the human body.

Passing from physiological sensibility to the more complex operations of the mind, Diderot accepts the standard sensationalist view of man, placing particular importance on the memory as the crucial factor in converting sensations into thought – though he realized that memory too was a result of physical organization, perhaps, he suggested, a kind of vibrating fibre. At the same time, he recognized the inadequacy of the usual accounts of the transition from physical sensations to thought, of the kind provided by Helvétius. Faced with the problem of explaining how the sensations received by individual organs come to be co-ordinated, he could only suggest the existence of some kind of central function, a 'common centre', which registers all the sensations, but which, being endowed with memory, its own special attribute, makes comparisons and provides the sense of continuity and of identity. Once again he resorted to an analogy to illuminate his explanation – though again it is more striking than philosophically enlightening: just as a spider at the centre of its web is immediately aware of the slightest movement in any of its strands, so the 'common centre' is informed of the impressions received in any part of the body by means of a 'network of imperceptible threads' ([9.5], 2: 141).

As ever with Diderot, it is difficult to know how literally he means us to take the analogy, but it is clear that he believed in the existence of a 'mind' separate from the sensations. It is equally clear, though, that thought was for him a totally physiological function, an automatically determined result of sense impressions, however complex the process might be. His own view of man was no doubt more subtle than Helvétius's, but it was certainly no less materialist and no less determinist, and if he found Helvétius's demonstration that judgement and will are merely forms of feeling simplistic, he none the less shared his conclusion that freedom was an illusion. The eponymous hero of

Diderot's novel *Jacques le fataliste* (written during the 1770s), clearly here the author's mouthpiece, was convinced that all our behaviour is determined by a necessary (if immensely complicated) series of physical causes and effects. So that the will is the result of conditioning, nothing but 'the last result of everything one has been since birth up to the present moment of existence' ([9.5], 2: 175). As Diderot had explained in 1756 in a letter to the author Landois, 'the word "freedom" is devoid of meaning; there are no free beings, nor can there be'. If we acquire the illusion of freedom, it is partly because of the 'prodigious variety of our actions', but mainly because we are in fact conditioned by our experience to believe that we are free ([9.5], 19: 435–6).

Because Diderot's materialist and determinist theories are often presented as tentative, and in the context of a debate, they contrive to appear less dogmatic and distinctly more subtle than those of some of his contemporaries. Yet they offer some striking similarities with the thought of d'Holbach, which is so lacking in subtlety that at least one modern historian of ideas has dismissed it as little more than crude anti-religious propaganda (Goyard-Fabre [9.21], 159). The two men were indeed close friends, and Diderot's correspondence bears witness to frequent lively discussions and arguments between them: there seems good reason to suppose both considerable mutual influence, and a greater identity of thought than is usually allowed.

The aggressively atheistic philosophy of Paul Thiry, Baron d'Holbach (1723–89), presented in a number of works but principally in the *Système de la Nature* (1770), is more comprehensive and more overt than that of either La Mettrie or Helvétius. He gives an unambiguous (if wordy and repetitive) account of a totally materialist position, an integrated 'system' in which all things, matter, the universe, man, society and government, form part of a cause-and-effect chain of necessity. D'Holbach's universe is, like Diderot's, an ever-changing one, with suns and planets continually dying and being born. It is composed of matter, which is eternal and eternally and necessarily in movement, behaving according to fixed laws, such as what d'Holbach calls 'conservation' (Newton's inertia), though he recognizes that not all these laws are yet understood. This is something he stresses repeatedly: everything that is and happens, is and happens necessarily, and if we see what appears to be evidence of chance, or still worse, of supernatural forces, it is because we do not understand the true links in the cause-effect chain – d'Holbach invokes the scientific explanations of the miracles and marvels of the past, such as earthquakes and meteors, and looks forward to a time when posterity will unravel still more of the secrets of nature.

Animate beings, since they are composed of matter, necessarily follow the same physical laws as the rest of the universe: plants and animals are made up of an aggregation of parts, held together by 'attraction continuelle'. And since the moral is only a different way of considering the physical, man as a moral being, too, is subject to the same rule of necessity and follows the same laws of nature. D'Holbach is careful to point out, however, that when he speaks thus of 'laws of nature', it is no more than a convenient way of referring to the 'essence' of things, by which he means the necessary result of the properties they possess. It is of the essence of a stone to fall, and similarly, of the essence of a sentient being to seek pleasure and to avoid pain. The law of inertia or 'conservation' affecting all matter becomes self-preservation or self-love in man.

Anticipating Diderot's determinist Jacques, d'Holbach thus saw the life of a man as 'a long sequence of necessary and connected movements' ([9.10], 1: 71), caused by his physiology and its interaction with his environment. All the intellectual 'faculties' are derived from the faculty of sentience, and d'Holbach's explanation of sentience is reminiscent of La Mettrie's: it is 'a consequence of the essence and properties of animate beings' just as gravity and magnetism are of other bodies, and no more (or less) inexplicable ([9.10], 1: 102). But like Diderot, he points to the ease with which inanimate matter such as milk and bread can become animate through the simple process of ingestion, and discusses the possibility that, as 'some philosophers think', sentience may be a universal quality of all matter, 'live' or 'inert' as the case may be ([9.10], 1: 104).

D'Holbach uses the same analogy as Diderot of the spider in its web to explain how the brain acts as the co-ordinator of sense data from different parts of the body, at the same time denying that it has any autonomous activity. Even more than Diderot, and recalling rather Helvétius and La Mettrie, he emphasizes the physicality of the so-called soul, demonstrating that thinking and even willing are only forms of feeling, automatic despite all appearances to the contrary. To will is to be disposed to action: thus, 'the sight of fruit on a tree modifies my brain in such a way that it causes my arm to move to pick the fruit' ([9.10], 1: 115).

D'Holbach, however, was just as aware as Diderot of the implications for morality of the denial of human freedom, and it is in truth misleading in both their cases to consider their scientific materialism and determinism separately from their moral and political thought. However great the interest of both these thinkers in science, their principal preoccupations were with man as a moral and social being, and this, rather than on scientific grounds, was why they were hostile to Christianity. Both of them saw Christianity as fundamentally anti-human and therefore as a force for social evil, and their materialist-based atheism was as much a consequence of this hostility as a cause of it. The priorities shared by Diderot and d'Holbach were in fact characteristic of the French Enlightenment in general. The move towards a greater understanding of the universe triggered by the discoveries of Newton, the development of a scientific approach to the understanding of human psychology stemming mainly from Locke, the enormous strides that were being made in the understanding of the animal world due to the work of Buffon and other contemporary naturalists and scientists, all this led to a new and exciting vision of the world, in which authority (especially that of religion) no longer held sway and every territory was available for exploration. But once the old certainties were dethroned, frightening possibilities were laid bare, and to thinkers who were above all anthropocentric in their concerns, it might well seem that there were far more pressing matters to be examined than, for example, the structure of the universe, the differences between animate and inanimate matter, or even the origin of life. It had become essential to re-examine the very fundamentals of human life, the nature of morality and the rules governing human behaviour and social organization, and it is to the discussion of these that the next chapter is principally devoted.

❧ BIBLIOGRAPHY ❧

Eighteenth-century Works

9.1 d'Alembert, Jean le Rond *Essai sur les Elements de Philosophie*, ed. R. N. Schwab, Hildesheim, Olms, 1965.

9.2 Buffon, Georges-Louis Leclerc, Comte de *Histoire naturelle*, Paris, 1749–1804.

9.3 Condillac, Abbé Etienne Bonnot de *Oeuvres philosophiques*, ed. Le Roy, 3 vols, Corpus Général des philosophes français, Paris, Presses Universitaires, 1947–51.

9.4 —— *Cours d'Etudes*, Parma, 1769–73.

9.5 Diderot, Denis *Oeuvres complètes*, ed. J. Assézat and M. Tourneux, Paris, Garnier Frères, 1875–7.

9.6 —— *Correspondance*, ed. G. Roth and J. Varloot, Paris, Editions de Minuit, 1955–70.

9.7 du Châtelet, Mme Gabrielle-Emilie *Institutions de physique*, London, 1741.

9.8 *Encyclopédie*, ed. Diderot and d'Alembert, Paris, 1751–80.

9.9 Helvétius, Claude-Adrien *De l'esprit*, Marabout-Université, Verviers, Gérard, 1973.

9.10 d'Holbach, Paul Thiry, Baron *Le Système de la Nature*, London, 1770, Slatkine Reprints, Geneva, 1973.

9.11 la Mettrie, Julien Offroy de *Textes choisis*, Les Classiques du peuple, Paris, Editions sociales, 1954.

9.12 Maupertuis, Pierre-Louis Moreau de *Oeuvres*, Lyon, 1768.

9.13 Raynal, Guillaume *Histoire philosophique et politique des deux Indes*, Geneva, 1780.

9.14 Rousseau, Jean-Jacques *Oeuvres complètes*, Bibliothèque de la Pléiade, Paris, Gallimard, 1959–69.

9.15 Voltaire, *Oeuvres complètes*, ed. L. Moland, Paris, Garnier, 1877–85.

9.16 —— *Traité de métaphysique*, ed. H. T. Patterson, Manchester, Manchester University Press, 1937.

General Surveys

9.16 Cassirer, E. *The Philosophy of the Enlightenment*, trans. F. C. A. Koellen and J. P. Pettegrove, Princeton, NJ, Princeton University Press, 1951.

9.17 Crocker, L. G. *An Age of Crisis*, Baltimore, John Hopkins Press, 1959.

9.18 —— *Nature and Culture, ethical thought in eighteenth century France*, Baltimore, John Hopkins Press, 1963.

9.19 Gay, P. *The Enlightenment: an interpretation*, 2 vols, London, Weidenfeld and Nicolson, 1966–9.

9.20 Goyard-Fabre, S. *La philosophie des lumières en France*, Paris, Klincksieck, 1972.

Critical Studies on Aspects of the French Enlightenment and Individual Authors

9.21 Crocker, L. G. *Diderot's chaotic order: approach to synthesis*, Princeton, NJ, Princeton University Press, 1974.

9.22 —— *Diderot the embattled philosopher*, London, N. Spearman, 1955.

9.23 Duchet, M. *Anthropologie et histoire au siècle de lumières*, Paris, Maspero, 1971.

9.24 France, P. *Diderot*, (Past Masters) Oxford, Oxford University Press, 1983.

9.25 Hermand, P. *Les idées morales de Diderot*, Paris, Presses Universitaires, 1923.

9.26 Knight, I. F. *The Geometric spirit: the Abbé de Condillac and the French Enlightenment*, New Haven and London, Yale University Press, 1968.

9.27 Lefèbvre, H. *Diderot*, Paris, Editeurs Réunis, 1949.

9.28 Proust, J. *Diderot et l'Encyclopédie*, Paris, A. Colin, 1962.

9.29 Roger, J. *Les Sciences de la vie dans la pensée française du XVIIIe siècle*, 2e édition, Paris, A. Colin, 1971.

There are also numerous relevant articles in the following specialist journals:

9.30 *Diderot Studies*, Syracuse, then Geneva, Droz, 1949–.

9.31 *Studies on Voltaire and the Eighteenth Century*, Geneva, then Oxford, 1955–.

CHAPTER 10

The French Enlightenment II: deism, morality and politics

Peter Jimack

One of the most striking features of the French Enlightenment was its hostility to Christianity, especially as represented by the Catholic Church, a hostility which went far beyond the mere loss of faith produced by the scientific and philosophical developments discussed in the previous chapter. To some extent it was on social and humanitarian grounds. First and foremost, the principle of religious intolerance and the practice of imprisoning or even burning dissidents were abhorrent to most Enlightenment thinkers. Many, too, condemned the Church for its vast wealth and the financial privileges it enjoyed, at the same time as it damaged the country's economy by removing so many men from the workforce, and even (at a time when population was perceived as a measure of prosperity) by preventing them from having children. There were even those like d'Holbach (1723–89), who, in works such as *La Contagion sacrée* (1768), anticipated the Marxist view of religion in seeing the Church as having always been in league with oppressive rulers to help keep the people in a state of submission. Some of these criticisms were no doubt unfair, and related more to excesses and abuses than to the essence of Christianity. But excesses and abuses aside, it may be argued that the Church stood for everything the Enlightenment was struggling to liberate itself from. The Church represented authority and restriction; it expounded a doctrine that could not be questioned, it told men what to believe and imposed on them a fixed view of the world and of their role in it. Whereas Enlightenment thinkers enthusiastically sought knowledge and gloried in the achievements and capacities of man, Christian morality was based on the original sin of tasting the fruit of the tree of knowledge, condemned the sin of pride and appeared to deplore most of man's natural inclinations.

It must not be forgotten, however, that rejection of Christianity did not necessarily mean rejection of God. While it is true that some of the more daring eighteenth-century thinkers saw atheist-materialism as the inevitable consequence of the new scientific thinking, the two great predecessors of the Enlightenment, Newton and Locke, had been able to reconcile their scientific and philosophical convictions with belief in God, and it was this kind of deism which seemed to most Enlightenment intellectuals to offer an acceptable compromise between the narrow authoritarianism of the Christian Church and the extreme of atheist materialism.

There were of course various deistic positions, ranging from the belief in a remote God who created the universe but is totally unconcerned with man, to a providential and personal God, such as Jean-Jacques Rousseau's, very closely modelled on the God of Christianity. Rousseau (1712–78) indeed claimed he was a Christian. He accepted the sensationalist view of man, but was very conscious of the dangers of atheism and materialism, and saw himself as defending Christianity against the materialists; in the event, he managed to achieve the unique distinction of incurring the hostility of both Church and *philosophes*. The particular characteristic of his religion – expounded in the 'Profession de foi du vicaire savoyard', part of his work on education, *Emile*, – was the emphasis he placed on 'conscience', a divinely inspired interior voice in every individual which obviated the need for a church and its priests. In fact, Rousseau's religion became immensely popular: his trust in conscience, his scepticism about miracles, his admiration for Christ combined with hesitation about his divinity, such views made it particularly attractive to Christians who had become converts to the anthropocentric rationalism of the Enlightenment.

But the best representative of what one might call standard eighteenth-century deism is Voltaire (1694–1778), who was in many respects the dominant personality of the French Enlightenment, even if he was not a particularly original thinker. Voltaire, as we saw in the last chapter, kept abreast of developments in science, and was largely responsible for the popularizing in France of the thought of Newton and of Locke. But he took from them selectively, and in particular, if he welcomed Newton's defence of the existence of God, at the same time he played down his tendency towards a certain mysticism. For this was Voltaire's own position: despite a number of fluctuations in his thought, he maintained a firmly deistic stance, deeply opposed to atheism and materialism, while at the same time hostile to Christianity and largely impatient with metaphysics and any form of mysticism – so much so that critics have occasionally seen him (wrongly in my view) as a crypto-atheist.

Shortly after he returned from exile in England, in 1734, Voltaire began to set down in one of his few theoretical works, the *Traité de métaphysique*, his views on a range of philosophical topics, starting with the demonstration of the existence of God. The first of his two proofs was the watchmaker argument, which had been used by Newton: if a watch implies the existence of a watchmaker, the manifest order of the universe surely implies an intelligent creator; and if we accept that the hands of the watch have been constructed to show the time, it is reasonable to accept that the eyes, for example, have been designed by the intelligent creator for seeing. Voltaire's second proof was the first cause argument: I exist, therefore something exists, therefore something has always existed; for either what exists is necessary and eternal, in which case it is God, or its being has been communicated to it by something else, to which the same argument applies. Since the material world is manifestly neither eternal nor unchanging, it is not necessary by itself but contingent, and must owe its existence to a being which *is* necessary, i.e. God. Similarly, movement, thought and feeling must all have been communicated to matter by God.

Despite the apparent rigour of this argument, Voltaire was clearly much more attracted by his first proof, based on the marvellous order of the universe and the plausibility of final causes. He was not alone. It might be seen as paradoxical that the great strides that were being made in the natural sciences during the eighteenth century, while they contributed on the one hand to the undermining of theological explanations of the universe, at the same time generated an often mystical awe before the wonders of nature. Even more perhaps than the Newtonian order of the universe, it was the other end of the scale – the study of maggots, worms, insects – that seemed to reveal the admirable wisdom and ingenuity of God. The distinguished physicist and entomologist Réaumur (1683–1757), for example, especially in his *Mémoires pour servir à l'histoire des insectes* (1734–42), saw the organization and behaviour of insects as nothing short of miraculous, leading inescapably to admiration for their creator. Even Diderot was at first greatly attracted by this kind of argument, suggesting in the *Pensées philosophiques* ([10.3]) that the mere wing of a butterfly, let alone the whole universe, surely offers compelling evidence of an intelligent creator – though, as we saw in the last chapter, he soon abandoned it in favour of the creation by chance theory.

Voltaire was particularly attached to the final cause argument as compelling evidence of the existence of a beneficent God (though it may be that it was a prior conviction that God was beneficent that made final causes seem so plausible). He recognized that the argument was not logically conclusive, it is true, but he saw it as providing a high indication of probability, constituting an appeal to common sense which it was only reasonable to accept – an approach to philosophy which he particularly favoured. To the objection that there is no proof, for instance, that stomachs are made for digesting, he retorted in the *Traité de métaphysique* that there is certainly no proof that they are not, and that common sense would surely suggest that they are.

In short, in the *Traité* and other works of the same period, Voltaire pictured a universe created by a God who was, if not concerned solely for the welfare of the human race, at least benevolently disposed towards it along with the rest of his creation. As a corollary, too, this deist God had endowed all men with both an awareness of moral good and a disposition to act in accordance with it. Concern for morality had in fact been a central feature of Voltaire's deism from the first, and belief in a universal innate moral sense, consisting of an injunction to obey an absolute 'natural law', was an article of faith to which he clung determinedly. In the face of a considerable body of apparent evidence to the contrary, he wriggled uncomfortably and unconvincingly: anthropological evidence of cannibalism, for instance, was explained away, and if in some tribes people ate their parents, it was no doubt to save them from being eaten by their enemies, or just a way (admittedly misguided) of honouring them. As for all the criminals in history, they were all secretly unhappy.

But then, however, Voltaire's faith in a benevolent God concerned with man and in the efficacity of a universal moral sense began to crumble, a development which was revealed particularly in a group of so-called 'philosophic tales' written from 1747 onwards. In *Micromégas* ([10.16]), for example, a gigantic traveller from the star Sirius is used as a vehicle for mocking the pretensions of the tiny inhabitants of this tiny planet, who wildly exaggerate their own importance in the universe. More frequently, however, this detachment was replaced by an expression of what sounds like Voltaire's disappointment at the fact that God was less concerned with man, and man less inclined to be good, than he had previously believed.

The Lisbon earthquake disaster in 1755, in which tens of thousands of people were killed, finally dealt a crucial blow to Voltaire's belief in the perfect order of the universe, or at least confirmed his suspicions that the order that existed was neither relative nor relevant to man; and the outbreak of the Seven Years War the following year undermined still further his faith in a God-given universal moral sense. His most famous work, *Candide* (1759) ([10.16]), is the embodiment of this revised philosophical position. Conceived ostensibly as an attack on Leibnizian Optimism (though directed in practice rather at the popularized version of it in Pope's *Essay on Man* (1733–4)), it proceeds by ridicule rather than refutation, continually mocking the doctrine of 'the best of all possible worlds' as it is taught by Candide's tutor Pangloss, who is a disciple of Leibniz, and not only stupid, but too obstinate to admit that he is wrong about the best of all possible worlds, even when the grotesque disasters that befall him make him realize he is. Beneath the savage humour, however, Voltaire is making the serious point, consistent with the ideological approach of the Enlightenment, that experience should take precedence over metaphysics, and that experience of this world soon demonstrates that it is not the best of all possible worlds. We witness earthquake, war, rape, murder, and all kinds of brutality, ample evidence of an uncaring God and of the apparent absence, in many men at least, of any moral sense.

Of course, the fact that everyone is not happy in the real world and that Candide and his friends suffer dreadful misfortunes in no way impinges on Leibniz's principle of Optimism, or even, as Voltaire knew full well, on the notion that the universe as a whole is harmonious and ordered. But again adopting a standpoint characteristic of the Enlightenment, he is protesting that he is concerned with man rather than the universe; the benevolent God who is concerned with the universe rather than man is as irrelevant to man as man is to him. The point is made succinctly in the final chapter of *Candide* when the travellers go to consult a Turkish sage: in answer to their question about the existence of evil in the world, he asks them whether, when the King sends a ship on a voyage, he is worried about the mice in the hold.

But this affirmation of man's insignificance in the eyes of God was by no means Voltaire's last word on the subject. It was difficult to use such a remote God as the foundation for a moral code which would fill the gap created by the rejection of Christianity, and Voltaire was becoming increasingly worried by the spread of atheism and materialism among the *philosophes*, and the dangerous moral consequences that would ensue if the loss of religion became more widespread. It seems likely that it was principally this preoccupation with morality that prompted him after *Candide* to return pragmatically to the God intimately concerned with man he had depicted in his earlier works, and even to the doctrine of final causes, which he had particularly ridiculed in *Candide*, and which amounted to saying that the world was arranged by God specifically for the convenience of man. In works such as *Des Singularités de la Nature* (1768) ([10.16]), totally resisting the current of evolutionary ideas that were beginning to be voiced and staying closer to Linnaeus than to Buffon, he expressed his conviction that there had been a once-and-for-all creation in which all things had been given their allotted place and purpose: just as the organs of the body had obvious functions, so too the mountains and the rivers (providing drinking water) were also evidence of divine providence. In return for this benevolence, God required obedience to the uncomplicated moral law of 'Worship me and be good', and rewarded and punished accordingly. Voltaire seemed to be convinced that without belief in this kind of punitive God, the moral order of society was gravely threatened. In short, 'If God did not exist, he would have to be invented' ([10.16], 10: 403). Voltaire's fear of the disastrous moral consequences of atheism was summed up with a wit that should not be mistaken for levity: 'I want my lawyer, my tailor, my servants, even my wife to believe in God, and I suspect I shall thus be less robbed and less cuckolded' (*L'ABC*, [10.16], 27: 399–400).

Voltaire's assumption that atheists were more likely to be wicked than believers may not have had any empirical basis, but it was a deeply-held and widely-shared prejudice – despite Bayle's demonstration as long ago as 1682 that it was without foundation. And the theoretical moral implications of atheist-materialism did indeed seem to be disturbing. More than anyone else, it was Diderot who, explicitly and repeatedly, spelled out these implications. As we saw in the last chapter, despite his reservations about Helvétius's view of man, he did not demur from his conclusion that moral freedom is an illusion. And if this is the case, man cannot be held responsible for his actions: 'if there is no freedom, there are no actions which deserve praise or blame. There is neither vice nor virtue, nothing which calls for reward or punishment' (letter to Landois, [10.3], 19: 436). The wicked man cannot be blamed for his wickedness, which is a determined characteristic like any other, the result of physical organization and environmental conditioning. The point is made with forceful clarity in an unsigned addition to the *Encyclopédie* article 'Vice', most probably by Diderot: 'Can a man help being pusillanimous, voluptuous, or just irascible, any more than squint-eyed, hunch-backed or lame?'.

It was the awareness of this apparent moral abyss which had initially deterred Diderot from wholeheartedly accepting the atheist materialism to which he was intellectually attracted, and which later led him to refrain from publishing his more daring works (such as the *Rêve de d'Alembert*). He illustrated the problem graphically in an incident in the allegorical *Promenade du sceptique* ([10.3]), written in 1747; Athéos, an atheist philosopher, and a man of virtue, convinces the symbolically blindfolded Christian of the error of his beliefs, and as a result the Christian throws off all moral restraint along with his blindfold, burns down Athéos's house and steals his wife. The anxiety manifested in this little story is not dissimilar from Voltaire's, and was probably shared by most of the *philosophes*. But the very expression of the anxiety paradoxically revealed their own attitude to virtue: it went without saying that they shared the same moral standpoint, that philosophers were virtuous, and that their atheism and materialism had not made them socially destructive. The problem was, then, other people: what would happen if those who were not philosophers should become converted to atheism?

In fact, the Enlightenment view of man was an ambiguous one. Although Rousseau might be described as a kind of Enlightenment maverick, his philosophy was in this respect a distilled and emphatic version of that of most of his contemporaries: when he said that man was naturally good, he was referring to the essence of man, or to a primitive, pre-social man, long since vanished; as for actual existing men, that was a very different matter, as he felt he had all too good reason to know, and much of his work is devoted to analysing the unhappiness and corruption of the members of a modern society. Whatever other thinkers thought about the essence of man, they mostly seemed to agree that men in practice were inclined to be bad, in the sense of anti-social, or at least that a sufficient proportion of them were to constitute a moral and social problem. On the other hand, if Enlightenment thinkers attached so much importance to the liberation of man from the oppression of Christianity and the doctrine of Original Sin, it was because one of their fundamental principles was the right of man to happiness – Diderot indeed went so far as to say: 'There is only one duty, and that is to be happy' ([10.4], 320). Which was implicitly to approve of the self-interested behaviour identified by the materialist analysis of man. What had to be demonstrated was that self-interest was not necessarily anti-social.

One approach was simply to claim that man was so constituted that he was *naturally* virtuous, in the sense of benevolently disposed towards his fellow men (or 'bienfaisant', as Diderot preferred to call it). In other words that self-interest led men, more or less automatically, to behave virtuously. This was in fact the thesis put forward in *L'Homme machine* (1748) by Julien Offroy de la Mettrie (1709–51): if he saw man as a machine, it was a very sophisticated machine, with a built-in moral sense and capacity for remorse, so that wrong-doers suffer as automatically as they do wrong. Remorse and conscience are, like thought, attributes of matter, and we distinguish good from evil as mechanically as we distinguish blue from yellow. La Mettrie's well-intentioned attempt to resolve the problem was decidedly simplistic – one might have answered him that there seemed to be a great many faulty machines on the market – but rejection of the doctrine of Original Sin and its repressive consequences led most materialists to express views which were not fundamentally very different. Diderot continued throughout his life to reiterate the view he had expressed so baldly at the very beginning of his career, that 'without virtue there is no happiness', even though at the same time he accepted, realistically if regretfully, that he was speaking only for a portion of the human race. Arguing that the terms 'virtuous' and 'wicked', which imply moral responsibility, should be discarded, he classified people into two categories, the 'fortunate by birth' ('heureusement nés') and the 'unfortunate by birth' ('malheureusement nés'). Whether one was constitutionally disposed to behave helpfully or harmfully to society was all a matter of chance.

But this was clearly an unsatisfactory position, and Diderot continued to cling to the conviction that the 'heureusement nés' were the norm, even though they might not be in the majority, and that the 'malheureusement nés' were in some way deficient – which was not very different from Rousseau's belief that man was 'naturally good'. In practice, along with most of the other *philosophes*, although he demonstrated that people's moral standards were acquired from experience rather than absolute, Diderot clearly believed in the existence of certain fundamental absolute moral criteria – very much like the universal morality which deists like Voltaire saw as coming from God. In reply to Helvétius, one of the few who steadfastly maintained that absolute justice and injustice do not exist, he asserted that the author of *De l'esprit* would have realized his mistake if he had paid more attention to the nature of man, and reflected that 'anywhere in the world, he who gives something to drink to the man who is thirsty, and something to eat to the man who is hungry, that man is good' ([10.3], 2: 270). Such absolute moral criteria were determined by 'the laws of nature'; for, as Diderot wrote in his *Entretien d'un père*, 'nature has made good laws since the beginning of time' ([10.3], 5: 297). He and the other *philosophes* were very much given to attributing a will and intentions to nature in this way. To some extent, no doubt, it was no more than a linguistic convention, a convenient way of talking about the evolution of the material world; but it frequently verged on a quasi-mystical divinization of nature, which atheists like Diderot sometimes seemed to seize on as a replacement for the God they had dispensed with.

However, the belief in some kind of absolute and universal code of morality still left unexplained the existence of so many who appeared to remain insensitive to it, the 'malheureusement nés'. Diderot tended to see the attractiveness of virtue as a kind of aesthetic truth, accessible only to those who had appropriate taste. In a letter to Voltaire, he explained that atheists 'could not, if they had good taste, put up with a bad book, nor listen patiently to a bad concert, nor tolerate on their wall a bad picture, nor commit a bad action' ([10.5], 1: 78). So that those who were capable of bad actions were lacking in 'normal' aesthetic sensitivity. Just such a one was Rameau, the materialist protagonist in Diderot's brilliant dialogue *Le Neveu de Rameau*, and his interlocutor, the virtuous philosopher 'I', asks him how it is that despite his great sensitivity to 'the beauties of the art of music', he should be 'so blind to the beauties of morality, so insensitive to the charms of virtue' ([10.3], 5: 468). (Rameau replies, of course, that it is all the result of environmental conditioning, heredity and physical constitution.)

D'Holbach too saw it as a question of moral blindness. For him, the virtuous man has the inestimable reward of self-esteem, as he surveys his actions with the same pleasure that others would feel 'if they were not blinded' ([10.8], 1: 321). But such explanations seem if anything to make the problem even more irreducible, for how can the morally blind be made to see? Fortunately, Diderot and d'Holbach both believed that virtuous behaviour brought with it advantages that could be perceived even by those who where not naturally inclined to love it – and it must be emphasized that it was behaviour rather than motivation that they were concerned with. In his letter to Landois, the very one in which he described so vividly the moral implications of materialism, Diderot claimed that wicked actions never go unpunished, because they lead inevitably to 'the contempt of one's fellow-men', and that is 'the greatest of all evils' ([10.3], 19: 435). The importance of the respect of other people was a point he came back to repeatedly, and he clearly believed that their disapproval was a deterrent to which all men were susceptible. D'Holbach's view was much the same. Because his actions are seen as despicable by his fellow-men, or would be if they were known to them, the wicked man is always in his heart ashamed and unhappy, however great the material advantages of his wickedness ([10.8], 1: 235–6). Conversely, the man who habitually behaves virtuously is motivated by the desire for the esteem of others, and for the consequent pleasure of self-esteem; but the force of habit becomes so strong that self-esteem alone will suffice to deter him from wicked actions, even if he could be sure of their remaining hidden, just as the person who has acquired the habit of cleanliness hates getting dirty (the choice of analogy speaks for itself ([10.8], 1: 313–14).

So that the wicked man is indeed blind, not just to the beauty of virtue, but to his own true interest; which is why we should pity him rather than blame him: 'You pity a blind man; and what is a wicked man if not someone who has short sight and cannot see beyond the present moment?' (*Encyclopédie* article 'Vice'). But if he remains resolutely blind despite the experience which should have opened his eyes, what is to be done? The answer is obviously that he must be modified. Now this pragmatic solution had a sound philosophical basis. If, as the materialists argued, man's behaviour is no more than the product of his physical organization and environmental conditioning, then it is clearly possible to modify it by modifying the conditioning. In the discussion of the subject in his humorous novel *Jacques le fataliste*, Diderot explains that Jacques 'became angry with the unjust man; and when you objected to him that he was behaving like the dog who bites the stone that has hit him, he would reply: ' "Not so, the stone bitten by the dog will not change its ways; the unjust man will be modified by the stick" ' ([10.3], 6: 181).

No doubt the stick was the most obvious way of modifying men's behaviour. Although the *philosophes* all criticized the repressive nature of the society they lived in, they nevertheless recognized that even a just society would need punishments for the anti-social citizen. But it was consistent with their humanitarian attitude that they should put far more emphasis on methods other than the stick of modifying men's behaviour. It was the human environment that was crucial. Rameau's nephew, in Diderot's work, suggests that one of the reasons why he is good at music but bad at morality may be that he has 'always lived among good musicians and wicked people' ([10.3], 5: 468). The materialists all emphasized that habit was supremely important in human development. 'Nature', said Helvétius (1715–71), 'is nothing other than our first habit', and he reminded his readers that if they are horrified by the Romans' enjoyment of gladiatorial combats, it is only as a result of their different upbringing, and that if they had been born in Rome, 'habit' would no doubt have made them find the same spectacle agreeable ([10.7], 191). It was then upbringing and education that, by inculcating habits, provided the principal means of modifying human behaviour.

But it did not need Helvétius' materialism to convince people of the importance of education and of the need to reform current practice. From the middle of the century onwards, in fact, discussion of the subject was very much in vogue, and it was a few years after *De l'esprit*, in 1762, that there appeared one of the most important works in the history of educational thought, Rousseau's *Emile ou de l'éducation*. In many ways, *Emile* reflected the prevailing currents of Enlightenment thought. Rousseau's enthusiasm for the goodness of nature was in general shared by most of the *philosophes*, despite their many ambiguities on the subject, and although the work was theoretically based on the natural goodness of man, he used this proposition as a way of demonstrating that education should consist above all in protecting the child from the corrupting influences of society – corresponding in practice to the programme suggested by Helvétius and d'Holbach. Rousseau accepted fully a sensationalism very close to Condillac's (though he explicitly refuted the extreme position adopted by Helvétius), and the education of the young child reflected this, with much emphasis being laid on the development of each of the five senses, and especially on the relationship between sight and touch, in a manner very reminiscent of the *Traité des sensations* (see above, Chapter 9, pp. 239–40). In one important respect, however, *Emile* diverged from the thought of the other *philosophes*: much as he admired the virtuous citizens of ancient Greece and Rome, Rousseau declared at the outset that such an ideal was impossible to recreate in a corrupt modern society, and the aim of the work was the formation of an independent, self-sufficient individual rather than a citizen who functioned primarily as a constituent part of a social whole.

But the reform of education, precisely because it accepted the structures of society as it then existed, was necessarily limited. The idea that man in contemporary society was *necessarily* corrupt was frequently expressed by the *philosophes*: Rousseau had demonstrated it in his *Discourse on inequality* in 1755, and when thinkers such as Diderot and d'Holbach attacked social and political injustice, they tended to adopt the same position, though in their case it was probably more of a polemical device than a deeply held conviction. But even if they held less extreme views than Rousseau on the subject, they shared his view about the urgent need for political reform, without which educational reform might seem to be little more than a palliative; Helvétius for example asserted that the two were so closely linked that it might well be impossible to make major changes in education without making corresponding changes 'in the very structure of states' ([10.7], 492).

Political thought is fundamentally different from what one is tempted to call 'pure philosophy' in that it is rarely if ever concerned principally with the objective quest for truth (even when it purports to be), and is always dominated by a response to actual contemporary conditions. In the case of the *philosophes*, this response was, it is true, determined by certain humanitarian convictions, the right to happiness, usually seen as inseparable from freedom (variously defined, as we shall see), equality before the law, and so on, all arguably following logically from their moral anthropocentrism. At the same time, however, their political thought was first and foremost shaped by the abuses of the *ancien régime*, the manifest injustice of the extremes of wealth and poverty, the existence of privilege, inequality before the law, religious intolerance... , and in some cases, the consciousness of the urgent need for practical reform took precedence over theoretical considerations about the nature of government and the structure of society.

It was above all Voltaire who came into this last category. He made virtually no attempt to systematize his political thought, which consisted largely of a series of pragmatic reactions to specific social problems. He shared the other *philosophes*' humanitarian convictions about human rights, and hated injustice, oppression and intolerance; but his principles were always tempered by a sense of realism, even expediency. Early in his career, largely due to his exile in England following a quarrel with a powerful nobleman, he conceived great enthusiasm for the English system of constitutional monarchy (somewhat idealized). But when it came to the actual situation in France, he firmly supported an absolute monarchy, even though he recognized the risk of absolutism degenerating into despotism. For the only intermediate powers between King and people were the clergy, the aristocracy, and the Parlements (regional high courts with considerable powers, including the right to block legislation), all of which Voltaire saw as defending sectional interests and the abuse of privilege. His ideal was a strong enlightened monarch, but given the actual problems of government, the strength was perhaps more important than the enlightenment. In the conflict between the throne and the Parlements which dominated the latter years of the *ancien régime*, Voltaire was emphatically on the side of the throne, which he continued to see as offering the best chance both of initiating reform and of averting revolution.

It is true that Voltaire's very real sympathy for the sufferings of an oppressed people was always accompanied by the fear of popular disorder, and ultimately revolution, which underlay his desire for strong government as much as did his desire for reform – paralleling his belief in the need for a policeman god to discourage his tailor from robbing him. But behind his anxiety about disorder – shared by practically all the *philosophes* – his works reveal a fundamental desire to preserve existing social institutions, suitably reformed. He advocated religious toleration, freedom of the press, and the reform of criminal law, but the main burden of his political thought was the defence of the freedom and rights of the middle classes, inseparable from the protection of their property. Certainly he believed in kindness to the poor, but if he advocated equality before the law, he was not keen on too much social equality. Society could not exist, he argued in his *Dictionnaire philosophique* (article 'Egalité'), without 'a vast number of useful men who have no possessions at all' ([10.16], 18: 476), for who would till our fields and make our shoes if there were no poor? Fortunately most of the poor are too busy working to notice their plight, though when they do, this just leads to wars which they inevitably lose, ending up in a worse state than before. Nevertheless, one must bear in mind the essentially pragmatic nature of Voltaire's thought and the practical limitations of contemporary society, and it could well be argued that his vigorous protests against oppression, his realism and his concentration on practical issues did more for suffering humanity, even in the long term, than the utopian schemes of some of his contemporaries.

The most important work on political science in the eighteenth century was surely *De L'esprit des lois*, published in 1748, by Charles de Secondat, Baron de Montesquieu (1689–1755). Although Montesquieu's thought was no doubt triggered by the consciousness of contemporary problems, which he saw as largely the legacy of the arbitrary government of Louis XIV, he went further than anyone else in the century towards establishing a theoretical basis for the subject. Although he dismissed as absurd the notion that the world could have been produced by 'a blind fatality', seeing it as self-evident that intelligent beings must have been created by an intelligent God, his approach was in other respects very similar to that of the scientific materialists who sought to discover the underlying laws governing the behaviour of matter – indeed he also rejects as absurd the possibility of God operating on the world other than through these invariable laws. While recognizing that 'the intelligent world' was much less well governed than the physical world, Montesquieu believed nevertheless that it too had its underlying laws (Diderot's 'laws of nature'), preceding all laws made by men: with rather dubious logic, he argued that just as the radii of a circle were all equal before anyone had ever drawn a circle, so the notions of just and unjust (and by implication the obligation to behave justly) existed independently of any man-made laws.

Rejecting Hobbes's view of a wolf-man in a state of war, Montesquieu argued that primitive man would have been characterized by the consciousness of his weakness rather than by feelings of aggression, and he imagined the origin of society as lying in a natural sociability. But once societies had been formed, positive laws were needed to embody and supplement the fundamental laws, and these positive laws had to vary with the enormous variety of local circumstances. They must be appropriate to differences in climate and soil, in the situation and size of societies, in the way of life of peoples, their religion, their temperament, traditions, and so forth. It was the relationships between laws and all these different factors that Montesquieu proposed to study in the *Esprit des Lois*.

There were, he observed, three forms of government, the republican, subdivided into democratic and aristocratic, the monarchic and the despotic, each with their distinct characteristics and guiding principles. He gave despotism, which he saw as based on fear, very short shrift, whereas, sharing as he did in the general Enlightenment enthusiasm for ancient Greece and Rome, he found much to admire in the republic, particularly in its democratic form. The guiding principle of the republic was virtue, which Montesquieu defined as love of the law, involving a preference for the public interest over private interest.

But his admiration for the democratic republic was very theoretical, and he saw it as extraordinarily difficult to realize, even in the very small states to which alone it was suited. In practice, his clear preference was for monarchy, which has no need for virtue in the above sense, being based instead solely on 'honour', in other words on the pursuit of personal ambition and the desire for distinction, both natural traits. Love of the 'patrie' and self-sacrifice are simply replaced by laws, so that 'each person works for the common good, believing he works for his individual interests' (III, 7, [10.11], 27). When he visited England in 1729–30, Montesquieu had discovered what he saw as the ideal constitutional monarchy, based on the separation of legislative, executive and judicial powers, and this separation of powers was to become the guiding principle of his own proposed scheme of government. His criterion was political liberty (in contrast to the equality which characterized democracies): but since 'any man who has power is led to abuse it' (XI, 4, [10.11], 155), the only way political liberty can be safeguarded is by a system of checks and balances, based on the separation of powers.

Montesquieu's political thought has been described as a mixture of Cartesianism and empiricism. Certainly it contained a number of a priori elements, and proposed a mechanistic model of society, in which he seemed to have made the mistake of applying to human behaviour the invariability of cause-effect relationships characteristic of the material world, though in this he could be said to be closer to Condillac and Helvétius than to Descartes. Montesquieu's great importance and originality, however did not lie in the model of government he proposed, but rather in his empirical, analytical approach to the subject. No doubt he was given to unwise generalizations and over-simplifications about the effect of climate and soil, etc., but in recognizing the relativity of truths about human nature, and in trying to discover the various laws determining the formation, structure and functioning of different kinds of society by observing and analysing actual societies (despite the inadequacies of his historical and anthropological knowledge), he was putting politics on a modern scientific footing and virtually creating sociology.

It is true that, politically speaking, Montesquieu defended the privileges of the aristocracy and his system of checks and balances seemed to produce an equilibrium which was essentially static, militating against any kind of change. But as far as France was concerned, this model represented for him a vast improvement over the degenerate government of Louis XV, and he certainly shared the humanitarian hostility of the *philosophes* to injustice and oppression. He fiercely attacked despotism and even more slavery, especially of the blacks: how can we believe that 'god, who is a very wise being, should have put a soul, above all a good soul, in a body that was entirely black'?, he asked ironically (XV, 5, [10.11], 250). And he did believe in the possibility of progress and reform, in the ability of a good government to modify its citizens. When he described the effects on men of different climates, for example, his attitude was far from passive: if the effects were bad (when, for instance, an extreme climate led men to be lazy or women immodest!), it was up to the legislator to correct them. 'Bad legislators', he wrote, 'are those who have favoured the vices of the climate and good ones are those who have opposed them' (XIV, 5, [10.11], 236).

The influence of *De l'Esprit des Lois* on Montesquieu's contemporaries seems to have been immediate, widespread and very selective. While the *philosophes* welcomed his scientific approach to politics, they tended to reject precisely the innovative political sociology, based on relativism and the introduction of variables. Human nature for Condillac, Helvétius and even for the more subtle Diderot, had fixed characteristics (always and everywhere the same needs and desires) and was thus modifiable in an entirely predictable way: a given cause would always produce a given effect. So politics became a simple extrapolation from scientific psychology: all the legislator had to do was construct society in accordance with human nature. Now if 'virtue', in the form of a preference for the general good over personal good, is indeed natural, as Diderot, for example, sometimes claimed, this will present no problem. The real difficulty for the organization of society is the existence of the morally blind or defective citizens, and the solution, as with personal morality, is provided by the modifiability of man inherent in sensationalist psychology.

Civic virtue can of course be stimulated by the same means used to encourage virtuous behaviour at the personal level, and especially by the formation of good habits by education. The point was made repeatedly by Helvétius, as well as by d'Holbach, for whom education was the principal way of 'giving to the soul habits which are advantageous for the individual and for society' ([10.8], 1: 287). And Morelly, in his utopian *Code de la Nature*, saw moral transformation by education as a prerequisite for the creation of the ideal society.

But even without moral transformation, there are qualities in men condemned by conventional (Christian) morality, which, properly used, can be socially constructive. Instead of trying to suppress human passions such as ambition and the desire for wealth, said d'Holbach, society (as in Montesquieu's ideal monarchy) should make the most of them and turn them to its advantage ([10.8], 1: 147); and in the *Supplément au Voyage de Bougainville*, Diderot showed that the sexual drive, far from being anti-social, made an invaluable contribution to society if, as was then generally believed, prosperity was dependent on population size. In any case, people will behave virtuously if they can see that it is in their own interests. So society, by using the carrot rather than the stick, should make it worth people's while to behave virtuously. The trick, as Diderot pointed out in one of his dialogues, is to construct society in such a way that 'the good of individuals is so closely linked to the general good, that it is almost impossible for a citizen to harm society without harming himself' ([10.3], 2: 517). D'Holbach too stressed that in the well-governed society, each citizen would be convinced that the 'well-being of the parts could result only from the well-being of the body as a whole' ([10.8], 1: 319). And

Helvétius also had made much the same point. A recurrent theme in *De l'esprit* had been that 'the virtues and vices of a people are always a necessary effect of its legislation' ([10.7], 325): Helvétius quoted many examples to demonstrate that the extraordinary incidences of civic virtue in the history of Ancient Rome and Sparta were the result of 'the skill with which the legislators of these nations had linked individual interest to the public interest' ([10.7], 324). Indeed, it was precisely the absence of such a link in the modern state (in other words France) which caused the alienation of modern man vividly described by d'Holbach, a man who had no feeling of involvement in the society in which he lived, and who, in the words of both Diderot and Rousseau, was 'neither man nor citizen'.

As for the actual political structure of society, the confidently rationalist approach of the *philosophes*, tending to make them see truth as absolute and indivisible, led them to reject Montesquieu's checks and balances and to see an absolute indivisible monarchy as the only logical ideal; intermediate bodies, they argued, would represent sectional interests, which might well differ considerably from the interest of the community as a whole. The intellectual objectivity of this theoretical analysis might, however, be seen as highly suspect, given that it coincided conveniently with the view that the *philosophes* shared with Voltaire that the principal source of injustice and oppression in France was the abuse of power and privilege on the part of the Church, the aristocracy and the Parlements. Diderot, in the *Encyclopédie*, and d'Holbach both maintained that sovereignty belonged to the people as a whole, and was entrusted by them to a ruler by a kind of contract, explicit or tacit; sovereignty acquired without the consent of the people was merely a usurpation, which would last only as long as the superiority of strength which initiated it. Furthermore, the two *philosophes* argued, the consent could never be unconditional: the object of government could only be the well-being and happiness of the governed, and the use by a sovereign of the powers entrusted to him to make a people unhappy was, in Diderot's words, 'a manifest usurpation' (*Encyclopédie*, article 'Souverains'), or, as d'Holbach put it, 'nothing but banditry' ([10.8], 1: 336).

But history convinced the *philosophes* that this, alas, was all too likely to happen, and that, to quote d'Holbach again, this time echoing Montesquieu, 'man is always tempted to abuse power' ([10.8], 1: 145). Having rejected Montesquieu's solution of the separation of powers, they opted instead for assemblies representing the people to advise the monarch, since, as the *Encyclopédie* article 'Représentants' (by Diderot or possibly d'Holbach – scholarly opinion is divided) explained, this is the only way the good sovereign can be made aware of the needs of all his subjects. And to avoid the representatives themselves losing sight of their responsibilities, they would have to be regularly elected. But only by those subjects who own property: 'it is property which makes the citizen: every man who owns something in the State is interested in the good of the State'. Diderot, d'Holbach, Helvétius were all agreed that those who did not own property in a state could not possibly have a serious interest in its prosperity, and should not therefore have any say in its government, just as, conversely, one of the first responsibilities of a ruler or ruling body must be the safeguarding of private property. The general interest of a society lay for d'Holbach in the three advantages which just laws should guarantee for the majority of its citizens, liberty, property and security – and even the latter was defined as the right to protection by the laws of a law-abiding citizen's person and property.

Private property was also at the very centre of the system proposed by the physiocrats, a school of thinkers who had come together as a group by about 1760, and who saw economics as the key to politics. Like the *philosophes*, they believed that the organization of society was governed by the same kind of fixed 'natural' laws as the material world, but for them these laws related essentially to trade. The founder of the school, François Quesnay (1694–1774), himself a doctor, saw the circulation of wealth in society performing the same function as the circulation of blood in the body. Their system involved the simplest form of government, an absolute monarchy, and a minimum of laws: starting from the premise that agriculture, and thus ownership of land, constituted the original source of all wealth, their implicit optimism concerning human nature led them to believe that the complete freedom of trade would result in the self-regulating balance of supply and demand as men realized their interdependence, creating prosperity and happiness for all.

Rather than Quesnay, however, it was Anne-Robert-Jacques Turgot (1727–81), a distinguished civil-servant and subsequently statesman, who gave these ideas their most lucid expression, and whose version of them was the most perceptive. In a remarkable anticipation of both Adam Smith and Marx, as well as twentieth-century theories of entrepreneurial capitalism, his *Reflections on the Formation and the Distribution of Wealth* (written 1766–7) developed an economic system firmly based on an historical sociological analysis which showed that societies operated according to predictable laws of cause and effect. The economic cycle begins with the surplus produced by the 'Husbandman' 'over and above his personal needs' ([10.15], 122), and the continued cultivation of land, the industry and the commerce necessary for the health of a society all depend on the circulation of money, which occurs in various ways. And it was an essential feature of Turgot's system that the different uses of capital will tend 'naturally' to achieve the ideal equilibrium necessary for the maximum benefit to society, though this will only occur where trade is untrammeled by restrictive laws, especially in the form of taxes.

Turgot's belief that man is so constituted that society tends naturally to perfect itself was not confined to the sphere of economics. In his *Discourse On Universal History*, he showed how, driven to action and thus to progress by the passions, in other words the urge to satisfy needs, and passing through violent fluctuations in its fortunes, 'the human race as a whole has advanced ceaselessly towards its perfection' ([10.15], 72). It is true that he had rather more confidence than most of his contemporaries in a natural evolution of society towards something like perfection, though the *philosophes* in general were optimistic about the future of mankind. But the most systematic exponent of the perfectibility of human society was Antoine-Nicolas de Condorcet (1743–94), whose *Esquisse d'un tableau historique des progrès de l'esprit humain*, was written, ironically, while he was in hiding after his proscription by the Revolutionary government consequent on his own involvement in politics. The *Esquisse* divided the history of man into successive ages, revealing a story of continual progress achieved over the centuries despite an unending battle with the forces of reaction, represented mainly by the Church. But now, as scientific knowledge of man and the universe continued to increase, and as men became progressively more enlightened, Condorcet believed, with what now looks like touching simplicity, that the end of the battle was at last in sight. It would be achieved by a mixture of natural development and positive legislation. He accepted to some extent Turgot's vision of a self-regulating economic system based on free trade, but he also believed in the necessity of governmental intervention to protect the weak and the poor. In fact, the removal of social and even natural inequalities was central to his idea of progress: he attacked slavery, argued for the equality of women (very much an exception during the Revolutionary period), and above all advocated universal education, on which his ideas (free elementary education for both sexes, teaching children to think for themselves, the independence of teachers, etc.) were admirably enlightened even by late twentieth-century standards.

Whereas Condorcet thought optimistically that society was already well on the road to perfection, however, there were in the second half of the eighteenth century a number of egalitarian political thinkers whose utopias involved a far greater transformation of society (though not, usually, a violent one) than was to be brought about merely by the French Revolution. The earliest and most interesting of these was Morelly (about whom virtually nothing is known), who envisaged in his *Code de la Nature* (1755) a gradual return, facilitated principally by a reform of moral education, to the ideal natural state in which men had been motivated solely by the benevolence produced in them by an awareness of mutual need. In modern society, 'natural probity' has become debased by the growth of avarice, man's one fundamental vice from which all others derived; and it was avarice that led to the existence of private property, which was, as Morelly emphasized throughout, the root of all social evil. In the ideal society, all land and all products of the land would remain common, all other goods would be distributed by laws according to need.

These principles were embodied in the 'Modèle de législation conforme aux intentions de la Nature' which concluded the *Code de la Nature*. Nothing would be sold or exchanged, but all produce would be taken to the Market Place, where people would simply take whatever they needed. All citizens would engage in agriculture from twenty to twenty-five; and all would marry as soon as they reached puberty, with celibacy permitted only after forty. There would be a minimum of penal laws, but life imprisonment would be the punishment for serious crimes such as murder, or any attempt to introduce 'la détestable propriété' ([10.12], 323).

The eccentric Benedictine, Dom Léger-Marie Deschamps (1716–74), whose ideas impressed both Diderot and Rousseau, also focussed on property as the source of all moral evils. In *Le Vrai Système*, written about 1770, he contrasted society as it is, which he described as the state of laws, based on property, with the utopian state of 'moeurs', the state of morality. In the absence of private property, all land, all women would belong to all (all men, too, though he makes less of this); even mothers and children would be common, with those women who were able to suckling any babies, or indeed any old men, 'who would grow strong and be rejuvenated from their milk' ([10.2], 171). In the state of 'moeurs', all would be equal and completely united, with the good of society as their only aim. Every factor in society causing differences between individuals would be suppressed: children would not be taught to read or write, all books would be burned, all works of art destroyed. Without desires or passions, through days that were always the same, people would live in total tranquillity, with no personal attachments, indifferent to death, never laughing or crying. The individual would become totally subsumed in the general, existing in a mystical state of harmonious oneness.

Now it was a characteristic of virtually all the political thinkers we have been discussing that they glossed over the conflict between the individual's natural desire for liberty and the political need for the individual to be subordinated to the state, by assuming that it was in some way natural for a naturally sociable man to prefer the general interest to his own, or at least that an enlightened reason would lead him to realize that his own interest was dependent on that of the state.

Rousseau, whose political thought is discussed in detail elsewhere in this volume, was the exception in seeing natural man and social man or the citizen as diametrically opposed. In his *Second Discourse* (1755) Rousseau had argued that the origin of inequality among men, and thus of their corruption and unhappiness, had been the introduction of private property, which led to rivalry and the replacement of natural self-love (*amour de soi*) by self-preference (*amour-propre*). But he always recognized that the state of primitive innocence was irrecoverable, and postulated two alternative solutions to the woes of alienated modern man: one, the aim of *Emile*, was to attempt to create by education a modern version of natural man, adapted to live in society as it is; the other was a total reorganization of society, to create a democratic republic inspired principally by the city states of the ancient world, which he described in his *Social Contract* (1762). Self-oriented natural man would have no place in such a society; the ideal citizen, said Rousseau, must lose all sense of self and be concerned only with the common weal. There was nothing natural about this abnegation, which must be inculcated by the laws and civic education. Political freedom consisted for Rousseau in willing the general good, so that some people will have to be forced to be free by the laws which embody the general will. Nothing contrary to the general will must be permitted, so there can be no freedom of thought in the usual sense of the term. There will be a state religion and no other, decreeing the sanctity of the laws and outlawing intolerance (!): anyone unwilling to accept its doctrine will be banished, and anyone who, having accepted it, behaves as if he had not, will be executed.

It seems highly probable that this highly theoretical construct represented nothing more for Rousseau than a systematic logical application of a number of speculative principles, and the dichotomy in his thought between a theoretical ideal and the possibilities of the real world was reflected in one way or another in the political ideas of most of the *philosophes*. In considering the ideal society, they could not escape from the realization that the existence of private property, the defence of which was for them a cardinal principle of political freedom, was incompatible with real (and not just political) equality. From time to time, Diderot indulged in utopian egalitarian flights of fancy, clearly influenced by Morelly and Deschamps, as for instance in the idealized Tahitian society of the *Supplément au Voyage de Bougainville*. In reality, though, he recognized that this kind of thinking was pie in the sky, and just like Voltaire, d'Holbach, Helvétius and indeed Rousseau, he continued to see the protection of private property as a *sine qua non* of the just and healthy society. Not only must property be a prerequisite for citizenship, but it was indispensable for the material prosperity, based on commerce and industry, which the Enlightenment thinkers were so enthusiastic about. The ideal of most of the *philosophes* was a materially prosperous property-owning democracy with a minimum of inequalities, and though they talked much about the sovereignty of the 'peuple', it was clear that in the majority of cases what they meant by 'peuple' was the bourgeoisie rather than anything like the Marxist proletariat.

Be that as it may, the *philosophes* were none the less vigorously opposed to injustice and oppression, and more specifically to the political regime they lived in. The Enlightenment was fundamentally a movement of intellectual challenge to authority on every level, and nothing any longer was sacred, especially not religion. But the far-reaching practical implications of the challenge to political authority made it a rather different matter from, say, rejecting the Church's doctrine on free-will or virtue, and at least to begin with, the *philosophes* were opposed to violent revolution. They wanted change, but peaceful, structured change. However, as hope for constitutional change in France seemed to recede and the enlightenment of Frederick the Great and Catherine of Russia looked more and more like a façade, the theme of the legitimacy of revolt against the abuse of power appeared ever more frequently in the works of Diderot and d'Holbach. The notion of the sovereignty of the people, and the associated one of a contract between people and ruler led directly to the conclusion that when the contract was broken by the ruler, the people were entitled to overthrow him. As d'Holbach wrote in 1767: 'Since the Government draws its power only from the society, and is established only for the latter's good, it is obvious that the society can revoke this power when its interest dictates, and change the form of its government' ([10.8] 1: 141). Yet this justification of revolution was always a reluctant one, on Diderot's part at least, and the overriding concern for the rule of law which he and others had expressed in the *Encyclopédie* never left him. In his *Supplément au Voyage de Bougainville*, having demonstrated that the laws governing the structure of society in a country like France were nonsensical, he nevertheless concluded by urging conformity to them, since 'the worst form of society' is the one in which 'the laws, good or bad, are not observed' ([10.3], 2: 240).

Most of the major thinkers of the French Enlightenment had died by the outbreak of the Revolution, but it is tempting to wonder what they would have written about it if they had survived. Condorcet, despite ending up its victim, still wrote a work expressing his faith in progress and the perfectibility of man, but one suspects that the humanitarian advocates of freedom and tolerance would for the most part have been somewhat disappointed, at least by the savage later stages of the Revolution. Whether or not their confidence in the progress of science and knowledge would have survived twentieth-century strides in the destruction of the environment and creation of weapons of mass destruction must remain open to conjecture.

❧ BIBLIOGRAPHY ❧

Eighteenth-century Works

10.1 Condorcet, Antoine-Nicolas de *Esquisse d'un tableau historique des progrès de l'esprit humain*, Garnier-Flammarion, Paris, Flammarion, 1988.

10.2 Deschamps, Dom Léger-Marie *Le Vrai Système*, ed. J. Thomas and F. Venturi, Geneva, Droz, 1963.

10.3 Diderot, Denis *Oeuvres complètes*, ed. J. Assézat and M. Tourneux, Paris, 1875–77.

10.4 —— *Oeuvres politiques*, ed. P. Vernière, Classiques Garnier, Paris, Garnier, 1963.

10.5 —— *Correspondance*, ed. G. Roth and J. Varloot, Paris, Editions de Minuit, 1955–70.

10.6 *Encyclopédie*, ed. Diderot and d'Alembert, Paris, 1951–80.

10.7 Helvétius, Claude-Adrien *De l'esprit*, Marabout-Université, Verviers, Gérard, 1973.

10.8 d'Holbach, Paul Thiry, Baron *Le Système de la Nature*, London, 1770, Slatkine Reprints, Geneva, 1973.

10.9 La Mettrie, Julien Offroy de *Textes choisis*, Les Classiques du peuple, Paris, Editions sociales, 1954.

10.10 Montesquieu, Charles de Secondat, Baron de *Oeuvres complètes*, Paris, Editions Nagel, 1950.

10.11 —— *The Spirit of the Laws*, trans. and ed. A. M. Cohler, B. C. Miller and H. S. Stone, Cambridge, Cambridge University Press, 1989.

10.12 Morelly, *Code de la Nature*, ed. G. Chinard, Paris, R. Clavreuil, 1950.

10.13 Raynal, Guillaume *Histoire philosophique et politique des deux Indes*, Geneva, 1780.

10.14 Rousseau, Jean-Jacques *Oeuvres complètes*, Bibliothèque de la Pléiade, Paris, Gallimard, 1959–69.

10.15 Turgot, Anne-Robert-Jacques *On Progress, Sociology and Economics*, trans. and ed. R. L. Meek, Cambridge, Cambridge University Press, 1973.

10.16 Voltaire, *Oeuvres complètes*, ed. L. Moland, Paris, Garnier, 1877–85.

10.17 —— *Traité de métaphysique*, ed. H. T. Patterson, Manchester, Manchester University Press, 1937.

General Studies

10.18 Cassirer, E. *The Philosophy of the Enlightenment*, trans. F. C. A. Koellen and J. P. Pettegrove, Princeton, NJ, Princeton University Press, 1951.

10.19 Cobban, A. *In Search of Humanity*, London, Cape, 1960.

10.20 Crocker, L.G. *An Age of Crisis*, Baltimore, John Hopkins Press, 1959.

10.21 —— *Nature and Culture, ethical thought in 18th century France*, Baltimore, John Hopkins Press, 1963.

10.22 Gay, P. *The Enlightenment: an interpretation*, 2 vols, London, Weidenfeld and Nicolson, 1966–9.

10.23 Goyard-Fabre, S. *La philosophie des lumières en France*, Paris, Klincksieck, 1972.

10.24 Leroy, M. *Histoire des idées sociales en France*, vol. 1, Paris, Gallimard, 1946.

10.25 Martin, K. *French Liberal Thought in the 18th Century*, ed. J. P. Mayer, London, Turnstile Press, 1962 (first pub. 1929).

10.26 Talmon, J.L. *The Origins of Totalitarian Democracy*, New York, Norton, 1970.

Critical Studies on Individual Authors

10.27 Benot, Y. *Diderot, de l'athéisme à l'anticolonialisme*, Paris, Maspero, 1970.

10.28 Burgelin, P. *La philosophie de l'existence de Rousseau*, Paris, Presses Universitaires, 1952.

10.29 Carcassonne, E. *Montesquieu et le problème de la Constitution française au XVIIIe siècle*, Paris, Presses Universitaires, 1927.

10.30 Crocker, L. G. *Diderot's chaotic order: approach to synthesis*, Princeton, NJ, Princeton University Press, 1974.

10.31 —— *Diderot the embattled philosopher*, London, N. Spearman, 1955.

10.32 *Diderot, les dernières années*, ed. France and Strugnell, Edinburgh, Edinburgh University Press, 1985.

10.33 France, P. *Diderot*, Past Masters, Oxford, Oxford University Press, 1983.

10.34 Gay, P. *Voltaire's Politics: the Poet as Realist*, Princeton, NJ, Princeton University Press, 1959.

10.35 Hermand, P. *Les idées morales de Diderot*, Paris, Presses Universitaires, 1923.

10.36 Lefèbvre, H. *Diderot*, Paris, Editeurs réunis, 1949.

10.37 Mason, H. T. *Voltaire*, London, Hutchinson, 1975.

10.38 Mason, S. *Montesquieu's idea of justice*, The Hague, Nijhoff, 1975.

10.39 Pomeau, R. *La religion de Voltaire*, Paris, Nizet, 1956.

10.40 Proust, J. *Diderot et l'Encyclopédie*, Paris, A. Colin, 1962.

10.41 Strugnell, A. *Diderot's Politics*, The Hague, Nijhoff, 1973.

There are also numerous relevant articles in the following specialist journals:

10.42 *Diderot Studies*, Syracuse, then Geneva, Droz, 1949–.

10.43 *Studies on Voltaire and the Eighteenth Century*, Geneva, then Oxford, 1955–.

CHAPTER 11
The Scottish Enlightenment
M. A. Stewart

❧ INTRODUCTION ❧

The term 'Scottish Enlightenment' is used to characterize a hundred years of intellectual and cultural endeavour that started around the second decade of the eighteenth century. Our knowledge of the period is changing, as scholars investigate more of the manuscript deposits and publishers reissue more of the scarcer printed sources. Although I am here concerned with philosophical developments, the Enlightenment was not narrowly philosophical. Scottish historical, legal and medical writers responded to the influence of philosophical debate; philosophers themselves did pioneering work in social science; and the natural sciences and the arts reached new heights of national and international distinction.[1] The Enlightenment should not, however, be defined solely in terms of innovation. There were significant continuities with the previous century, while the challenge of criticism brought a new quality to the work of the best defenders of orthodox tradition.

The controversy surrounding the replacement of the Catholic King James by the joint monarchy of William and Mary in 1688 had reawakened interest in the nature and basis of civil government, and fuelled a certain amount of idealism about the reform of the institutions of state to re-establish ancient ideals of public and personal virtue.[2] The Scottish universities were caught up in this mood of reform, while constrained by the preparedness of those involved to subscribe the Westminster Confession of Faith. William III, faced with the rival claims of episcopacy and presbytery to the control of the Scottish Church, awarded the contest to the presbyterians on the understanding that they appoint 'moderate' persons to positions of influence, persons who would avoid pulpit demagoguery and theological witchhunts. The mandate was more easily fulfilled in the universities, where there was greater influence over appointments than in the Church, though an attempt in the 1690s to steer the universities into a uniform national syllabus failed. One reform, introduced piecemeal over the following century, contributed to a temporary superiority of the Scottish over the English universities: the institution of Dutch-style specialist appointments in the different branches of the curriculum.

Scotland was unusual in the degree to which developments in philosophy occurred within, rather than in opposition to, the universities.[3] The main exception is in the work of David Hume (1711–76), who was twice barred, by clerical opposition, from university appointments, at Edinburgh in 1745 and Glasgow in 1752. But Hume interacted with the intellectual establishment, and it will be convenient to build the following account round some of this interaction.

The curriculum was dominated by the three traditional divisions of philosophy: logic and metaphysics, moral philosophy, and natural philosophy.[4] Logic in the early part of the century was still substantially Aristotelian, sometimes recast in the language of 'ideas', but half a century later Alexander Gerard, Thomas Reid and George Campbell could write of this formal training as largely discredited. Meanwhile rhetoric, another traditional component, was being transformed into the study of belles lettres.[5] A certain amount of epistemology, Cartesian and later Lockean, whose methodology ran counter to that of syllogistic logic, might be added.[6] Metaphysics, even after the decline of Aristotelianism, remained primarily the study of ontology. This could extend, particularly in later usage and among medical writers, to the nature of mind and its modes of operation.[7] The latter was traditionally called 'pneumatology' and was regarded as the foundation for moral philosophy. Moral philosophy was not confined to ethics, for ethics had to be grounded in a thorough understanding of human nature. A century earlier, this had been the prerogative of the theologians, whose emphasis on humanity's fallen state had encouraged a strictly biblical view of moral teaching. The Enlightenment changed this ethos, but the aim of instruction remained one of instilling principles of virtue and good citizenship within a context of general piety.[8]

As for natural philosophy, Cartesianism and the controversies it brought in its wake had become the staple of most universities by the later seventeenth century, but gave way to the science of the early Royal Society by the turn of the century. This was presented in different ways in different institutions, according to the experimental facilities and mathematical expertise available. Some stressed the experimental or at least data-gathering basis of the new science, some its inherently systematic character in reducing diverse phenomena to a body of laws; while all of them in some degree saw the different branches of philosophy as sharing a common methodology.[9]

❧❧ THE AGE OF HUTCHESON ❧❧

The official face of reform appears in the increasing use of classical Stoic sources for teaching purposes.[10] These offered a morality attractive enough to the moderate Calvinist mind to satisfy the pedagogical requirement that secular writings should not endanger the faith. Cicero was frequently studied as a Stoic resource, and Scottish editions of Seneca, Epictetus and Marcus Aurelius were reprinted throughout the eighteenth century. Francis Hutcheson (1694–1746) and James Moor (1712–79) collaborated on an annotated translation of Aurelius which was promoted as an antidote to sectarianism.[11] Along with this went a revived interest in natural law – a field where ethics and epistemology converge. Because these studies traditionally related to natural religion, for which the advances in science appeared to be opening up spectacular new vistas, the arts faculties at last found themselves with an integrated agenda for the post-scholastic era, in which, even if they continued to respond to the religious climate of the day, they could re-establish their independence from dogmatic theology.

The natural religion which was particularly in vogue was that of the Dutch Remonstrant tradition of the previous century, which ran from the jurist Hugo Grotius – on whom Hutcheson used to give public Sunday lectures – to the theologian-journalist Jean LeClerc. It had received expression in English through the work of Henry More, John Wilkins, John Tillotson and other English divines close to the early Royal Society; while their defences of the biblical revelation had received additional support in the writing of Locke. Locke had argued that the existence of God could be rationally demonstrated, though his handling of the arguments of natural religion was relatively cursory and dogmatic for someone working in the heyday of the Design argument; and he had developed a defence of revelation from his own historical researches. Believers in revelation appeared to have two lines of recourse. They could appeal to personal experience and claim to have been favoured with individual revelations. This, for Locke, gave carte blanche to the 'enthusiast' or fanatic, hence to sectarianism and social division. A personal faith impervious to rational arbitration was a kind of madness.[12] The alternative appeal was to the public revelation of the written, ultimately spoken, doctrine of the Scriptures, validated by the miraculous events contained within their history. But here the same difficulty recurred: when can a miracle story be believed? A rational test was found in the criteria for 'weighing' historical evidence by reference to the quantity and quality of ancient witnesses.[13] One Scot who was influential in insisting on the rational credentials of revelation was Hutcheson's teacher John Simson (1667–1740), who was prevented by the Church from carrying out his office as professor of divinity at Glasgow after 1729.[14]

Besides these overt trends in the curriculum, there was a more clandestine debate, particularly among the students of divinity and law. We find it in the graduate clubs, some of whose members go on to form the nucleus of the professional literary and scientific societies of the mid-century. Four not entirely separate interests can be documented, almost contemporaneously – a sharpened political consciousness, and a fascination with the imported philosophies of Shaftesbury, the deists, and Berkeley.

Politically, it was the Ulster students at Glasgow who made the running. Their disabilities at home made them sensitive to authoritarian administration. Some came, too, with a hostility to theological regimentation, at a time when other young intellectuals, some of them trainees for the ministry, were questioning the Church's continuing role in the oversight of the universities and arguing that religion could as easily corrupt morals as promote them.[15] If they and their fellow students found Shaftesbury's ironic attitude to religious and educational institutions attractive, they were particularly receptive to his argument that religion presupposes morality rather than the reverse; and if that means there has to be an instinctive moral feeling – particularly if it can be shown that this is also the impetus to all that is best in art and literature – then there must be a brighter side to human nature than either traditional theology or recent philosophy had proposed. Gershom Carmichael (1672–1729), the first designated professor of moral philosophy at Glasgow, was no follower of Shaftesbury, but he nevertheless laid the groundwork for this reception, by emphasizing the social nature of humanity, and putting it on a new philosophical footing, as part of a theory of rights founded in the love of God rather than the fear of man.[16]

More radical free-thinkers were also discussed, such as John Toland (himself a Scottish graduate), Anthony Collins, and Matthew Tindal. George Turnbull (1698–1748), who taught at Aberdeen in the 1720s, had gone through a deist phase when he sought to engage Toland, and Toland's patron, Lord Molesworth, in correspondence. His contemporary in Divinity school, Robert Wallace (1697–1771), who was avowedly utilitarian in his thinking, subjected religious doctrine to moral tests and questioned the intended universality of some Bible precepts. But both used the deist challenge to test the limits of acceptable belief rather than to go beyond them, and both responded to Tindal with defences of the Christian dispensation.[17] The one committed Scottish deist of the period was William Dudgeon (1706–43), who has no known academic connections. He published tracts in the 1730s defending a natural religion whose content was purely ethical. He accepted an afterlife, but denied the reality of sin. In the divinely ordained order, conduct is fully determined by motive, but no motive is inherently evil: error, which is the by-product of our necessary imperfection, can be corrected by self-discipline.[18]

Dudgeon combined this with a Berkeleyan metaphysic which reduced a causally inoperative 'matter' to 'ideas' caused immediately by God, the only autonomous substance, on whom finite intelligences depend. Turnbull also wrote, in the work which grew out of his Aberdeen lectures, as if matter is reducible to perceptions (the dissolution of bodies in death is the end of certain ideas, and the effects of matter upon matter are no more than perceptions excited in our minds). But what he rejected, like many of his contemporaries, was active matter. Its indestructibility as a *passive* object, operations upon which are linked to our minds by laws, is a prerequisite for his argument for immortality.[19]

Thomas Reid (1710–96), Turnbull's most distinguished pupil, is the only individual for whom we can document an initial attachment to outright immaterialism.[20] For others of the period, what caught their fancy was Berkeley's theory of vision – until it was subjected to influential criticism by the physician William Porterfield[21] – and his theological voluntarism: the laws by which the objects of our experience are related are seen as direct evidence of God's sustaining power. These notions were sufficiently congenial that, when Berkeley attacked their other hero, Shaftesbury, in *Alciphron* in 1732, it provoked one former admirer, William Wishart (1692–1753), to violent satire.[22] By this time, however, Edinburgh students were hearing in their logic class that Colin MacLaurin in his natural philosophy lectures had invalidated Berkeley's metaphysics.[23] Andrew Baxter's (1686–1750) defence of the conventional two-substance view of the creation was also influential: he challenged the assimilation of perception with the object of perception and established the stereotype of Berkeley as a Cartesian doubter who never found the way back to reality.[24]

Turnbull's engagement with all these new trends in a single body of writing – deism, Berkeleyanism, liberty in religion, the reform of education, the moral basis of art, moral law, the restoration of civic virtue – has given him an interest for modern scholars which he could not claim in his lifetime, when most of his books were remaindered. Binding them together is a consistent methodology in which all studies can be reduced to laws by a combination of historical and experimental study. Turnbull was already practising this before Hume conceived his own project of 'introducing the experimental method of reasoning into moral subjects', but, significantly, both were pupils of the same 'professor of natural philosophy and ethics' in Edinburgh, Robert Steuart.[25]

Hutcheson was less flamboyant but more influential, a charismatic teacher whose Ulster background contributed to his strong interest in natural and civil rights. The common good is enjoined by the law of nature, and there is a natural right to engage in whatever mode of action advances this common good. The conventions of social organization are all subordinate to this purpose. Hutcheson's arguments against undue authority in every form made him a leading campaigner, not only for toleration, but against slavery, hereditary power, and so-called 'rights of conquest'.[26] It was probably Hutcheson's version of the contract theory of civil authority, entitling the governed to resist, and if necessary to separate from, whatever power threatened the common good, that had most influence in the American colonies. But what Hutcheson defended as the rights of colonies he also identified as the rights of 'provinces'.[27]

Our concern for the common good and the rights that it entails both reflects and reinforces an instinctive philanthropy that shows itself when we look self-critically at the happiness and misery brought about by different kinds of behaviour. It excites in us an 'esteem' or 'perception of moral excellence' of any action motivated by benevolence. Not all action is so motivated, nor is all appraisal moral; but Hutcheson was best known in his lifetime for this theory of moral appraisal and its aesthetic analogue. He developed it in the four treatises, in two books, composed while he kept an academy in Dublin in the 1720s, before he succeeded Carmichael at Glasgow in 1730.[28]

Moral practice was for Hutcheson a matter as much of the heart as of the head, and his work is concerned with both analysing and cultivating the appropriate 'affections'. We have a sense of beauty, which shows itself not only in our appreciation of the arts and mathematics, but in our response to the whole creation as a manifestation of infinite wisdom. The humane affections are as much part of this creation – as much inherent in human nature and independent of social artifice – as size and shape, and almost as readily detectable; and that they are is evidence in turn of the benevolence and intention of their designer.

Hutcheson's account is built round his theory of a moral sense, which is less well articulated than its place in his system requires. The aesthetic analogy drops out in his later writing. Hume believed he had a similar account, when he argued that virtue is a quality of action or character that promotes in persons of normal sensibility a distinctive 'pleasing sentiment of approbation';[29] its being virtuous lies in its promoting such a sentiment, and he then seeks to analyse the sentiment (a kind of love) and its causes (the benefit of those affected). Both agreed we may feel such sentiments even when the act runs counter to our interests. Hutcheson, however, in a work published after Hume's *Treatise of Human Nature*, insists that 'the good approved is not this tendency to give us a grateful sensation' but is independent of and prior to it: it lies in the *source* of the sentiment, which for him is the benevolent affections of the agent.[30]

The St Andrews theologian Archibald Campbell (1691–1756) agreed with Hutcheson that we have an instinctive tendency to social bonds, but instead of attributing this to benevolent motives, he attributed it to the feature Hutcheson disdained: self-love.[31] To some degree this was a verbal dispute, since self-love for Campbell is not a form of selfishness and is not a consideration of advantage. It includes self-esteem, or respect, but it can be gratified through the esteem of others, because the 'self' in question is the 'self' of Aristotle's theory of friendship, whereby another person can be 'self' to oneself; indeed self-love on this account motivates God as much as humans. Moral virtue is brought about through the love and respect that self-love prompts us to desire and deserve of others, who desire and deserve it of us, creating an amicable society in which there is mutual esteem. While the phrasing is not ideal, there is a substantive point at the back of it, picked up later by Hume and Kames: benevolence on its own is not enough to engage an agent to any particular action.

Elsewhere, Campbell threatened to challenge the rational religion of the Enlightenment. In *The Necessity of Revelation* (1739), he adopts a basically Lockean epistemology, but takes issue with the idea that the existence of God, the soul's immortality, and the conduct necessary to eternal happiness, can be proved without revelation. God's existence is provable to those who see the evidence. But this evidence was unavailable until within living memory – the Design arguments of antiquity were naive – whereas the foundations of religion must have been open to persons of ordinary comprehension at all periods. The mass of mankind, surveying nature, ascribe supernatural powers to everything, and it requires a revelation to see, with modern science, that that is a mistake. Neither do ordinary persons understand the essence of matter, or how to abstract from experience to form the idea of another immaterial, indissoluble, substance. In section III of this work, Campbell rejects Plato's arguments for immortality as sophistries, and contends that no other of the ancients suspected the soul was immaterial: 'all the great ends of morality and religion are well enough secured without it'. The data of comparative religion suggest that no one attained a doctrinally sound monotheism and its associated morality by reason alone.

But if we are dependent on revelation, we face Locke's problem afresh: how is a revelation to be identified? We cannot simply assume a Deity, or fall back on the word of a being whose existence is in contention. Campbell's solution, in section VII, is bafflingly brief and unimpressive, though a variant on the argument from testimony: he conjectures that an angel 'led on the human mind by rational proofs and arguments' which were communicated in turn to posterity, the moral probity of the source being the factor that carried conviction. We have the evidence of Mosaic history that such a revelation, once given, was corrupted and lost. Campbell is happy to count Pierre Bayle as one of his authorities.

Campbell's strategy had been anticipated by another Scottish theologian, Thomas Halyburton (1674–1712). The deists, Halyburton claimed, cannot pretend that mankind in general subscribe to natural religion: experience is plainly against it. Some have been steered into it by the authority of a small group of thinkers, but on what principles did they recognize the authority of their evidence? Appended to his *Natural Religion Insufficient* was *An Essay concerning the Nature of Faith*, where Halyburton specifically attacked Locke's argument to found faith in reason. It does not fit the scheme of knowledge as intuitive, demonstrative, or sensitive, and conflicts with Locke's claim to accord revelation the highest degree of assent. The external signs (miracles) to which Locke appealed in confirmation of an original revelation did not serve that function. They might deepen the hearers' faith, but most biblical doctrine was delivered without such signs. To do without them is not to fall back on 'enthusiasm': enthusiasm is irrational and at some point conflicts with the evidence of sense and reason. The prophets did not need external signs to recognize God's hand. They had it by an 'irresistible Evidence', like someone who knows an author's style well enough to recognize it in anonymous instances.[32]

❦ HUME'S CRITIQUE OF RATIONAL ❧ RELIGION

While this native sceptical tradition was grist to his mill, Hume's own critique of prevailing trends grew out of a wider background, in British and French thought of the previous hundred years and in the main traditions of antiquity; and it is from that background that we must understand his disagreements with Hutcheson.[33] Hume was introduced to Hutcheson in 1739 between the publication of Books II and III of *A Treatise of Human Nature*, and their ensuing correspondence shows an unsuccessful attempt at a meeting of minds. Hutcheson was probably behind at least one of the cautiously critical reviews of the *Treatise* which appeared in the *Bibliothèque raisonnée* in 1740–1. Hume responded to the reviewer's criticisms of his theories of belief, power and the self through the Appendix to the *Treatise*, while in the body of the text he tried to address problems raised by Hutcheson in correspondence, problems which the later reviewer seized on afresh to scotch any suggestion that Hume was Hutchesonian in his moral philosophy. Hume was seen to derive morality from a strictly secular view of human nature, and to analyse it with the unengaged aloofness of a pure metaphysician. He reduced the moral sense to a limited sympathy, and seemed to turn justice into a Hobbesian conventionalism.[34]

These charges returned to haunt Hume in the mid-1740s, when an alliance of clerical interests helped defeat his attempt to succeed John Pringle (1707–82) as professor of moral philosophy at Edinburgh.[35] Hutcheson and another Glasgow colleague worked to avert Hume's election, as did Wishart, principal of Edinburgh University and a life-long supporter of Hutcheson's philosophy. The sceptical aspect of Hume's thought – his stress on the limitations of reason – attracted most attention. He was seen as rejecting the operation of causes and the reality of moral distinctions, indeed as denying our ability to believe the existence of anything; and this despite the lengths he went to, to explain how we all, including himself, unavoidably come to such beliefs. The main target of attack was the supposed implications of his tenets for religious and moral conviction. Hume complained that his philosophy had been traduced, and denied there were anti-religious implications (meaning implications for personal faith) in the argument of the *Treatise*.[36] In rebuilding his defences in *An Enquiry concerning Human Understanding* (1748), he finally addressed the applications of his philosophy to both revealed and natural religion which had been suppressed in bringing the *Treatise* to publication, and this helped provoke some of the first published responses to his philosophy.[37] A fuller critique of natural religion appeared posthumously.

Hume's target is the Lockean scenario presented above, which claimed a *rational* foundation for revealed and natural religion. Hume, like Locke, has no time for the 'enthusiast', and ignores the attempts to immunize personal revelation against criticism.[38] He builds his critique of revealed religion round the question of the historical credibility of the miracle stories associated with the foundation of the main theistic systems.[39] The key concepts in the debate – probability and testimony – link his discussion to Locke. Locke had distinguished the general evidence we have in experience for specific types of phenomena from the quality of the evidence in the particular case – the number and skill of the witnesses, the consistency and circumstances of the report, the purpose of the reporter, and the nature and extent of contrary testimony. The importance of the particular evidence is in inverse proportion to the strength of the general evidence. Where testimonies conflict with experience, or with each other, we should 'proportion' our assent after weighing the circumstances, and any signs of passion, interest or confusion in the telling.[40]

This epistemology is taken over by Hume in a way that defeats

Locke's attempt to plead a special case for biblical miracles. To believe in a one-time exception to the order of nature, we must be aware of an exceptionless order to constitute the law from which the departure occurred. The type of evidence needed to establish the norm destroys our ability to identify the exception, for which the evidence is at best derivative.[41] And yet Hume is not impugning the *concept* of miracle. A miracle is 'a transgression of a law of nature by a particular volition of the Deity, or by the interposition of some [other] invisible agent'.[42] The laws are what operate (by God's general providence) in the absence of such transgressions (or particular providences). The problem is one of detectability.

Hume presents it as a problem of matching proof against proof. He accepts with Locke that the regular sequence of cause and effect offers the highest degree of empirical proof. So we have proof of tomorrow's sunrise from uniform past experience, though there is no logical absurdity in suggesting it will not rise; and we have comparable proof of any law of nature from comparable natural uniformity. In this sense there is 'proof' against any miracle.[43]

The potential counter-proof cannot claim direct evidence of divine intervention. It consists in looking for evidence of the reliability of historical witnesses – witnesses with as much proven reliability as other people's experience of the laws of nature. Hume depicts it as an outweighing in numbers, calculated by subtraction, and illustrates it by the way that witnesses to one side in a legal case can offset those for the other side. It is difficult to make sense of this notion of subtraction for the case in hand, and some of his criteria remain clearly qualitative.[44] Appealing to all the weaknesses that Locke identified in human testimony, Hume argues that there is no case where the quantity and quality of the witnesses have met the required standards. One hypothetical case would give him pause: if people came in sufficient numbers from all corners of the earth testifying to a week's darkness, he would accept that as evidence of something unusual. But he would not leap to a supernatural explanation.[45]

Locke could make that leap, because he accepted the tradition, established by Bacon, that miracles were not intended to convert athe-ists. The theist has already accepted the arguments of natural religion, and considered that these lead to a being who would wish to communi-cate with the sentient creation. Miracles are there to establish a particu-lar system, within an existing framework of belief. Hume challenged this strategy on two fronts. First, a miracle can 'never be proved, so as to be the foundation of a system of religion'. No matter how worthy the witnesses, they could not show that an appeal to supernatural power – an appeal necessarily outside our experience – was our only recourse.[46] Secondly, reason is incapable of establishing the kind of Deity whose revelation is being postulated.

This brings us to the second limb of Hume's critique of rational religious belief: the critique of natural religion. Because his fullest treatment of this is presented as a dialogue sequence, one must be alive to the limitations of the genre.[47] The views that Hume sets up for critical scrutiny are little more than stereotypes. But a number of factors support the verdict of his contemporaries that the character of Philo in the *Dialogues concerning Natural Religion* is more than a 'careless sceptic' and is predominantly Hume's mouthpiece, even sharing his characteristic irony. In the first state of the manuscript, some 60 per cent of the work was assigned to Philo; 85 per cent of the subsequent revision belongs to Philo, including the additions of Hume's last months.[48] He invested his labour overwhelmingly in Philo's side of the case. Furthermore, even at the time of the *Treatise*, he had sketched out a narrative study, in which he developed in his own person an argument similar in structure to Philo's in the *Dialogues*, and identical in substance on the one topic where comparison is still possible – the problem of evil.[49]

All parties to the *Dialogues* accept the existence of a 'first cause', but this does not commit them to a meaningful theism.[50] It opens up the debate over whether anything can be known of the attributes of an entity so removed from experience. The main focus of discussion is the Design argument, espoused by the character Cleanthes, and presented in the form of an analogy. The world is an integrated system of interacting 'machines', in that their essential feature is 'the adaptation of means to ends' through an 'order, proportion, and arrangement of every part' according to regular laws. From a similarity of effects (the adaptation of means to ends both in artefacts and in the works of nature) Cleanthes infers a similarity of causes (reason and intelligence).

'Machines' here does not have narrowly mechanistic associations.[51] The emphasis is on organic nature – the structure of legs and eyes, and biological, psychological and social circumstances that combine to support human reproduction. Cleanthes, under pressure, goes on to try to make a virtue of the logical weaknesses exposed by Philo, by self-consciously emphasizing the 'irregularity' of the argument – that is, its power to carry more conviction than its logic warrants. The 'idea of a contriver' strikes us 'with the force of sensation' when we dissect the eye.[52] It is like hearing or reading a familiar language, where the recognition of intelligence is, or would be, instantaneous even in bizarre conditions. Everyone sees that the recognition in the linguistic case is sound, and this should inspire our confidence in the other. Although the analogies of immediate recognition are offered by Cleanthes, at the beginning of Part III, as so many 'illustrations, examples, and instances' to reinforce the 'analogy between their causes', they are better seen as a commentary on it, and as a rhetorical attempt to circumvent Philo's insistence on case-by-case assessment.

The discussion develops round a distinction between God's natural and moral attributes. The natural attributes relate to intelligence and power, and would pertain to a Deity in any circumstances, whether there had been a creation or not. The moral attributes arise from a freely chosen relationship with sentient creatures. Most of the debate is over the natural attributes, and involves three contentious issues.

First, most fundamental, is whether 'order, arrangement, or the adjustment of final causes' is the 'proof of design' that the argument requires. Philo contends that we cannot see things in cosmic perspective and can only infer design in the kinds of cases we know from experience; order and arrangement are not, themselves, *kinds* of cases. But if it is a condition that the manifestations of design be recognizably analogous to that in human artefacts, we shall end up ascribing human characteristics to divinity.[53]

Second, we cannot from experience prove the ultimate priority of ordering mind over ordered matter. Perhaps mind needs to be and can be explained in turn through natural causes; while this is contrary to a common assumption of the time, it is a live issue for those who admit that the essence of matter and mind is unknown.[54]

Third, the evidence of experience is that there are many 'springs and principles' in nature, and different kinds of order. There is an absurdity in taking any singly as the model for all nature. If we do, we have no worse reason to see the world as an ordered animal, or vegetable, than to see it as an artefact; while even a disordered world must have its parts so structured that they would in due course shake out into some sustainable pattern.[55]

To these challenges to God's natural attributes, Philo adds a version of the problem of evil. In reasoning from experience we cannot attribute to the cause qualities that are not provable by the effects, and the calamities of human and animal life give no support to belief in the moral attributes of the creator. The committed theist can accommodate this problem, but what is at issue is what we can infer without that commitment. Hume argues through Philo, and in his own person in the early fragment, that the balance between the frequency of pleasures and intensity of pains is such that no determination of whether there is moral purpose in nature is possible.[56]

Thereafter, in the final Part of the *Dialogues*, Philo somewhat relents, and concedes that, whatever the limitations of our understanding, the psychological pressures to believe in *something* are very considerable. But it is a qualified concession, and nowhere more so than in the longest paragraph of the work, the only significant addition from

Hume's last weeks of life, and thereby his dying testament to posterity.[57] The dispute between theist and atheist, it is argued, is 'verbal'. The theist grants the nature of God's mind to be incomprehensible; the atheist concedes a remote analogy between the orderings of nature and intelligence – not, however, moral intelligence in the human understanding of the phrase. Each from their opposite position must consider the analogy so attenuated that neither has the means to make it more precise or useful.

The critical arguments of the *Dialogues* have found most of their admirers in the twentieth century, but only after Darwinism changed scientific attitudes to the study of nature. In the short term, Hume's critique stimulated a number of forceful apologists, of whom the most successful was the English theologian William Paley. Modern commentary portrays Paley's *Natural Theology* (1802) as a reactionary work written in ignorance of Hume, but careful study of the language and logic of his opening chapter shows it is a systematic riposte, item by item, to many of Hume's moves. Because Paley builds into his exposition of the Design argument the limitations that Hume's critique imposes, Hume's criticisms have no particular target in his work.

As for Hume himself, where we fail to find adequate reasons for a belief we may still explain its causes. The belief in God is not one of those fundamental to 'common life', where the mechanisms of the mind compensate automatically for the deficiencies of reason. Indeed, the ordinary mind does not have the synoptic view of nature that – unlike Paley – Hume supposes essential to the theistic perspective. Hume explores the roots of religious belief in *The Natural History of Religion*, which presents a logical reconstruction of popular thought in the guise of a series of historical steps.[58]

Hume argues that humanity develops from a state of ignorance motivated by hope and fear. This hope, and more particularly fear, is directed to the unknown causes of human fortune, which come to be personified as unseen rulers. Hence polytheism. From that arises the idea of a chief ruler, to whom virtues are ascribed by way of flattery, while their servants amass exaggerated honours. There is a 'flux and reflux' in the popular mind, between polytheism and monotheism, the former tending towards toleration and social virtues, the latter towards authoritarian control and a moral abasement that runs contrary to human nature.[59] This 'vulgar' superstition is contrasted with the sophisticated insight of the minority – Hume ironically includes Adam in Paradise – who appreciate the connected order of nature and derive from it a more fitting and consistent view of the divine character.

Though written from a contrary perspective, Hume's account of 'vulgar' religion is largely consistent with contemporary Calvinist teaching about human belief since the Fall, where it was a commonplace, as we have seen, that monotheism is not a position that comes naturally to the unaided mind.[60] His writing was a greater challenge to those who favoured the claims of natural religion, because he seemed to show that they could never carry the bulk of mankind with them. But it had a direct influence on William Robertson (1721–93), leader of the Moderate Party in the Scottish Church, whose accounts of primitive religions follow Hume's specification.[61]

One frequent element in religious belief, which commonly links it to moral practice, is the belief in immortality. Hume examines this in a posthumous essay, 'Of the Immortality of the Soul', which first recapitulates the argument on immateriality in the *Treatise*.[62] Philosophers had often contended that thought, as immaterial, must inhere in an immaterial substance, which by its nature lacked the power to disperse. Hume responded that we have no experience of the substance of anything, so cannot show that any given properties are essential to it; while the doctrine of an indivisible soul-stuff seems to carry with it the implication of an undivided substance throughout nature – a thesis beset with paradox. In the essay, he adds further objections. Assuming the orthodoxy that immortality is bound up with reward and punishment (which liberal thinkers already disputed), he focuses on the apparent disproportion between the petty conduct of most human life and the eternal after-effects. Furthermore, all the analogy of nature is against there being something that resists the processes of change; indeed, we have the evidence of experience that the mind declines as well as the body, and in parallel with it.

❦ THE RESPONSE TO HUME ❦

The first significant response to Hume's philosophy within Scotland came with the *Essays* of Henry Home, Lord Kames (1696–1782), in 1751. Its criticism was sufficiently muted that some contemporaries saw little to choose between them, despite Kames's support for natural religion. A flurry of pamphlets in the 1750s, aimed at both thinkers and their circle, repeated the charge that Hume's philosophy, and now Kames's, was a threat to morals and religion, but it failed to advance the debate philosophically. On the periphery of this controversy was another dispute with theological ramifications, between Kames and John Stewart, natural philosophy professor at Edinburgh, over whether Newton's admission of mechanical forces was tantamount to conceding activity to matter.[63]

Kames's reading of Newtonianism as a necessitarian system seemed to open the way to fatalism and the denial of providence, particularly when he characterized the sense we have of human liberty as a kind of divine 'deceit'.[64] Within this framework, Kames nevertheless offered a balanced picture of human motivation. 'Self-love operates by means of reflection and experience' and belongs to the calculating part of our nature, guided by considerations of pleasure and pain. But our appetites and affections do not directly correlate with pleasure and pain. Grief and compassion move us alike in real life and in the arts, and our ability to be drawn to what is painful, and be stimulated by it to delicate feelings, is a sure sign of our social nature. This nature forms the basis of the laws to which we are subject, and which we discover through the instinctive responses of our moral sense to the beauty or deformity of human character and action.[65] Kames thought, however, that neither Hutcheson nor Hume gave sufficient attention to the sense of duty and justice, which he traced to a distinctive feeling, without which the trust that holds society together could never have arisen.

Kames considered the deceptiveness of moral liberty no different in principle from the 'unreality' of secondary qualities. It is consistent with the great design that God should present things in the way best suited to his purposes for mankind, while still enabling us to discover the underlying reality. Berkeley, who might have contemplated a similar argument, was one of his targets here, and Hume another. For Kames it would be more than divine deceit – it would be a totally pointless assignment of useless faculties – if our senses did not put us in touch with a material world. Our perceiving observable qualities as aspects of a whole is proof that we have a sensory impression of substance, that is, of 'independent and permanent existence'. Equating belief with a simple, unanalysable feeling, he considers there is no appeal against our sense of the externality and power of observed objects; if they are indeed external, and have the power they appear to us to have, no better way of conveying this can be conceived than the way we actually experience them.[66] Our sensitivity to the presence of God in nature is accounted for on similar principles.[67]

Kames's appeal to a 'feeling' which opposes any philosophical scepticism with regard to an objective order – an appeal, in fact, to the concurrent operation of external and what he sometimes calls 'internal' senses – has been seen as an extension into the metaphysics and epistemology of Hutcheson's concept of an inner sense in morals. If so, it is a stage towards the 'common sense' theory developed among the members of the Aberdeen Philosophical Society, in part, again, in reaction to the scepticism of Hume.[68] Because the 'common sense' theory is a theory that accounts for those fundamental convictions which both parties placed outside the province of reason, and which Hume attributed in certain cases to 'natural instinct', the difference between them has sometimes seemed merely verbal. But natural instinct in Hume

– as it relates, for example, to belief in the self and the external world, the identification of purposive behaviour, and the operation of causes – is something brought about by the natural processes of the mind *consequent* to experience, and is not inherent in that experience; and it does not extend to a religious instinct.

The first salvoes against Hume's philosophy to be publicly fired from Aberdeen originated from the pulpit. George Campbell's (1719–96) *Dissertation on Miracles* is intended to demonstrate the rational basis of revealed religion. Its two parts match the sections of Hume's critique, assessing first the a priori case, then the a posteriori case, for miracles.

Campbell argues that 'testimony hath a natural and original influence on belief, antecedent to experience', but we learn, by experience, to regulate our confidence in it. The predisposition to accept testimony is a feature of our 'common sense', one of the original 'grounds of belief, beyond which our researches cannot proceed, and of which therefore 'tis vain to attempt a rational account'. Belief in the uniformity of nature, and in the prima facie reliability of memory, is of this kind. 'If we had not previously given an implicit faith to memory, we had never been able to acquire experience', notwithstanding that memory, like testimony, can be corrected by experience.[69]

The unusualness of an event, Campbell concedes, may be a presumption against its authenticity, but cannot always be so. If I have had two thousand experiences of a ferry boat making a safe and regular crossing, then one day meet a stranger who gravely reports he has just seen it lost with all on board, I am likely to give more credence to this than Hume's simple subtraction formula would authorize. This holds until sufficient counter-evidence is found, either from other witnesses about the fact, or from witnesses about the witness. Hume had tried to weigh incommensurables; and whether past experience is a sound guide to a new case depends not only on how far relevant circumstances are the same, but on whether they are known.[70] Hume himself ran into inconsistency in exploiting testimony to help establish the laws of nature while discounting it in cases of alleged violations, and in dismissing untested any reports that he considered religiously motivated.[71] Campbell scores some sound points against Hume's logic, but sometimes misreads his irony, and is less effective on the decisive question of how one would identify divine intervention.[72]

Thomas Reid likewise criticized Hume from common-sense principles, but took as his target Hume's critique of natural rather than revealed religion. He claims to detect 'first principles of necessary truths', principles 'of which we can give no other account but that they necessarily result from the constitution of our faculties', in grammar, logic, mathematics, taste and morals, but he is mostly concerned with metaphysics.[73] Hume properly showed that we cannot derive, either from experience or reason, the belief in material and mental substance, the principle of universal causation, or the certainty 'that design and intelligence in the cause may be inferred from marks or signs of it in the effect'. Any attempt to do so already assumes the principles in question, so, argues Reid, they must be self-evident. In regard to other intelligence, the case for the existence of God is no different from the case for other minds generally.[74] Hume had argued in *Enquiry* XI that we cannot infer an intelligent cause for the universe because we have had no experience of the origin of other universes. Reid retorts that 'according to this reasoning, we can have no evidence of mind or design in any of our fellow-men', either, since we have never been able to match their wisdom against its visible signs. The role of these signs is not, therefore, to form the premises for inductive argument. It is part of the providential design for human life that they are transparent.

Hume got into the sceptical impasse, in Reid's view, because he was obsessed with the principle that there are no ideas without preceding impressions, and no impressions appropriate to the case. Hume's failing is, however, part of a broader failing of the philosophical tradition since Descartes, which Reid castigates as the 'theory of ideas'. This is the attempt to build up an account of human knowledge entirely through an account of the atomic contents of experience. But these contents in themselves never reach to the world of which we claim the knowledge, so the project is self-defeating. Reid draws a clear distinction between the study of the body and its relations with other bodies, which may give us a natural history of the senses, and the anatomy of the mind, by which we obtain a history of human consciousness;[75] and he sees an obvious absurdity in supposing either that the second is in some way a representation of the first, or – if the absurdity of that is granted – that the first is then beyond our reach. There are limits to our knowledge of the physical world, and to our knowledge of the mind, but there is a kind of philosophical 'madness' in confusing the one with the other.

In place of the theory of ideas, Reid postulates a distinction between sensation and perception. His formulation of this remains obscure, and has been adapted to serve the interests of different modern theorists. Sensation is an affection or feeling of the mind, quite unlike any physical quality: it can exist only in a sentient being. (Thus the sensation we feel from impact with a hard body is merely a sign. It has nothing about it that corresponds literally to the compactedness of the particles of that body.) But it 'suggests', or brings about a 'conception and belief of', an external reality. The notion of suggestion is taken from Berkeley's philosophy of vision, but Reid rejects any idea that it is an acquired association: there is no way such an association could arise if it is not inherent in our make-up, although he does allow that the way we learn to judge specific sizes, shapes and distances by sight takes time. Perception is the awareness we have of the existence of external objects by our senses.

Reid's work is imbued with a pleasant wit. Of the principal items that make up his *Philosophical Works*, his *Inquiry into the Human Mind* (1764), in which he first stresses the distinction between physical and mental enquiry, is a minor classic, while his *Essays on the Intellectual Powers of Man* (1785), completed after his move to, and retirement from, Glasgow, is a comprehensive study on a grand scale. Of the other members of the Aberdeen circle, the moralist and belletrist James Beattie (1735–1802) made most noise in his day by his fast-selling *Essay on the Nature and Immutability of Truth*, which incurred the censure of Kant. This attack on scepticism, largely targeted at Hume, is vaguely concerned more with the criteria than the nature of truth: he vacillates between conceiving truth as something eternal, and as a variable property ('certain truth', 'probable truth') of individual judgements. We attain truth in proportion to the degree to which we believe what the 'constitution of human nature determines' us to believe. Sometimes this comes from reasoning or evidence; sometimes (where those can add nothing to what is already there) 'by an instantaneous, instinctive, and irresistible impulse; derived neither from education nor from habit, but from nature'. This, again, is 'common sense', upon whose axioms all proof is founded and to which all truth is conformable.[76] Beattie does not follow Reid deeply into the theory of perception, and his work is coarser in tone, sniping at the 'irreligion' and 'licentiousness' he sees ensuing, once the defences of common sense are breached by philosophical scepticism.

The common-sense tradition itself, by its apparent preoccupation with the anatomy of the mind, came to be criticized on similar grounds, by a logic that is now difficult to reconstruct. It was left to Reid's most gifted student, Dugald Stewart (1753–1828), an inspirational teacher who was professor of moral philosophy at Edinburgh from 1785 but ceased to be active after 1810, to redeploy this philosophy just as the infiltration of Kantian ideas (still ill understood) began to have its impact; but Stewart's most original work was in political economy.[77] The 'Dissertation' which he contributed to the fourth and later edition Supplements to the *Encyclopaedia Britannica* from 1816 was a history of metaphysics since the Renaissance, and included research into documents now lost. As a historian Stewart could not shake off the standpoint of the 'Scottish' philosophy, and indeed used the history of philosophy as a means of vindicating that tradition. In doing so he helped perpetuate certain stereotypes that have outlasted his own philosophy. One is the view that Hume subscribed to a 'constant conjunction' analysis of causation which denied any necessitation in nature. Stewart willingly endorsed this, as a death-blow to Spinozism.[78] He also approved Hume's demonstration that there can be no proof of universal causation or of the uniformity of nature, since this gave the common-sense philosophy its needed opening. So when there was opposition to a mathematical appointment at Edinburgh in 1805 because the nominee, John Leslie, had endorsed Hume's supposedly irreligious view of causality in natural philosophy, Stewart was active in his support. (So were the evangelical party in the Church, who accepted Hume's proof that faith was beyond reason.) Stewart contended, indeed, that Hume's analysis was not only commonplace, but had been commonplace before Hume.[79] But this needs qualification. What Stewart favoured was the view of Clarke and Berkeley that the active agents are minds, and what is popularly conceived as agency in nature is no more than constant conjunction according to the laws of a lawgiver. As Reid had already expressed it, 'We perceive no proper causality or efficiency in any natural cause; but only a connection established by the course of nature between it and what is called its effect. Antecedently to all reasoning, we have, by our constitution, an anticipation that there is a fixed and steady course of nature: and we have an eager desire to discover this course of nature'.[80]

Stewart's deputy after 1810, Thomas Brown (1778–1820), had also contributed to the Leslie controversy, with a tract on the 'nature and tendency' of Hume's doctrine. He supports a constant-conjunction account of cause, but also endorses Hume's view that whatever account is given of physical causation applies equally to mental causation. He denies that we have any distinct sense of mental power. However, that the relation of cause and effect is not discoverable a priori, or by reason, but is an object simply of 'belief' (that is, a belief with regard to future contingencies), he sees as compatible with the common-sense appeal to an 'instinctive principle of faith'.[81]

Brown's defence of Hume called forth the talents of the principal woman writer to have a place in the philosophy of the Scottish Enlightenment – Lady Mary Shepherd (1777–1847), daughter of the third Earl of Rosebery. After a book on causality she published another primarily on perception, where additionally she addresses the views of Berkeley, Reid and Stewart.[82] She is anxious to obviate any threats to theism, whether from a revisionist view of causation or from doubts about material existence, and she seeks to restore to human reason whatever Hume had attributed to associative instinct and others to common sense. Try to conceive an effect that was not necessarily linked to (in Shepherd's terms, 'inherent in') its cause. Can it, then, begin its own existence? But such beginning is an action, and an action can only be the action of something already existing. An effect is a difference occurring in an existing situation, but it cannot begin of itself if there is nothing to 'make' a difference: by 'reasoning upon experiment', whether in laboratory study or ordinary life, we establish a difference in the attendant circumstances. Single experiments are often sufficient, except to narrow down the circumstances in which the cause is operative, since it is contradictory to conceive that the course of nature might change.[83] However, the factors we observe are strictly effects or signs of the underlying reality, and it is the latter that is subject to the laws of nature: Hume's mistake in conceiving laws of nature as generalizations from experience undermines his strategy over miracles.[84] Her second book tries to show why we must accept that there are efficacious but unknown causes that do not have the character of mind. Mind, she holds, supplies the conditions for sensation in general, but only when there is something else that acts upon it does sensation actually occur.[85]

The common-sense tradition had also involved itself in moral theory. The intellectual powers were traditionally paired with the active (or 'active and moral') powers in that analysis of human nature which was the propaedeutic to moral instruction; and the textbooks and lecture courses of the day all surveyed the nature of human action, the role of appetite, desire, affection and passion, the nature of the moral faculty, the principles that influence moral conduct, and those that regulate it. This was considered an essentially scientific enterprise. The language of a 'moral sense' is retained, if by some, like Stewart, apologetically. Reid equates it with conscience, and introduces it into the discussion of the sense of duty, rather than, as in Hutcheson, the sense of good. His account echoes his account of 'common sense':

> All reasoning must be grounded on first principles. This holds
> in moral reasoning as in all other kinds. There must, therefore,
> be in morals, as in all other sciences, first or self-evident
> principles, on which all moral reasoning is grounded, and on
> which it ultimately rests.

Thus there is no reasoning with someone who does not acknowledge the Golden Rule: you can appeal to his sense of interest, but not his sense of duty.

> To reason about justice with a man who sees nothing to be just
> or unjust, or about benevolence with a man who sees nothing
> in benevolence preferable to malice, is like reasoning with a blind
> man about colour, or with a deaf man about sound.[86]

But we may reason about specifics, for example for and against particular family arrangements. By this time, however, the focus of interest in moral psychology had shifted to the analysis of agency, and to the attempt to understand human power as the ability to act in conformity with judgement.[87]

It was outside the common-sense tradition that Scottish moral philosophers in the eighteenth century made their strongest mark. Adam Smith (1723–90) at Glasgow and Adam Ferguson (1723–1816) at Edinburgh – both of whom would become widely travelled scholars with an international circle of acquaintance – carried the analysis of human nature well beyond its customary applications in the moral sphere.[88] Breaking the taboo on the analysis of self-interest, Smith made a landmark contribution to the study of the workings and place of economic forces in society, albeit with a normative purpose – the defence of freedom of action, including freedom of competition and freedom of trade. However, although he advocated governmental regulation only in matters relating to the protection of society, he did not deny the duty of government to provide basic public services. Where Smith's researches into moral and economic conduct led him into two complementary studies, Ferguson had space to integrate the subjects into a single work, in which he saw the existence of moral sentiment as foundational to society. Ferguson's work is always informed by a strong sense and knowledge of history, whether real or conjectural, and particularly in his conscious rehabilitation of the social ideals of antiquity, which he forcefully distinguished from modern book-learning about them.

In his own moral theory, Smith had laid great weight on the classical notion of sympathy as the source of social ties.[89] Hume had already revived this idea, in seeking a more convincing mechanism than the instinctive philanthropy of Hutcheson. Smith considered that we are endowed by nature with a twofold sympathy which is reflected in moral judgement. We may sympathize with agents who act from a virtuous motive, and thereby approve their conduct. We may also sympathize with the gratitude of the person who benefits from the virtuous conduct (or if it is not virtuous, we may sympathize with their resentment). This is not the same as simply sharing their sentiments, although we naturally seek to do so. It is an exercise of imagination, and can therefore vary in degree from individual to individual.[90] But it can also be trained, in the way that we naturally adapt to the responses of others. (This does not entail blind conformity: we can be out of step with popular sentiment where we have a better, or worse, command of the facts of the case.) But if it were simply a matter of thinking ourselves in other people's shoes this would not explain how we can also assess our *own* actions. We do this by becoming 'impartial spectators', seeing ourselves as others would see us, if they were fully apprised of the facts. Society therefore serves as a mirror through which we come to scrutinize our own conduct. And in the interaction generated by the operation of sympathy we learn to develop two characteristics essential to the moral life – self-command, and compassion or sensibility.

❧ NOTES ❧

The following abbreviations are used in the notes:

D   David Hume *Dialogues concerning Natural Religion*, in [11.42].

E   David Hume *An Enquiry concerning Human Understanding*, in [11.43].

HHC M. A. Stewart and J. P. Wright (eds) *Hume and Hume's Connexions* [11.122].

PSE   V. Hope (ed.) *Philosophers of the Scottish Enlightenment* [11.96].

SPSE M. A. Stewart (ed.) *Studies in the Philosophy of the Scottish Enlightenment* [11.104].

1 Sher [11.103], 329–76, offers an excellent bibliographical guide to this wider field.
2 One form of this idealism is found in the 1690s in the political pamphleteering of Andrew Fletcher (1655–1716), a Scottish correspondent of Locke, whose experience in exile led him to favour a Dutch type of confederacy for Britain. Fletcher's extolling of a mythic 'Gothic' past in which there was sufficient balance of political power to ensure the liberties of the subjects is a forerunner of early Enlightenment attitudes. But he represented an idiosyncratic nationalism that was out of line with the anglicizing stance of most eighteenth-century Scottish intellectuals.
3 There were five universities. St Andrews, Glasgow, and King's College, Aberdeen, were late medieval papal foundations. Edinburgh and Marischal College, Aberdeen, were local political creations of the post-Reformation period. Present information is sparsest on eighteenth-century St Andrews.
4 There were, additionally, foundational studies in classical languages, seen also as a source of moral instruction; and mathematical training became increasingly important as a requisite for natural philosophy. During the eighteenth century, civil history, often considered as an extension of natural history, came to be regarded as a significant source of data for the study of morals.
5 George Campbell [11.22] runs somewhat against this trend. His work is distinctive for founding its discussion of eloquence and the grounds of conviction in the study of 'human nature', and for three chapters on logic, both formal and informal.
6 Duncan's popular tutorial manual [11.27] provides an example of this synthesis.
7 J. P. Wright, 'Metaphysics and Physiology', SPSE, 251–301.
8 R. B. Sher, 'Professors of Virtue', SPSE, 87–126.

9 R. L. Emerson, 'Science and Moral Philosophy in the Scottish Enlightenment', SPSE, 11–36.

10 M. A. Stewart, 'The Stoic Legacy in the Early Scottish Enlightenment', in M. J. Osler (ed.), *Atoms, Pneuma, and Tranquillity* (Cambridge, Cambridge University Press, 1991), pp. 273–96. See also the editors' introduction to Smith [11.72], 5–10. Stoicism had already attracted some seventeenth-century Scots, like the emigré radical Robert Ferguson in his *Sober Enquiry into the Nature, Measure and Principle of Moral Virtue* of 1673 (Allan [11.87], 115–18).

11 Hutcheson [11.49], introduction.

12 John Locke, *An Essay concerning Humane Understanding*, 4th edn, 1700, IV. xix. Hume developed further the associationist psychology on which Locke based his analysis. See C. Bernard, 'Hume and the Madness of Religion', HHC, 224–38.

13 It is significant that as history comes to be established in the Scottish curriculum, it is a synthesis of classical and biblical sources.

14 Simson [11.69], 3–5, 12–13, 20; see also 'Mr. Simson's Answers to Mr. Webster's Libel' in *The Case of Mr. John Simson*, 1715, pp. 254–63. For contemporary criticism see James Hog, *A Letter to a Gentleman concerning the Interest of Reason in Religion*, 1716; John McLaren, *The New Scheme of Doctrine contained in the Answers of Mr. John Simson*, 1717, ch. 12; Alexander Moncrieff, *Remarks on Professor Simson's First Libel and his Censure Considered*, 1729, pp. 43–59.

15 M. A. Stewart, 'Rational Dissent in Early Eighteenth-Century Ireland', in K. Haakonssen (ed.), *Enlightenment and Religion* (Cambridge, Cambridge University Press, forthcoming). Cf. Wishart [11.85], 221–6.

16 J. Moore and M. Silverthorne, 'Natural Sociability and Natural Rights in the Moral Philosophy of Gerschom Carmichael', PSE, 1–12.

17 Turnbull [11.74]; Wallace [11.83]. See M. A. Stewart, 'George Turnbull and Educational Reform', in Carter [11.90], 95–103; and M. A. Stewart, 'Berkeley and the Rankenian Club', *Hermathena* 139 (1985): 25–45.

18 Dudgeon, *The State of the Moral World Consider'd*, 1732 and *A Catechism Founded upon Experience and Reason*, 1739, in *Works* [11.25]. Cf. Carabelli [11.112], 197–206. Raphael [11.145], 36, suggests that Adam Smith was also a deist. So, almost certainly, were some of the philosophically minded scientists in the later part of the century, like William Cullen (1710–90) and James Hutton (1726–97).

19 Turnbull [11.80], ch. 9. Turnbull's examples reappear in George Wallace [11.82], 42.

20 Reid [11.62], 162.

21 Porterfield [11.57], 214–33. Rejecting Berkeley's view that our judging of distance by sight is due to 'custom and experience', Porterfield sees as the only alternative an acknowledgement of 'an original connate and immutable Law, to which our Minds have been subjected from the Time they were first united to our Bodies'. Such a law is already implicit in Berkeley's appeal to touch; and if we accept it in relation to one sense, it is more, not less, economical to accept it for a second. So, he supposes, the mind 'traces back its Sensations' through the retina along the 'perpendicular Lines' described in optics – never addressing the difficulties Berkeley found in this suggestion. The language of ideas

obscures the fact that Berkeley must hold that vision causes us only to *imagine*, not detect, a tangible distance. Porterfield's analysis of the problem led Reid to his distinction between sensation and perception, discussed below.

22 Wishart [11.86]. Patrick Hardie of Aberdeen, the first Scot to mention Berkeley in print (1719), and perhaps the first to discuss him in the classroom, was an exception to the view of Berkeley as a friend to religion: Wood [11.106], 38.

23 Stewart, 'Berkeley and the Rankenian Club' (above, n. 17).

24 Baxter [11.6], vol. 2, sect. II.

25 On Steuart, see M. Barfoot, 'Hume and the Culture of Science in the Early Eighteenth Century', SPSE, 151–90. On Turnbull, see J. Laird, 'George Turnbull', *Aberdeen University Review* 14 (1926–7): 123–35; Norton [11.120], ch. 4; Stewart, 'Turnbull and Education' (above, n. 17).

26 Hutcheson, *System* [11.50], Bk. III. He first published these views in a Latin class manual, translated posthumously as *A Short Introduction to Moral Philosophy*, 1748; but the underlying theory of rights was already developed by 1728, in the second edition of the *Inquiry concerning Virtue* [11.48], sect. VII. The political argument against hereditary guilt also challenged the theological doctrine of original sin.

27 C. Robbins, ' "When it is that Colonies may Turn Independent" ', *William and Mary Quarterly*, 3rd series, 11 (1954): 214–51. In his *System* (vol. 2, p. 232), Hutcheson even allows release from the obligation to comply with a policy implemented by consent, if its effect is contrary to the one intended.

28 These are reprinted as vols 1–2 of Hutcheson's *Collected Works*, Hildesheim, Olms, 1990.

29 Hume, *Treatise* [11.45], III. i. 2, which he could reasonably consider modelled on Hutcheson's remarks on beauty, *Inquiry* [11.48], sect. I.

30 Hutcheson, *System* [11.50], 1: 53. Cf. *Illustrations* [11.46], sect. IV. The difference between Hutcheson and Hume here is a difference over their interpretation of the theory of secondary qualities – whether in the mind or in the object – to which virtue and vice are being assimilated.

31 Archibald Campbell [11.19]. For Hutcheson, benevolence and self-love were conflicting motives, the one moral, the other amoral. It required rational reflection and self-discipline to cultivate the one and counteract the other.

32 The ultimate authority here would have been Calvin's *Institutes of the Christian Religion*. A similar orthodox defence of inspirational religion, seen as distinct from enthusiasm, was developed by Moncrieff (above, n. 14). 'The Miracles of Christ and his Apostles are to be believed, because contained in the Scriptures, and not the Scriptures because of them' (*Remarks*, p. 56). Otherwise Moncrieff could not be sure why the miracle reports in Josephus were ridiculous, and those in the Gospels not.

33 J. Moore, 'Hume and Hutcheson', HHC, 23–57; L. Turco, 'Hutcheson nel terzo libro del *Trattato sulla natura umana*', in M. Geuna and M. L. Pesante (eds), *Passioni, interessi, convenzioni*, Milano, Angeli, 1992, pp. 77–93. Norton [11.120], 87–92, stresses the 'providential dimension of Hutcheson's thought'; contrast Hume, as presented in the same author's 'Hume, Atheism, and the Autonomy of Morals', in Hester [11.115], 97–144.

34 M. A. Stewart and J. Moore, 'William Smith (1698–1741) and the Dissenters' Book Trade', *Bulletin of the Presbyterian Historical Society of Ireland* 23 (1993):

20–27. For further discussion of Hutcheson's ethics in relation to Hume's, see S. Darwall, 'Hume and the Invention of Utilitarianism', HHC, 58–82.

35 On Pringle see Stewart, 'Stoic Legacy' (above, n. 10).

36 See *A Letter from a Gentleman* [11.40], a pamphlet hastily assembled by Henry Home, adapting material by Hume.

37 English clerics were first off the mark. See Thomas Rutherforth, *The Credibility of Miracles Defended against the Author of Philosophical Essays*, 1751.

38 J. Passmore, 'Enthusiasm, Fanaticism and David Hume', in Jones [11.99], 85–107.

39 For recent scholarship see Gaskin [11.113], ch. 8; Houston [11.116]; Jones [11.118], ch. 2; M. A. Stewart, 'Hume's Historical View of Miracles', HHC, 171–200; D. Wootton, 'Hume's "Of Miracles" ', SPSE, 191–229.

40 Locke, *Essay*, IV, xv–xvi. On 'proportioning assent', cf. E, 110.

41 Hume is emulating the strategy adopted against transubstantiation by Tillotson, in a sermon 'The Hazard of being Saved in the Church of Rome'.

42 E, 115n.

43 E, 56n., 115; cf. 127.

44 E, 122. Cf. George Campbell [11.21], 21–30.

45 Hume used similar tests, elsewhere, to appraise the claims to inspiration made on behalf of Joan of Arc and the claims to historical authenticity made on behalf of the Ossian forgeries. Another who felt the need to defeat whatever threatened established regularities was Pringle [11.58], who contested the evidence for meteorites.

46 E, 121, 129.

47 Carabelli [11.112], esp. ch. 3; M. Malherbe, 'Hume and the Art of Dialogue', HHC, 201–23; M. Pakaluk, 'Philosophical Types in Hume's *Dialogues*', PSE, 116–32.

48 I owe these calculations to Ruth Evelyn Savage.

49 M. A. Stewart, 'An Early Fragment on Evil', HHC, 160–70.

50 Hume sometimes calls this minimal belief and the practice of virtue 'true religion'. This is not a body of doctrine, or a practice of worship. The same lip-service to the traditional cosmological argument in *Dialogues* Part II is consistent with the speakers' subsequent disagreement over the 'demonstrative' formulation of such an argument in Part IX. See M. A. Stewart, 'Hume and the "Metaphysical Argument *A Priori*" ', in A. J. Holland (ed.), *Philosophy, its History and Historiography*, Dordrecht, Reidel, 1985, pp. 243–70; E. J. Khamara, 'Hume *versus* Clarke on the Cosmological Argument', *Philosophical Quarterly* 42 (1992): 34–55.

51 D, 45. Such associations were expressly repudiated by George Cheyne [11.23], 2, the Scottish Newtonian from whom Hume drew the description.

52 This formulation (D, 56) draws on another Scottish Newtonian, MacLaurin [11.53], 381, and foreshadows Reid [11.62], 460.

53 D, 47, 50, 52, 58, 68–71. Hurlbutt [11.117] has introduced an influential misunderstanding into Hume's exegesis by suggesting a sense of 'design' in which the detection of design becomes a *premise* of the Design argument. This reduces it to triviality. The argument scrutinized by Hume takes as its premise the existence of a certain kind of *order* in nature, and seeks to show, by analogy, that order of this kind is evidence of design.

54 D, 62–6, 84–5.

55 D, 72–3, 78–9, 85–7. Cf. Hume's account of polytheism, as a response to the diversity of phenomena, *Natural History* [11.42], 139.

56 D, 96–7, 102–3. This was always for Hume the main obstacle to theism; and as his correspondence with Hutcheson shows, he had problems understanding what it could mean, on his own secular analysis of morals, to ascribe virtues to the Deity. An alternative interpretation of the preponderance of pain is found in Baxter [11.6], who used it as evidence for a compensating immortality.

57 D, 119–21.

58 Hume himself disparaged one common application of this technique, the 'contract' theory of society. Dugald Stewart later recommended the practice as offering a truer insight into the nature of human institutions than a correctly documented narrative history. He called it 'conjectural history' and cited Hume's *Natural History* as a paradigm. It is important to see, however, that Hume was speculating not on the first origins of religion, but on its recurrent origin in human nature, wherever it occurs. Cf. S. Evnine, 'Hume, Conjectural History, and the Uniformity of Human Nature', *Journal of the History of Philosophy* 31 (1993): 589–606; R. A. Segal, 'Hume's *Natural History of Religion* and the Beginning of the Social Scientific Study of Religion', *Religion* 24 (1994): 225–34.

59 A similar picture of historical religion is found in Hume's *History*. See Bernard (above, n. 12).

60 Hume used the same tactic, ironically, in concluding his discussions of miracles and of immortality.

61 William Robertson, *History of America*, 1777, *Historical Disquisition concerning the Knowledge which the Ancients had of India*, 1791. In the appendix to the latter, Robertson's depiction of the 'Stoicism' of the Brahmins has Humean echoes.

62 Hume, *Essays* [11.44], 590–98; *Treatise* [11.45], I. iv. 5. The essay is partly targeted against Joseph Butler's *Analogy of Religion*, 1736.

63 Wright [11.123], §16.

64 Henry Home, *Essays* [11.39], 1st edn, 207–18.

65 Ibid., Pt I, essays 1–2.

66 He supports this by comparison of the different senses: because some involve contact with the object sensed and others do not, we have intuitive evidence of the distinction between perception and the object perceived.

67 Ibid., Pt II, essays 1–4, 7. For the Hume-Kames relationship, see Norton [11.120], ch. 4; Stewart, 'Hume and the "Metaphysical Argument"' (above, n. 50).

68 On this Society, see Ulman [11.54]. In spite of the occasionally acerbic rhetoric, several of his critics relished the challenges posed for them by Hume's philosophy. For a wider view of Aberdeen philosophical activity, see Wood [11.106]; Wood, 'Science and the Pursuit of Virtue in the Aberdeen Enlightenment', SPSE, 127–49. The Aberdeen philosophers constituted a loosely knit fraternity with varied interests. The herding of them into a monolithic 'school' derives from later German and French commentary, but has its roots in Joseph Priestley's *Examination of Dr. Reid's Inquiry, etc.* of 1774. Priestley, an advocate of David Hartley's materialism, castigated Reid, Beattie and Oswald as a reaction-

ary coterie, cut off from the mainstream. Of these, James Oswald (1703–93), whose interests were predominantly theological, repudiated any association with Kames.

69 George Campbell [11.21], 14–16, 22, 18.

70 Ibid., 26, 33.

71 Ibid., 45, 72–7.

72 A fuller discussion of common sense occurs in Campbell [11.22], I. v. 3, where it is one of three sources of 'intuitive evidence' (evidentness). It is the basis upon which we recognize that whatever has a beginning has a cause, that where the parts of something serve a common end there was intelligence in the cause, and that there are other intelligent beings besides oneself. If we have not implicitly recognized these and other principles – the third is perhaps the most striking – we have nothing on which to base other knowledge.

73 Reid, *Intellectual Powers*, VI. vi (*Works* [11.62], 452–61).

74 Cf. Berkeley, *Principles*, §148.

75 P. B. Wood, 'Hume, Reid and the Science of the Mind', HHC, 119–30.

76 Beattie [11.10], 41, 142. Beattie left in manuscript a second, satirical, attack on scepticism. See King [11.107], ch. 5; E. C. Mossner, 'Beattie's "The Castle of Scepticism" ', *Texas University Studies in English* 27 (1948): 108–45. For a reassessment of the relation of Reid and Beattie to Hume, see Somerville [11.108].

77 K. Haakonssen, 'From moral philosophy to political economy', PSE, 211–32.

78 Dugald Stewart [11.73], 1: 441. For a searching critique of this reading of Hume, see Wright [11.123], ch. 4.

79 Stewart [11.73], 3: 417–24. Cf. I. D. L. Clark, 'The Leslie Controversy', *Records of the Scottish Church History Society* 14 (1960–3): 179–97; J. G. Burke, 'Kirk and Causality in Edinburgh, 1805', *Isis* 61 (1970): 340–54; Carabelli [11.112], ch. 12.

80 Reid [11.62], 199.

81 Brown [11.12], 2nd edn (1806): 44–7, 51–5, 80, 94.

82 Another projected treatise on Berkeley has not been traced.

83 Shepherd [11.67], 33–4, 39–43, 28.

84 Shepherd [11.68], essay 8.

85 Ibid., ch. 2.

86 Reid, *Active Powers*, III. iii. 6 (*Works* [11.62], 590–1). A better picture of Reid's substantive ethics is to be obtained from his manuscripts. See *Practical Ethics* [11.63], including Haakonssen's substantial introduction.

87 Rowe [11.138].

88 Smith [11.71]; Ferguson [11.28]. Hume, principally in his *Essays* [11.44], also worked on topics in political economy. See A. S. Skinner, 'David Hume: Principles of Political Economy', in D. F. Norton (ed.), *Cambridge Companion to Hume*, Cambridge, Cambridge University Press, 1993, pp. 222–54.

89 Smith [11.72], I.i.1. For significant new scholarship on Smith the philosopher, see Skinner [11.146] and Jones [11.143].

90 Smith learnt from Hume the constructive role of the imagination in the workings of the mind. For his application of this to scientific systems, see A. S. Skinner, 'Adam Smith: Science and the Role of the Imagination', in W. B. Todd (ed.), *Hume and the Enlightenment*, Edinburgh, Edinburgh University

Press, 1974, pp. 164–88; D. D. Raphael, ' "The True Old Humean Philosophy" and its Influence on Adam Smith', in G. P. Morice (ed.), *David Hume: Bicentenary Papers*, Edinburgh, Edinburgh University Press, 1977, pp. 23–38.

❧ BIBLIOGRAPHY ❧

(Asterisked titles are available in modern photographic reprints)

Original Works

11.1   *Alison, Archibald *Essays on the Nature and Principles of Taste*, 2 vols, Edinburgh 1790; 6th edn, 1825.

11.2   Arthur, Archibald *Discourses on Theological and Literary Subjects*, Glasgow, 1803.

11.3   *[Balfour, James] *A Delineation of the Nature and Obligation of Morality*, Edinburgh, 1753; 2nd edn, 1763.

11.4   *—— *Philosophical Dissertations*, Edinburgh, 1782.

11.5   [——] *Philosophical Essays*, Edinburgh, 1768.

11.6   *[Baxter, Andrew] *An Enquiry into the Nature of the Human Soul*, London, 1733; 3rd edn, 2 vols, 1745. *Appendix*, ed. J. Duncan, London, 1750.

11.7   —— *The Evidence of Reason in Proof of the Immortality of the Soul*, London, 1779.

11.8   *Beattie, James *Dissertations, Moral and Critical*, London, 1783.

11.9   *—— *Elements of Moral Science*, 2 vols, Edinburgh, 1790–3.

11.10   *—— *An Essay on the Nature and Immutability of Truth, in Opposition to Sophistry and Scepticism*, Edinburgh, 1770; 6th edn, 1777.

11.11   Brown, Thomas *Lectures on the Philosophy of the Human Mind*, 4 vols, Edinburgh, 1820.

11.12   *—— *Observations on the Nature and Tendency of the Doctrine of Mr. Hume, concerning the Relation of Cause and Effect*, Edinburgh, 1805; 3rd edn, retitled *Inquiry into the Relation of Cause and Effect*, 1818.

11.13   Brown, William Laurence *An Essay on the Existence of a Supreme Creator*, 2 vols, Aberdeen, 1816.

11.14   —— *An Essay on the Folly of Scepticism*, London, 1788.

11.15   —— *An Essay on the Natural Equality of Men*, Edinburgh, 1793.

11.16   Bruce, John *Elements of the Science of Ethics, on the Principles of Natural Philosophy*, Edinburgh, 1786.

11.17   [Burnett, James, Lord Monboddo] *Antient Metaphysics, or the Science of Universals*, 6 vols, Edinburgh, 1779–99.

11.18   *[——] *Of the Origin and Progress of Language*, 6 vols, Edinburgh, 1773–92.

11.19   Campbell, Archibald *An Enquiry into the Original of Moral Virtue*, Edinburgh, 1733. (A pirated edition was issued by Alexander Innes, Westminster, 1728.)

11.20   —— *The Necessity of Revelation*, London, 1739.

11.21   *Campbell, George *A Dissertation on Miracles*, Edinburgh, 1762; 3rd edn, 1796.

11.22   *—— *The Philosophy of Rhetoric*, London, 1776.

11.23   Cheyne, George *Philosophical Principles of Religion, Natural and Revealed*, London, 1715; 5th edn, 1736.

11.24   *Crombie, Alexander, *An Essay on Philosophical Necessity*, London, 1793.

11.25   Dudgeon, William *Philosophical Works*, n.p., 1765.

11.26   *Duff, William *An Essay on Original Genius, and its Various Modes of Exertion in Philosophy and the Fine Arts*, London, 1767.

11.27   Duncan, William *Elements of Logick*, London, 1748; 4th edn, 1759.

11.28   Ferguson, Adam *An Essay on the Origin of Civil Society*, ed. D. Forbes, Edinburgh, Edinburgh University Press, 1966.

11.29   *—— *Principles of Moral and Political Science*, 2 vols, Edinburgh, 1792.

11.30   [Fordyce, David] *Dialogues concerning Education*, London, 1745–8.

11.31   *—— *The Elements of Moral Philosophy*, London, 1754.

11.32   Gerard, Alexander, *Dissertations on Subjects relating to the Genius and the Evidences of Christianity*, Edinburgh, 1766.

11.33   *—— *An Essay on Genius*, London, 1774.

11.34   *—— *An Essay on Taste*, London, 1759; 3rd edn, Edinburgh, 1780.

11.35   —— *Plan of Education in the Marischal College and University of Aberdeen, with the Reasons of it*, Aberdeen, 1755.

11.36   [Gregory, John] *A Comparative View of the State and Faculties of Man, with those of the Animal World*, London, 1765.

11.37   Halyburton, Thomas *Natural Religion Insufficient, and Revealed Necessary to Man's Happiness in his Present State*, Edinburgh, 1714.

11.38   *[Home, Henry] *Elements of Criticism*, 3 vols, Edinburgh, 1762; 5th edn, 2 vols, 1774.

11.39   *[——] *Essays on the Principles of Morality and Natural Religion*, Edinburgh, 1751; 3rd edn, 1779.

11.40   *[—— (ed.)] *A Letter from a Gentleman to his Friend in Edinburgh*, Edinburgh, 1745.

11.41   *[——] *Sketches of the History of Man*, 2 vols, Edinburgh, 1774.

11.42   Hume, David *Dialogues concerning Natural Religion, and The Natural History of Religion*, ed. J. C. A. Gaskin, Oxford, Oxford University Press, 1993.

11.43   —— *Enquiries concerning Human Understanding and concerning the Principles of Morals*, ed. L. A. Selby-Bigge, rev. P. H. Nidditch, Oxford, Clarendon, 1975.

11.44   —— *Essays, Moral, Political and Literary*, ed. E. F. Miller, Indianapolis, Liberty Classics, 1985.

11.45   —— *A Treatise of Human Nature*, ed. L. A. Selby-Bigge, rev. P. H. Nidditch, Oxford, Clarendon, 1978.

11.46   *Hutcheson, Francis *An Essay on the Nature and Conduct of the Passions and Affections. With Illustrations on the Moral Sense*, Dublin, 1728; 3rd edn, 1742.

11.47   —— *On Human Nature*, trans. and ed. T. Mautner, Cambridge, Cambridge University Press, 1993.

11.48 *—— *An Inquiry into the Original of our Ideas of Beauty and Virtue; in Two Treatises*, Dublin, 1725; 4th edn, 1738.

11.49 [Hutcheson] *The Meditations of the Emperor Marcus Aurelius Antoninus. Newly Translated from the Greek: With Notes, and an Account of his Life* [by Francis Hutcheson and James Moor], Glasgow, 1742.

11.50 *—— *A System of Moral Philosophy*, 2 vols, Glasgow, 1755.

11.51 Hutton, James *An Investigation of the Principles of Knowledge and of the Progress of Reason, from Sense to Science and Philosophy*, Edinburgh, 1794.

11.52 Jameson, William *An Essay on Virtue and Harmony, wherein a Reconciliation of the Various Accounts of Moral Obligation is Attempted*, Edinburgh, 1749.

Kames, Lord, see Home, Henry.

11.53 *MacLaurin, Colin *An Account of Sir Isaac Newton's Philosophical Discoveries*, London, 1748.

11.54 *The Minutes of the Aberdeen Philosophical Society*, ed. H. L. Ulman, Aberdeen, Aberdeen University Press, 1990.

11.55 Ogilvie, John *An Inquiry into the Causes of the Infidelity and Scepticism of the Times*, London, 1783.

11.56 [Oswald, James] *An Appeal to Common Sense in Behalf of Religion*, 2 vols, Edinburgh, 1766–72.

11.57 Porterfield, William 'An Essay concerning the Motions of our Eyes: Part I', in *Medical Essays and Observations, Revised and Published by a Society in Edinburgh* 3 (1735): 160–261.

11.58 Pringle, John 'Some Remarks upon the several Accounts of the Fiery Meteor (which appeared on *Sunday* the 26th of *November, 1758*), and upon other such Bodies', *Philosophical Transactions of the Royal Society* 51(1) (1759): 259–74.

11.59 Ramsay, Andrew Michael *The Philosophical Principles of Natural and Revealed Religion*, 2 vols, Glasgow, 1748–9.

11.60 Reid, Thomas 'Of Common Sense', ed. D. F. Norton, in Marcil-Lacoste [11.137], 179–208.

11.61 [Reid.] *The Philosophical Orations of Thomas Reid*, ed. D. D. Todd, trans. S. D. Sullivan, Carbondale, Ill., S. Illinois University Press, 1989.

11.62 *—— *Philosophical Works*, ed. W. Hamilton, 8th edn, 2 vols, Edinburgh, 1895; repr., with introduction by H. M. Bracken, Hildesheim, Olms, 1967.

11.63 —— *Practical Ethics*, ed. K. Haakonssen, Princeton, NJ, Princeton University Press, 1990.

11.64 [Reid.] *Thomas Reid on the Animate Creation: Papers relating to the Life Sciences*, ed. P. B. Wood, Edinburgh, Edinburgh University Press, 1995.

11.65 Scott, Robert Eden, *Elements of Intellectual Philosophy*, Edinburgh, 1805.

11.66 —— *Inquiry into the Limits and Peculiar Objects of Physical and Metaphysical Science, tending Principally to Illustrate the Nature of Causation*, Edinburgh, 1810.

11.67 [Shepherd, Mary] *An Essay upon the Relation of Cause and Effect, Controverting the Doctrine of Mr Hume, concerning the Nature of that Relation*, London, 1824.

11.68   —— *Essays on the Perception of an External Universe, and Other Subjects connected with the Doctrine of Causation*, London, 1827.

11.69   [Simson.] *A True and Authentic Copy of Mr. John Simson's Letters to Mr. Robert Rowen, Late Minister at Penningham*, Edinburgh, 1716.

11.70   Smith, Adam *Essays on Philosophical Subjects*, ed. W. P. D. Wightman *et al.*, Oxford, Clarendon, 1980.

11.71   —— *An Inquiry into the Nature and Causes of the Wealth of Nations*, ed. R. H. Campbell and A. S. Skinner, Oxford, Clarendon, 1976.

11.72   —— *The Theory of Moral Sentiments* [1759; 6th edn, 1790], ed. D. D. Raphael and A. L. Macfie, Oxford, Clarendon, 1976.

11.73   *Stewart, Dugald *Collected Works*, 11 vols, ed. W. Hamilton and J. Veitch, Edinburgh, 1854–60.

11.74   [Turnbull, George] *Christianity neither False nor Useless, tho' not as Old as the Creation*, London, 1732.

11.75   —— *A Discourse upon the Nature and Origin of Moral and Civil Laws; in which they are Deduced, by an Analysis of the Human Mind in the Experimental Way, from our Internal Principles and Dispositions*, London, 1741.

11.76   [——] *An Impartial Enquiry into the Moral Character of Jesus Christ*, London, 1740.

11.77   [——] *Justin's History of the World translated into English. With a prefatory discourse . . . By a gentleman of the University of Oxford*, London, 1742; 2nd edn, 1746.

11.78   —— *Observations Upon Liberal Education, In all its Branches*, London, 1742.

11.79   —— *A Philosophical Inquiry concerning the Connection between the Doctrines and Miracles of Jesus Christ*, London, 1726; 2nd edn, 1732; 3rd edn, 1739.

11.80   *—— *The Principles of Moral and Christian Philosophy*, 2 vols, London, 1740.

11.81   *—— *A Treatise on Ancient Painting*, London, 1740. Reprinted without plates, introd. V. M. Bevilacqua, München, Fink, 1971.

11.82   Wallace, George *A System of the Principles of the Law of Scotland*, Edinburgh, 1760.

11.83   Wallace, Robert *The Regard Due to Divine Revelation, and to Pretences to it, Considered*, London, 1731; 2nd edn, 1733.

11.84   *—— *Various Prospects of Mankind, Nature and Providence*, London, 1761.

11.85   Wishart, William *Discourses on Several Subjects*, London, 1753.

11.86   [——] *A Vindication of the Reverend D— B—y, from the Scandalous Imputation of being Author of a Late Book, Intitled, Alciphron, or, The Minute Philosopher*, London, 1734.

Secondary Works

(There is not space to itemize individual articles of significance, many of which are included in the collections listed here, or can be traced through other references in the following books or in the preceding notes.)

11.87   Allan, D. *Virtue, Learning and the Scottish Enlightenment*, Edinburgh, Edinburgh University Press, 1993.

11.88   *Bryson, G. *Man and Society: The Scottish Inquiry of the Eighteenth Century*, Princeton, NJ, Princeton University Press, 1945.

11.89   Campbell, R. H. and Skinner, A. S. (eds) *The Origins and Nature of the Scottish Enlightenment*, Edinburgh, Donald, 1982.

11.90   Carter, J. J. and Pittock, J. H. (eds) *Aberdeen and the Enlightenment*, Aberdeen, Aberdeen University Press, 1987.

11.91   Davie, G. E. *The Scottish Enlightenment and other Essays*, Edinburgh, Polygon, 1991.

11.92   —— *A Passion for Ideas*, Edinburgh, Polygon, 1994.

11.93   *Grave, S. A. *The Scottish Philosophy of Common Sense*, Oxford, Clarendon, 1960.

11.94   Haakonssen, K. *Natural Law and Moral Philosophy, from Grotius to the Scottish Enlightenment*, Cambridge, Cambridge University Press, 1995.

11.95   Hont, I. and Ignatieff, M. (eds) *Wealth and Virtue: The Shaping of Political Economy in the Scottish Enlightenment*, Cambridge, Cambridge University Press, 1983.

11.96   Hope, V. (ed.) *Philosophers of the Scottish Enlightenment*, Edinburgh, Edinburgh University Press, 1984.

11.97   *Jessop, T. E. *A Bibliography of David Hume and of Scottish Philosophy from Francis Hutcheson to Lord Balfour*, Hull, Brown, 1938.

11.98   Jones, P. (ed.) *Philosophy and Science in the Scottish Enlightenment*, Edinburgh, Donald, 1988.

11.99   —— *The 'Science of Man' in the Scottish Enlightenment*, Edinburgh, Edinburgh University Press, 1989.

11.100 Kuehn, M. *Scottish Common Sense in Germany, 1768–1800*, Montreal and Kingston, McGill-Queen's University Press, 1987.

11.101 *M'Cosh, J. *The Scottish Philosophy*, London, Macmillan, 1875.

11.102 Olson, R. *Scottish Philosophy and British Physics, 1750–1830*, Princeton, Princeton University Press, 1975.

11.103 Sher, R. B. *Church and University in the Scottish Enlightenment*, Edinburgh, Edinburgh University Press, 1985.

11.104 Stewart, M. A. (ed.) *Studies in the Philosophy of the Scottish Enlightenment*, Oxford, Clarendon, 1990.

11.105 Turco, L. *Dal sistema al senso commune: Studi sul newtonismo e gli illuministi britannici*, Bologna, Il mulino, 1974.

11.106 Wood, P. B. *The Aberdeen Enlightenment: The Arts Curriculum in the Eighteenth Century*, Aberdeen, Aberdeen University Press, 1993.

Additional Secondary Works on Individuals

Beattie

11.107 King, E. H. *James Beattie*, Boston, Massachusetts, Twayne, 1977.
11.108 Somerville, J. W. F. *The Enigmatic Parting Shot*, Aldershot, Avebury, 1995.

Ferguson

11.109 Kettler, D. *The Social and Political Thought of Adam Ferguson*, Columbus, Ohio, Ohio State University Press, 1965.

Home (Kames)

11.110 McGuinness, A. E. *Henry Home, Lord Kames*, New York, Twayne, 1970.
11.111 Ross, I. S. *Lord Kames and the Scotland of his Day*, Oxford, Clarendon, 1972.

Hume

(Select list: see also bibliographies to Chapters 6 and 7 above)

11.112 Carabelli, G. *Hume e la retorica dell'ideologia*, Firenze, La Nuova Italia, 1972.
11.113 Gaskin, J. C. A. *Hume's Philosophy of Religion*, 2nd edn, London, Macmillan, 1988.
11.114 Hanson, D. J. *Fideism and Hume's Philosophy*, New York, Lang, 1993.
11.115 Hester, M. (ed.) *Hume's Philosophy of Religion*, Winston-Salem, N. Carolina, Wake Forest University Press, 1986.
11.116 Houston, J. *Reported Miracles: A Critique of Hume*, Cambridge, Cambridge University Press, 1994.
11.117 Hurlbutt, R. H., III *Hume, Newton, and the Design Argument*, rev. edn, Lincoln, Nebraska, University of Nebraska Press, 1985.
11.118 Jones, P. *Hume's Sentiments*, Edinburgh, Edinburgh University Press, 1982.
11.119 Leroy, A. *La Critique et la religion chez David Hume*, Paris, Alcan, 1930.
11.120 Norton, D. F. *David Hume: Common-Sense Moralist, Sceptical Metaphysician*, Princeton, NJ, Princeton University Press, 1982.
11.121 Penelhum, T. *God and Skepticism*, Dordrecht, Reidel, 1983.
11.122 Stewart, M. A. and Wright, J. P. (eds) *Hume and Hume's Connexions*, Edinburgh, Edinburgh University Press, 1994.
11.123 Wright, J. P. *The Sceptical Realism of David Hume*, Manchester, Manchester University Press, 1983.
11.124 Yandell, K. E. *Hume's 'Inexplicable Mystery': His Views on Religion*, Philadelphia, Temple University Press, 1990.

Hutcheson

11.125 Blackstone, W. T. *Francis Hutcheson and Contemporary Ethical Theory*, Athens, Georgia, University of Georgia Press, 1965.

11.126 Leidhold, W. *Ethik und Politik bei Francis Hutcheson*, München, Alber, 1985.

11.127 MacIntyre, A. C. *Whose Justice? Which Rationality?* London, Duckworth, 1988.

11.128 *Scott, W. R. *Francis Hutcheson, his Life, Teaching and Position in the History of Philosophy*, Cambridge, Cambridge University Press, 1900.

11.129 Smyth, D. (ed.) *Francis Hutcheson*, Supplement to *Fortnight* 308, Belfast, 1992.

Oswald

11.130 Ardley, G. *The Common Sense Philosophy of James Oswald*, Aberdeen, Aberdeen University Press, 1980.

Reid

11.131 Barker, S. F. and Beauchamp, T. L. (eds) *Thomas Reid: Critical Interpretations*, Philadelphia, University City Science Center, 1976.

11.132 Dalgarno, M. and Matthews, H. E. (eds) *The Philosophy of Thomas Reid*, Dordrecht, Kluwer, 1989.

11.133 *Daniels, N. *Thomas Reid's 'Inquiry': The Geometry of Visibles and the Case for Realism*, New York, Franklin, 1974.

11.134 Gallie, R. D. *Thomas Reid and 'the Way of Ideas'*, Dordrecht, Kluwer, 1989.

11.135 Lehrer, K. *Thomas Reid*, London, Routledge, 1989.

11.136 Manns, J. W. *Reid and his French Disciples*, Leiden, Brill, 1994.

11.137 Marcil-Lacoste, L. *Claude Buffier and Thomas Reid, Two Common-sense Philosophers*, Montreal and Kingston, McGill-Queen's University Press, 1982.

11.138 Rowe, W. L. *Thomas Reid on Freedom and Morality*, Ithaca, NY, Cornell University Press, 1991.

11.139 Schulthess, D. *Philosophie et sens commun chez Thomas Reid (1710–1796)*, Berne, Lang, 1983.

Smith

11.140 Campbell, T. D. *Adam Smith's Science of Morals*, London, Allen and Unwin, 1971.

11.141 Haakonssen, K. *The Science of a Legislator*, Cambridge, Cambridge University Press, 1981.

11.142 Hope, V. *Virtue by Consensus*, Oxford, Clarendon, 1989.

11.143 Jones, P. and Skinner, A. S. (eds) *Adam Smith Reviewed*, Edinburgh, Edinburgh University Press, 1992.

11.144 Lightwood, M. B. *A Selected Bibliography of Significant Works about Adam Smith*, London, Macmillan, 1984.
11.145 Raphael, D. D. *Adam Smith*, Oxford, Oxford University Press, 1985.
11.146 Skinner, A. S. and Wilson, T. (eds) *Essays on Adam Smith*, Oxford, Clarendon, 1975.

CHAPTER 12

The German Aufklärung and British philosophy

Manfred Kuehn

INTRODUCTION

The German Enlightenment was not an isolated phenomenon.[1] It was closely connected with developments in other European countries and in North America. Like the thinkers in other countries, the Germans were advocating a new ideal of knowledge. They were concerned with a critical examination of previously accepted doctrines and institutions from the point of view of reason. Though the German Enlightenment had its own distinctive voice, it would have been very different without influences from abroad. Two countries were especially important in shaping the German Enlightenment, namely France and Great Britain. It is perhaps not too much of an exaggeration to say that the German Enlightenment would have been impossible without these British influences. The following chapter will investigate the influence of British philosophers on the German Enlightenment.

It would be easy to enter into a dispute as to when the Enlightenment actually began. Some scholars have argued that the family of ideas and attitudes that characterize what we today call 'the Enlightenment' originated in the second half of the seventeenth century, others have argued that it was essentially an eighteenth-century phenomenon.[2] There are even good reasons for the claim that the 'enlightenment' as we understand it today really began to flower only at the middle of the eighteenth century.[3] However, it would be very easy to exaggerate the importance of such periodizations. There is no 'real chasm' between the Enlightenment and the period that preceded it. As Ernst Cassirer has pointed out, the new ideal of rationality developed 'steadily and consistently from the presuppositions which the logic and theory of knowledge of the seventeenth century . . . had established' ([12.19], 22). There is a change in emphasis, not a radical break. While such seventeenth-century philosophers as Descartes, Leibniz, and Spinoza were rather optimistic in believing that all knowledge could actually be reduced to rational principles and thus be raised to a strict science, the eighteenth-century Enlightenment thinkers were more sceptical about how this could be done. There is a move away from the principles to the phenomena, and from the general to the detail, but no abandonment of the goal of rational explanation. For this reason, we should expect difficulties in determining who did or did not 'belong' to the Enlightenment, but for the very same reason we must say that not much rides on such classifications.[4]

In any case, it is much easier to determine the beginning (and the end) of the Enlightenment in Germany than in most other countries. It clearly has its beginnings in the disputes between the followers of Christian Thomasius (1655–1728) and Christian Wolff (1679–1754) early in the eighteenth century at the University of Halle. The pietistically influenced Thomasians strongly opposed Wolff's rationalistic philosophy on religious grounds and they ultimately were successful in having Wolff not only expelled from the University, but even from Prussia (in 1724). Wolff's formal address to the University of Halle 'On the Practical Philosophy of the Chinese' of 1721 may be taken to be the culmination of this dispute, and it may also be taken as the starting-point for the discussion of the history of the Enlightenment in Germany. Wolff argued in this address that ethics was not dependent on revelation, that Chinese ethics and Christian ethics were not fundamentally different, that happiness need not have a religious basis, and that reason was sufficient.[5]

Wolffian philosophy became the dominant force at German universities after 1720. Its influence began to wane only after the middle of the century. However, when Wolff died in 1754, it was no longer at the centre of the philosophical discussion. From about 1755 on the Germans opened up more to external influences, and the Enlightenment in Germany began to resemble more closely the Enlightenment in France and Great Britain. This lasted until the early 1790s. With the first successes and transformations of Kantian philosophy Germans turned inwards again. This change also marks the end of the German Enlightenment. Accordingly, it will be convenient to divide the German Enlightenment into two different periods, namely that of the early Enlightenment, or 'The Wolffian Period', which lasted from about 1720 to 1754, and that of the late Enlightenment or of 'popular philosophy', lasting from about 1755 to 1795.

❧ THE EARLY ENLIGHTENMENT ❧

The years between 1720 and 1754 are characterized mainly by the religious dispute between the Wolffians and Thomasians. While the Thomasians, deeply influenced by Pietism, advocated an almost mythical view of nature, the Wolffians were, on the whole, not religiously inclined and motivated by scientific concerns ([12.46]). Though both groups knew the major works of British philosophers, and especially those of John Locke, neither one had any deep affinities for them, and the influence of British philosophy on German thought during the Wolffian period was rather peripheral.

The Thomasians

Thomasius and his followers did not have much to offer by way of original thought addressed to philosophical problems.[6] They regarded most of the classical problems of perception and knowledge as sceptical quibbles of no consequence, believing that ultimately these problems could all be explained as the result of the Fall upon man's faculty of knowledge. Accordingly, they also believed that if the influence of the evil will were to be eliminated, everything would find its proper place and perspective. The Thomasian epistemology was therefore rather meagre. Its most distinctive characteristics are: (i) an extreme sensationalism, and (ii) a correspondence theory of truth, and (iii) the subordination of the faculty of knowledge to that of the will, and thus (iv) the subordination of philosophy to theology. Many of their psychological views exhibit a great resemblance to Locke's theories. And while Locke definitely had an influence on their theories, these influences are not very interesting. In fact, everything that makes Locke philosophically interesting and important, namely his detailed investigations of particular epistemological problems and their consequences for metaphysics, is almost completely absent from the works of Thomasius and the Thomasians.[7] When they were not engaged in criticizing particular doctrines in Wolff, most of them excelled in general discussions of commonplaces.

Crusius, one of the last adherents of this way of thinking, is usually regarded as the most important of all the Thomasians. Following the earlier Thomasians, Crusius criticized rationalism from a pietistic point of view, objecting strongly to the optimistic faith in the omnipotence of reason. He argued that reason is limited and can be shown to be more dependent upon sense perception than the Wolffians wanted to admit. While he no longer accepted Thomasius's simple-minded sensationalist account of the origin of knowledge, and tended toward some sort of compromise between the rationalist belief in innate ideas and principles and Thomasian sensationalism, he is far from being clear on the details. Thus he did not want to reject entirely the doctrine of innate ideas, and he left the matter undecided. The following passage is perhaps typical:

> At the occasion of external sensation the ideas of certain objects arise. We then say that we sense these objects. There are two possible explanations for this. Either the ideas themselves already lie in the soul, and are made lively by these concurring conditions . . . or we have only the immediate cause and the power to form them at the moment of the concurrent condition and in accordance with it. We cannot know for certain which of these two possibilities is true. But we assume less, if we assume the latter.
>
> ([12.5], 153)

According to Crusius, rationalism was not necessarily wrong, though it may be presumptuous.

Crusius was at his strongest when he criticized Wolff and at his weakest when he tried to develop his own theory. Indeed, this can be said of all the Thomasians. Though they found in Locke a welcome ally in criticizing Wolff, they hardly ever went beyond him. Furthermore, their strong theological convictions usually got in the way of their philosophical arguments, making it very difficult for them to appreciate Locke's more subtle philosophical analysis. Accordingly, most of the similarities between the German sensationalists and British philosophers were incidental and remained without significant philosophical consequence.

The Wolffians

The Wolffians were philosophically more interesting.[8] However, since their philosophical project was essentially defined by the attempt to work out in a clearer and more systematic fashion the ideas of Leibniz, they had little use for such philosophers as Hobbes and Locke. Believing that the Leibnizian principles of contradiction, of sufficient reason, of the identity of indiscernibles, and of pre-established harmony were essentially correct, they also thought that philosophy was well on its way to becoming an exact science by following the 'mathematical model'. The British philosophers, who emphasized the role of sensation in all of knowledge, appeared to be of little use in this context.

However, they were not dismissed. Wolff was clearly not a 'rationalist' in the sense of discounting empirical observation altogether. In fact, empirical observation formed for him the very starting-point, even 'foundation', for philosophy because he thought that by 'means of the senses we know things which are and occur in the material world'. Yet philosophy is not so much concerned with establishing and describing things as they exist, or as we may be acquainted with them by the senses. For Wolff, things 'which are or occur possess a reason from which it is understood why they are or occur', and philosophy is the enterprise of finding these reasons and putting them into systematic order by demonstrating how they are connected. Put differently, whatever exists or occurs is by that very fact possible. Philosophy's task is to show how they are possible. Accordingly, 'philosophy is the science of the possibles insofar as they are possible'. It must demonstrate from 'certain and immutable principles' and with 'complete certainty' why 'those things which can occur actually do occur' ([12.13] 3–20). Once this has been done, we have also demonstrated the 'reality' of the concepts of these objects, and we have gone from mere sensible and 'historical' knowledge to true philosophical understanding. In demonstrating why the things that can occur do occur, Wolff follows essentially Leibnizian lines, appealing to the principles of contradiction and sufficient reason. It is obvious that such philosophers as Locke could not be of much help in that enterprise. However, they could be important in determining what things exist or occur. Accordingly, one can find references to Locke in Wolff's discussion of 'empirical psychology'. He also appears to have made use of Locke in his moral philosophy. Some of his comments on Locke are negative, but many were much more positive than one might expect.[9]

Yet it would be easy to exaggerate the importance of Locke for Wolff. Though he could use some of the ideas of this British philosopher to his own end, he was ultimately more interested in developing his own metaphysics, i.e. in demonstrating the possibility of things and the reality of concepts. This was the part of his work that he considered to be most important. In fact, it was only this part that he considered to be truly philosophical. Locke entered really only into the pre-philosophical or 'historical' parts of his system. Even later, when such Wolffians as Baumgarten attempted to develop an aesthetic theory on Wolffian principles, this did not change. Aesthetics remained an attempt to show how beauty only appeared to be sensible, and that it was really also rational or conceptual. Accordingly, British philosophy could be for them, at best, marginally important.[10] It was only with Wolff's death and the end of the conflict between the Wolffians and the Thomasians that the Germans began to open up to British philosophers.[11]

❧ THE LATE ENLIGHTENMENT AND ❧ POPULAR PHILOSOPHY

Moses Mendelssohn (1729–86), one of the best-known and most important philosophical talents of the second period, described the philosophical situation during the 1750s as one of 'general anarchy', in which philosophy, 'the poor matron', who according to Shaftesbury had been

> banished from high society and put into the schools and colleges ... had to leave even this dusty corner. Descartes expelled the scholastics, Wolff expelled Descartes, and the contempt for all philosophy finally also expelled Wolff; and it appears that Crusius will soon be the philosopher in fashion.[12]

This crisis was not a special German phenomenon, but one of European thought in general. In fact, it clearly was largely imported. While in Britain empiricism and rejection of ambitious all-inclusive speculative systems could already look back on a long and distinguished tradition, during the early part of the Enlightenment most German philosophers were still engaged in attempting to develop and work out such systems. In France, the mood had already changed under the British influence. Thus Condillac was asking in his *Treatise on Systems* (1749) for a synthesis of the positive or empiricist approach with a more systematic or rationalistic one, differentiating between the 'ésprit systématique' and the 'ésprit de système', rejecting the latter, while advocating the former. Voltaire had previously published his *Lettres philosophiques* (1743) and his *Elements de la philosophie de Newton* (1738), in which he attacked Cartesianism and argued for Newton's approach. Diderot, in his *On the Interpretation of Nature* (1754), advocated the experimental method and gave expression to his belief that mathematics had run its course and could not develop further. Rousseau's *Discourse on the Arts and Sciences* was published in 1750, and Buffon began to exert great influence when the first volume of his *Natural History* came out in 1749. Given the fact that most educated Germans could speak French and looked to France for literary and cultural models, it was inevitable that these developments would also have profound effects upon these Germans. Furthermore, since this empiricist turn in France was closely connected with a new appreciation of British natural science and British philosophy (indeed with an enthusiasm for anything British), the same also had to happen in Germany.

When Frederick the Great assumed power in 1740, he almost immediately began to work at reorganizing the Berlin Academy of Sciences. His intent was to raise its status, and to make it at the very least a worthy rival of the French Academy. To achieve this goal, he appointed to the Academy two of the leading Newtonians of the time, namely the French natural philosopher Pierre L. M. Maupertuis (1698–1759) and the gifted Swiss mathematician Leonhard Euler (1707–83). The perpetual secretary of the Academy, J. B. Merian, was also a Newtonian and therefore also anti-Wolffian. The King also invited promising Wolffians because he wanted a balance of Wolffians and Newtonians in the Academy.[13] However, between 1744 and 1759, it was clearly the Newtonians who had the upper hand. The questions for the regular prize essays were designed to discredit Leibniz-Wolffian philosophy, and to advance the course of Newton in Germany ([12.48]). This also involved close attention to British philosophy. The anti-Wolffians in the Academy knew and appreciated not only Locke, but also such thinkers as Berkeley and Hume ([12.50]) And Hume appears to have played an especially important role in the dispute between the Wolffians and the Newtonians at the Academy. Though it is not clear that the Newtonians always understood Hume correctly, they did invoke him against Leibniz and Wolff.[14] Indeed, both the German and the French translations of Hume's *Essays* clearly were occasioned by the interest of the Newtonian members of the Academy.[15]

This clearly had important consequences. As one of the earliest historians of this period put it:

> Around the middle of the century ... German scholars
> familiarized themselves more and more with other languages
> and especially with the beautiful and philosophical literatures of
> the French and the English. This ... not only made them aware
> of the deficiencies and imperfections of the German language
> and the German national taste in the sciences and fine arts; and
> created not only the most lively passion to educate, to refine the
> sciences and the arts, and to compete with the foreigners in all
> kinds of beautiful representations, but it also made the Leibniz-
> Wolffian method of the school hitherto followed distasteful to
> the better talents. The strict systematic form, which the Wolffians
> had accepted, appeared to put oppressing chains upon the free
> flight of philosophical genius. Moreover, in a number of
> philosophical works by foreigners they also found
> thoroughness and systematic spirit, but no pedantry and
> coercion ... even the textbooks of foreign philosophers were
> much more readable than those of the Germans.[16]

What looked at first like philosophical anarchy gave rise, under the influence of British models, to a new way of philosophizing. In the following I would like to say more about these effects.

Philosophical Style and Method

Hume's first *Enquiry* appeared in German as the second volume of the *Vermischte Schriften* in 1755. Johann Georg Sulzer (1720–79), the editor of the German translation of the first *Enquiry*, gave Hume high praise as a philosophical writer. He found that Hume could write clearly and elegantly about the most profound and difficult problems of metaphysics. Indeed, he claimed that in Hume 'thoroughness and pleasantness seem to fight for priority', and he praises Hume's work as the model for a truly popular philosophy, expressing his hope that the Germans would imitate Hume in this regard.[17] Closely connected with the problem of a popular philosophical style is for Sulzer – as well as most of his contemporaries – the problem of common sense. In fact, popular expression is seen only as the external expression of the principle of common sense ([12.14]). Therefore, Hume's philosophy could also be a model for philosophers who want to combine philosophical reasoning with common sense. However, one of Sulzer's most important reasons for publishing the translation was his belief that philosophers who are uncritically received become lax and superficial, and that the German philosophers are in this situation. They had allowed their weapons to become blunt and rusty 'during the long peace' of the Wolffian period.[18] Hume could be useful as a critic of German philosophers. Sulzer hoped that 'the publication of this work will interrupt their leisurely slumber and give them a new occupation'.[19]

Mendelssohn

One of the philosophers who was most impressed by Hume's style was Mendelssohn. In fact, he openly emulated it in his own works. Thus in his anonymous 'Letter of a Young Scholar in B'. he spoke of

> the beautiful philosophical writers, those who have noticed that the systematic way of representation is not always the best, those like Leibniz, Shaftesbury, Hume or the author of the *Letters on Sensation*, who often digress, but who always get back to the point.[20]

According to most Germans of the period, Mendelssohn succeeded admirably. They praised the elegance and thoroughness of his writings – comparing them explicitly with those of Hume. This shows that Hume provided these Germans with a new model for writing philosophy.

Garve

However, it would be a mistake if it were thought that this was a *merely* stylistic manner. We can see this clearly in another philosopher, who found Hume important for his style of writing, namely in Christian Garve (1742–98). Differentiating between a number of methods of thinking, he called special attention to what he called the method of observation.[21]

> It starts neither from the most general principles nor from
> common experiences; it is neither a systematic deduction of the
> appearances from rational concepts, nor a Socratic ascent from
> facts to the ideas and principles of reason. The philosopher ...
> leads his readers ... right into the materials, allowing necessary
> and preparatory ideas to flow in at certain occasions.

The philosopher who follows this method does not represent himself as a teacher among students. Rather, he presupposes that his readers know what any well-educated person knows about the subject, 'and his only goal is to add to the common stock of knowledge some new discoveries from his experience, and to fill in, or even discover some gaps'. According to Garve it is natural that 'all such new ideas ... are only fragments'. He thought that the essays of David Hume were full of such fragmentary ideas. Furthermore, Garve argued that the value of these fragments was enhanced by Hume's sceptical approach. As a sceptic, Hume evaluates both reasons for and against any view under consideration. Since this is done in a masterful fashion by Hume, both in his *History* and in his philosophical writings, Hume could serve as the model for a new way of philosophizing. While his philosophy may have a bad name for some 'ever since its aim has been identified as empirical', it need not be contradictory to systematic philosophy. Indeed, such a philosophy of observation can itself be systematic, and 'an investigation that consists only of observations can possess true philosophical thoroughness as Hume's and Montesquieu's works which are written in this spirit prove'. Hume's cautious and methodological scepticism became an alternative to the dogmatic way of doing philosophy, and many Germans followed Hume without ever openly referring to him.

Feder and Meiners

Similar methodological considerations also motivated the Göttingen philosophers Johann Georg Heinrich Feder (1740–1821) and Christian Meiners (1747–1810). Though both opposed radical scepticism, they also considered themselves as moderate sceptics. In fact, Feder described himself as having 'wavered between Wolffian dogmatism and scepticism' early in his life, and he further characterized his early scepticism as having been 'unrefined', 'unchecked' and 'without system'. His later thought consists exactly of a refined or checked scepticism, or a scepticism with a system. The same may also be said of Meiners. His *Revision der Philosophie* of 1772 relied mostly on the 'wise Locke' and the 'brave and good-natured Hume'. He also found that for strict or 'esoteric' philosophy 'no other method is as favourable as the sceptical method'. This scepticism towards all philosophical theories brought Feder and Meiners into the proximity of such common-sense philosophers as Thomas Reid. Like Reid, they felt that philosophers aimed too high in their conception of philosophy, attempted to obtain knowledge out of reach for human beings, and believed that 'whatever else man may try, he can only think with *his own* understanding' and not with some superhuman faculty of thought which grants absolute certain knowledge. Our understanding is very limited and not the best we can imagine, but it is all we have: 'to despise it for this reason, or not to be satisfied with it . . . would be neither philosophy nor wisdom'. According to Göttingers, philosophy had to become more modest. It had to learn from common sense, which is stronger than philosophical speculation. Indeed, the circumstance that common sense and the principles of morals, upon which human happiness depends most, have been conserved in spite of all the many artificial webs of error shows the beneficial frame of nature, which does not allow us to drift too far from these wholesome truths in the course of exaggerated speculation. Obscure feelings indicate them for us and instinct leads us always back to them. Accordingly, for the Göttingers the real task of philosophy could only be to establish these principles of common sense and morality more clearly and to defend them against the exaggerated speculations of certain philosophers.

However, their works had a tendency to become what Kant called a mere 'critique of books and systems'. Rather than concentrating on analyzing philosophical problems and solving them on their own, they collected all the different theories others had advanced with regard to them. While their philosophical approach is therefore usually characterized as 'eclecticism' or 'syncretism', it is perhaps better to call it 'indifferentism' or 'methodical scepticism', for the Göttingers did not set out simply to give a collection of different philosophical opinions, but they tried to develop a consistent philosophical system. Their study of different philosophical theories was no end in itself, but a methodological tool. As Feder put it, for instance: 'In order to protect myself from the delusions of one-sided representations and to reach well-founded insights it is necessary to compare different ways of representation and to study several systems'.

This approach to philosophy became very influential during the latter half of the eighteenth century. Indeed, most popular philosophers followed this approach.[22] At least partially as a result of this tendency to mere eclecticism, most did not succeed in making interesting contributions to the discussion of philosophical problems, and their works deteriorated into a mere listing of different philosophical opinions.

New Problems in Metaphysics and Ethics

The increased attention to the observations and problems raised by British philosophers also had definite influence on what these Germans viewed to be the philosophical problems that needed to be solved. The early Wolffians had been occupied mainly with the rational side of man, or with logic and metaphysics, and they had neglected almost completely our sensitive side (or, like Baumgarten, simply treated it 'in analogy to reason'). The works of the British philosophers brought the importance of man's sensitive nature most forcefully home to them. Accordingly, the younger German philosophers tried to supplement the Wolffian theory by relying on British observations, or they simply rejected Wolffianism altogether. Psychology and anthropology, aesthetic and educational theories based upon more empirical methods began to replace logic and rationalistic metaphysics as the key disciplines for an understanding of the world and man's place in it. The discipline of metaphysics itself was transformed by this. While the Wolffians had already differentiated between an 'empirical' and a 'rational' or 'pure' discipline within metaphysics, they had also clearly emphasized the work of pure metaphysics as the most distinctive and fundamental occupation of philosophy. During the second part of the German Enlightenment, the empirical part became more and more decisive. Yet only few were willing to give up pure metaphysics altogether. In their heart of hearts, most of these philosophers remained Wolffian.

Mendelssohn

One of the philosophers who most resisted the move in this direction, while at the same time paying a great deal of attention to incorporating British observations into aesthetics and ethics was Mendelssohn.[23] Brought up on Wolffian logic and ontology, *rational* theology and *philosophia practica universalis*, he had early discovered that this way of philosophizing was exhaustive neither of the world nor even philosophical discussion. He found that British philosophers also had something to offer. The works of Locke, Shaftesbury, Hutcheson, Hume, and almost every other British philosopher of note were full of problems that needed solution and observations that needed to be explained, if German philosophy of the traditional sort was to succeed, and most of these problems seemed to have do with the analysis of sensation in theoretical, moral, and aesthetic contexts. Mendelssohn had formulated a new problem or task for himself (and the other Germans). This task was conceived by him – at least at first – as one of incorporating British 'observations' in a comprehensive theory. As he noted at the occasion of a review of Edmund Burke's *A Philosophical Enquiry into the Origin of our Ideas of the Sublime and Beautiful*:

> The theory of human sensations and passions has in more recent times made the greatest progress, since the other parts of philosophy no longer seem to advance very much. Our neighbours, and especially the English, precede us with philosophical observations of nature, and we follow them with our rational inferences; and if it were to go on like this, namely that our neighbours observe and we explain, we may hope that we will achieve in time a complete theory of sensation.[24]

What was needed, he thought, was a *Universal Theory of Thinking and Sensation*, and such a theory would explain the relation of sensation and thinking in theoretical, moral and aesthetic contexts.[25] It would use British 'observations' and German (speak: Wolffian) 'explanations'.

Mendelssohn had also definite ideas about the general approach that had to be followed. It had to be shown that the phenomena observed by British philosophers and traced by them to a special sense are really rational. Thus it was wrong, he argued, to follow certain British philosophers in speaking of a special 'moral sense' or 'common sense', for instance. Though they may appear to be independent faculties of the mind, they must be reduced to reason. Though he admitted that this reduction to reason is difficult in the case of moral judgements, since our moral judgements 'as they present themselves in the soul are completely different from the effects of distinct rational principles', he did not think that this means they could not be analysed into rational and distinct principles.[26] Our moral sentiments are 'phenomena which are related to rational principles in the same way as the colours are related to the angles of refraction of light. Apparently they are of completely different nature, yet they are basically one and the same'.[27] Moral phenomena are phenomena in the Leibnizian sense, but they are also *'phenomena bene fundata'* because they are ultimately founded in something rational. In this way Mendelssohn also set for himself and others a most important task, namely the task of explaining how the rational principles are related to what appear to be the completely different moral sentiments, for the colour analogy, though very suggestive, does not explain anything about the actual relation between rational principles and moral judgements. It was precisely this task that defined one of the central concerns of German metaphysicians and moral philosophers during the second half of the eighteenth century, namely to show how 'sense' could be reduced to 'rational principles', or how British observations could be incorporated into a framework that remained more or less Wolffian. Most philosophers in Germany between 1755 and 1790 were working on this problem in some way or other. In the following I shall briefly summarize two of the most important and influential attempts, namely those of Johann Nicolaus Tetens and Immanuel Kant.

Tetens

Johann Nicolaus Tetens may well be the German philosopher of this period who learned most from British thinkers. He is sometimes referred to as the 'German Locke', but he might also have been called the 'German Reid', for Tetens always starts his own discussion of philosophical issues at the point where Reid left off, and his epistemological theory is deeply influenced by the Scottish analysis of the problem of perception. Dissatisfied with the state of German speculative philosophy as he found it, Tetens turned to observational psychology for his method and to common sense for the subject-matter of his philosophy. Thus he declared that the method he has used 'is the method of observation; the one which Locke and our psychologists have employed in their empirical psychology', and that 'the cognitions of common sense are the field which must be worked in philosophy'. Yet even Tetens did not believe that Locke's method could exhaust all of philosophy. Rather, he believed that even if we were to succeed in determining and describing all the principles of the human mind 'in accordance with the analytic method, used by Locke, Hume, Condillac, and others (including some German philosophers)', there would still be much more work to be done; we would have to go on to develop a basic science that has to do with the 'universal reason' of things. Though Tetens spent most of his efforts pushing further along the lines of Locke, Hume, Reid and Condillac, he argued that speculative philosophy is not only possible, but even desirable. Ultimately, his work was meant to show that, once the human mind had been correctly described, and its fundamental concepts and principles had been catalogued, metaphysics could be freed from the contradictions which make up such a large part of it. Metaphysics would then be able to progress without further difficulties. In fact, Tetens believed that a metaphysics is possible even without a complete delineation of the basic features of the human mind. That this is possible is shown by the fact that there 'exist already, at present, many particular speculative theories from general concepts, which our metaphysicians have developed, and which secure for the understanding that knows how to use them great, extensive and fertile vistas just as they are'. We need only to develop further these fragments of metaphysics that exist in order to arrive at the truths that define the fundamental science of metaphysics.

These truths will, according to Tetens, be objective truths, not merely subjective convictions. Since Locke's analytic method can yield at best 'subjective necessity which forces us to think in accordance with universal laws of the understanding', he must show how objective necessity arises, or how it is that we can legitimately ascribe 'what we cannot think otherwise' to properties in the objects themselves. Tetens tries to accomplish this by first showing that this question can only mean 'whether the laws of thought are only subjective laws of our own faculty of thought or whether they are laws of any faculty of thought whatsoever'. After these reformulations, Teten's answer to the question concerning the objectivity of knowledge has become surprisingly simple. Since we cannot think any other faculty of thought than our own – for if there were such a faculty of thought with other laws, it could not be called 'thought' in the same way as our faculty – the truths of reason 'are objective truths, and the fact that they are objective truths is just as certain as the fact that they are truths in the first place. We cannot doubt or deny the former, just as we cannot doubt or deny the latter'.

Kant and the end of the Enlightenment

It was in this philosophical situation that Kant first conceived of the problem of a critical philosophy and began to work towards his *Critique of Pure Reason*. His own work owes just as much to such philosophers as Locke, Hume, Reid, Hutcheson and Smith as it does to the earlier German discussions of their theories. Indeed, Kant's ultimate theory is in one important sense no different from the reactions of his German contemporaries. He is also concerned with developing a universal theory of thought and sensation. He also wanted to show that the mere subjective necessity of sense that appeared to be sufficient for British philosophers to speak of certainty, can be shown to be objective. Furthermore, he also followed the lead of the other Germans in trying to show that sense-perception presupposes concepts. Though his account of how the senses presuppose concepts is different from those given by his contemporaries, it owes a great deal to them, and it alone does not radically differentiate his position from theirs. His a priori 'categories and principles of understanding' are closer relations of Tetens's 'laws of the understanding'.[28] However, what differentiates him from his contemporaries is that he was willing to take a step they apparently could not make, namely to accept as true Hume's principle of significance, or the claim that we cannot possibly know anything that goes beyond what can be experienced through our senses. Sensations without concepts may be blind, but concepts without sensations are empty. Kant argued that metaphysics in the traditional sense was a dead end and an illusion, while they were all trying to revise or repair it so that it could take into account sense-perception in a better way than traditional Wolffian metaphysics had allowed it.

One might say that Kant finished the task that Mendelssohn had earlier formulated. The (British) observations had been incorporated into a (German) theory. His *Critique of Pure Reason* is, at least by intention, the kind of *Universal Theory of Thought and Sensation* that Mendelssohn was asking for and that most of the Germans of the period were trying to develop. But when the *Critique* appeared it was not seen as the solution of that problem, but rather as a problem itself. Indeed, it was seen to give rise to a great number of problems. During the 1790s, Germans began to concentrate more and more on the problems posed by Kant. Though British philosophers were still mentioned, their views were hardly ever discussed. In this context we find such oddities as a review of a German translation of Hume's *Treatise* that neither says anything about the contents of the work nor about the quality of the translation, but offers just a discussion of Kant's deduction of causality as an a priori principle.[29] British philosophy had become irrelevant for the problems the Germans were discussing now. This turn-away from British sources coincided with the end of the Enlightenment in Germany.

❧❧ NOTES ❧❧

1 This chapter should be compared with the fuller treatment of the Enlightenment given by Lewis White Beck in [12.17].
2 Hazard [12.27], suggests such an early beginning. See also [12.28], xvi. Beck, [12.16], 243, suggests '1687–1688, the publication of Newton's *Principia* and the Glorious Revolution' as a convenient date for its beginning and '1790–1793, the publication of Kant's last *Critique* and the Reign of Terror' as the date for its end. I shall follow Beck's suggestion.
3 This is suggested by Cassirer in [12.19].
4 See also [12.21].
5 I agree with Beck that both Thomasius and Wolff are important for the German Enlightenment. However, I am not sure that it is quite correct to refer to the two as the 'two founders of the German Enlightenment', and that besides the rationalistic form of the Enlightenment of Wolff, there was also a Pietistic version of it. (See [12.16], 243ff.) I am dubious as to whether Thomasius and

his followers really should be viewed as belonging to the 'Enlightenment' per se. In many ways they are better characterized as belonging to the enemies of the Enlightenment. It is not insignificant that Wolff gave this address when he had to leave Halle because of pressure from the Thomasians.

6 The most important members of this school are Christian Thomasius, Johann Franciscus Budde (1667–1729), Joachim Lange (1670–1744), Andreas Rüdiger (1673–1731), and very remotely A. F. Hoffmann (1703–41) and Christian August Crusius (1715–75). Johann Jakob Brucker (1696–1770) also deserves to be mentioned. His influential *Historia critica philosophiae* is said to have been the source of Diderot's articles on the history of philosophy in the *Encyclopédie*. See [12.26], 1: 346–8.

7 For details (and a more positive account) see [12.45], 33–72.

8 The names of the Wolffians are legion. They are too numerous to mention, since they held positions at almost every institution of higher learning in Germany. Some of the most important are Ludwig Wilhelm Thümmig (1697–1728), Bernhard Bilfinger (1693–1750), Friedrich Christian Baumeister (1709–85), Gottsched (1700–66), Georg Friedrich Meier (1718–77), and especially Alexander Gottlieb Baumgarten (1714–62).

9 Wolff clearly also knew of Berkeley and Collier, and he found it necessary to offer a refutation of idealism that is meant to refute them along Leibnizian lines. It is not clear how well he knew Berkeley.

10 Nationalist historians of philosophy have attempted to show that the Germans never took British philosophy seriously, and that the entire eighteenth century can be explained by German sources alone. Dessoir, for example, tried to show in [12.22], 53, that 'the basic direction of this development [of German thought in the eighteenth century] can be understood even without referring to England' by relating Kant to the later Thomasians and especially Crusius. And Max Wundt argued that Kant's critical problem arose 'from a connection of the subjective and psychological approach of Thomasius with the objective and ontological principles of Wolff', claiming that Kant's 'transcendental logic must be derived from this tension within German philosophy and not from foreign influences' ([12.43], 250 and 254).

11 The following can trace only the rough outline of the German-British relation. It would take several monographs to do it justice. Above all, Shaftesbury, Hutcheson, Lord Kames, Hume, and Reid and Ferguson were found to be extremely important by the Germans. For Shaftesbury, see [12.41]. For Henry Home, Lord of Kames, see [12.42], [12.32] and [12.65]. For a general account of the state of discussion concerning Home's influence in Germany see [12.37]. On Ferguson not very much work has been done. But see [12.24]. See also Pascal [12.65]. For Reid see [12.30] or [12.31] and for Hume see [12.29].

12 Mendelssohn, *Briefe, die neueste Literatur betreffend* 1 (1 March 1759): 129–34.

13 See [12.51]. See also [12.49].

14 See, for instance, [12.8]. See also [12.9]. Both are discussed in [12.53], 70ff. Merian's interest in Hume did not decline. Thus on 16 December 1763 Mr. Merian read 'une Piece traduite de Hume "Sur l'Eloquence"' ([12.52], 282). For the 1790s see [12.10].

15 Thus the translator of [12.15] with the first *Enquiry* as volume I, was the perpetual secretary of the Berlin Academy, J. B. Merian. The writer of

the Preface was another prominent member of this institution namely J. H. S. Formey, and the entire enterprise is said to go back to a suggestion by Maupertuis, the president of the Berlin Academy. Johann Georg Sulzer, a prominent Wolffian in the Academy thought that Hume was important for precisely the same reasons that Maupertuis, Merian and Formey believed him to be important. He also believed that Hume's scepticism constituted a most significant objection to Leibnizian philosophy, and it was for that reason he thought that the *refutation* of Hume was most important. Thus he became the editor of the German translation of the first *Enquiry*, and took the occasion to provide this dangerous work with an introduction and a running commentary, designed to refute Hume's theories.

16 See [12.4], 4: 503f., see also [12.4], 5: i-x, and [12.6], 1: 289.

17 [12.14], Vorrede. That Sulzer is not the translator is clear from the following: 'Es haben mich zwei Gründe zu der Bekanntmachung dieser Übersetzung bewogen, die ich durch einen blossen Zufall in die Hände bekommen habe'.

18 Sulzer obviously did not think that the criticisms put forward by the Thomasians were serious objections to Wolff.

19 Kant later in the *Prolegomena* seems to allude to just this passage when he says that he was awakened by Hume from his 'dogmatic slumber', and that this gave his enquiries a 'new direction'. See also [12.72] and [12.74].

20 [12.2], 524f. Since Mendelssohn himself was the author of the *Letters on Sensation*, he explicitly identifies himself as a Humean in so far as writing is concerned. He goes on to wonder whether Shaftesbury and Hume followed 'a single line of inferences', but he declines to answer the question because this exegetical question can only be answered by a closer study of the actual texts. Shaftesbury was also important. The *Philosophische Gespräche*, for instance, are patterned after a dialogue of Shaftesbury (see [12.53], 1f. and [12.54], 37ff.). His 'Briefe über die Empfindungen' are even more indebted to Shaftesbury's style ([12.53], 86–90). Mendelssohn also began a translation of Shaftesbury's essay on the *sensus communis* because he liked that work so much. What he seems to have appreciated the most was Shaftesbury's suggestion that ridicule could serve as a test of truth ([12.54], 109–12). Hume's *Enquiries* also played a large (though mainly negative) role in Mendelssohn's thought. In fact, his essay 'Über die Wahrscheinlichkeit' is, at least in part, an attempt to answer Hume's doubts about experiential judgements and their basis in analogy and induction (see [12.16], 321n. and [12.53], 233).

21 Actually, he differentiates six methods. 'The first is the method of education or the systematic method, the second, the method of invention or the Socratic method, the third the historical, the fourth the method of refutation, the fifth the method of commentary, and the sixth that of observation.' As the best example of the systematic method he mentioned Descartes. It is the method of those who already know what they want, and who want to get to their goal as efficiently as possible. The second method was for him that of the inventors of ideas. He mentioned Franklin and Plato as examples. The third, fourth, fifth and sixth methods are really only subgroups of the second. The third is really the methods of genetic explanation. It is either that of an individual of a species and either true or fictional. The method of refutation might be thought to be

the one he assigns to Hume, but he doesn't. It is for him really a German method. Leibniz and Kant are characterized by it. As he puts it:

> Leibniz, whose name honours that of Germany found his way to most of his truths by refuting or correcting the concepts of Locke and Descartes. And even that philosophy by which our age will distinguish itself for posterity and which begins to communicate its form, though not always its spirit to German writings in all different kinds really is the fruit which developed from the germ of an examination and refutation of the skeptical claims of Hume and the dogmatic assertions of Leibniz.

22 The most important philosophers in this group are Dietrich Tiedemann (1748–1803), Christian Lossius (1743–1813), and Ernst Platner (1744–1818). Their theories are in many ways not much more than the stricter application of the principles of Feder and Meiners. In fact, some of them, like Tiedemann, for instance, actually studied in Göttingen. Others, like Platner, Irwing and Lossius, were more independent. But in general, it may be said that while the Göttingers were content with a careful consideration of various theories and often suspended final judgement, the sensationalists had a strong bias towards physiological explanations. They were convinced that sensation and its basis in human physiology was the key for understanding human nature and thus for putting philosophy on a scientific basis. They all rejected Wolffian rationalism as being fundamentally mistaken and leading to a form of idealism. But they were by no means radical materialists. For they denied neither the existence and immortality of the soul nor the existence of God. Though they tended even further towards empiricism and sensationism than either the Berliners or the Göttingers, their general aim may still be described as the attempt to achieve a synthesis of British and German thought. And no matter how far they go in the direction of empiricism, they still remain deeply influenced by Wolffianism.

23 Mendelssohn is sometimes grouped together with other thinkers as belonging to the 'Berlin Enlightenment'. This group includes such names as Gotthold Ephraim Lessing and Mendelssohn. But there are also such lesser known figures as Sulzer (1720–79), Johann August Eberhard (1739–1809), Johann Heinrich Lambert (1728–77), Thomas Abbt (1738–66), Freidrich Gabriel Resewitz (1728–1806), and a number of even more minor thinkers. Because they all remained to a significant degree Wolffians they have also been called 'neo-Wolffians' by some historians.

24 *Bibliothek der schönen Wissenschaften und der freyen Künste* II, 2 (1759), I quote from the 2nd edn of 1762, pp. 290f.

25 This is the title of a book by Eberhard (Berlin, 1776). The book was a response to a question by the Prussian Academy, asking for a more precise theory of thinking and sensation. Eberhard reports that the question specifically demanded that '(i) one precisely develop the original conditions of this twofold power of the soul as well as its general laws; thoroughly investigate how these two powers of the soul are dependent on each other, and how they influence each other, and (iii) indicate the principles according to which we can judge how far the intellectual ability (genius) and the moral character of man depends upon the degree of the force and liveliness as well as on the increase of those two mental faculties'. (p. 14f).

26 [12.3], 2: 183.
27 [12.3], 2: 184.
28 Compare [12.17].
29 [12.7], 4 (1791): 155–69. Feder's only reference to the work reads: 'The many merits of this work have without doubt already been decided for most readers. Therefore I do not think it necessary to say anything about it'.

❧ BIBLIOGRAPHY ❧

(This should not be viewed as a complete bibliography of the subject, but only as a supplemented bibliography of 'works cited'. For more comprehensive bibliographies see especially [12.17], [12.29], [12.30], [12.35], [12.36], and [12.40].)

Primary Sources

(i) Complete and Selected Works

12.1 Garve, Christian *Gesammelte Werke*, ed. K. Wölfel, Hildesheim, Olms, 1985–.

12.2 Mendelssohn, Moses *Gesammelte Schriften*, 7 vols, ed. G. B. Mendelssohn, Leipzig, 1843–5.

12.3 —— *Gesammelte Schriften. Jubiläumsausgabe*, 20 vols, ed. I. Illbogen, J. Guttmann, E. Mittwoch. Continued by Alexander Altmann *et al.*, Berlin, 1929–. (Now Stuttgart, Frommann and Holzboog.)

(ii) Separate Works and Articles

12.4 Buhle, Johann Gottlieb *Geschichte der neuern Philosophie seit der Epoche der Wiederherstellung der Wissenschaften*, 6 vols, Göttingen, 1800–5.

12.5 Crusius, *Weg zur Gewissheit und Zuverlässigkeit der menschlichen Erkenntnis*, Leipzig, 1747.

12.6 Eberstein, Wilhelm L. G. von *Versuch einer Geschichte der Logik und Metaphysik bey den Deutschen von Leibniz bis auf die gegenwärtige Zeit*, 2 vols, Halle, 1794–9.

12.7 Feder, J. G. H. (ed.) *Philosophische Bibliothek*, 4 vols, Göttingen, 1788–93.

12.8 Merian, J. B. 'Sur le principe des indiscernables', *Histoire de l'Academie Royale des Sciences et Belles Lettres, Année 1754*, Berlin, 1756.

12.9 —— 'Réflexions Philosophiques sur la Ressemblance', *Histoire de l'Academie Royale des Sciences et Belles Lettres, Année 1751*, Berlin, 1752.

12.10 —— 'Sur le phénomisme de David Hume', *Histoire de l'Academie Royale des Sciences et Belles Lettres, Année 1793*, Berlin, 1793.

12.11 Tetens, Johann Nicolaus *Philosophische Versuche über die menschliche Natur und ihre Entwicklung*, 2 vols, 1777 (repr. Hildesheim, Olms, 1979).

12.12 —— *Über die allgemeine speculativische Philosophie 1775*.

Translations

12.13 Wolff, Christian *Preliminary Discourse on Philosophy in General*, trans. R. J. Blackwell, Indianapolis, Bobbs-Merrill, 1963.

12.14 Hume, David *Philosophische Versuche über die Menschliche Erkenntnis*, Hamburg and Leipzig, 1755.

12.15 —— *Oeuvres philosophiques*, ed. J. B. Merian, 5 vols, Preface J. H. S. Formey, 1758–60.

General Surveys and Background Materials

12.16 Beck, L. W. *Early German Philosophy, Kant and His Predecessors*, Cambridge, The Belknap Press of Harvard University Press, 1969.

12.17 —— 'From Leibniz to Kant', *The Routledge History of Philosophy*, vol. VI, *The Age of German Idealism*, ed. Robert Soloman and Kathleen Higgins, London, 1993, ch. 1.

12.18 Brandt, R. and Klemme, H. *David Hume in Deutschland. Literatur zur Hume-Rezeption in Marburger Bibliotheken*, Marburg. Universitätsbibliothek, 1989.

12.19 Cassirer, E. *The Philosophy of the Enlightenment*, Princeton, NJ, Princeton University Press, 1951.

12.20 —— *Das Erkenntnisproblem in der Philosophie und Wissenschaft der neueren Zeit*, vol. 2, Berlin, 1907 (repr. Darmstadt, Wissenschaftliche Buchgesellschaft, 1974).

12.21 Crocker, L. G. 'Introduction' in *The Blackwell Companion to the Enlightenment*, Oxford, Blackwell, 1991, pp. 1–10.

12.22 Dessoir, M. *Geschichte der neueren Psychologie*, 2nd edn, 1902.

12.23 Erämtsae, E. *Adam Smith als Mittler englisch-deutscher Spracheinflüsse*, Helsinki, 1961.

12.24 Flajole, E. S. 'Lessing's Retrieval of Lost Truths', *Proceedings of the Modern Language Association* 74 (1959): 52–66.

12.25 Ganz, P. F. *Der Einfluss des Englischen auf den deutschen Wortschatz*, Berlin, 1957.

12.26 Gay, P. *The Enlightenment*, 2 vols, London, 1967, 1971.

12.27 Hazard, P. *The European Mind, 1680–1715*, trans. J. Lewis May, Cleveland/ New York, The World Publishing Co., 1963.

12.28 —— *European Thought in the Eighteenth Century, From Montesquieu to Lessing*, trans. J. Lewis May, New Haven, Yale University Press, 1954.

12.29 Kreimendahl, L. and Gawlick, G. *Hume in der deutschen Aufklärung*, Stuttgart, Frommann and Holzboog, 1987.

12.30 Kuehn, M. *Scottish Common Sense in Germany, 1768–1800: A Contribution to the History of Critical Philosophy*, with a Preface by Lewis White Beck, Kingston and Montreal, McGill-Queen's University Press, 1987.

12.31 —— 'The Early Reception of Reid, Oswald and Beattie in Germany', *Journal of the History of Philosophy* 21 (1983); 479–95.

21.32 Neumann, W. *Die Bedeutung Homes für die Aesthetik und sein Einfluss auf die deutschen Aesthetiker*, Halle, 1894.

12.33 Oppel, H. *Englisch-deutsche Literaturbeziehungen*, 2 vols, Berlin, 1971.

12.34 Popkin, R. H. 'New Views on the Role of Skepticism in the Enlightenment', *Modern Language Quarterly* 53 (1992): 279–97.

12.35 Price, L. M. *The Reception of English Literature in Germany*, Berkeley, 1932.

12.36 Price, M. B. and Price, L. M. 'The Publication of English Humanioria in Germany in the Eighteenth Century', *University of California Publications in Modern Philology* xliv (1955).

12.37 Randall, H. W. *The Critical Theory of Lord Kames*, Northampton, Mass., Smith College Studies in Modern Languages, 1964.

12.38 Stäbler, E. *Berkeley's Auffassung and Wirkung in der deutschen Philosophie bis Hegel*, Tübingen, 1935.

12.39 Walz, J. A. 'English Influences on the German Vocabulary of the 18th Century', *Monatshefte* (Madison) 35 (1943): 156–64.

12.40 Waszek, N. *The Scottish Enlightenment and Hegel's Account of Civil Society*, Dordrecht/Boston/London, Kluwer Academic Publishers, 1988.

12.41 Weiser, C. F. *Shaftesbury und das deutsche Geistesleben*, Leipzig und Berlin, 1916.

12.42 Wohlgemuth, J. *Henry Homes Ästhetik und ihr Einfluss auf deutsche Ästhetiker*, Berlin, 1893.

12.43 Wundt, M. *Die Schulphilosophie im Zeitalter der Aufklärung*, Tübingen, 1945. (repr. Hildesheim, Olms, 1984).

12.44 Yolton, J. W. *The Blackwell Companion to the Enlightenment*, Oxford, Blackwell, 1991.

12.45 Zart, G. *Einfluss der englischen Philosophie seit Bacon auf die deutsche Philosophie des 18. Jahrhunderts*, Berlin, 1881.

Wolff and the Thomasians

12.46 Becker, G. 'Pietism's Confrontation with Enlightenment Rationalism: An Examination of Ascetic Protestantism and Science,' *Journal for the Scientific Study of Religion* 30 (1991): 139–58.

12.47 Biller, G. 'Die Wolff-Diskussion von 1800 bis 1985. Eine Bibliographie', in *Christian Wolff, 1679–1754*, 2nd edn, Werner Schneiders, Hamburg, Meiners, 1986, pp. 321–46.

The Berlin Academy

12.48 Buschmann, C. 'Philosophische Preisfragen und Preisschriften der Berliner Akademie, 1747–1768. Ein Beitrag zur Leibniz-Rezeption im 18. Jahrhundert', *Deutsche Zeitschrift für Philosophie* 35 (1987): 779–89.

12.49 Calinger, R. S. 'The Newtonian-Wolffian Controversy (1740–1759)', *Journal of the History of Philosophy* 30 (1969): 319–30.

12.50 Gossman, L. 'Berkeley, Hume and Maupertuis', *French Studies* 14 (1960): 304–24.

12.51 Harnack, A. von *Geschichte der Königlich-Preußischen Akademie de Wissenschaften zu Berlin*, 4 vols, Berlin, 1900.

12.52 Winter, E. *Die Registres der Berliner Akademie der Wissenschaften, 1746–1766; Dokumente für das Wirken Leonhard Eulers in Berlin*, Berlin. Akademie Verlag, 1957.

Mendelssohn

12.53 Altmann, A. Moses Mendelssohns *Frühschriften zur Mataphysik*, Tübingen, J. C. B. Mohr (Paul Siebeck), 1969.

12.54 —— *Moses Mendelssohn; A Biographical Study*, Alabama, University of Alabama Press, 1973.

12.55 Pinkuss, F. *Moses Mendelssohns Verhältnis zur englischen Philosophie*, Würzburg, 1929.

12.56 —— 'Moses Mendelssohns Verhältnis zur englischen Philosophie', *Philosophisches Jahrbuch der Görres Gesellschaft* 42 (1929): 449–90.

Feder and Meiners

12.57 Brandt, R. 'Feder and Kant', *Kant-Studien* 80 (1989): 249–64.

12.58 Röttgers, K. 'J. G. H. Feder – Beitrag zu einer Verhinderungsgeschichte eines deutschen Empirismus', *Kant-Studien* 75 (1984): 420–41.

12.59 Zimmerli, W. C. ' "Schwere Rüstung" des Dogmatismus und "anwendbare Eklektik". J. G. H. Feder und die Göttinger Philosophie im ausgehenden 18. Jahrhundert', *Studia Leibnitiana* 15 (1983): 58–71.

Hamann, Herder and Jacobi

12.60 Beck, H. 'Introduction. To Friedrich Heinrich Jacobi', *David Hume über den Glauben: über den Glauben oder Idealismus und Realismus*, Breslau, 1787 (repr. New York and London, Garland, 1983).

12.61 Merlan, P. 'From Hume to Hamann', *The Personalist* 32 (1951): 11–18.

12.62 —— 'Hamann et les *Dialogues* de Hume', *Revue de Metaphysique* 59 (1954): 285–9.

12.63 —— 'Kant, Hamann-Jacobi and Schelling on Hume', *Rivista critica di storia filosofia* 22 (1967): 343–51.

12.64 Pascal, R. 'Herder and the Scottish Historical School', *Publications of the English Goethe Society* 14 (1939): 23–42.

12.65 Shaw, L. R. 'Henry Home of Kames: Precursor of Herder', *Germanic Review* 35 (1960): 116–27.

Kant

12.66 Beck, L. W. *Essays on Kant and Hume*, New Haven and London, Yale University Press, 1978.

12.67 Gracyk, T. 'Kant's Shifting Debt to British Aesthetics', *British Journal of Aesthetics* 26 (1986): 204–17.

12.68 Henrich, D. 'Hutcheson und Kant', *Kant-Studien* 49 (1957–8): 49–69.

12.69 Janitsch, J. *Kants Urteile über Berkeley*, Strassburg, 1879.

12.70 Justin, G. D. 'Re-relating Kant and Berkeley', *Kant-Studien* 68 (1977): 77–9.

12.71 Kreimendahl, L. *Kant – Der Durchbruch von 1769*, Köln, Jürgen Dinter, 1990.

12.72 Kuehn, M. 'Kant's Conception of Hume's Problem', *Journal of the History of Philosophy* 21 (1983): 175–93.

12.73 —— 'Kant's Transcendental Deduction: A Limited Defense of Hume', in *New Essays on Kant and Hume*, ed. den Ouden, New York and Bern, Peter F. Lang Publishing Company, 1987, pp. 47–72.

12.74 —— 'Hume's Antinomies', *Hume Studies* 9 (1983): 25–45.

12.75 —— 'The Context of Kant's "Refutation of Idealism" in Eighteenth-Century Philosophy', in *Man, God and Nature in the Enlightenment*, ed. D. C. Mell, T. E. D. Braun, and L. M. Palmer, East Lansing, Colleagues Press, Inc., 1988, pp. 25–35.

12.76 —— 'Reid's Contribution to "Hume's Problem" ', in *The Science of Man in the Scottish Enlightenment: Hume, Reid, and Their Contemporaries*, ed. P. Jones, Edinburgh, Edinburgh University Press, 1989, pp. 124–48.

12.77 Lovejoy, A. 'Kant and the English Platonists', *Essays, Philosophical and Psychological in Honor of William James*, London, 1908.

12.78 Oncken, A. *Adam Smith and Immanuel Kant*, Leipzig, 1877.

12.78 Piper, W. B. 'Kant's Contact with British Empiricism', *Eighteenth-Century Studies* 12 (1978–9): 174–89.

12.79 Smith, N. K. 'Kant's Relation to Hume and Leibniz', *Philosophical Review* 24 (1915): 288–96.

12.80 Swain, C. 'Hamann and the Philosophy of David Hume', *Journal of the History of Philosophy* (1967): 343–51.

12.81 Walsh, W. H. 'Kant and Empiricism', in *200 Jahre Kritik der reinen Vernunft*, ed. J. Kopper and W. Marx, Hildesheim, Gerstenberg Verlag, 1981, pp. 385–42.

12.82 Wentscher, E. *Englische Wege zu Kant*, Leipzig, 1931.

12.83 Werkmeister, W. H. 'Notes to an Interpretation of Berkeley', in *New Studies in Berkeley's Philosophy*, ed. W. E. Steinkraus, New York, Holt, Reinhart and Winston, 1966.

12.84 Winter, A. 'Selbstdenken, Antinomien, Schranken. Zum Einfluss des späten Locke auf die Philosophie Kants', *Eklektik, Selbstdenken, Mündigkeit*, ed. N. Hinske [vol. 1 of *Aufklärung*].

12.85 Wolff, R. P. 'Kant's Debt to Hume via Beattie', *Journal of the History of Ideas* 21 (1960): 117–23.

331

CHAPTER 13
Giambattista Vico
Antonio Pérez-Ramos

Faire, c'est se faire.
S. Mallarmé

Giambattista Vico's (1688–1744) contribution to the history of western thought is both difficult to identify and still harder to evaluate. So much so that the overall characterization of his philosophy should perhaps be made chiefly by way of negatives: Vico is no empiricist, no experimentalist, no scholastic, no idealist, no positivist, no rationalist and so on. In fact, any philosophical classification would be a misnomer for the purported creator of a New Science, the self-appointed critic of Cartesianism, the passionate vindicator of a 'topical' versus a 'critical' pedagogy, the putative discoverer of a novel criterion of truth etc. This historiographic problem – i.e. the difficulty of classifying such a many-sided figure into a well-established canon – becomes further compounded by at least three complementary considerations: Vico's purported isolation as an eighteenth-century thinker, the not yet corrected imbalance between his reputation in Italy (where he tends to be considered the country's greatest philosopher) and his reputation abroad; and, more generally, the fact of his being perceived as a precursor, which conjures up the whole panoply of unresolved tensions related to that status. Vico himself made much of the first of these factors in his *Autobiography* of 1725–8 and in his private letters, where he grossly exaggerated his loneliness as a thinker in his native Naples; and since that time many critics and scholars have repeated the implied corollary of that book, i.e. the picture of a gigantic figure without direct forerunners or disciples. Thus, nationalistic motivations and the fervour of Neapolitan exiles in the early nineteenth-century began to cement a cult which elevated Vico to the pedestal of a cultural hero in the age of the Risorgimento – a situation which with all due modifications still prevails today.[1] And, finally, the status of a precursor is particularly difficult to assess in this instance, for it sends us back to a much discussed question in the history of ideas and of philosophy proper. Such a question could be formulated in this manner: are influences the result of direct acquaintance whenever we are talking of intellectual affinities, or is there a collective wealth of patterns of thought which the human mind is compelled to resort to whenever confronted with the same or similar type of issue? Vico, for example, has been lyrically hailed as, among other titles of glory, containing the nineteenth century in embryo,[2] of fathering or at least prefiguring the whole of German idealism,[3] and of being the fountain-head of modern anthropology and psycho-analysis.[4] Though most of these claims appear today vastly exaggerated if taken at face value, there is a sense in which the radically atypical traits in Vico's thought are linked to further developments in western speculation, with or without direct acquaintance from author to author. It is for this reason that any historiography worth its salt should try to asses such purported affinities, or, at least, to outline the tantalizing contours of similarities and incompatibilities.

Vico's starting-point as a philosopher is his criticism of Cartesianism, both as a philosophy and as a philosophically-inspired pedagogy. From the early inaugural orations that Vico had to deliver in his capacity as Professor of Rhetoric at the University of Naples, he emphasized time and again the putative sterilizing result of applying the analytical method of thinking (as epitomized by the Cartesians Arnauld and Nicole in their *Port Royal Logic*) against the old *ars topica*, that is, the ancient canon of specific questions and answers that the prospective learner had to ask about any subject whatsoever in order to attain a plausible (though not necessarily true) opinion in the matter in question.[5] This debate ('topical' versus 'critical' philosophy) has led some students to see Vico as a fundamentally old-fashioned figure, propounding a superseded method of thinking in the tradition of rhetoric instead of embracing the novelty of contemporary doctrines in natural philosophy. As it stands, this criticism is unfair, for a reading of Vico's inaugural lessons prefigures his great discovery, i.e. the *verum factum* formula in *De Antiquissima Italorum Sapientia* of 1710, as a key to an understanding of contemporary physical science. So we can read in the oration *De Nostri Temporis Studiorum Ratione* of 1708:

> Modern physicists resemble those who have inherited mansions
> where no luxury is lacking, so that they only need to move
> around the many pieces of furniture or embellish the house with
> some ornaments in accordance with the tastes of their time;
> and these learned men hold that the physical doctrines are
> Nature herself . . . That is why every thing that on the strength
> of the geometrical method is shown in physics as being true is
> only probable /ista physicae quae vi geometricae methodi
> ostenduntur verae, nonnisi verisimilia sunt/ and from geometry

has got the method, but not the demonstration. We demonstrate geometrical entities because we make them; if we could demonstrate physical truths, then we would be their authors / geometrica demonstramus qua fecimus; si physica demonstrare possemus, faceremus/.[6]

Now there are three main components in these compressed lines of the young Vico, lines belonging to a chapter tellingly entitled 'Of the Disadvantages of Introducing the Geometrical Method into Physics'. The first factor we should consider pertains to what in our idiolect is termed 'the philosophy of science'. Vico's radical and at the same time original position amounts to this: he is expressly rejecting the realist understanding of the 'mechanization of the word-picture' (roughly: of Newtonian mechanics) as the true and objective portrait of the physical world. Further yet, this rejection is made extensive to any physical system whatsoever. Instead, Vico proposes to consider the so-called mechanical philosophy as a useful or expedient fiction, whose certainty is solely based on the method deployed (i.e. mathematics), but falls short of the supposed objectification of reality which a widespread realist self-understanding of modern science would claim for itself.[7] Naturally, this approach may strike a conventionalist or fictionalist chord, and resembles Locke's para-doxical dictum in the *Essay* iv. 12. 10: 'Natural philosophy is not capable of being made a science'. But Vico's philosophical acumen in reaching that conclusion is all the more remarkable coming as it does from the rhetorical tradition and being, by and large, alien to the great philosophical debate that the new science had unleashed. The second point to stress in the above passage concerns Vico's view of pure mathematics as precisely the only *true* science conferred on man, because in it author and knower coincide: the mathematician, Vico holds, knows his truths by making, doing or bringing forth the elements with which or upon which he works. This is the first embryo of Vico's celebrated *verum ipsum factum* principle as a criterion for gauging human knowledge, and the cornerstone of his own constructivist theory, to which I shall shortly return. And, finally, the above passage characterizes Vico's own response to the *crise pyrrhoni-enne* or sceptical challenge, the reaction to which, according to Pierre Bayle, serves to document the rise of modern philosophy and science.[8] Vico's answer to that challenge, moreover, establishes a certain hierarchy in the forms of human knowledge which he is going to develop and modify in his mature work. Let us consider Vico's response to scepticism with some more detail.

Mathematical knowledge, we said, is provenly certain (*verum*) because it is produced, realized, constructed or made (*factum*) by the knowing subject himself: 'We demonstrate geometrical entities because we make them'. Now if mathematics thus typifies human cognition at his

best, would it not be the case that it does so because it is precisely
embodying the only criterion of truth that man can follow? Here begins
Vico's systematic critique of the other great foundationalist movement of
the age, namely, Cartesianism, a critique to which he partially devoted the
so-called *liber metaphysicus* of 1710, i.e. the *De Antiquissima Italorum
Sapientia*.⁹ In this book Vico's quasi-fictionalist or conventionalist understanding of physical science is expressly coupled with a full-fledged constructivist theory of truth whose further implications for the classification
of the sciences are clearly delineated. In so doing, however, Vico considerably draws on the Aristotelian doctrine that to know means to know *per
causas* as a way of exposing the putative fallacy and incoherence of the
Cartesian cogito. Thus, he programmatically asserts that 'science is
the knowledge of the genus or the mode by which a thing is made /scientia
sit cognitio generis seu modi, quo res fiat/ ... by means of which the
mind, at the same time that it knows the mode because it arranges
the elements, makes the thing /dum mens cogitat, rem faciat/'; and consequently: 'Human truths are those of which we ourselves arrange the
elements'.¹⁰ So the first adumbration of Vico's great epistemic canon in
De Nostri Temporis Studiorum Ratione reaches maturity and becomes
fully developed in his criticism of Cartesian metaphysics: the true and the
made are convertible, and the ego which the cogito is supposed to discover
or establish as the firmest truth is not that piece of rock-bottom knowledge from which other verities can be inferred in a deductive chain.
According to Vico, the notionally unchallengeable ego has no causal
underpinnings whatsoever, that is to say, it is not constructed or fabri-
cated, made by the thinking mind. In fine, the Cartesian cogito 'I think,
therefore I am' is therefore a form of *coscienza* (or very vivid mental
content, as a Humean 'impression'), but it can never attain to the status of
scienza or proven knowledge as constructed by the inquiring subject.
Again, the anti-sceptical tenor (even as Descartes emphasized in the case
of his own cogitation) of Vico's purported discovery is expressly stressed:

> To be sure, there is no other way in which scepticism can indeed
> be refuted, except that the criterion of the true should be to
> have made the thing itself. ... Those truths are human truths,
> the elements of which we shape /fingamus/ for ourselves, which
> we contain within ourselves, and which we project ad infinitum
> (to infinity) through postulates; and, when we combine them,
> we make the truths that, by thus combining them, we come to
> know. And because of all this we get hold of the genus and form
> by which we make these things.¹¹

At this point Vico also invokes a theological sanction for this criterion,
given that 'Divine Knowledge is the norm of human knowledge' (ibid.).
The starting-point of his reflection here, however, seems to be an

awkward philological doctrine, namely, the putative synonymity of the words *verum* and *factum* in classical Latin. Indeed, Vico's opening gambit in chapter 1 of the *De Antiquissima* runs:

> For the Latins *verum* /the true/ and *factum* /what is made/ are interchangeable, or to use the customary language of the Schools, they are convertible /Latinis verum et factum reciprocantur, seu, ut Scholarum vulgus loquitur, convertuntur/ . . . . Hence it is reasonable to believe that the ancient sages of Italy entertained the following belief about the true: 'The true is precisely what is made' /verum ipsum factum/.[12]

Vico's resort to the Latin language in order to bolster up his gnoseological position was soon criticized on linguistic grounds in the review of his book which appeared in the learned publication *Giornale de' Letterati d'Italia*. In his *First Response* to those criticisms, Vico tried to defend his philological thesis by quoting Plautus and Terence, but in his *Second Response* (following a rejoinder in the journal) he wisely retreated from the terrain of pure lexicography and explained that

> etymologies which the grammarians draw largely from the Greek language of the inhabitants of the Ionian coast serve me only as evidence that the ancient Etruscan language was diffused among all the peoples of Italy, as well as in Magna Graecia. *They have no other use for me*. I have tried to figure out the reasons that the concepts of these wise men became obscure and were lost to sight as their learned speech /i loro dotti parlari/ became current and was employed by the vulgar.[13]

So the *verum factum* criterion, stripped of its philological clothing, is now presented as possessing the character of an absolute and self-evident truth – the touchstone of *any* conceivable human truth. To make this position even clearer, Vico condenses much of his constructivist ideal under a theological cloak which recaptures most of the topics we have been considering, that is, the nature of mathematics, the criticism of Descartes's claim about the self-certainty of clear and distinct ideas, the *verum factum* topos as exemplified not only in mathematics qua constructs but in any facet of human cognition, and finally his own hierarchy of knowledge. For this reason, Vico's *Second Response* to the learned journal deserves extensive quotation:

> The criterion for possessing the science of something is to put it into effect /è il mandarla ad effetto/ and proving from causes is making what one proves. And this being is absolutely true because it is convertible with the made and its cognition is identical with its operation. This criterion is guaranteed for me

by God's science, which is the source and standard of all truths. This criterion guarantees me that the only human sciences are the mathematical ones, and that they only prove from causes /e ch'esse unicamente pruovano dalle cause/. Beyond that, it gives me the way of classifying the non-scientific disciplines /notizie/ that are either certain on the basis of indubitable signs, or probable on the basis of good argument, or truelike on the basis of powerful hypotheses. Do you wish to teach me a scientific truth? Grant me the cause which is completely contained within me so that I invent a name at my will, and I establish an axiom regarding the relation that I set up between two or more ideas of things which are abstract and which are, consequently, both contained in me. . . . You could tell me, 'Make a demonstration of the assumed theorem', which is tantamount to 'Make true what you want to know'. And in knowing the truth that you have proposed, I shall make it; so that there will not remain for me any ground to doubt it because I myself have made it. The criterion of the 'clear and distinct perception' does not assure me of scientific knowledge. As used in physics or ethics, it does not yield a truth that has the same force as the one it gives me in mathematics. The criterion of making what is known gives me the /logical/ difference here: for in mathematics I know truth by making it; in physics and the other sciences the situation is different.[14]

This long quotation may help us to approach two *questiones vexatae* that have exercised the mind of a host of philosophers and Vichian scholars. These are: (a) in how far is Vico's thought original, i.e. is his constructivist criterion really new, as he never tires to repeat?; (b) is it philosophically sound to uphold that criterion and what are its historical credentials?

The first question has been dealt with with some acerbity, given Vico's reputation in Italy. Thus the great philosopher and Vichian scholar Benedetto Croce maintained that Vico's originality was beyond dispute, although *formal* precedents of his criterion could be found.[15] More recent research, however, makes it impossible to share Croce's view and tends to regard Vico's *Grundsatz* as one of the various formulations, perhaps the most felicitious one, of a whole family of ideas: the maker's knowledge tradition, or in Amos Funkenstein's phrase, the 'ergetic ideal'.[16] Its barest outline would be roughly as follows.

A tradition which goes back to Antiquity postulates that objects of knowledge are in an essential sense objects of construction, that knowing is a form of making, and that the human knower is such as maker or doer. This gnoseological principle has been advanced not so much as a method but as a mode of thinking or as an archetype of thought, and its polemical rejection is to be found in many significant places of ancient philosophical writing. Both Plato and Aristotle, for example, considered that ideal worth criticizing and consistently saw the human knower as a privileged beholder or enlightened user, never as a maker.[17] But there are some traces of this tradition that classical speculation was unable to erase. Thus in the theological reflections of Philo of Alexandria and in the mathematical thought of Proclus we encounter the notion that knowing implies making or is a kind of making and vice versa.[18] God's knowledge of the world, for example, is pre-eminently knowledge by doing, i.e. knowledge *qua* Creator, and, as Christian theology gradually asserted itself, the difference between divine and human knowledge began to be perceived more and more as quantitative rather than as qualitative: God possesses infinite knowledge, but man's knowledge of some privileged truths contained in God's mind (i.e. mathematics) approaches that of the Deity. We know about the circle almost in the same way as God does, though we know much less; yet allegedly in the discovery of the pertinent mathematical truths we proceed discursively or step by step, whilst God's mind encompasses all cognitive operations in a single all-embracing intuition. In the same vein, Proclus argued that the mathematician projects his figures out of his own mind into a kind of imaginative space, where he proceeds to arrange his elements. He is therefore knower *qua* maker of mathematicals. Now, these ideas gained much favour in the fifteenth century with Nicholas of Cusa (1401–64), who systematically dwelt on mathematics as a form of human and divine creation.[19] Later on, the new scientific movement made its own use of these notions under the guise of a legitimizing or metatheoretical topos – an undercurrent in philosophical thought which has rarely been spotted. Men like Cardan, Vives, Sanchez, Bacon, Galileo, Descartes, Mersenne, Gassendi, Pascal, Kepler, Locke, Boyle and many minor figures embraced the new, yet elusive but immensely powerful ideal that knowledge is achieved through doing or construction and gave to it different emphases and interpretations.[20] Thus, the understanding of this principle and the stress laid on its implication by each individual thinker was sometimes vastly different and even opposite (for instance, as regards the question whether this kind of knowledge by making referred exclusively to mathematics or also to the material fabrication or construction of a model of man and the universe), although the tenor of the ideal is perceptible in the most unlikely sources, sometimes with a sceptical slant. To confine ourselves to English figures, Joseph Glanville (1630–80) wrote that 'the Universe must be known by the same art whereby it was made', obviously meaning thereby that to know physical things amounts to being able to reconstruct them at a minute scale as far as it is humanly feasible.[21] Thomas

Browne (1605–82) in *Religio Medici* (1642, written *c.* 1630) expressly calls God Artifex 'wise because he knows all things, and he knows all things because he made them all'.[22] With yet another aim in view, Thomas Hobbes (1588–1679) wrote that

> Of arts, some are demonstrable, others undemonstrable; and the demonstrable are those the construction of the subject whereof is in the power of the artist itself, who, in his demonstration, does no more but deduce the consequences of his own operation. The reason whereof is this, that the science of every subject is derived from a precognition of the causes, generation and construction of the same; and, consequently, where the causes are known, there is a place for demonstration, but not where the causes are to seek for. Geometry therefore is demonstrable, for the lines and figures from which we reason are drawn and described by ourselves. But because of natural bodies we know not the demonstration, but seek it from the effect, there lies no demonstration of what the causes be we seek for, but only of what may be.[23]

This is fairly similar to some of Vico's pronouncements above, especially if we compare it to Vico's hierarchy of knowledge as presented in *De Antiquissima*:

> Mechanics is less certain than geometry and arithmetics, because it deals with motion, but with the aid of machines; physics is less certain than mechanics, because mechanics, treats the external motion of circumferences, whereas physics treats the internal motions of centres; morality /moralis/ is less certain than physics because the latter deals with those internal motions of bodies which are by Nature certain, whereas morality examines the motions of minds /motus animorum/ which are most deeply hidden /penitissimi/ and arise mostly from desire, which is infinite /et ut plurimum a libidine, quae est infinita, proveniunt/.[24]

Now it is highly unlikely that, with the possible exception of Proclus' *Commentary on the First Book of Euclid's Elements* translated into Latin by Francesco Barozzi (Padua, 1560), Vico had really come across an articulated intimation of the *verum factum* topos. This may be an excellent instance, therefore, of the kind of progress philosophy sometimes has in store, namely, the growth in tension and self-awareness in certain opaque areas, or the making finally explicit of a pattern of thought which philosophers had been utilizing on various occasions without properly identifying the common denominator of much of their thinking. Hence, one of Vico's claims to greatness lies surely here: he abruptly opens *De Antiquissima Italorum Sapientia* with the formulation of the epistemological canon so many thinkers in his age were unwittingly using. According to D. P. Lachterman, that canon stands for nothing else but 'the Mark of the Modern', that is, the idea that the human mind should be compared to a pair of hands instead of to a faithful mirror – a notion which will eventually make a construct of 'reality' itself.[25] Of course, it would be utterly preposterous to claim that the convertibility of the true and the made can be unqualifyingly predicated of all of man's cognitive facets. But, since we do not know whether such an all-embracing formula exists or can exist, we may well greet the Vichian topos as a historically exact identification of one of the leading ideals of man's self-reflecting rationality. So much for the philosophical soundness of his principle.

Let us glance back at Vico's last quotation above. The 'moral science' had been demoted to the lowest rank in his epistemological hierarchy because the 'motions of minds' were supposedly inscrutable. Now it is surprising that what has been called since Croce's studies 'the second form of Vichian gnoseology' should take its starting-point precisely from the reversal of that position, that is, from the contention that it is man *qua* constructor or creator of human institutions ('the motions of minds') that should enjoy pride of place in the architecture of Vico's magnum opus, i.e. the *Scienza Nuova*.[26] Though nowhere termed 'principle' or 'corollary' (*degnità*) in the language that Vico adopts in that work, the *verum factum* topos is expressly expounded in three paragraphs (334, 349, and 374) as though it were a reminder of the epistemological pillar on which the new science is erected. Further yet, any attempt to salvage the cognitive credentials of natural science in the domain of the maker's knowledge tradition (as in *De Antiquissima Italorum Sapientia*) disappears altogether, and to the later Vico the foundation of this knowledge of human affairs or *cose umane* entails a radical scepticism about the possibility of man's ever achieving a science of Nature. In Vico's own words:

> In the night of thick darkness enveloping the earliest antiquity, so remote from ourselves, there shines the eternal and never failing light of a truth beyond all question /*questo lume eterno, che non tramonta, di questa verità*/: that the world of civil society has been made by men, and that its principles are therefore to be found /*ritruovare*/ within the modifications of our own human mind. Whoever reflects on this cannot but marvel that the philosophers should have bent all their energies to the study of Nature, which, since God made it, he alone knows; and that they should have neglected the study of the world of the nations, or civil world, which, since men have made it, men could come to know.[27]

Now it is important to realize that the Italian *ritruovare* in this paragraph may mean to find *again*, since many misunderstandings have arisen from it being translated as simply 'to find'. This sentence somehow implies that the human mind is posited by Vico as containing in its present and civilized stage all the patterns of thought that it has deployed or projected into the surrounding world, first in the process of humanization and then in the setting-up of the multifarious panoply of human institutions, social structures and political systems. So Vico is not simply asserting that it is men that make their history, but upholding a rather strong thesis as to the rationale of man's capacity to grasp that very history, even when he is not its direct author. Yet, critically considered, here lies one of Vico's most serious weaknesses, for he offers no proof as to the possibility of that *ritruovare* in the required gnoseological sense. In fact, the difficulty can be further pressed, for the 'motions of the mind' are most of the time an act of epistemic self-deception, as Lachterman argues and Vico seems to recognize in several places.[28] How can a rational mind – say, the historian's – run the gamut of all the irrational or non-rational moves that in Vico's own narrative of the origins of mankind have played so decisive a part? Besides, what counts as 'rational' in the mind of a Vichian historian? For example, the invention of what he considers the three master institutions of humanized life (religion, marriage and burial) did not arise from any kind of rational computation that we could understand and exactly reproduce in our own minds with absolute certainty. Simply to attribute them to our feelings of fear and of shame, as Vico does, appears a rather jejune thesis, given the vast plurality of forms that such feelings may take and may have in fact taken in man's psychological make-up:

> [M]an in his ignorance makes himself the ruler of the Universe, for in the examples cited /[i.e. those related to the origin of language and metaphor]/ he has made of himself an entire world. So that, as rational metaphysics teaches that man becomes all things by understanding them /homo intelligendo fit omnia/ this imaginative metaphysics shows /dimostra/ that man becomes all things by *not* understanding them /homo non intelligendo fit omnia/ and perhaps the latter proposition is truer than the former, for when man understands, he extends /spiega/ his mind and takes in /comprende/ the things, but when he does not understand, he makes the things out of himself and becomes them by transforming himself into them.
>
> [(*Sc. N.* par. 405)]

If this is really so and the possibilities of error become less and less frequent as we advance towards those stages of humanity which are supposed to resemble ours, then a good case could be made for arguing that Vico had in fact adumbrated the concept of *Verstehen*, that is to say, of cognitive empathy or imaginative understanding which man can use solely when handling the things that belong to man: motivations, fears, feelings and so forth. This is a mode of knowing (sometimes understood as a method of sorts) proper to the human sciences or *Geisteswissenschaften*, a mode or perhaps a method that by definition natural sciences lack.[29] This interpretation is suggested by, amongst others, Isaiah Berlin in his essays on Vico and the *Scienza Nuova*. According to Berlin, Vico discovered a hitherto 'unrecognized sense of knowing basic to all humane studies'. In his own words, this sense of knowing is no other but the sense

> in which I know what it is to be poor, to fight for a cause, to belong to a nation, to join or abandon a church or a party,
> to feel nostalgia, terror, the presence of a God, to understand a gesture, a work of art, a joke, a man's character or that one is transformed or lying to oneself.

One has to note, however, that in the above examples no time or place provision is made, so that it would appear that the experience of being poor – to quote one of his illustrations – is fundamentally the same in twentieth-century Britain and in tenth-century China: But it is highly unlikely that the notion of 'poverty' has remained unaltered throughout history and geography. Be that as it may, such things are known, Berlin continues,

> in the first place ... by personal experience, in the second place because the experience of others is sufficiently woven into our own to be seized quasi-directly ... and in the third place by the working (sometimes by a conscious effort) of the imagination. This is the sort of knowing that participants of an activity claim to possess as against mere observers; the knowledge of the actors as against that of the audience, of the 'inside' story as against that obtained from some 'outside' vantage point: knowledge by 'direct acquaintance' with my inner states or by sympathetic insight into those of others.[30]

Berlin's suggestion and description is indeed valid for much of Dilthey's, Weber's or Collingwood's theorization of the method and aim proper to the human sciences or to history. In the initial mist to which Vico's efforts belong, however, that characterization turns out to be far too clear, though undoubtedly Berlin is looking in the right direction. There is something else, in fact, that would make possible the operations of *Verstehen* in Vico's *Scienza Nuova*. Let us see how it might work.

The other key idea which Vico resorts to when attempting to guarantee the exactness of our re-entering into other men's minds or when trying to engage cognitively with the most remote past is the notion of Providence. This, as shall be shown, *semi*-secular idea would guide the course of nations according to specifical, intellectually grasp-able patterns (Vico's *corsi* and *ricorsi*), constituting the so-called *storia ideale eterna* of that which 'was, is, and shall be'. Needless to add, in Vico's speculation the 'motions of the human mind' are to follow suit, over and above the personal will of the historical actors themselves. Now, this notion, no less than the *verum factum* topos, enjoys a reputable pedigree from the prophet Isaiah 10:5–8, to Maimonides's 'cunning of God', Mandeville's 'private vices, public benefits', Kant's 'hidden plan of Nature' (*verborgener Plan der Natur*) and, of course, Hegel's 'cunning of Reason' (*List der Vernunft*) – the last ones being wholly secular ways of translating an old theologoumenon. Amos Funkenstein has identified and richly documented this family of ideas. He has dubbed it 'the invisible hand explanations' in history, alluding to Adam Smith's celebrated simile in economics.[31] Now, Vico is quite amenable to this description in his explanation of history and of the manner man is capable of grasping it in the *Scienza Nuova*. Thus, while describing at length the slow process by which man has forged his own civil nature out of an initial brutish existence, Vico rejects all forms of diffusionism in the spreading of civilization and insists on a spontaneous process taking place in each nation and place. Yet, he emphasizes again and again that mankind is willing one thing and invariably achieving another, and that the oblique route that the nations follow (their *corso* and *ricorso*) is, as it were, guaranteed in its intelligible uniformity by a non-conscious effort of the historical subjects:

> For, though men have themselves made this world of nations . . .
> it has without doubt been born of a mind often unlike /diversa/,
> at times quite contrary to /tutta contraria/ and always superior
> to, the particular ends these men had set themselves. . . . Thus
> men would indulge their bestial lust and forsake their children,
> but they create the purity of marriage, whence arise the families;
> the fathers would exercise their paternal powers over the clients
> without moderation, but they subject them to civil power,
> whence arise the cities; the reigning orders of nobles would
> abuse their seigneural freedom over the plebeians, but they fall
> under the servitude of laws which create popular liberty; the
> free people would break loose from the restraint of their laws,
> but they fall subject to monarchs. . . . By their always acting
> thus, the same things come to be.[32]

Yet, this Providence is hardly a religious, not to say a Catholic, concept, for it is in-built in the very process of humanization (the birth of nations) and does not leave any room for any form of transcendence. Mankind would behave in that way with or without the supervision of an all-powerful Deity and, for this reason, Vico's Providence is, so to speak, a Providence without a God.

In the end, the five books and the 1,112 paragraphs of the final version of the *Scienza Nuova* of 1744 may seem to prove unequal to the gigantic task Vico had glimpsed himself accomplishing. For one thing, it was necessary to command far more philological and anthropological scholarship, and especially to be in possession of a more worked-out methodological thought as regards its organization and presentation.[33] Nevertheless, truncated as it now appears, Vico's accomplishment in the *Scienza Nuova* is admirable in terms of its originality in the role that he (perhaps unwittingly) attributed to the non-rational in man's protracted search for his own social being: the inquiry into 'truth' in its historical dimension, into the creation of the city and of civilized existence, and into the capacity we possess – or we lack – of grasping other men's expectations and fears. In a word, Vico was trying to formulate the credentials we can legitimately attribute to historical knowledge of any sort. If neither the *verum factum* canon nor the labyrinthine expositions of the *Scienza Nuova* appear to us wholly satisfactory, we should perhaps remember that the theory of truth, like the Greek Argos of old, has a hundred eyes. The merit of having spotted several of them, and not the feeblest ones, is the indisputable basis of Vico's intellectual achievement.

❦ NOTES ❦

1 Cf. Jules Chaix-Ruy, 'La fortune de G. B. Vico', in [13.16], 124–52. The myth of Vico's isolation in Naples has been exposed, among others, by Nicola Badaloni in his two books, [13.26] and [13.27] and in his article 'Vico nell 'ambito della filosofia europea', [13.12], 233–66. Badaloni stresses Vico's links with the Accademia degli Investiganti and other local circles of the Neapolitan Enlightenment. Cf. also G. Bedani, *Vico Revisited. Orthodoxy, Naturalism and Science in the Scienza Nuova*, Oxford, 1989, pp. 7–32, and A. Battistini, 'Momenti e tendenze degli studi vichiani dal 1978 al 1985', *Giambattista Vico. Poesia, Logica, Religione*, ed. G. Santinelli, Brescia, Morcelliana, 1986, pp. 27–102.

2 [13.47], 'Conclusione', 219–26: 'egli fu né più né meno che il secolo decimonono in germe' (p.226).

3 B. Spaventa, *La filosofia italiana nelle sue relazioni con la filosofia europea*, Bari, Berg, 1908, pp. 31, 60.

4 Cf. E. Leach, 'Vico and the Future of Anthropology', [13.20], 149–59; J. H. White, 'Developmental Psychology and Vico's Concept of Universal History', [13.20], 1–3; Silvano Arietti, 'Vico and Modern Psychiatry', [13.20], 81–94 (on Vico and Freud).

5 Cf. [13.77], esp. 24–89, and 105–15; Gustavo Costa, 'Vico and Ancient Rhetoric', *Classical Influences on Western Thought*, ed. R. R. Bolgar, Cambridge, Cambridge University Press, 1979, pp. 247–62; E. Grassi, 'Critical Philosophy or

Topical Philosophy? Meditations on the *De Nostri Temporis Studiorum Ratione*',
[13.18], 39–50 (Italian version in [13.3], 108–21).

6 [13.3], 68–9 (my trans.). Cf. [13.22], 31–45. This is the first recorded formulation
of the *verum factum* principle.

7 On the young Vico's scientific background, cf. P. Rossi's historical account,
'Ancora sui contemporanei di Vico', *Rivista di filosofia* 76(1985): 465–74; M.
Torrini, 'Il problema del rapporto tra scienza e filosofia nel pensiero del primo
Vico', *Physis* 20(1978): 103–21. J. Barnouw has reviewed the different trends of
research in [13.29], 609–20. Barnouw's thesis does not refer specifically to the
De Antiquissima Italorum Sapientia, but the author maintains that 'Vico's
development . . . supports the view that the new sciences of the 17th century,
from Galileo on, provided the crucial inspiration and model for the formation
of the human sciences' (p.609). This is more or less the route Comte took, but
it hardly squares with the methods of Vico in the *Scienza Nuova*, despite his
own claim that he is applying Bacon's method (par. 163; cf. also 137, 359). Cf.
n. 33 below.

8 Cf. Richard Popkin, *A History of Scepticism from Erasmus to Spinoza*, rev. edn.
London, University of California Press, 1979, Preface, p. xvii.

9 *De Antiquissima Italorum Sapientia* was also called *liber prius metaphysicus*; in
Vico's original project, a *liber secundus physicus* and a *liber tertius moralis* were
to follow. Some notes prepared for the second book were published fifty years
after Vico's death, assembled as a monograph entitled *De Aequilibrio Corporis
Animantis*, a book now lost. Vico appears to have begun working on the *Scienza
Nuova* fairly soon after the publication of the *De Antiquissima*. Cf. [13.8],
Introduction.

10 Vico stresses that the cogito is a *sign*, but not a *cause* of my being. Vico uses
here the Greek term *tekmērion*, a word of Stoic echoes. This is Vico's sceptic
reply to Descartes:

> The dogmatist . . . would allow that the sceptic acquires knowledge of his
> being from awareness of his thinking, since the unshakable certainty of
> existence is born from his awareness of thinking. And, of course, no one
> can be wholly certain that he exists unless he makes up his own being out
> of something he cannot doubt. Consequently, the sceptic cannot be certain
> that he is because he does not gather his existence from a wholly undoubted
> principle. To all this the sceptic will respond by denying that knowledge of
> being is acquired from consciousness of thinking. For, he argues, to know
> (*scire*) is to be cognizant (*nosse*) of the causes out of which a thing is born.
> But I who think am mind and body, and if thought were the cause of my
> being, thought would be the cause of the body. Yet there are bodies that do
> not think. Rather, it is because I consist of body and mind that I think; so
> that body and mind united are the cause of thought. For if I were only body
> I would not think. If I were only mind, I would have /pure/ intelligence.
> In fact, thinking is the sign and not the cause of my being mind. But the
> sure sign (*techmerium*) is not the cause, for the clever sceptic will not deny
> that certainty of sure /rational/ signs, but just the certainty of causes.
>
> ([13.8], 55–6; [13.6], 72–5)

11 [13.8], 57; *De Antiquissima*, I, iv [13.6], 74f. This subchapter is entitled 'God is

the comprehension of all causes – Divine Knowledge is the norm of human knowledge'.

12 [13.3], 63–4; [13.8], 45f. (italics added). Cf. also the following: 'Amongst human sciences only those are true which ... have elements which we coordinate and are contained within ourselves ... and when we put together such elements, we are becoming authors of such truths /et cum ea componimus, vera quae ... cognoscimus, faciamus/ [13.3], 62f, 68f, 73f.

13 [13.3], 149; [13.8], 157. In [13.3], 155 Vico recognizes that the value of every thing he is proposing does not stem from 'the force and evidence of the reasons advanced', for in lexical questions usage and authority overshadow the innermost meanings of speech.

14 [13.8], 167; [13.3], 156.

15 [13.48], 233–59. Cf. also G. Gentile, *Studi vichiani: Lo svolgimento della filosofia vichiana* (1912–15), *Opere Complete*, vol. xvi, Florence, Sansoni, 1963³.

16 Amos Funkenstein, *Theology and the Scientific Imagination from the Middle Ages to the Seventeenth Century*, Princeton, NJ, Princeton University Press, 1986, 290–345; esp. 296–9; R. Mondolfo, *Il verum factum prima di Vico*, Bari, Guida, 1969, and the criticisms levelled against this book by Maria Donzelli, 'Studi vichiani e storia delle idee. (A proposito di un saggio di Rodolfo Mondolfo)', *Filosofia* 21(1970): 33–48; and A. Pérez-Ramos, *Francis Bacon's Idea of Science and the Maker's Knowledge Tradition*, Oxford, Clarendon, 1988, pp. 48–62, 167–96.

17 In Aristotle's *Politica* 1282a17ff. we read:

> About some things the man who made them would not be the only nor the best judge, as in the case of professionals whose products come within the knowledge of lay men also (hoi mē echontes tēn technēn): to judge a house, for instance, does not belong only to the man who built it, but in fact the man who uses the house (the householder) will be an even better judge of it, and a steerman judges a rudder better than a carpenter, and the diner judges a banquet better than the cook.
>
> [(Loeb edn, trans. H. Rachman, 227)]

Plato resorted to the same sort of confutation in several places (*Euthydemus* 289A–D, *Cratylus* 390 B, *Meno* 88 E), and especially in *Republic* 601 E–602 A:

> The user of anything is the one who knows most of it by experience, and he reports to the maker the good and bad effects in the use of the thing he uses. As, for example, the flute-player reports to the flute-maker which flutes respond and serve rightly in flute-playing, and will order the kind that must be made and the other will obey him.... The one, then, possessing knowledge (epistēmēn) reports about the goodness or badness of the flutes, and the other, believing, will make them.... Then, in respect to the same implement, the maker will have right belief (pistin orthēn) about its excellent and defects from association with the man who knows, ... but the user will have true knowledge.
>
> [(Loeb edn, trans. P. Shorey, 445–7)]

It is tempting to perceive in these statements a dim reflection of social conditions amongst the Greeks.

18 Cf. Philo of Alexandria (*floruit c.* AD 40), *Quod Deus Immutabilis sit*, in *Complete Works* I, 22–3, (Loeb edn, trans. F. H. Colson and G. H. Whittaker, repr. 1960); cf. also *De Opificio Mundi* I, 20–1. For a treatment of this topic by mediaeval Jewish and Christian philosophers, in the context of God's self-knowledge *qua* Creator, cf. A. Funkenstein, *Theology and the Scientific Imagination*, p. 291f. For mathematics, cf. Proclus' *Commentary on the First Book of Euclid's Elements*, ed. and trans. P. R. Morrow, Princeton, NJ, Princeton University Press, 1970, Prologue 11–12 and 64. The soul is equipped with mathematical patterns (*paradeigmata*) which it brings forth as projections (*probolai*) of its own making. Proclus' Platonism is fairly similar to Vico's in that both purport to find the seeds of truth hidden in man's creative mind.

19 Cf. [13.24], 321ff., Hans Blumenberg, ' "Nachahmung der Natur": zur Vorgeschichte des schöpferischen Menschen', *Studium Generale* 10 (1957): 266–83), and *Cusanus und Nolanus*, Frankfurt-on-the-Main, Suhrkamp, 1973.

20 Cf. Vinzenz Rüfner, 'Homo secundus Deus. Eine gestesgeschichtliche Studie zum menschlichen Schöpfertum', *Philosophisches Jahrbuch* 63(1955): 248–91; A. Funkenstein, *Theology and the Scientific Imagination*, pp. 290–345; Jürgen Klüver, *Operationismus. Kritik und Geschichte einer Philosophie der exakten Wissenschaften*, Stuttgart, Frommann-Holzboog 1971, pp. 38–52; and A. Pérez-Ramos, *Francis Bacon's Idea of Science*, pp. 135–98.

21 Joseph Glanvill, *Plus Ultra, or the Progress and Advancement of Learning*, London, 1668, p. 35.

22 *Religio Medici* I, 13 (1642/43, written in the mid-1630s), ed. with Introduction and notes by C. A. Patrides (Harmondsworth, Penguin, 1977, repr. 1984), p. 74.

23 'Six Lessons to the Savillian Professors of Mathematics', *English Works*, ed. W. Molesworth, London, 1838–45, VI, pp. 183–4; repr. Scientia Verlag, Aalen 1961–6. Cf. Arthur Child, *Making and Knowing in Hobbes, Vico and Dewey*, Los Angeles, University of California Press, 1953, pp. 271–83, and W. Sacksteder, 'Hobbes: the Art of the Geometricians', *Journal of the History of Ideas* 18(1980): 131–46, and his 'Hobbes: Geometrical Objects', *Philosophy of Science* 48(1981): 573–90. Mathematics was not, however, the sole direction in which Hobbes developed his constructivist stance. As with the later Vico, there is a second interpretation of this topos, once it is realized that the State, no less than mathematicals, is a man-made product:

> To men is granted knowledge only of those things whose generation depends upon their own judgement. Hence the theories concerning quantity, knowledge of which is called geometry, are demonstrable. There is a geometry and it is demonstrable because we ourselves make the figures. In addition, politics and ethics, namely, knowledge of the just and the unjust, of the equitable and the unequitable, can be demonstrated a priori: in fact its principles, the conception of the just and the equitable and their opposites, are known to us because we ourselves create the causes of justice, that is, laws and conventions.
>
> *De Homine* II, 10, *Opera Philosophica quae latine scripsit* (same edn) II, pp. 92–4; cf. also *De Cive* XVII and *De Corpore* XXV

24 [13.3], 68–9; [13.8], 52. Vico, however, tries to provide a rationale for successful explanation in physics:

> Those theories /ea meditata/ are approved in physics which have some similarity with what we do /simile quid operemus/. For this reason, hypotheses about the natural order are considered most illuminating and are accepted with the fullest consent of everyone, if we can base experiments on them, in which we make something similar to Nature.
>
> (ibid.)

25 Cf. D. P. Lachterman, *The Ethics of Geometry. A Genealogy of Modernity*, London, Routledge, 1989, pp. 1–24. For other expositions of the *verum factum* topos, cf. W. Vossenkuhl, *Wahrheit des Handels. Untersuchungen zum Verhältnis von Wahrheit und Handeln*, Bonn, Bouvier, 1974, pp. 1–43; Stephen Otto, 'Vico als Transzendentalphilosoph', *Archiv für Geschichte der Philosophie* 62(1980): 67–80, and 'Interprétation transcendentale de l'axiome "verum et factum convertuntur" ', *Archives de Philosophie* 40(1977): 13–39. Against this interpretation, cf. F. Fellmann, 'Ist Vicos "Neue Wissenschaft" Transzendentalphilosophie?', *Archiv für Geschichte der Philosophie* 61(1979): 68–76. Many points of this debate are summarized in J. C. Morrison, 'Three Interpretations of Vico', *Journal of the History of Ideas* 39 (1978): 511–18.

26 The *Scienza Nuova* is a rather ambitious work. It purports to contain: (a) a 'civil and rational theory of Providence', i.e. a demonstration of the way Providence supposedly acts in social life; (2) a 'philosophy of authority', or on the origins of property (*auctores*); (3) a 'history of human ideas', especially the oldest ones in the religious field; (4) a 'philosophical critique' of the most remote religious traditions; (5) an 'eternal ideal history', showing the always-repeated route the nations run; (6) a 'system of natural law of the nations', based on primitive necessity and usefulness; and (7) a science of the oldest and darkest beginnings or principles of 'universal human history', where Vico tries to interpret the hidden truth of mythological fables. All in all, Vico aims at what we might call an exploration of the 'savage mind' in the age of gods and heroes. In this sense the *Scienza Nuova* purports to advance a rational theory of the *mondo civile*. Cf. K. Löwith, *Meaning in History*, Chicago, University of Chicago Press, 1949, ch. vi.

27 Par. 331. [13.3], 461; [13.5], 96. Vico, however, does not forget the theological sanction of the *verum factum* topos in par. 349:

> For the first indubitable principle posited above /par. 331/ is that this world of nations has certainly been made by men, and its guise /la guisa/ must therefore be found within the modifications of our own human mind /le modificazioni della nostra mente umana/. And history cannot be more certain than when he who creates the things also narrates them. Now, as geometry, when it constructs the world of quantity out of its elements, or contemplates that world, is creating it of itself, just so does our science / create for itself/ the world of nations/, but with a reality greater by just so much as the institutions having to do with human affairs /gli ordini d'intorno alle faccende degli uomini/ are more real than points, lines, surfaces and figures are. And this very fact is an argument, O reader, that these proofs are of a kind divine and should give thee a divine pleasure, since in God knowledge and creation are one and the same thing.
>
> Cf. [13.3], 467; [13.5], 104f.

28 'Vico and Marx: Notes on a Precursory Reading', [13.21], 38–61, esp. 51.

29 Cf. Karl-Otto Apel, *Die Erklären-Verstehen Kontroverse in transzendeltalprag-matischer Sicht*, Frankfurt-on-the-Main, Suhrkamp, 1979; J. R. Martin, 'Another Look at the Doctrine of Verstehen', *British Journal for the Philosophy of Science* 20 (1969): 53–67; W. Bourgedis, 'Verstehen in the Social Sciences', *Zeitschrift für allgemeine Wissenschaftstheorie* 7 (1976): 26–38.

30 I. Berlin, 'Vico's Concept of Knowledge', in [13.18], 375f. For a criticism of Berlin's views cf. [13.84], 159ff.

31 A. Funkenstein, *Theology and the Scientific Imagination*, pp. 202–89, esp. pp. 279–89. Vico's secularized Providence and the autonomy he attributes to the course of human history bears a strong resemblance with some of Spinoza's doctrines, despite Vico's claims about man's free will. Cf. A. Pons, 'L' idée de développement chez Vico', in *Entre Forme et histoire*, ed. O. Bloch, B. Balan and P. Carrive, Paris, Méridiens Klincksieck, 1988, pp. 181–94; [13.77], 49–68; J. Samuel Preus, 'Spinoza, Vico and the Imagination of Religion', *Journal of the History of Ideas* 49 (1988): 71–93.

32 *Sc. N.* par. 1108; [13.5], pp. 700f. Cf. also par. 341:

> But men, because of their corrupted nature, are under the tyranny of self-love, which compels them to make private utility their chief guide. Seeking everything useful for themselves and nothing for their companions, they cannot bring their passion under control /porre in conato/ to direct them towards justice. We thereby establish that man in the bestial state desires only his own welfare /la sua salvezza/; having taken wife and begotten children, he desires his own welfare along with that of the nation; when the nations are united by wars, treaties of peace, alliances, and commerce, he desires his own welfare along with that of his family; having entered upon civil life, he desires his own welfare along with that of his city; when its rule is extended over several peoples, he desires his own welfare along with that of the whole human race. In all these circumstances man desires principally his own utility. Therefore, it is only by divine providence that he can be held within these institutions /dentro tali ordini/ to practice justice as a member of the society of the family, the city, and finally of mankind. Unable to attain all the utilities he wishes, he is constrained by these institutions to seek those which are his due: and this is called just. That which regulates all human justice is therefore divine justice, which is administered /ministrata/ by divine providence to preserve human society.
>
> (*Scienza Nuova*, par. 341, [13.5], pp. 101f.)

Because of that, Vico adds in the next paragraph (342) that his science must be a rational civil theology of divine providence (cf. also par. 385). On this question, see S. R. Luft, 'A Genetic Interpretation of Divine Providence in Vico's *New Science*', *Journal of the History of Philosophy* 30 (1982): 151–69. On the method of the *Scienza Nuova* Vico is impenetrably opaque. He claims (n. 7 above) that he is deploying Bacon's method in human affairs (par. 163), but Vico mentions the somewhat atypical *Cogitata et Visa* insted of, as expected, the *Novum Organum*. E. McMullin has studied this question in 'Vico's Theory of Science', in [13.20], 60–89. He terms Vico's method 'hypothetico-suggestive' (p. 83).

∿ BIBLIOGRAPHY ∿

Works in Italian and English

13.1   *Opere di Giambattista Vico*, ed. with textual and historical notes by Fausto Nicolini, in collaboration with Giovanni Gentile (vol. i) and Benedetto Croce (vol. v), 8 vols, Bari, Laterza, 1911–41.

13.2   *Opere di Giambattista Vico*, ed. with an Introduction and notes by F. Nicolini, Milan and Naples, Ricciardi, 1953.

13.3   *Opere Filosofiche*, texts, translations and notes by Paolo Cristofolini, with an Introduction by Nicola Badaloni, Florence, Sansoni, 1971.

13.4   *Opere Giuridiche*, ed. Paolo Cristofolini with an Introduction by Nicola Badaloni, Florence, Sansoni, 1974.

13.5   *The New Science of Giambattista Vico*, trans. with an Introduction by T. G. Berlin and M. H. Fisch, Ithaca and London, Cornell University Press, 1948, repr. 1988.

13.6   *The Autobiography of Giambattista Vico*, trans. T. G. Bergin and M. H. Fisch, Ithaca and London, Cornell University Press, 1944, repr. 1975.

13.7   *On the Study Methods of Our Time*, trans. with an Introduction and notes by Elio Gianturco, Indianapolis, Bobbs-Merrill, 1965.

13.8   *On the Most Ancient Wisdom of the Italians, Unearthed from the Origins of the Latin Language, Including the Disputation with the Giornale de' Letterati d'Italia*, trans. with an Introduction and notes by L. M. Palmer, Ithaca and London, Cornell University Press, 1988.

13.9   *Vico: Selected Writings*, ed. and trans. L. Pompa, Cambridge, Cambridge University Press, 1982.

Bibliographies and Journals

13.10 Croce, B. *Bibliografia vichiana*, with additions by F. Nicolini, 2 vols, Naples, Ricciardi 1947–8.

13.11 Donzelli, M. *Contributo alla bibliografia vichiana* (1948–1970), Naples, Guida, 1973.

13.12 Tagiacozzo, G., Verene, D. P. and Rumble, V. *A Bibliography of Vico in English*, 1884–1984, Philosophy Documentation Center, Ohio, Bowling Green State University, 1986.

13.13 *Bolletino del Centro di Studi Vichiani*, Naples, 1971–.

13.14 *New Vico Studies*, New Jersey, Humanities Press, 1983–.

13.15 *Studi Vichiani*, Naples, Guida, 1969–.

Collective Works of Criticism

13.16 *Campanella e Vico*, Publications of the *Archivio di filosofia*, Padua, CEDAM, 1969.

13.17 *Omaggio a Vico*, Naples, Morano, 1968.

13.18 *Giambattista Vico: An International Symposium*, ed. G. Tagliacozzo and H. V. White, Baltimore, Johns Hopkins University Press, 1969.

13.19 *Giambattista Vico's Science of Humanity*, ed. G. Tagliacozzo and D. Verene, Baltimore, Johns Hopkins University Press, 1976.

13.20 *Vico and Contemporary Thought*, ed. G. Tagliacozzo, M. Mooney and D. P. Verene, New Jersey, Humanities Press, 1979, 2 vols; two vols in one, 1981.

13.21 *Vico and Marx: Affinities and Contrasts*, ed. G. Tagliacozzo and D. P. Verene, New Jersey, Humanities Press, 1983.

Books and Articles

(Those articles to be found in *Collective Works of Criticism* (above) are excluded.):

13.22 Amerio, F. *Introduzione allo studio di Giambattista Vico*, Turin, Società Editrice Internazionale, 1947.

13.23 —— 'Vico e il barocco', *Giornale di metafisica* 3(1948): 157–63.

13.24 Apel, K. O. *Die Idee der Sprache in der Tradition des Humanismus von Dante bis Vico*, Bonn, Bouvier Verlag, 1980 (3rd edn).

13.25 Auerbach, E. 'Sprachliche Beiträge zur Erklärung der der *Scienza Nuova* von Giambattista Vico', *Archivum Romanicum* 21(1937): 173–84.

13.26 Badaloni, N. *Introduzione a Giambattista Vico*. Milan, Feltrinelli, 1961.

13.27 —— *Introduzione a Vico*, Roma-Bari, Laterza, 1984.

13.28 Barnouw, J. 'The Relation between the Certain and the True in Vico's Pragmatist Construction of Human History', *Comparative Literature Studies* 15(1978): 242–62.

13.29 —— 'Vico and the Continuity of Science: the Relation of his Epistemology to Bacon and Hobbes', *Isis* 71(1980): 609–20.

13.30 Battistini, A. 'Vico e l'etimologia mitopoietica', *Lingua e Stile* 9 (1974): 31–66.

13.31 Bellofiore, L. *La dottrina della Provvidenza in Vico*, Padua, CEDAM, 1962.

13.32 Berlin, I. *Vico and Herder: Two Studies in the History of Ideas*, New York, Viking Press, 1976.

13.33 Burke, P. *Vico*, Oxford, Oxford University Press, 1985.

13.34 Cantelli, G. *Mente, corpo, linguaggio. Saggio sull'interpretazione vichiana del mito*, Firenze, Sansoni, 1986.

13.35 Caponigri, A. *Time and Idea. The Theory of History in Giambattista Vico*, London, Routledge and Kegan Paul, 1953.

13.36 —— 'Vico and the Theory of History', *Giornale di Metafisica* 9(1954): 183–97.

13.37 Chaix-Ruy, J. *La Formation de la pensée philosophique de Giambattista Vico*, Gap, L. Jean, 1943.
Giambattsita Vico et l'illuminisme athée, Paris, Del Duca, 1968.

13.38 Child, A. *Making and Knowing in Hobbes, Vico and Dewey*, Berkeley, University of California Press, 1953.

13.39 Ciardo, M. *Le quattro epoche dello storicismo: Vico, Kant, Hegel, Croce*, Bari, Laterza, 1947.

13.40 Corsano, A. *Giambattista Vico*, Bari, Laterza, 1956.

13.41 —— *Il pensiero religioso italiano dall'umanesimo al giurisdizionalismo*, Bari, Laterza, 1937.

13.42 —— *Umanesimo e religione in Giambattista Vico*, Bari, Laterza, 1953.

13.43 Costa, G. *Le antichità germaniche nella cultura italiana da Machiavelli a Vico*, Naples, Bibliopolis, 1977.

13.44 —— 'Giambattista Vico e la "natura simpatetica" ', *Giornale critico della filosofia italiana* 47(1968): 401–18.

13.45 —— *La leggenda dei secoli d'oro nella letteratura italiana*, Bari, Laterza, 1972.

13.46 —— 'Vico and Ancient Rhetoric', *Eighteenth Century Studies* 11(1978): 247–62.

13.47 Croce, B. *La filosofia di Giambattista Vico*, Bari, Laterza, 1911; 6th edn 1962. Trans. R. G. Collingwood as *The Philosophy of G. B. Vico* London, 1913; repr. New York, Russell and Russell, 1964.

13.48 —— 'Le fonti della gnoseologia vichiana', *Studio sullo Hegel*, Bari, Laterza, 1912, 1967, pp. 233–59.

13.49 De Mas, E. 'Bacone e Vico', *Filosofia* 10(1959): 505–59.

13.50 —— 'On the new Method of a New Science: A Study of Giambattista Vico', *Journal of the History of Ideas* 32(1971): 85–94.

13.51 De Santillana, G. 'Vico and Descartes', *Osiris* 21 (1950): 565–80.

13.52 Fassò, Guido, 'Genesi storica e genesi logica della filosofia della *Scienza Nuova*', *Rivista internazionale di filosofia del diritto* 25(1948): 319–36.

13.53 Fellmann, F. *Das Vico-Axiom: Der Mensch macht die Geschichte*, Freiburg und Munich, Verlag Karl Alber, 1976.

13.54 —— 'Vicos Theorem der Gleichursprünglichkeit von Theorie und Praxis und die dogmatische Denkform', *Philosophisches Jahrbuch* 84(1978): 259–73.

13.55 Flint, R. *Vico*, Edinburgh and London, W. Blackpool and Sons, 1884.

13.56 Focher, F. *Vico e Hobbes*, Naples, Giannini, 1977.

13.57 Fornaca, R. *Il pensiero educativo di Giambattista Vico*, Turin, G. Giappichelli, 1957.

13.58 Fubini, M. *Stile e umanità di Giambattista Vico*, 2nd edn, Naples, Ricciardi, 1965.

13.59 Funkenstein, A. *Theology and the Scientific Imagination from the Middle Ages to the Seventeenth Century*, Princeton, NJ, Princeton University Press, 1986.

13.60 Garin, E. 'Cartesio e l'Italia', *Giornale critico della filosofia italiana*, 4(1950): 385–405.

13.61 —— *Storia della filosofia italiana*, 3 vols, Turin, Einaudi, 1966.

13.62 Gaukroger, S. 'Vico and the Maker's Knowledge Principle', *History of Philosophy Quarterly* 3(1986): 29–44.

13.63 Gentile, G. *Studi vichiani*, 3rd enlarged edn as vol. xvi of the *Opere*, Florence, Sansoni, 1968.

13.64 Grassi, E. *Rhetoric as Philosophy*, University Park, Pennsylvania State University Press, 1980.

13.65 Haddock, B. 'Vico's Discovery of the True Homer: A Case Study in Historical Reconstruction', *Journal of the History of Ideas* 40(1979): 583–602.

13.66 —— *Vico's Political Thought*, Swansea, Mortlake Press, 1986.

13.67 Hess, M. B. 'Vico's Heroic Mataphor', *Metaphysics and Philosophy of Science in the 17th and 18th Centuries. Essays in Honour of Gerd Buchdahl*, ed. R. S. Woolhose, Dordrecht, London and Boston, Kluwer Academic Publishers, 1988.

13.68 Iannizzotto, M. *L'empirismo nella gnoseologia di Giambattista Vico*, Padua, CEDAM, 1968.

13.69 Klemm, O. *Giambattista Vico als Geschichtsphilosoph und Völkerpsycholog*, Leipzig, Engelman, 1906.

13.70 Lilla, M. *G. B. Vico, The Making of an Anti-Modern*, Cambridge, MA and London, Harvard University Press, 1931.

13.71 Löwith, K. *Meaning in History: the Theological Implications of the Philosophy of History*, Chicago, Chicago University Press, 1949.

13.72 —— *Vicos Grundsatz: Verum et factum convertuntur: seine theologische Prämisse und deren säkularen Konsequenzen*, Heidelberg, C. Winter, 1968.

13.73 Mali, J. *The Rehabilitation of Myth: Vico's New Science*, Cambridge, Cambridge University Press, 1992.

13.74 Manno, A. G. *Lo storicismo di Giambattista Vico*, Naples, Istituto editoriale del Mezzogiorno, 1965.

13.75 Manson, R. *The Theory of Knowledge of Giambattista Vico: On the Method of the New Science concerning the Common Nature of the Nations*, Hamden, Conn., Anchor Books, 1969.

13.76 Meinecke, F. *Die Entstehung des Historismus*, 4th edn, Munich, Oldenbourg, 1959.

13.77 Mooney, M. *Vico in the Tradition of Rhetoric*, Princeton, NJ, Princeton University Press, 1985.

13.78 Morrison, J. C. 'Vico and Spinoza', *Journal of the History of Ideas* 41(1980): 49–68.

13.79 —— 'Vico's Doctrine of the Natural Law of the Gentes', *Journal of the History of Philosophy* 16(1978): 47–60.

13.80 Nicolini, F. *Commento storico alla seconda Scienza Nuova*, 2 vols, Rome, Storia e letteratura 1949–50; repr. Rome, Storia e letteratura, 1978.

13.81 —— *Saggi vichiani*, Naples, Giannini, 1955.

13.82 O'Neill, J. 'Vico on the Natural Workings of the Mind', *Phenomenology and the Human Sciences*, 117–25 (suppl. to *Philosophical Topics* 12, 1981).

13.83 Pérez-Ramos, A. 'La emergencia del sujeto en las ciencias humanas', *La crisis de la razón*, M. Foucault *et al.*, Murcia, Pub. Universidad de Murcia, 1986, pp. 163–202.

13.84 Pompa, L. *Vico: A Study of the New Science*, Cambridge, Cambridge University Press, 1975; 2nd edn 1990.

13.85 —— *Human Nature and Historical Knowledge: Hume, Hegel and Vico*, Cambridge, Cambridge University Press, 1990.

13.86 Rossi, P. *Le sterminate antiquità: Studi vichiani*, Pisa, Nistri-Lischi, 1969.

13.87 —— *I segni del tempo. Storia della terra e storia delle nazioni da Hooke a Vico*, Milan, Feltrinelli, 1979.

13.88 Vasoli, C. 'Topica, retorica e argomentazione nella prima filosofia di Vico', *Revue Internationale de Philosophie* 33(1979): 188–201.

13.89 Verene, D. P. *Vico's Science of the Imagination*, New York, Cornell University Press, 1981.

13.90 Viechtbauer, H. *Transzendentale Einsicht und Theorie der Geschichte: Überlegungen zu G. V. Vicos "Liber Metaphysicus"*, Münich, Fink, 1977.

13.91 Vossenkuhl, W. *Wahrheit des Handels. Untersuchungen zum Verhältnis von Wahrheit und Handeln*, Bonn, Bouvier Verlag, 1974.

13.92 Werner, K. *Giambattista Vico als Philosoph und gelehrter Forscher*, 1879; repr. New York, Burt Franklin, 1962.

CHAPTER 14

Rousseau and Burke

Ian Harris

Those who thought about the social and political order directed their attention to a new centre of interest towards the end of the seventeenth century. It was not that speculation about political authority was forgotten, but rather that it came to be complemented with a concern for the social order. This concern was primarily political, in the sense that it focused on how people might live well in groups. Sometimes this addressed their morals (the french term *moeurs*[1] captures this meaning) and sometimes their prosperity. To put the matter generally, where the political theorists of the preceding century had looked at politics with an eye chiefly to preserving the citizen and his interests, their successors in the eighteenth century looked much more at how people might live well. Public morals, civic culture, social justice, education (including aesthetic education), 'improvement' in its manifold forms and political economy were their preoccupations.

The change may be read not least in theorists' use of reason. Reason was supposed more versatile then than some think it is now. It was supposed to disclose ethical truths and to be instrumental in governing conduct. It is easy to see how the former doctrine took hold: those who thought about morals in terms of natural faculties (as opposed to the information provided by revelation) tended to make use of natural law thinking. Natural law, being concerned in part with the benefits of acting in certain ways, focused on the correlation of means and ends. Hence good and evil would tend to be conceived in terms of reason. By the same measure it was easy to think of reason selecting courses of action, which the will then executed. Of course, not all thinkers were ethical rationalists: but it was true, too, that sentimentalists (not least Hutcheson) supposed that reason, if not the source, was a central element in moral thought and practice.[2] The point appeared clearly in Locke, who indicated that God 'having given Man an Understanding to direct his Actions, has allowed him a freedom of Will, and liberty of Acting, as properly belonging thereunto'.[3]

This implies that the understanding was a means of virtue. Where reason in politics had been directed primarily towards matters of preservation it was now directed also towards virtue. Robert Wallace illustrated this when he remarked that

> the more clear and extensive Views Men have of the exact Regularity ... that obtains in all the Works of Nature, they must be more sensible of the Excellency, Beauty and Advantages of that Order, that reigns ... they must admire it in general more highly, and be less disposed to transgress the Laws of Order in any particular Case.

It was not only nature that would stand approved, but the human world too, for 'the Order of the natural will lead them to love and admire the Order of the moral World, and the Laws which regulate Society and human Commerce'.[4] Thus knowledge and virtue were taken to be correlated.

Burke began as a representative of this cast of mind. If that had been his destination as well as his beginning, he would not have been a very remarkable thinker. But even initially there was more to him than that and, in the course of his speculations he encountered a thinker who held diametrically opposed views. That was Rousseau. It was the way in which Burke developed his special views, including his response to Rousseau, and the way in which Rousseau developed his own line of speculation that marked them as important thinkers.

❧ I ❧

Edmund Burke was born in 1729 or 1730, the a son of an Irish attorney. After education at Trinity College, Dublin he crossed St George's Channel and thereafter rose rapidly in English society, first obtaining a considerable reputation as a writer and then as a politician, becoming a member of the House of Commons, a privy counsellor and, on two occasions, a minister just below cabinet level. He is best known to posterity for his *Reflections on the Revolution in France* (1790), but this work was the product not least of his thought over the preceding forty years, especially that of the 1740s and 1750s. What sort of thinker was he? His mind was equal to a wide range of concerns – theology, aesthetics, moral philosophy, history and political theory. These interests were intimately connected. Burke's theoretical writings suggested that the world was patterned unequally.

When Burke was an undergraduate at Trinity, he and his friends founded a society devoted to improving themselves and the world. We discover from the club's minute book and from the writings which Burke published at the same period that he concerned himself especially about three matters: the revealed word and its effectiveness; aesthetics and virtue; and the possibilities of power and wealth for the good of society.

The first concern was expressed in 'an extempore commonplace of the Sermon of Our Saviour on the Mount' and was amplified when Burke asserted 'the superior Power of Religion towards a Moral Life'.[5] For the second Burke assumed that the arts and virtue went together, as 'the morals of a Nation have so great Dependence on their taste . . . that the fixing the latter, seems the first and surest Method of establishing the former'.[6] In January, 1748 he asked, 'who . . . is so audacious as to affirm Knowledge begets Vice?'. Wealth and power entered into a debate on the merits of the lord lieutenant of Ireland, in which Burke observed that 'the opportunity a man can have of promoting ye good of his Fellow creatures, is proportionate to his wisdom, his wealth, or his power'. He dwelt later on the necessity of property – 'a man's property's his life' – and on how the gentry of Ireland could improve their estates and so benefit the whole community. In March 1748 he descanted on the example of 'a Gentleman of Fortune' who had used his wealth for the good of his dependants through improvement. He had introduced manufacturing onto his estate, so that 'his Tenants grew rich, and his Estate increased daily in Beauty and Value'. Burke looked to the propertied order for the good of his country, moral and economic (though lamenting on occasion that they usually did not provide it).[7] These concerns, diverse as they seem, came to be related in one theory.

Burke embraced these three into a single understanding through the idea of inequality. Let us start with the revealed word. How could revelation – of all things, one might ask – fit this description? The answer lies in deism.

Deism may be defined as the view that the information mankind requires as a condition of salvation is obtained from natural means alone. By natural was meant what could be collected through human faculties, especially reason, as distinct from revelation. It was revelation, in fact, about which the deists had qualms. For they assumed that God willed that everyone in principle could be saved. This implied that each person had the minimum means needed for salvation. This could not include revelation, for the Bible had not been available to all people at all times. It followed that the revealed word was at the very least superfluous to salvation and at worst not actually of divine authorship. The deists considered that mankind's own faculties, especially his reason, could supply him with the information he needed.

Burke found deism obnoxious. His observations on the Sermon

on the Mount[8] declared a preference for revelation, arguing that it was superior to reason as a means of salvation. Shortly afterwards he suggested that Dublin's deists were really enemies to morality.[9] For if revelation was integral to God's design of saving man, to deny its authenticity was a denial of His plan.[10] To deny God's providence might in itself be held to signify atheism, or scepticism about revelation might be felt to reflect a complete unbelief. At any rate whilst Burke could later distinguish deists from atheists,[11] he was not ultimately much concerned about the difference.[12]

To uphold revelation in the face of deism implicitly was to prefer a pattern of divine conduct involving inequality. To make revelation necessary to salvation is to found it on a form of inequality, for historically revelation was diffused over only a limited part of the globe: God's favour was not extended equally to all. As such, revelation implies the concession that at least one part of God's government was conducted on unequal lines. Since that part, the business of salvation, was obviously the most important to man and God was held to work in a constant fashion, we might expect that others would conform to the same pattern. So we find in Burke's views on the social order.

Before turning to them, it is as well to turn to what Burke rejected. Again deism figures, this time not merely for itself but in the logic Burke read into it. Deism, in his view, opened up unpleasant implications for society. One deist in particular might be read in this way. The posthumous publication of Bolingbroke's works was a literary event and one especially interesting to Burke. For to provide deism with a conceptual guarantee one had to reject God's particular Providence – His concern with individual destinies – for that obviously embraced revelation. Most deists were not so thorough: but Bolingbroke was.[13] His view was objectionable on wider grounds. Besides discounting revelation it implied that God exercised no direction over specific cases. Individual events and institutions would not reflect His intentions. The social order, on this reading, need not answer to any beneficial purpose. Such a view would be unlikely to appeal to Burke, who at Trinity had sensed benevolent possibilities in the unequal order of his day.

Yet to understand the form taken by Burke's argument about the social order, we need to consider another thinker. For shortly after Bolingbroke's *Works* were issued there appeared a work which attributed a range of miseries to just the form of social order that Burke approved. This was Rousseau's *Discourse on the Origin and Foundations of Inequality amongst Men*, a work of cardinal importance for understanding both Burke and Rousseau.

∾ II ∾

Jean-Jacques Rousseau had been born at Geneva in 1712. His early life was marked not least by dependence and by the practice of the fine arts. Dependence appeared first in his being apprenticed to an engraver, Rousseau's father having come down in the world; next, in a more agreeable but ultimately unsatisfactory manner, in the bounty of Madame de Warens; and then in a role as secretary to the Comte de Montaigu, France's ambassador to Venice, who ultimately dismissed Rousseau and refused to pay his salary. Thereafter he enjoyed success as a man of letters, writing musical criticism and composing operas. If it were necessary to seek a biographical reference for his doctrines, we could say that his dislike of dependence outweighed his desire to be applauded for his artistic and intellectual prowess.

For the central assumption of Rousseau's thought in the earlier 1750s was that the supposed correlation between knowledge and virtue was mistaken. Accordingly the view of things that followed from it was mistaken too.

Rousseau's *Discourse... on ... the Arts and Sciences* studied the moral effect of knowledge and was submitted in a competition for an essay prize sponsored by the Academy of Dijon in 1750.[14] Rousseau argued that virtue and ignorance were correlated and so were vice and knowledge: that 'our minds have been corrupted in proportion as the arts and sciences have been improved'. He considered that knowledge had been deployed to make people behave pleasingly rather than virtuously. He assumed that the disposition of a human being, as it came from the hand of nature, would be read in its behaviour. Here he assumed that a condition of an action's being good was that it manifested the disposition of the agent, preferably a disposition to do good. But knowledge, Rousseau continued, showed us how to mould our actions in order to hide our dispositions. Thus knowledge concealed the truth. In effect natural people were truthful and sophisticated ones were deceivers. Rousseau went on to suggest that knowledge was encouraged by vice. It was not merely that knowledge concerned vice (legal science was parasitic on crime, for instance), but more especially that those forms of knowledge that pandered to vice (or were unconnected with virtue at any rate) were favoured and those that encouraged virtue were discountenanced. The accomplishments for which people were rewarded were not devoted to any good end, so the 'question is no longer whether a man is honest, but whether he is clever'. The Academy awarded the prize to Rousseau, perhaps intimidated by his asseveration that 'there are a thousand prizes for fancy discourses and none for virtuous conduct'.[15]

Rousseau's inverse correlation between virtue and knowledge, however, lacked something. It lacked an explanation of how this situation had arisen. In order to produce one, Rousseau took himself to the resources of natural law thinking and transformed them.

Natural law thinking had emphasized not only reason but interdependence, whether in the form of sociability or weakness. That is to say it had considered the human agent in abstraction from society and government and made two sorts of judgement. One of these was that man was a rational creature, capable of deciding what conduced to certain ends, what was right and how to act. The end that the agent had in mind, primarily, was self-preservation. The other judgement was that reason adverted to the dependent character of the species. This might take the form of suggesting that people were dependent on God, as in Locke. More generally it suggested that they were not constituted to subsist independently of each other, for instance because they were too weak to subsist individually in the face of their physical environment.[16] An instinct for the company of other human beings produced a similar inference: that if each agent was to obtain the ends he required other people were necessary. Hence the dependent nature of man suggested society.

The same line of reasoning suggested that government was needed, in order to secure the benefits of society. For despite their needs for others, people tended to conflict, largely over the possession of resources. They were sociable but not peaceable: and this was part of what Kant intended by describing the human condition as a social sociability.[17] Hence government was required to restrain human aggression.

Rousseau proceeded to stand these judgements on their head in the interest of explaining his inverse correlation of virtue and knowledge. He asserted that by nature mankind was neither sociable nor weak, but rather asocial and strong; not dependent but independent. Neither was man given to aggression, but rather peace.[18] If these assertions were made out it followed that society and government did not arise as the products of rational reflection on the human condition. They might be the outcome of something rather more unacceptable.

To make out his case, Rousseau evolved a dramatic sequence of history, running from mankind's natural condition to civil society. Rousseau needed to conduct two stories to achieve his ends. He wished to link virtue with ignorance and vice with knowledge. So he had to explain both the transition from virtue to vice and the growth of knowledge. To achieve these goals he needed to posit a figure of virtue and ignorance, to show the loss of virtue and to explain how knowledge accompanied that loss.

The first requisite was achieved in the exemplary figure of the savage, who also provided a way of pointing to the effects of knowledge. The savage embodied at once virtue and ignorance. He was virtuous in that he gave full rein to his natural sentiments and 'all' that comes from nature 'will be true'[19] Rousseau said. These comprised powerful instincts for self-preservation and for compassion. We should note in particular that from compassion flowed the 'social virtues' and that the savage's compassion was very strong. So he had the seeds of virtue. On the other hand he lacked the characteristics which would lead him to develop a knowledge that would encourage vice. The savage did not reason. Why? The savage, who was strong, had no need of others to assist him in self-preservation. Besides, he had no instinct for the society of other humans. He was therefore solitary.

But if a man was weaker he would need others. Needing them he would have to combine with them; and being constantly exposed to their company he could not but compare himself with them. This, of course, was an act of reason. Reasoning thus cultivated in each individual a sense of his distinctness from others. Under these conditions, if a man prospered, he would have little regard for others, whom he would see as significantly different from himself. So reasoning was a condition of the weakening of compassion. To compare one's situation with that of the pitiable, Rousseau thought, dried up mercy and led a man to say 'Perish if you will, for I am secure'.[20] So where there was ignorance there was virtue: and knowledge was a condition of the reverse of virtue, a regard only for oneself.[21]

How did Rousseau fill out the condition under which the latter would flourish, namely the prosperity of one and the inferiority of another? Obviously he required people to enter society, which made comparison possible. He also needed to make one person inferior or, more exactly, dependent on another. The first was a condition of the second, for 'it is impossible to make any man a slave', he noted, 'unless he be first reduced to a state in which he cannot do without the help of others'.[22] The transition was accompanied through a loophole in the savage's independent isolation.

Rousseau supposed that the species faced difficulties that encouraged thought and with thought co-operation and enmity. The savage was soporific and unreflective by nature, living off the fruits of the earth. But competition for those resources from other animals or from other people (for Rousseau mysteriously assumed an increase in population) encouraged reflection on how to overcome his circumstances. In part this meant inventing tools and in part associating with other humans to gain benefits unobtainable individually. But, at any rate, human society became established. Now Rousseau did not suggest that society as such was reprehensible or that the acquisition of knowledge was itself vicious. He did indicate, however, that society soon assumed an unequal, indeed hierarchical form in which knowledge became the instrument of vice and misery.

Once in society, comparison made one person eager to excel another. Soon human intelligence devised instruments by which a man could outstrip others in accumulating property. This was achieved through the discovery of agriculture and iron, for the art of iron working facilitated extensive cultivation. This required many hands: and it precipitated a state of inequality and, thereby, dependence. 'From the moment one man began to stand in need of the help of another', Rousseau wrote,

> from that moment if appeared advantageous to any one man to have enough provisions for two, equality disappeared, property was introduced, work became indispensable, and vast forests became smiling fields, which man had to water with the sweat of his brow and where slavery and misery were soon to germinate and grow up with the crops.[23]

Slavery and misery grew up because there were, on the one hand, those who had acquired property, and on the other those who had not and, of course, here was the condition under which a knowledge of one's own prosperity dried up one's compassion for others: 'the privileged few . . . gorge themselves with superfluities, while the starving multitude are in want of the bare necessities of life'. So the poor, in the face of a lack of compassion, lacked the necessities of life.

The rich, however, were also miserable. The withering of compassion and the triumph of self-regard made a man ask, not what it was right for him to do, but what should he do to impress others with his importance. Thus he became dependent on the opinion of others and was only happy when he captured their attention; in which, since they were as much absorbed by their self-regard as he was by his, was a search for happiness in vain. Meanwhile, in order to show their magnificence, the rich multiplied their trinkets, contrivances and all the apparatus of living far beyond their real needs. It was to satisfy these superfluous wants, of course, that the arts and sciences laboured.[24] We need hardly insist that the bad effects of the arts and sciences were now obvious, for 'from society and the luxury to which it gives birth arise the liberal and mechanical arts, commerce, letters, and all those superfluities which make industry flourish, and enrich and ruin nations'.[25] The essential point was that man ran sharply away from his natural sentiments and moral conduct to unnatural affections and that these unnatural feelings fed on social inequality, particularly in property.

Thus we have Rousseau's *Discourse on the Origin and Foundations of Inequality amongst Mankind* (1755). This piece, like its predecessor, was occasioned by the Dijon Academy. The subject prescribed was whether natural law authorized inequality. Rousseau took over self-preservation from established thinking about natural law: but had altered much else in order to show that society had developed as the violation rather than the product of human nature. This time he did not win the prize.

~~ III ~~

Rousseau did not impress Burke during his visit to England in 1766. Burke, who 'had good opportunity of knowing his proceedings almost from day to day', was sure that 'he entertained no principle either to influence his heart, or to guide his understanding but *vanity*', and in fact described him as 'the great professor and founder of *the philosophy of vanity*'.[26] This was a distaste conditioned by an intellectual origin. For the references to vanity suggest that Burke thought Rousseau knew that what he was saying was wrong, as in the declaration of Burke's friend Dr Johnson that 'a man who talks nonsense so well, must know that he is talking nonsense'.[27]

Burke had good reason to remark upon Rousseau. The Genevan's arguments inverted his own assumptions. With Rousseau knowledge accompanied vice and the growth of property produced neither 'Beauty' nor 'Improvements'. When Burke had asked who would affirm knowledge begot vice he could hardly have guessed that someone would be 'senseless' enough to assert 'its Opposite Quality' that 'Ignorance should be the Parent of Virtue'.[28] No doubt he attributed vanity to Rousseau because this seemed the only explanation for the paradoxical denial of what he took to be unexceptional truths.

Certainly Burke attributed views of the 'Opposite Quality' to Rousseau. *A Vindication of Natural Society* illustrated the logic of Bolingbroke's deism, which had asserted the sufficiency for salvation of the truths which man could learn from his natural faculties, by pushing its position to the Rousseauvian extreme. If man's natural endowments sufficed for that purpose, why not every other? If revelation was needed, why was civilized learning necessary? And if it were superfluous perhaps it was positively evil? Burke's parody takes Rousseau's course: man's great error in association, the establishment of inequality by the ambitious, and the miseries it brought on everyone are all present. The pseudo-Bolingbroke was made to observe that 'the original Children of Earth lived with their Brethren . . . in much Equality' and that the 'evils' of society were 'not accidental' for 'whoever will take pains to consider the Nature of Society, will find that they result directly from its Constitution' because 'as *Subordination* . . . is requisite to support these Societies', there result 'the worst and blackest Purposes'.[29] Whilst Burke was mistaken in thinking that Rousseau decried all society, as opposed merely to the course which modern society had taken, he was right in seeing that Rousseau's views were radically incompatible with his own. An answer was obviously required.

Rousseau's *Discourse* in effect embodied two claims about modern European society. One was that its hierarchical form implied a perversion of man's moral feeling. That feeling, which by nature took the form of compassion, the regard for those less fortunate than ourselves, would be stifled by the regard for those above us engendered in the social order. The compassion which man had by nature would be lost in the emulation he assumed in society. Rousseau's second claim was that a society so constituted, because unnatural, produced a range of economic and social miseries. Both claims condemned social inequality in the name of nature.

A mere denial of all this would not do. Burke could not be unimpressed by Rousseau's case, disagreeable though it was. After all his own view that the rich ought to work for the common benefit sprang from the common assumption that property existed for that end. With Locke, for instance, property existed to increase the fruits of the earth so that it could support people, just as political authority did not exist for the benefit of kings alone. 'Our modern Systems hold, that the Riches and Power of Kings are by no means their Property, but a Depositum in their Hands, for the Use of the People', Burke wrote, adding, 'And if we consider the natural Equality of Mankind, we shall believe the same of the Estates of Gentlemen, bestowed on them at the first distribution of Properties, for prompting the Public Good'. But that, in fact, was just what 'Gentlemen' in Ireland had omitted. Despite Burke's hopes, instead of making the people happy they seemed rather to have impoverished them. So much was this so that civilization wore a strange countenance, for 'it is no uncommon Sight [Burke wrote] to see half a dozen Children run quite naked out of a Cabin, scarcely distinguishable from a Dunghill, to the great Disgrace of our Country with Foreigners, who', Burke thought, 'would doubtless report them Savages'. Here, at the least, was a disturbing resonance in Rousseau's paradox of the misery of civil society. Indeed the indifference of the gentry seemed to bear out his psychological analysis. Burke asked,

> Is it not natural for a Man, who rides in his Coach on a bitter
> Day, or lies on his Velvet Couch, secured from all the
> Inclemencies of the Weather, to reflect with Pity on those who
> suffer Calamities equal to his Enjoyments?

but their indifference seemed to say it was natural no longer.[30]

A Philosophical Enquiry showed how nature gave rise to inequality. Burke did not dispute the standard view that men were by nature equal, though he did little to illuminate it. He indicated instead how passions that were entirely natural would give rise to a graduated social order. For Burke divided the passions which 'served the great chain of society' under three heads – sympathy, imitation and ambition. These linked men in society and linked them so as to make inequality natural. Sympathy was a 'bond' which made men never 'indifferent spectators of almost anything which men can do or suffer'. Sympathy by itself did not make for inequality, but it concurred with the passions which did. 'For as sympathy makes us take a concern in whatever men feel', Burke wrote, so imitation 'prompts us to copy whatever they do'; and imitation was complemented by ambition, which gave 'a satisfaction arising from the contemplation of excelling his fellows' to a person.[31] So it was natural for the ambitious to lead and for the imitative to follow. Hence inequality in society would be established. The bonds of civil society were the causes of inequality: and inequality arose from nature.

An unequal society in Burke's view was not only natural but also progressive. If men were devoted to imitation alone, 'it is easy to see that there never could be any improvement amongst them' and it was 'to prevent this' that God instilled ambition into man.[32] 'Improvement' implies human artifice, and Burke was quick to show how human invention lay in the pattern of nature. Nature could extend to artifice and to a specific form of artifice. For 'nature' in Burke's hands included the best adaptation of the artificial to the ends that man's nature suggested. The content of 'nature' would be presented to best advantage not in a primitive condition, as Rousseau had seemed to suggest, but in the perfection of artifice. 'Art is man's nature', Burke wrote, because 'man is by nature reasonable; and he is never perfectly in his natural state, but when he is placed where reason may be best cultivated'.[34] At one level this view enlarged upon the view that man required society to flourish, for 'without which civil society man could not by any possibility arrive at the perfection of which his nature is capable, nor even make a remote and faint approach to it'.[33] At another, it authorized the distinct version of civil society Burke intended. For the author of *A Philosophical Enquiry* believed that society could produce 'a true natural aristocracy'. Nature culminated in artifice. In Burke's own words, 'the state of civil society, which necessarily generates this aristocracy, is a state of nature'.[34]

Thus, Burke found no reason to think that modern society necessarily involved moral perversion. He wrote of humanity, without deliberation, that 'we love these beings and have a Sympathy with them'.[35] But did society involve the misery of man? We may assume that social inequality could involve an unequal distribution of benefits. But the point is less a state of affairs than how it is considered. We have seen that Burke could be scarcely more restrained about contemporary conditions than Rousseau: but he viewed society in a different light. He would argue that society depended for its prosperity on inequality: so that to undermine the latter was to strike at whatever benefits the poor might receive.[36]

We have seen that for Burke the divine worked through inequality. Revelation was an unequal mode of distributing information. It involved a further inequality, because God issued it, who was man's superior: and this superior directed man through his passions. 'Religion' showed that God was also the author of a morality discoverable by reason, just as *A Philosophical Enquiry* had emphasized the passions which tended to establish a social inequality.

We need not suppose that Burke's general stance implies an indiscriminate approval of all graduated dispensations. He could say that 'all who administer in the government of men . . . stand in the person of God himself':[37] but this scarcely implies that those who were like God in power were like Him also in goodness. To put the matter another way, some modes on inequality might be better than others. In order to distinguish which, Burke's focus had to move from the general to the particular. Most of his writings after *A Philosophical Enquiry* assess individual regimes. He turned first from his native Ireland in his *Abridgement of English History*.

When the undergraduate Burke discussed the possibilities of wealth for good, he had not forgotten power. In fact he thought that power might be more important for good than wealth. Power too required vindication, for among the inversions Burke attributed to the pseudo-Bolingbroke was the claim that any government, in its nature, was an instrument of evil. For just as Rousseau had told a story in which man was corrupted by society, Bolingbroke's account of history suggested that the liberty found amongst the Saxons in England was subsequently under threat from government and that one of its other enemies was the church.

The accounts of Rousseau and Bolingbroke in their different ways suggested that the motif of European and English history was decline, whether in the loss of virtue through society or in the problems of liberty after the Saxons. A writer offering an antidote might prefer to place his accent on progress. Where Bolingbroke's account questioned whether English liberties had grown since the Saxons and implied with a deistic sneer that the church was against political liberty,[38] an alternative would suggest that liberty had grown, not diminished, and that the church had assisted it. Since Bolingbroke argued that the early Middle Ages had seen a virtual extinction of political liberty, it would also be fitting to suggest that it was then that it was established.

Burke's *Abridgement* did not suggest the direct intervention of

God, save at one point, but showed how desirable results occurred gradually without any human having insight into His plans. By the same token the results did not reflect deliberate human activity. Burke emphasized the themes of inequality, improvement and liberty. Fundamentally, he thought, the structure of Saxon and Norman society was sound in that it reflected nature by instancing inequality. Further, whether under the indistinct forms of Saxon society or under the feudalism of the Normans, the subordination of one man to another, reaching to the king, was uncoerced. Therefore kings felt sufficiently secure, on the whole, to govern through laws rather than by force. These monarchs, too, favoured Christianity, which secured the benefits of improvement. Literacy and good manners were nurtured. So Burke could see the Middle Ages as the period in which the bearers of religious and social inequality secured blessings to England.

These reflections formed the basis of Burke's view of how government by opinion arose. Government by force ceased to be necessary when the ruler and the ruled could trust each other. This happened under the feudal system, which embodied the loyalty of subject to sovereign and which Burke would describe eventually as 'the old feudal and chivalrous spirit of *Fealty*, which by freeing kings from fear, freed both kings and subjects from the precautions of tyranny'.[39] Under this condition force would be replaced by opinion as a mode of government. This feudalism both necessitated and provided. It was necessary because leaders were followed freely (the sovereign 'was only a greater lord among great lords')[40] and supplied by the code of honour feudalism embodied ('the soft collar of social esteem').[41]

Improvement flourished under the same conditions. Burke thought that 'the rudeness of the world was very favourable for the establishment of an empire of opinion' and the body most fitted to form opinion was the Church. As 'the asylum of what learning had escaped the general desolation'[42] she imparted knowledge to the world. Hence the 'ground-work' of intellectual improvement was a 'Gothic and monkish education', because the Church had been the agent 'preserving the accessions of science and literature, as the order of Providence should successively produce them'.[43] Thus the agents of revelation complemented the beneficiaries of social hierarchy in God's design.

This story was common to Europe and England, for both had been feudal, but there was one feature peculiar to England. Political liberty arose through the coincidence of the growth of order, the church, and the precise structure of Norman society. Executive government extended its power. But it was balanced when the aristocracy was encouraged by the church to resist. Since the aristocracy was not sufficiently strong on its own to prevail, it sought to enlist popular support by claiming liberty for all. In this fashion it was ensured that liberty was not merely won but won on a general basis.[44] We could perhaps say that because Burke's story gives out at *Magna Carta* it is that unclear what would happen next; and that his story concerned chiefly England. But a passage in *Reflections* made it clear that to his mind the civilization and manners of modern Europe as a whole were the children of church and hierarchy:

> Nothing is more certain, than that our manners, our civilization, and all the good things which are connected with manners, and with civilization, have . . . depended for ages upon two principles; and were indeed the result of both combined; I mean the spirit of a gentleman, and the spirit of religion.[45]

Inequality in society, in short, was the bearer of the fruits of civilization.

Thus Burke's view of the social order began not merely from a position opposed to Rousseau's, but also developed in a diametrically different direction. Where for Rousseau inequality in society was unnatural, it was natural for Burke; where history showed a declension for one, for the other it showed a providential improvement. Rousseau was not the only piece of grit in the Burkean oyster: but neither was he insignificant. At any rate, whatever the causation, the result was two irreconcilable theories of the social order.

⚬⚬ IV ⚬⚬

It would be wrong to present Burke as an uncritical admirer of contemporary institutions. His middle life (let us say 1760 to 1789) was preoccupied with the abuses of English government and politics, whether at home or in the colonies. Neither did he suppose that the European order was without serious defects.[46] But essentially these were criticisms of policy and a recognition of problems rather than a call for wholesale reconstruction. Burke's view that inequality was the pattern of nature suggested that the hierarchical social order he contemplated had within it the fundamental ingredients of rightness.

Rousseau's attitude, of course, was quite different. To insist that inequality was a moral perversion in the context of an hierarchically constructed society was a radical criticism. Rousseau proposed quite a different standard.[47] It has come down to us as *The Social Contract*.[48] This embraced two central items, the general will and the means establishing it institutionally. Both of these transcended inequality. The general will implied an equality of treatment for all citizens *ceteris paribus* and Rousseau's means of instantiating it excluded the dependence of one person on another.

The concept of the general will has a transparent meaning and an unusual institutional form. By 'general will' Rousseau meant a measure which 'tends always to the preservation and welfare of the whole and of every part'.[49] More specifically he had in mind a measure implying the same treatment for all members of a community. In his own words, each person 'submits . . . to the conditions he imposes on others'.[50] This, no doubt, explains why Rousseau referred to it as justice,[51] for justice implies that each person be treated in the same manner as the next, unless there is some reason in their nature or circumstances that requires a difference should be made. In the words of his *Letters from the Mountain* under the general will 'all want conditions to be equal for all, and justice is only this equality'.[52]

The general will stood in contrast with the particular will. Where the general will prescribed an identical treatment for all persons under consideration, the particular preferred the interests of one agent alone. Rousseau assumed that each agent would seek his or her own advantage, writing of 'the individual's own will, which tends only to his particular advantage'.[53] To illustrate the difference very simply, suppose one were faced with the task of distributing 200 sweets amongst 100 persons (including oneself). The solution fitting the particular will would be to allot all 200 to oneself and none to the others, whilst that matching the general will would distribute two sweets to each person in the group.

Rousseau, in effect, proposed that each individual should regard himself or herself in precisely the same manner as others, other things being equal. This principle that one should pay a significant regard to others is embodied deeply in almost all European moral thinking. Those who hold a different view, such as Nietzsche, are in defiant isolation. It appears as a form close to Rousseau's in the Christian precept to 'love they neighbour as thyself'.[54] Whilst in Rousseau's time this principle would have found general acceptance, most would have restricted its application. No one would have doubted that some principle of this kind applied to moral conduct. Rousseau, in a like mood, conceived that acting according to the general will was virtuous:[55] but it was his application of the concept to politics that was striking.

For Rousseau meant to transpose his attitude to inequality from a critical to a constructive key. He had diagnosed inequality as a central constituent in the malaise of modern society. He meant to show how a rather better society could be constructed, one which avoided what he took to be the core of inequality, namely undue distinctions between persons and the dependence of one person upon another. That is to say, Rousseau sought a situation in which people would be treated in an identical manner and one in which personal dependence was not possible. Let us look first at identity of treatment.

Beginning with matters of institutional form, we find that the political body that Rousseau conceived to bear the general will had an unusual character. To understand that character we should adduce the requirements for fulfilling the general will. If we take it that each person should be treated in the same manner as the next, *ceteris paribus*, and wish to move to Rousseau's position that people *are* to be treated in the same manner, we must fill out the *ceteris paribus* clause in a way that admits of no difference amongst the people under consideration. This implies, amongst other things, that they must be juridically equal. How as Rousseau to satisfy this condition? He thought that people were not equal in terms of strength and other natural endowments, and was painfully aware that they did not all have the same status in modern society. Neither of these could provide the means of satisfying Rousseau's requirements. Hence people would have to *acquire* equality of standing.

This acquisition was provided for through Rousseau's conception of the political body. Rousseau supposed that people would *place* themselves upon a footing of equality. This was achieved by each agent totally alienating his person and his rights. A *total* renunciation was necessary, for prior to it people were unequal in various ways and to reserve something might perpetuate that condition. Hence the foundation of a body capable of bearing the general will was 'the total alienation of each associate and all his rights', 'for ... each giving himself entirely, the condition is the same for all'.[56] That is to say, people set themselves all on the same footing.

But to what did they alienate themselves and their rights? It may sound as if people created a body, rather like Hobbes's, which was endowed with all of their attributes. So it was, but the crucial question was the composition of this body. With Hobbes the sovereign was juridically distinct from the agents that created it: they transferred rights to it. With Rousseau the sovereign body was composed of those who created it.[57] They alienated their persons and rights to a body whose members they became. Indeed it is in precisely this act that we can locate their equal standing: people placed themselves on the same footing *as* members of the body, as citizens. To put the matter another way, Rousseau conceived people as equal because he identified sovereignty with citizenship. This may seem an excessively simple move, but great intellectual innovation is often distinguished by a masterly simplicity.

Thus people obtained an equal status. But we may ask how they were able to do so? Rousseau assumed that nature did not imply the subordination of one to another. His account here, as in his second discourse, transformed the resources of preceding speculation, this time those of absolutism. Neither parentage nor force provided a title to direct others, he thought, thus bypassing Filmer and Hobbes respectively.[58] On the contrary, the make of nature suggested that each agent was concerned for *self*-preservation and therefore that it was appropriate to exercise his or her capacity for self-direction, including free will. Of course, the quest for self-protection might be supposed to lead to subordinating oneself to another person without reservation. Grotius (amongst others) had conceived this. Rousseau rejected the suggestion, like Locke before him, but for a different reason. Where Locke had supposed that people were bound to do God's will, Rousseau argued that to be free was integral to being a moral agent and therefore freedom could not be surrendered.[59] At any rate, it is evident that people would be free to create a body politic.

Rousseau's suggestion that freedom could not be surrendered raises questions about the advantages of his political exercise. Did not setting up a sovereign involve a total surrender of person and rights? It did, but the process produced corresponding advantages, including a freedom more extensive than the one enjoyed previously.

Rousseau continued to argue through self-preservation. He supposed that people's chief means to this goal lay with their force and their freedom. Agreeing with preceding thought for once, Rousseau saw co-operation as a means of increasing the force on which each individual could call. But what of liberty? Rousseau indicated that the question was how to reconcile the advantages of co-operation with the continuance of self-direction. His answer was that in his political body the latter would continue through what he termed conventional liberty, notwithstanding that natural liberty would be surrendered.[60]

This requires some explanation. Had each agent not surrendered his or her means of independence to the sovereign? They had; and freedom in the sense of independence, therefore, was gone. But in a body answering to the general will there arose conventional or civil liberty. This was a condition in which no agent was dependent on another. For the direction of such a community came from rules that accorded with the general will: that is to say from rules treating each person's interests with the same consideration as the next's. It follows that under this scheme of justice or equal dealing no agent's liberty would be defined in a way that conflicted with another's or with another's interests. But why should liberty on this model be an advantageous exchange for the independence given to people by their natural powers? The answer is that Rousseau supposed that people by nature were entitled to whatever they could get. This neo-Hobbesian supposition, it scarcely needs saying, rather suggests that in this condition life would not be very tolerable and it was rational to institute political order – a point Rousseau himself made.[61] Hence it was worthwhile to exchange an insecure independence for a protected liberty. Rousseau suggested in his *Letters from the Mountain* that it was misleading to 'confuse independence and liberty. These two things are so different that they exclude each other', he continued: that was to say that, 'liberty consists less in doing one's own will than in not being subject to another's' and that 'in the shared liberty no one has a right to do what the liberty of another forbids him to do'. Hence liberty implied the presence of the general will, 'liberty without justice is a veritable contradiction'.[62] Civil liberty meant a liberty prescribed by the measure of justice contained in the general will.

In Rousseau's political body the possibility of personal dependence was removed. For man became more fully master of himself in a political condition. In the first place he was released from direction by his appetites. For though not directed by another people, natural man was dependent on nature, being moved by appetites and instincts. Another direction succeeded, for, in the second place, though no longer independent, he was dependent on laws prescribed by the general will. Third, to depend on such laws was preferable to depending on other people. Rousseau believed that dependence on persons was dangerous. For it was not regulated by any moral norm and so admitted vagaries of conduct. As he put the matter in *Emile*:

> There are two kinds of dependence: dependence on things, which belongs to nature; dependence of men, which belongs to society. Dependence on things, having no morality, is not harmful to freedom and does not engender vices; dependence on men, being uncontrolled, engenders them all, and it is through this dependence that master and slave become mutually depraved. If there is some means of curing this evil in society, it is through substituting law for men,

and more precisely by substituting laws founded on the general will.[63] Fourth, direction by the general will to Rousseau's mind meant direction by self-legislated measures. Thus, guided by the general will the agent was directed by morality and by himself, rather than by nature and by other people. As master of himself in this way, he was genuinely free.

Much else could be said about *The Social Contract* which only considerations of space prevent. But one matter requires attention. That is Rousseau's civil religion. This cult would propound a doctrine which, without prejudicing other beliefs consistent with it, was meant to reinforce the political body by teaching congruent with the activity and the regard for others implied in the general will. This was to be contrasted with Christian doctrine, which for Rousseau preached patience and indifference to the world, as well as drawing people's allegiance away from their proper loyalty to the state.[64] If Rousseau had studied Burke as Burke had studied him he would have discovered that

Christian belief might match the sort of unequal order that *The Social Contract* was meant to supersede.

❧ V ❧

Burke's views had dwelt on inequality in manifold forms. He had begun by emphasizing the importance of revelation, which was a message distributed unevenly. He had developed a view of man which stated that the inequality between leaders and followers was natural. Social hierarchy, property and government too stood on an unequal basis. The bearers of social and religious inequality, aristocracy and church, had achieved liberty and improvement for England in the Middle Ages. After nearly twenty-five years in Parliament Burke held that good government was still secured by some of the bearers of inequality. So when the French Revolution came it touched a live nerve. For Burke a movement which made *égalité* its watchword implied the destruction of the conditions on which society existed and prospered. To his mind it would involve not merely the destruction of legal privilege but the destruction of inequality in society and everything which went with it.

Burke believed that 'the true actuating spirit' of 'the whole' of the initial policies of the Revolution belonged to 'a cabal'. The character of the cabal, that it had the pretension of 'calling itself philosophic',[65] is a hint to what he thought he saw was the spirit of the revolutionaries, namely that they were deists or, as Burke preferred to insinuate, atheists:

> It is not with you composed of those men, is it? whom the vulgar, in their blunt, homely style, commonly call Atheists and Infidels? If it be, I admit that we too have had writers of that description, who made some noise in their day. At present they repose in lasting oblivion. Who, born within the last forty years, has read one word of Colins, and Toland, and Tindal, and Chubb, and Morgan, and that whole race who called themselves Freethinkers? Who now reads Bolingbroke? Who ever read him through?

The destruction of inequality would be a congenial task for the enemies of revelation to Burke's way of thinking.

To whom did Burke suppose the revolutionaries looked for inspiration, apart from deism? They were alleged to have taken for their 'canon of holy writ', 'standard figure of perfection' and 'pattern' Rousseau.[65] In Rousseau Burke had early found a great challenge to social inequality and to society itself.

The forces Burke had conceived early in life as the enemies of revealed religion and civil society respectively were now combined. Deism had no use for revealed theology. The civil society which Burke recognized revealed theology to need in order to perfect man's condition was the object of Rousseau's enmity. So Rousseau and the deists appeared to him as alike parts of a pattern of rejection of God's will. With God's will went the order of modern Europe which embodied the conditions on which progressive civilization was to be had. In other words revealed theology and social inequality or, as Burke said, 'the spirit of religion' and 'the spirit of a gentleman', stood or fell together.

Reflections on the Revolution in France divides into two parts, arranged in dramatic contrast with one another. The first contains an account of a properly regulated society, interwoven with a description of the attack upon it. It displays a providential order. The succeeding part provides a sharp contrast, dwelling on the results of working by human foresight alone – inadequacy. The inadequate nature of the revolutionary institutions is underlined by an appreciation of British recognition of mankind's limitations and proper reliance on God. The divine order and its opposite stand in pointed contrast.

The French Revolution was the worst of nightmares for Burke. The programme he attributed to it implied the destruction of everything he thought valuable in society. Yet by the same token it was the greatest opportunity to expound his views. It had never before fallen to him to deploy his political opinions in concentrated form. Are those views eccentric? All interesting political theory makes connections others have overlooked. This prize is likely to fall to one whose stance is out of the ordinary. Burke's point of view, formed, we have seen, out of an amalgam of inequalities, was the fruit of a particular origin and experience. No doubt Burke's perspective is unusual, as is Rousseau's in a different way, but one of the objects of historical study is to explain how unusual doctrines are natural enough to their creators.

❧ NOTES ❧

1 Convenient but hard to translate into English. Whilst the latin *mores* is a good equivalent it has become a term of sociological art; *manners* has connotations of politeness; *morals* connotes ethical distinctions. *Moeurs* suggests something that is embodied in conduct and in institutions.

2 See [14.55] for a closely observed account of Hutcheson's ethics and the place of reason in them.

3 [4.6], II.vi.58: 324.

4 [14.36], 9.

5 See Burke's 'Extempore Commonplace on our Saviour's Sermon on the Mount' in [14.27], 3; *The Reformer* no. 11 (7 April 1748) in [14.26] p. 324.

(Dates for British and Irish events before Lord Chesterfield's Act are given according to the old style, but with the year beginning on 1 January).

6 *The Reformer* no.1 (28.1.1748), in [14.26], 297.

7 *Minute Book* (26.5.1747) of Trinity College debating society, [14.26], 248; *Minute Book* (2.6.1747), *ibid.* (3.7.1747), *The Reformer* no. 7 (10.3.1748) in [14.26], 263, 289, 317.

8 [14.27], 3.

9 *The Reformer* no. 11 (7.4.1748), [14.26], 323.

10 Cf. *Speech on Toleration Bill, 17th March 1773*, [14.18], ii: 387f.

11 [14.18], ii: 389.

12 [14.25], 185f.

13 Bolingbroke, [14.31], v: 414, 'The truth is that we have not in philosophical speculation, in any history except that of the Bible, nor in our own experience, sufficient grounds to establish the doctrine of particular providences'.

14 For the Dijon Academy and the circumstances of the 1750 competition, see [14.37].

15 [14.2], pt i in [14.1], iii: 9. I have not relied implicitly on any particular translation of Rousseau and have made my own renderings where it seemed needful, but the reader will recognize an extensive debt to those listed in the bibliography (see [14.9–15]).

15 [14.2], pt i in [14.1], iii: 17, 25.

16 See for the whole line of thought the concise statement of [14.34], in [14.35]:

> the end for which men enter into society, is not barely to live ... but to live happily; and a Life answerable to the dignity and excellency of their kind. Out of society, this happiness is not to be had, for singly we are impotent, and defective, unable to procure those things that are either of necessity, or Ornament for our lives, and so unable to defend and keep them when they are acquired. To remedy these defects, we Associate together that what we can neither joy nor keep, singly, by mutual benefits and assistances one of another, We may be able to do both ... That ... by which we accomplish the ends of a Sociable life, is our subjection, and submission to Laws, these are the Nerves and Sinews of every Society or Common-wealth.

17 Immanuel Kant, *Ideas for a Universal History with Cosmopolitan Purpose*, 4th proposition in [14.33], 44f.

18 [14.3], pt i in [14.1], iii: esp. 135–40.

19 [14.3], preamble to pt i, [14.1], iii: 132f.

20 [14.3], preface and pt i, [14.1], iii: 126, 155f.

21 *amour propre* in Rousseau's vocabulary.

22 [14.3] dedication, pt i, pt ii; [14.1], iii: 111, 162, 171.

23 [14.3], pt ii, in [14.1], iii: 192f.

24 Ibid.

25 [14.3], i: ix n., [14.1], iii: 206.

26 [14.21] in [14.19], iv: 298.

27 For Johnson, see [14.32], 405, 30 September 1769.

28 *The Reformer*, [14.26], 298.

29 [14.20], [14.19], i: 8, 22. For a convincing array of parallels see [14.56], 97–114.

30 *The Reformer*, [14.26], 315, 316.
31 [14.24] (since the text is the same in both editions of [14.24], it is cited here only by book and chapter number), I.xii, xiii, xvi, xvii.
32 [14.24], I.xvii.
33 [14.25], 196f.
34 [14.22] in [14.19], v: 101.
35 'Religion', [14.27], p. 82.
36 *The Reformer* (10 March 1748) in [14.26], 314–17; 'Thoughts and Details on Scarcity' (written 1795), [14.19], vi: 4, 9, 11; [14.25], 372.
37 [14.25], 189.
38 [14.31], especially *A Dissertation on Parties*, letter xvi; *Remarks on the History of England*, letter iv; *Letters on the Study and Use of History*, nos v and vi.
39 [14.23] esp. I.ii, II.i-ii, vii; III.iii, viii, [14.25], 172.
40 [14.23], III.i.
41 [14.25], 170.
42 [14.23], III.i.
43 [14.25], 199.
44 [14.23], III.viii.
45 [14.25], 173.
46 [14.25], 193, on the 'defects, redundancies and errors' of existing jurisprudence; p. 141 on 'hereditary wealth, and the rank which goes with it, are too much idolized by creeping sycophants'; p. 197 on 'the wealth and pride of individuals at every moment makes the man of humble rank and fortune sensible of his inferiority, and degrades and vilifies his condition'; p. 372 on the 'body of the people' who 'must respect that property of which they cannot partake'.
47 That is a standard, see [14.6] in [14.1], iv: 836f.
48 For Rousseau's larger design, see [14.7], ch. x ([14.1], i: 516) and [14.6], ch. v ([14.1], iv: 836–49).
49 [14.4], [14.1], iii: 245; cf. [14.5], II.iii ([14.1], iii: 371); [14.5], IV.i ([14.1], iii: 437).
50 [14.5], II.iv, [14.1], iii: 374.
51 [14.4], [14.1], iii: 251.
52 [14.8], no. 9, [14.1], iii: 891.
53 [14.5], III.ii, [14.1], iii: 400. cf. [14.5], I.vii, [14.1], iii: 383 and [14.6], ch. v, [14.1], iv: 843.
54 For Rousseau's views on ethics, note his view that 'La grande Société, la Société humaine en général, est fondée sur l'humanité, sur la bienfaisance universelle', letter to Leonhard Usteri, 18 June 1763 no. 2825 in [14.16], xvii: 63, and for a qualification see [14.8], no. 1, [14.1], iii: 706.
55 [14.4], [14.1], iii: 252.
56 [14.5], I.vi, [14.1], iii: 361. The distinction of private and public will be found in [14.6], II.xiii.151: 386.
57 [14.5], OC, iii: 361f.
58 [14.5], I.ii-iii, 14.1 iii 352–5; for Hobbes and Filmer, see 'Locke's Political Theory' ch. 4, supra, pp. 97, 117; [14.5], I.iv, [14.1], iii: 352.
59 [14.5], I.iv, cf. [4.6], II.ii-iv; for all this see 'Locke's Political Theory', pp. 106–8.
60 [14.5], I.vi, [14.1], iii: 360.
61 [14.5], I.vi, [14.1], iii: 360f.

62 [14.8], no. 8, [14.1], iii: 841–2.

63 [14.6], ii, [14.1], iv: 311.

64 [14.5], IV.viii, [14.1], iii: 460–9; for Rousseau's view of religion more generally, see the texts assembled in [14.13] and for commentaries see [14.34] and [14.37].

65 [14.25], 185, [14.21], in [14.19], iv: 297. Cf. [14.25], 181.

❧ BIBLIOGRAPHY ❧

Primary Works

(i) Rousseau

All Rousseau's works cited here will be found in

14.1 *Oeuvres Complètes de Jean-Jacques Rousseau*, ed. B. Gagnebin and M. Raymond, 4 vols, Paris, Bibliothèque de la Pleiade, 1959–69. The most important texts for our purposes are 14.2–14.8:

14.2 *Discours sur les sciences et les arts*

14.3 *Discours sur ... l'inégalité*

14.4 *Discours sur l'économie politique*

14.5 *Du contrat social*

14.6 *Emile*

14.7 *Confessions*

14.8 *Lettres écrites de la montagne*. Helpful translations include.

14.9 *The Social Contract and Discourses*, trans. G. D. H. Cole, London, Dent, 1913. revised J. H. Brumfitt and J. C. Hall, London, 1973.

14.10 *First and Second Discourse*, trans. V. Gourevitch, New York, Harcourt Brace, 1986.

14.11 *The Social Contract*, trans. M. Cranston, Harmondsworth, Penguin, 1968. Other relevant texts by Rousseau include:

14.12 *Rousseau on International Affairs*, ed. S. Hoffman, and D. Fidler, Oxford, Oxford University Press, 1991.

14.13 *Religious Writings*, ed. R. Grimsley, Oxford, Oxford University Press, 1970.

14.14 *Reveries*, trans. P. France, Harmondsworth, Penguin, 1982.

14.15 *Lettre à D'Alembert*, trans. A. Bloom as Politics and the Arts, Glencoe, Free Press, 1960.

His letters have been printed as

14.16 *Correspondence Complète*, ed. R. A. Leigh *et al.*, 50 vols, Geneva and Oxford, Institut et Musée Voltaire, the Voltaire Foundation, 1965–91.

(ii) Burke

14.17 *A Notebook of Edmund Burke*, ed. H. V. F. Somerset, Cambridge, Cambridge University Press, 1957.

14.18 *The Writings and Speeches of Edmund Burke*, ed. P. Langford, *et al.*, 5 vols so far, Oxford, Oxford University Press, 1981–. For works yet to appear in this edition, see

14.19 *Works*, 6 vols, Oxford, Oxford University Press, 1906–7. This includes 14.20–14.22:

14.20 *A Vindication of Natural Society*

14.21 *A Letter to a member of the National Assembly*

14.22 *An Appeal from the New to the Old Whigs*

14.23 *An Abridgement of English History.* Helpful editions include

14.24 Boulton, J. T. (ed.) *A Philosophical Enquiry into the Origin of our Ideas of the Sublime and Beautiful*, London, Routledge and Kegan Paul, 1958; 2nd edn, Oxford, Oxford University Press, 1986.

14.25 O'Brien, C. C. (ed.) *Reflections on the Revolution in France*, Harmondsworth, Penguin, 1968. Burke's early writings are printed in

14.26 Samuels, A. P. I. *The Early Life, Correspondence and Writings of . . . Edmund Burke*, Cambridge, Cambridge University Press, 1923. See also

14.27 Harris, I. (ed.) *Edmund Burke: Pre-Revolutionary Writings*, Cambridge, Cambridge University Press, 1993. Burke's letters are printed in

14.28 Copeland, T. W. *et al.* (eds) *The Correspondence of Edmund Burke*, 10 vols, Cambridge, Cambridge University Press, 1958–78.

Bibliographies of Primary Works

14.29 Todd, W. B. *Edmund Burke*, London, Hart-Davis, 1964.

14.30 McEachern, J.-A. E. *Bibliography of the writings of Jean-Jacques Rousseau to 1800*, Oxford, Oxford University Press, 1989.

(iii) Other Primary Sources

14.31 St John, Henry, Viscount Bolingbroke *Works*, 6 vols, London, 1754.

14.32 Boswell, James, *Life of Johnson*, ed. R. W. Chambers, rev. J. D. Fleeman, Oxford, Oxford University Press, 1970.

14.33 Kant, Immanuel *Political Writings*, trans. H. B. Nisbet, 2nd edn, Cambridge, Cambridge University Press, 1989.

14.34 [Sexby, Edward] *Killing No Murder*, n.p., 1657, published in:

14.35 Ward, A. C. (ed.) *A miscellany of Tracts and Pamphlets*, Oxford, Oxford University Press, 1927.

14.36 Wallace, Robert, *Ignorance and Superstition a Source of Violence and Cruelty*, Edinburgh, 1746.

Secondary Writings

Helpful works about our subjects and related matters include:

14.37 Bouchard, M. *L'Académie de Dijon et le premier Discours de Rousseau*, Dijon, Université de Dijon, 1950.

14.38 Cameron, D. R. *The Social Thought of Rousseau and Burke*, London, Weidenfeld and Nicolson, 1973.

14.39 Canavan, F. P. *The Political Reason of Edmund Burke*, Durham, Duke University Press, 1963.

14.40 Chapman, G. *Edmund Burke: the practical imagination*, London, Harvard University Press, 1967.

14.41 Davy, G. *Thomas Hobbes et Rousseau*, Oxford, Oxford University Press, 1952.

14.42 Dérathé, R. *Rousseau et la science politique de son temps*, Paris, Presses Universitaires de France, 1950.

14.43 Dreyer, F. A. *Burke: A study in Whig Orthodoxy*, Waterloo, Ontario, Wilfred Laurier University Press, 1979.

14.44 Grimsley, R. *Rousseau and the Religious Quest*, Oxford, Oxford University Press, 1968.

14.45 *Rousseau*, Brighton, Harvester Press, 1983.

14.46 Leigh, R. A. 'Liberté et autorité dans le *Contrat social*' in *Rousseau et son temps: Problèmes et recherches*, Paris, Vrin, 1964, pp. 231–47.

14.47 *Rousseau and the Problem of Toleration*, Oxford, Oxford University Press, 1978.

14.48 MacCunn, J. *The Political Philosophy of Burke*, London, Edward Arnold, 1913.

14.49 Morley, J. *Burke: a critical study*, London, Macmillan, 1867.

14.50 Plamenatz, J. P. ' "Ce qui ne signifie pas autre chose, sinon qu'on le forcera d'être libre". A commentary', *Annales de philosophie politique* 5(1965): 137–52.

14.51 Pocock, J. G. A. *Politics, Language and Time*, London, Methuen, 1972.

14.52 *Virtue, Commerce and History*, Cambridge, Cambridge University Press, 1985.

14.53 Riley, P. *The General Will before Rousseau*, Princeton, Princeton University Press, 1986.

14.54 *Will and Political Legitimacy*, Harvard, Harvard University Press, 1982.

14.55 Scott, W. R. *Francis Hutcheson*, Cambridge, Cambridge University Press, 1900.

14.56 Sewell jr, R. B. 'Rousseau's Second Discourse in England, 1755 to 1762', *Philological Quarterly* 17(1938): 97–114.

14.57 Starobinski, J. *Jean-Jacques Rousseau*, London, Chicago University Press, 1988.

14.58 Talmon, J. L. *The Origins of Totalitarian Democracy*, London, Secker & Warburg, 1952.

14.59 Tisserand, R. *Les concurrents de J. J. Rousseau à l'Academie de Dijon pour le prix de 1754*, Paris, Flammarion, 1936.

14.60 Toulmin, S. *An Examination of the Place of Reason in Ethics*, Cambridge, Cambridge University Press, 1950.

14.61 *Annales de la société Jean-Jacques Rousseau*,

14.62 *Studies in Burke and his Time* (formerly *The Burke Newsletter*), as their titles suggest, have carried numerous essays on our subjects.

Glossary

absolutism: (a) In political philosophy, an 'absolute' government is one whose rule is subject to no (human) restraint, for instance by a parliament or a constitution, and answerable (if at all) only to God. Contrasted with 'bounded' government (q.v.). (b) Elsewhere 'absolutism' is contrasted with some form of 'relativism'. For instance an absolutist about space will hold that it exists independently of matter.

a posteriori: what is knowable, if at all, through experience. Contrasted with 'a priori' (q.v.).

a priori: what is known, if at all, independently of experience. Contrasted with 'a posteriori' (q.v.).

bounded government: bounded government is government that is limited by human laws. Belief in bounded government is contrasted with 'absolutism' (q.v.).

Cabala: literally 'tradition', specifically an esoteric tradition of interpreting Scripture supposed to have been handed down in secret by Moses to certain select disciples and by them in turn. There was considerable Christian interest in the Cabala during the Renaissance and, though it was discouraged by the Catholic Reformation, this continued to be expressed by Neoplatonists in Protestant countries into the eighteenth century.

Calvinism: the theology of the French Protestant theologian John Calvin (1509–64) which was influential in England in the seventeenth century and in Scotland throughout the period covered by this volume. Calvin subscribed to an austere doctrine of predestination according to which the future salvation or damnation of any individual soul has been predetermined for all time. The Calvinistic emphasis on the corruption of human nature led to a stress on faith rather than fallible human reason. It was opposed by those who believed in natural theology or rational religion.

Cartesianism: the doctrines associated with the philosophy of René Descartes: especially, in the context of this volume, the belief that events in the natural world are determined by invariant mechanical laws. Descartes claimed to know a priori that the essence of matter consisted in extension and Cartesianism was associated with a physics that was partly a priori. Descartes's radical separation of the material world from that of the mind and his endorsement of innate ideas encouraged some to interpret him as sympathetic to Christian Platonism.

cause: a cause has often been understood to mean that, in the presence of which some event *must* occur. If, however, this means that there would be a contradiction in supposing that the cause occurred but not its effect, it seems there

379

are few causes in this sense. As the occasionalists (q.v.) recognized it was only in the case of God willing something to happen that there would be a contradiction (since God is by definition omnipotent) in supposing it not to happen. From this it seems as if a natural cause is nothing more than a phenomenon that is regularly found to be followed by events of the kind in question. Empiricist (q.v.) accounts of causation stress this regularity or, in Hume's phrase, 'constant conjunction'.

certainty, moral: what is morally certain had the highest degree of probability and is certain for the purposes of practical life. It is distinguished from theoretical certainty or *scientia*. (q.v.)

common notions: these are notions that are universally imprinted on humans and make possible a universal consent to certain propositions. The existence of such notions was a matter of controversy during the period covered by this volume. See 'innate ideas'.

consensus gentium: a mode of argument for the truth of a proposition from the existence of universal consent to it. This mode of argument was attractive to those who believed in common notions (q.v.).

constructivism: opposed, for example to realism in mathematics, those who hold this view argue that truths are not so much discovered as constructed. This view was advocated by Vico. See Chapter 13.

contract, original: the obligation to obey the ruler was supposed by some theorists to be based upon a contract made at the founding of political society. In return for the promise of the people to obey the sovereign, the ruler undertook for his part to protect the people and their rights.

contradiction, principle of: every self-contradictory statement must be false and its denial must be true.

corpuscular philosophy: the view, associated with Gassendi, Boyle and Locke, that the world is made up of tiny particles of matter.

correspondence theory of truth: the theory that a proposition is true if, and only if, there is some (corresponding) state of affairs or set of facts in the objective world in virtue of which it is so.

deism: a point of view embracing belief in a Creator but hostile to revealed religion. Deists characteristically disbelieved in miracles and tended to be anti-clerical. Though they sometimes believed in a general Providence and even in a deity who punishes the wicked and rewards the virtuous, they did not regard the sacraments as necessary to salvation.

demonstration: a logical term for an argument whose conclusion follows from its premises, i.e. where it would be inconsistent to accept the premises and reject the conclusion. Demonstrations, so defined, have been admired as the strongest possible form of argument. Deductive logic is concerned with valid forms of demonstrative or deductive inference.

deontology: the science of duty, usually associated with the view that we are bound by certain absolute duties, which we can know, and which are not affected by circumstances.

design, argument from: an argument based upon the orderliness observed in nature which is intended to establish the existence of an intelligent and purposive cause of the natural world. This argument became very popular in the eighteenth century, though it was severely criticized in Hume's *Dialogues Concerning Natural Religion*.

determinism: the view that every event (including every human action) has a cause and that there is no chance in the universe. Determinists usually interpret the existence of a cause as meaning the event could not fail to occur and that human actions, when caused, are not 'free'. Some determinists, however, have claimed not to deny free will and have maintained, on the contrary, that the absence of a cause of a human action would bring free will into question in a way that the presence of a cause does not.

divine right (of kings): an absolutist (q.v.) doctrine according to which kings are appointed by God and are not answerable to their people for their actions.

eclecticism: a term used of the tendency of some philosophers to take elements from several different sects or schools rather than adhere consistently to a single one. Eclectics are usually liberal and anti-sectarian.

egoism, ethical: the view that what I morally ought to do is to promote my own interests.

egoism, psychological: a theory according to which individuals are motivated to action only by concern for their own interests.

egoism, rational: the view that I only have good reason to do those actions which promote my own interests.

emanation: a characteristically Neoplatonic (q.v.) doctrine in which the world is conceived as a kind of over-flowing of the divine nature. Everything that is of the spirit, comes from the divine light, thus emanates from God. Evil is simply the privation of this and so is present in anything which is not pure divinity. Evil and good, darkness and light, matter and spirit, passivity and activity, are all treated in analogous ways. So the material world, though it is fundamentally spirit-like, was conceived as having fallen into a torpid state from which, according to some, it will eventually be restored to its true nature.

empiricism: the view that all our knowledge about the nature of things is derived from experience. Usually contrasted with rationalism (q.v.).

Enlightenment: the name given to a period in European history which was marked by an emphasis on reason and a distrust of mystery and authority. Though there were many connections across national boundaries, the circumstances of the intellectual élite in each country were different and so what may be true of the Enlightenment in one country may not be in another.

epistemology: theory of knowledge. Concern with the nature of human knowledge and its limitations became, as a result of Locke's *Essay*, a major concern of eighteenth-century philosophy.

fideism: from the Latin word for 'faith', this term is used to refer to the view that there is no basis in reason for religion and that its basis can only be that of faith.

final cause: that for the sake of which something is done. In that sense the final cause or 'end' of taking exercise may be health. The term goes back to Aristotle. According to the mechanical philosophy final causes were not to be used in physics.

form, substantial: a scholastic (q.v.) term deriving ultimately from Aristotle. The substantial form of a thing is what makes it the kind of thing it is. Any change in the state of a thing which is not caused externally is referred to its substantial form.

general will: a term of French social thought, signifying the collective will of society or the will of an individual insofar as that person is public-spirited. The term is probably theological in origin, deriving from a contrast between God's general will (which results, for example in the laws of nature) and His particular wills (on specified occasions, for example in performing a miracle). As applied to individual humans a general will contrasts with a self-regarding 'particular will'.

gnoseology: another term for epistemology (q.v.).

hedonism: the view that pleasure is the greatest good.

hedonism, psychological: a theory according to which human beings are primarily motivated by the prospect of their own pleasure.

humanism (Renaissance): the movement is associated with the *studia humanitatis* and with promoting the 'humanities' through the recovery and establishment of the classical texts – particularly of ancient Roman but also of Greek authors. The humanities, so understood, included grammar, rhetoric, poetics, moral philosophy and history. Humanists were opposed to the scholastic curricula which predominated in universities until the end of the seventeenth century. But their ideas influenced the education of the aristocratic laity and remained influential throughout our period.

humanism (Erasmian): usually associated with the project of applying humanistic disciplines to the texts of the Bible. This was opposed, on the one hand, to the authoritarian view that the Bible meant what the Church determined that it meant and, on the other hand, to the subjective interpretations of 'enthusiasts'. Erasmian humanism may be seen as paving the way for the more rational approaches to religion that emerged in the seventeenth century.

idea: the term originates with Plato for whom the ideas or forms constituted a transcendent realm of archetypes. Christian Platonists located these ideas in the mind of God. Descartes extended this use to allow that the human mind is also furnished with 'ideas' and the use of the term to refer to what is before our minds when we think, imagine, dream, etc., became established in the writings of later philosophers, such as Locke and Berkeley.

idealist: originally contrasted with 'materialist' and used of philosophers such as Plato, the term is readily applicable to philosophers like Berkeley who denied the existence of 'matter' and who affirmed that the sensible world was dependent on (the divine) mind. It was not until after Kant that 'idealist' came to be contrasted with 'realist' and to be associated with the view that the physical world is in some way the product of (the human) mind.

indiscernibles, identity of: a principle of Leibniz's, that there are no two things in the universe that differ only numerically, hence if A and B are exactly alike then A is identical with B. Leibniz inferred this principle from the principle of sufficient reason (q.v.) since God could have no reason to create A and B as separate individuals.

induction: a process of arguing from particulars to an a posteriori (q.v.) conclusion, characteristically a statement about the future, a generalization or a claim about an unobserved member of a class.

innate ideas: these are ideas (such as the idea of God) with which human beings were supposed to have been born and in virtue of which they are able to have a priori knowledge of how things are. Locke's *Essay* played an important part in bringing innate ideas into disfavour during the eighteenth century and in encouraging explanations of ideas in terms of origins in sense experience.

intuition/intuitive knowledge: commonly regarded as the highest form of knowledge by seventeenth-century philosophers, intuitive knowledge involves a total understanding of why something that is so, has to be so. This kind of knowledge, rare in humans, was thought to be characteristic of God's knowledge of the world. See also under *scientia*.

materialism: the view that the basic metaphysical entities of the universe are material and that there is no independent world of mind or spirit. Hobbes and Spinoza were read as materialists, Locke was suspected of it and a number of the French *philosophes* openly advocated materialism.

mechanical philosophy: the view that all the interactions in the physical universe are to be understood as like the interactions of parts of a mechanism such as a clock. Advocates of the mechanical philosophy rejected explanations in terms of 'occult qualities' (q.v.) or unintelligible 'influences'. Their rejection of action 'at a distance' led the mechanical philosophers to develop their own theories of gravitation, magnetic attraction, etc. They also rejected the use of final causes in physics.

metaphysics: as used in this volume, the supposed a priori (q.v.) science of what really exists. Metaphysics goes beyond what can be discovered by the empirical sciences. It purports to demonstrate, for instance, the immortality of the soul or the existence of God and perhaps even the nature of a 'hidden' world beyond the world of phenomena. What is generally called 'rationalism' (q.v.) by philosophers is favourable to metaphysics, whereas empiricism (q.v.) is generally anti-metaphysical.

microcosm/macrocosm: the view that Man is a microcosm of the Cosmos (the macrocosm) was quite widely held in the sixteenth century and persisted through the seventeenth. It is associated with Renaissance Neoplatonism (q.v.) and had a range of applications from design to medicine. In a scientific context it assumed interactions that were excluded by the mechanical philosophy (q.v.).

monad: Neoplatonic term for 'one'. In the seventeenth century some Neoplatonists used the term 'monad' to describe the equivalent in their system of atoms in materialistic systems. Their monads were, however, never merely material and were sometimes conceived of (for example by Leibniz) as essentially non-extended, albeit always having some connection to matter.

moral sense (theory): the view that the ability of human beings to distinguish right from wrong depends, not on their reason, but on the fact that they are disposed to find certain actions (and characters) pleasing and others displeasing.

naturalism: a word with a wide range of variously related meanings but used in this volume (in connection with Hume) to refer to the view that our beliefs are arrived at by natural processes rather than by the operation of abstract Reason.

natural law: a moral code, laid down by God but based on created human nature, for instance on the urge for self preservation and the need to live in society. Natural law was supposed to be known through human reason.

Neoplatonism: this term is used in the first place of the revival of an eclectic Platonism between the third and sixth centuries AD. The most important figure of this movement was Plotinus. During the Renaissance there was a revival of this Neoplatonism when Ficino produced Latin editions from Plato, Plotinus and others. See Vol. IV in this series, pp. 25–36.

occasionalism: a theory according to which God is the only true cause, hence that the apparent causes of the changes in the world should be regarded as no more than 'occasions' for God's acting to bring the changes about. On this view we should not say, strictly speaking, that striking a match is the cause of its lighting but that it is the 'occasion' on which God causes the match to light. See Vol. IV in this series, Ch. 10.

occult qualities: scholastic philosophers regarded certain qualities such as attraction as 'occult'. Adherents of the mechanical philosophy sought to do away with such 'occult qualities' and the phrase became, for them, a term of abuse.

ontological argument: one kind of argument for the existence of God, according to a classification that derives from Kant. Such arguments begin with a premiss about the nature or essence of God or definition of 'God' and seek to demonstrate that such a being must exist. Some of these arguments are still found impressive, as they were by Descartes, Spinoza and Leibniz. Such a priori arguments were not in favour in the eighteenth century, however, when the argument from design (q.v.) became the main argument used to support belief in God.

parsimony, principle of: the principle that, other things being equal, simpler hypotheses should be preferred to more complex ones.

peripatetics: Aristotle was reputed to have walked around whilst lecturing and the term 'peripatetics' (literally, 'those who walk round and round') came to be used in an uncomplimentary way of his followers, eventually of the scholastics (q.v.).

philosophe: French word for 'philosopher' but used especially of the intellectual figures of the French Enlightenment.

philosophia perennis: literally 'perennial philosophy'. It is a reference to that body of ancient wisdom in which Renaissance philosophers believed and which they sought to revive. See also under *prisca theologia*.

pietism: a devotional movement within the Lutheran Church in Germany. Founded by P. J. Spener (1635–1705), pietism encouraged Bible Study and advocated love rather than argument in dealing with dissenters and unbelievers.

positivism: the view that there is no knowledge to be obtained of the nature of things except by following the methods of the natural sciences.

predestinarianism: the theological theory that each individual's capacity for good or ill (and destiny of salvation or damnation) is totally dependent upon a divine grace whose distribution has been determined for all eternity. This theory is part and parcel of the Calvinist (q.v.) view of human nature as wholly 'fallen' and corrupt. It was opposed by those who thought human nature was basically good, as for instance did the Cambridge Platonists.

pre-established harmony: Leibniz, like the occasionalists, rejected the idea of an external causal action by one substance on another. He proposed instead that each substance had been so designed from the Creation that everything that would happen to it would emerge spontaneously from its own 'nature' but in perfect harmony with what was taking place in other substances. Leibniz himself referred to his proposal as a 'hypothesis' or, more commonly, as his 'system' of 'pre-established harmony'.

premiss: a logical term for a proposition put forward at the beginning of an argument, particularly in a formal demonstration (q.v.).

prisca theologia: literally 'ancient theology'. Renaissance Neoplatonists such as Ficino sought to recover the wisdom of ancient sages such as Hermes Trismegistus (a legendary Egyptian priest), Zoroaster and Orpheus. They assumed that the thoughts of the ancient theologians were harmonious with one another and with both Platonism and Christianity.

qualities, primary and secondary: an old distinction certain seventeenth-century philosophers took over in order to separate those qualities of bodies that were essential from those that were not. The exact formulation of the distinction varied and was controversial. Locke, for instance, characterized primary qualities (like shape) as ones which produced ideas in us that resembled their causes as they are in bodies. In the case of secondary qualities (like colour), on the other hand, there is no resemblance between the ideas they produce in us and their causes in bodies. For Locke these qualities are all powers in bodies, whereas Berkeley offered a radically different account of qualities which rejected such powers and material bodies (so understood).

rationalism: a term used in a number of senses, for instance to signify opposition to any reliance on mystery or the arbitrary will of God in religion. Its main use in this volume is for the view, as opposed to empiricism (q.v.), that true certainty is grounded in reason ('intuition', q.v.) and that we can have a priori knowledge of the nature of things, of our duties, etc. See Introduction.

realism, moral: a theory in ethics according to which there are distinctively moral facts.

relativism: (a) in ethics, the view that there are no absolute moral standards but that these vary from one society to another. (b) about space and time, that they are nothing ('absolute') in themselves, but ways in which phenomena and events are ordered.

scepticism: most generally the view that knowledge of any sort is unobtainable. Commonly used for the view that knowledge of an objective world is unobtainable.

scepticism (moral): strictly the view that we have no knowledge of objective moral truth but often also for the view that there is no objective moral truth, in the sense of moral realism (q.v.), and that moral distinctions are conventional or subjective.

scholasticism: the style of philosophy associated with the Church schools and universities of the medieval period. The status according to Aristotle by the scholastics is indicated by their referring to him simply as 'the philosopher'. But, although they operated within a broadly Aristotelian framework, the scholastics elaborated a technical vocabulary of their own. The humanists attacked the 'barbarity' and the Moderns the 'obscurity' of this language. Scholasticism lost its dominance in universities around the end of the seventeenth century.

scientia: the term means 'knowledge' but is used to refer to an Aristotelian ideal of knowledge widely shared by philosophers in the seventeenth century. According to this view *scientia* is of 'that which is necessary' and 'cannot be otherwise'. Ultimately knowledge depends upon 'intuition' (q.v.), on this view, but demonstration (q.v.) was seen as the key process for arriving at new knowledge.

sensationalism: the view that all human knowledge derives from the senses.

sentimentalism: an ethical theory according to which moral distinctions are discerned not by reason but by feeling or sentiment.

Stoicism: one of the ancient Greek Schools of philosophy which spread to Rome, where it was adopted by Cicero and other figures who were widely admired during the seventeenth and eighteenth centuries. Stoics tended to pantheism, believing that events in the natural world are part of an interconnected whole. Though it was sometimes liberally interpreted as a Christian philosophy the Stoic virtue of steadfastness in the face of necessity did not sit easily with belief in a personal providence or in a God who acts freely. At the same time philosophers with a tendency to deism (q.v.) were not necessarily deterred from accepting Stoic ideas by such a consideration.

subjectivism: in ethics, the view that a moral judgement does no more than express the speaker's feelings, for example of approval.

sufficient reason, principle of: a favourite principle of Leibniz's, admitting of many formulations, including: for every statement that is true there is a sufficient reason (though not always know to us) why it is true. Leibniz denied that there could be any two things in the universe that were exactly alike since God would not have a sufficient reason to create both of them.

system: a theory such as the Copernican theory but also a speculative a priori metaphysical theory. It is in the latter sense that the term 'system' was often used during the Enlightenment in a disparaging way, especially by Condillac.

utilitarianism: a view according to which the rightness or wrongness of an action was to be decided by reference to question whether its consequences were beneficial or harmful. The term was first adopted by J. S. Mill in the nineteenth century but utilitarian thinking had become more common during the eighteenth century. Earlier theological utilitarians had credited God with a commitment to securing the greatest amount of human happiness possible in the long term. But utilitarian thinking in Hume, Helvétius, Bentham and others was distinctly secular and often anti-religious.

verstehen: a cognitive empathy or imaginative understanding peculiar to human understanding of personal activities, for example of motives, etc. This view is associated with the rejection of attempts to model the human on the natural sciences.

voluntarism (theological): any of several views that stress the will of God, among them (a) the view (endorsed, for instance by Descartes) that the so-called 'eternal truths' depend for their truth upon the will of God, who could have willed that they are false. On this view the natural order is good simply because God created it. God did not create the world the way He did in conformity with some standard of goodness that is independent of His will: (b) the view (held by Berkeley among others) that the continuing existence of the sensible world depends on God's continuing causation and that the constancy of the laws of nature are dependent on the constancy of the divine will.

Index of subjects

Index of names